D1175579

The global evolution of

industrial relations

ABOUT THE AUTHOR

Bruce E. Kaufman is Professor of Economics and Senior Associate of the W.T. Beebe Institute of Personnel and Employment Relations at Georgia State University in Atlanta, GA. He has written or edited fourteen books and numerous scholarly articles on labour economics, industrial relations and human resource management. His book **The Origins and Evolution of the Field of Industrial Relations in the United States** won the 1992 Richard Lester prize for "Best Book in Labor Economics and Industrial Relations". Professor Kaufman is past president of the University Council of Industrial Relations and Human Resources Programs (US) and is currently co-chair of the IR Theory and IR as a Field Study Group of the International Industrial Relations Association.

"Kaufman's book is a tour de force. It is a thoughtful and analytical history of the evolution of international and comparative industrial relations as a field of study. It is an insightful overview of the links between industrial relations and institutional economics and a passionate (and in my view correct) argument for why we need to maintain and strengthen these linkages. It will be an extremely valuable resource as we take up the challenges facing our field today and tomorrow."
Thomas A. Kochan, MIT Sloan School of Management, Institute for Work and Employment Research, USA

"This is the best work ever written on the historical development of industrial relations."
Tadashi Hanami, Professor Emeritus, Sophia University, Tokyo, Japan

"...an indispensable source of knowledge for anyone interested in the field of industrial relations, in the work of the ILO and in the activities of the IIRA."
Prof. Dr. Manfred Weiss, Johann Wolfgang Goethe University, Frankfurt, Germany

The global evolution of

industrial relations

EVENTS, IDEAS AND THE IIRA

Bruce E. Kaufman

 International Labour Office • Geneva

Kaufman, B.
The global evolution of industrial relations: Events, ideas and the IIRA
Geneva, International Labour Office, 2004

Labour relations, history, trend, developed country, developing country, UK, USA.
13.06.1

ISBN 92-2-114153-5

ILO Cataloguing in Publication Data

Typeset by Magheross Graphics, France & Ireland *www.magheross.com*

Printed in Switzerland   SRO

Dedicated to Sidney and Beatrice Webb, John R. Commons and
John D. Rockefeller, Jr., founders of the field of industrial relations

FOREWORD

The initial impetus for this book was the desire of the International Industrial Relations Association (IIRA) to provide an institutional history recording the contributions of the Association during the nearly four decades of its existence. However, as the author shows convincingly in this book, the origin and role of the IIRA are part of a larger story of the globalization of industrial relations, whose roots were in the United Kingdom, evolved in the United States and then spread to continental Europe and other societies. A detailed and exhaustive phase-by-phase account of this evolutionary process is synthesized by the author, demonstrating the beginnings of industrial relations in the nineteenth century as a response to the Labour Problem, and recounting and explaining its later emergence as an academic and professional field.

The book admirably presents the inspirational role of the International Labour Organization (ILO), right from its founding in 1919 to date, in mobilizing the expertise of scholars, practitioners and policy-makers in the promotion of employment and labour values around the world. The author also demonstrates that the founding of the IIRA in 1966 complemented part of ILO's global campaign for a rights-based labour policy.

Thus the story of the IIRA and its symbiotic relationship with the ILO is embedded within the globalization of industrial relations. The book makes clear the enormous influence of the ILO in the promotion of industrial relations worldwide, notably in the developing countries, and provides a thorough analysis of its role in promoting fair labour practices and social justice in the world of work among the emerging democracies of Africa, Asia, Eastern Europe and Latin America. As the book suggests, it is hardly an exaggeration to say that that without the ILO and the IIRA, the spread of the field of industrial relations in these regions would not have attained its present significance.

Through archival records and direct interviews with key actors, Professor Kaufman provides an original, systematic account of the beginning of industrial relations and the methods by which the ILO and IIRA promote industrial relations as a field of study and practice worldwide. It is noteworthy that the world congress of the IIRA is in its fourteenth session, while regional congresses have been taking place in the various regions of the world for about 20 years. The congress study groups have become a forum for serious intellectual discourse of theoretical and practical issues of industrial relations in our contemporary world, just as the special seminars have evolved as important mechanisms for addressing challenges in the practice of industrial relations. These forums provide a unique opportunity for scholars and practitioners of various callings to debate and exchange ideas on employment and labour market issues. The publications from the various mechanisms of the IIRA have contributed no less to the story of the globalization of industrial relations.

Readers will learn in this book about some of the prime catalysts in the transplanting of industrial relations to other parts of the world. Of important note is the evidence that some of those who have contributed to the development of industrial relations as a field of scholarship in various parts of the world have also been behind the IIRA. Today IIRA affiliated membership of over 5,000 worldwide is spread across 40 national associations, 60 institutional members and about 1,000 direct individual members. The organization continues to expand its membership, not only in these numerical terms, but also across several occupational and professional endeavours. The IIRA of today boasts the leading scholars and thinkers in the field of industrial relations, and is pleased to see a growing spread of membership among practitioners in industry, labour and public administration, and among judges, labour law practitioners and arbitrators.

There are challenges for the field of industrial relations, as there are for the ILO and the IIRA. The world of work is changing, with the globalization of markets and other environmental factors continually influencing or dictating the course and context of the labour market and labour relations. There have also been significant developments in the status and orientation of the labour market institutions and actors, as there have been in industrial relations and its own institutions and processes. But responses to these challenges are unfolding. The ILO, for example, has recently refocused its mandate around a Decent Work Agenda as an integrated approach to the changing world of work and contemporary labour issues. The IIRA too is part of this phenomenon of change and response.

Based on his analysis, the author offers a menu of these challenges and possible response options for the key protagonists and institutions that have played and will continue to play an important role in industrial relations.

Our Association notes the author's perspectives on the challenges and opportunities, and commends them to all parties.

A book on a topic such as this is undoubtedly a pioneering work, but one which is not likely to escape questions about its account, methodology or interpretation of the origin and sequence of events that led to the evolution of industrial relations. This will be a welcome debate and it is our anticipation that any intellectual discourse will contribute to the unfolding story that the book has initiated. Needless to emphasize here that while the book was commissioned by the IIRA and has been reviewed and approved by the IIRA officers, the positions and point of view in this book are those of the author and do not represent the position or point of view of the IIRA or its officers.

On behalf of the Executive Committee of the IIRA, indeed the membership of the IIRA worldwide, we want to express our appreciation to Professor Kaufman, whose enthusiasm in providing this account exceeds our expectation. We would also like to convey our thanks to the former officers of our Association, particularly Professor Manfred Weiss in whose presidency this book was initiated. Though in retirement, they readily embraced the idea of a book on this subject and enthusiastically provided their individual perspectives on the role of our Association in this international phenomenon.

Luis Aparicio-Valdez   *Tayo Fashoyin*
IIRA President   *IIRA Secretary*

CONTENTS

PREFACE

I never intended to write this book; once started I sometimes thought it would never end. The genesis was a telephone call I received in April 2002 from Tayo Fashoyin, Secretary of the International Industrial Relations Association (IIRA). Tayo and I had never met or corresponded so I had no idea what the call was about. Tayo said that the officers of the IIRA wanted someone to write up the official history of the Association and my name had been recommended. I later found out that the recommendation came from Anil Verma, my good friend and an IIRA Executive Committee member.

My initial reaction was lukewarm, partly because my plate was already full with other research commitments and partly because I did not see that this project promised much of an audience or exciting intellectual challenge. Also complicating things, I had recently promised Diane, my partner and significant other, to cut back on work and try to lead a more balanced life. However, on the plus side were several considerations: the book was intended to be short (75–125 pages), the project was a natural extension of my previous work on the history of industrial relations in the United States, I would get an opportunity to broaden my intellectual horizons and name recognition beyond my home country and I would perform a useful service activity for the IIRA and the field of industrial relations. All of these considerations inclined me to say yes, and the opportunity to accompany me on research trips to the IIRA headquarters in Switzerland swung Diane's vote. So I called Tayo back and agreed to do it as a short-run "overload" assignment. Had any of us only known!

We travelled to Geneva for nine days in mid-August 2002. In our free time, Diane and I explored all the towns around Lake Geneva and had a perfectly wonderful time – luckily so, because these fond memories had then to sustain us over what turned out to be the most gruelling, all-consuming 18 months of my life. Back in Geneva, I discovered in the archives and from talks with several of the past and present officers that the history of the IIRA was more interesting than I had first thought and, indeed, the story of the IIRA might have broader intellectual significance. That week I conducted in-depth telephone interviews with three past presidents, Tadashi Hanami, Ben Roberts and Manfred Weiss, and each recounted the important role the IIRA played in the birth and development of the industrial relations field in their countries. These conversations raised the curtain on a subject I had never really given much thought to: how had the industrial relations field come to diverse countries such as Germany, Japan and the United Kingdom, and how was it both similar to and different from the industrial relations field I knew in Canada and the United States?

After returning to Atlanta, and facing a March 2003 deadline for the manuscript, I quickly set to work. The more I dug into the subject, however, the more I realized that to really communicate the extent and significance of the Association's contributions, the IIRA's history and activities needed to be placed in a larger historical and institutional context. I also saw the need to provide not only a description of events and trends but also an *explanation*.

For example, I soon discovered that up to the early 1960s the industrial relations field was largely limited to three countries: Canada, the United Kingdom and the United States. After the founding of the IIRA in 1966, however, industrial relations quickly spread to several dozen more countries, witnessed by the founding of industrial relations associations in Argentina, France, Germany, Israel, Japan, Nigeria, Sweden, and numerous other nations around the world. To my mind, this story cried out for a more in-depth exploration of key issues. Why did the industrial relations field start in North America and the United Kingdom, and not other regions or countries? What kept industrial relations largely confined to these countries until the early 1960s, particularly since the objects of study in industrial relations (labour problems, trade unions, human resource development) were well represented in many other nations of the world? Who were the first scholars in each country to take an active role in developing the field of industrial relations and to what degree were they influenced by the IIRA and Anglo-American model? Why has the industrial relations field experienced a serious decline in some countries in the last two decades but continued growth in others? Added to all of these considerations was yet one other vital subject: the International Labour Organization (ILO). In the intended short volume I would be able to give only a few pages of attention to the role and contributions of the ILO, centred principally around the fact that the ILO is the headquarters' home of the IIRA. As my research progressed, however, I came to realize that the birth and subsequent development of the ILO and industrial relations field were closely intertwined and that this important connection had not heretofore been documented.

After several months had elapsed, I went back to Tayo and the IIRA officers and told them that I wanted to expand and broaden the book substantially and make it a fully fledged historical survey of the global development of the industrial relations field. The prospective gain I put before them was that a larger historical work would not only attract many more readers but would also provide a more powerful and in-depth account of the contributions of the IIRA and the ILO. They agreed to this modification, although neither they nor I yet realized just how large this "modification" would eventually grow into. The end result was that instead of having the manuscript completed in February 2003 it was not finished until over a year later and had grown from a few short chapters of perhaps 100 pages to 13 chapters and more than 600 pages.

The reader will have to judge the value of these additional pages. I can state, however, what my objectives were in writing them.

The first objective was historical and descriptive: to produce the most comprehensive, well-crafted and insightful account of the birth and development of the industrial relations field that was in my power to create, given the rather tight time constraints I had to operate under. Thus, starting in Chapter 1, I describe the "pre-history" of the field, starting in the 1770s and extending up to the First World War period, followed by a detailed exposition of the emergence and growth of industrial relations in each major region of the world, extending in chronological order from Chapter 2 (the birth of industrial relations in North America in 1920) to Chapter 11 (the most recent developments at the ILO and IIRA). This account is meant to be a straightforward recitation of the facts regarding the major people, events, ideas and institutions that have guided the development of the industrial relations field across time and nations.

The second objective was intellectual and conceptual: to delineate and describe the subject matter and body of knowledge encompassed within the field of industrial relations and to articulate and describe its theoretical foundation, major positive and normative premises, and alternative schools of thought (or "paradigms"). As the reader will discover, to the present day considerable disagreement exists over the boundaries and core subject matter of industrial relations. In part my purpose in this book is simply to bring these competing perspectives into fuller view to facilitate a more informed discussion and debate, but in part I also use these chapters as an opportunity to let the historical record speak on what is the correct definition and demarcation of the field. As most readers also know, the industrial relations field is largely an applied area of problem solving, and theoretical development has rather badly lagged behind. In these chapters I endeavour to push theorizing forward by describing in some detail the underlying theoretical models of the founders of the field and important theoretical contributions of later generations of scholars. In particular, I present in Chapter 2 a description of the "three faces" of industrial relations (science building, problem solving, ethical/ideological) and provide for each a detailed account of their major premises and points of view. Also provided in Chapters 1–3 are the most detailed, in-depth expositions available of what I perceive are the major theoretical wellsprings of industrial relations: the German historical/social economics of the late nineteenth century, the heterodox economics of Sidney and Beatrice Webb of England, and the early twentieth-century American institutional economics of John R. Commons and the Wisconsin school. Also occupying a central role in the development of industrial relations is Frederick Taylor and the application of "social Taylorism" to workplace reform, while Karl Marx is a constant if today often unacknowledged presence in the shadows of the field.

The third objective was interpretative: to use the history in this volume to understand and explain the pattern of development of the industrial relations field, the reasons for the field's declining fortunes in many countries in recent decades, and its prospects in the years ahead. In many countries the pattern of development of the industrial relations field represents an inverted V, characterized by a period of expansion in the first several decades after the Second World War and then, in the last decade or two, a period of contraction. Advanced in this book are six factors that account for this pattern, as well as its absence in some other countries. Also advanced is a relatively optimistic conclusion that industrial relations in generic form most certainly will survive in the years ahead since a capitalist system cannot function without it.

A fourth objective was to examine the development of industrial relations in a truly comparative, cross-national manner. Numerous books have examined the comparative development of national systems of industrial relations – that is, the development of national labour movements, the institutions of collective bargaining, the legal framework governing labour relations, and so forth – but none that I am aware of has done the same for the academic *field* of industrial relations. An important lesson that emerges from these pages is that the production and organization of knowledge is socially constructed, giving rise across countries to different conceptualizations and interpretations of the subject of industrial relations, different approaches to research in terms of theory and method, and different disciplinary emphases regarding economics, law and sociology. Interestingly, this book shows that the way the academic field of industrial relations in each country is structured and practised tends to mirror the structure and practice of industrial relations in the world of business and industry.

Several features of the book deserve brief comment. The greatest obstacle and largest danger in writing a book such as this is ethnocentrism. Every one of us is to some degree a prisoner of our national experience and there is no escaping these shackles. For this author, ethnocentrism means that the content and interpretations contained on the following pages are inevitably filtered and shaped by the American cultural lens through which I experience and perceive the events and ideas in other countries. Certainly one could say with some merit that Atlanta, Georgia, is not the most "centred" location from which to write a balanced, value-neutral account of industrial relations in the other nations of the world. Compounding the problem, my only language is English and thus most of the non-English literature on industrial relations is inaccessible to me. (However, I had certain key articles translated from German, French and Spanish.)

I have been very sensitive to these limitations and have struggled mightily to avoid as much ethnocentric bias as possible. Among other methods, I have made extensive use of personal interviews with scholars from other countries in order to learn first-hand their perspective and point of view on industrial relations. I have then asked them to review critically draft chapters in order to alert me to problematic statements and propositions. But let's be honest and openly recognize that to some degree – modest I hope – this book is inevitably written from an American point of view. As a small but telling example, one will read in these pages that a certain political position or ideology is "left wing" or "radical". As readers in other countries have told me, what is left wing or radical to an American is mainstream in these countries and it is the American position that is "right wing" and "managerialist". Since I am an American, these matters tend to be framed as the former; if I were from a different country they would probably be framed as the latter. Caveat emptor!

While on this subject, I should note that several readers of the manuscript felt I devoted too much attention to the development of industrial relations in the United States, and they particularly objected to starting the history of the field with the United States (Chapter 2) rather than United Kingdom (placed as Chapter 3). My counter-response is that the field of industrial relations as a formal institutionalized entity started in the United States, not the United Kingdom (despite the pioneering work of the Webbs), and until the 1960s the United States was without rival as the centre of the field of industrial relations. Although the American experience is given extensive coverage, I nevertheless endeavour to balance the treatment in two respects: first, by standing back at places and taking a critical view of American developments and, second, by giving a full and complete history of the field in numerous other countries. Certainly it is my impression that the historical account presented here for countries such as Germany, Japan, Mexico and the United Kingdom is the most in-depth and detailed available.

Due to limitations of space and time, not all countries could be included in this volume, or were only given very brief mention. To the people of these countries I express my sincere apology and regrets.

Note should also be made that in certain places the history presented in this volume and the implications and conclusions drawn from it are revisionist or iconoclastic with respect to the conventional wisdom. To a degree that even I did not heretofore fully appreciate (having in a previous book drawn attention to this theme), the early field of industrial relations pioneered in the United States started out in the 1920s with a substantial managerialist orientation. Illustrative is the evidence presented in Chapters 2 and 3 that the person who did the most to promote industrial relations directly in both industry and academia in the 1920s was industrialist John D. Rockefeller, Jr. – a person whose name is conspicuous by its absence in the modern industrial relations literature – while the indirect influence of Frederick Taylor through the concept of "social Taylorism" was likewise far larger than currently recognized in the field. Also noteworthy, one often encounters the assertion that human resource management is "unitarist" and industrial relations is "pluralist", and the two fields are thus to a large degree separate and rivalrous. This bifurcation may arguably be true today (since it is now so widely professed), but this book documents that when the field started in the 1920s industrial relations was broadly conceived to incorporate *both* the unitarist and pluralist models and to include *both* human resource management and labour–management relations. Finally, this book also suggests that the well-known transformation thesis popular in the current industrial relations literature may need to be reconsidered. The argument is that the field of industrial relations largely originated in the 1930s in the United States with the New Deal and was mainly concerned with unions and collective bargaining. The substantial decline of the union sector in the 1980s-90s in the United States and other countries is framed, in turn, as the "transformation of industrial relations" and the rise of a new non-union, human resource management employment model is frequently dubbed the "new industrial relations". If the earlier and oft-neglected 1920s American model of industrial relations is used as the baseline, the New Deal abandonment of welfare capitalism and embrace of collective bargaining becomes the *real* transformation: the subsequent decline of the union sector is more of a regression to the mean (a return to the 1920s baseline after the huge exogenous shock of the Great Depression and New Deal) and the corresponding rise of a non-union, "high-performance" human resource management model is a return to a revised and expanded version of the *original* industrial relations model pioneered by Rockefeller, Commons and other participants in early industrial relations. Indeed, the evidence shows that industrial relations in the 1920s was widely considered to represent and subsume that era's version of *strategic* human resource management!

I now come to the most important task: the acknowledgements. It is trite sounding but so very true that this book is made possible only with the very generous cooperation and help of dozens of people from around the world.

I want to start by recognizing a small group of individuals who in my opinion went far above the call of duty in the help and guidance they gave me. It is literally the case that their help made the difference between success and failure in putting together the history of industrial relations in their respective countries. They are (arranged alphabetically): Luis Aparicio-Valdez (Latin America), Isabel da Costa (France), Paul Edwards (United Kingdom), Tayo Fashoyin (Africa), Tadashi Hanami (Japan), Richard Hyman (United Kingdom and continental Europe), Berndt Karl Keller (Germany), Diana Kelly (Australia), Kazutoshi Koshiro (Japan), Walther Müller-Jentsch (Germany), Michael Byungnam Lee (Korea), Young-Myon Lee (Korea), C.S. Venkata Ratnam (India).

Next in the list of acknowledgements and appreciations are all those people who shared their time and expertise with me through one or more in-depth personal interviews. Much of the information I gleaned about the field of industrial relations in the countries discussed in this book is not available in print in any language. Rather, it came from the collective knowledge of the many people I interviewed who have been witnesses to the historical development of our field. I owe them a huge debt of thanks for sharing their recollections.

Particularly meaningful to me were the interviews with the "veterans" of the field – the people now in their late 70s, 80s and even 90s who were the pioneer scholars in industrial relations after the Second World War. I conducted two interviews with John Dunlop, one shortly before his death. He was feisty to the end. (I also requested an interview with Clark Kerr but his health had deteriorated too far.) Also noteworthy and gratifying was an extended interview with Ben Roberts, one of founders of industrial relations in the United Kingdom and a co-founder of the IIRA. It is my pleasure to be able to relate his contributions in this book. Another veteran I interviewed was Jean-Daniel Reynaud, the founding father of French industrial relations. Reynaud is well into his 80s and now blind, but he still remembers vividly when he formed the French Industrial Relations Association in the late 1960s and the representatives of the unions and employers refused to sit at the same table. Perhaps most poignant, I tracked down a person from Asia who served as a research assistant to one of the "four horsemen" (Kerr, Dunlop, Harbison and Myers). He is now in a nursing home and barely able to speak, but I could tell that it was a treasured moment to be able to share his memories of those long-distant events and his contributions to the field of industrial relations.

Organized by country, region, or institution (affiliated past or present) are the people I interviewed. Africa: Sonia Bendix and Tayo Fashoyin; Australia/New Zealand: Alan Geare, Diana Kelly, Russell Lansbury and Kenneth Walker; Belgium: Roger Blanpain; Canada: Jean Boivin, John Crispo, Morley Gunderson, Gregor Murray, Richard Chaykowski, Marcel Simard, Daphne Taras, Mark Thompson and Anil Verma; France: Isabel da Costa, Jean-Daniel Reynaud and Jacques Rojot; Germany: Friedrich Fürstenberg, Berndt Karl Keller, Walther Müller-Jentsch and Manfred Weiss; United Kingdom: George Bain, Paul Edwards, John Kelly and Ben Roberts; India: Subbiah Kannappan, C.S. Venkata Ratnam, E.M. Rao and C.P. Thakur; ILO/IIRA: Johanna Boixader, Arturo Bronstein, Giuseppe Casale, Robert Cox, Gert Gurst, Tayo Fashoyin, Alan Gladstone, Kate Mennie-Cecconi, Margaret Kearns, Gerry Rogers, Johannes Schregle; Israel: Ozer Carmi, Michal Frenkel; Italy: Tiziano Treu; Japan: Tadashi Hanami, Kazutoshi Koshiro; Mexico: Enrique De la Garza Toledo and Sebastian Sansberro; South America: Luis Aparicio-Valdez, Hector Lucena, Emilio Morgado and Hélio Zylberstajn; United States: Maria Cook, John Dunlop, Peter Feuille, John French, Harry Katz, Thomas Kochan, Edward Lawler, Barbara Lee, Solomon Levine and Paula Voos.

In addition to interviews, a number of people (including many of those listed above) sent me detailed information and answers to questions by email. Also quite valuable were the comments and suggestions received from people who reviewed draft chapters. The list includes: Peter Ackers, Roy Adams, Carlos Aldao-Zapiola, Luis Aparicio-Valdez, George Bain, Willy Bendix, Richard Block, William Brown, Ozer Carmi, Efrén Cordova, Isabel da Costa, Robert Cox, Clifford Donn, John Dunlop, Paul Edwards, Oscar Ermida Uriarte, Tayo Fashoyin, Martheanne Finnemore, Carola Frege, Friedrich Fürstenberg, Tony Giles, Alan Gladstone, Howard Gospel, David Guest, Morley Gunderson, Tadashi Hanami, Robert Hebdon, Juan Carlos Romero Hicks, Richard Hyman, Joe Isaac, Dan Jacobsen, Sandy Jacoby, Harish Jain, Timo Kauppinen, Brian Keeling, Tom Keenoy, Berndt Karl Keller, Diana Kelly, John Kelly, Thomas Kochan, Kazutoshi Koshiro, Russell Lansbury, Michael Byungnam Lee, Young-Myon Lee, David Levine, Hector Lucena, Ray Markey, Richard Miller, Martha Monsalve, Sylvia Montreuil, Walther Müller-Jentsch, Gregor Murray, Enrique Pistoletti, Horacio Quiros, C.S. Venkata Ratnam, Udo Rehfeldt, Malcolm Rimmer, Alberto Rimoldi, Jacques Rojot, Sebastian Sansberro, James Scoville, Daphne Taras, Carol Thornby, George Strauss, Manfred Weiss, Paula Wells, Mark Westcott, Keith Whitfield and Hélio Zylberstajn. (Throughout I follow Western tradition and put surnames last.) To anyone who I have forgotten to list, it is inadvertent and regretted.

I also want to take this opportunity to expressly thank the officers and staff of the IIRA for inviting me to write this book and for their unstinting trust, support and cooperation. I am particularly indebted to Tayo Fashoyin, who opened many doors, gave much encouragement, and successfully shepherded the entire project from beginning to end. He also somehow managed to remain relatively calm as the volume steadily expanded while a succession of deadlines came and went.

Also of great assistance throughout this project was Johanna Boixader, administrative assistant of the IIRA. Besides being charming and gracious, she had all the archival records of the IIRA effectively organized and waiting for me when I arrived in Geneva and helped get me started on interviews and fact-gathering. Then, over the next eighteen months she sent to Atlanta a steady stream of documents, archival records, organizational statistics and contact names, all very efficiently done.

My appreciation also goes to Rosemary Beattie and Charlotte Beauchamp of the Publications Bureau of the ILO, in the former case for expeditiously getting the book through the review and publishing process and in the latter for doing an expert job editing the manuscript under intense time pressure.

When I began working on this book I described the subject to one of my colleagues at another university and she commented, "Sounds kind of boring." Another person who read an early chapter draft wished me well but called the effort "an heroic but impossible task". My worst nightmare is that I have shown both of them to be right. A third person, on hearing what the book was about, remarked, "You'll make Jack Barbash proud." This goal is the one I hope I have accomplished, even if he might not agree with everything.

In closing, I wish to express my deep gratitude to and affection for my soulmate, Diane, and two wonderful children, Lauren and Andrew. They were incredibly understanding and supportive and generously gave me the time and emotional space needed to complete this book. As the project unfolded, what became known as "the book" gradually came to dominate family life to the point it *was* family life – week after week after week. After much forbearance, toward the end Diane in particular became so frustrated with the all-consuming, never-ending nature of the beast that she wanted to throw my computer and over 700 library books (and probably me!) out the window. No one could blame her, but luckily love and patience and hope for the future triumphed. I greatly respect and admire Diane, and my children, for their selfless commitment, and feel eternal gratitude for their presence in my life. So that these sentiments are more than just lofty words, I pledge in print before the world to never again let a book so usurp our time and emotional energy for each other.

ABBREVIATIONS

AALL	American Association of Labor Legislation
ABET	Brazilian Association of Labour Studies
ACAC	Australian Conciliation and Arbitration Commission
ACIRRT	Australian Centre for Industrial Relations Research and Training
ACRIP	Asociación Columbiana de Relaciones Industriales y Personnel
ACTU	Australian Council of Trade Unions
ADP	Asociación de Administradores de Personal
ADRIL	Asociación Dirigentes de Relaciones Industriales del Litoral
AEA	American Economics Association
AFL	American Federation of Labor
AFL–CIO	American Federation of Labor and Congress of Industrial Organizations
AIRROC	Association of Industrial Relations, Republic of China
ALLR	*American Labor Legislation Review*
ALP	Australian Labour Party
AMA	American Management Association
APERT	Asociación Peruana de Trabajo
ARI	Industrial Relations Association of Peru
AWIRS	Australian Workplace Industrial Relations Survey
BUIRA	British Universities Industrial Relations Association
CCL	Canadian Congress of Labour
CEROP	Centre for Employment Relations and Organizational Performance
CESIT	Center of Studies on Unions and Labor
CF&I	Colorado Fuel and Iron Company
CIA	Central Intelligence Agency
CIO	Congress of Industrial Organizations

CIR	Centre for Industrial Relations (Canada)
CIRA	Canadian Industrial Relations Association
CIREM	Centre D'Iniciatives i Recerques Europees a la Mediterrània
CNRS	Centre national de récherche scientifique
CTM	Confederación de Trabajadores de México
DGB	German Trade Union Confederation
EIRO	European Industrial Relations Observatory
ELS/ISS	Employment and Labour Studies Programme, Institute of Social Studies
EU	European Union
FAOS	Forskningscenter for Arbejdsmarkeds-og Organisationsstudier
FIDAP	Interamerican Federation of Personnel Management
FLSA	Fair Labor Standards Act
GIRA	German Industrial Relations Association
GM	General Motors
HRM	human resource management
IALL	International Association for Labour Legislation
IERA	International Employment Relations Association
IILR	Institute of Industrial and Labor Relations (Israel)
IILS	International Institute for Labour Studies
IIRA	International Industrial Relations Association
ILE	institutional labour economics
IMF	International Monetary Fund
INSORA	Institute of Business Administration, Chile
INTUC	Indian National Trade Union Congress
IPL	Fondazione Istituto per il Lavoro
IRAA	Industrial Relations Association of America
IRASA	Industrial Relations Association of South Africa
IRC	Industrial Relations Counselors, Inc.
IRES	Institut de recherches économiques et sociales
IRI	Industrial Relations Institute
IRRA	Industrial Relations Research Association
IRRAI	Industrial Relations Research Association of Israel
IRRU	Industrial Relations Research Unit, Warwick
ISLE	Indian Society of Labour Economics
ISLLSL	International Society for Labour Law and Social Legislation
IST	Institut des sciences du travail
IWW	Industrial Workers of the World
JIL	Japan Institute of Labor

JIRA	Japan Industrial Relations Association
KLI	Korea Labor Institute
LEST	Laboratoire d'économie et de sociologie du travail
MERCOSUR	Mercado Común del Sur
MIT	Massachusetts Institute of Technology
NAFTA	North American Free Trade Agreement
NAM	National Association of Manufacturers
NATO	North Atlantic Treaty Organization
NBER	National Bureau of Economic Research
NGO	non-governmental organization
NICB	National Industrial Conference Board
NIR	National Industrial Recovery Act
NIWL	Arbetslivsinstitutet
NLRA	National Labor Relations Act
NPA	National Personnel Association
NWLB	National War Labor Board
NYSSILR	New York State School of Industrial and Labor Relations
OB	organizational behaviour
OD	organizational development
PM	personnel management
PRF	Personnel Research Federation
RELASUR	Industrial Relations in the Southern Cone
SCC	Special Conference Committee
SPD	Social Democratic Party
SSRC	Social Science Research Council
TLC	Trades and Labour Congress
TUC	Trades Union Congress
UCLA	University of California, Los Angeles
WEP	World Employment Programme
WERS	Workplace Employment Relations Survey
WTO	World Trade Organization
YMCA	Young Men's Christian Association

INTRODUCTION: THE ROAD AHEAD

The subject of work and the relations between those who manage it and those who perform it is as old as human civilization. It is only in the last 200 years, however, that these matters have become objects of significant social concern and government policy, and only in the last century have they emerged as a separate, well-recognized area of study and research in educational institutions. This book is a chronicle of this evolution, and the field that subsumes it – widely known today as *industrial relations*.

The phenomena of industrial relations are found in all countries where people work for others in paid employment. As a generic subject, therefore, industrial relations is ubiquitous. The field of industrial relations, on the other hand, is one particular approach to studying these phenomena and solving the problems that arise from them. It is only one of a variety of possible ways to produce and organize knowledge, and as such it has a unique frame of reference and its own theories and concepts, techniques and practices, and ideological commitments.

Through a complex and somewhat unlikely set of circumstances, the field of industrial relations was born in the United States in the late 1910s. Over the next eight decades it slowly spread to other countries, reaching first other English-speaking nations and then later extending to countries across Africa, Asia, Europe and Latin America. Today, at the beginning of the twenty-first century, industrial relations is found across the world.

The field of industrial relations was born out of a confluence of events and ideas associated with the rise of industrial economies and democratic governments in the Western world of the late nineteenth and early twentieth centuries. It emerged from both negative and positive impulses.

In its negative aspect, industrial relations was a reaction against the waste, human suffering and social injustice associated with unrestrained profit making and employer power in nineteenth- and early twentieth-century capitalism. As described in a later chapter, these evils led to deplorable conditions and many hardships for a large bulk of the workforce, precipitating considerable political agitation, mounting class conflict between capital and labour, and a rising tide of labour strikes and protest. Out of these tensions and conditions grew a number of revolutionary and reform movements, with the more radical groups dedicated to the overthrow of capitalism and the wage system, while the more moderate ones sought to work within capitalism but soften and humanize its rough edges.

Industrial relations was part of the reform wing. Its founders were critical of the callous and exploitative treatment of labour and believed the existing relations between capital and labour were seriously unbalanced and inequitable. These conditions arose, in turn, from socially pernicious economic and legal doctrines and associated business practices. Among the most objectionable, for example, were the "labour as a commodity" theory, unabridged freedom of contract, the policy programme of laissez-faire and the monarchial or "employer autocracy" model of workforce governance. Measured against prevailing social opinion of the day in the United States, industrial relations occupied a position in the progressive centre to moderate left on issues of politics and economics, spanning a diverse and not entirely consistent range of opinion with liberal business leaders on the more conservative side of the field and moderate socialists on the more radical side. Few Marxists and revolutionary socialists, on the other hand, participated; indeed, the desire to find an alternative solution to Marxist class revolution was a sustaining impulse behind the birth and growth of the field. The anti-Marxist hue of industrial relations, combined with the fact that the United States was positioned distinctly toward the right end of the political/social spectrum in the years following the First World War, gave industrial relations a more conservative and business-oriented cast from the vantage point of Europe and was one factor limiting its movement outside of North America for many years.

In its positive aspect, industrial relations arose from a conviction that the conditions of work and the relations between bosses and bossed could be improved progressively through a combination of scientific discovery, education, legal reform, institution building, and appeal to a higher sense of ethics and social responsibility. Key work-related objectives shared by early participants in the field were closer cooperation and harmony between employers and workers; more secure, stable and plentiful jobs; a better balance of bargaining power between company and employee and improved wages, hours and conditions of employment; and provision of basic democratic rights and processes in workforce governance.

Imbued with a desire to promote social progress and impressed with the potentials of science and rational administration, the early participants in industrial relations approached the reform of capital–labour relations as a task of social engineering. In their tool kit were a variety of new practices, institutions and theories. Principal among them were trade unions, collective bargaining, protective labour legislation, social insurance programmes, arbitration and conciliation tribunals, personnel management, shop committees and work councils, industrial welfare programmes, countercyclical macro-economic policies, greater market regulation, and (in some cases) public ownership of key industries and some form of technocratic or socialist economic planning. Many of these ideas and practices had earlier been developed and implemented in Europe and Australasia and were imported to the United States, while several others were home grown or a domestic adaptation. These new reform methods and institutions, it was believed, would materially reduce labour problems and conflict and, thus, lead to improved industrial relations. The social pay-off, in turn, was believed to be a win–win of increased efficiency in production, enhanced equity in the workplace, improved opportunities for human self-development, and a more humanized, democratic and stable society.

These two impulses came together in the late 1910s and led to the creation of a new field of study and vocational area of practice in industry called industrial relations. In industry, the term industrial relations developed a broad, generic meaning connoting the tenor or state of relations between the different parties to the employment relationship. The relationship between employer and employees was of course central to this concept, but also included were other relations such as between work groups in the enterprise and between trade unions and employers' associations.

Industrial relations also developed other, more specific meanings. The term, for example, also came to connote the corporate employment department and personnel policies and practices used to coordinate, control and motivate labour. Going further, the term also came to signify one particular approach or strategy to labour management, generally associated with a progressive labour policy and, in particular, methods of joint dealing and collective employee voice. Since most firms of that era were wedded to traditional employment methods resting on the commodity conception of labour, unregulated markets and employer autocracy, the corporate practitioners of industrial relations were typically found in the liberal or progressive wing of the business community, such as the American Welfare Capitalism movement of the 1920s.

Industrial relations in the early 1920s also became a field of teaching and research in colleges and universities. As in industry, the term industrial relations soon took on multiple meanings and ideological shadings. Defined most broadly, the term industrial relations encompassed the study of all aspects of work and employment, thus spanning all industries, types of employment relationships, and topics and problems related to labour. The field was, in this version, also explicitly interdisciplinary, reflecting the fact that the employment relationship had distinct economic, legal, social, psychological, organizational and ethical dimensions and thus crossed the boundaries of numerous established branches of knowledge.

As taught in the classroom and written about in textbooks, however, industrial relations often had a somewhat narrower and less neutral perspective. In this version, industrial relations became the study and resolution of labour problems, where labour problems were typically portrayed as the dysfunctional and undesirable behaviours and outcomes generated by modern capitalist industry. One inevitable tendency of the "problems" perspective was to highlight the shortcomings of capitalism and employers and to cast trade unions and labour law in a more positive light; a second was to shrink the perimeter of the field from "all aspects of employment" to a narrower range of labour problems and solutions thereto.

But the term industrial relations in academia took on yet a third and still more specific meaning. In this version, industrial relations still subsumed the study of labour problems, but it gave priority of attention to one particular strategy or institution for solving these problems – the trade union and the practice of collective bargaining. This conception of industrial relations, in its early American version, emphasized the inherent conflict of interest that exists between employer and employee, the oft superior bargaining power of the employer, and the autocratic nature of workplace governance in the traditional firm. Influenced by the philosophy of voluntarism (minimal government intervention in labour–management relations), proponents of this view of industrial relations concluded that these problems are most effectively addressed by fostering widespread trade unionism so that collective bargaining can equalize bargaining power in wage determination and provide a measure of industrial democracy in the enterprise. While this form of industrial relations gave nominal attention to all aspects of work and all solutions to labour problems, in practice the focus was on collective forms of relations between unions and employers, often called labour–management relations.

In these various guises the field and practice of industrial relations has since grown and evolved in numerous ways, directed and shaped by a combination of events, new ideas, influential people and institutions. From its original North American base in the 1920s, industrial relations spread to the United Kingdom in the 1930s, to the countries of the British Commonwealth in the 1950s, and to the countries of Africa, Asia, Europe and Latin America in the 1960s and afterwards. As all participants in the field know, however, the path has been anything but smooth and linear and in recent years the growth line has reversed course in a number of countries. Perhaps not unexpectedly, the different and sometimes contradictory self-concepts of industrial relations enumerated above figure prominently in the explanation of these divergent trends.

The purpose of this book is to chronicle the birth and development of the industrial relations field – its ups, downs, challenges, transformations and differing fortunes across countries. The book is more than just a chronicle of events, however, for it also presents an *intellectual* history of the field. Toward that end, I spend considerable time in the early chapters tracing the intellectual roots of the field and describing the fundamental ideas, theories and principles underlying industrial relations, as advanced by the founding fathers (and mothers). But there is yet more to the history of industrial relations than events and ideas. There are also people and institutions. All the major players in the history of the field of industrial relations parade across these pages, as do hundreds of the supporting actors. One contribution of the book is thus to present what is in effect the family tree for the field. Also central to the development of industrial relations have been the institutions that have helped organize, promote and fund teaching and research in the field, including industrial relations programmes and institutes in universities, professional associations and a wide variety of government agencies and foundations connected to industrial relations.

The justification for undertaking this type of history is simple – no one else has yet told the story in any depth and there is much to be learned from a more complete understanding of our past and how the field got to where it is today.[1] Indeed, history not only illuminates the path already taken but also shines light on where we are headed and the strategic choices facing industrial relations in the years to come. An additional benefit of this type of work is that it helps draw together the worldwide community of scholars in industrial relations, separated as we are by different national boundaries, languages, institutional traditions and research interests.

Besides an intellectual history, the book also provides an interesting study in the comparative and international aspects of industrial relations. It is well known to scholars in the field that the institutions and practices of industrial relations vary considerably across nation states and that no single form or archetype of industrial relations system exists. Although reference is sometimes made to "French exceptionalism" or "American exceptionalism", in reality every country's industrial relations system is exceptional in the sense of having numerous unique practices and institutions. A lesson provided by this book is that the academic study of industrial relations – how the concept is defined and investigated and the structure and institutions of research and teaching – exhibits the same national diversity and exceptionalism. Thus, just as there is no one system for organizing industrial relations in the work world, so also is there no one system for organizing industrial relations in the academic world. What is particularly telling is that many of the unique features of each nation's academic system of industrial relations mirror and arise from corresponding unique features of its larger system of industrial relations in the national economy. Understanding one system thus provides insights about the other.

These features of the book will appeal most directly to scholarly participants in industrial relations. But other objectives of a broader and sometimes more indirect nature are also served.

People interested in the history and epistemology of the social sciences will, for example, find this account a useful case study, particularly since the analysis is comparative and cross-national. Why, for example, did industrial relations start in the United States, rather than England, Germany or Japan, and why did it spread more quickly to some countries than others? These questions direct attention to the forces that shape and direct the social production and organization of knowledge. In this book I endeavour to identify the most important of these forces. Some will be immediately recognizable to economists, such as division of labour and the role of consumer demand (a "paying audience"). Others fall in the domain of sociology, political science and other fields, such as the role played by class interests and ideologies, the political agenda of governing elites, and cross-national differences in cultures, social histories, the institutional structure of universities and the denseness of professional networks.

This account will also have value for those people interested in the larger history of industrialism and capitalist development. One of the most important social phenomena growing out of the Industrial Revolution and spread of capitalism was the development of a large wage-earning labour force, the emergence of a self-conscious and aggrieved working class, and the spread of trade unionism, industrial conflict, and radical social and political movements. These events became collectively known as the Labour Problem, viewed in many countries in the late nineteenth and early twentieth centuries as the most fundamental and threatening of all domestic crises. The birth and development of industrial relations was essentially a strategy and set of tactics developed by social reformers to vent the steam building up in the Labour Problem and keep it from boiling over into destructive class struggle and a Marxian-inspired overthrow of capitalism and representative democracy. A history of industrial relations is thus a glimpse into this fascinating and pivotal chapter in the history of modern industrial societies and brings into sharp relief not only one of capitalism's deepest and most threatening fault lines but also the struggle it engendered between the advocates of industrial reaction, reform and revolution. As this saga is retold in these pages, also receiving historical treatment are the plethora of reforms and innovations advanced by the advocates of industrial relations to bridge, stabilize and ultimately integrate capital and labour. Among these reform measures are trade unions, human resource management, protective labour laws, social welfare programmes and full employment policies.

And, finally, these pages offer insights on understanding not only the past but also the future of labour problems and employer–employee relations. To many people it appears that the Labour Problem of the late nineteenth–early twentieth century is a largely vanquished and bygone relic of an earlier era of robber barons, dark satanic mills and sweatshops. As these evils of the past fade into history in modern societies, so too fades in many people's minds the social rationale for the workplace institutions built up in earlier decades to provide workers protection and security, such as trade unions, protective labour laws and the modern welfare state. Further, in the minds of these people is the fact that the fast-proceeding pace of globalization appears to undercut the viability of these institutions, leading many instead to put their faith in the power of competitive and increasingly unrestrained market forces. Naturally, accompanying these suppositions is also a growing question about the social rationale and value added of the academic field of industrial relations that is devoted to studying and often promoting and defending these institutions and practices.

History cannot predict the future but it can provide some signposts that help anticipate the path ahead. Out of this study emerge several such signposts: unrestrained competition can easily become dysfunctional with respect to economic efficiency and human values; a market economy needs a degree of central management and buffering by social institutions in order to work effectively; and lack of jobs and stark inequalities breed social discontent. As we look around the world in the early twenty-first century, these signposts appear to be sending out a bright warning light. Globalization is undercutting coordination and central guidance in national economies, the gulf between rich and poor within nations and between nations is growing, and hundreds of millions of people in the world wake up each day without decent jobs, any form of social protection or security from the hazards of life. These conditions, it happens, were exactly those that accompanied capitalist development in the industrializing nations during the first age of globalization in the late nineteenth century, spawning in their wake the great Labour Problem and, some would argue, the First World War. So, as the second age of globalization proceeds one may wonder if the Labour Problem in advanced nations is completely dead or perhaps ready to stir to life again, albeit in different dress and form. Meanwhile, in the several dozen poorest countries of the world the first phase of industrialism has hardly started, sweatshops and child labour remain a stark reality, and labour problems of the most elementary form are legion.

The history in this book suggests, therefore, that while the contemporary study and modern-day institutions of industrial relations are currently challenged and in some decline, one would greatly err to write their obituary. Indeed, the lesson of these pages is that without a programme of industrial relations – conceived in this volume to represent the rules, institutions and practices that humanize, professionalize, democratize, stabilize and balance the labour market process and employment relationship – the global capitalist system will turn dysfunctional and quite possibly self-destruct.

Plan of the book

The origins and evolution of the field of industrial relations is a long story, particularly when told in a comparative, cross-national context.

To begin, I start in the next chapter with what others have called the "pre-history" stage of the field (Kelly, 1999). By pre-history is meant the formative, embryonic period of development for the field – when the seed was planted and grew but before industrial relations emerged as a self-contained, articulated body of ideas and practices.

Although others may date it differently, I start the pre-history period with two epochal events spaced within a few years of each other in the late eighteenth century – the beginning of the Industrial Revolution and the publication of Adam Smith's *The wealth of nations* (1776). The pre-history stage is then developed along two separate branches – developments in the realm of ideas and in the realm of events. In the former are well-recognized names such as Karl Marx, Frederick Taylor, Emile Durkheim and Max Weber, and various schools of thought, such as German and English historical economics, French syndicalism, industrial psychology and classical political economy. The realm of events is equally rich and varied. Crucial to the development of industrial relations, for example, are nineteenth-century events such as the rise of the factory system and large corporations, the emergence and growth of an urban-based wage labour force, the appearance and spread of trade unions, the growing crescendo of labour conflicts and violence, the spread of political democracy, the development of a professional class of business managers and the emergence of the first modern universities.

The next two chapters, Chapters 2 and 3, describe the birth and early development of the field of industrial relations. The transition from pre-history to formal beginnings and institutionalization took roughly twenty years, starting in the last decade of the 1800s and coming to fruition in the last years of the 1910s. The beginning point of this transitional period occurred in England and was principally initiated by the husband and wife team of Sidney and Beatrice Webb. Their two books, *A history of trade unionism* (1894) and *Industrial democracy* (1897), effectively laid the foundation for the new field of industrial relations. But, interestingly, while the Webbs set in motion the birth process of the industrial relations field, they were not the ones who actually brought it to fruition as a formal institutionalized entity. The actual birth of the field took place in the United States of America, and its "midwives" were the unlikely duo of industrialist John D. Rockefeller, Jr. and university economist and labour investigator John R. Commons.

For the next two decades, industrial relations remained a primarily North American phenomenon, becoming a small but recognized part of university curricula and a significant new area of management practice in industry. In the United Kingdom, by way of contrast, industrial relations had a distinctly peripheral, almost shadow existence in both industry and academia before the Second World War, while the concept and practice of industrial relations in the rest of the world was virtually unknown.

Chapters 4 and 5 take up the history of industrial relations from the end of the Second World War to the early 1960s. This period is dominated by events in the United States but with significant developments also occurring in Australia, Canada, New Zealand and the United Kingdom. The spread of mass unionism across most of American industry, and the associated problems of contract negotiation, strikes, grievance settlement, and wage-push inflation, gave a tremendous impetus to industrial relations in the country. Within a decade several dozen new industrial relations programmes were established in major universities, a new professional association was created, as was a new academic journal. Teaching and research in industrial relations boomed and, in hindsight, the period stands out as a "golden age" for the field in America. Outside of America, industrial relations was also entering the first stage of a distinct growth phase in several other Anglophone countries. For the first time industrial relations gained a secure foothold in Australasia, Canada and the United Kingdom, witnessed by the creation of new faculty positions in industrial relations and the expansion of industrial relations courses, and the establishment of several new centres and degree programmes.

Chapters 6 to 11 of the volume continue the history of industrial relations from the early 1960s to the end of the century. The chapters both move forward chronologically and outward geographically to a wider and wider group of countries. It is the latter process that is of particular interest.

The globalization of industrial relations – the spread of the field beyond its Anglo-American roots – occurred in stages and formed successive ripples outward from North America and the United Kingdom. After 1945, the field of industrial relations first sprouted in former British colonies, such as Australia, India, New Zealand and South Africa. Later it spread to Continental Europe, Japan, Scandinavia, and many of the developing nations in Africa, Latin America and East and South Asia. With the collapse of the communist regimes in the Soviet Union and central and eastern Europe in the late 1980s and early 1990s and the liberalization of communist rule in China, industrial relations began to sink roots in these countries too.

It is an interesting but heretofore largely untold story how this globalization process unfolded, and the important events and people behind it. The story, as recounted in Chapters 6 through 11, rests on four pillars: the International Labour Organization (ILO), the International Industrial Relations Association (IIRA), the leading role in industrial relations played by the United States in the years after the Second World War, and the spread of industrialism, market economies, trade union movements and democratic forms of government to many non-Western nations.

Established in 1919 as part of the League of Nations, the ILO has done more than any other institution to promote the protection of basic human rights in the workplace and to improve workplace conditions and relations between managers and workers in nations across the world. In an important way, therefore, the ILO opened the door and prepared the way for the spread of the industrial relations field to the many other countries outside the Anglo-American group. But the link between the ILO and the industrial relations field is much closer than this. An examination of the history of the ILO and the field of industrial relations reveals that the two are practically fraternal twins, in the sense that they were born at the same time, were born of the same events (fear of the Labour Problem, a reform movement to improve the conditions of labour), and share many of the same basic intellectual, policy and ideological principles. The ILO in the world community has thus helped directly to promote the field of industrial relations by being a global mouthpiece for many of its core ideas – freedom of association, bilateral and trilateral mechanisms for representation and voice, minimum standards for wages and labour conditions, and respect for the human essence of labour.

The second actor in the globalization of industrial relations is the IIRA. Although the ILO had brought to international attention the cause of improved labour conditions in the workplace, in the world community of the early 1960s teaching and research on workplace issues in many countries was still fragmented and often largely non-existent. Further, no forum existed to promote cross-national research and dialogue on workplace issues, leaving scholars largely isolated in their home countries. The ILO was thus engaged in the practical and policy ends of workplace reform, but its leaders found they had a very small supporting foundation of academic research and applied policy analysis to draw upon. On the academic side, in the late 1950s and early 1960s a small group of prominent industrial relations researchers in North America and the United Kingdom began a series of research projects on cross-national comparisons of work systems and labour movements and quickly came to realize that the international dimension of industrial relations was woefully neglected.

In 1966 the two sides came together and established the IIRA. On the ILO side, Robert Cox, director of the International Institute for Labour Studies (IILS) in the ILO, was the prime mover; on the academic side, Ben Roberts from the London School of Economics was his counterpart. A significant contribution was also made by Gerald Somers, acting as a representative of the American-based Industrial Relations Research Association (IRRA), while in the background other important scholars, such as Arthur Ross, Jean Daniel Reynaud and Ichiro Nakayama, also participated. The IIRA was chartered to promote cross-national dialogue and exchange of ideas. With headquarters at the ILO in Geneva, Switzerland, the four founding institutional members of the IIRA were the British University Industrial Relations Association (BUIRA), the IRRA (United States), the Japan Institute of Labor (JIL) and the IILS. The Association organized tri-annual World Congresses, which brought together scholars and researchers from around the world and actively promoted the establishment of industrial relations programmes, conferences, and national associations in individual nations. Illustrative of its success, the number of institutional members in the IIRA grew from the original four in 1966 to 60 in 2004, while individual membership grew to nearly 1,000, drawn from more than 80 countries.

The third catalyst in the globalization of industrial relations is the dominant economic and intellectual position played by the United States in the post-Second World War world community. As a formal institutionalized entity, industrial relations was born in the United States and remained largely an American phenomenon into the 1950s. The field could easily have remained confined to the United States, except that the nation emerged from the Second World War as the undisputed world power and economic and intellectual leader of the non-communist bloc.

Seeking to rebuild their universities and labour–management systems, countries of war-torn Europe and Asia looked to the United States for models, expertise and training. The model the United States had to share was industrial relations, and numerous European and Asian academics, government officials, union leaders and employee relations managers came to the United States to obtain training and oftentimes an industrial relations degree from one of the new industrial relations centres and institutes. Naturally, when they returned to their home countries they helped propagate the field and practice of industrial relations there.

Also at work was another, quite different influence. The goal of the United States was to stabilize and democratize the countries of Europe and Asia as part of the Cold War battle against Soviet communism. Fearful that the Soviets would exploit labour radicalism and conflict, the American government saw industrial relations as a useful weapon in this battle. Thus, through scholar exchange programmes, foreign aid, targeted research funding and other measures, the United States government proactively encouraged the transference of the American industrial relations model to a wide range of other countries as part of its larger geopolitical strategy.

The globalization of industrial relations was also stimulated by a fourth important factor – the spread of industrialism, market economies, trade union movements and political democracy. While work is ubiquitous to human life, the topic areas within industrial relations – the organization and management of work, the terms and conditions of work, the impact of the work experience of employees, and the role of labour unions and governments in mediating and improving the relations between employers and employees – only come to the fore in nation states that have moved beyond the traditional economic base of agriculture, family labour, handicrafts and personal services. Thus, as national economies in Africa, the Asia Pacific, Latin America and the Middle East progressively develop modern industry, an urban-based wage labour force and trade union movements, and become increasingly exposed to national and international market forces, these countries also develop greater interest in the field of industrial relations and seek to become more involved in it through education, research, business and policy-making.

The spread of greater political democracy and protection of human rights among countries on all continents has also helped spur the internationalization of the industrial relations field, given the latter's normative commitment to certain core ethical principles, such as freedom of association, freedom of speech, and the sanctity of law and due process. Where political regimes are authoritarian and repressive, industrial relations is seldom welcomed.

In the concluding chapter, Chapter 12, I summarize the main themes contained in the preceding chapters and draw conclusions and implications about the past, present and future of industrial relations as a field of study. Perhaps of most interest, this book necessarily deals at some length with the challenges and threats facing the industrial relations field and the reasons for its substantial decline in a number of countries in recent years. Paradoxically, while the globalization of industrial relations extended the field's reach and number of participants to many new countries, at the same time the membership base and intellectual vitality of the field was seriously eroding in the country of its birth – the United States – and was under significant threat in the rest of its original Anglo-American base. Indeed, so severe had this threat become in some countries that IIRA president John Niland was moved to observe in his 1994 presidential address, "It is not being overly dramatic to wonder whether the discipline will survive much beyond the year 2000."

The contributing factors behind the decline of the industrial relations field are well known – the long-term downward trend in union density and political power in many countries, a diminution of class conflict and major forms of labour unrest, the rise of human resource management as a rival field of study, the ascendancy of free-market, neoclassical economics, the rise of individualism and neo-liberalism in national and world politics and the concomitant retreat of the various "social" and "coordinated" forms of economic organization (e.g., the American "New Deal" model, the European social-democratic and social-market economy models). These forces are not equally present in all countries and, indeed, industrial relations continues to prosper and grow in some, but the overall trend is unmistakable and worrisome.

How did a field that once claimed jurisdiction over "all aspects of work" get into this predicament? What is the outlook for industrial relations, and can the field stabilize or even rebound and grow in the years ahead? Are there core intellectual ideas and institutions in industrial relations that retain their centrality to the modern world of work and employment? The remaining chapters seek to provide evidence and insight on these important and much debated questions, and I draw the threads of the argument together in the final chapter to provide answers and implications. Getting from here to there, however, requires spanning a period of more than 200 years of history and developments and events in several dozen countries.

Notes
  [1] Short but useful comparative accounts of the development of the industrial relations field are given by Adams (1993a) and Elvander (2002).

THE ROOTS OF INDUSTRIAL RELATIONS
1

Industrial relations did not emerge as a recognized field of study and area of vocational practice in industry until approximately 1920, appearing first in the United States. Its roots go back 150 years, however, to the dawn of the Industrial Revolution in Great Britain. In this chapter, I sketch the historical antecedents of industrial relations, describing important events, people and ideas that contributed to the birth of the field. The focus is almost entirely on Europe and North America, since industrialism was either largely non-existent or quite new in the rest of the world.

The Industrial Revolution

A field of industrial relations would not exist except for the combined effect of three interrelated "revolutions" that spanned the late eighteenth and nineteenth centuries. The first is the Industrial Revolution.

The beginning date of the Industrial Revolution is a matter of debate among historians, but one commonly cited candidate is 1769 – the year James Watt filed a patent for the steam engine and Richard Arkwright one for the cotton-spinning waterframe (Kindleberger, 1990: 104). What is not a matter of debate is that the country of origin of the Industrial Revolution was England.

Before the Industrial Revolution, the great share of economic activity and population in all nations of the world was in agriculture. Urban areas were small and the workforce engaged as artisans, tradesmen, common labourers, and domestics and servants. As a result, most of the workforce was dispersed, working as tenant farmers or peasants on a small plot of land, at home spinning thread or weaving cloth, in a small workshop with a handful of other craftsmen or out on the street peddling goods. Even at this time a significant number of people worked for wages, but the relationship between employer and employee was generally personal and often close – as between a master craftsmen, the journeymen and apprentices in his shop. People worked long hours, were exposed to harsh conditions and treatment, and many lived close to the margin of subsistence, but many also had considerable autonomy in their work, close personal contact with family and workmates, and opportunities for time off due to seasonal slow periods, religious holidays and personal predilections.

Over the next century and a half, the Industrial Revolution completely transformed economic and social life in northern Europe and North America, and began to do so in other countries, such as India, Italy, Japan and Russia, to which it had been recently introduced. With respect to understanding modern industrial relations, there are four aspects of the Industrial Revolution that deserve emphasis.

The first is that across all nations and periods the Industrial Revolution contained certain common features. At its core, the Industrial Revolution was driven by a series of interconnected developments in technology and organization (Crouzet, 2001). On the technology front, core characteristics were a cumulative process of invention and innovation, the substitution of machinery for human labour, the discovery of new chemical and metallurgical processes, and the harnessing of new forms of energy to production. The Industrial Revolution was also an organizational revolution. The epitome was the emergence of the factory and, somewhat later, the large corporation. In contrast to the small workshops of traditional industry, a factory brings together in one place a large concentration of fixed capital, hundreds and even thousands of workers, a central power source, and a tightly coordinated, interdependent production process featuring control by a hierarchy of management and a detailed division of labour on the factory floor. The corporation allows the pooling of capital from thousands of investors, making possible the development of giant steel companies, cross-national railways and multinational trading companies.

The second important feature of the Industrial Revolution is the spread and development of free labour markets and a contract-based employer–employee relationship. As industrialization progressed, social and economic relations passed from one of "status" to "contract", labour became a commodity, albeit a human one, and was increasingly bought and sold in markets (Polanyi, 1944; Biernacki, 1995). Accompanying the growth of labour markets was labour mobility, evidenced in large-scale movements of people from rural to urban areas and waves of emigration from the Old World to the New World. As factories and corporations developed, so too did the employer–employee relationship and the proportion of people working for wages. As home production and artisanal workshops gave way to large-scale mines, mills and factories, hundreds and thousands of workers were grouped together in one enterprise under the centralized control of an owner and cadre of managers.

The third important feature of industrialism and the Industrial Revolution is the diversity in national experiences and development profiles. While the Industrial Revolution had common core elements, no two countries followed the same path of industrial development over the nineteenth century. One element of diversity was the timing of industrialization – the United Kingdom began first, followed by France and the United States and, later in the nineteenth century, by Germany. By the end of the nineteenth century, however, the United States was the industrial leader, and in many areas Germany had surpassed the United Kingdom (Mathias and Postan, 1978). A second element of diversity was the role of the state in industrial development. More so than continental Europe, the United Kingdom and the United States followed not only in theory but also in practice a policy of laissez-faire, emphasizing individualism, volunteerism, private ordering and the primacy of market forces. Although Germany and France in the first half of the nineteenth century were also attracted to the model of economic liberalism, over the rest of the century they (and other countries, such as Japan) gravitated toward a more state-guided model of capitalism in which the free play of market forces and individualism were more highly regulated and structured by government, employers' associations, trade unions and industrial cartels.

Finally, a fourth feature of industrialism important for understanding the development of industrial relations is its concentration in a relatively small handful of countries. One hundred years after its birth, industrialism was still a feature limited primarily to northern Europe and North America. At the beginning of the twentieth century, for example, 80 per cent of the world's industrial production was concentrated in four countries with less than 10 per cent of the world's population: Germany, France, the United Kingdom and the United States (Rostow, 1978: 49). Today, as we start the twenty-first century, there are still dozens of countries that have only started or part-way progressed with the industrialization process.

The democratic revolution

Accompanying the Industrial Revolution was a parallel revolution in political governance and social concern for human rights. Like the Industrial Revolution, the roots of the democratic revolution first took hold in England, stretching back several centuries to the Magna Carta and, thereafter, the slow but cumulatively significant devolution of sovereignty from monarch to House of Commons. Although the British started the movement toward democracy, the transformative break point (or revolution) in the theory and practice of political governance took place in France and the United States in the late eighteenth century.

In an act of rebellion against the British, the American colonists issued the Declaration of Independence in 1776. It proclaimed to the world a startlingly new doctrine: "We hold these truths to be self-evident, that all men are created equal, that they are endowed by their Creator with certain unalienable Rights, that among these are Life, Liberty and the pursuit of Happiness. That to secure these rights, Governments are instituted among Men, deriving their just powers from the consent of the governed." Slightly more than a decade later, France also embarked on revolution, aimed not against a tyrannous foreign power but an oppressive social oligarchy of king, nobility and Church. In terms of influence on other countries, the French Revolution was of far greater significance and its manifesto of personal liberty and freedom, contained in the Declaration of the Rights of Man (1789), had a more galvanizing effect on the peoples of Europe. It declared "Men are born and remain free and equal in rights ... The aim of all political association is the preservation of the natural and imprescriptible rights of man."

Today democracy is deeply institutionalized and a core value in many countries of the world; in numerous others the words of the two Declarations are honoured neither in principle nor practice. If democracy is an incomplete project in the current age, in the years preceding the American and French Revolutions it was a completely unknown and untried idea, regarded by many as dangerous, foolhardy and utopian. At the time, Great Britain alone had an elected House of Parliament, though suffrage was restricted to the wealthy and landowners and the executive power remained in the hands of King George III. Across the rest of the world, including the other European powers, governance was invested in kings, emperors, czars, maharajas and other potentates who exercised autocratic, largely unrestricted power on the basis of heredity, religious appointment, military conquest or personal power. To these leaders, the land and people were under their dominion, existed to serve the needs and interests of themselves and the ruling elite, and could be taxed, conscripted, confiscated or killed as deemed appropriate. Justice was personal, arbitrary and often tilted in favour of the powerful – a political system of absolutism, constrained to a degree by a web of social and religious obligations but at bottom operating according to principles of "might makes right" and "rules by men, not law".

In many nations of the world, tyranny and political subjection went even further. Since the beginning of human history, serfdom and slavery have been widely practised and accepted as a natural order of affairs (Friedlaender and

Oser, 1953; Stanley, 1998). Serfdom still existed in eastern and southern Europe in the first half of the nineteenth century, and in various forms was widespread in East Asia and Latin America. Slavery was also widely practised, particularly in the New World into the 1880s, where more than ten million black Africans were forcibly brought to work on plantations and agricultural estates. The idea that slavery was immoral and a fundamental affront to human rights only first surfaced in a significant way with the abolitionist movements in the United Kingdom and the United States in the early 1800s, and was seen by many as an equally radical and utopian notion. The British Abolition of the Slave Trade Act (1807) and Slavery Abolition Act (1833), and the Emancipation Proclamation (1863) issued by President Lincoln, stand in this regard as additional landmarks on the path to democracy and human rights.

The pace and extent of democratization varied widely in the Western world over the nineteenth century, while other regions of the world remained in the grip of absolutism and feudalism of various forms and proportions. Crucial to the story of industrial relations is that the implementation of political democracy and representative government developed earliest and most widely in two particular nations of the West: the United Kingdom and the United States. The United States does not have a feudal past and the rigid patterns of class hierarchy, inequality and political hegemony of a hereditary elite that go with it – with the notable exception of the slavery of black Africans. Great Britain also made considerable progress in moving beyond its feudal heritage through a 300-year process of incremental reform. Without armed struggle, the United States had granted universal white male suffrage by the 1830s, while the British moved progressively in this direction with acts of Parliament in 1832, 1867 and 1884. Both countries, by 1920, had universal suffrage (Sturmthal, 1953: 20). By these actions, the United Kingdom and the United States gave a measure of political influence to the lower strata of the social hierarchy, such as wage earners, who earlier had no effective voice other than direct acts of violence and street protest. With political liberalization, and the development of industry and trade, also came another crucial development – the emergence and growth of a middle class.

In continental Europe, the pace and spread of democracy over the nineteenth century was considerably slower and less complete. In most other parts of the world, democracy was largely unknown even at the beginning of the twentieth century.

In continental Europe, the democratic process began in France but was largely aborted when Napoleon declared himself emperor and, after his defeat at Waterloo in 1815, the country returned to a limited form of monarchy. In the 1820s, only 80,000 Frenchmen out of an electorate of 27 million had voting rights, while the three traditional estates of nobility, clergy and burghers retained their privileged and largely impermeable social position (Friedlaender and Oser, 1953: 8). In 1848, the French attempted another revolution, deposed Louis Philippe, and four years later had another emperor, Napoleon III. France had yet another attempt at revolution in 1871, led by leftist radicals and centred on the short-lived Paris Commune. It was brutally repressed, with 20,000 dead and 50,000 sent to trial. With the founding of the Third Republic, France began to inaugurate a limited form of parliamentary democracy.

Democracy was also very slow in coming to Germany in the nineteenth century. The German principalities in the early 1800s were ruled by monarchs, the peasants were not freed from serfdom in Prussia until 1807, and remnants of feudalism did not disappear until mid-century. Like France, Germany experienced a revolutionary revolt against absolutism in 1848, which after much bloodshed was defeated. Only with the establishment of the Second Empire in 1871 was Germany united, governed by a hereditary monarch Emperor (Kaiser) Wilhelm I, an appointed Chancellor, Prince Otto von Bismarck, and an elected parliament (Reichstag). Parliament, however, had weak powers and the electoral system gave most voting power to the landed aristocracy (the Junkers).

In Belgium, manual workers did not gain suffrage rights until 1893 and the electoral rules were gerrymandered in favour of the upper and middle classes; in the Austro-Hungarian Empire, the government remained in the hands of aristocrats until the First World War; Italy was only united and gained parliamentary democracy in the 1860s; Sweden was ruled by a monarch and only substantially extended the suffrage in 1902 after a mass political strike; Spain in the late 1800s was governed by a monarch and parliament tightly controlled by a landed oligarchy; and Russia was under the autocratic control of a czar, with Russian society divided between a small but wealthy aristocracy and a large peasant population only barely out of feudalism.

Although the actual establishment of democracy was slow and halting in these countries, the idea of democracy gradually spread and gained irresistible momentum throughout the West. It also changed the way people looked at the world of work. In the early part of the nineteenth century, according to E.P. Thompson (1964: 90), Thomas Paine's radical political tract, *Rights of man* (1791–2), was "a foundation-text of the English working class". These once heretical ideas gradually spread and deepened as institutions of political democracy took hold, leading workers to question the juxtaposition of democratic rights in the political sphere but continued autocracy and denial of basic human and civil rights in the mill and factory. It appeared that the "divine right of kings" was passing from the scene, while the "divine right of capitalists" still reigned unchallenged. Thus, the Industrial Revolution and democratic revolution slowly joined together, creating toward the end of the nineteenth century a growing awareness of and demand for *industrial democracy*. One early proponent explained it as (quoted in Montgomery, 1993: 28) "the conscious or unconscious effort on the part of workers to extend into the industrial field the political democracy which we have, as a result of the struggle of ages", while another (ibid., p. 25) said of it "Industry, like government, exists only by the cooperation of all, and like government, it must guarantee equal protection to all."

The capitalist revolution

A third revolution starting in the late eighteenth century that fundamentally shaped the origin and history of industrial relations is the emergence and rise of capitalism and the spread of a market economy.

Capitalism and a market economy are distinct but nonetheless tightly linked by their common foundation on the social instruments of private property and freedom of contract. Private property is a foundation stone of capitalism for the system is based on private ownership of the means of production and their use for personal profit. Freedom of contract, in turn, is essential to profit making for it allows private individuals to exploit new economic opportunities and reap gains from trade through unimpeded exchange of property rights. Such exchange is, in turn, greatly facilitated by the creation of markets so buyers and sellers of property rights can meet, negotiate and consummate mutually advantageous trades.

The birth of capitalism is not marked by a single event or book, but the birth of a market economy can more easily be dated. And, by remarkable coincidence, the birth year is 1776 – the same year as the American Declaration of Independence. The key event is the publication of Scotsman Adam Smith's book *The wealth of nations*. The Declaration of Independence was at once a revolt against the abuse and injustice of monopoly power exercised by monarchs and the aristocratic elite in the political sphere and a manifesto for the benefits to be had from the alternative system of representative democracy. Smith's *The wealth of nations* performed the same dual role in the economic realm – a penetrating critique of the waste, injustice and denial of liberty inherent in the mercantile system of economic monopoly and state regulation, accompanied by brilliant exposition of the individual and social benefits to be reaped from allowing self-interest, profit making and market forces to have relatively free play. One document makes the case for political liberalism, the other for economic liberalism.

As described in a later part of this chapter, whether a capitalist market economy works with the social beneficence claimed by Smith was a highly contested issue in the nineteenth and early twentieth centuries and remains controversial today. Few people then or now would dispute, however, that the new capitalist system quickly undermined the remains of the old feudal order and ushered in an era of historically unprecedented growth. Even Marx and Engels, in their radical critique contained in the *Communist manifesto*, pay tribute to capitalism and competitive markets, saying of the former (Feuer, 1959: 12): "The bourgeoisie [owners of capital], during its rule of scarce one hundred years, has created more massive and more colossal productive forces than have all preceding generations together", and of the latter (p. 8): "Modern industry has established the world market. ... This market has given an immense development to commerce, to navigation, to communication."

Equally important, the confluence of capitalism, a market-ordered economy and industrialism together created the fundamental social relations and conditions that were to later become the core organizing concepts and raison d'être for the field of industrial relations.

Most central is the employment relationship. Neither in feudalism nor in an agricultural and handicraft economy of self-employed farmers and artisans is there an employment relationship. Such an economy will have commercial relations but not industrial relations, at least as that term is generally conceived. The employment relation is a natural outgrowth of capitalism, for in such a system the means of production are privately owned by one group (or class) of people, acting as employers, who pay another group of people, the employees, to provide labour in the form of work. The employers then take the output and sell it for profit. As the process of industrialism proceeds, the size of capitalist enterprise increases, leading to a concomitant expansion of the employment relationship and number of people who earn their living by working for others.

Also central to a capitalist, industrial, market economy are the labour market and wage relation. In an industrial enterprise, the capitalist's own labour is not sufficient to produce the needed scale of output so they must obtain additional labour elsewhere. The institution that mediates between the employer's demand for labour and the worker's supply of labour is the labour market. The labour market may be a physically constituted place, or a geographical area over which competition for labour takes place, but in either case it is the locus for trade in labour. All forms of trade involve a process of bargaining, negotiating and "higgling", and the operation of the labour market is no different. In the bargaining process, the consideration usually given most prominence is the price of labour – the wage – whose level is affected by all those variables that influence the bargaining power of the two parties, such as financial resources, range of alternatives in the market, and costs of failing to reach agreement. In the employment relation, the wage is the cost of labour to the employer and affects production cost and profit, while to the employee the wage is the sole or predominant source of income and means of survival. In its economic dimension, therefore, the employment relation is also a wage relation.

When labour is traded in markets, it inevitably takes on the character of a commodity, like wheat or steel. As with wheat or steel, capitalists desire to obtain labour at the lowest possible price, while the suppliers of labour – like the suppliers of wheat and steel – desire to sell at the highest possible price. Intrinsic to the employment relationship, therefore, is a conflict of interest between the two parties, which creates an adversarial relation between employer and employee and an inevitable "win–lose" (zero-sum) dimension to the wage determination process. Both parties are, of course, also aware that they gain from cooperation, since only through cooperation is a product produced and profits earned and wages paid (a "win–win" or positive sum). Thus, in general, the employment relation is a combination of these two elements, conflict and cooperation (or a "mixed motive").

Although labour is traded in markets much like any other commodity, it is in certain respects a unique commodity because the labour is embodied in and inseparable from the human being who supplies it. Once suppliers of inanimate objects such as wheat and steel sell their goods, they have no reason to care if the wheat is stored in a cold or hot place or the steel is treated with dignity or harshness by the new owner. The situation is very different for the seller of labour, however. The seller of labour is inseparable from the labour itself and must be physically present at the point of production and personally experience whether the work is onerous or pleasant, the room is hot or cold and the employer is fair or grasping. This fact makes the labour exchange far more complex, as many additional considerations enter into the negotiations between buyer and seller, and of far greater social significance since flesh-and-blood people are being utilized in production.

The human essence of labour creates yet another unique aspect in the capitalist employment relation. What the employer buys with the wage is a certain amount of time of the employee; however, it is not time that produces output and earns a profit but the amount and intensity of physical and mental effort (or work). The amount of work provided by the employee, however, is to some degree discretionary, whatever may have been the agreements and understandings on this matter at the time of hiring. There is, consequently, a potentially large divergence between the labour input bought by the employer and the actual labour power provided by the employee. Part of the employer's goal is thus to manage the labour process (the conversion of labour input into labour power and a product) as efficiently and effectively as possible, given that doing so adds to profit. To obtain maximum efficiency in the labour process, the employer will use various methods and practices, such as close supervision, incentives and bonuses, and threats and penalties. These generally fall under the rubric of personnel/human resource management. Because the employment relation inevitably rests on an incomplete contract, a certain amount of implicit jockeying and bargaining always takes place between employer and employee, while room for misunderstandings and opportunistic behaviour abounds.

A final important feature of the capitalist employment relation is that it establishes between the employer and employee an asymmetric authority relation. When bargaining in the labour market, the employer and employee are legal (if not economic) equals and, thus, one party cannot compel agreement by the other. Once the employment contract is concluded, however, the relationship changes and the employer becomes the legal superior and the employee the legal inferior (or subordinate). Expressed differently, the employer becomes the boss or "order giver" and the employee becomes the "order taker".

In nineteenth-century British common law, the nature of the authority relation was well captured by the term "master and servant". Evidently, therefore, the employment relation embodies both an economic relation between employer and employee (coming from the labour market and wage bargain) and a political relation grounded on the employer's authority to command performance and set the rules, terms and conditions of work. In early capitalism, prevailing legal thought and popular opinion held that the workplace was the private property of employers, thus giving them relatively unrestricted authority to hire, fire and run the workshop as they pleased. Despite the growing democratic impulse in the nineteenth century, the traditional governance system remained one of industrial autocracy – sometimes exercised in a harsh and inhumane way and in other cases in a more paternalistic or enlightened manner, but always at the discretion and command of the employer.

Class, conflict and unions

The Industrial Revolution and the spread of capitalism and a market economy brought with them many pluses and minuses for workers and society. On the plus side, over the long run, industrialism led to a marked increase in a number of basic indicators of well-being. Over the nineteenth century, for example, average life expectancy substantially increased, real per capita income doubled and tripled, hours of work declined from 12–14 per day to 9–10, and working conditions noticeably improved (Floud and McCloskey, 1994). It seems fair to state that few workers in the steel mills and coal mines of 1900, even given the onerous and poorly paid nature of their labour, would have voluntarily chosen to return to the work conditions of 100 years earlier.

Paradoxically, therefore, all of the industrial countries of western Europe and North America were gripped in the late 1800s and early 1900s by a wave of labour conflict, growth of far-left political parties of various socialist, communist and syndicalist stripes, and open talk of abolishing capitalism and the wage system through a worker-led revolution (Geary, 1981). How could the apparent success of industrialism and capitalism spawn such a backlash?

The answer forces one to look at the many negative features of industrialism and capitalism, as perceived and experienced by working people. From the very beginning, the Industrial Revolution brought with it a variety of abuses and hardships on workers. The early decades of the nineteenth century were widely known as the "age of pauperism" because of the vast poverty and lack of work (Beck, 1995). According to contemporary estimates (cited in Thompson, 1964: 249–50), one-third to one-half of the workforce in England in the 1830s did not have regular gainful employment. Living conditions in cities of France in this period were so wretched that one contemporary observer stated (quoted in Pillbeam, 2000: 24), "At 20, people thrived, or they were dead."

Those lucky enough to have jobs faced very onerous conditions. One father testified to factory commissioners in England that his two sons (aged 10 and 13) left home at half-past five in the morning, had a 30-minute dinner break, and regularly worked until nine or ten at night, and yet brought home pay only one-half that of an agricultural labourer (Knight et al., 1928: 396). Regarding work conditions in the textile mills, a medical doctor stated in the early 1830s (Kay, 1970: 7):

> The operatives are congregated in rooms and workshops during the twelve hours in the day, in an enervating, heated atmosphere, which is frequently loaded with dust or filaments of cotton ... They are drudges who watch the movements, and assist the operations, of a mighty material force ... The persevering labour of the operative must rival the mathematical precision, the incessant motion, the exhaustless power of the machine.

Conditions such as these were not unique to England or the early nineteenth century and were slow to disappear even after a half-century of economic development and progress. Illustrative are these reflections of an American employed as a factory hand at the Detroit Stove Works in 1898. He states (Lescohier, 1960: 32–3):

> Working in factories during the 1890s, or indeed, up to the time of the First World War, was very different from working in factories today. In the first place, the method of hiring the unorganized was for foremen to come to the front gate of the plant around 7a.m., look over the gang of men congregated outside the gate, pick out men he knew or thought he wanted, or motion to this man or that, without interviewing, to come through the plant gate. It was a good deal like a butcher picking out particular animals from a herd.
>
> When he got as many as he wanted he led them to his department, assigned them their work, with perhaps momentary interviews to find out whether they had any experience in the kinds of work in his department. Ordinarily a man hired in this process did not know what his pay would be until he got his wages on payday. If you asked the foreman that question when you were hired you would, ordinarily, be shown the gate. Complete submission of unorganized workers to the company was the expectation of the Detroit Stove Works. Like hundreds of other common labourers I had heard the foreman say to me: "Put on your coat," which meant that you were fired. You did as he said.
>
> In the basement of the building where I worked at that time was a grinding room. The only artificial light was old fashioned gas lights, one above and between each pair of grinding wheels. It was in almost complete darkness – say dark twilight – since the gas flames gave so little light. You had to walk slowly and keep a hand out in front of you to avoid falling over a truck handle or other obstruction.
>
> The stock room where I worked was a corner partitioned off from the metal polishing department. On the side toward the polishing room were large removable windows which allowed light to come through the stock room to the polishers – who were skilled, union men. The windows also let in the south and southwest summer breezes. The polishers asked to have the windows opened each day during the summer so they could feel those breezes. The company refused. The polishers went out on strike to force the company to remove the windows. When one union struck, they all did. So a plant with 2500 employees was tied up for three days over this simple grievance. But striking was the only grievance procedure the men had and only the union men had that.

The conditions described above were, in actual fact, far from the worst. Nor were they confined to the industrial countries of the West. After a violent strike at the Ashio Copper Mining Company in 1907, the Japanese government conducted an investigation. According to the official account (quoted in Sumiya, 1990: 27),

There were few officials who did not wield their authority in arbitrary fashion, and lead lives of mounting luxury, always greedy for bribe money. All the worse were those among them who went out and actively sought bribes and, on the strength of the money received, altered a worker's pay or the degree of ease or hardship of his job. If, unable to bear the injustice, a worker refused an official's order, he would be dismissed from work on the spot, sent away from the mine, and so at once lose his means of livelihood. The workers had no choice but to submit to the hard labor, wiping their tears and choking back their voices. They did this for these long years – which had pushed the bitter resentment, for which they had no outlet, almost to the breaking point.

Without denying the many benefits both individual and social that accrued over the nineteenth and early twentieth centuries from the spread of industrialism and capitalism, one can still appreciate from these quotations that for tens of millions of workers daily life was deeply insecure, harsh and unjust. This common experience led to three mutually related developments of fundamental importance for the future field of industrial relations. They were the growth and emergence of working-class consciousness, worker-led protests and strikes, and worker-created trade unions. The common denominator among them is resort to collective action.

According to Thompson (1964: 9), class consciousness arises when "some men, as a result of common experiences (inherited or shared), feel and artic-ulate the identity of their interests as between themselves, and as against other men whose interests are different from (and usually opposed to) theirs". In the early nineteenth century, social divisions in the United Kingdom and Europe were sharp and well recognized, but were still in flux from a feudal order to a capitalist order. Thus it was common to differentiate between the "upper classes" and the "lower classes", and perhaps to identify working people as part of the "productive class", but the concept of a "working class" had not yet formed. Even well into the nineteenth century, it should be noted, feudal class distinctions remained strong in eastern and southern Europe, where most people were still peasants, in Japan, where feudalism only ended in the 1860s, and India, where the caste system continued well into the twentieth century. Of all nations in the world, the United States had the weakest social divisions, reflecting its republican and immigrant heritage and wide-open frontier.

Over the course of the nineteenth century, as capitalism and industrialism proceeded, a distinct working class emerged, defined both objectively in terms of common attributes (e.g., a wage earner) and (more importantly) in terms of individual consciousness and perceived experience. Furthermore, central to the working-class consciousness was not only a sense of being separate and distinct but also excluded, exploited and repressed. Speaking of the growing class divisions among the British, future prime minister Disraeli (1845) wrote that the nation was "divided, as nearly as possible, into two classes – the very rich and the very poor", while Thompson (1964: 198) states, "We can now see ... some of the reasons why the English working class took form in these years. The people were subjected simultaneously to an intensification of two intolerable forms of relationship: those of economic exploitation and of political oppression." Five decades later Sidney and Beatrice Webb (quoted in Dickman, 1987: 104) state, "What the workers are objecting to ... is a ... feudal system of industry, ... of the domination of the mass of ordinary workers by a hierarchy of property owners." Explicit in the statement of the Webbs is the view that feudalism had not disappeared but only changed form.

Class lines were even more firmly drawn in continental Europe. Illustrative are these words of Adolf Sturmthal (1972: 4):

> To regard the European capitalistic society as riddled with class privileges and organized to keep the worker in his place required no profound social analysis; it corresponded with the everyday experience of the worker. The dominant institutions of the European society in which modern industry developed emphasized the virtue of submission to its hierarchical order. Not only was it difficult to move up the social order, it was unbecoming as well.

Even in America, where class lines were least sharply drawn, by the end of the nineteenth century it was widely recognized that a large working class had formed and that it festered with discontents and grievances. Socialist Daniel DeLeon articulated the feelings of many when he said (Dickman, 1987: 109), "The working class and the employing class have nothing in common. ... The condition of the Working Class is one of hunger, want and privation, that from bad it is getting worse and ever worse." Although America's democratic political institutions were intended to bridge class lines and provide participation and influence to workers, they did so only imperfectly for, in the pithy words of Thorstein Veblen (1904: 286), "representative government means, chiefly, representation of business interests".

Accompanying the growth of a working class in the industrializing countries was a parallel growth in conflict and violence in industry and the haunting spectre of working-class revolution. Prior to the birth of capitalism and industrialism, large-scale protests and outbreaks of violence on the part of commoners were generally not directed at employers or the workplace per se, but more often took the form of food riots or mob actions against hated landlords and tax collectors (Rudé, 1964). With the development of industry in the nineteenth century and a growing body of wage earners, the locus and form of conflict shifted. Increasingly, conflict came spilling out of the workshops and factories as workers came to locate their major source of grievance and injustice in conditions of work and the actions of the capitalist employers.

Often, the conflict at the end of the century resembled that of earlier decades in that it tended to take the form of relatively spontaneous and disorganized protests and mob action. The early nineteenth century had seen the machine-smashing binge of Ned Ludd and associates in England; another is the unannounced walk-outs and street demonstrations staged by French workers, the latter done less to win a particular demand than to warn their employers "We can only be pushed so far!" (Sewell, 1986). As the century progressed, industrial conflict became more frequent, more organized, and conducted on a larger scale. Geary (1981: 105) states, for example, "there can be no doubt that industrial disputes reached unprecedented proportions after the turn of the century. Britain saw massive strikes on the railways and in the docks, ... in France the first effective industry-wide strikes were staged in 1902 [and] ... in 1905 no fewer than three-quarters of Ruhr miners downed their tools in the same dispute." Also illustrative is the Pullman railroad strike in 1894 in the United States, involving 150,000 strikers and spanning 27 states.

Organized labour strikes and protests also grew in violence and political radicalism as the nineteenth century progressed. Some of these strikes started out as workplace disputes and escalated into pitched battles or "labour wars", sometimes resulting in large loss of life, destruction of property and use of armed militia to restore order (Lens, 1974; Clegg, 1985). The Cambrian Coal Mining Strike of 1911 in Wales and the Homestead Steel Strike of 1892 in the United States are exemplars. In other cases, large-scale strikes were staged for overtly political and even revolutionary goals, sometimes led by socialists or communists preaching class struggle and proletarian overthrow of the capitalist system. Belgium and Sweden both had nationwide general strikes around the turn of the century over overtly political demands, resulting in the case of Belgium in half of the industrial workforce taking to the streets and an escalation of conflict into rioting and bloodshed (Slomp, 1990: 51). A series of general strikes called by socialists and anarchists also roiled France, Italy and Spain in the late 1800s and early 1900s, while in 1905 the general strike in Russia was a key stage in the revolution to overthrow the czar.

Accompanying class and conflict in the nineteenth century was the development and growth of trade unions and national labour movements. Although workers' trade societies antedate the Industrial Revolution, it was only after 1800, with the spread of industrialism and a market economy, and the divorce of capital of labour, that trade unions started to appear in more or less modern form (Webb and Webb, 1894; Kendall, 1975). The classic definition of

29

a trade union is provided by the Webbs (1894: 1): "A Trade Union, as we understand the term, is a continuous association of wage earners for the purpose of maintaining or improving the conditions of their employment." In this role, the principal activity of a trade union is collective bargaining, a term also coined by Beatrice Webb.

As Richard Hyman (2001a) points out, this conception of trade unions reflects British (and American) experience at the time and does not fully capture their different roles and activities, particularly in other countries and continents. Unions, in his view, seek to advance their members' interests at three levels: market, class and society. Their market (economic) function is to represent and advance the employment interests of their members through collective bargaining and workplace representation, gaining improved wages and conditions and providing workers with voice and protection in the shop. In their class function, unions battle for the rights and interests of all workers in society, attempting to increase their status, power and opportunity in the nation's economic and political system. Often seeing the social system as dominated by the rich and powerful, and set up so workers are in a subordinate position, unions in their class function seek through broad-based reform or revolution to bring greater freedom and power to labour. In this sense, they are in effect leaders of a workers' emancipation or even liberation movement. In their social function, unions work within the system to improve workers' overall social quality of life and promote greater social justice and inclusion, such as through improved schools, health care, environmental protection, and programmes to fight poverty and discrimination.

The trade unions of the early nineteenth century in all the countries of Europe and North America largely started out as economic-oriented bodies, pursuing a primitive form of collective bargaining with employers to establish minimum rates of pay and a limit on hours. Most were local-based craft unions, formed by printers, shoemakers and other skilled workers in a particular occupation or trade – hence the name trade union. Helga Grebing (1969: 17) states of Germany, for example:

> Before 1850 many factories, particularly, smaller ones, had a hard struggle to survive. The burden of this struggle was generally borne by the workers, whose social conditions continued to deteriorate: the working day was increased to 13 or 14 [hours] ... spent in appalling conditions; falling wages had to be made up by women and children going out to work.

Under these conditions, workers sought some method to protect themselves and naturally were led to combine into trade unions, realizing that collective action could possibly better their position when individual action was largely hopeless. However, only the skilled workers had sufficient market power, on account of the scarcity of their skills, to maintain their new organizations and win improvements in the face of employer opposition.

The early trade unions were viewed with considerable hostility in all countries, and governments and courts took a repressive stance toward them. In the United Kingdom and the United States, for example, unions in the early nineteenth century were declared under the common law to be illegal conspiracies, while in Germany and France unionists were jailed and their organizations broken up by police and courts. As industrialism and capitalism gathered speed, so also did the ranks of the wage-earning class and their propensity to form unions. At this point occurred a historic inflection point in the labour histories of the Anglo-American countries and the countries of the European continent (Lieberman, 1986; Breuilly, 1992).

Although imperfectly done and resisted at many points, the United Kingdom and the United States from the 1830s onward chose the road of political and economic accommodation with labour, gradually extending the suffrage to the working class (more rapidly in the United States than in the United Kingdom) and removing the legal restraints on unions and collective bargaining (the United Kingdom more than the United States). By extending suffrage, all social groups knew that the wage earners, because of their size, would gain greater political power and use it to shift law and wealth in their favour, per the British trade unionists' refrain of the 1830s – "From the laws of the few have the existing inequalities sprung; by the laws of the many shall they be destroyed" (Thompson, 1964: 822). Most capitalists and wealthy landowners naturally opposed liberalization and reform, but were induced to accept it in steps by a combination of factors: relatively weak central governments which precluded effective repression, a respect for constitutionalism and democratic traditions and a fear of an even worse fate – a revolution from below and a new state built on "confiscatory Socialism" (Fox, 1985).

Also crucial was the pressure from the middle classes to accommodate labour, done partly out of progressive moral and political instincts but equally because they feared the threat that class war posed to their own newly found prosperity and social position. As a result, over the nineteenth century the United Kingdom and the United States took the road of incremental reform, gradually giving labour a greater voice in the national polity and giving trade unions enough legal space to grow and practise collective bargaining for at least a portion of the workforce. Although it remained true, in the words of one contemporary observer (quoted in Pipkin, 1927: 7), that "millions of English people feel that they have no place and no stake in their country", the process of reform and inclusion was nonetheless sufficient to keep the mainstream of the labour movements relatively pragmatic and economic-oriented, and uninterested in radical communist and socialist political solutions. The American labour movement, as a consequence, never formed a labour party, while the British Labour Party eschewed fighting for a new model of society and focused on winning greater freedom and autonomy to practise collective bargaining.

Developments in continental Europe (and, later, other countries such as Argentina, India and Japan) played out in a different direction. Feudalism and absolutism had a stronger grip in the early nineteenth century, capitalism and market economies arrived later, societies were more deeply split along class, religious and linguistic lines, and the middle classes were smaller and less liberal in outlook. As a result, Sturmthal (1972: 3) says, "Discrimination [against manual workers] extended into every phase of social life." These societies, therefore, started the process of industrialization with a more polarized and locked-in social structure, less developed and open markets and political institutions, and an employer class more steeped in elitism and authoritarianism (Spencer, 1984). As already described, one consequence was that democracy came much later to these countries; another was that governments practised much greater repression and violence against working-class political movements and trade unions; and yet another was a greater sense of class division and antagonism. As late as 1878, Germany enacted an Anti-Socialist Law that banned all political meetings and trade unions associated with socialist groups, while France banned or heavily repressed labour unions during most of the nineteenth century (Lieberman, 1986; 1970; Berger, 2000). Thus the avenue of reform and social integration was more thoroughly blocked, leading to greater political radicalization, working-class solidarity, and distrust or disdain for the promises of liberal capitalism and democracy. For these reasons, socialism and anarcho-syndicalism had far greater appeal to the working classes on the continent. The bulk of labour unions subordinated their economic and bargaining function in favour of winning socialism through political action and alliance with some form of social democratic party, and the frightened and insecure middle classes allied themselves with the landowners and industrialists, choosing the protection and order of the status quo over the risks of transferring a measure of power and legitimacy to workers and their unions (Slomp, 1996; Kocka, 1999).

The Labour Problem and the Social Question

As industrialism and capitalist development proceeded over the nineteenth century, public attention was increasingly drawn to the problems enumerated above: the low wages, long hours and deplorable conditions of manual workers; the appearance of a deepening divide and hostility between the classes of capital and labour; the growth of unions and strikes, and the rising spectre of socialist revolution. Although these problems were discussed and debated in newspapers, parliaments, learned societies and churches during the first half of the nineteenth century, they had not yet become of sufficient gravity or threat to merit being distinguished in public discourse by a new name or descriptive term of reference. This situation changed near mid-century, however, in Europe and North America and signals the earliest intellectual roots of what was seven decades later to become the field of industrial relations.

Although discussion of capital–labour relations goes back much further, the first time the topic was addressed explicitly in English-language books was the early 1850s. The most notable example is *An essay on the relations between labour and capital*, published in 1854 by Englishman Charles Morrison (a wealthy financier and businessman). Not only does the title squarely encompass what later became known as industrial relations, Morrison also develops in the book several themes and concepts of considerable significance. In the very first sentence of the book, for example, Morrison states (ed., 1972: 2, emphasis added):

> The following Essay is intended as a contribution towards the solution of the great *social problem* which has exercised so many minds in the present age, and is likely to give occupation to those of more than one succeeding generation – the discovery of the most efficacious means of improving the condition and elevating the character of the working majority of mankind. The particular part of this great subject which is treated in it is the examination of the relations between the working class and the class of employers.

An important aspect of this quotation that deserves attention is Morrison's use of the term "social problem". Relatively soon thereafter, usage of this term was modified by changing the beginning letters of each word from lower case to upper case so it became Social Problem. Illustrative is American journalist Horace Greeley's book *The Social Problem* (1856) and Englishman Charles Williams' series of four published lectures, *The great Social Problem: Four lectures on labour, capital, and wages* (1859). In continental Europe and later Japan, the corollary term Social Question was more widely used (*Soziale Frage* in German, *Question sociale* in French, and *Shakai Mondai* in Japanese), and in Europe began to appear in the 1840s (Pankoke, 1970; Pillbeam, 2000). The Social Problem in the Anglo-American countries and Social Question in Europe and Japan (and other countries) came to represent the broadest and most encompassing terms for discussions of the problems of labour and capital–labour relations. The term Social Question remained in widespread use in continental Europe until well into the twentieth century, while the term Social Problem was relatively quickly displaced in the Anglo-American countries by the alternative and more narrowly constructed term "Labour Problem" (or Labour Question). This difference in terminological usage between the Anglo-American and continental European countries – Labour Problem in the former and Social Question in the latter – is of profound importance for understanding the divergent development of the field of industrial relations in the two regions, as explained below.

The Labour Problem is the more narrow and delimited of the two concepts. Of all the different human relationships in society and problems they produce, the Labour Problem focuses attention on just one area – the labour sector and, in particular, the problems that grow out of the relations between employers and employees. As used in the nineteenth century, the Labour Problem was a term representing the fundamental clash between two powerful groups in society, capital and labour, and the strikes, violence and discord that result. By calling it *the* Labour Problem and putting the first letter of each word in upper case, writers were indicating that the clash between capital and labour is deep, fundamental and widespread, calling into question the core principles on which the relationship is built, and that it threatens major disruption to society. But by using the word "Labour" in the term, writers also separated the problem of labour and capital from other social issues and from the higher-level debate about the pros and cons of the social system as a whole. Thus it became possible in the United Kingdom and the United States to discuss the Labour Problem as a quasi-autonomous subject and substantially to separate labour policy from social policy. I emphasize the word "possible", however, for this is not a hard and fast rule. Certainly many critics of the Labour Problem in the late nineteenth century believed that only the abolition of capitalism would end the exploitation and marginalization of labour (Barnes, 1886; Dickman, 1987). In this instance, the Social Question and Labour Problem remain effectively joined, making it impossible to divorce "politics" from industrial relations. But, on the other hand, the Labour Problem concept also opens up the possibility that a significant degree of separation may be possible, particularly if the problems of capital and labour originate largely within the labour sector, can be largely solved at that level, and do not require wholesale change in the larger social system. In this situation an autonomous field devoted to the study of labour policy and capital–labour relations also becomes feasible from both an intellectual and policy perspective.

Recognizing this contingency, it remains the case that the Social Question by construction encompasses a larger intellectual space and breadth of issues than does the Labour Problem, and inevitably draws greater attention to the functionality and legitimacy of the overall social system. In Germany and France of the nineteenth century, people spoke of the Labour Problem (in German, *Arbeiterfrage*, and loosely in French, *Organization du travail*) just as they spoke of other problems, such as the National Problem and Race Problem (Ascher, 1963; Fischer, 1973). The key difference, however, is that in continental Europe all of these disparate problems were more widely regarded as inseparable and inextricably linked to the legitimacy and functionality of the overall political, economic and legal structure of society. So viewed, it is far more difficult to separate the Labour Problem from the larger Social Question, to treat the subject of labour policy as something autonomous from social policy and to look at a solution to the Labour Problem in terms of concrete, practical measures (as opposed to systemic and often revolutionary measures). Thus, in countries where the problems of capital and labour are submerged in the Social Question, an autonomous field of study devoted to labour policy and the problems of capital–labour relations inevitably appears too constrictive, narrowly conceived, and politically and ideologically committed to the status quo.

Contemporary evidence suggests that the distinction between continental Europe's "social" perspective and the Anglo-American "labour" perspective was not just a nineteenth-century phenomenon but retains explanatory power today. Thus the social partners in continental Europe become unions and employers in the Anglo-American countries, while the term "labour movement" in the latter is narrowly construed to mean the organized trade union movement but is broadly construed in the former to include all groups seeking to advance the position of labour, such as political parties, workers' social organizations and churches (Sturmthal, 1972: 1). Finally, as Hyman (2004) notes, the Anglo-American term employment relationship suggests a bilateral relationship between employer and employee, while the nearest French equivalent, *rapport salarial*, connotes a more complex relation of employer and employee within a web of social and legal obligations.

Anticipating future chapters, it is in the United Kingdom and the United States where the field of industrial relations first emerged, largely as an intellectual and policy effort to defuse and contain the Labour Problem. In continental Europe, industrial relations as a field did not emerge until after the Second World War, when these countries were able to reconstruct their social systems and effectively dispose of the Social Question (at least in its traditional form). Although the field of industrial relations did not actually appear in the United Kingdom in a formal way until the 1930s, the transition from the Social Question to the Labour Problem in the several decades after mid-century in the 1800s was crucial for preparing the way both by narrowing the subject area to labour and increasing the possibility of practical, non-revolutionary solutions. This fact is clearly evident in this statement at the beginning of the *Final report of the Royal Commission on Labour*, chartered to investigate the cause of strikes and labour–management conflict. The report states (1894: 5):

> We have not desired to restrict our inquiry within too rigid lines. At the same time it should be understood that we do not intend in this Review to survey the whole of what has been termed the 'social question,' or to undertake an examination of the fundamental causes of wealth and poverty, or to discuss the remedies by which evils and misfortunes, not directly connected with or bearing upon industrial disputes, can be met. Thus we have felt it to be our duty to examine proposals put forward for obviating the clash of industrial interests [and] our attention has chiefly been directed towards the amelioration of the relations of employers and employed.

Having marked out the distinction between the Labour Problem and Social Question, it is now useful to examine the concept of the Labour Problem in more depth. To use a French term, the Labour Problem defined the *problématique* (problematic) for what later became the field of industrial relations. A better sense for the nature of this *problématique* can be gained by returning to Morrison's pioneering book (1854).

As cited earlier, Morrison states that his central objective is "the discovery of the most efficacious means of improving the condition and elevating the character of the working majority of mankind". Then, further in the Preface, Morrison tells us that the study of capital–labour relations forms (p. v) "one division of the science of Political Economy". Moving on, the next key part of the *problématique* mentioned by Morrison rests on his observation that cooperation and good feelings between labour and capital are essential for both sustained economic progress and political stability. Thus he states (p. 2), "The incessant and energetic cooperation of labour and capital in productive industry is the condition on which the dense populations of civilized communities live: and the degree of energy and efficiency, to which their joint action attains, is a measure of the degree of progress of these populations in comfort and material civilization." He further observes that where capital and labour fail to cooperate the result is likely to be (p. x) "confusion and carnage, to end in despotism".

Ominously, Morrison goes on to observe that the actual relations between capital and labour are full of mistrust and bitterness, thus threatening to undermine effective cooperation. In this regard he states (pp. 3–4):

> A very general disposition prevails among them [the workers] to believe, that the relations between themselves and the capitalists are less advantageous to themselves, than is either just or necessary … [and this] tends to produce feelings of

ill-will and distrust on their part towards their employers. At the best it can hardly fail to prevent the growth of the active feelings of good will and mutual confidence, which ought to exist between the two classes, who have to live in such constant and intimate connection with each other.

The challenge facing society, therefore, is how to improve capital–labour relations and industrial cooperation or, as Morrison states it (pp. 3–4), whether "by some regulation of these [relations], for which the power to exact and enforce only is wanting, a great and permanent improvement might be effected".

Synthesizing these diverse observations, the *problématique* raised by the Labour Problem contains the following parts: how to improve simultaneously the conditions and welfare of workers; integrate labour as class into the polity and economy so it no longer feels alienated, disenfranchised and exploited; replace bitterness and conflict between capital and labour with trust and goodwill; and generate greater economic advance, social improvement and political stability through improved cooperation and harmony between capital and labour.

Finally, Morrison also captures one other part of the *problématique* – whether achieving the above-stated goals is best accomplished by reform methods, such as trade unions and protective labour legislation, that preserve capitalism but make it work more efficiently and equitably or, alternatively, by revolutionary methods that replace capitalism with an alternative political and economic system such as socialism or communism. Thus he observes (p. 2) that "political agitators and leaders of all kinds, and from all classes of society, abound; numerous plans and theories of social improvement are put forth in all degrees of importance, from regulations for the management of a Trades Union to the extreme Communist doctrines".

Whether framed as the Labour Problem or the Social Question, the conflict between capital and labour in the 40-year period between 1880 and 1920 was widely perceived to be the number one domestic policy issue facing governments in the industrializing countries. In Germany, Chancellor Otto von Bismarck (quoted in Heclo, 1995: 666) remarked, "Germany's unity has developed so much new energy and created new interests and points of view. But oh! The social question! It makes all governments shudder." In the United Kingdom, Prime Minister Disraeli stated (Sheehan, 1966: 25): "The working class question is the real question and that is the thing that demands to be settled," while a writer in the *Fortnightly Review* declared in 1880, "The Labour Problem, the one problem which, above all others, demands solution in an age described not without reason as 'the age of the working man'" (Davidson, 1985: 34). In the United States, President Theodore Roosevelt observed in a speech to Congress (quoted in Baker, 1904) that the "tangle of far-reaching questions which we group together when we speak of 'labour' [is] the most vital problem with which this country or, for that matter, the whole civilized world, has to deal". Also illustrative is this statement by Noburu Kanai (quoted in Pyle, 1974: 144), Japan's foremost early twentieth-century scholar on the Social Question:

> The two great political responsibilities for the modern nation are foreign policy and social policy ... Ultimately the highest object of social policy in modern times is to bring back together again the various social classes which are daily becoming more and more separated; and it must establish a socially cooperative life based on intimate relations of mutual help and interdependence.

Given the seriousness of the Labour Problem and Social Question, the focus naturally moved to the identification of their causes and solution. This endeavour engaged scholars and thinkers in many countries for well over a century. It is to this evolution of thought that I now turn.

Antecedent ideas

Industrial relations had roots not only in the development of the Labour Problem and Social Question in the nineteenth century but also in the growing body of writing and theorizing about the cause of labour problems and methods to improve capital–labour relations. These theories and ideas not only influenced the development of labour practice and policy in the twentieth century but also provided an intellectual foundation for the field of industrial relations.

The beginning: Adam Smith

People had thought about and written on work and how to effectively organize it since the time of the early Greek philosophers. A theme of Xenophon and Plato, for example, was that success in war, business or civil government is more likely when people cooperate with each other, the group has an effective leader and everyone feels committed to a common goal (Laistner, 1923; Kaufman, 2003b).

Modern thought on the employment relationship, and the cause of problems therein, did not start, however, until the Industrial Revolution began to transform traditional society and work arrangements. Over the nineteenth century a variety of new ideas were advanced that had an impact on thinking about the Labour Problem and, later, the field of industrial relations. It all began with Adam Smith, the Scottish moral philosopher and founder of modern economics.

In *The wealth of nations*, published in 1776, Smith articulated for the first time the modern perspective on the employment relationship and put forward several elements of the positive and normative rationale for what would later become the field of industrial relations. Summarized below are the salient points made by Smith.

According to Smith, the original and enduring cause of a nation's wealth is its people – their number, skill, dexterity, work ethic, inventiveness and character. People, more than land, natural resources, capital, or gold and silver, determine why some countries are rich and others poor. Smith thus points to two important features of labour – first, labour is a strategic asset for economic development and, second, it can be made more productive through investment in human capital.

Smith also highlights the critical role in economic growth played by division of labour. Division of labour promotes greater productivity, stimulates development of machinery and spurs development of new skills and trades among workers. Smith also recognized, however, that division of labour has human costs – costs that arise because labour is embodied in people, not machines or inanimate natural resources. As an example, Smith observes (pp. 734–5), "the great body of the people come to be confined to a few very simple operations. ... The man whose whole life is spent in performing a few simple operations ... has no occasion to exert his understanding ... and generally becomes as stupid and ignorant as it is possible for a human creature to become."

Division of labour also gives rise to the employment relationship. As division of labour and capital investment proceed, it becomes more efficient to shift from an economy of self-employed artisans to large-scale industry with a wage-labour force. The employment relationship, according to Smith, is best viewed as a contract, both economic and legal. And because the interests of the employer and employee are at least partially divergent, the negotiation of the contract inherently gives rise to an adversarial relationship between the two parties. On this matter Smith states (p. 66), "What are the common wages of labour, depends every where upon the contract usually made between those two parties [employers and employees], whose interests are by no means the same. The workmen desire to get as much, the masters to give as little as possible."

In economic affairs, Smith favours a system of "natural liberty" as much as possible. In general, he believes that minimal government intervention in markets is desirable, and that the operation of self-interest will lead "as if by an invisible hand" to outcomes that not only benefit the individual but also society. In all areas of economic activity, therefore, his predilection is to favour freedom of contract and competitive market outcomes.

Interestingly, however, Smith appears to qualify his support of laissez-faire when it comes to the wage bargain. In the negotiation of the labour contract, the employer in the normal state of affairs, states Smith, is in a superior bargaining position to the individual worker and can obtain the advantage with respect to wages and other terms and conditions of employment. Smith states in this regard (p. 66):

> It is not, however, difficult to foresee which of the two parties must, upon all ordinary occasions, have the advantage in the dispute, and force the other into a compliance with their terms. ... In all such disputes the masters can hold out much longer. ... In the long-run the workman may be as necessary to his master as his master is to him, but the necessity is not so immediate.

Also, Smith notes, "Masters are always and every where in a sort of tacit, but constant and uniform combination, not to raise the wages of labour. ... The masters, being fewer in number, can combine much more easily; and the law, besides, authorises, or at least does not prohibit their combinations."

For these reasons, Smith observes that wages for labour are often lower than would prevail in a truly free market. He notes that there is a lower limit on the wage bargain, since in the long run wages cannot sink below the level necessary for the maintenance and propagation of the workforce. He does not believe, however, that a subsistence level of wages is good for workers or society. On efficiency grounds, he claims, higher wages are beneficial because (p. 81) "Where wages are high, accordingly, we shall always find the workmen more active, diligent, and expeditious, than where they are low." But Smith also supports higher wages on equity grounds, stating (p. 79), "It is but equity, besides, that they who feed, clothe and lodge the whole body of the people, should have such a share of the produce of their own labour as to be themselves tolerably well fed, clothed, and lodged."

For both efficiency and equity reasons, therefore, Smith favours higher wages than what labour markets may yield. What are the solutions? One possibility is for workers to form trade unions, thus offsetting employer market power with their own market power obtained through combination into unions. Smith is relatively agnostic about this solution, although he appears to give it some legitimacy in cases when they are used for what he calls "defensive" purposes (p. 67). On the other hand, he appears critical of trade union tactics, noting that unions "have always recourse to the loudest clamour, and sometimes to the most shocking violence and outrage" and perceives them to be relatively ineffectual, since they "generally end in nothing, but the punishment or ruin of the ring-leaders".

Smith also notes several other approaches to increasing the wages of labour. He observes (p. 75), for example, that one reason employers often have an advantage in negotiating the labour contract is that most workers are relatively immobile and cannot easily leave one local labour market for another ("man is of all sorts of luggage the most difficult to be transported"). Measures to increase labour mobility would, therefore, promote more competitive labour markets and wage determination. Another solution is to promote faster economic growth in the economy, since at full employment (p. 68) "the scarcity of hands occasions a competition among masters, who bid against one another, in order to get workmen, and thus voluntarily break through the natural combination of masters not to raise wages". A third solution is to increase workers' bargaining power by augmenting their skills through public policies that promote greater training and education.

English classical and neoclassical economics

After Smith, theorizing about wages, conditions of labour, and relations between capital and labour steadily advanced over the nineteenth century in the United Kingdom. Although numerous people from all walks of life and professions participated in this dialogue, certainly the dominant influence came from the field of political economy. This contribution is divided, in turn, into two distinct phases. The first stretches roughly from 1805 to 1870 and is the period of English classical economics. It begins with Malthus and Ricardo, includes Cairnes, McCullogh and Senior, and ends with Mill. The second phase began in 1870 with the birth of neoclassical economics, a school of thought that not only continues today but has come in the post-Second World War period to dominate the science of economics around the world. Neoclassical economics is associated with the marginalist revolution pioneered by Jevons (British), Walras (French) and Menger (Austrian) in the 1870s, but found its best-known and most influential exposition in Alfred Marshall's *Principles of economics* (1890, 1st cd.). Classical and neoclassical economics differ in a number of significant respects, but are considered together here because they share important features regarding scientific theory and method in labour research and implications for labour policy and measures to improve capital–labour relations. In a number of ways, the future field of industrial relations, when it emerged in the early 1920s, was a reaction (or rebellion) against the classical and neoclassical schools, so understanding both is important for the story that follows.

Exemplified in the writings of David Ricardo, English classical economists started with a sparse set of assumptions and purported "economic laws" and used deductive logic to build up a general theory that describes the determinants of economic growth and the functional distribution of income. Key components of English classical economics were belief in the self-interested nature of human beings (following Smith in this matter) and three theoretical constructs: the law of diminishing returns, the Malthusian population theory and the wage-fund theory (Hollander, 1987).

In combination, these assumptions led to several predictions or implications concerning labour. One is that the level of wages will be driven down to the subsistence level in the long run – termed the "iron law of wages". Ricardo (1817: 90), for example, states, "The natural price of labour is that price which is necessary to enable the labourers, one with another, to subsist and to perpetuate their race, without either increase or diminution." This prediction rests on the Malthusian theory of population. In this theory, population growth – in conjunction with a fixed amount of land and the law of diminishing returns – leads to a decline in per capita income until wages fall to the subsistence level, the death rate balances the birth rate and population growth comes to an end, and the economy enters a "stationary state".

Not only did the English classical economists perceive that subsistence-level wages were the long-run tendency in an economy; they thought low wages actually were beneficial on several counts. One reason is based on the wage-fund theory. This theory holds that at the end of one production period (e.g., the annual harvest of agricultural goods in the autumn) the rate of saving determines the amount of goods consumed and the amount remaining to support next year's production. Of this "wage fund" carried over from one year to the next, the greater the share devoted to new capital investment the greater will be next year's production, while the greater the share devoted to paying wages the lower will be investment and growth. Thus low wages are in this theory crucial to rapid capital accumulation and growth. This conclusion is buttressed by the belief popular at the time that low wages and the whip of economic necessity were the only things that kept the working class productive and leading abstemious lives. Illustratively, one British writer on political economy remarked (quoted in Ekelund and Hébert, 1997: 46), "Everyone but an idiot knows that the lower classes must be kept poor or they will never be industrious."

Finally, the wage-fund theory also leads to the conclusion that trade unions are pernicious and often futile (McNulty, 1980). Unions are pernicious because they divert part of savings from capital accumulation to wages, and also because they foment strikes and industrial discord. Other classical economists saw unions as futile, since once capital investment funds are taken from the production surplus at the end of the production period the remaining portion of the wage fund is a fixed amount to be divided among the working class. Thus success by a union in claiming a larger share for one group of workers can only come at the expense of a smaller share for unorganized workers.

More so than Adam Smith, who introduced throughout his work various real-world qualifications and moralistic and humanitarian concerns, the English classical economists took a more "scientific" approach to economics (i.e., abstract, formalistic and doctrinaire) and, as a result, also took a stronger stance in favour of competition and minimal state intervention in the economy, generally subsumed under the term laissez-faire. Laissez-faire in mid-nineteenth-century England was most ardently preached by economists of the Manchester school, so named because they were located near Manchester which at the time was the centre of British industry and the export trade, and in later years the two terms became synonyms. The fact that certain unalterable economic laws mandated harsh working conditions and low wages for the mass of common labour was seen by them as regrettable on humanitarian grounds but not a basis for soft-headed and often counter-productive ameliorative actions, such as trade unions, labour laws and employer or community welfare activities. Furthermore, reform efforts appeared pointless if economic laws predetermined the long-run outcome. To the degree that classical economics offered a solution to low wages and other labour problems, it was an admonition for people to be strong of character and watchful of their self-interest, and use the competitive market to get ahead through industriousness and hard work and for society to foster rapid capital accumulation, law and order, and a strong work ethic.

Classical economics went into sharp decline after 1870. Two developments were crucial. The first was John Stuart Mill's abandonment of the wage-fund theory. Not only did this remove one of the theoretical pillars of the paradigm but it also opened the door to the idea that government and unions could improve the workers' lot. According to Mill, the production side of the economy is still governed by deterministic economic law but the distribution side is dependent on laws and institutions made by people and thus can be altered to change relative income shares. Any "artificial" rise in wages is still suspect, however, on grounds that it reduces profits and thus slows capital accumulation and long-term growth.

The second development was the rise of marginalist economics in the United Kingdom and continental Europe. Marginalist economics, later called neoclassical economics (a label coined by institutional economist Thorstein Veblen) – represented an entirely new approach to economic theory in one important respect – it grounded economic theory and the method of economics on the marginal concept. The marginal concept paved the way for development of the single most important theory in economics: the model of price determination by demand and supply in a competitive market. It also provided a unifying approach for analysing and modelling all economic phenomena. Thus Marshall (1890; 9th ed., 1961: 526) states, "The normal value of everything, whether it be a particular kind of labour or capital or anything else, rests, like the keystone of an arch, balanced in equilibrium between the contending pressures of its two opposing sides; the forces of demand press on the one side, and those of supply on the other." Illustrative of the use of marginal reasoning, Marshall goes on to say about wages (p. 532), "Wages tend to equal the net product of labour; its marginal productivity rules the demand-price for it; and on the supply side, wages tend to retain a close though indirect and intricate relation with the cost of rearing, training, and sustaining the energy of efficient labour."

Several features of neoclassical economics deserve to be highlighted as they have relevance for the development of industrial relations. Like its classical economics' forebear, neoclassical economics is an enemy of mercantilism and a strong, interventionist state and seeks to minimize both. The project of mercantilism is to use well-placed market regulation and state guidance to support domestic producers, build a strong economic base and move the nation to a higher position in the international division of labour. It is a version of "producer economics" (Thurow, 1988). Neoclassical economics, on the other hand, believes that the welfare of the nation is nothing but the welfare of its individual citizens; free markets best serve individual welfare by promoting personal freedom and maximum production; consumers' interests should take precedence over producers' interests ("consumer economics"); and the best government is the one that intrudes the least in economic affairs.

With regard to method, neoclassical economics also follows classical economics in that it is largely based on deduction from a small set of abstract "canonical" assumptions. These assumptions, such as the maximization principle and law of diminishing returns, are generally taken as both a given (not requiring or based on empirical verification) and of universal applicability. Neoclassical economics is thus a-historical and a-cultural. More so than classical economics, neoclassical economics also abstracts from broader issues of political economy, such as class relations, private property, and institutions of capitalism, and focuses more narrowly on the operation of the market system and how prices coordinate economic activity and allocate resources. Also, while recognizing that economic behaviour is diverse and complex, early neoclassical economists also followed in the classical tradition by abstracting from most non-economic influences and "realistic" considerations, particularly those that are the province of other academic disciplines. (Marshall, as with Adam Smith, was more eclectic than his followers in this matter.) The orientation of neoclassical economics is thus toward an insular, unidisciplinary and "imperialistic" science rather than a holistic, multidisciplinary science. Another characteristic of the neoclassical school is to cast economic theory in the mould of physics rather than in the direction of "human"-oriented disciplines such as biology, the social sciences and law (Mirowski, 1989). The economy is thus modelled, in the core theory, as a collection of atomistic traders operating without constraint of social relations and obligations. Neoclassical economics also eschews consideration of justice and fairness in both positive and normative analysis. In positive analysis (theory) this is because of the individualistic and a-social model of people and because the market is believed able to generate efficient outcomes independent of "who gets what" (the fundamental welfare theorem and Coase theorem in modern neoclassical theory). In normative analysis (policy) it is rejected on grounds that fairness and justice are metaphysical concepts outside the realm of scientific inquiry and are too often introduced to justify partisan rent-seeking and income redistribution. And, finally, neoclassical economics assumes as the baseline in theory building and policy analysis that markets are competitive and market failure is relatively infrequent.

These properties of neoclassical economics are well illustrated in one of the seminal books of the field – Leon Walras' *Elements of pure economics* (1874). He states (p. 73): "this pure theory of economics is a science which resembles the physico-mathematical sciences in every respect", and (p. 84) "Our task then is to discover the laws to which these purchases and sales tend to conform automatically. To this end, we shall suppose that the market is perfectly competitive, just as in pure mechanics we suppose, to start with, that machines are perfectly frictionless."

Core components of the neoclassical school of economics, therefore, are self-interest, individualism, rationality, equilibrium, competitive markets and the application of the marginalist principle to all economic analysis. Although in certain respects a marked departure from the earlier classical school, the central animating ideas of neoclassical economics come directly from Adam Smith – the virtues of economic liberalism, competition and a market economy, all guided by the force of the invisible hand.

Five propositions of fundamental importance flow from this theory. The first is that a competitive market economy is self-regulating – that the free play of demand and supply and flexible price adjustments will bring markets back to an equilibrium, which in the labour market is equivalent to a position of full employment. The second proposition is that a competitive market economy maximizes economic efficiency – that relative prices and the pursuit of individual gain lead all resource owners to squeeze the most value possible from given endowments of land, labour and capital. The third proposition is that the outcomes of a competitive market economy are not only efficient but by at least one standard also equitable. (This point, although not ostensibly a concern of the paradigm, emerges as a happy coincidence.) The most damning indictment levelled at capitalism by Marx and other late nineteenth-century critics was that it can only reproduce itself by exploiting workers – where exploitation arises because the employers pay the workers wages that are less than the value of their contribution to production (absconding with the rest as "surplus value"). In a major theoretical coup, American neoclassical economist John Bates Clark demonstrated with the newly developed marginal productivity theory that in a competitive market economy land, labour and capital receive an income share that is commensurate with their contribution to the value of production (Bronfenbrenner, 1971). Clark's conclusion suggests, in turn, that labour is not exploited in capitalism and, furthermore, that wages for labour are fair because they reflect the market's impersonal evaluation of the economic value workers add to production ("marginal productivity justice"). The fourth proposition is the efficacy of free trade in both domestic and international markets, for free trade spurs innovation and work effort, captures the gains from comparative advantage, and leads to mutual gains outcomes ("all sides gain from trade"). The fifth proposition is the virtue of minimalist government interference in the economy. Because markets are largely self-regulating, efficient and meritocratic, government should confine itself to establishing the institutional infrastructure for a competitive market economy, devising and enforcing efficiency-maximizing "rules of the game" (contract law, for example), and intervening in the market process only in those limited cases where clear and compelling evidence exists of market failure.

When applied to the analysis of labour, the corpus of neoclassical economics gives rise to a number of implications. Both in the late nineteenth century and now, the focus in neoclassical economics is on the labour market, how wages and working conditions are determined by demand and supply, and how situations of disequilibrium are corrected by changes in wage rates. Larger issues of political economy central to discussions of the Labour Problem, such as labour's inferior legal and economic position, thus tend to remain in the background. Furthermore, the physics-like character of neoclassical economics means that labour is modelled in most respects as similar to other inanimate commodities – to be bought and sold on markets and employed and paid a wage as determined by demand and supply. Also, the individualistic and a-social construction of the theory means that concepts such as working class and social justice are generally downgraded or omitted, while the assumption of competitive markets leads to the presumption that labour exploitation is not serious or long lasting, hours and working conditions are the product of voluntary choice and thus socially acceptable, and unemployment and other maladies will self-correct or require only modest and selective government intervention. In a neoclassical world, therefore, industrial relations boils down to a species of commercial relations in which both sides gain from trade as long as government protects property rights, contract law and competition. And, finally, the neoclassical theory leads to a negative view of trade unions, seeing them as a form of labour monopoly that leads to inflated wages, restrictions on productivity, and economic gains for a few at the expense of the many, while protective labour laws are in most cases viewed with suspicion as expensive obstructions to competition that cost jobs and raise prices (Booth, 1995; Kaufman, 2004a).

In 1886, Simon Newcomb – one of America's most respected economists and a disciple of the classical/neoclassical school – published a book *A plain man's talk on the Labor Question*. He justifies the competitive organization of the economy with these words (p. 190): "We now see very clearly that the policy to which individuals were led merely by following their own interests, and acting as circumstances dictated, was wiser, and tended more to the public good, than any system which had received the sanction of government", and says of labour policy (p. 192) "Is it possible to get through Congress any legislation on the labor problem which will not be inimical to the interests of the labourers? Judging from the past, the outlook is not encouraging." With regard to trade unions, Newcomb (pp. 41 2) states this rule: "Every kind of action which gives the public at large a better supply of the necessaries and comforts of life promotes our prosperity; everything which diminishes that supply retards our prosperity. We have, therefore, only to inquire whether more or less service is rendered to the public." He then concludes (p. 47), "I have seldom, if ever, heard of their [unions] combining to render better service to the public. Such of their rules as I have seen are rather in the direction of rendering as little service to the community as they conveniently can." Thus, based on this reasoning and the application of what might be called "Newcomb's Rule", not only are trade unions held to be anti-social but by implication so also are many forms of protective labour legislation, such as child labour and occupational safety laws.

Marxian economics

Another classical economist is Karl Marx, although his theory is sufficiently distinctive that it is generally separated from the theories of Ricardo and his followers. The implications of classical economic theory for the long-run course of wages and living standards were so gloomy that early political economy became known as the "dismal science". Marx took many of the classical economic laws, revised some and added others, and deduced an even more dire portrait of workers' fate under capitalism. His theory of capitalist economic development proved to be one of the most influential ever written and had a profound impact on thinking across the world concerning labour and industrial relations. Indeed, part of the driving force behind the development of neoclassical economics was to find an effective answer to Marx.

Much more so than the English classical economists, Marx (German born and educated but later a resident of the United Kingdom) made a core part of his theory the fact that labour is embodied in the human being who supplies it (Mandel, 1968; Hollander, 1987). According to Marx, while the employment relationship is based on a buying and selling of labour, as if labour were a commodity, in fact what the employer purchases is potential labour power – the ability and willingness of the worker to exert physical and mental effort in the production process. An implication is that work is a daily life experience for the employee, since the provision of labour power cannot be separated from the person providing it, while to the employer it is only a means to an end – greater profit. Another is that a key aspect of the employment relationship is the methods used to transfer labour power from the worker to the employer, given that labour power is volitionally provided. Thus the employer is confronted with the challenge of using a mix of "carrots and sticks" to extract the maximum of labour power. A further implication of this interpretation is to contradict Mill's assertion (also later made by Walras) that the production side of economic theory can abstract from institutions and ethics, and that it yields determinate outcomes (via the production function) based on technological laws and quantity relations.

From a Marxian perspective, the employment relationship has an inherent adversarial nature. The goal of the employer is to obtain as much labour power as possible at the lowest cost, while the goal of the employee is to conserve labour power and gain as high a wage as possible. But not only is the employment relationship under capitalism adversarial, according to Marx; it is also fundamentally unjust and inhumane.

Marx, for example, adopted from Ricardo a labour theory of value. Marx maintained that all economic value comes from labour but that in capitalism the wages workers receive only pay back a portion of the value they have created: the remainder is appropriated by capitalists as "surplus value" or profit. From a Marxian point of view, the wage system is thus unjust since workers suffer from exploitation – they receive a wage that is less than their contribution to the value of production, while employers receive an "unearned" income stemming from having legal title to the instruments of production (themselves created by labour).

The employment relationship is also inhumane, according to Marx. As capitalism develops, production becomes concentrated in ever larger factories and mills, featuring a finer division of labour and disintegration of work skills. Workers thus make the transition from skilled craftsmen and artisans, with good pay, considerable control over the work process and involvement in the entire production process, to unskilled or semi-skilled machine operatives and labourers doing one small, repetitive task under the tight control of management and speeded up by the relentless pace of the machinery. Workers thus suffer greater alienation, exhaustion and subordination (Gorz, 1976).

Marx also gave much greater emphasis to the role of class in the unfolding of capitalist society than did Smith and the English classical economists. Marx saw society divided into two antagonistic classes, based on their relationship to the means of production. One class, the capitalists, owns the means of production and lives off surplus value produced by workers; the other class is the proletariat or working class, who sell their labour to capitalists in return for wage income and use the employer's capital to produce goods and services.

According to Marx, the laws of economic motion of capitalism lead to a growing separation of classes, a growth in the working class, a gradual impoverishment of workers and eventual rebellion and revolution. In the *Communist manifesto*, for example, Marx and Engels (quoted in Feuer, 1959: 8) declare that "society as a whole is splitting up more and more into two great hostile camps, into two great classes directly facing each other: Bourgeoisie and Proletariat". The gradual concentration of capital leads to the development of monopolies and trusts that restrict production, drive out smaller firms, reduce profit margins (because more capital-intensive forms of production yield less surplus value from labour), and lead to "the absurdity of over-production" and a growing reserve army of the unemployed. Capitalist nations thus suffer from secular stagnation, growing unemployment and periodic economic crises.

In the short run, Marx believed that workers can gain some protection from these negative forces by forming trade unions and using the strike to wrest better wages and conditions from employers. These gains are likely to prove ephemeral in the long run, however, as the competition for jobs among the growing mass of unemployed workers and the growing pressure on capitalists to find new sources of surplus value force down wages and conditions to a subsistence level. From a Marxist perspective, therefore, the ameliorative function of trade unions is at best a stopgap and at worst a barrier to and diversion from their larger historical mission. This larger historical mission is political, not economic, and requires trade unions to mobilize workers for revolutionary resistance, promote class solidarity and class struggle in industry, and work toward social revolution and the end of private property and the capitalist industry. Thus, in the short run Marxists are prone to take a critical and even hostile view of reformist projects such as industrial relations. Industrial relations props up an inherently unjust and exploitative system and promotes collaboration with the enemy, while in the long run the very concept becomes meaningless because workers own the means of production, and capitalist employers and the employment relationship cease to exist.

Faced with the fact that by the turn of the century the proletarian revolution was not unfolding as Marx and Engels predicted, Lenin modified the theory in two important ways. The first was to argue that capitalists in the advanced industrial countries, in league with their class allies in government, are driven to practise intensified forms of imperialism and colonialism in order to find new markets and sources of surplus value. Countries in the industrial periphery become a captive source of raw materials for the advanced industrial economies and a dumping ground for their excess production. Imperialism thus extends and intensifies capitalist exploitation to subject people in Africa, Asia and Latin America.

Lenin also modified the theory of class revolution. The working class, to the distress of Marxists, showed worrying signs of succumbing to "economism" and "labourism" – that is, abandoning class struggle and revolution for short-run economic gains obtained through pragmatic trade unionism and legislative enactment. Thus, in his famous article "What is to be done?" (1902), Lenin says (quoted in Middlemas, 1980: 20), "Left to themselves, the workers can only arrive at trade union consciousness." To carry forward the class struggle and socialist revolution, Lenin had to find a different group that would serve as the vanguard of the movement and lead the working class to communism. The group he chose was intellectuals. He concludes, "There can be no revolutionary movement without revolutionary theory, and that revolutionary theory is not arrived at spontaneously by the working class but is brought to them from outside by revolutionary intellectuals." Professors and other intellectuals thus become the leading edge of working-class liberation, and universities and scholarship become political and ideological instruments for promoting class consciousness and socialist transformation.

Anarcho-syndicalism

Marxism was not the only solution to the Labour Problem (and larger Social Question) to come from the revolutionary Left. A variety of other theories of socialism and communism also vied with Marxism, leading to a socialist "Tower of Babel" in the last half of the nineteenth century and great struggles among the factions for leadership.

Of the varieties of socialism, the one that proved to be the greatest challenger to Marxism was anarcho-syndicalism. Anarcho-syndicalism is centred in the Latin countries and has its roots in France. Early influences on the development of anarcho-syndicalism were the works of French socialists of the 1820s and 1830s, such as Charles Fourier, Simonde de Sismondi and Claude Henri de Saint-Simon. The pivotal contributions came during the next three decades, however, in the writings and proselytizing of men such as Pierre-Joseph Proudhon, Auguste Blanqui and Michael Bakunin (Ridley, 1970).

The theory of anarcho-socialism is tied up with the history and experiences of the Latin countries, especially France. After the revolution of 1789, France had three more revolutions (or attempts at revolution) in the nineteenth century, in 1830, 1848 and 1871, all of which took the form of a mass uprising from below against an oligarchic elite entrenched in power and privilege. Although the suffrage was extended and representative legislatures established, it appeared to many people in the lower ranks of French society that the bourgeois middle class, once given access to power, forgot their commitment to democracy and social reform and joined ranks with the old elite to use the power of the state for their own aggrandizement. As one example, despite promises to the contrary the successive governments reverted to a policy of repression of trade unions, including a legal ban on their activities. The feeling among many manual workers and other groups in the lower part of the social hierarchy, therefore, was that democratic-led reform was an empty promise, politicians and parliamentary parties could not be trusted and acted only in their own self-interest, and the state was inevitably subverted to benefit the few at the expense of the many.

The theory of anarcho-syndicalism was never as fully developed as Marxism and splintered into different versions. As contemporary historians of anarcho-syndicalism also stress, to a degree it was less a theory than a plan of action – a revolutionary call to man the barricades (Ridley, 1970; Pillbeam, 2000). As a theory, however, it sought to develop a blueprint for a classless society giving maximum political and economic freedom to the common person. The method is suggested in the term anarcho-syndicalism – a term formed by the joining together of two antecedent concepts: anarchism and syndicalism.

Anarchism suggests absence of government and prevalence of civil disorder but this is not what the French writers had in mind, except perhaps at the revolutionary moment. As exemplified in the writings of Proudhon, the ideal of anarchism is to decentralize responsibility for civil order to the lowest possible level, accomplished by organizing society into a multitude of self-governing communes, cooperatives, and mutual aid societies. Like Marx, Proudhon advocated abolition of private property. But while Marx wanted to centre ownership of all property in the state, Proudhon opposed this, seeing it as opening the door to even greater tyranny and exploitation.

Proudhon's vision of a decentralized civil society was then joined with a similar vision of a decentralized economic order. Here enters the concept of syndicalism. A *syndicat* is the French term for a workers' association. Although a *syndicat* can be a trade union in the modern sense, in the theory of syndicalism the *syndicat* generally takes the form of a producer's cooperative. The means of production are thus collectively owned by the members of the *syndicat* and operate for the benefit of all. The *syndicat*, in effect, becomes the local basis for both production and government. In this form of society, political and economic freedom are maximized and problems of industrial relations – the relations between employer and employee – are eliminated, for no class of employers or employees exists (Lieberman, 1986).

Proudhon advocated a non-violent transition to the anarcho-syndicalist society and only late in life gave the working class a leading role in this process (reflecting his earlier attachment to the artisan and peasant classes). The anarcho-syndicalists who followed Proudhon, such as Blanqui and Bakunin, were on the other hand avowed revolutionaries and saw the proletariat as the revolutionary force in society. Their contribution to anarcho-syndicalism was less in the realm of theory than in their plan of action for revolution. The *syndicats* became the local cells for fostering working-class consciousness and revolutionary fervour and their purpose is not ameliorative collective bargaining but organizing workers for direct action – such as general strike – against the state and private property. Thus a hallmark of anarcho-syndicalism is rejection of collective bargaining, seeing it as ineffective and a collaboration with the exploiters, and resort to strikes and violence as political and revolutionary instruments to be used against both employers and their state allies.

German historical–social economics

The study of labour and capital–labour relations was widely regarded in the nineteenth century as falling within the broad field of political economy, as indicated in the previously cited quotation from Morrison. Within political economy, however, existed different schools of thought. Two of the most important were the English classical/neoclassical school and the Marxian/socialist school. These schools can be looked at as endpoints on a spectrum of theory and policy, with the former anchoring the right (a capitalist employment relationship, free markets, laissez-faire) and the latter anchoring the left (abolition of capitalism and the employment relationship, worker-owned and managed industry). We now come to a third school of political economy: the German historical–social school. Often, the economists in this group are referred to as the German historical school. This practice, however, masks the diversity of thought among them and, in particular, hides the existence of two distinct intellectual premises (Lehmbruch, 2001). The first premise is that economics is like a historical process; the second is that economic behaviour is always and everywhere socially embedded. Sometimes this branch of economic thought is also called the German ethical school (Koslowski, 1995), because these economists also emphasize that all economic behaviour is structured and regulated by ethical belief systems. Yet another name applied to the German economics of the nineteenth century is the national school, referring to the contention of these economists that government should design economic policy to promote the strategic national interests of the state. A final term applied to them is the realist school of economics, for they sought to base economics on the facts of real life rather than deductive abstractions (Barnes, 1925). The German historical–social school occupies a middle position in the spectrum of theory and policy on labour and it is in the German school – and its English and American branches – that the field of industrial relations has its most significant intellectual roots.

The conventional wisdom today is that England was the primary home of economic science in the nineteenth century. In point of fact, economics also thrived in Germany in the last half of the nineteenth century and, indeed, Germany had far more university chairs in the subject than did England (Hodgson, 2001: 57). German universities were also widely regarded at this time as the best in the world, attracting hundreds of graduate students from other countries. In 1872, German social scientists founded the Verein für Sozialpolitik (Society for Social Policy). This organization had more influence on issues of economic policy than any other during the late nineteenth century and was soon imitated in America, Japan and Sweden.

The German economics of the historical–social school is conventionally divided into a first generation (old) and second generation (new) (Perlman and McCann, 1998). The beginning point of the old historical–social school is the 1840s, such as the publication of *Principles of political economy* (1843) by Wilhelm Roscher and Friedrich List's book *National system of political economy* (1841).[1] The new historical–social school begins a half-century later and is associated with (among others) Lujo Brentano, Gustav Schmoller, Werner Sombart, Adolf Wagner and Max Weber. Schmoller is more representative of the historical branch of thought, while Weber represents the social branch, although both elements are contained in each person's work. The German historical–social school continued into the twentieth century but then went into decline, due in part to perceived intellectual weaknesses, association with German nationalism and militarism, and the damage done to German universities by fascism and two world wars. Its legacy, however, has been absorbed and extended by other heterodox schools of thought, such as institutional economics, social economics and various theories about political economy and "coordinated economies". The Verein für Sozialpolitik also continues today as the principal professional association for German-language economists.

Up until the 1860s economic liberalism and Smithian economics maintained a strong following in Germany. By the early 1880s, however, economic liberalism was largely displaced and the newly unified German government pursued an alternative programme of "state socialism". State socialism does not mean, however, socialism in the classic sense of state ownership of the means of production, but rather a state-coordinated and -regulated market economy with a social safety net of welfare programmes. State socialism was also the policy programme of the German historical–social economists, as well as earlier writers such as Lorenz von Stein, and the Verein was the major professional group of economists utilized by Chancellor Bismarck for economic advice and policy formulation.

Several factors were responsible for the abandonment of Smithian economics and the ascendancy of state socialism. It is not coincidental, for example, that at the same time as state socialism was displacing economic liberalism the German economy was also going through a deep economic slump. This period saw large-scale industrial bankruptcies and unemployment, severe downward pressure on prices and wages from cut-throat competition, and growing suffering and unrest among the working class. Not only did the behaviour of the economy not seem to match the self-regulating "best of all worlds" version of Smithian economics, but the government came under mounting pressure from all economic groups to stabilize the market and protect them from ruinous competition domestically and internationally (Sheehan, 1966; Rueschemeyer and van Rossem, 1996).

Also operating at the time was a resurgence of German national pride and feeling of rivalry with England. The unification of the German states in 1871 under the leadership of Prussia fulfilled a long-held goal of many Germans and contributed to an up-swelling of nationalist sentiment and celebration of the unique aspects of German culture and thought. To many Germans, classical English political economy was heavily ethnocentric in its assumptions and construction and did not fit either the German situation or mentality (Ascher, 1963; Lehmbruch, 2001). The English, for example, glorified individualism, acquisitiveness and commercialism, and limited government, while the Germans were attracted to organization, collectivism, romanticism and a strong state. Furthermore, as Germany began its industrialization drive it came to feel growing rivalry and enmity toward England, believing that England was deliberately trying to keep Germany in a subordinate position and that English doctrines of free trade were an intellectual prop in this geopolitical strategy.

Also playing a central role in the transition to non-liberal economic policy was the Social Question and Labour Problem (Streeck and Yamamura, 2001). England had the good fortune of being able to gradually develop democratic institutions and a social integration of classes over several hundred years. While this project was far from complete, and the English had their own Labour Problem to worry about, the English nation was nonetheless largely free from the threat of revolution and class war. In Germany, on the other hand, the entire process of nation building and industrialization was telescoped into the last part of the nineteenth century. Moreover, it was built on a far stronger and more immediate heritage of authoritarian rule and political repression, class dominance and social division, and an agricultural economy only a half-century removed from the vestiges of feudalism.

As the industrialization process picked up speed in Germany, the rumblings of the Labour Problem quickly emerged, as they did in England. But they emerged in a far more threatening form and on a larger scale in Germany, represented by the growth and militancy of socialist, Marxist and anarchist political parties, and working-class movements dedicated to replacement of both the existing political regime and capitalistic economic regime (Geary, 1981). The centre of this movement was the Social Democratic Party and its various branches and subdivisions, all of which in the late nineteenth century espoused elimination of capitalism and some form of socialist working-class state. The German historical–social economists, on the other hand, were middle- and upper-class social reformers, often drawn from the ranks of Christian democracy or Christian socialism. They regarded the burgeoning Labour Problem and class conflict with deep apprehension because it threatened to rip the newly formed German nation apart in bloody civil strife.

Part of the inspiration for the founding of the Verein, therefore, was to craft and propagate new social policy that would solve the Labour Problem. At the first meeting of the Verein, for example, Schmoller (quoted in Rueschemeyer and van Rossem, 1996: 118) said that the group's founders were concerned about the "deep cleavage that cuts through our society, the conflict that pits entrepreneur against worker, the owning against the propertyless classes, the possible danger of a ... social revolution". He goes on to add (p. 96), "Now that the national task [political unification] is about to be accomplished, it is our foremost duty to contribute to solving the social question." Their strategy for solving the social question, in turn, is based on "the re-establishment of a friendly relationship between social classes, the removal or modification of injustice, a nearer approach to the principle of distributive justice, with the introduction of a social legislation which promotes progress and guarantees the moral and material elevation of the lower and middle classes" (quoted in Dawson, 1973: 3). Also illustrative of their point of view is this statement of principles crafted by the founders of the Verein (Herbst, 1965: 144–5):

> We are convinced that the unrestricted play of contrary and unequally strong private interests does not guarantee the common welfare, that the demands of the common interest and of humanity must be safeguarded in economic affairs, and that the well-considered interference of the state has to be called upon early in order to protect the legitimate interests of all. We do not regard state welfare as an emergency measure or as an unavoidable evil, but as the fulfilment of one of the highest tasks of our time and nation. In the serious execution of this task the egotism of individuals and the narrow interest of classes will be subordinated to the lasting and higher destiny of the whole.

The emergence of the Verein and the second generation of historical–social economists was thus partly motivated by a desire to construct a new a body of economic theory more congruent with German conditions and cultures. The more important reason, however, was to serve as a tool for guiding state policy in solution of the Social Question. And the fact that the German economists were oriented toward applied problem solving, rather than building abstract theories of the capitalist growth process such as done by Marx and the English classical economists, gave their type of economics a special flavour in terms of both method and concept. Both Marx and the classical economists attempted to deduce the "laws of motion" of capitalism from a small subset of assumptions that were highly simplified and largely unverified with empirical data. Not only was the resulting product of little use for solving concrete problems, but both theories also reached the pessimistic conclusion that no socially constructed improvement in class relations and labour conditions was possible because these matters were largely determined by inexorable economic laws. The German economists, therefore, set off to develop an economics that was at once more realistic and useful for state policy-making.

They began by abandoning deductive theorizing built on "armchair assumptions" and opting instead for an inductive form of theorizing where assumptions are derived from the lessons and facts of history (Koslowski, 1995; Shionoya, 2001). In this vein, Carl Knies – a German professor who had future American institutional economists, such as Richard Ely and Henry Carter Adams, as graduate students – stated that economic theory must be "based on the facts of historical life", while Bruno Hildebrand states, "The history of economic culture in connection with the history of all political and juridical development of nations is the only sure basis on which a successful development of economic science seems possible" (both quotes from Hodgson, 2001: 60).

Grounding economics on history has several significant ramifications. One is that its eschews mathematics and model building for in-depth case studies, historical narratives, and investigations of institutions. From the time of its founding to the First World War, for example, the Verein published 134 volumes of historical and statistical research on an immense range of subjects spanning agriculture, industry, banking, and labour and social conditions. Synthesizing this mass of historical evidence and deriving generalizations proved very difficult, however, and for the most part the German economists failed at this task (Schumpeter, 1954).

A history-based approach to economics also precludes the development of a body of universalistic theory that applies to all places and all times, or at least with much explanatory power. The German economists believed that all economic relations take place within specific cultural and institutional settings and that these background factors significantly shape the outcomes generated by supply and demand and other such economic forces. The law of diminishing returns, for example, may be applicable to the production of farm commodities in an agricultural economy but not to the production of steel in large mechanized mills, while a higher wage may elicit greater work effort in modern societies but less in traditional societies. Economic theory thus becomes highly contingent. As one example, the German economists believed that capitalist economies progress through distinct historical stages characterized by unique modes of production and market relations. A nineteenth-century example is the progression from industrial capitalism to banker capitalism; a contemporary version is the transition from the regime of Fordism to post-Fordism (Boyer and Saillard, 2001). A second example concerns the applicability of the doctrine of free trade. List (1841) maintained that the theory of free trade is valid for countries at a similar level of economic development, but when applied to countries at different stages of industrialism, such as Germany and the United Kingdom in the mid-nineteenth century, it loses validity because free trade then serves largely to maintain the underdeveloped, dependent condition of the less developed country.[2]

Another feature of the German historical approach is a commitment to a holistic, social-science (interdisciplinary) approach to economic analysis. The practice of historical scholarship inevitably leads the analyst to try to bring into the picture all the relevant factors and considerations that shape events. For this reason, the German historical economics was hardly "economics" as that term is conceived today but rather a broad-based melange of social-science perspectives drawn from economics, sociology, law and ethics, with historical analysis uniting these disparate parts (Hofer, 2000). In the words of Schmoller (quoted in Herbst, 1965: 152), these disciplines are "partial ingredients of an interrelated whole". Not surprisingly, the German economists were quite dismissive of the classical school's model of "economic man" because it focused so narrowly on pecuniary motives and self-interest. So, part of their efforts was to use historical studies to develop a more realistic portrayal of people in economic life, leading them to emphasize the social and cultural embeddedness of behaviour. Also given much greater emphasis in German economics was the role of institutions, since institutions determine the rules and norms that govern economic relationships and shape people's habitual modes of thought. For these reasons, Schumpeter (1954: 783) called German economics "economic sociology" and leads me henceforth to broaden the label from historical economics to historical–social economics.

German historical–social economics also gives emphasis to the organic nature of society and the importance of collective organization and behaviour in economics. Society is not simply a collection of individuals, and institutions cannot be explained as the sum of choices made by their members (methodological individualism). From the German perspective, each social institution and nation state has a separate, independent existence and "spirit" (*Geist*) and should be treated in economic theory as akin to a "living being" with a will and goals of its own. The German economists also take a top–down view and see institutions as the fundamental social fact within which individual behaviour unfolds and develops (methodological collectivism). Reflective of this perspective, Commons (1934a) was later to define an institution as "control, liberation, and expansion of individual action". Their organic view of society also made it easier for the German economists not only to give a prominent place in economics to various types of institutions but to regard a corporate form of economy (an economy of collective groups and organizations) as beneficial to social balance and national development.

The German historical–social school peaked in influence in the 1880s and then after the turn of the century went into significant decline. Two criticisms loomed large that a century later would be aimed at industrial relations. The first was in the area of theory or, more precisely, the lack of theory. As seen by its detractors, the German school was bogged down in endless fact-gathering and case studies. It was perceived as having lost sight of the economics forest amidst the trees of history, sociology and law, and failing at the essential task of science – that of developing theoretical generalizations to help interpret and explain reality. A famous war of words, called the *Methodenstreit* (battle of methods), erupted in the 1880s when Austrian economist Carl Menger published a stinging critique of the theoretical weaknesses of the historical school (Schumpeter, 1954). Schmoller published an equally vigorous defence, but most economists concluded that Menger had the better part of the argument and the empiricist strategy of the historical–social school was largely a scientific dead end.

Then, a second line of attack was launched on the scientific methods of the historical–social approach, this time aimed at the "problem of value judgements" (*Werturteil*). The position of the German economists was that the purpose of economics is to provide guidance on improving the social welfare of the nation through better laws and institutions and, thus, economic analysis has to be informed and guided by ethical considerations of "what should be". In the eyes of critics, however, introducing values into academic scholarship transforms it from "science" (an objective, neutral pursuit of truth) to an instrument of partisan persuasion and politics. The historical–social school was thus tagged with two significant liabilities in the academic community – a reputation for lack of theory and partisan bias.

Because of their interest in reform and finding solutions to the Social Question, the German economists were generally supportive of trade unions and government and corporate welfare programmes to help labour. The centrepiece of Bismarck's programme to wean the working class from socialism, for example, was a series of social insurance laws, such as health insurance (1883), accident insurance (1884) and old-age pensions (1889). These measures were strongly endorsed by the historical–social economists (Ascher, 1963), which caused their liberal critics to label them *Kathedersozialisten*, or ivory-tower socialists.

With regard to trade unions, the most notable writer among the German economists on this subject is Lujo Brentano. According to Brentano's biographer (Shehan, 1966: 40), he "wanted progress within the framework of the existing social structure" and was attracted to unions (p. 41) "because he saw them as offering an essentially conservative, gradualist solution to the social question" and (p. 38) "would equalize but not destroy the free market economy".

The influence of the German political economists spread to many other countries, including the United Kingdom and the United States, as well as Japan (but not France). In the United Kingdom, a historical–social school of economics developed that challenged Marshall and neoclassical economics. The centre of the "economic dissenters" was the new London School of Economics, founded in 1895 by Sidney and Beatrice Webb. The Webbs will be discussed in more detail in Chapter 3, but it is important to note here that they were solidly in the camp of the historical–social economics, believing in the "practicability and urgent necessity of a concrete science of society implemented through historical research, personal observation, and statistical verification".

German economics also had a major impact in America. Numerous American graduate students travelled to Germany to do graduate work in economics in the 1880s and 1890s. The most important figure was Richard Ely. Ely returned to the United States and became the most ardent and influential proponent of what became known as the "new economics" (Ely, 1938; Fine, 1956). The new economics was of the "realistic, inductive, and ethical" kind Ely had learned in Germany. To promote the new economics, he set out to organize an association of economists modelled along the lines of the German *Verein*. The new association was established in 1885 and called the American Economics Association (AEA). The statement of principles Ely drafted for the AEA contained this declaration (quoted in Rader, 1966: 35):

> We regard the State as an educational and ethical agency whose positive aid is an indispensable condition of human progress. While we recognize the necessity of individual initiative in industrial life, we hold that the doctrine of laissez-faire is unsafe in politics and unsound in morals; and that it suggests an inadequate explanation of the relation between the State and citizens. ... We hold that the conflict of labour and capital has brought to the front a vast number of social problems whose solution is impossible without the united efforts of Church, State and Science.

Ely went on to write the first scholarly book on the history of the American labour movement, *The labor movement in America* (1886), and in it argued that trade unions are a beneficial force in economic life because they equalize competition between labour and capital and promote social justice. In 1905, Ely also took the lead in founding the American Association for Labor Legislation (AALL) – a social reform group that became the nation's most influential research and lobbying organization for protective labour law and social insurance programmes (Moss, 1996). In 1894, Ely left Johns Hopkins University for the relatively new and unknown University of Wisconsin. In 1904, he hired his former student, John R. Commons, to serve as a professor in the Department of Economics. Commons, in turn, became the nation's leading labour scholar in the early part of the twentieth century, a founder of the industrial relations field in America, and co-founder of the institutional school of economics, as discussed in detail in Chapter 2 (Kaufman, 1997a, 2003c). Under Ely and Commons, the state of Wisconsin (with a large German-born population) became a laboratory for progressive social legislation. The influence of the German tradition in economics is indicated in these words by Charles McCarthy in his book *The Wisconsin idea* (1912: 30–31):

German professors have come repeatedly to Wisconsin and have been surprised by the German spirit in the university. Therefore it is only natural that the legislation of Wisconsin should receive an impetus from men who believe that laws can be constructed as to lead to progress and at the same time preserve to the fullest all human betterment; that the advice of scholars may be sought; that what has made Germany happy and prosperous may be duplicated in America. ... If Wisconsin is a prosperous state to-day, there is no doubt that is it largely because of German ideas and ideals, early instituted in the state.

Sociology

Although political economy was the dominant intellectual home during the nineteenth century for the study of labour and labour–capital relations, contributions also came from a number of other fields and disciplines. The most important of these was sociology.

Sociology began to form as a distinct discipline in the social sciences in the late nineteenth century. The term *sociologie*, and vision of sociology as a grand science of society, comes from the writings of Frenchman Auguste Comte in the 1840s (Turner, Beeghley and Powers, 1989). Sociology as an intellectual subject area is concerned with the structure of society, social relations among people, the formation and behaviour of social groups and the influence of social forces (such as norms, culture, class) on individual behaviour. In the early years sociology was defined very broadly to, in effect, cover all the social sciences, including economics. In the early twentieth century, however, economics and sociology gradually split apart and became separate disciplines. This bifurcation was promoted by the ascendancy of neoclassical economics after 1900, both because it tends to narrow the focus of economics from political economy to market exchange and resource allocation and because its core assumptions of individualism and labour as a commodity leave little intellectual space for sociology. The opposite tack was taken by the various branches of historical economics, and later institutional economics. Seeking to be holistic, and perceiving that all economic relations – including the process of work and buying and selling of labour – are relations between people and embedded in constructed social and legal institutions, these economists sought to marry economics and sociology into "economic sociology". Thus many of the earliest contributors to industrial relations, such as Commons, Ely and the Webbs, considered themselves to be both sociologists and economists, and their work in the field might well be characterized as the "economic sociology of labour".

Among early contributors to sociology, four Europeans – two German, one English, and one French – stand out with respect to their influence on the future field of industrial relations. Also important to the development of sociology, but appearing several decades later, was the work of Italian Vilfredo Pareto.

One of the Germans is Karl Marx. Although Marx saw himself as a political economist, in the long run his impact has been greater on sociology than economics, particularly regarding concepts and theories of class, social stratification and the labour process (Barbalet, 1983).

Marx's theory of sociology is "materialist" in that it posits that the social relations of production reflect and are shaped by the underlying mode of production. In the workplace, for example, social relations among workers are shaped by the structure of the labour process. Important variables are technology, which determines the division of labour, and property rights over capital, which give employers a relation of authority over workers. Beyond the workplace, Marx saw society at large as stratified into separate classes, with class affiliation largely determined by ownership over the means of production. Thus capitalist societies feature a large working class, or proletariat, that are propertyless and work for wages, and a small capitalist class, or bourgeoisie, that own the factories and mills and live off profit. In early capitalism, a middle class, or petit bourgeoisie, also exists, such as artisans and shopkeepers, but over time competition and the concentration of capital cause them to lose their small property holdings and fall into the proletariat.

From a Marxist perspective, capitalist ideology holds that competition and free labour markets give workers economic freedom but, in reality, they are "wage slaves" with no choice in life but to compete daily with each other for scarce, low-paying jobs (Glickman, 1997). Furthermore, workers have little chance from escaping from the proletariat since social institutions, such as institutions of marriage and education, are structured in ways to largely block upward class mobility and perpetuate the hegemony of the elite. A consequence of the presumed rigid class lines between capital and labour, and common experience of exploitation under capitalism, is that the working classes in each country develop a shared sense of oppression and solidarity, thus extending the class struggle on to the world stage.

The second German who made a marked impact on sociology is Max Weber. Weber was a renaissance man in the intellectual world of the late nineteenth and early twentieth centuries, for he made major contributions to the study of sociology, history, economics, law, administration and religion (Kronman, 1983). Early in his career Weber was a member of the historical school of economics and later switched to the study of law. He is considered a sociologist, however, for in his best-known works – for example, *The Protestant ethic and the spirit of capitalism* (1904) and *Economy and society* (1968) – the central focus is "the interpretative understanding of social action".

Two areas of Weber's sociological work are most relevant to the field of industrial relations. The first is his inquiries into the development of capitalism. Weber rejected Marx's materialistic and deterministic theory of capitalist development and his apocalyptic vision of class struggle and revolution. Rather than argue with Marx on the level of abstract theory, however, Weber followed the historical approach. He conducted a painstaking empirical study of the roots of capitalism in the West and, in several other books, the reasons for capitalism's failure to develop in Oriental countries (as of the early twentieth century). While not denying the importance of economic factors such as capital accumulation, Weber nonetheless concluded that the origin and triumph of capitalism in the West was not preordained by economic laws but was in significant measure an accident of history arising from unique cultural and institutional developments associated with the Protestant Reformation. According to Weber, Protestantism made capitalism possible because it gave social sanction to a new set of values and modes of behaviour without which capitalism cannot thrive (Hamilton, 2000). Among these are the virtues of work for its own sake and frugality and postponement of pleasure; social approval of acquisitiveness, commerce and profit; and the identification of righteousness with personal initiative and the exercise of rationalism and order in life's pursuits and dealings with others. The key to capitalism and industrialism, therefore, is a spiritual (cultural) transformation in which traditional (feudal, non-rational) modes of thought and values give way to a society based on rationalism, order, science and commerce.

Weber's second important area of contribution was in the analysis of organizations. In a seemingly odd remark, Wren (1994: 197) states, "Weber was the Adam Smith of Germany." How can Smith's pioneering work on the operation of a market economy be equated with Weber's equally pioneering work on the structure and operation of large organizations? The answer is to recognize that every society can coordinate economic activity through two mechanisms: the use, respectively, of prices and markets and of command and formal organizations. For historical and cultural reasons, England chose to use the market economy and Smith brilliantly described the virtues of this system, while for other historical and cultural reasons Germany chose to emphasize an organizational (or "corporate") economy and Weber brilliantly described its virtues. As portrayed by Weber, industrialism leads to the development of large business firms to take advantage of division of labour and economies of scale and scope. These large firms in effect "internalize" market relations, replacing coordination through the invisible hand of price with coordination through the visible hand of command as exercised by the owners and hired managers. Part of this internalization process is the replacement of continuous buying and selling labour on the external (spot) labour market with a longer-term employment relationship in which employees are attached to a firm for some indefinite time.

The challenge, as Weber observed, is how to manage these large organizations efficiently and, in particular, how to manage the workforce in the most rational, well-ordered (and, hence, profitable) manner. Toward this end, he developed the concept of *bureaucracy* and described how a bureaucracy should be structured to promote efficiency. Principles advanced by Weber include, for example, a clear chain of command, positions in the bureaucracy allocated on the basis of technical qualifications, and job tasks clearly delineated to promote division of labour. Another key concept advanced by Weber was the notion of authority. Every bureaucracy has to be under the command of a superior person who has the authority to set goals and direct the performance of production. While Marx portrayed the authority of the capitalist employer as tyrannous and exploitative, Weber argued that efficiency and profit instead required that authority be recognized as legitimate by subordinates, and legitimacy, in turn, requires that authority be based on "rational–legal" criteria. Although Weber thought large organizations were in general a great accomplishment of capitalist societies, they also had their downsides. He noted, for example, that workers inside a large bureaucracy can feel trapped in an "iron cage" and thus powerless and alienated.

The great English contributor to the development of sociological thought is Herbert Spencer. Spencer's writings reflected the individualism and rationalism of British society, and borrowed heavily from and reinforced the economic philosophy of laissez-faire earlier developed by Adam Smith (Turner, Beeghley and Powers, 1989). In this respect, Spencer's writings in sociology influenced industrial relations in the negative sense of providing a model of society the field did not want to emulate. Like the German historical economists, however, Spencer also viewed society as a body or organism. But Spencer then went in a completely different direction in his theorizing.

According to Spencer, just as every part of the human body has a functional purpose, so too does every part of the social organism. Further, the forces of evolution lead these parts of the human body and social organism to be best adapted for their purpose – an outcome Spencer labelled (preceding Darwin) "the survival of the fittest". According to Spencer, individuals should be allowed to pursue their self-interest and to seek happiness as long as it does not infringe on others' rights to do so. The appropriate role of government is thus a minimalist one – to provide public necessities and enforce the rule of law, particularly property rights and the sanctity of contracts. Division of labour creates social differentiation and interdependence, necessitating specialization and trade, while self-interest and competition are the coordinating force in society and the spur that drives people to act. In the ensuing process of survival of the fittest – causing Spencer's doctrines to later become known as "social Darwinism", some people succeed handsomely in the competitive struggle and rise to the top of society with great riches and positions of authority, while others – through personal character defects or the misfortunes of birth or bad luck – sink to the bottom of society and endure lives of poverty and hardship. From a Spencerian perspective, therefore, many of the evils of industrialism can be rationalized as the unfortunate but inevitable and even necessary consequences of social progress through evolution. Spencer's ideas were highly influential in the last third of the nineteenth century, even among labour scholars such as the Webbs and Commons.[3]

The fourth great sociologist of the late nineteenth and early twentieth centuries is Emile Durkheim of France. Durkheim became an internationally recognized scholar in sociology, despite the fact that French universities (dominated by clerics) were hostile to the subject and refused to offer courses in it. Durkheim made contributions in both sociological theory and method (Parkin, 1992). With regard to method, Durkheim sought to put sociology on a more scientific grounding by emphasizing Comte's theory of "positivism" – knowledge should be based on fact and observation and not philosophical speculation or religious doctrine. In terms of theory, Durkheim was heavily influenced by the social and political upheavals experienced in France since the revolution, so he devoted his life to studying the social forces that hold together and integrate society. On this subject he held a middle position between Spencer and Marx, believing society would disintegrate if the only social forces allowed free rein were competition, contract and self-interest, but also believing that revolution and class struggle as advocated by Marx was equally destructive of social order and progress. Durkheim provided an alternative perspective, starting with his first book *The division of labor in society* (1893). He argued that the social glue that holds societies together and coordinates the actions of self-interested individuals is a sense of shared solidarity inculcated by common social norms, cultural sentiments and moral philosophy. When people lose contact with the "collective conscience" they develop a condition of "anomie" (rootlessness and alienation), leading to a variety of socially dysfunctional forms of behaviour.

To Durkheim, therefore, the solution to labour problems begins with reintegrating people into the social order by building a sense of common purpose and shared social commitments. This line of thought later figured as a central precept in the writings of Australian-turned-American Elton Mayo and the human relations school of the 1930s.

Management

Management as a separate area of study in universities did not develop until well into the twentieth century. Indeed, the most influential early writings on management were by business people and engineers. Well into the 1930s, therefore, business administration (or "commerce") was often regarded as an applied offshoot of economics and the study of management was seen more as a vocational "art" than a science (Bossard and Dewhurst, 1931; Kaufman, 2000b). Nonetheless, in the nineteenth century several people wrote important works on management that strongly influenced thinking on labour problems and the subsequent development of industrial relations.

Two early contributors were from the United Kingdom, Robert Owen and Charles Babbage. Owen was a Welsh mill owner in the 1810s and became a convert to social reform and industrial uplift. In various writings, he deplored the neglect employers gave to their human resources (employees) and argued that improving work conditions and the treatment of workers would more than pay for itself through higher productivity and lower turnover (Follows, 1951).

Babbage was an inventor and self-taught engineer. In his book *On the economy of machinery and manufactures* (1832), Babbage put forward in embryonic form two ideas that would later be made famous by Frederick Taylor. The first is that factory efficiency can be increased by a rational, scientific approach to equipment layout, the flow of materials, and methods of control and coordination; the second is the proposition that employers and employees really have a harmony of interests and that conflict can be overcome by appropriate methods of administration and compensation. With respect to the latter idea, Babbage proposed a profit-share form of pay so the interests of employees and employers are aligned on the goal of greater efficiency and sales. Babbage was not opposed to unions, but thought they would become unnecessary if his proposals were adopted. In this regard he states (p. 258),

> Another advantage ... would be the total removal of all real or imaginary causes for combinations. The workmen and the capitalist would so shade into each other, – would so evidently have a common interest ... that instead of combining to oppress one another, the only combination which could exist would be a powerful union between both parties to overcome their common difficulties.

Thus both Marx and Babbage thought unions unnecessary in the long run, but for opposite reasons.

Frederick Taylor's name has already been mentioned, and without question he ranks as the most influential writer on management in the nineteenth century – and possibly the twentieth century too. Taylor was an engineer in an American steel company and became convinced that improved methods of management held out the promise of a win–win outcome – greater profits for employers, higher wages for workers and a solution to the Labour Problem. He first outlined his ideas in 1895 in a paper entitled "A piece-rate system, being a step toward partial solution of the Labour Problem", and then later further developed them in a book *The principles of scientific management* (1911). In the first paper, he proposed to solve the Labour Problem by a new piece-rate method of compensation. He states (p. 856), "The ordinary piece-work system involves a permanent antagonism between employers and men, and a certain punishment for each workman who reaches a high level of efficiency." He goes on to say "The system introduced by the writer, however, is directly the opposite .... It makes each workman's interests the same as that of his employer." His new system rests on three parts: determination of piece-work prices through time and motion study of each part of the production process, a differential piece-rate that pays a high price per unit when the work is finished in the shortest possible time, and paying employees on day work according to the skill and energy devoted to the job and not according to the position filled.

In his later book, Taylor lays out a more complete statement of the philosophical principles and methods of scientific management. He states the philosophical principle to be (p. 10) "Scientific management ... has for its very foundation the firm conviction that the true interests of the two [employers and employees] are one and the same", while the four underlying pillars of scientific management are (p. 130) "the development of a true science, the scientific selection of the workman, his scientific education and development, and intimate friendly cooperation between the management and the men". If successfully implemented, Taylor claims that the result is increased efficiency and productivity, which yields higher profits for employers, higher wages and better, more secure jobs for workers, and (p. 139) "justice for all parties through impartial scientific investigation of all the elements of the problem".

Taylor and "Taylorism" proved to be among the most influential and controversial forces shaping the development of the twentieth century both inside and outside industry. Many analysts of scientific management have concentrated their attention on Taylorism's effects on work and workers on the shop floor. Few subjects have drawn a more divided opinion (e.g., Braverman, 1974; Nyland, 1998). Illustrative are the diametrically opposed viewpoints offered by two early Japanese observers of scientific management (quoted in

Tsutsui, 1998: 26). One characterized Taylorism as "a convenient tool for capitalists to squeeze the last drop of blood from the workers", while the other said "the employers get greater production, the workers get better wages, and both end up being very contented".

One criticism immediately levelled against Taylor was that he ignored the human element of labour and treated workers as machines. Another was that he was anti-union and his system was meant to drive organized labour out of industry. Yet a third was that scientific management is inherently elitist and undemocratic. Controversy has swirled around these charges with evidence adduced for and against (Haber, 1964; Nelson, 1975; Burawoy, 1979). Sometimes missing from these debates, however, is the fact that even at the time of Taylor's death (1915) his followers were busily revising the doctrine and practices of scientific management to overcome these real or perceived problems. Future American Supreme Court judge Louis Brandeis, for example, delivered the memorial address at Taylor's funeral and his remarks were later published under the title "Efficiency by consent: To secure its active cooperation labour must be consulted and convinced in regard to changes". A similar theme was struck by consultant Robert Valentine in an article in the November 1915 *Bulletin of the Taylor Society* (organized that year) entitled "The progressive relation of efficiency to consent". Brandeis, an architect of the 1910 "protocol of peace" agreement between the unions and employers in the New York City garment industry, sounded this decidedly democratic and participative note (Brandeis, 1918):

> In the task of ascertaining whether proposed conditions of work do conform to these requirements [of scientific management], the labourer should take part. He is indeed a necessary witness ... the participation of representatives of labour is indispensable for the inquiry which essentially involves the exercise of judgement ... truth can only rule when accompanied by the consent of men.

The effort to democratize and humanize scientific management became a central mission of the progressive reformers who formed the core of the Taylor Society in the 1920s.

Also sometimes missed in debates about the legacy of Frederick Taylor are the larger social and industrial relations ramifications of Taylorism, which go beyond the shop floor. Part of Taylor's huge influence was that he sought to put capital–labour relations on an entirely different basis. Taylor saw that politics, ideology and arbitrariness separated employers and workers and bred conflict and low productivity, so he sought to banish them by substituting rationality, expert administration and strict observance of the law of the shop, thus removing enmity and uniting employers and workers in the common pursuit of prosperity. Paradoxically, while he sought to banish ideology his doctrines became a powerful ideology, and while he sought to banish emotionalism with rationalism his followers soon discovered that the key to success was to harness emotionalism in the pursuit of rational goals.

Finally, Taylor's "mental revolution" also had a dramatic impact on the entire approach to social policy. For centuries, people had sought to find ways to harmonize society and foster cooperation instead of conflict, looking to devices such as religion, enlightened monarchs and workers' cooperatives. Taylor's concept of scientific management quickly crystallized in people's consciousness two potentially revolutionary ideas that had been brewing but were not yet fully grasped and appreciated (Maier, 1979; Merkle, 1980; Tsutsui, 1998).

The first of these new ideas is that the laws of science and the application of the scientific method can be used to solve social problems. Industrial engineering thus led to social engineering, and the development of the physical sciences was joined by the need to develop the social sciences. The importance of having trained engineers and technicians to make the production system run smoothly was joined by the need to have trained social scientists and social administrators to make the social system run smoothly.

The second revolutionary idea was that through rational design and the application of science, social problems can be solved in ways that lead to positive-sum outcomes. Suddenly the way opened up to move beyond the conflict-laden zero-sum distributional battles waged by competing social classes and economic groups, and to design new institutions and methods that can bring about more peace and progress though the power of mutual gain. These ideas, an application of what might be called social Taylorism, developed in the years immediately preceding the birth of industrial relations and had great effect on it.

Law

The subject of law is also central to the development of industrial relations. The evolution of the science of law (or jurisprudence) in the nineteenth century also reflected a mix of common trends and unique national characteristics. All countries of Europe and North America sought in the nineteenth century to codify their national law into one coherent body of legal rules and principles, inspired both by the pioneering example of the French under Napoleon and the necessity of cementing national political unity and economic progress. Reflective of their different national identities and environments, however, the doctrines of law they developed toward this end differed considerably (Allen, 1964; Stromholm, 1985).

In the United Kingdom, and later North America, British common law was the primary source of legal doctrine and principles. It is heavily based on custom, accepted practice and precedent, and in the British case this reflected concerns with rights of property, freedom to make contracts, and aversion to restraints on trade. In the United Kingdom and North America, therefore, the science of law tended to reinforce philosophies of individualism and laissez-faire, with the effect that protective labour laws and trade unions were often overturned on the grounds that they restrained trade and acted as conspiracies against the welfare of the public.

In continental Europe, on the other hand, the ancient law of Rome carried greater weight and, particularly in the Romance countries (e.g., France, Spain, Italy), the legal code was based on civil law (law enacted by government), not common law. Likewise, in Germany and France the philosophy of law was heavily influenced by ideas and national events quite different from those in the United Kingdom. German law in the nineteenth century also came under the sway of the nationalistic impulse ("*Ein Volk, Ein Reich, Ein Recht*", or one people, one empire, one law) and the writings of Friedrich Savigny and exponents of a "historical school" of jurisprudence (Ebke and Finkin, 1996). Following their colleagues in political economy, German legal scholars argued that the law of each country should be regarded as a reflection of its national spirit – thus precluding the development of universal legal principles – and crafted to promote the national interest. Since the Germans were far more concerned than the English with social stability, order and use of collective institutions to promote national progress, this "relativistic" theory of law was used to construct a different legal regime governing commerce and labour relations. German law in the late nineteenth century, for example, was far more lenient toward cartels than was British law, but was repressive of trade unions. The former were perceived to promote the national interest by contributing to market stability and national industrial power, while the latter worked in the opposite direction.

Until the late nineteenth century, the law of labour and the employment relationship were not considered a distinct area of legal teaching and practice in any of the major industrial countries. According to Birk (2002), the first use of the term "labour law" was in an academic treatise written in Germany in 1876, but a separate field of labour law was slow to emerge for several more decades. In large part this was because legal issues surrounding labour and employment were widely assumed to fall under the general corpus of contract and commercial law. Thus the conventional view of the courts and legal profession at this time was that labour commanded no special treatment under the law, was not intrinsically distinct from other commodities in trade, and the employment relation was not in principle different from other species of commercial relations. This view led the courts in most countries to take a hostile stance toward unions and their activities for they appeared in this guise as conspiracies, restraints of trade, and an abridgement to freedom of contract. The two countries where labour law emerged first were Germany and the United States. In the first decade of the 1900s two major treatises on labour law were published in Germany by Phillip Lotmar and Hugo Sinzheimer (Birk, 2002), while in the United States the subfield of labour law appeared after 1900 as part of the effort of Progressive-era reformers to gain passage of protective labour legislation and a degree of legal immunity for trade unions (Hoevenkamp, 1990). One marker of the birth of the new field of labour law was the publication of the textbook *Principles of labor legislation* by John Commons and John Andrews (1916). In other countries, such as Canada, Japan and the United Kingdom, labour law only became a well-recognized subject area in universities after the Second World War (Arthurs, 2002; Davies and Freedland, 2002; Araki, 2002).

Another legal development that played a significant role in the birth of the field of industrial relations was the slow but persistent campaign for international labour standards (Engerman, 2003). The movement began in the early 1800s with employer and reformer Robert Owen. Owen sent appeals to the great powers of Europe to legislate uniform labour protections for workers, noting that only by a common upward movement could each country avoid being put at a competitive disadvantage. The campaign for international labour standards was later picked up by others, such as Jérôme Blanqui, a French professor of political economy, and Daniel LeGrande, an Alsatian manufacturer. LeGrande lobbied the governments of Europe for common labour laws, stating (quoted in Follows, 1951: 31):

> Long hours for which the worker sacrifices his moral fibre, his health and rest, and the free development of the spiritual and physical faculties of his children, lie like a curse upon industry. ... Can the redress of such terrible abuses, practices under deplorable conditions, become a subject of negotiation between the governments of all industrial countries?

Only late in the century, however, was there concrete action (Solano, 1920). In 1889, the Swiss government proposed for the first time that an international labour conference be convened, and such a conference was subsequently held in 1890 in Berlin with 14 governments represented. Ten years later, another labour conference was held in Paris and in 1901 an International Association for Labour Legislation was created to promote labour legislation through research, lobbying and public education. National associations were soon chartered, such as the AALL in the United States. Then, in 1919, the drive to develop a code of international labour law took another major step forward with the creation of the ILO, discussed in greater detail in Chapter 3.

Psychology

Rounding out the list of academic disciplines with an early impact on industrial relations is psychology. Of the various fields and disciplines reviewed here, psychology is the youngest and, for that reason, had the least impact on nineteenth-century and early twentieth-century thinking about the Labour Question.

Certainly the study of human psychology goes back to the time of the Greeks, but most of this was based on non-scientific methods of personal observation and introspection. Relevant to the nineteenth century, for example, is the utilitarian theory of British philosopher Jeremy Bentham. Bentham argued that human behaviour is driven by the desire to maximize pleasure and minimize pain (Mack, 1969) He adduced no scientific proof for this assertion other than appeal to its obvious agreement with real life and common sense. Classical and early neoclassical economists incorporated this idea into British and American political economy, per the assumption that the individual's goal is to maximize "utility", where utility was portrayed as a generalized form of pleasure called "satisfaction" and pain took the form of "disutility".

As an empirical and theoretical science, the psychology of work and industry began in Germany, and centred around the pioneering work of Wilhelm Wundt. Wundt opened a laboratory in 1879 and conducted experiments on the relationship between boredom, work rhythm and fatigue. The central focus of early German psychological research was not on fatigue, however, but *Arbeitsfreude* – translating into English as "joy in work" and corresponding loosely to what today would be called job satisfaction (Campbell, 1989). Also attracting attention was the work of Sigmund Freud. The importance of Freud for the study of work and industrial relations is that his emphasis on the subconscious and id and ego suggested that human behaviour is, in fact, shaped and guided by numerous, sometimes conflicting motives – rather than one unifying motive as conceived by Bentham. Shortly thereafter, the concept of "instinct" was developed, leading psychologists such as William James of America to contend that people's behaviour could be explained as the product of (in his theory) 28 different instincts (Wren, 1994). These theories were then applied to understand the motives and behaviours of people at work. Bentham's utility theory, for example, predicts that people choose to work only when the bribe of extra money outweighs the pain of the work experience, while Thorstein Veblen counter-argued that people have an intrinsic motivation to work which comes from an innate "instinct for workmanship" and, thus, will exert work effort as long as the work is deemed satisfying and worthy (Reisman, 1995).

The actual birth of the field of industrial psychology did not occur, however, until the early part of the twentieth century. The seminal work was by Hugo Münsterberg, who trained in Germany under Wundt but later emigrated to the United States and took a chair at Harvard. His book *Psychology and industrial efficiency*, published in 1913, is widely considered to have inaugurated the academic field of industrial psychology. Münsterberg proposed to use psychology much as Taylor had used engineering – to achieve maximum efficiency and harmony in the workplace. Illustratively, his book is divided into three parts: "The best possible man", "The best possible work", and "The best possible effect".

Social Christianity

Although of a non-academic nature, one of the most influential bodies of thought that shaped nineteenth-century discourse and policy on capital–labour relations came from what has been called "Social Christianity" (Fine, 1956).

In all countries of the West, the Christian Church and clergy of the first half of the nineteenth century were generally indifferent or even hostile to the problems of labour and capital–labour relations. Many Church leaders did not think it was appropriate for the Church to get embroiled in economic and political issues, particularly when they had radical implications, as did the Labour Problem. The Church as an institution, and many of its clergy, were also closely allied with the ruling governments, property owners and social elites, and thus were motivated to take a distinctly conservative and sometimes reactionary position on trade unions and strikes. Further, Church doctrine also provided a powerful prop to the status quo, teaching the virtues of obedience, deference and acceptance of one's lot in life. For these reasons, in the first half of the nineteenth century the Church steadily lost influence among large swathes of the working class (Thompson, 1964), while it was roundly attacked by socialists and Marxists. Engels stated, for example, that "the first word of religion is a lie" and Marx claimed "The idea of God must be destroyed" (quoted in Peabody, 1900: 16).

As the century progressed, important groups within both the Catholic and Protestant Churches shifted position, taking on the problems of the working class and articulating a message of social reform. The Methodists were among the first group to do this in early nineteenth-century England, gaining a large membership among the working class. Only after the second half of the century, however, did the mainline Catholic and Protestant Churches come to play a significant role in shaping debate about the Labour Problem. The impetus was in part defensive. As socialism and socialist political parties grew in numbers and power across Europe, the Church felt increasingly threatened on several counts. Socialism, for example, professed godlessness and was thus leading the working class away from the Church, while socialist political victory could only spell disaster for the Church as an institution. Forward-looking motives also entered, however, as a growing number of Church leaders and clergy became convinced that the message of Christ required a more activist programme of social reform to end suffering and poverty and restore brotherhood.

Important figures in the Protestant Church in both Europe and America began to write on the Labour Problem, with such titles as *Die Arbeiterfrage und das Christenthum* (Ketteler, 1864) and *Jesus Christ and the Social Question* (Peabody, 1900). In Europe, the reform impulse among Protestants was largely channelled into the Christian Democracy and Christian Socialist movements, while in America reform-minded Protestants launched the "social gospel" movement. I start with the latter.

The social gospel movement began about 1870 in America and grew to the end of the century (Fine, 1956). These Protestants believed that the Kingdom of God should be built on Earth and people committed to the Christian faith must take personal responsibility for realizing this vision. This mandate led them to examine the cause of the many social ills afflicting the nation, including the plight of workers and the cause of the Labour Problem. In doing so, they were brought face to face with the prevailing system of laissez-faire capitalism and its primary intellectual defenders, the classical and neoclassical economists. Over time the social gospellers took an increasingly critical stance on both, arguing that treating labour as a commodity, glorifying self-interested individualism, practising "dog eat dog" capitalism and sanctioning the pursuit of unbridled materialism were all antithetical to the Christian religion and responsible for the growing conflict between social classes. Said one Protestant minister (Fine, 1956: 173), the "existing competitive system is thoroughly selfish, and therefore thoroughly unchristian", while another claimed "Christianity means cooperation and the uplifting of the lowliest; business means competition and the survival of the strongest."

Turning to solutions to the Labour Problem, the social gospellers counselled a middle course between laissez-faire and socialism – the path of the "golden mean" and "midway between two opposing errors" (p. 186). Much of the conflict between labour and capital was caused, in their view, by the injustice and poverty experienced by workers, leading them to campaign for more enlightened management of labour, profit sharing and other forms of industrial cooperation, and trade unions in order to provide a "just wage". Of significance for the future development of industrial relations, Ely, Commons and a number of other progressive labour scholars were active in the social gospel movement, reinforcing their belief (gained from historical economics) that ethical principles and practices could not be divorced from the study of economics and labour (Gonce, 1996). Ely, for example, promoted his brand of economics as "sound Christian political economy" (Hoeveler, 1976: 295).

Shifting to Europe, during the latter part of the nineteenth century important wings of both the Protestant and Catholic churches became active in promoting a middle-road solution to the Labour Problem. This movement led to the creation of Christian Democratic parties throughout the nations of Europe and the political and economic doctrine of Christian Socialism. The purpose of Christian Democracy and Christian Socialism is to use Christian principles to construct a society that promotes individual self-development, social justice and brotherhood (Fogarty, 1957). Based on these general principles, and interpreted through historical experience and Church teachings, Christian Democrats and Christian Socialists have a commitment to democracy, a mixed economy, vertical and horizontal pluralism, the principles of subsidiarity (devolution of problem solving to the lowest practical level of social organization, with state intervention reserved for cases where autonomous private action is ineffective) and social solidarity (policies that maintain and foster social cohesion) and systems of joint consultation in industry. A Christian Socialist thus favours social regulation of the economy but is opposed to classical socialism or communism.

The Christian Democrats and Socialists saw the Labour Problem and the growth of Marxist-oriented Social Democracy in Europe as a threat to these principles. Like the social gospellers in America, they sought to promote a "middle course" of reform, preserving democracy and capitalism but making them work more effectively by promoting greater cooperation, social justice, and respect for human values (Shanahan, 1954). Initially Church leaders disapproved of trade unions but, later in the nineteenth century, changed course and sanctioned them as a way to promote the goals of democracy, cooperation and justice. Beginning in the 1870s, a small but significant non-socialist Christian trade union movement developed in the various countries of Europe.

The most influential statement by the Catholic Church on the subject of labour, and the greatest impetus to the formation of trade unions, was the encyclical *Rerum Novarum* (Letter on the condition of labour) issued by Pope Leo XIII in 1891. In it he states (reproduced in Bakke, Kerr and Anrod, eds.,

1967), "The great mistake that is made … is the idea that class is naturally hostile to class; that rich and poor are intended to live at war with one another. … The exact contrary is the truth. … Each requires the other: capital cannot do without labour nor labour without capital." The Pope continues, saying "Let it be granted that, as a rule, workman and employer should make free agreements, and in particular, should freely agree to wages; nevertheless there is a dictate of nature … that the remuneration must be enough to support the wage earner in a reasonable and frugal comfort." He also sanctions trade unions as long as they "draw the two orders [capital and labour] more closely together" and states it is "greatly desired that they should multiply and become more effective".

Hundreds of books and articles have been written by scholars on the rise of Social Democracy and socialism/Marxism in late nineteenth-century Europe, compared to a relative handful on Christian Democracy and Christian Socialism. When searching for the roots of the industrial relations field, this imbalance can give a misleading picture, for the field has a closer association to the latter movement than the former. In late nineteenth-century Germany, for example, most of the historical economists belonging to the Verein were connected to Christian Socialism. Likewise, the Christian trade unions espoused a pragmatic, workplace-centred form of collective bargaining, rather than the more political and ideological model promoted by the socialist unions. Not until after the Second World War did the German Social Democratic Party and the main German trade unions renounce their commitment to some form of planned economy and socialization of industry, while the model of a "social market" economy was first promoted by the Christian Democrats. A social market economy is a middle-of-the-road choice between laissez-faire and socialism and thus consistent with the "golden mean" espoused by early founders of industrial relations.

To round out the record, it should be noted that Christianity also played an important role in fostering labour reform and, eventually, industrial relations in countries outside the West. In India, Japan and Latin America, for example, Catholic missionaries and Jesuit priests were among the first to teach the subjects of labour rights and labour unions, while in Japan many of the earliest Japanese labour scholars and union activists had earlier converted to the Christian faith.

Christianity, of course, is also not the only religion or moral teaching to advance the cause of better relations between employers and workers. In Asia, the Confucian tradition has also played this role with its principles of mutual obligation and social harmony. Islam and Judaism lay heavy emphasis on the principle of justice in social dealings, including at the workplace. The teachings and personal example of Mahatma Gandhi in India were also instrumental in settling bitter labour disputes in the early twentieth century and fostered a "Gandhian" philosophy of labour relations (Smith, 1959; Bose, 1956). Hanami (2002a) underlines, however, that the religions and social values of the East were not as conducive to the birth of the fields of industrial relations and labour law because they did not give emphasis as did Christianity and the Western tradition (albeit quite imperfectly and slowly) to one important core concept: universalism – the moral precept that all people enjoy certain basic, inalienable human rights.

The prelude to industrial relations: The First World War

Despite the impressive advance in living standards in the Western industrializing countries over the nineteenth century, the parallel advance of popular suffrage and representative government, enactment of selected social reform measures and the outpouring of new thinking and ideas on labour, the Labour Problem refused to go away. Indeed, in the years before the First World War the Labour Problem continued to rank in most of the countries of Europe and North America as the greatest domestic challenge facing civil society. Illustratively, a British newspaper told its readers in 1909 (quoted in Ridley, 1970: 86–7), "Englishmen lately returned from Paris tell us that respectable French people are alarmed at the frequency and viciousness of labour riots, shake their heads at the signs of the times, and speak of another revolution." In Germany, trade union membership increased from 300,000 to 7 million between 1880 and 1914 and the Social Democratic Party – committed in its official programme to Marxist class struggle and abolition of capitalism – steadily expanded until at the eve of the First World War it was the largest political party in the nation (Adams, 1995a). A swing toward socialism and labour radicalism also seemed to be occurring in the United Kingdom, marked by a fivefold increase in union membership, the birth of the Labour Party (1906), and an increasing number of militant strikes – producing in the words of Fox (1985: 256) "acute alarm among the middle and upper classes". Likewise, the United States government, alarmed by growing labour violence and support for socialist political parties, appointed an investigative commission on labour. The commission declared in 1916 in its final report that the Labour Problem (quoted in Kaufman, 1993: 3) "is more fundamental and of greater importance to the welfare of the Nation than any other question except the form of government".

It seems fair to say, therefore, that in the decade leading up to the First World War the traditional economic order of largely unregulated, laissez-faire capitalism was under increasing challenge. The centre of disaffection, in turn, was in the growing ranks of the working class and took its most visible form in the union organizing, strikes and socialist politics spawned by the Labour Problem. Resolving the Labour Problem was thus paramount, but whether the status quo, repression, reform or revolution would win was an issue still undecided in each country. On the answer to this question hung the future of industrial relations, for the field would only come to life if one of these four options were chosen – the path of labour reform.

The unexpected outbreak of the First World War in 1914 suddenly made the status quo option untenable, for the Western nations faced the daunting task of mobilizing their economies, maintaining labour peace, and enlisting their workers' cooperation and support for all-out production. Because of these pressing necessities, governments and employers were forced to shift position and embrace labour reform in both the political and economic realms, hoping also to avoid the even worse fate of labour-led revolution.

In the economic realm, the war soon created full-employment conditions in the industrial countries and a pressing need for greater production of war goods. But workers responded to scarcity of labour and rising inflation rates with a wave of strikes and union organizing, unprecedented rates of job quitting, and demands for shorter hours and higher wages (Jacoby, 1985; Kendall, 1975; Clegg, 1985). Seeing that the traditional employment model was broken, employers in large numbers started to look about for a new model. With labour scarce and rebellious, suddenly employers awoke to the defects of the "commodity" and "autocracy" approach to managing labour and became interested in reform. Welfare programmes were expanded, discontent was assuaged with higher wages, the first personnel programmes were initiated, and shop councils and other forms of joint consultation were established.

Governments also suddenly switched from an indifferent-to-repressive stance toward labour to one of accommodation and support. Equally effective, they also beat the drum of nationalism to overcome class divisions and unite unions and employers in a common fight against a foreign enemy, social unitarism. In Europe, to the dismay of Marxist internationalists, the socialist-oriented political parties and trade unions swiftly closed ranks with the governments and employers they earlier sought to replace. All the major combatant nations implemented some form of wartime economic controls programme and sought labour's pledge to promote production and avoid strikes. To gain labour's cooperation, however, the governments could no longer treat unions as an "outsider" or "outlaw" but had to bring labour within the governing councils of the nation, give it a measure of legitimacy and voice, and meet some of its demands (Conner, 1983; Fox, 1985; Gordon, 1987). Among these demands, three stood out: labour can no longer be treated as a commodity, unions must have organizational security, and employees' democratic rights in the workplace must be protected.

The pressures for change in work relations set off by the wartime economic conditions was then greatly amplified by political events. Across the Western world many people saw the war as the fault of autocrats and privileged elites who were unaccountable to and unconcerned with the common person. A groundswell of reaction against authoritarianism thus emerged, coupled with growing demands for democracy and self-determination – fuelled, for example, by the propaganda campaign in the United States to "make the world safe for democracy". But the insistent demand for democracy did not stop at the ballot box. Workers also wanted democracy in the workplace and the term industrial democracy became a "national byword" (Brody, 1980: 56) and the movement for industrial democracy a "great flaming religion" (Mathew Woll, quoted in McCartin, 1997: 72). Even many employers were moved by the spirit of industrial democracy, setting up shop committees and works councils in their plants.

Perhaps the greatest impetus for change came, however, from events in Russia and the long shadow of revolution they cast across the rest of Europe and North America (Lieberman, 1986). In late 1917, the Bolsheviks seized control of the Russian government and proclaimed a socialist workers' state. Suddenly, the "haunting spectre of communism", announced by Marx and Engels in the opening sentence of the *Communist manifesto*, was very real and caused a wave of panic in the corridors of power and among the middle classes. These fears were further inflamed by the outbreak of workers' revolt in Germany in the summer and autumn of 1918, culminating in the formation of workers' soviets to run industrial enterprises and the overthrow of the imperial German government. With the proclamation of a Soviet republic in Bavaria and Hungary, vast strikes and uprisings across Europe and North America, and an assassination attempt on the French premier, the possibilities of socialist revolution seemed a real and growing danger.

To observers at the time, it appeared that the labouring masses were becoming increasingly radicalized and mobilized and represented the true revolutionary threat. To forestall revolution, employers, governments and middle-class electorates looked in two directions. One was repression, evidenced by use of armed force to quell the most threatening strikes and by police raids on radical organizations and their leaders. The other impulse was to implement meaningful labour reform so that workers had better wages, conditions of employment, voice and protection in the workplace, and security from unemployment and other threats to their livelihood. The specifics of reform differed across countries, but one common element was greater toleration of and even support for collective forms of worker voice. The United Kingdom established joint labour–management councils at the industry level (Whitley Councils), Germany passed legislation setting up works councils, and the United States government during the war ordered established several hundred shop committees and forbade employers to practise union discrimination (Fox, 1985; Kaufman, 2000c; Sturmthal, 1964). Another common element among the industrialized countries was high-level government commissions and investigations on labour reform. Similarly, all recognized that some form of international cooperation and regulation of labour standards was needed, and out of this conviction the ILO was born.

The years during and immediately following the First World War thus brought to a head broad-based labour problems that had started 150 years earlier and developed in tandem with the Industrial Revolution. Although these labour problems took many forms and had many specific causes, they found their common expression and revolutionary potential in the workers' collective sense of *social injustice*. As these labour problems grew to crisis proportions, the opportunity opened for meaningful, comprehensive reform of work and employment relations. From this was born the field of industrial relations – the result, in part, of a defensive response to save the industrial countries from socialism and civic disorder and partly a recognition among progressive elements that a more scientific, humane and regulated employment relationship would benefit all social parties.

Notes

[1] It is worth pointing out that List lived in the United States for several years and drew many of his theoretical ideas in favour of trade protection from American economist Henry Carey (1837), whom Commons (1934b) identifies as the first American economist in the institutional line.

[2] Ricardo pointed out, for example, that by the law of comparative advantage Portugal should produce wine and England should manufacture textiles. But, asked List, does this arrangement not also lock in England's economic superiority and lead to a cumulative disparity between the two countries over time?

[3] Spencer was a personal friend and mentor to Beatrice Webb, and Commons (1934b) states in his autobiography that as a child he was raised on "Hoosierism, Republicanism, Presbyterianism, and Spencerism".

THE BIRTH AND EARLY DEVELOPMENT OF INDUSTRIAL RELATIONS: NORTH AMERICA

2

This chapter tells the story of industrial relations' birth and early years of development. The time span is roughly the two decades from the early 1910s to the first half of the 1930s. The birthplace of industrial relations is the United States of America, although Canada also enters the picture at key places. Described in this chapter are the major events, ideas and people involved in the founding and early institutionalization of industrial relations, as well as the emergence of two alternative and partially rival schools of thought with regard to research and practice in industrial relations. After emerging in North America in the late 1910s, industrial relations next appeared in the United Kingdom in the early 1930s – a subject reserved for the next chapter.

Setting the stage

As recounted in the previous chapter, the Labour Problem reached crisis proportions during and immediately following the First World War, certainly in people's consciousness and to a significant degree in fact. All the industrial countries experienced mounting labour unrest and militancy, a burst of union organizing and strikes, and talk of socialism's impending triumph over capitalism – a prospect made palpable by the Bolshevik Revolution in Russia. Also putting the Labour Problem at the centre of attention was the war itself. All the combatant nations realized that military victory hinged on effectively marshalling their domestic industries to the production of war goods, a task made impossible if capital and labour were engaged in their own battle.

Several key concepts thus rose to the centre of public discourse during the late 1910s. One was *efficiency* – the job of organizing and operating the industrial system for maximum output. Spurred by economic rivalry and new creeds such as scientific management, formally organized efficiency (or rationalization) movements and an ideology of efficiency arose in the Western nations and Japan prior to the war and, on outbreak of war, became matters of national urgency (Searle, 1971; Nolan, 1994; Tsutsui, 1998).

The quest for efficiency then turned the public spotlight on a second concept: *cooperation*. All parties to industry, including the most hard-bitten employer and the most radical labour leader, realized that the industrial machine functions most effectively when everyone involved works as a team, pulls in the same direction and works with energy and commitment. This idea was decades if not centuries old, but the war not only made cooperation between capital and labour imperative; it showed that it could be attained through social engineering.

In the case of the United States, President Wilson suspended free markets when the nation entered the war in 1917 and established a large number of government agencies, such as the War Industries Board and the National War Labor Board (NWLB), to manage production and stabilize wages, prices and strikes (Conner, 1983; McCartin, 1997). In a path-breaking and highly symbolic decision, he gave American Federation of Labor (AFL) president Samuel Gompers and other union leaders equal seats with employers and members of the public on the NWLB and several other agencies, in one stroke transforming labour from an outsider in the polity to an insider and cementing the principle of tripartism in the formulation and administration of national labour policy. The NLWB also, for the first time, forced employers to deal with unions, and in hundreds of cases ordered the establishment of shop committees.

Wilson's aim in creating these new agencies was far less to promote the cause of labour than it was to promote greater cooperation and, above all, *industrial peace*. Avoiding crippling strikes and labour unrest was essential if the nation's industries were to meet the challenge of all-out war production. Under the old laissez-faire theory, industrial peace was presumed to be the natural state of affairs. The parties to the employment relationship were considered free and able to protect their own interests, and this freedom in bargaining was believed sufficient to ensure that workers and employers would deal justly with each other and amicably resolve their differences (Feis, 1927). Faith in this creed had already been shaken in the years up to the war by the growth of large-scale, sometimes bitter and violent conflicts between well-organized trade unions and equally well-organized employers; when the war broke out and strikes and labour unrest multiplied, this theory looked increasingly bankrupt. Facing a crisis, Wilson reversed course and actively used the government to engineer industrial peace by making organized labour a partner in the war effort, giving trade unions greater organizational security and using the government wartime agencies to promote mediation and negotiation of disputes.

Besides efficiency, cooperation and industrial peace, the events of the First World War put at centre stage yet a fourth idea: *industrial democracy*. The term industrial democracy began to be used in the 1880s, being given meanings as diverse as worker ownership of industry, trade unionism and profit sharing (Derber, 1970; Lichtenstein and Harris, 1993). Until the late 1910s, however, it was not a mainstream term and had a somewhat radical flavour. The term, as described at the end of the last chapter, suddenly burst forth into the public consciousness at the end of the First World War and became a full-blown social movement, espoused not only by trade unionists and social reformers but by many employers. Two decades earlier, for example, the ideology of private property rights and "divine right of capitalists" were sufficiently well entrenched that a railway magnate could declare without fear of public clamour (quoted in Commons, 1913: 63), "The rights and interests of the laboring man will be protected and cared for, not by the labor agitators, but by the Christian men to whom God in his infinite wisdom has given control of the property interests of the country." At the end of the war in 1918, sentiments had shifted so far that industrialist John D. Rockefeller, Jr. was moved to state (quoted in Selekman and van Kleeck, 1924: 32): "On the battlefields of France, this nation poured out its blood freely in order that democracy might be maintained at home and that its beneficent institutions might become available in other lands as well. Surely, it is not consistent for us as Americans to demand democracy in government and practice autocracy in industry."

The specifics of industrial democracy remained a highly contested concept even among its supporters and a deep fault line ran down their middle, defined by the issue of independent trade unionism. More important in the larger picture, however, is that the notion of industrial democracy had moved from a fringe topic in American intellectual and political circles to the mainstream. With this came the legitimation of the core idea that people at work have a fundamental right to voice, representation and due process, just as in the political life of their country: a concept as revolutionary in its implications as those contained in the Declaration of Independence a century and a half earlier.

The quest for efficiency, cooperation, industrial peace and industrial democracy bubbled up in all the industrial countries of the late 1910s and became a matter of national strategic concern. Concern was then turned into a sense of crisis by the fear of revolution and communism unleashed by the Bolshevik revolution in Russia and an outbreak of general strikes in some cities, such as Seattle and Winnipeg. Thus, to contemporary observers the Labour Problem seemed to reach its critical moment in the year 1919. Illustrative of this sentiment, Commons (1919a: 1) noted with alarm, "If there is any one issue that will destroy our civilization, it is this issue of labor and capital." Having won the military war, the Allied governments were now confronted with the challenge of preventing industrial war. Hurriedly, Canada, the United Kingdom and the United States all formed high-level government commissions in the late 1910s to investigate the causes of labour unrest and make recommendations for change in public policy. Perhaps the clearest signal of change, however, was on the world stage when the Allied powers agreed in the Treaty of Versailles to create an "international parliament" for labour, called the International Labour Organization (the ILO).

With the Labour Problem at crisis stage, the time was ripe for the birth of a new field of study in universities devoted to capital–labour relations and the fourfold problems of efficiency, cooperation, conflict and industrial democracy. Since all industrial nations were grappling with these problems, this new field of study could have emerged in any one of them, or in all of them. But, for interesting reasons of history and happenstance, it emerged in only one: the United States.

If any country was destined to be the birthplace of industrial relations, one would think it was the United Kingdom, with its longer history of industrialism, organized labour and labour legislation (Rodgers, 1998). Furthermore, the first great writers in industrial relations, Sidney and Beatrice Webb, were English, and it was they "who laid the foundation of labour history and opened the way to the systematic study of labour institutions and of industrial relations" (Harrison, 2000: 217). Moreover, the United Kingdom is home to the London School of Economics and Political Science, founded by the Webbs and the oldest institution of its kind. History went in a different direction, though, and with some surprising turns along the way. Industrial relations was instead born in the United States. At first industrial relations was no more than a new shorthand term for the old phrase "relations between capital and labor in industry". But soon industrial relations took on more complex meanings, connoting a new vocation in industry, a new field of teaching and research in universities and a new approach and philosophy to solving labour problems. Likewise, it was not the London School of Economics that became the first academic home of industrial relations but the University of Wisconsin in the agricultural heartland of North America. And, while the Webbs were the world's most influential intellectual figures in the study of labour and trade unions, it was a Wisconsin professor, labour economist John R. Commons, who first introduced the subject of industrial relations into a university and became its most influential early academic exponent. Certainly in an American context Commons deserves the appellation "founder of industrial relations", although, more broadly viewed, he and the Webbs share this claim. Then there is the greatest surprise of all. More than any other person, it was John D. Rockefeller, Jr. – the son of the world's richest capitalist – who in this early period did the most to institutionalize industrial relations in both American industry and American universities. For this reason, he also should be considered a founder.[1]

Why did industrial relations develop first in the United States and not the United Kingdom? When was it born, who were the most important people and what were the key ideas animating this new field? Here are the answers.

Industrial relations' birth and early development

The first event in the birth of industrial relations as a field of study took place in 1912. That year President Taft established a Commission on Industrial Relations. The idea and impetus for the commission came from social reformers and "college men" affiliated with *The Survey* magazine, the nation's leading publication for progressive social policy (Adams, 1966). The membership of the commission was tripartite, with nine representatives from organized labour, employers and the public. One of the public members was John R. Commons, while the chair was Frank Walsh, a pro-labour attorney. An editorial in *The Survey* remarked of the commission (ibid., p. 25): "It is somewhat as if, in the period prior to the Civil War, a President had appointed a Commission on Slavery."

The commission arose from national dismay and outrage with the growing crescendo of labour violence and strikes and the concern of many progressives that capital–labour relations were spiralling out of control. A particular object of concern and fear at this time was the growth and activities of the Industrial Workers of the World (IWW), an anarcho-syndicalist labour union that preached class struggle and overthrow of capitalism. The precipitating event in the formation of the commission was the 20 deaths in 1910 that resulted from the dynamite bombing of the *L.A. Times* building by two leaders of the Structural Ironworkers Union (protesting against the company's use of non-union construction labour).

The commission conducted two years of much-publicized hearings across the nation, helping to give "industrial relations" both currency and importance. In the end, the commission could not agree on a consensus final report and issued a majority report (by the labour group with Walsh) and two minority reports (the employer representatives and public members). The majority report put most of the blame on employers, argued that only through trade union organization could workers receive justice, and concluded (United States Commission on Industrial Relations, 1916: 66):

> The fundamental question for the Nation to decide … is whether the workers shall
> have an effective means of adjusting their grievances, improving their condition, and
> securing their liberty, through negotiation with their employers, or whether they
> shall be driven by necessity and oppression to the extreme of revolt.

The public members (Commons and Florence Harriman) refused to sign the majority report because the recommendations (ibid., p. 171) "are directed at making a few individuals scapegoats, where what is demanded is serious attention to the *system* that produces the demand for scapegoat" (emphasis added). The general principle Commons and Harriman put forward for reforming the (industrial relations) system was recognition that "the struggle between capital and labour must be looked upon, so far as we can see, as a permanent struggle. … But there are certain points where the interests of capital and labour are harmonious or can be made more harmonious" (p. 172). To reconcile the duality of permanent struggle and potential for increased harmony, their major proposals were to encourage voluntary collective bargaining; create tripartite state-level industrial commissions that would be "above politics" and lay down mutually agreeable employment standards in industry; and restrict immigration. The minority report of the employers endorsed the public members' report but strongly opposed the secondary boycott, closed shop[2] and any programme that would force unionism on employers where work relations were satisfactory.

The commission and its work gave a first and permanent imprint to the term industrial relations and helped establish in the American context six connotations or associations that have lasted in varying degrees to the present time. The first is an association with conflict and labour problems, and a general sense that industrial relations comes to the fore in times of strikes and labour unrest. The second is an emphasis on the term relations, suggesting that while the subject of industrial relations is broadly related to the subject of work, its core focus is the relations between employers and employees. The third is the virtue of workplace voice and interest representation, kept at a bilateral workplace level where possible but taking a tripartite form for government labour boards and investigative committees. The fourth is the mixed nature of interests in the employment relationship, including both conflict of interest and harmony of interest. The fifth is the deep divide over the desirability and social consequences of trade unionism and the difficulty of forging a compromise between its proponents and opponents. The sixth is the desire to find methods to reconcile capital and labour and thus de-politicize the workplace.

The commission also set another precedent that would be repeated in other countries and at other times. Not only did the commission focus public attention on the subject of employer–employee relations; it also helped legitimate the academic study of labour, helped create a "brains trust" of talented scholars who would later become the backbone of the American industrial relations field, and led to a substantial increase in funding for labour research by government and private foundations. Before the formation of the commission, labour research was viewed with considerable scepticism and hostility, since many people regarded it as politically motivated and dangerously radical. Commons convinced fellow commission members to allocate considerable funds to conduct a wide-ranging research programme (directed by Charles McCarthy), arguing that educating the public on the conditions of labour was a prerequisite to winning political support for legislative reform. As a result, numerous graduate students and professors were recruited to do field investigations and write reports for the commission. Among them were George Barnett, William Leiserson, Don Lescohier, David McCabe, Selig Perlman, Sumner Slichter, Edwin Witte and Leo Wolman – people who later became well-known labour and industrial relations scholars (Derber, 1967: 32). Also appearing at this time were numerous books and articles that helped create a foundation for industrial relations, such as Hoxie's *Scientific management and labor* (1915) and Lescohier's *The labor market* (1919).

While the commission was conducting its investigations, one other event happened that was to have a substantial impact on the development of the field of industrial relations in the United States. In 1913, the Labour Problem spawned another violent confrontation between capital and labour, this time in the coalfields of southern Colorado (Gitelman, 1988). Miners and employers were locked in a long and bitter strike. It finally ended when the state militia stormed a miners' tent colony and burned it to the ground, in the process killing a dozen women and children. The event became known as the Ludlow Massacre and generated intense nationwide attention and condemnation. The focal point of the criticism was John D. Rockefeller, Jr., who, in partnership with his father, was the principal stockholder of the largest company in the dispute, the Colorado Fuel and Iron Company (CF&I). Rockefeller initially defended the management of the company, blamed the trouble on union agitators and radicals, and washed his hands of responsibility because he had delegated all aspects of the company's labour practices to local management. Much of the public viewed it otherwise, and Rockefeller was excoriated as the archetypical capitalist interested only in greater profit no matter the human toll on the workers and their families.

Rockefeller was subpoenaed to appear before the Commission on Industrial Relations and it was widely expected that Walsh would use every opportunity to cast Rockefeller in a bad light. Embarrassed, threatened and knowing nothing of labour matters, Rockefeller hired as his personal industrial relations consultant Canadian labour expert William Lyon Mackenzie King. King had studied labour problems at Harvard, mediated numerous labour disputes in Canada, and served as Minister of Labour in the Canadian federal government. King took Rockefeller to Colorado to spend a week with the miners and personally experience life in the coal camps. He also counselled Rockefeller on an entirely new philosophy and programme of employee relations, later expounded in his book *Industry and humanity* (1918). Rockefeller became a "born again" convert to progressive labour management and emerged as its most influential American spokesman and supporter (Rockefeller, 1923; Kaufman, 2003a). As described shortly, this philosophy became one of the two main branches of thought in American industrial relations.

Usage of the industrial relations term gradually spread and then spiked upward in the crisis year of 1919. The term "employment relations" also appeared at this time but did not subsequently catch on (Kaufman, 1993; Morris, 1997). The idea of industrial relations was also given further impetus by the decision of the American and Canadian governments to again conduct public hearings and investigations on the troubled state of employer–employee relations. The title of the American group, appointed by Wilson in 1919, was the President's Industrial Conference; the name of the Canadian body was the Royal Commission on Industrial Relations. The official report of the Canadian Commission declares (1919: 5), "The upheaval taking place throughout the world, and the state of men's minds during this critical period, make this the time for drastic changes of the industrial and social systems ... A new spirit of partnership is therefore essential."

The American conference ultimately broke down over the issue of collective representation and bargaining, and failed to make a recommendation (Gitelman, 1988). Most of the employers insisted on maintaining a system of individual representation and an open shop (non-union) policy, while the labour group insisted on collective bargaining by independent trade unions. Rockefeller, acting as spokesman for the public group, proposed a middle course. He moved that national labour policy endorse the principle of employee representation but leave it open to the workers to decide what form of representation (if any) they prefer. Thus representation is encouraged but workers have the option of no representation, a company-created plan (of the kind Rockefeller and King earlier installed at CF&I), or union representation. This proposal was also defeated, so the status quo prevailed by default.

Much the same outcome emerged in Canada. The commission divided into majority and minority groups and issued separate reports. On most issues the two groups were in agreement, but they were divided over the majority group's recommendation that government protect the right to organize and collective bargaining. The majority report (Royal Commission on Industrial Relations, 1919: 6) enumerated ten causes of labour unrest and identified unemployment as the most serious. Others included the workers' desire for shorter hours and higher wages, denial of collective representation and bargaining, lack of confidence in constituted government, and restrictions on freedom of speech. Regarding the development of a "new spirit of partnership" in industry, the majority report states (p. 9):

> To a considerable extent in the past labour has been regarded as a commodity to be bought and sold in the open market, the price to be paid being determined by the supply and demand. We believe that labour should no longer be so regarded, but that greater recognition should be given to human rights and human aspirations, and that the chief consideration of industry should be the health, happiness and prosperity of the workers and service to the community.

Although the minority group (employer representatives) opposed legal recognition and protection of the right to organize trade unions, they supported a declaration in favour of collective representation through various forms of shop committees and joint industrial councils. As in the United States, the commission's recommendations generated a great deal of commentary and public discussion but failed to generate legislation (MacDowell, 2000).

While government commissions were putting industrial relations in the news in North America, so too was the business press. Starting in 1917 and growing in number, articles began to appear in management-oriented periodicals, such as *Industrial Management*, on the new management function of industrial relations. In late 1919, this trend gave rise to an entirely new business publication, called *Industrial Relations: Bloomfield's Labor Digest*. The editors were business consultants Daniel and Meyer Bloomfield, who had taken the lead in founding in 1912 the Boston Employment Managers' Association – the first group in the United States specializing in what at that time was called labour management. The term labour management metamorphosed into employment management, which soon thereafter evolved into personnel management or personnel administration or industrial relations management (Bloomfield, 1917).

By 1919, personnel management was conceived as part of a broader management function dealing with industrial relations. Cowdrick (1924: 3) states, for example, "Labor needs of the war period found the employment managers and the welfare director already established in many business institutions. They were promptly drafted into the new vocation of industrial relations management." Not only did industrial relations supersede personnel management, it also represented a much-expanded and more strategic version of it. Illustratively, Cowdrick states (pp. 3–4),

> In many companies the duties of the labour manager had little visible connection with management in general. The personnel man was not expected to have much knowledge about – sometimes not even much sympathy with – the business affairs of the employer ... . The result [of the industrial relations movement] has been an enlarged conception of labor management as an essential part of general management, not to be separated from the other policies of the corporation.

Business writer and consultant Dudley Kennedy (1919: 358) also notes this change, stating that, "employment management is, and always must be, a subordinate function to the task of preparing and administering a genuine labor policy, which is properly the field of industrial relations". In modern language, Kennedy is saying that industrial relations not only subsumes personnel management but represents the strategic component of it (Kaufman, 2001b).

The actual birth of the field, as I date it, occurred in the year 1920. It is marked by two events. The first is the formation of the first academic programme devoted to industrial relations. At the University of Wisconsin, the economics department, chaired by Professor Commons, created a "course" or area of specialization for students wishing to study industrial relations. This area of specialization entailed taking classwork on four related subjects: labour legislation, labour history and industrial government, labour management, and causes and remedies of unemployment (U.S. Bureau of Labor Statistics, 1921).

The next event is the founding in 1920 of the Industrial Relations Association of America (IRAA). The IRAA had formerly been the Employment Managers' Association and was composed largely of business people and consultants with an interest in personnel management. Many of these people's job titles included the term industrial relations, such as William Larkin, vice-president of industrial relations at Bethlehem Steel and the association's second president. The association had more than 2,000 members and several dozen local chapters in its first year. Among its activities, the IRAA published a monthly journal entitled *Personnel*. The IRAA later evolved into the American Management Association (Lange, 1928).

In the next year, Commons (1921a) published an edited book of readings on labour, *Trade unionism and labour problems* (revised ed.), and the introductory chapter was titled "Industrial relations". This chapter is, as far as I am aware, the first research-oriented article written by an academic person to feature industrial relations in the title. The article was a revised version of a speech Commons had delivered in 1919 to the annual meeting of the Employment Managers' Association.

The next step on the path of development of industrial relations is in 1922, when the first autonomous centre devoted to industrial relations was established at Princeton University. This centre was called the Industrial Relations Section and was created as a separate unit housed within the Department of Economics (Industrial Relations Section, 1986). Impetus for the creation of the section came from Clarence Hicks. Hicks had earlier been hired by Rockefeller to run the employee representation plan at CF&I, and was at this time executive in charge of industrial relations at Standard Oil of New Jersey, one of the nation's leading corporate advocates of industrial relations, and chair of the Special Conference Committee – a group of ten leading welfare capitalist companies (Hicks, 1941; Scheinberg, 1986; Kaufman, 2003a). Funding of the section was contributed by Rockefeller, principal shareholder of Standard Oil. The section was headed by Professor J. Douglas Brown of the Economics Department. Hicks describes his motivation as a combination of bringing a more balanced view to the teaching of industrial relations and a desire to promote development of the field (Hicks, 1941). The section did not offer classes or provide a degree in industrial relations but sought to promote improved industrial relations through research and publication, conferences and executive education (e.g., an annual conference for high-level industrial relations managers), and creation of a library with a comprehensive holding of materials in the employment field.

A year earlier, it should be noted, an Industrial Research Department at the Wharton School of Finance and Commerce at the University of Pennsylvania had been established (Wharton School, 1989). Although its primary focus was industrial relations research, other economic studies of industry were also occasionally undertaken. The director was Joseph Willits, an officer of the IRAA and member of the Rockefeller-connected network of labour reformers (Domhoff, 1996; Harris, 2000).

Moving forward, the next major institutional development for the field is the creation of the world's first consulting and research organization devoted exclusively to industrial relations practices – Industrial Relations Counselors, Inc. (IRC). IRC was established in 1926 in New York City by Rockefeller, and was financially supported by him through large gifts (Kaufman, 2003a). The firm was operated on a non-profit basis, employed over a dozen research and consulting staff, and conducted in-depth audits of industrial relations practices and policies at companies and carried out research studies on selected industrial relations issues in industry. IRC was widely regarded at the time as doing some of the best industrial relations research in the nation and played a leading role in the development of the American systems of unemployment insurance and social security (Burton and Mitchell, 2003). IRC was also a major advocate of plans of employee representation, did much to promote and extend the welfare capitalist employment model in industry, and helped develop personnel management techniques such as job evaluation methods and foreman training.

Since the United States decided in 1919 to remain outside the League of Nations, Rockefeller provided funds so that the IRC could maintain an office in Geneva, Switzerland, giving the United States informal representation and communication with the ILO (Tipton, 1959; Gunderson and Verma, 2003). The IRC also donated funds to support the activities of the ILO, per the observation of the ILO's Director-General David Morse (1969: 18):

> In 1929, thanks to assistance from Industrial Relations Counselors of New York, I.L.O. staff members began to visit important industrial and commercial undertakings in Europe and North America and to prepare reports on labour–management relations within those undertakings. These reports, which were published by the I.L.O., proved to be very popular.

Yet another sign of development for the field was in 1928 when the Social Science Research Council (SSRC, a non-profit group funded, in part, with Rockefeller foundation money) commissioned Herman Feldman of Dartmouth University to write up a comprehensive report on the subject area and research literature of industrial relations (SSRC, 1928; Fisher, 1993). Advising Feldman was a 12-person advisory board, including academics such as Commons and Willits and representatives of both the labour movement and the more liberal wing of the business community. The final product, *Survey of research in the field of industrial relations*, ran over 100 pages in length and included within its purview a vast range of subjects broadly related to work, drawn from contiguous disciplines such as psychology, anthropology, engineering, economics and ethics. The fact that one of the gatekeeper organizations of the American social sciences commissioned the report indicates that this new subject of industrial relations had gained recognition and professional legitimacy as a distinct body of knowledge.

In the late 1920s, industrial relations won further recognition when Harvard University, using funds donated by the family of Jacob Wertheim, published a book entitled *Wertheim lectures on industrial relations* (Harvard University, 1929).[3] This book is important because it brought together a notable and diverse group of scholars, including Commons and Elton Mayo, and also because it was the first of several dozen other industrial relations books published under the auspices of the Wertheim Lectures, under the editorship of John Dunlop for more than half a century.

During the 1920s, industrial relations also slowly made its way into university curricula. Although no American university I am aware of established a separate degree programme in industrial relations until the 1940s (a small Jesuit school, Rockhurst College in Kansas City, was the first to do so in 1944), a number created courses in industrial relations and several, such as Columbia University and the University of Michigan, created some kind of industrial relations major or concentration (Industrial Relations Counselors, Inc., 1949). Among the 1,398 faculty members in 42 accredited business schools in 1930 (Bossard and Dewhurst, 1931: 314), 14 listed industrial relations as an area of specialization, while 31 did so for personnel management and 48 for labour (suggesting that labour and employment issues had by this time a presence in American business schools, but not a large one).

The 1930s witnessed the establishment of four other quasi-independent industrial relations units in American universities, and the establishment of the first industrial relations unit at a Canadian university (Kaufman, 1993). All of these industrial relations units, modelled along the lines of the Princeton Industrial Relations Section, were established at the instigation of Hicks and funded with financial gifts from business people, including Rockefeller-connected foundations and companies. Most were housed within a business school. The four American universities were the Massachusetts Institute of Technology (MIT), Stanford, Michigan, and the California Institute of Technology. An Industrial Relations Section was also established at Queen's University in Canada (Kelly, 1987). According to Hicks, the University of Wisconsin also agreed to establish an industrial relations section in the late 1930s, but for unknown reasons it never materialized (Hicks, 1941). Only three of these industrial relations centres remain active today: Princeton, Queen's and MIT (renamed the Institute for Work and Employment Research).

Compared to the rapid expansion experienced in the decade after the Second World War, these early events and developments in the American industrial relations field were relatively modest sized and formative in nature. When compared to the rest of the world, however, the development of industrial relations in the United States in this early period was innovative and trend setting. Testimony on this point is provided by Englishman Harold Butler (1927), at that time Deputy Director of the ILO, who states (p. 107, emphasis added),

> The study of industrial relations is nothing but the study of human nature in the setting of modern industry, and that setting is largely similar everywhere. It is a subject to which comparatively little attention has been devoted, despite its great and growing importance to the general welfare of society in the present industrial age. The attempt which is now being made in America to raise it to the dignity of a science comparable to the study of politics or economics is in itself both significant and important. ... *The American literature on the subject during the last ten years probably exceeds that of the rest of the world put together.*

What is industrial relations?

What was this new subject of industrial relations that suddenly appeared on the American scene in the late 1910s and then gradually spread in industry and universities? When closely examined, the answer is complex since from the very beginning industrial relations was never a unitary construct. Rather, the field contained three distinct and partially divergent dimensions or "faces". I call these the science-building, problem-solving and ethical/ideological faces.

Before considering each of these faces in more depth, it is useful to map out in a general way the subject domain and boundaries of industrial relations as they were perceived to exist in the 1920s. Evidence on this question is available from a variety of sources.

The earliest known document is a pamphlet published in 1919 by the Russell Sage Library entitled *Industrial relations: A selected bibliography*. The reading list is divided into two major parts: employment management and participation in management. The former covers various subjects related to labour/personnel management; the second covers what today would be called methods of workforce governance. The latter includes readings on trade unionism, shop committees, plans for guild socialism, and wartime joint labour–management committees.

A second piece of evidence comes from Feldman's 1928 survey of the industrial relations field done for the SSRC. The report states that (p. 19, emphasis added): "the focal point of the field [of labour/industrial relations] is the *employer–employee* relationship". Amplifying on the subject area of industrial relations, Feldman goes on to say that the field deals principally with five topics: factors in human behaviour with special reference to industry, workers in relation to their work, workers in relation to their fellow workers, workers in relation to their employer, and workers in relation to the public. Finally, the report also clearly indicates that at that time industrial relations was conceived of as a multidisciplinary field of study, rather than a self-contained discipline of its own. The report contains a "Map suggesting a field of research" (reproduced in Kaufman, 1993: 14–17) that identifies 18 other areas of the social and physical sciences (e.g., biology, ethics, economics, psychology) that contribute to an understanding of industrial relations.

A third piece of evidence comes from university curricula. As already mentioned, the specialization in industrial relations at Wisconsin contained four areas of coursework: labour legislation, labour management (personnel management), labour history and industrial government (including trade unionism), and causes and remedies of unemployment. This pattern was widely repeated, with variations. The industrial relations programme at Columbia

University, for example, required courses in law of the employment of labour, labour administration, adjustment of labour disputes, and personnel and employment problems (U.S. Bureau of Labor Statistics, 1930). A further indicator comes from the industrial relations course Sumner Slichter taught at Harvard University. The lecture notes survive and reveal that approximately half of the course was devoted to employers' labour policies (personnel management, employee representation, benefits programmes, etc.) and half to trade unionism and labour policy (Kaufman, 2003e).

A final testament on the subject matter of industrial relations comes from the report *Industrial relations: Administration of policies and programs* (1931) by the National Industrial Conference Board. The report declares (p. 1): "In the broadest sense, the term 'industrial relations' comprises every incident that grows out of the fact of employment."

Summing up, one may conclude from these four sources that industrial relations as an intellectual enterprise circa the 1920s covered the subjects of work, labour and the employment relationship, and gave particular attention to relations in the work world. It also subsumed both employers' methods of work organization and personnel management and the employees' individual and collective response to the work experience, including strikes, trade unions and collective bargaining, and took a multidisciplinary perspective, including attention to legal, psychological, technical, sociological, economic, ethical, historical and administrative forces. Moreover, it focused on both public policy issues concerning labour and workplace practices and outcomes.

This list of topics is quite broad and covers the entire world of work. Taking the word "relations" seriously suggests, however, that the fundamental construct that underlies the field is the *employment relationship*. In its most general form, therefore, industrial relations is the study of the employment relationship and all the behaviours, outcomes, practices and institutions that emanate from or impinge on the employment relationship. Industrial relations could thus be more accurately called *employment relations*.

The science-building face

Industrial relations is partly an intellectual project, partly an applied programme of problem solving, and partly a moral and ideological commitment. This section explores the intellectual or science-building dimension.

Science building is largely an academic endeavour aimed at explaining and understanding the major features and consequences of the employment relationship. The tools of science building are theory and research methods and the goal is to derive useful generalizations and insights about the operation of the world of work. Numerous books and articles have been published over the years detailing and debating the theory and methods of industrial relations. My aim here is not to repeat any of this. Rather, the goal is to return to the original source materials and reconstruct the theory and methods of industrial relations, starting from first principles as described by the founders of the field. I do this in considerable detail, since the issue of theory (and perceived lack thereof) is fundamental in current industrial relations, and contemporary policy and problem-solving programmes of industrial relations drift rudderless without theoretical guidance and justification. Moreover, no one else has undertaken this task.

In its American version, industrial relations is largely coterminous with the labour branch of the institutional school of economics, particularly the stream pioneered by Commons and colleagues of the Wisconsin school (Cain, 1993; Barbash, 1994; Budd, 2004). As described below, Commons is considered one of the founders of institutional economics and, as noted earlier in this chapter, he is also widely considered to be the academic father of American industrial relations – suggesting a tight linkage between the two streams of thought. Furthermore, nearly all the most influential names in early industrial relations, such as Douglas, Hoxie, Leiserson, Millis, Perlman and Slichter, were broadly affiliated with the institutional approach (McNulty, 1980).

By way of background, the institutional school of economics arose in the United States as an outgrowth and adaptation of German and British historical– social economics, albeit with some greater receptivity to theory (of a heterodox kind), greater effort to integrate ideas and concepts from law and sociology, and a movement away from the more overt aspects of German nationalism and statism (Jacoby, 1990; Perlman and McCann, 1998; Yonay, 1998). American institutional economics then lost almost all connection with German economics with the outbreak of the First World War.

As a formally recognized entity, institutional economics dates from the early 1920s. The term "institutional economics" was coined by Walton Hamilton (1919), and the field was sometimes referred to as the "new economics" or the economics of control (Knight, 1932). The roots of the field go back four decades earlier, however, to a group of American graduate students, including John Bates Clark, Henry Carter Adams, Richard Ely, Simon Patten and Edward Seligman, who travelled to Germany to study economics (described in the previous chapter) and came back to the United States committed to establishing an alternative to the dominant classical/neoclassical school (Fine, 1956). The writings of Ely and colleagues in the 1880s and 1890s gave significant attention to labour and labour–capital relations (e.g., Ely, 1886), but also included many other aspects of economic and public policy. As conventionally portrayed by historians of economic thought, the founding members of the institutional school come from the following generation of economists and include Commons, Wesley Mitchell and Thorstein Veblen (Dorfman, 1959). Their writings include labour but also deal with numerous other subjects, such as public utility regulation, monetary policy and industrial pricing (Commons), business cycles (Mitchell) and the theory of business enterprise and conspicuous consumption (Veblen).

The conventional wisdom among contemporary economists (e.g., Blaug, 1997; Boyer and Smith, 2001) is that the institutional school was largely an exercise in dissent and criticism, which failed at the larger and more constructive task of theory development. They see it as having been eclipsed by modern neoclassical economics not only because the latter has succeeded at developing an insightful body of theory but also because this body of theory has over the years been extended and modified to explain the various deviant observations (e.g., the existence of rigid wages and involuntary unemployment) noted by the institutionalists. An objective observer must give these criticisms significant credence. Indeed, even some committed practitioners have admitted that institutional economics lacks a coherent body of theory – perhaps by the very nature of the project. Industrial relations, being the child of institutional economics, has inherited all of these problematic features.

On this theme, Walton Hamilton states in his original essay, "The institutional approach to economic theory", for example, that (1919: 318), "Its [institutional economics'] concern with reality, its inability to ground a scheme of thought upon a few premises, its necessity of reflecting a changing economic life, alike make its development slow and prevent it from becoming a formal system of laws and principles. It must find in relevancy and truth a substitute for formal precision in statement."

Likewise, Edwin Witte, one of Common's closest students and later a president of the American Economic Association, states (1954: 133):

> Institutional economics, as I conceive it, is not so much a connected body of economic thought as a method of approaching economic problems. ... In seeking solutions of practical problems, they [the institutionalists] try to give consideration to all aspects of these problems: economic (in the orthodox use of that term), social, psychological, historical, legal, political, administrative, and even technical.

A more recent commentator, Rodney Stevenson, states in his presidential address to the Association for Evolutionary Economics (2002: 263): "Institutional economics is about problem-solving" and (p. 276), "Rather than envisioning ourselves as social scientists, institutional economists should reconceptualize themselves as social physicians." What all of these statements point to is that institutional economics shares both the priorities and shortcomings of its intellectual forebear, the historical–social school of economics and, in particular, the emphasis on holism, realism and applied problem solving and concomitant lack of formal (or perhaps "analytical") theory.

While the "lack of theory" viewpoint must be given its due, to claim that institutional economics during its early formative years (the 1920s and 1930s) was bereft of a conceptual framework and body of theory for purposes of science building would be inaccurate and misleading. This is the case I set out to demonstrate by examining two levels of institutional theory. The first is the general theoretical corpus or framework of institutional economics; the second is the institutional theory of labour economics – that is, industrial relations.

To start the discussion, I first examine the institutional method of theorizing, for this heavily influences the nature of the theory itself. In this regard, the institutional economists were very much in the German and British historical tradition. Every early institutional economist was united in the belief that neoclassical theory was a seriously incomplete and biased view of human nature and economic activity and, thus, an inaccurate and misleading tool for purposes of understanding and prediction. The origins of this problem, from their perspective, are threefold. The first is that the neoclassical economists of their day followed in the tradition of Ricardo and sought to develop, using deductive reasoning, a universally applicable body of formal theory built on a small base of unverified a priori axioms and economic laws. Since these assumptions were in important respects unrealistic – in the sense of being a poor first approximation to the facts of real life – the predictions of the theory were likewise often thought to be inaccurate. The second was the penchant of these economists to model economics along the line of physics, treating people as "individualistic atoms" guided and constrained only by impersonal and invisible forces of competition with no role for social interactions or national cultures and histories (Mirowski, 1989). The third problem was taking for granted the institutional framework within which markets and competition operate, neglecting the fact that much economic activity takes place within formal organizations (as well as markets) and that markets are themselves regulated by a complex web of property rights, laws, social norms and customs (Schmid, 1987).

The methodology of institutional economics seeks to solve or avoid these problems. Institutional economists (at least many of them) are not averse to theorizing, but insist that the theory be grounded in the facts of real life and take into account the historical, social and political environment in which economic activity takes place. Realism is a virtue in institutional economics and, to ensure realism, the institutional method insists that the person building the theory gain contact with real-life aspects of the subject through "go and see" methods of field investigation, personal interviews and case studies. Illustratively, Slichter took a summer job in a factory of the International Harvester Company to gain insight into the causes of factory turnover, while Commons had his students tour nearly two dozen firms before they collectively wrote the book *Industrial government* (1921b). Commons and other institutionalists also had close relationships with trade union leaders, such as Samuel Gompers, and business executives, such as Henry Dennison, and incorporated their insights and writings (Bruce, 2004).

One virtue of "go and see" methods of research is that they acquaint the researcher with the real nature of the problem; another is that they provide facts and insights on construction of realistic assumptions and generalizations for purposes of theory building. In this respect, the institutionalists practised a modified form of inductive theory development in which they constructed the premises, assumptions and "laws" of a theory from regularities revealed in empirical research and personal observation. Stated another way, institutional economics demands that theorizing start with empirically informed priors. Of course, empirically informed priors are not only closer to the truth but also likely to be more complex and contingent, thus complicating and sometimes preventing more abstract, formal and deterministic types of theory building. As an example, early institutional economists rejected the economic man of neoclassical theory as too unrealistic and narrowly constructed and sought to substitute in its place a broader "social" and "behavioural" model, drawing insights from fieldwork and ideas and theories from psychology and sociology. Veblen (1899), for example, argues that emulation and status seeking are as powerful as self-interest (forms of social interaction typically excluded from the model of economic man), while Perlman (1928) explains the origin of job-control trade unionism as the workers' response to the insecurity of the marketplace. As a third example, Commons (1934a) argues that human decision making is not perfectly rational as presumed in neoclassical theory but is instead heavily constrained by "stupidity, ignorance, and passion" – insights later taken by Nobel laureate Herbert Simon and developed into the theory of bounded rationality (Simon, 1982: 449; Kaufman, 1999c). Status seeking, security and bounded rationality, while evidently powerful forces in human behaviour, are nonetheless difficult to build into a composite model of human behaviour that is analytically tractable for purposes of model building.

Another methodological consequence of realism is that theory building in institutional economics is necessarily multidisciplinary. The strategy of neoclassical economics is "imperialistic", in that it always begins with the standard model of microeconomics (e.g., assumptions of rationality, maximization, competitive markets, equilibrium) and uses it – without reference to ideas or concepts from related disciplines – to model and explain all forms of human behaviour (Becker, 1976; Lazear, 2000). From an institutional perspective, the result is a caricature of real life: a theory that may accurately capture a slice of reality (like a Picasso painting) but which misses or misrepresents many aspects of the larger picture. Believing that economic behaviour stems not only from the standard economic assumptions of microeconomics but also from influences and motives emphasized in sociology, psychology, law and ethics, institutionalists are naturally drawn to build theories that also include ideas and concepts from these other disciplines. In this vein, Commons (1934a: 56) states that the goal of institutional economics is to "correlate economics, law, and ethics". An alternative description of institutional economics (Schumpeter, 1954), as noted in the previous chapter, is that it represents "economic sociology".

Also noteworthy from a methodological point of view, institutional economics downgrades (but does not eliminate) the central analytical device of neoclassical economics – marginal analysis and differential calculus. The reasoning is that many economic and social institutions and relations have large elements of indivisibility, non-convexity and path dependency and are thus incompatible with these techniques (Potts, 2000). A form of non-convexity, for example, is increasing returns of scale which institutionalists regard as ubiquitous in economic relations (because of the ubiquity of fixed cost and learning by doing), while a form of path dependency is a social phenomenon called history or, more precisely, the idea that future events are contingent on (or partially predetermined by) past events. The latter phenomenon is ruled out of neoclassical economics by the continuity assumption that allows economic agents (as in Walrasian general equilibrium models) to make fully contingent contracts that incorporate all possible future states of the world (Clower and Howitt, 1997). In these situations, alternative mathematical techniques have to be used, such as game theory, lattice theory and computer simulations, or, more frequently, resort is made to comparative, literary, and historical methods of theory construction. Marginal analysis and equilibrium are not completely ruled out of court, however, for institutionalists recognize that these techniques have pragmatic usefulness and fit the requirement of realism in a certain subset of economic activity.

Finally, institutional economics shares with historical–social economics one other methodological attribute – a predisposition to mix positive and normative considerations in scholarly research. This predisposition comes from two sources. The first is that in nearly all cases the early American institutional economists were social reformers and, to varying degrees, critics of existing economic relations. For them, theory and academic research could not be divorced from the social obligation facing every scholar to work toward the improvement of the human condition and elimination of injustice. Since injustice is always present and the human condition never reaches its highest development, every generation of social scientists faces the same calling. The second is their belief that all theorizing in the social sciences inevitably has a normative component. The normative component enters in the choice of assumptions and decision rules included in the theory. Why, for example, did Adam Smith build his model of the invisible hand on certain assumptions, such as self-interest and competitive markets, and not on others? The answer, as Smith is frank to admit, is that he sought to demonstrate a normative proposition – that a system of natural liberty is superior to a system of mercantilism. One may also ask: why do neoclassical economists favour the welfare rule of Pareto optimality and not another, such as the greatest good for the greatest number (utilitarianism)? Marx, on the other hand, used different assumptions, such as a labour theory of value and the reserve army of the unemployed, to derive quite different normative conclusions. Thus, from an institutional point of view the choice of assumptions is never "innocent" but always has a purpose in mind, and this purpose is inevitably tainted with normative considerations. In this spirit, Barbash (1991: 107) observes, "In the final analysis differences in method are typically metaphors for differences in underlying ideology. Institutional labour economics and industrial relations sought to advance equity in the employment relationship. Economics has been used mostly to resist it."

The above-described methodological positions of institutional economics are, in almost all respects, also the methodological positions of industrial relations in its science-building mode. Numerous examples in succeeding pages and chapters will demonstrate this point. Having covered methodology, I now turn to the issue of theory itself.

The issue at hand is whether the new field of industrial relations, as it emerged in the 1920s and 1930s, started life with any discernible theoretical framework or mode of theorizing or, alternatively, was it entirely descriptive (fact-gathering) and prescriptive? Again, one must note that some famous scholars in industrial relations have taken the negative position on this matter. An example is Dunlop's well-known complaint (1958: vi) that, "[g]reat piles of facts are lying around unutilized" and "a systematic and theoretical discipline of industrial relations is still to be established". Recognizing that opinions vary greatly on this matter, and that sometimes writings and ideas look more coherent with the advantage of hindsight, I nonetheless argue that Dunlop is incorrect on this issue and that, in fact, industrial relations had in this early period a nascent theoretical framework, albeit in certain respects largely inchoate and in other respects not well articulated and formalized.

As earlier stated, the theoretical framework of industrial relations, to the degree it existed at this early time, was largely derivative from American institutional economics and the antecedent German and British historical–social economics. Furthermore, the theory of institutional economics plays out at three levels – the grand, meta-level of institutional theory that attempts to explain the choice of economic systems; the middle, meso-level of institutional theory that attempts to explain the operation of a particular type of economic system (e.g., the price system of markets or command system of organizations); and a micro-level pertaining to the individual human agent. The micro-level theory has already been described – a behavioural/social model of the human agent, so attention is focused on the meta- and meso-dimensions.

In searching for the theoretical perspective of institutional economics writ large, one place to begin is Hamilton's article (1919), where the concept of institutional economics is first advanced. In it, he identifies five characteristics of institutional economics. The theory (1) unifies economic science and explains different economic systems (patterns of economic organization), (2) is relevant to the modern problem of social control of industry and economy (as opposed to laissez-faire, which presumes no active social control), (3) deals with the proper subject matter of economics, which is institutions (recognizing that all economic activity takes place within socially constructed institutions, such as firms and markets), (4) is concerned with matters of process, dynamics and evolution, and (5) is based on an acceptable (realistic, empirically informed) theory of human behaviour.

If there is one person in these early, pre-Second World War years who tried to pull these five attributes together and develop a theory of institutional economics, it is Commons in his magnum opus *Institutional economics: Its place in political economy* (1934a).[4] It must be freely admitted that this book, both when published and up to the present day, has had a negligible influence on industrial relations. To the best of my knowledge, Jack Barbash and Neil Chamberlain, perhaps with Milton Derber, are the only American industrial relationists to have exhibited in their writings any substantial influence from the theory expounded in *Institutional economics*. One reason for this minimal effect is that Commons' style of exposition is so dense and convoluted that it defies all but the most determined readers; another is that Commons covers several hundred years of history, the detailed evolution of economic doctrines, and theoretical concepts in a wide range of other fields; and yet another is that his theoretical ideas were considerably ahead of his time. Given these caveats, it is nonetheless instructive to examine in more detail the ideas contained in this book for they can be considered to provide the intellectual backbone for both institutional economics and industrial relations. Furthermore, as indicated below, many of the basic ideas and points of view explicated by Commons had earlier entered into economics discourse among other institutional economists, even if not through the pages of *Institutional economics*.

Scarcity, Commons says, is the elemental fact of economic life, and to overcome scarcity every society must devise methods to resolve conflict, deal with interdependence and create order. Institutional economics, like Durkheimian sociology, thus takes as its problematic "the problem of order" and, in particular, the creation of institutions to effectively coordinate human beings in the acts of production, distribution and consumption, and resolve the disputes that arise therefrom. In this spirit, Commons (1934a: 6) states: "In my judgement this collective control of individual transactions is the contribution of institutional economics to the whole of a rounded out theory of Political Economy." In modern language, institutional economics is thus the study of alternative regimes of social coordination and control, including as a subset "varieties of capitalism" (Hall and Soskice, 2001). In this sense it clearly satisfies Hamilton's first characteristic: unifying economic science and explaining different economic systems.

Commons proceeds to consider different social coordination and control systems, such as capitalism, fascism and communism. The two ends of the spectrum of economic organization, he states, are economies of "extreme individualism" and "extreme collectivism". In modern language, these two end points are models of "perfect decentralization" and "perfect centralization", represented in the former case by the competitive "invisible hand" economy of general equilibrium theory and in the latter case by a top-to-bottom centrally planned economy (Kaufman, 2003d). In a perfectly decentralized economy, all economic activity is coordinated by price through markets; in a perfectly centralized economy all economic activity is coordinated by command through organizations. Of course, in real life all economic systems are mixed economies and occupy some place in the middle of the spectrum and feature coordination by both price and command.

Commons observes that every economic system can be thought of analytically as an industrial government or a governance system. A governance system, in turn, is defined and structured by a web of rules – called by Commons the "working rules of collective action", such as laws, court decisions, business and trade union rules, social norms, ethical principles and customs, that in totality delineate the opportunities and constraints of each person. All of these working rules, both formal and informal, are property rights (or simply "rights") in the sense that they give individuals control over scarce resources, including their physical self and political liberties. An economic system is thus a series of institutions, including governments, markets and firms, which coordinate human economic behaviour by creating property rights, establishing rules for the exchange of property rights, and enforcing the rules and resolving conflicts. The degree to which this "system of order" functions effectively is determined, in turn, by the characteristics of the people in it (e.g., their rationality, intelligence, social behaviour) and the degree to which the web of working rules is effectively formulated, aligned and administered in light of environmental conditions.

Armed with this insight, the question is how societies determine the type of economic system they use. Since each economic system, such as a decentralized market economy and centralized command economy, represents a quite different configuration of working rules, the issue is to determine why one configuration of rules is used over another. Toward this end, Commons notes that production and distribution of economic goods requires exchange and that exchange rests on property rights and contract law – important elements in the totality of working rules. Thus he is led to define the *transaction* as the most fundamental unit of analysis for institutional economics. A transaction is (p. 55) "the legal transfer of ownership". He specifies three types of transactions: the bargaining transaction (exchange of property rights through market exchange), the rationing transaction (exchange of property rights commanded by a legal superior) and the managerial transaction (the exchange of the worker's property rights over his or her labour power with the employer). The bargaining transaction represents market coordination of economic activity through price; the rationing transaction represents organizational coordination of economic activity through command; and the managerial transaction represents the use of command to separate the worker and his or her labour power during the labour process (the worker's time and physical presence are obtained by the employer through a bargaining transaction in the labour market, the labour power is then obtained through the managerial transaction).

As later explicated by Ronald Coase (1937), Oliver Williamson (1985) and other "new institutional" economists, the choice of organizations and command coordination or markets and price coordination – or, to use a modern phrase, the choice of "make versus buy" – turns on the relative benefits and costs of using each type of transactional mode. This line of thought has led to the concept of transaction cost, which may be defined as the ex ante and ex post costs of transferring the ownership of property rights. New institutional economists have shown that when transaction costs are zero – made possible by neoclassical assumptions such as perfect human rationality, perfect information, perfect divisibility of property rights and zero costs of legal enforcement, all contracts are complete and fully contingent and, accordingly, all economic activity takes place through product markets in a system of perfect decentralization (Furubotn and Richter, 1997). In such a system, only single-person firms exist (family farms and self-employed artisans and independent contractors), implying that there are no labour markets nor employment relationships and thus no rationale for a field of industrial relations (Dow, 1997; Kaufman, 2004g). When transaction costs are non-zero, however – made possible by non-neoclassical assumptions of bounded rationality, imperfect information, incomplete markets and costly enforcement of contracts – economic activity takes place through a mix of markets and organizations, including large hierarchial firms with an employment relationship (Kaufman, 2004d).

Without going into further detail about the meta-theory of institutional economics, several points deserve emphasis.

First, the field of industrial relations is predicated on the existence of an employer–employee relationship, generally assumed to be embedded in a capitalist economy. Although scarcely developed and understood in the 1920s and 1930s, from the vantage point of today the theory of institutional economics, as described above, does provide conceptual tools for under-standing and predicting the central problematic of industrial relations: the nature, structure and performance of the employment relationship. Thus one may conclude that industrial relations has a theoretical foundation – it is the labour economics of positive transaction cost.

Second, positive transaction cost implies that markets can never be self-regulating or fully efficient. To assume such is to assume a utopia that cannot exist, much like communism. With positive transaction cost, all contracts are incomplete, markets and price cannot fully coordinate economic activity, and some markets will be missing altogether. Labour markets must thus be regulated by other institutional controls and in many cases replaced altogether by more efficient governance systems (e.g., large corporations) and coordinating mechanisms (e.g., human resource management).

Third, institutional economics and industrial relations are inherently multidisciplinary (as the disciplines are conventionally defined). With positive transaction cost, every economic system will be a "mixed economy" of different types of economic institutions, such as firms, markets, governments and non-profit agencies. To understand the operation of the economy, therefore, one must know how price and markets work but also how command and organizations work, as well as the law and government policy that regulate them. Management theory is thus just as much a part of economics as is price theory, and the theory of general market equilibrium and theory of scientific management are in reality a theoretical unity: one seeks optimal efficiency through price and the coordinating mechanism of markets and the other seeks optimal efficiency through command and the coordinating mechanism of formal organization. Further, since contracts are incomplete, society must invent other ways to enforce contracts and coordinate exchange. Examples include social norms, cultural values, religious principles, statute law, court rulings, company policy and collective bargaining agreements. Sociology, law, history, political science, management, organization theory, ethics and other such disciplines and fields of study are thus essential to institutional economics.

A fourth point is that the theory of institutional economics makes different assumptions about the welfare criteria that are used to judge the performance of the economy. Neoclassical economics judges economic performance with reference to one welfare criterion, that of economic efficiency. According to this criterion, the best economy is the one that produces the most output at the least cost. The group this criterion favours is consumers – consumers are the "sovereign" power in the economy, firms are perfect agents in that competitive prices guide them to produce the optimal quantity and quality of goods and services demanded by consumers, and labour and all other inputs are utilized to their maximum and for only as long as needed in the pursuit of consumers' satisfaction.

Institutional economics, on the other hand, uses a broader set of welfare criteria. One goal is efficiency for, clearly, human welfare rises with greater material abundance. But material abundance is hardly the sole desideratum for the "good life" (Lane, 1991; Budd, 2004). According to the early institutionalists, also crucial are two other welfare criteria: the achievement of equity (social justice) and expanding opportunities for development of the self. Equity captures the idea that satisfaction with life comes from not only maximizing the size of the pie but also from a subjective feeling that both the process used to make the pie and the distribution of the pie are fair and meet a collective sense of being just or reasonable. Development of the self captures, in turn, the idea that people gain satisfaction in life from more than fulfilment of self-interest. Also as important, if not more so, is the fulfilment of other concepts, such as self-esteem, self-respect, self-efficacy and self-actualization. Besides gaining the maximum of goods and services, for example, people also want to be treated with dignity and respect; feel valued for their own intrinsic worth as human beings rather than an instrumental means to an end; to have a measure of voice and control in matters that concern them; and have a life situation that provides rewarding experiences, new opportunities and challenges for personal growth and development, and freedom from fear and insecurity. In effect, the neoclassical school bases economic welfare only on the bottom level of Maslow's hierarchy of needs, while the institutionalists use the bottom, middle and top levels (Lutz and Lux, 1979).[5]

With this expanded social welfare function, economic performance can no longer be judged solely on the basis of maximum production at least cost but must also consider equity and self-development. With this addition, the neoclassical conclusion that a competitive free market economy maximizes social welfare (the fundamental welfare theorem) no longer holds, as some contributors to well-being at work have a public goods quality and are underproduced, such as pleasant working conditions and fair treatment, while in other cases competitive markets create conditions that directly subtract from well-being, such as insecurity and social anomie (Rothstein, 2002). Equally important, these expanded welfare criteria justify counting the producer interests of workers in the social welfare function as well as the interests of consumers – since fair treatment and self-development opportunities at work affect life satisfaction, in addition to the amount of goods and services – and rationalize trading off higher prices in consumption for improved conditions at work. Differently stated, a certain degree of "protectionism" for workers now gains social legitimacy.

A fifth point is that institutional economics, and thus industrial relations, is always at its meta-level an exercise in political economy. Commons emphasizes that the corpus of economic institutions and fabric of legal relations governing and embedding economic relations of production and buying and selling are always determined by the rulers of the sovereign nation-state. Thus he states (1934a: 522–3): "The subject matter of institutional economy ... is not commodities, nor labour, nor any physical thing – it is collective action which sets the working rules for proprietary rights, duties, liberties, and exposures." Political science, law and the ethical considerations of the social good are thus inseparable from the study of economics and industrial relations. The exercise of political sovereignty by the rulers of the nation (and rulers of lower-level industrial governments, such as firms and unions, and international agencies) is the most basic of all determinants of the industrial relations system, since it is sovereignty that determines the web of working rules, individual resource endowments and the social trade-off between efficiency, equity and human self-development.

A sixth point is that institutional economic theory singles out labour for special treatment since labour is not assumed to be a commodity, as in neoclassical economics, but is explicitly modelled as residing in a human being. The human essence of labour, combined with incomplete contracts, means that the workplace is always a "contested terrain" and a place of moral significance. The labour process (managerial transaction) is largely ignored in neoclassical theory, where a unit of commodity-like labour is purchased on the market and via the production function yields a determinate output. But, as

107

Commons and Marx before him emphasize, what the employer purchases is an hour of a person's time, while what produces output is labour power. The labour process – the process by which the labour power is separated from the worker – is thus the most personal and direct location of the conflict of interest in the employment relationship. It is also the site of considerable indeterminacy in the labour contract regarding how much work, sweat, stress, self-respect and so forth is to be exchanged for money. Because of this indeterminacy, a process of implicit and explicit bargaining (the wage/effort bargain) at the point of production is ongoing and endemic. The neoclassical labour demand (marginal product) curve thus becomes ill defined. This indeterminacy also creates the need for a human resource management function to use carrots and sticks to gain as much labour power as possible at least cost (Kaufman, 2004e).

A seventh point is that it is impossible to separate ethics and economics even on purely "positive" grounds of prediction and understanding. With incomplete contracts, self-interest can quickly turn dysfunctional and anti-social. Because of bounded rationality, imperfect information and lock-in from fixed costs, economic agents have an incentive to cheat, lie, misrepresent, renege and extort both in the ex ante process of making a contract and the ex post process of contract implementation. This corruption of the economic exchange process can cause markets to self-destruct and bring great injury to the exposed party. In an imperfect world, legal sanctions can never fully eliminate such behaviour and, indeed, legal sanctions can be used by the powerful to exploit the weak. Thus, crucial to a well-functioning economy, and thus to economic theory, is a commonly accepted and observed moral code that protects the contracting process from breakdown and abuse. Also crucial to economic theory is one particular ethical value – justice (equity). Neoclassical economics neglects justice on the grounds that it is a metaphysical concept or non-scientific value judgement. Real people, however, judge economic transactions by not only price but also fairness, and transactions that are deemed unfair lead to predictable negative consequences, such as quitting, holding back work effort, striking and forming a union. Thus institutional economics recognizes, not as a matter of special pleading but as a statement about how the world works, that free trade in property rights must also be fair trade and that exchanges that violate the canon of fairness will introduce their own form of inefficiency and welfare loss.

Finally, an eighth point is that theory in institutional economics and industrial relations must also have an evolutionary and historical component since institutions make economic development path-dependent, and the social, legal and technical relations that market exchange rests on are continually changing over time. It is not a coincidence, therefore, that the institutional labour economists specialized in historical labour research, exemplified by

Commons' famous article on "American shoemakers" (1909) and multi-volume *History of labor in the United States* (1918).

Although *Institutional economics* did not have significant influence at the time of its publication, the general point of view and many of the basic ideas contained in it were already known to and appreciated by the institutional economists who formed the core group active in industrial relations. The clearest example is provided by Sumner Slichter of Harvard University. (Slichter was a master's student at Wisconsin and then obtained his Ph.D. at the University of Chicago.) It is noteworthy, for example, that in his book *Modern economic society* (2nd ed., 1931), the title of Chapter 1 is "The control of economic activity". This chapter is then followed by nine chapters in Part 2 that deal with the organization and operation of industry (the "command" economy), followed by 13 chapters in Part 3 that deal with markets (the "price" economy).

Focusing on Chapter 1, Slichter states several themes that are directly related to the points just enumerated from Commons. For example, regarding social control of industry and ethical values Slichter tells his readers (p. 16), "Our ultimate concern is with the problem of social control, with how to bring our methods of making a living into harmony with our conceptions of a good life", and (p. 14):

> Here we are undoubtedly face to face with the kernel of the problem of industrial control – namely, how to prevent industry from unduly molding our opinions, how to prevent our ideals, our scales of values, from being too much affected by the standards of the market-place, how, in short, to protect life itself from being too completely dominated by the process of getting a living.

Regarding the subject of economics and the role of institutions and human relations, he states (pp. 11–12, emphasis added):

> Economics studies industry, not as a technological process [i.e., neoclassical production function], but as a complex of *human practices and relationships*. ... It is vitally concerned with how human interests are affected by the *institutions* of slavery, serfdom, or the wages system. ... In brief, economics is simply the study of industry from the standpoint of the human practices and organizations which make the process of getting a living what it is.

Concerning human nature, he states (p. 8) "[h]uman cupidity and stupidity are dangerous in proportion to the power which men have at their disposal", while the performance of a free market system is likewise portrayed as subject to great limitations because (p. 5) "[a]mong the most extraordinary economic phenomena of the age are the periods of unemployment and depression. ... Under existing economic arrangements, most enterprises must normally restrict

109

output [i.e., are not competitive firms]", and (p. 10) "it is difficult to avoid the conclusion that man, in no small degree, is a slave to his creations, dominated by industry instead of making it serve his ends". Finally, he concludes that the problem of social control and organization of industry are (p. 9) "more difficult than the problems of political organization because, in the case of industry, it is a matter of giving a balanced representation to a broad range of interests without seriously impairing the efficient operation of complicated and delicate economic machinery".

The science-building face of early American industrial relations was significantly influenced by this meta-theoretical perspective and approach to research methodology of its intellectual parent, institutional economics. The greater source of intellectual influence, however, was more immediate and occurred at the level of meso-theory – the institutional theory of labour markets and organizations as developed during the early twentieth century. This level of institutional economics in modern nomenclature would be called labour economics, although the conception and boundaries of the institutional version of this subject (i.e., industrial relations) are considerably different from the neoclassical version.

As with the meta-level of institutional economics, most modern-day economists believe that the early institutional economists also failed at the meso-level to develop theory or useful generalizations, implying that the science-building face of industrial relations was in its early days largely an empty intellectual space. Illustrative of this point of view, Boyer and Smith (2001: 201) state:

> Institutional labor economics emphasized the word *labor*. This approach was fact-based, its methodology largely was inductive, and it generally relied on a case study approach toward data-gathering. From the intensive, often historical, study of individual cases or events came detailed *descriptions* of various labor-market institutions or outcomes. Followers of this institutional approach differentiated 'descriptive economics' from 'economic theory,' and saw their role as providing 'data sufficiently concrete, definite, and convenient to form a basis for analysis, discussion, and criticism.'

This statement, and similar views, capture a portion of truth about the early institutional labour economists. Certainly their research, reflecting its roots in historical economics, emphasized the inductive and historical method, eschewed abstract and formal forms of theorizing, and devoted great effort to "digging up the facts". To dismiss this line of research, however, as descriptive economics or otherwise barren of theoretical generalization is quite inaccurate.

The beginning point for the institutional analysis of labour is the observation (already drawn from the meta-level of theory) that economic activity involving labour takes place within two distinct types of institutions: labour markets coordinated by price and formal organizations coordinated by command. The job of meta-level institutional theory is to determine the split or "division of labour" between the two institutions. At the level of meso-theory, this split is taken as a "given" and institutional analysis proceeds to theorize separately about each form of institution. I start with theorizing about labour markets, as contained in the writings of the early institutional labour economists, and then turn to formal organizations.

The institutional theory of labour markets builds on and incorporates the larger methodological and theoretical principles already articulated. But, naturally, this theory goes deeper into the construction and operation of labour markets. Perhaps the first point to note is that the early institutionalists did not entirely reject the orthodox supply and demand model of labour markets. Their position is that orthodox theory has useful insights but that it is nonetheless defective because it takes a too narrow and mechanistic view of the matter. Thus Commons (1919b: 5) states, "Demand and supply determines wages. ... The ebb and flow of the labour market is like the ebb and flow of the commodity market." He goes on to say, however, that (p. 17, emphasis added) "the commodity theory of labor is not false, it is *incomplete*".

In their science-building mode, therefore, the early institutional economists sought to explicate an alternative, more complete and accurate (or realistic) model of labour markets. The greatest source of inspiration came from Sidney and Beatrice Webb and their monumental book *Industrial democracy* (1897). Leo Wolman, a prominent institutional labour economist of the 1920s and 1930s, attests to the influence of the Webbs when he states (1961: 55): "[T]he labor view [was] first and most effectively developed by the Webbs, where they set out, in a literary way, to develop the whole notion of inequality of bargaining power, and there wasn't a man in the United States – or in the world – who taught this stuff, or any writers of textbooks in succeeding generations, who didn't say this." The depiction and reasoning about labour markets set out by the Webbs was thus the foundation for early American institutional labour economics, albeit one to which they added elaborations and qualifications.

The Webbs' labour theory in *Industrial democracy* is examined in detail in the next chapter so I mention only the key points here. First, wage determination is looked at as a bargaining process. The Webbs propose that in most situations of individual bargaining the worker typically suffers from an inequality of bargaining power due to market imperfections and considerable unemployment, which in turn depresses wages and working conditions below competitive full employment levels. Trade unions can promote efficiency and equity by raising wages, thus restoring a balance in wage determination, motivating employers to improve plant operations and invest in new capital, and making sure firms pay the full social cost of labour. This is best achieved by using market-wide collective bargaining to set a uniform floor (or "common rule") of labour cost, thus taking wages out of competition. In this view, trade unionism not only provides a balance to the employer's market power over labour but also a balance to the employer's power over the worker in internal firm governance, thus promoting democracy in industry. The conceptual framework developed by the Webbs was adopted by the American institutionalists and then expanded and elaborated.

The institutional theory of labour markets starts by considering the end goal(s) towards which economic activity is meant to contribute. As previously noted, these goals are the trilogy of efficiency, equity and self-development. Commons (1934a) sought to incorporate equity into labour theory through the concepts of reasonable value and fair competition. The former represents the notion that all labour market outcomes (e.g., wages, hours) must pass the test of "reasonableness" in the eyes of society or they lose moral legitimacy and are not likely to be allowed to exist as long-run equilibrium values, while the latter holds that competition may be free but unfair if one side has much greater bargaining power (options and alternatives) than the other. With respect to self-development, the institutionalists felt that orthodox theory makes production of goods and services the goal of economic activity and turns workers into mere instruments (or "inputs") to accomplish this end. Properly viewed, however, the economic system should serve humankind, including people's needs to grow and develop as personalities and spiritual beings. In this vein, Ely (1886: 3) argues that labour markets should promote "the full and harmonious development in each individual of all human faculties".

A second principle that flows from the first is that economic theory should include in people's utility functions not only consumption goods but also variables representing the conditions and experience of work, and that where efficiency and the two other goals (justice, self-development) conflict, a trade-off should be made. Commenting on the orthodox point of view, Commons (1919b: 33) states workers are treated "as commodities to be bought and sold according to supply and demand", while in the institutional perspective "they are treated as citizens with rights against others on account of their value to the nation as a whole". Slichter (1931: 651–2) arrives at the same idea when he says "it is vitally important that the methods of production shall be planned not only to turn out goods at low costs but to provide the kind of jobs which develop the desirable capacities of the workers".

A third principle is that in economic theory the human agent should be modelled as purposive and self-interested, but with two significant amendments.

The first, previously noted, is to incorporate a theory of bounded rationality. The second is to also incorporate interdependent utility functions, noting that many human emotions (e.g., injustice, hatred, love, envy) arise from interactions or comparisons with other people. This fact is another reason why orthodox theoretical constructs, such as indifference curves and labour supply and demand curves, are not stable functions (Slichter, 1931: 625–7; Kaufman, 1999b; 2004c).

A fourth principle is that most labour markets contain significant imperfections, such as limited information, mobility costs and externalities, and these imperfections most often work to the disadvantage of labour. As Commons' student Harry Millis (Millis and Montgomery, 1945: 364–5) states, for instance: "Industry affords an abundance of evidence that a competitive demand for labour does not go far to protect the workers against long hours, excessive overtime, fines, discharges without sufficient cause, and objectionable working conditions." An example often cited by the institutionalists was the American steel industry where even a nationwide strike in 1919 was unable to induce employers to abandon the 84-hour work-week.

Fifth, the market imperfections just cited create an inequality of bargaining power for many workers, particularly the less skilled and educated and in periods of less than full employment (Kaufman, 1989). One consequence is that wages for many workers are market determined only within an upper and lower limit, and within these bounds they are determined by either administrative fiat or bargaining. Because wages are often administered prices, Commons (Commons and Andrews, 1916, 4th ed.: 372) notes that "today 'individual bargaining' in any real sense [in the sense of a "give and take"] cannot exist" and that without union or government help "the inequality in withholding power between employer and employee is so great that the term bargaining is a misnomer [i.e., is "take it or leave it"]". Reminiscent of the Webbs, he further states (p. 373), "It is obvious that the individual labourer is at a great disadvantage in bargaining with the employer. ... It is a case of the necessities of the labourer pitted against the resources of the employer." Out of such conditions grow overt exploitation and sweatshops.

A sixth principle is that ordinarily most labour markets have more people wanting work than there are jobs. The result is to add to the employer's bargaining advantage, put downward pressure on wages and working conditions, and obviate the need of employers to pay fully compensating wage differentials for things such as safety risks and long hours. "This competition," states Slichter (1931: 294), "if unrestricted, is likely to result in low wages, a killing speed of work, an excessively long working day, and hazardous and unhealthy shop conditions." Another consequence of excess labour supply, according to the institutionalists, is that it leads to a labour market version of Gresham's Law in which bad employment practices drive out good. States Commons (1913: 411), "It is an application of the well-known principle of political economy that the competition of the worst employers tends to drag down the best employers to their level." This type of downward pressure on established labour standards can also arise from large-scale immigration or the extension of markets, such as described in Commons' (1909) classic study of American shoemakers. If the overhang of excess labour supply or cheaper labour is large and persistent, a condition of destructive competition may ensue where labour market conditions spiral downward in a race to the bottom.

A seventh principle is that often wage rates are unable to equilibrate demand and supply and clear labour markets. One reason is that the wage rate performs a dual role in labour markets – it allocates labour, as in neoclassical theory, but is also used by firms to motivate labour (Slichter, 1931: 592–650). The wage rate (or change in the wage) that meets one objective often does not meet the other, leading to non-market-clearing outcomes. A second reason is that wage cuts are often unable to eliminate involuntary unemployment due to insufficient aggregate demand. The early institutionalists were "proto-Keynesians" in that they believed that the level of output and labour demand was primarily a function of the level of purchasing power and, thus, they concluded that wage cuts often exacerbate the level of unemployment (Slichter, 1931: 490–91). Of all the defects of capitalist labour markets, Commons (1921a: 1–16; 1934b: 67) and the institutionalists believed that unemployment is the most serious and debilitating for good industrial relations.

Eighth, the early institutionalists believed that on net workers do not receive the full value of their marginal product (Slichter, 1931: 616–39; Douglas, 1934: 94). One reason is that firms often face a rising supply curve of labour even in relatively competitive labour markets (because inframarginal workers face positive costs of mobility and can be paid less than is necessary to attract new workers from the labour market), giving rise to an upward-sloping marginal cost of labour schedule and an equilibrium wage that is less than the workers' marginal revenue product (Manning, 2003; Mitchell and Erickson, 2004). In addition, specific on-the-job training, and other sources of bilateral monopoly, create an area of indeterminacy in wage rates and thus open the door to wage determination through bargaining. Given that workers (particularly the less skilled) suffer an overall inequality of bargaining power, they are likely to be underpaid relative to their productivity. Worker bargaining power is also undercut by involuntary unemployment in labour markets, which allows firms to pay a wage lower than a truly competitive value marginal product.

Ninth, and finally, the institutionalists noted that competitive labour markets contain an inherent contradiction that sabotages both their efficiency and sustainability. The essence of a real-life competitive labour market is intense rivalry, no security in a job, and constant change in wages. These conditions have no effect on a commodity such as wheat or steel but people tend to be averse to them. For this reason, as labour markets become very competitive – particularly when "more competitive" includes not enough jobs for everyone who wants one – workers develop deep feelings of fear, insecurity and "scarcity consciousness" and take actions to protect themselves (Perlman, 1928). These actions, all restrictive in nature, include forming trade unions, the closed shop, "going slow" on the job, excluding women and minorities from desirable employment and lobbying politicians to keep out immigrants and foreign goods. Too much competition can thus lead to a protective response that not only curbs competition but may actually lead to the replacement of the market altogether – seen by the growth and development of trade unionism and radical politics particularly in those periods and places where market insecurity is the greatest (Commons, 1922; Polanyi, 1944).

Described to this point is the early institutional view of labour markets. But labour markets are only one institution used to allocate, coordinate and organize productive activity. In modern industrial economies, formal organizations such as firms, unions and employers' associations also perform these functions. Other institutions, such as families and clans, also perform these functions, particularly in less developed economies.

Orthodox economics also includes these organizational entities, albeit generally in highly artificial and narrow terms. The firm, for example, is represented as a production function, while the trade union is typically treated as a labour market monopoly. The early institutional labour economists did not reject these formalizations out of hand, believing instead that they also capture a portion of truth. But, again, they sought to introduce more realism and holism and to reach outside of economics proper for conceptual ideas.

Following the Webbs, the early institutionalists noted that organizational entities such as firms and unions have not only an economic dimension (or function) but also a political dimension and it is the political dimension that they gave precedence to in terms of conceptual analysis. Writing much later, Chamberlain and Kuhn (1965: 49–65) call these functions the marketing and governmental dimensions. According to Commons, for example, both firms and unions are economic entities because firms enter into contracts through bargaining transactions with workers to buy labour services, and unions represent their members in the sale to firms of labour services through bargaining transactions. In general, he and the other institutionalists saw this

115

arrangement in conceptual economic terms as some type of bilateral monopoly arrangement. Typically, non-union firms have some market power in the buying of labour services (per the inequality of bargaining power idea), while trade unions act as a form of labour market cartel – substituting joint marketing of labour for individual bargaining (Kaufman, 2000a). The outcome is to shift the terms and conditions of employment in favour of employees and, most often, also in the direction of a more efficient, socially advantageous utilization of labour (on account of unions offsetting market imperfections, internalizing social costs and balancing the employers' superior bargaining power). Of course, the institutionalists also recognized that in some cases powerful unions can dominate small, competitive employers and then capital suffers from an inequality of bargaining power.

The early institutionalists argued that firms and unions (and other institutions) are also political entities and have political functions. Just as nation-states are governance structures defined by a web of working rules established through collective action and the exercise of sovereign power, so too are all forms of economic organization. Thus firms, unions, employers' associations and the like are viewed as industrial governments, for "they are, indeed, governments, since they are collective action in control of individual action through the use of sanctions" (Commons, 1950: 75). The sanctions (physical, economic, moral) are not exercised, however, by a political president or prime minister but by a chief executive officer, president of a trade union, or leader of a work team. Thus a firm is more than a production function: it is a hierarchial organization with superiors and subordinates and a chain of command. When viewed from a neoclassical perspective, the web of rules is irrelevant in a substantive sense since competitive market forces structure the terms and conditions of employment and give equal power to both employer and employee. From a political perspective, however, the fact that a firm is a governance structure creates an inherently unequal and asymmetric power and authority relation between employer and employee. Similarly, a trade union is not simply a labour market analogue of a monopolist firm that sets a price (wage) to maximize some quantity. Rather it is an instrument used by workers to democratize the governance system of the workplace, replacing a system of industrial absolutism with a system that provides workers with representation, voice, due process and a measure of joint determination of the web of rules.

The problem-solving face

In addition to science building, early American industrial relations had two other "faces". The second is problem solving – the application of knowledge and expertise to solving practical problems in the work world – a method highlighted in Dale Yoder's statement "The most widely accepted approach to the study of industrial relations is one which involves an examination of the phenomena that are usually described as Labour Problems."

Both this chapter and the last have described how the Labour Problem was the central driving force in the birth of the field of industrial relations. Understanding the Labour Problem from an intellectual or scholarly angle was certainly one attraction bringing the first group of academics into the field. In the larger picture, however, most early participants were drawn to industrial relations for more practical and socially and politically motivated reasons (Derber, 1967: 5). Looking back on his career, for example, Commons (1934b: 170) observed: "What I was trying to do, in my academic way, was to save Wisconsin and the nation from politics, socialism, or anarchism, in dealing with the momentous conflict of capital and labor." Toward this end, Commons participated in an immense range of problem-solving activities, including serving on the Wisconsin Industrial Commission, administering the unemployment insurance fund for the Chicago garment trades, drafting numerous pieces of legislation, serving on the Commission on Industrial Relations and other investigative bodies, and performing as arbitrator and mediator in numerous labour disputes. Symbolic of his dual roles as intellectual and problem solver, he had two offices – one at the university and another at the state capital.

Other academics active in early industrial relations were also drawn to the field by the attraction of problem solving. William Leiserson, for example, was a graduate of the Wisconsin programme, became a professor of economics at Antioch College, and wrote several well-recognized books and articles on industrial relations. It was not scholarship, however, that was Leiserson's greatest passion and contribution. Rather, he became the nation's foremost mediator of labour disputes and the chair of numerous high-level labour policy boards, including the National Mediation Board and National Labor Relations Board. States Leiserson's biographer (Eisner, 1967: 5): "Although Leiserson was rooted in the new economics and institutionalism, he was not an 'institutionalist' or a member of any formal school of thought. He was a pragmatic reform economist who was concerned with individuals and their problems and not with economic theory."

While the science-building approach to early industrial relations brought mainly academics to the field, the problem-solving approach also attracted many practitioners from the ranks of business, law, government and social reform groups. Like the academics, they were also repelled by the waste, conflict and human suffering they saw in the work world and attracted by the opportunity to make things better through enlightened leadership and industrial reform. Among business people, the "dean of industrial relations men" was Clarence Hicks. Hicks (1941: 15) states in his autobiography *My life in industrial relations* that he intended to become a lawyer but instead chose a career in industrial relations, because "the law was too far removed from people and their everyday problems to satisfy an urge the good Lord had given me. The next step brought me close to my goal, a life spent working with people, helping them in the job of earning a living and making it worthwhile."

Another practitioner who became involved in industrial relations was Thomas Spates. Spates served as vice-president of personnel at General Foods Corporation, spent several years in Geneva, Switzerland, as the IRC representative to the ILO, wrote numerous articles on industrial relations in publications for the American Management Association, and later retired from business life and became a professor of personnel administration at Yale University. In his autobiography, Spates (1960: 50) states:

> Up to the time of my going into the army in the First World War, most of my employment experiences followed a pattern of mistrust, goldbricking, sabotage, petty theft, and a severe economic waste, as expressions of resentment against inconsiderate leadership. ... It was about then, while reflecting upon my employment experiences, that I resolved to devote my remaining time to trying to improve the lot of my fellow man on the job.

A final example comes from Canada. Although his contributions do not receive adequate recognition today, one of the most influential figures in early industrial relations was William Lyon Mackenzie King. In the Introduction to the 1973 edition of *Industry and humanity*, Bercuson (p. xvii) writes, "It was this desire to work for Christian reform of society which led King into settlement and city mission work and brought him, for a brief time, to Hull House. This, in turn, led to a desire to work for the amelioration of the 'unfortunate' and unprotected members of the working class."

The advancement of labour reform was thus an animating impulse for the early industrial relationists and a central goal of problem solving. Also important is how they approached problem solving.

The labour reformers were part of a wider movement for social reform in the United States called the Progressive Movement, dating from the turn of the century to 1920 (Hoffstadter, 1963). The leaders of the Progressive Movement were primarily drawn from a new generation of people with higher education, middle-class backgrounds, and professional careers in business, government, academia, social services and journalism.

A significant number of the movement's prominent members were women (Rodgers, 1998; Tonn, 2003; Gilson, 1940). They came to the Labour Problem through a variety of channels, such as social reform groups (Florence Kelly of the National Consumers' League), foundations (Mary van Kleeck of the Russell Sage Foundation), independent consulting (Mary Follett, Lillian Gilbreth), industrial welfare work and personnel management (Gertrude Beeks of International Harvester Company and Mary Gilson of Joseph & Feiss Co. and, later, IRC), government (Frances Perkins), journalism (Ida Tarbell), and assistants to their labour-reforming husbands (Irene Andrews, wife of John Andrews, president of the American Association for Labor Legislation). Several women, such as Helen Sumner and Elizabeth Brandeis at Wisconsin, held academic positions, but their numbers were quite small and their influence limited.

Influenced by the development of the social sciences in the United States and the potential opened up by social Taylorism, the men and women of the Progressive Movement strongly embraced the promise held out for social reform by the application of science and expert administration to the problems of work and society. They thus approached social reform as an exercise in social engineering, best removed from the corruption of politics and irrational elements of mass control and entrusted to objective, impartial, but ethically enlightened experts. Says Bercuson (1973: xviii), "They [the progressive labour reformers] commonly believed, for example, that scientific investigation combined with the use of industrial and technological experts was the only proper way to manage society." To Commons (1919b), the task of the industrial relations scholar was to determine "the equilibrium of capital and labor" and the primary tools were theory, investigation, and what he called "utilitarian idealism" – the search for the best practical outcome. In the political spectrum, the early industrial relationists could thus be characterized as social liberals, placing them considerably to the centre (or right) relative to the European social democrats of that era.

Also central to the problem-solving approach of the scholars in early industrial relations was a commitment to non-ideological pragmatism and seeking truth through the facts of experience. In practice, this orientation made the early industrial relations scholars deeply distrustful of Marxist/radical solutions to labour problems, particularly as pronounced by left-wing intellectuals. The classic statement is by Perlman. He begins the Preface to *A theory of the labor movement* with these words (1928: vii–ix):

> Twenty years ago the author of this book, like most of his college generation in Russia, professed the theory of the labor movement found in the Marxian classics. 'Labor' was then to him – he realized afterwards – mainly an abstraction: an abstract mass in the grip of an abstract force. ... Shortly afterwards (having in the meantime transferred himself to the American environment), by an unusual stroke of good luck,

the author joined the research staff of Professor John R. Commons. Here he became acquainted with Professor Commons' method of deducing labor theory from the concrete and crude experience of the wage earners. ... In this approach the Hegelian dialectic nowhere occurs, nor is cognizance taken of labor's 'historical mission.' What monopolizes attention is labor combating competitive menaces – 'scabs,' 'green hands,' and the like; labor bargaining for the control of the job. ... Here he [Perlman] stumbled on the idea that there is a natural divergence in labor ideology between the 'mentality' of the trade unions and the 'mentality' of the intellectuals.

In its science-building mode, institutional economics provided the central organizing framework for research and teaching on industrial relations. Interestingly, a separate but complementary framework was developed to structure discourse and practice in the problem-solving aspects of industrial relations. Rather than focus on the configuration of alternative economic systems, the transaction concept and other intellectual esoterica, industrial relations scholars instead made labour problems the focal point for the problem-solving face of the field (Derber, 1967).

The concept of labour problems grew out of the earlier notion of the Labour Problem. Conceived as a unitary construct, the Labour Problem connoted the generalized struggle between labour and capital over the control of production and distribution of income, and the conflict and violence engendered by this struggle. After the turn of the century, however, usage began to change and the plural form of labour problems came into vogue (Leiserson, 1929). The ascendancy of the new term was heralded by the first university textbook devoted to the study of labour – *Labour problems*, written by Wisconsin professors Thomas Adams and Helen Sumner (McNulty, 1980).

As a generic construct, "labour problems" was used by early writers as a shorthand descriptor for all the various maladjustments, shortcomings and undesirable outcomes and behaviours arising in the work world. The term was significant for the development of industrial relations in several respects.

The pluralist version, for example, recognizes that labour problems take many different forms besides labour–capital conflict, that labour problems afflict both employers and employees, and that labour problems exist in both capitalist and socialist economies. Commonly cited examples of labour problems facing employers were high employee turnover, worker "soldiering" (loafing) and excessive waste and inefficiency in production, while labour problems affecting workers included insecurity of employment, low pay, child labour and unsafe working conditions. By breaking up labour problems into smaller, discrete topics, the subject became less "revolutionary" in scope and spirit, easier to organize teaching and research around, and gave recognition (albeit generally not in equal proportion) to the fact that employers as well as workers suffer from labour problems.

The labour problems concept also imparted a distinct critical, reformist air to the study of labour. Labour problems were often presented as a catalogue of "evils", such as child labour, sweatshops and excessive work-hours, and laid at the door of the present organization of industry. At a broad level of analysis, the source of labour problems was a lack of balance in the industrial relations system (Budd, 2004). This imbalance favoured employers and arose at three strategic locations in the industrial relations system: unequal bargaining power in external labour markets, unchecked management power in internal firm governance, and business domination of the nation's political processes and institutions. More specific causes were unregulated competition in labour and product markets; the practice of employers to view labour as a commodity; the employers' autocratic and insensitive conduct of employee relations; the pressure on workers exerted by poverty and unemployment to sell their labour at any price; and the lopsided advantage enjoyed by employers due to the skewed nature of wealth, property rights, laws and political influence. From this diagnosis flowed a twofold conclusion. First, the present industrial system is badly skewed to the disadvantage of workers and yields outcomes that are in important respects dysfunctional and anti-social. Second, the goals of efficiency, equity and human self-development are mutually served by an active, broad-ranging programme of social and industrial reform. It is in this spirit that Adams and Sumner conclude Chapter 1 of their textbook with this statement (p. 15): "The true ideal of society is not laissez-faire, but economic freedom, and freedom is the child, not the enemy, of law and regulation."

While the early participants in labour research and industrial relations were critical of laissez-faire and the present social order, they were hardly revolutionaries – at least as seen from today's perspective. Most were middle-class reformers and progressive technocrats, only a relative few (particularly in their mature years) leaned in the direction of socialism, and while they borrowed ideas and some critical perspective from Marx they also – contra Marx – saw a necessary and useful role for private property, capitalism and industrial management and strongly opposed the Marxian vision of class struggle and proletarian revolution. Emblematic of their position is Commons' (1934b: 73) statement, "It is not revolution and strikes that we want but collective bargaining on something like an organized equilibrium of equality."

Thus the "labourism" and "economism" of the workers and their trade unions that Lenin and fellow Marxists found so frustrating were exactly what Commons and fellow industrialists were appealing to in their reform strategy. Favourite tactics in this strategy were trade unions, expanded labour legislation, civil service reform, municipal ownership of utilities, women's suffrage, health insurance, restricted immigration and deficit spending on public works during recessions. However, this list of seemingly modest reform proposals was regarded by conservatives of that period as dangerously "socialistic" and caused a number of the labour academics, such as Carter Adams, Commons and Ely, to be either dismissed or threatened with dismissal from their university positions in the early part of their careers (Furner, 1975). Such experiences, not unexpectedly, exercised another moderating influence on them. The reform agenda of the labour progressives, with its corollary indictment of the present order, also led to perennial complaints from business people (e.g., Hicks) that the teachers of labour problems courses in universities were biased against employers and took a partisan position favouring labour unions and "collectivism".

When industrial relations emerged in 1920 as a formal field of study, it was quickly linked to the study of labour problems and the two subjects became virtually synonymous. In this guise, labour problems and industrial relations are opposite sides of the same coin – labour problems are the undesirable behaviours and outcomes generated by defects and maladjustments in the employment relationship, while industrial relations is the body of theory and methods that resolves or ameliorates these problems. This duality is suggested in the statement by Watkins (1928: 5) that "industrial conflict is often characterized as the greatest problem of industrial civilization, and that scientific administration of industrial relations is described as its most imperative need". Thus another reason that industrial relations and neoclassical economics are incompatible is that the nature of neoclassical theory largely rules out the existence of labour problems as a meaningful, widespread phenomenon (e.g., unemployment is voluntary; low pay reflects low individual productivity), robbing industrial relations of part of its intellectual and social raison d'être.

Although the concept of industrial relations and an associated research programme were introduced in American universities in the 1920s, courses in industrial relations were relatively rare and textbooks on the subject of industrial relations were unavailable. This lacuna does not mean, however, that industrial relations was absent from the classroom. The opposite is the case. Industrial relations in American universities was offered as a subject of study in two different contexts. The first and most frequent was as part of a "labour problems" course, typically offered through a department of economics. The second was in a college of business administration or commerce, typically as part of a course in personnel management. The former were taught by labour economists who often took a more theoretical and "social" perspective, while the latter were frequently staffed by adjunct faculty and part-time teachers drawn from the ranks of consultants and business people, and taught with a heavy descriptive and vocational slant (Kaufman, 2000b). Also sometimes used to teach the personnel course were industrial psychologists.

Adams and Sumner's *Labor problems* was the only textbook available for many years, but after the emergence of the industrial relations field in 1920 this genre expanded rapidly. These textbooks are interesting because they reveal how the problem-solving face of the field continued to evolve and develop. By the late 1920s, not only was industrial relations identified with the study and solution of labour problems; these texts organized the solution to labour problems into three distinct categories (Estey, 1928; Watkins and Dodd, 1940). These categories became, in turn, the central divisions of the problem-solving approach in industrial relations. Typically, the first several chapters of these books were devoted to a description of the various labour problems and evils. Then the remainder of the text was divided into three parts. The first part was devoted to what was called the *workers' solution* to labour problems and focused on topics related to trade unions and collective bargaining. The second part was devoted to what was called the *employer's solution* to labour problems and covered topics related to personnel management, profit sharing and employee representation. Then, the third part covered the *community's solution* to labour problems and dealt with various aspects of protective labour law and social insurance programmes, such as minimum wage laws and old-age pensions. This three-way division of the subject of industrial relations was later reflected in the curricula and degree programmes of many of the industrial relations programmes established after the Second World War.

Industrial relations also contained a fourth solution to labour problems, although it typically was not given much attention in labour textbooks. This solution involved macroeconomic stabilization of product and labour markets through countercyclical public works spending and monetary policy, and adoption of institutional devices such as the experience rating feature in unemployment insurance programmes. Commons, Douglas and Slichter all emphasized the importance of macroeconomic stabilization as a method to solve labour problems, and a number of articles on this subject appeared in the *American Labor Legislation Review*. Indeed, Commons considered macroeconomic stabilization the single most effective policy for promoting good industrial relations, as illustrated by his statement (Commons, 1921a: 4), "The first great method of importance in bringing about industrial peace is the stabilization of the dollar."[6]

While the science-building and problem-solving faces of industrial relations are distinct approaches to the subject, it is noteworthy that they are nonetheless highly complementary. The institutional theory of labour markets and firms, for example, clearly implies that labour problems will be rife due to inequality of bargaining power, market imperfections, persistent unemployment and employer autocracy. Likewise, the focus of institutional economics is on changing working rules and institutions to achieve a more efficient and equitable economic system. Not coincidentally, the major approach of industrial relations in its problem-solving face it to solve labour problems with some form of institutional change, such as a trade union, personnel management programme or minimum wage law. The emphasis on institutions thus comes from both the science-building and problem-solving sides of industrial relations and continues to this day to represent a defining characteristic of the field.

Finally, notice should also be taken of the fact that the problem-solving side to industrial relations reinforces another characteristic of the science-building aspect – the emphasis on a holistic, multidisciplinary approach to the subject. Based on their personal experiences, it was obvious to the early participants in industrial relations that successfully mediating disputes, drafting labour legislation and advising management on its personnel programmes require a broad base of knowledge that transcends traditional academic disciplines. For this reason, the founders of American industrial relations consciously structured the field to be a multidisciplinary "meeting place" of people and ideas – with economics, however, placed at centre stage. According to Gordon Watkins (1922: 7), for example, "the study of Labour Problems is fundamentally a part of the social science of economics, but it is related definitely to Sociology, History, Politics, Law, Ethics, and Psychology." J. Douglas Brown also spoke to this dimension of industrial relations when he commented on the founding of the Industrial Relations Section at Princeton, of which he was director (1976: 5, emphasis in original):

> It was the intention of the founders to broaden the scope of the field studied to include *all* factors, conditions, problems and policies involved in the employment of human resources in organized production or service. It was not to be limited to any single academic discipline. Nor was the term 'industrial relations' limited to activities within *private* enterprise but was assumed to cover the relations of governments and all other institutions with those people who constituted the working forces of the country.

The ethical/ideological face

Early industrial relations also had a third face, defined in terms of ethical values and ideological positions with respect to the performance of work, the structure of the employment relationship and the solution of labour problems. Science building, at least in concept, is value-free and seeks only to expand the domain of objective, factual knowledge. Problem solving, on the other hand, inevitably introduces normative considerations since problem solving, by definition, seeks an answer to the question "what should be?" The direction problem solving takes, as well as the intellectual questions raised in science building and the theoretical concepts and methodological tools used to answer these questions, is thus inevitably shaped by ethical values and ideology.

That the industrial relations field contains both a positive and normative dimension has long been recognized. A particularly clear statement is provided by Slichter (1928: 287):

> There are two ways of looking at labor problems. One is the scientific point of view. ... It is aspired to by the scientist who studies trade unions, child labor, unemployment, in order to find out what *is* or what *might be*, without speculating about what *should be*. ... To the vast majority of people, however, even to the economists and sociologists, the labor problem is more than this. It is also a matter of ethics, a matter not simply of what is or what might be, but of what should be ... From the ethical point of view, therefore, the labor problem is concerned with two principal things: with the effect of the prevailing institutions ... upon the conflict between life and work, and with the institutional change needed to harmonize men's activities as laborers with their interests as men.

Values and ideology are subjective features of consciousness that shape how people interpret reality, relate to each other, and respond to the problems they face and the conditions in the world around them. From a Marxist perspective, values and ideology reflect the underlying materialist conditions and relations in each society and thus are largely a refraction of objective circumstances. Early American industrial relations scholars rejected this position, seeing it as overly deterministic and materialist. As an earlier quote from Slichter reveals, they clearly recognized that people's attitudes and values are shaped and moulded by their environment – or, as Commons (1934a) phrased it, they come to social relations with an "institutionalized mind". But Commons and colleagues also believed in the power of human agency and free will, and thus gave subjective considerations of ideology and values independent power to shape events. Adopting this perspective, different national patterns of development in the industrial relations field are then determined by two elements: the differences in objective circumstances and the differences in subjective perceptions and consciousness. Commons (1921b: vi) referred to this dichotomy as "personality versus system".

The ideology of early American industrial relations was constructed on several different strata. To live in the United States and be American in the early twentieth century meant that one perceived and experienced an entirely different world from that of Europe or Asia. The United States was the land of opportunity, a wide-open frontier of economic and social mobility, where hard work, education and strong character mattered far more in life than one's class and social origins. Competition, money-making and individual striving, often seen as unseemly in Europe and Asia, were social virtues in the United States. The rags-to-riches stories of best-selling author Horatio Alger, although entirely fictional, were nonetheless very real in their message to Americans. Automobiles were also seen as a cultural and political statement in the United States, with Ford's mass-produced and inexpensive Model T symbolizing the wide-open American society, and the prestigious Rolls Royce and Mercedes-Benz representing the class-stratified nature of European societies (Helfgott, 2003). Also implanted deep in the American consciousness was the idea of democracy and freedom. While most other nations around the world were governed by kings, czars, emperors and dynastic elites, Americans took great pride in their country's democratic heritage and ethos, and elevated the concepts of liberty, freedom and democracy to the status of core values, along with competition, commerce and individualism. Also central to the American consciousness was a belief in science, rationalism and pragmatism.

These uniquely American values and predispositions exerted a strong influence on how American scholars, business people and workers looked at and interpreted the work world and relations between employers and employees. Had Selig Perlman never left Russia, it is doubtful he would have written a world-famous book extolling the virtues of "job conscious" trade unionism (Perlman, 1928); had Commons grown up in Germany rather than the United States, one may guess he would have found the cause of social democracy more appealing than industrial relations; and had Clarence Hicks worked for a British company, it is likely that his superiors would have quietly told him to forget newfangled management ideas like job evaluation plans and old-age pensions for, after all, "workers will always be workers".

While the new field of industrial relations reflected core American values and ideological beliefs, it was far from a carbon copy. Relative to the epicentre of social, economic and political opinion in the United States of the late 1910s, the people involved in promoting and building industrial relations were clearly in the progressive, liberal to left wing of the polity and from their respective social and occupational classes, and nearly all were social reformers. Moving them towards this position were a wide array of influences, some of a materialist nature and some entirely subjective.

A factor common to many of the early founders of American industrial relations, for example, was a deep commitment to a socially progressive version of Christianity. Ely and Commons were immersed in the Social Gospel movement in the early parts of their careers and both claimed to be Christian socialists (Commons, 1934b; Gonce, 1996). Likewise, Hicks, King and Rockefeller were all devout Christian practitioners (Rockefeller taught Sunday school each week) and were drawn to industrial relations by the Christian obligation to do good works.

Christian instincts were then reinforced for many of the founders of American industrial relations by early experiences with the realities of industrialism and employer–employee relations. Commons relates in his autobiography that early in life he served as a union printer while his brother worked as a non-union printer and he observed that both his wages and security were better than those of his sibling. His first real introduction to labour problems occurred when he served as an investigator for the United States Industrial Commission and spent six months documenting the urban poverty of immigrant workers, followed by a field investigation of the causes of a violent strike by anthracite coal miners. Several of his students experienced the same conversion to reform while working on other field investigations, such as John Fitch after his year-long study of steel workers for the Pittsburgh Survey of 1907–8.[7] The conversion of prominent business people to the cause of industrial reform was also often aided by personally confronting the Labour Problem. Rockefeller, for example, only became a convert to progressive management after the disaster of the Ludlow Massacre, while Hicks entered industrial relations work after witnessing the deplorable conditions of railroad workers during his work for the Young Men's Christian Association (YMCA).

Also important in shaping the ideology of industrial relations were left-of-centre ideas and theories, sometimes imported from Europe, that were not widely known or popular in the mainstream of American academic and social life. A number of the early industrial relations academics, such as Leiserson and Perlman, were socialists of various stripes as young adults. Perlman (1926: 51) recalls, for example, "When I first came to Wisconsin sixteen years ago, I immediately joined the socialist club." While none of the major figures in early industrial relations were Marxists, they nonetheless believed that Marx had captured important aspects of labour–capital relations. Also influential in these circles were the writings of heterodox economists, such as Englishman John Hobson and his theory of underconsumption. And, of course, the German influence was very large among the industrial relations group and, as earlier noted, led these scholars to take a much more positive view of the role of the state as an agent of social reform.

What was the ideology of early industrial relations? To answer this question one must find the core values that serve as the common denominator for all participants in the field. As detailed more fully in the next section, this task is made difficult in this early period because the field was split into two groups or schools of thought, one oriented around the business practitioners of industrial relations and the other around the academic institutional labour economists. They shared a number of common values but also diverged with respect to others.

To make progress on this matter, one approach is to focus on the two men of significant stature who most closely occupy the centre ground of North American industrial relations at the time of its birth. The first is Commons, the foremost academic aspect on the subject; the second is King, the most influential adviser and consultant to the business practitioners. A search for the ideological premises of early industrial relations thus involves looking for the shared values and moral commitments of King and Commons. King's views are expressed at length in his book *Industry and humanity*, while Commons' are scattered over many places. However, the three publications that most closely represent his views at the time of the founding of the field are the books *Industrial goodwill* (1919b), *Trade unionism and labor problems* (1921a, rev. ed.) and *Industrial government* (1921b).

Looking through these publications, certain core ethical and ideological premises are apparent. I express each of these in the form of a "should", reflecting the normative position being taken.

- Labour should not be treated like a commodity. The principle expressed here is that while labour is traded in markets, in the same way as wheat, steel and other commodities, it is fundamentally different because labour is embodied in human beings and thus the terms and conditions of employment gain a higher moral significance.
- Human rights should have precedence over property rights in the employment relationship. Both Commons and King recognize that protection of property rights is a fundamental function of government, but this ethical standard nonetheless affirms that in the final analysis people are more important than things.
- Workers should not be viewed solely as a means to an end but also as an end in themselves. This premise affirms that workers are more than a factor input or instrument for producing wealth and have independent, socially legitimate interests in the terms and conditions of employment that deserve to be counted in the social calculus.
- Workers should be given opportunities for voice, representation and due process in the workplace. Some form of industrial democracy or "constitutional government in industry" is highly desirable.

- A capitalist, market economy should be preserved. Both authors recognize that this type of economy creates numerous labour problems, but nonetheless believe that some regulated, humanized version of capitalism is the best economic system for promoting not only economic advance but also political freedom and personal initiative and responsibility.
- The right of management to direct the enterprise is legitimate, serves the social interest and should be protected. The management function (controlling, coordinating, risk taking) is crucial if industry is to grow and prosper, so the challenge is to make management work better, not to eliminate it.
- Cooperation between capital and labour should be promoted. A central task of industrial relations is to create conditions so capital and labour can more effectively cooperate, recognizing that cooperation is good not only because it leads to greater production but also because it enhances social relations and satisfaction from work.
- The causes of industrial conflict should be removed where possible and, where they cannot, conflict should be resolved through well-ordered negotiation, dialogue and third-party adjudication. A considerable amount of industrial conflict is avoidable through intelligent and ethical business and industrial relations practices, while the amount that is irreducible should be openly expressed and fairly resolved.
- Labour should have the right to collective representation. Commons and King agree that freedom of association is a fundamental human right and workers should have legal protection to form trade unions and collective bargaining if this is their preference.
- Workers should also have the right not to join a trade union, or to choose an alternative form of representation, such as a representation plan sponsored by an employer. Both authors hold that some form of collective voice should be readily available to workers, but that workers should be free to choose what kind of collective voice they want and whether they want any form at all.
- Government should set minimum standards for terms and conditions of employment so that no worker suffers wages, hours or other aspects of work that fall below the community's judgement of a minimum acceptable level. In the final analysis, moral principles and respect for the human essence of each person, not supply and demand, should set the baseline in the labour market and workplace.
- Government should also take steps to provide security of person and livelihood for workers, including the right to work, freedom from arbitrary dismissal, and protection from economic and social risks. This premise

reflects the shared judgement that security of person and livelihood is a fundamental social good; that markets and employers under-supply security through inadequate employment opportunities, protection from job loss, and protection from risks of unemployment, accident, old age and other such events; and that lack of security is a source of fear, violence, personal hardship and other anti-social effects.

- Capital, labour and the public are all stakeholders in the economic system and should be given interest representation in the development and administration of the rules that govern industrial relations. Various forms of tripartite representation are thus favourably viewed, albeit subject to the next principle.

- Private ordering, decentralized decision making and voluntary agreement should be encouraged whenever possible in industrial relations. Under this principle of voluntarism, government should "level the playing field", establish fair "rules of the game", and then move to the sideline and let employers and employees work out their own agreements. The preference was thus for a maximum of bilateralism in industry, supplemented by trilateralism on a modest network of government commissions and agencies.

- Social justice should be an explicit goal of policy in industrial relations. Not only is social justice a goal for its own intrinsic ethical worth; social justice is also a crucial ingredient for effective capital–labour cooperation and avoidance of industrial conflict and civil disorder. Free trade is welcome as long as it is also fair trade.

The schism in American industrial relations

The progressive reformers who started industrial relations in the United States were drawn together by fear, faith and commitment. The fear came from the menacing threat of the Labour Problem to civic order and the preservation of the American political and business system, the faith came from the belief that through science and institutional reform the Labour Problem could be defused, and the commitment arose from the desire to make the work world a better place through reform and uplift. These three drives provided a common base of understanding and motivation for establishing and participating in the new field of industrial relations, cemented together by the common ideological principles enumerated above.

If one looks below the surface, however, a fault line ran underneath the early coalition of industrial relations reformers that split them into two separate but partially overlapping camps or "schools of thought". In an earlier work

(Kaufman, 1993), I have called these two groups the *ILE school* (institutional labour economics) and the *PM school* (personnel management) of industrial relations. The two schools were largely united on certain principles and programmes of industrial relations but split on others. The most fundamental fault line centred on the issue of independent trade unionism and the ILE contention that more unionism would be good for the industrial relations system and the PM contention that more unionism would be detrimental.

During the first 15 years of the field's life, the forces uniting the PM and ILE schools were stronger than those pulling them apart and both groups worked together in the "house of industrial relations". Beginning in the 1930s, however, the pressure of developments accentuated and deepened the divisions between them and, finally, in the 1950s the house of industrial relations broke apart. What remained of American industrial relations was a narrow and truncated form of the ILE school, often called labour–management relations, while the PM school evolved after 1960 into the rival and largely separate field of personnel/human resource management.

The presence and identity of these two contrasting schools of thought is revealed in looking back at the two events previously cited as marking the birth of the field in 1920: the establishment of the first academic industrial relations programme at the University of Wisconsin and the founding of the Industrial Relations Association of America (IRAA). The former represents the core of the ILE school, the latter the core of the PM school.

So far in this chapter the discussion of the science-building and problem-solving faces of industrial relations has focused primarily on the writings of members of the ILE school. This same emphasis is repeated in nearly all historical accounts of the early years of industrial relations (e.g., Kochan, Katz and McKersie, 1986; Adams, 1993). Indeed, one may go further and say that in the eyes of many modern scholars the field of industrial relations and the ILE school are largely one and the same, the existence of an alternative PM school is either not acknowledged or treated as a marginal development, and the entire 1920s period is neglected.[8] A substantial part of the explanation for this rests with the fact that most members of the PM school were business people, consultants or industrial psychologists, who devoted their time to the practical aspects of industrial relations or relatively technical issues of employee testing, selection and fatigue. Although some wrote books and a number contributed short articles to professional journals and conference proceedings, the "paper trail" for the PM school is considerably shorter and shallower. Another factor entering the picture is that the bulk of the scholars writing on industrial relations in later decades have come from the ILE school and for reasons of disciplinary orientation, research interest and ideology have tended to bypass or downgrade the PM side of the field. One must also point out that the climatic events of the Depression and New Deal in the 1930s, as described in a later chapter, also drove a serious wedge between the PM and ILE schools and tended to wipe out the "collective memory" of later generations of ILE scholars regarding the formative 1920s period.

The PM school

At the time of industrial relations' birth in 1920 the IRAA formed the nucleus of the PM school. The majority of the 2,000-strong members of the IRAA were business practitioners who were involved in general management or personnel work, although some academics also belonged to the organization. These professionals were especially interested in the new field of personnel management, a subject many of them practised and a number wrote and lectured on. Since the IRAA had been founded to promote a more progressive and humane approach to labour management, its members tended to have a relatively liberal point of view.

The IRAA, however, was not the only organization with an interest in industrial relations, as various associations of employers were also involved in the PM school. In this regard, one must appreciate that the American business community in the 1920s was far from a monolithic body in its philosophy and approach to labour (Harris, 1982). In point of fact, a wide spectrum of opinion existed, extending from a very liberal position on the left to a conservative or even reactionary position on the right. The people interested and involved in industrial relations largely came from the progressive, left-of-centre end of the business community. At the time, they were sometimes referred to as "industrial liberals" (Kaufman, 2003a), while more recently Jacoby (1985) has referred to them as the "progressive minority" – a term that usefully highlights the fact they were a relatively small, albeit influential, group among employers.

Anchoring the liberal end of the employing class was the Taylor Society. The Taylor Society included a number of progressive industrialists, such as Henry Dennison, Richard Feiss, Edward Filene, Morris Leeds and Henry Kendall, and liberal business consultants and investigators, such as Morris Cooke, Mary Gilson, Ordway Tead, Robert Valentine and Mary van Kleeck. To the dismay of more conservative colleagues, these people not only advocated the various accoutrements of progressive management, such as personnel departments, shop committees and a measure of job security; they went further and also advocated a socially progressive (some said radical) labour policy, including minimum-wage laws, unemployment insurance programmes, and collaboration with AFL-like business unions. Illustrative of its liberal slant, the

Taylor Society not only invited AFL president William Green to address the group but also sought to work with the AFL to promote union–management cooperation programmes in industry.

Next in the spectrum of management thought were people and companies affiliated with Rockefeller, referred to by Domhoff (1990) as the "Rockefeller network". In the 1920s, Rockefeller was probably the single most powerful and influential capitalist in the world, partly through his vast family fortune, the family's ownership interests in numerous large companies and his web of philanthropic foundations (Magat, 1999). As already noted, two important conduits of Rockefeller's interest in industrial relations were the consulting firm IRC, and the Special Conference Committee (SCC). Both the IRC and the SCC were strong proponents of collective voice through employee representation. This movement was denounced by trade unionists and pro-labour academics as a sham method of industrial democracy and, paradoxically, by conservative industrialists as opening the door to trade unionism and socialism (Dunn, 1926; Ching, 1953), while the SCC has frequently been pictured by labour historians as a secret cabal of companies whose central object was union avoidance (e.g., Scheinberg, 1986; Gitelman, 1988). Certainly these companies had a strong desire to avoid AFL-style craft unionism and the closed shop, but the SCC's annual reports and few surviving records provide almost no evidence of overt anti-unionism (Jacoby, 1985; Kaufman, 2003a). Rather, after a detailed examination of the groups' records and activities, the LaFollette Senate investigative committee concluded (U.S. Senate Committee on Education and Labor, 1939: 16789), "Throughout the material in the files of the Special Conference Committee we find a constant emphasis on the necessity for cooperation between employers and employees in industry. The 'cooperative' methods appears as the desideratum of sound industrial relations."

Also in the liberal wing was a new group called the Personnel Research Federation (PRF). The PRF was founded in 1921, with the AFL as one of its charter members, and was directed by Henry Metcalf. Metcalf earned a doctorate in political science but become involved in personnel and industrial relations work with the government during the war. With co-author Ordway Tead, he published the first American textbook in personnel management, *Personnel administration: Its principles and practice*, in 1920. Like many progressives in the industrial relations movement, he was convinced that a significant part of the Labour Problem arose from haphazard and ill-informed management practices. He thus founded the PRF in order to bring the latest scientific research to bear on personnel issues. The organization sponsored many conferences, published the professional magazine *Personnel Journal*, and funded academic research, including Stanley Mathewson's (1931) influential book on restriction of output among unorganized workers. Metcalf also served as an industrial relations consultant for the IRC and did much to bring the work of management writer Mary Follett – now considered one of the seminal thinkers on management and administration in the twentieth century – to the attention of American businessmen (Metcalf and Urwick, 1942; Tonn, 2003).

Yet another group in the progressive minority is the YMCA. The YMCA became involved in industrial welfare work before the First World War. One of its first activities was establishment of YMCA clubhouses and dormitories for railroad crews away from home, with the intent of providing them with a more spiritually uplifting (or less corrupting) place to rest than the local saloons and boarding houses. The director of this programme for some years was Clarence Hicks. In the 1920s, the YMCA sponsored annual industrial relations conferences at Silver Bay, New York, where progressive management methods, such as employee benefits and employee representation, were prominently featured.

The American Management Association (AMA) was another of the more liberal groups. The AMA was a lineal descendant of the IRAA, the latter having evolved into the National Personnel Association in 1922 and then into the AMA in 1923 (Lange, 1928). The officers of the AMA, particularly in the early part of the 1920s, were heavily represented by academics, consultants and industrial relations professionals from the progressive wing of industry. Important names in the AMA were Edward Cowdrick (consultant and secretary of the SCC), Sam Lewisohn (co-author of a book with Commons and employers' representative to the ILO for the United States) and Arthur Young (director of IRC). According to Jacoby (1985: 185), the AMA was the leading exponent of the model of personnel management espoused by the SCC and the SCC, in turn, considered the AMA (quoting an SCC document) "the organization best qualified to give nationwide impetus to sound industrial relations policies".

Toward the middle of the spectrum of business opinion on labour policy was the National Industrial Conference Board (NICB). The NICB conducted several surveys of industrial relations practices among its many hundreds of corporate members in the 1920s and 1930s and these provide the best composite picture available of the extent and development of industrial relations practices at the national level. Also valuable are a variety of studies on individual aspects of industrial relations, such as employee representation. On matters of labour policy, the NICB lobbied on behalf of employers' interests, albeit from a moderate position, and generally opposed further government intervention in this area (Rodgers, 1998).

On the conservative side of the spectrum of business opinion on labour policy were a number of other groups. These might be called the "traditional majority" in the business community. These employers often came from large firms where employee morale or a union threat were not major concerns, small companies in highly competitive industries with low profit margins or a substantial union threat, and from small and medium-sized companies operated by the owner or controlling family. Examples include the National Association of Manufacturers (NAM), the United States Chamber of Commerce, and various industry associations, such as the National Metal Trades Association and National Erectors' Association. These groups also spoke of the great national threat posed by the Labour Problem and the need to restore class harmony and labour peace (Fine, 1995; Harris, 2000). The Labour Problem, from their point of view, was largely the work of radical unions and labour agitators bent on "dominating to a dangerous degree the whole social, political, and governmental system of the Nation", willing to commit "many acts of aggression and ruthless violation of principles", and using political power to "engraft upon the statute books its sprigs of socialism" (remarks of NAM president David Parry, quoted in Fine, 1995: 3–4). The focus of these employers was thus centred squarely on maintaining the open shop and fighting trade unionism with all available means, while they gave little attention to the constructive programme of personnel management and industrial relations – effectively placing them outside the field of industrial relations, at least on problem-solving and ideological grounds.

Most of the members of the PM school came from the ranks of managers and consultants. A few words should also be said, however, about the school's academic members. They were relatively few in number in the 1920s and did not have much influence on the development of industrial relations, at least until the Hawthorne experiments began to be publicized by Elton Mayo and colleagues of the Harvard Business School (discussed in Chapter 4). The bulk of the academic members of the PM school were industrial psychologists. Well-known names were Walter Bingham, Walter Dill Scott, Arthur Kornhauser and Morris Viteles. The United States Army hired Scott and colleagues to conduct selection and rating tests for new infantry recruits during the First World War and the results received wide publicity (Baritz, 1960). Soon employers were hiring Scott and other psychologists to construct similar tests for new employee recruits (Ling, 1965). During the 1920s, industrial psychologists also extended their research into employee fatigue, motivation and leadership, and David Houser (1927) conducted the first employee attitude surveys in American industry. The psychologists considered personnel management "applied psychology" and had some impact there. In the broader field of industrial relations, however, the influence of psychologists was quite modest because of their narrow focus on individual behaviour and technical issues concerning the construct validity of selection tests, the design of job evaluation plans and so forth (Kaufman, 2000b).

Having described the membership of the PM school, I now turn to a more detailed description of their particular philosophy and strategy of industrial relations. The industrial relations strategy of the PM school was shaped by an overriding consideration: the employer's labour policy had to contribute to (or at least could not unduly subtract from) competitive advantage and profit making if both were to survive in the long term. The case that the industrial liberals set out to make was that a progressive labour policy was not only the right thing to do from a moral, ethical point of view but was also the best option for long-run organizational performance and profit.

The case they built started with the shortcomings of the traditional labour policy used by employers up to the late 1910s. Before this time employers had no personnel function and nearly all aspects of hiring, firing, pay, job assignments and other such matters were left to the discretion of individual foremen (Jacoby, 1985). This system lacked any scientific rationale, formalization or standardization and led to a jumbled pattern of wage rates, haphazard job assignments, rampant opportunities for favouritism and discrimination, and lack of any channel for complaint or redress of grievances. Some firms provided "welfare" services, such as lunchrooms, libraries and a company nurse, but these practices were haphazard and often heavily tainted with paternalism (Tone, 1997). Furthermore, the prevailing model of work motivation was the "drive system", in which foremen used rough language, coercive supervision and the threat of termination to push workers to exert maximum effort. Workers who complained or tried to organize a union were often fired and sometimes blacklisted. One contemporary observer (Gilman, 1899: 10) described the relation of employer to employee as "a purely economic one – they [employers] considered them [employees] not as men, but as means of accumulating capital", while an employer said (quoted in Cummins and DeVyver, 1947: 218), "my policy is … to hit the head of the radical in my shop whenever he puts it up".

This system began to break down during the boom economy of the First World War, when the threat of unemployment disappeared and undercut the effectiveness of the drive system, the quest for greater wartime production exposed the inefficiencies and waste of the traditional model, employee turnover jumped to 300–400 per cent in many companies, unionism and strikes mushroomed, and the idea of industrial democracy began to take hold. Faced with a crisis, employers looked for a solution to their labour problems. Many reacted with short-run expedients, such as a sizeable wage increase to hold on to the employees, tolerating slack work effort or violations of discipline, and banding together in employers' associations to gain more leverage against unions. Others, however, concluded that the war had demonstrated the inherent flaws of the old model and searched for a superior model of labour management. Out of this search was born the field of industrial relations in the employer community, or what I have called the PM school.

The goal of the PM school was to construct a new model of labour management that simultaneously increases profits and competitive advantage, keeps out unions and government interference, and moves American industry to a higher level of ethical and social legitimacy. The core of this new model is what was called in university labour texts of the period the employer's solution to labour problems and what in the 1920s became known in industry as the model of welfare capitalism (Bernstein, 1960; Jacoby, 1997).

As it developed in the 1920s, the employer's solution (or industrial relations strategy) of welfare capitalism had four basic elements.

- *Personnel management.* The introduction of scientific and professional principles of personnel management, such as employee selection tests, job evaluation methods, and written employee handbooks, and the creation of a specialized staff function in the management hierarchy to plan, operate and supervise labour policy.
- *Employee welfare benefits.* The introduction of various employee welfare or "service" benefits, such as a company-provided doctor or nurse, clean and pleasant working conditions, employment security through promotion from within, old-age pensions and company-funded sports teams.
- *Human relations.* The introduction of the spirit and practice of "human relations" into the workplace, such as training foremen in the art of handling employees, non-punitive forms of discipline and employee recognition awards.
- *Employee representation.* The introduction of some form of representational organization for employee voice, involvement and dispute resolution, such as a works council, grievance committee or employee representation plan.

The leading American employers mixed and matched these practices to suit their particular competitive strategies and production processes. Whatever the package, all of these new features cost the employer money, but the expectation was that they would more than pay for themselves by fostering greater output, reducing cost, and protecting management autonomy and control from outside interference (Cohen, 1990). The route to this happy combination was to replace rule of thumb with science; instil employees with loyalty and confidence in the future rather than fear and insecurity; treat employees as people and not factor inputs; and replace autocracy with voice and due process. In practice, a good measure of enlightened and not so enlightened paternalism was also a key ingredient, such as the investigative and counselling activities of the Sociological Department in Henry Ford's auto plant (Meyers, 1981). Some writers, such as King (1918) and Rockefeller (1923), added to these measures the suggestion that employers need to move from a strict profit maximization model to a stakeholder model in which they seek to ensure a reasonable financial return to all contracting members of the firm.

Perlman (1928: 207) insightfully describes the transition from the 1910s to the 1920s as a change "from a 'demand and supply' capitalism to 'welfare capitalism'". The strategic thrust of the new model was to reap higher profit through a comprehensive programme aimed at de-commodifying labour. The linchpin idea was to replace the traditional adversarial model of employer–employee relations with one built on cooperation, unity of interest and mutual gain. It was, thus, a socialized and "welfarized" version of Taylorism (Nelson, 1997). Of course, this conception of a unitarist employment relationship was not new to the welfare capitalists for, as pointed out in the last chapter, earlier thinkers, such as Charles Babbage, had already articulated it. But the early PM members of industrial relations took the unitarist idea, further developed and humanized it, and brought it within the mainstream of American business (Kaufman, 2003b).

One of the most influential proponents of the unitarist concept was management consultant and writer Mary Follett. She states the gist of the idea this way (Follett, 1925a: 82): "When you have made your employees feel that they are in some sense partners in the business, they do not improve the quality of their work, save waste in time and material, because of the Golden Rule, but because their interests are the same as yours."

Clarence Hicks (1941: 93–4), arguably the leading practitioner exponent in American industry of this new philosophy, summed up the unitarist idea in these words:

> To the extent that American employers recognize the common interests of management and men and invite their employees to cooperate with them through representatives of their own choice [in a non-union employee representation plan], to that extent American industry will pass from the stage of autocracy and its counterpart antagonism, to one of friendly cooperation. … With an increasing emphasis on the unity of interest of all levels of employees, the effectiveness of American industry will provide a standard of work and living which will be as satisfying as its is secure.

He also adds, however, an important caveat (1941: 78, quoting Rockefeller): "It is idle wholly to deny the existence of conflicting interests between employers and employees. But there are wide areas of activity in which interests coincide. It is the part of statesmanship to organize an identity of interests where it exists in order to reduce the area of conflict." Thus the unitarist position does not assume (as sometimes stated today) an absence of conflict in organizations, as this is a utopian goal. Rather, the objective is to structure and manage the organization to, as much as possible, foster goal alignment, cooperation and creative conflict resolution, in order to reap mutual gain outcomes – as reflected in the title and message of Follett's (1925b) paper "Constructive conflict". The personnel (industrial relations) department, in turn, was the employer's self-designated mediator of conflicting interests (replacing the union) and, if possible, the designer of new methods to align interests. Viewed in this light, the unitarists' fundamental objection to trade unionism is that it has an organizational imperative that impels it towards perennial conflict and an adversarial "us versus them" posture that undercuts the trust and cooperation vital to high performance and competitive advantage.

Hicks implemented the unitarist model at Standard Oil of New Jersey in 1918, constructing what labour historian Irving Bernstein (1960: 166) calls "the most ambitious and enduring monument of the welfare capitalism of the 1920s". Looking back on Hicks' experiment in industrial relations, Gibb and Knowlton (1956: 578–9) observed of Hicks' new industrial relations programme: "No one of the many measures adopted in this first year of great transition was unprecedented, but the comprehensive scope and the total effect of all the efforts imparted to company policy an almost revolutionary character." They go on to say (pp. 594–5, emphasis added), "In labor relations as in technology the company deliberately set as its goal the attainment of an *entirely new performance level*" – language clearly evocative of the goals of today's high performance workplace model (Kochan and Osterman, 1994).

A further observation by Gibb and Knowlton says much about the industrial relations strategy taken by the PM school toward unions (p. 585): "There was a ready, if unspoken appreciation of the fact that the new plans and practices were suffocating by the sheer weight of generosity the forces of unionism within the company." In a similar vein, Perlman (128: 210) observes, "Unionism knew how to handle situations under the 'old' capitalism. But this 'new' capitalism which fights unionism with a far-sighted 'preventive' method rather than with the old 'remedial' one of breaking up the union by discharging agitators and imposing the 'yellow dog' contract, leaves it stunned and bewildered." The welfare capitalist employers chose to take the high road where possible and, thus, union substitution took the place of heavy-handed union suppression as the first line of union avoidance. One can look at the large "overhead" expense of welfare capitalism as the price the employers were willing to pay to buy labour peace and keep their massive capital investments and finely tuned production operations from being split up among competing craft unions and shut down by strikes and labour troubles.

Besides taking a unitarist perspective on solving labour problems, the PM school also took an "internalist" perspective (Kaufman, 1993). That is, the business people, consultants and industrial psychologists tended to look inside the firm for the causes of labour problems and the solutions thereto. In doing so, they also tended to omit or abstract from consideration forces outside the firm that affect employment relations, such as labour markets, the regime of labour law, and social class and culture. In this spirit, Lewisohn (1926: 48–9) states, "To approach labor unrest as if it were mainly due to peculiar defects of capitalism is thus a profound error. ... We should, therefore, focus our attention for a while on the individual plant where the daily contact between employer and employee takes place." He goes on to say (p. 202), "There is no escaping the conclusion that the most important factor in sound industrial relations is management." People writing on industrial relations in the PM tradition, therefore, were prone to identify factors such as faulty executive leadership, inappropriate organizational structure, poorly designed and administered personnel practices, and defective human relations as the cause of labour problems, while solutions were likely to entail corrections in these same areas. This perspective also accentuated the emphasis on knowledge areas such as management, organization and administration, psychology and the micro side of sociology, and tended to place responsibility for improving industrial relations in the hands of corporate executives and personnel officers rather than labour unions, government policy-makers or the Federal Reserve Board.

The ILE school

The second major school of thought in American industrial relations was centred on the institutional labour economists, located principally in American universities. The Wisconsin school represented the core of the ILE school, although a number of labour economists (e.g., Jacob Hollander and George Barnett of Johns Hopkins University, and Paul Douglas of the University of Chicago) took part in industrial relations but were outside the Wisconsin orbit. The ILE school was also not limited only to economists, or even academics. ILE-oriented people outside universities who played an influential role in labour research and policy development in the 1920s include Florence Kelly (National Consumers' League), Leo Wolman (Amalgamated Clothing Workers' Union), Louis Brandeis (attorney and Supreme Court Justice) and Father John Ryan (National Catholic Welfare

Conference). The closest publication to a "house organ" for the ILE school was the *American Labor Legislation Review*, edited by Wisconsinite John Andrews.

It was earlier noted that the institutional labour economists believed the problem with orthodox (neoclassical) theory was not that it is false but that it is seriously incomplete as an explanation of how markets work. They took a similar if somewhat less critical position regarding the PM school and its prescription for improved industrial relations.

In the years before the First World War, in particular, the ILE group tended to attract academics whose sympathies and interests were with labour and, indeed, the desire to "do something for labour" was perhaps the animating impulse bringing them to the field (Blum, 1925; Commons, 1934b). Given this mindset, a number of them not surprisingly expressed varying degrees of antipathy toward employers, free labour markets and the existing capitalist order. Leiserson (1922), for example, pejoratively referred to employers as the "royalists" and "Bourbon kings" of industry. Most also expressed frank sympathy for the cause of trade unionism and greater government regulation of markets and labour (Kaufman, 1997a; 2000c). One outside observer (Stockton, 1932: 224) described the ILE group as "[l]abor economics men who have the social point of view, coupled perhaps with an anti-management complex [and] look upon personnel management as a means of driving labor and eliminating trade unionism".

This predisposition of the ILE group to favour labour is well known. What is almost entirely neglected, however, is the noticeable shift in their opinion that occurred after the First World War and continued through the 1920s. A common viewpoint (e.g., Kochan, 1980: 8) is that the institutional labour economists largely neglected management in their writings and advocated that collective bargaining be as widespread as possible. Before the war this is an accurate generalization, but after the war it substantially errs (Kaufman, 2003c). Indeed, a veritable transformation occurs in their writings on labour, with Commons' *History of labor in the United States* published in 1918 marking the end of one period (the "trade union" period) and the publication of his *Industrial goodwill* in 1919 marking the start of the new (the "employment management" period). Not coincidentally, this transition point in 1919 also corresponds exactly with another key event – the birth of the field of industrial relations – and also follows in lockstep with two other important developments. The first of these is the emergence of the highly capital-intensive, finely tuned Fordist mass production model; the second is the transition of the Progressive-era social reform movement from an ameliorative, working-class-oriented "uplift" strategy to a social Taylorist strategy of management- or technocrat-led workplace reform through science-based social engineering. The combination of Fordism and Taylorism promised a revolutionary jump in industrial production and standard of living, but it also required a far more sophisticated and humanized employment management function, a flexible and committed workforce and labour peace.

The PM school's version of industrial relations sought to meet this challenge, but without much attention to external market conditions or the underbelly of the economy where "low-road" employers and miserable working conditions were rampant. The ILE school's post-First World War industrial relations strategy overlapped and included large parts of the PM school but also included other components that were largely missing and in some cases antithetical to the PM approach. The ILE school differed from the PM school in two important respects. First, the ILE group more clearly recognized that employers' industrial relations practices are highly contingent on market forces, such as the extent of unemployment in labour markets and the degree of cyclical boom and bust in the macro-economy, and thus made market stabilization and full employment important goals in their industrial relations programme. Second, they also recognized that the labour market has a dual character, with a top stratum of advanced, progressive employers and a bottom stratum of backward and exploitative employers, and that the existence of the latter is not only deplorable on social grounds but poses a direct competitive threat to the survival and spread of advanced firms with high labour standards. Another goal of their industrial relations programme, therefore, was to simultaneously encourage and propagate the "high-road" employment model of progressive firms while at the same time protecting workers and raising minimum labour standards at the backward "low-road" employers.

As of the early 1920s, tools for the task of policing labour conditions and raising standards in the low or middle end of the labour market – that is, trade unions and labour legislation – were already relatively well known and developed, albeit significantly undersupplied from the perspective of the ILE school, and thus did not represent the same new and exciting area of research that they had in the 1900–19 period. Furthermore, the opportunity to advance this part of the ILE programme seemed to wane seriously after 1920 due to adverse court rulings, the rise of conservative political forces, the declining energy and relevance of the craft-dominated labour movement, and the determined opposition of employers. With this avenue of social advance largely blocked, the centre of attention among the ILE group turned to the "new frontier" in employment reform and practice where more exciting things were happening and greater opportunity for social progress seemed to appear – the development and propagation of a new, high-road, high-performance employment model for the emerging mass production firms. In so doing, the group was led to reformulate and broaden the ILE model by incorporating a much greater PM component in it (leading to a "composite model" described in more detail shortly). Thus what brought union sympathizer Commons and rich industrialist Rockefeller together and led them to spearhead the introduction of the new field of industrial relations in the academic and business worlds was a common purpose and interest: the introduction and development of progressive labour management, including wherever possible some mechanism for collective employee voice.

This revised historical and intellectual sequence greatly helps understanding the place of the new field of industrial relations in the spectrum of that era's thought and practice and making sense of Commons' first book of the new industrial relations era, *Industrial goodwill* (1919b). Accustomed, for example, to thinking of industrial relations as largely focused on unions and the workers' point of view, modern American industrial relations scholars would understandably read with puzzlement Balderston's assertion in 1935 that (p. 305, emphasis added) "[i]n the literature dealing with the relations between employers and employees are a series of terms the use of which signifies whether the approach taken is that of *management* or of the workers. If the former, the phrases used are *industrial relations*, or personnel, or employment management; if the latter, labor economics." Further puzzling would be the juxtaposition of Commons' *Industrial goodwill* and his companion book *Industrial government* (1921b) with the conventional union-centred view of industrial relations, for both volumes are clearly managerialist in subject and tone. This fact perhaps explains why both are almost completely absent from modern-day accounts of the intellectual history and development of the American industrial relations field.

Industrial goodwill is a book on management and labour policy; today it would be categorized as "macro human resource management". As far as I am aware, it is the first academic treatise in the United States to espouse and describe the new industrial relations management model that came to form the basis in the 1920s for the PM school and welfare capitalism. It also provides the original statement of the core principles for what is today popularly called the high-performance or "mutual-gain" workplace (Kaufman, 2001b). In a book review, the *New York Evening Post* (26 April 1919) called *Industrial goodwill* "the most important book for the intelligent employer since Taylor's *Scientific management*".

The fundamental theorem of the book is stated on p. 74 in quite modern terms: "Goodwill is a competitive advantage." Commons goes on to explain (pp. 19–20; 25–8, emphasis in original):

> Goodwill is productive, not in the sense that it is the scientific economizing of the individual's capacities [e.g., the time–motion study of Taylorism], but because it enlists his whole soul and all his energies in the thing he is doing. ... It is *l'esprit de corps* ... the soul of a going concern, the value of the unity and collective personality that binds together all its parts in a living organism. ... Goodwill is valuable because ... it brings larger profits and lifts the employer somewhat above the level of competing employers by giving him a more productive labour force than theirs in proportion to the wages paid. ... But goodwill is fragile. ... It requires continuous upkeep through continuous repetition of service [by the employer]. ... For it is goodwill that converts the 'class struggle' of socialism into class harmony ... and builds up a harmony of interest, where both parties gain reciprocal advantage [mutual gain].

Industrial goodwill also outlines five different models of employment relations, providing in effect the first theory of strategic human resource management (or employment systems). The five models are the commodity, machine (Taylorism) goodwill, public utility (labour as a "human resource", a term used by Commons on p. 130), and citizenship. The "old" industrial relations system before the First World War is the commodity (demand and supply) model and autocracy (lack of citizenship) model. The "new" industrial relations system just being born – and the one which the term industrial relations was meant to personify – includes the machine model, but humanized and democratized with the goodwill, public utility and citizenship models. Reminiscent of today's literature on strategic choice and varieties of capitalism, Commons (p. 63) states, "The problem of goodwill is really the problem of finding out how far the different theories are true and necessary at a given time and place, under given circumstances and given facts."

Two other points from *Industrial goodwill* are important to mention. The first is that securing labour's goodwill requires that workers have a voice, and preferably a collective form of voice, in the governance of the enterprise. The collective form of voice can be of any kind, as long as it provides meaningful influence and the protection of due process in the resolution of disputes (pp. 112–21). The second is that it is the job of the industrial relations (personnel) function in the firm to win and maintain labour's goodwill through "continuous repetition of service". Commons adds (pp. 165, 167), "The personnel department ... is the department of industrial goodwill. ... It is more than scientific management, it is scientific justice. ... We see this new profession forming itself about us and beginning to fill the gap between capital and labor." Commons amplified on these themes in his next book, *Industrial government* (1921b), titling his concluding chapter "The opportunity of management".

Commons was not the only institutional labour economist to write on the new topic of labour management. Douglas, Leiserson, Lescohier and Slichter all wrote on the subject and became widely recognized as the leading experts in the area during the 1920s (Kaufman, 1998a; 2000b). In fact, in the early literature of personnel management Commons had more books and articles cited than any other academic author (Rossi and Rossi, 1925). In an earlier work (Kaufman, 1998a), based on this and other evidence, I conclude that Commons and the PM school duo of Tead and Metcalf arguably deserve to be considered the founders of the American field of personnel (industrial relations) management.

The new goodwill/industrial relations employment strategy was generally quite effective in the companies that fully implemented it, per the observation of Commons (1921a: 263) that, "from 10 per cent to 25 per cent of American employers may be said to be so far ahead of the game that trade unions cannot reach them. Conditions are better, wages are better, security is better, than unions can actually deliver to their members." He was speaking, of course, of the elite of employers, such as Standard Oil, DuPont and so on – or what was previously referred to as the "progressive minority" in the business community.[9] But Commons' quote raises the question: what about employment conditions in the other 75 to 90 per cent of employers – the "traditional majority"? This is where Commons and the other members of the ILE school thought the PM school was incomplete as a full programme of industrial relations.

When it came to improving labour conditions and fostering improved industrial relations at the firms in the traditional majority, the proponents of the PM school were caught in a dilemma. They readily agreed that some firms were exploitative and oppressive towards labour and that adversarialism, not cooperation, was widespread. But what should be done? One option was to try to spread the welfare capitalist or goodwill model to the firms in the traditional majority, such as through the consulting work of the IRC, the educational programmes and conferences of the AMA, and so on. A second option was to expand the coverage of collective bargaining, protective labour law and social insurance programmes in order both to give greater incentive to traditional firms to practise welfare capitalism and to protect the viability of the welfare capitalist firms from the competitive threat posed by low-road firms. However, only the most progressive business leaders in the PM school actively promoted this option (such as Rockefeller's support of unemployment and old-age insurance programmes and international labour standards through the ILO) and even then collective bargaining received very lukewarm and qualified support. A third option pursued in the 1920s was to form industry trade associations and use these to stabilize or cartelize product markets, thus reducing price competition from lower-cost rivals (Hawley, 1966; Gordon, 1994). Yet a fourth was to try to avoid the ruinous effect business cycles and extensive unemployment have on cooperative, mutual-gain employment systems by deliberately boosting mass purchasing power by paying above-market wages and tying wage increases to improvements in productivity, as promoted in the much-publicized "doctrine of high wages" (Williams, 1927; Raff and Summers, 1987) born from Ford's "five dollars a day" experiment in the late 1910s.

From the point of view of the institutional labour economists, these measures were inadequate, not only because they were practised by only a small proportion of the business community, but also because in real life a very large gap often exists between management rhetoric and shop-floor reality (Bendix, 1956). "Exhibit A" for the ILE group was the steel industry which until 1924 continued to operate with a 12-hour/7-day work schedule (and only gave it up after strong pressure from Washington). Also illustrative is the statement of Senator Wagner (Huthmacher, 1968: 64), after touring coal camps in the Appalachians, that "had I not seen it myself, I would not have believed that in the United States there were large areas where civil government was supplanted by a system that only can be compared with ancient feudalism". Another blight on the employment record of the United States was the several million children employed in mines, mills and factories. Not only were these labour conditions anti-social; the employers doggedly fought the workers' efforts to improve their lot through unionism. It was with these thoughts in mind that Commons (1920: 130) told the personnel managers at the 1920 IRAA convention:

> I have listened here to what seem to me to be the most marvellous and keen discussion of what employers could do, of what foremen could do, of what management could do, and I am firmly convinced that if these most informing discussions could be carried out ... the capitalist system could be saved, that there will be no need of either unionism or revolution. But we know that will not be done; we know that you are but a small number. ... There is, therefore, a need for unionism to supplement management.

Commons and associates of the ILE side thus devised an alternative strategy for improved industrial relations (Kaufman, 2003c). The objective was to substantially solve the Labour Problem in the United States through a three-part strategy: equalizing bargaining power, stabilizing markets and introducing constitutional government in industry (the institutionalists' term for industrial democracy). To accomplish this strategy they put forward a new programme of industrial relations that rested on four pillars of institutional change: the extension of the goodwill model of progressive management, trade unionism and collective bargaining, protective labour law and social insurance programmes, and the use of fiscal and monetary policy to maintain full employment.

The first pillar of their industrial relations strategy incorporated the unitarist welfare capitalism model as expounded in Commons' *Industrial goodwill*. However, for reasons already outlined they believed that in many employment situations it is not possible to achieve a substantial harmony of interests and, more generally, that the intrinsic nature of the employment relationship means that there will usually be a moderate to significant degree of opposed interests. The ILE advocates also perceived that in many situations the balance of power in both the labour market and the internal governance of the firm is typically skewed in favour of employers, resulting in the numerous labour problems previously described. When integrating interests in an equitable manner is not feasible, the alternative strategy is to put the competing interests on an equal footing and let them negotiate and bargain their way to an outcome that is fair to all sides. This idea is clearly evident in the quotation given earlier from the minority report Commons wrote for the Commission on Industrial Relations. He elsewhere expanded on the idea (1911: 466), stating:

> The employer's business is to attend to the increase in efficiency; the wage earner's business is to sell himself to do the employer's bidding. The two interests are necessarily conflicting. Open conflict can be avoided in three ways: by the domination of the employer, by the domination of the union; by the equal domination of the two interests. The first and second methods do not solve the problem, they suppress it. The third meets it in the same way that similar conflicts are met in the region of politics; namely, a constitutional form of organization representing the interests affected, with mutual veto, and therefore with progressive compromise as conflicts arise.

The resulting system is pluralist, in that outcomes are determined by bargaining and negotiation among two or more organized interest groups, with the outcome taking the form of a reasonable compromise both sides can live with. Cooperation is still a goal but relations are kept at arm's length, and the parties, in effect, sign a peace treaty agreeing to work together toward a common end that benefits both.

An essential part of a pluralist industrial relations system is, thus, a significant-sized labour movement and widespread collective bargaining in key industries and firms. For this reason, the American institutional economists advocated more extensive trade unionism in the economy (the workers' solution to labour problems) and a change in public policy to provide stronger legal protection of the right to organize. Although acknowledging that trade unions have shortcomings, the institutionalists nonetheless believed that outside the progressive minority of firms they promote efficiency on net and, more certainly, social welfare. They do this by promoting the three goals of equalizing bargaining power, stabilizing markets and introducing constitutional government in industry. Unions, for example, equalize bargaining power by introducing collective bargaining into wage determination, while they stabilize labour markets by taking wages out of competition. Unions also make labour markets work more effectively by prodding management to improve operational efficiency and invest in new capital equipment and technology, upgrade employee benefits and working conditions, and internalize social costs of labour. Another advantage is that unions democratize internal firm governance by giving workers voice and representation with management, provide the protection of due process in the settlement of disputes, and give labour as a class voice and influence in the national political system.

The ILE advocates in industrial relations also favoured a considerable expansion and strengthening of government labour legislation (the community's solution to labour problems). To promote labour law, they founded the American Association for Labor Legislation (AALL), an outgrowth of the International Association for Labor Legislation and itself a forerunner of the ILO. As with unions, most business people (and neoclassical economists) take a relatively unsympathetic, often critical stance on labour legislation, viewing it as an undesirable interference with management and market forces and a source of higher cost and inefficiency. From an ILE perspective, however, labour legislation has a valuable role to play in promoting improved industrial relations. One form of government regulation favoured by the ILE group is protective labour law, such as mandates on minimum wages, maximum hours, child labour, and health and safety conditions (Commons and Andrews, 1916; Kaufman, 1997a). In their view, without government protection the forces of superior employer bargaining power, imperfect markets and destructive competition will lower labour standards to a socially undesirable, below-competitive level. Labour law is thus an alternative institutional method to equalize bargaining power and stabilize markets through the device of the common rule. Also, just as the federal government uses its power to regulate the quality of firms' goods and services to protect consumers' welfare, so too is it in the social interest for the government also to promote workers' welfare by ensuring minimum standards in the workplace. Finally, unions are a complement to effective labour law since they give labour a voice in the larger political process of the nation so that legislation, judicial appointments and regulatory enforcement are more balanced and not prejudiced in favour of employers.

A second type of government labour law the ILE school promoted is social insurance programmes, such as unemployment insurance, workmen's compensation (workplace accident and injury insurance), health insurance and old-age insurance (Moss, 1996). One rationale for this type of legislation is that free labour markets will underproduce these forms of protection, or allow firms to shift the costs of unemployment or injuries to workers and communities (due to market imperfections, such as public goods and excess labour supply), thus necessitating public provision. A second is that relying on employer provision means that many workers will not be covered, workers become tied to firms so benefits become a source of monopsony power, and incomplete labour market coverage puts labour costs back into competition. A third is that for humanitarian reasons workers and their families should not be subjected to the financial insecurity and demoralization of character that happen without a safety net of protection.

A final element in the industrial relations strategy of the ILE school is macroeconomic stabilization and use of fiscal and monetary policy to maintain full employment. Laissez-faire economists believe the market economy is self-regulating and that freely fluctuating wages and prices work to keep the labour market at full employment. In this theory, the remedy for unemployment is a cut in wages and other components of labour cost so employers will find it attractive to hire more people. Many bankers and business people in the early part of the twentieth century also subscribed to this view. The economists of the ILE school took a different view. Presaging the later theories of British economist J.M. Keynes (1936), the institutional economists rejected the idea that a modern industrial economy is self-regulating. Further, they saw that substantial unemployment and the cyclical booms and busts of the economy destroy both the ability and incentive of firms to practise a progressive, welfare capitalist employment strategy: lay-offs and wage cuts destroy trust and harmony of interest, extensive training and job security provisions become too expensive and the threat of unemployment becomes a more effective and cheaper discipline and motivational method than fair treatment. For these reasons, Commons argued that the single most effective device for improved industrial relations is using the monetary and fiscal policies of the government to maintain full employment and that full employment must be a "managed equilibrium".[10]

It was earlier noted that the PM school took an internalist perspective on the cause of and solution to labour problems. As is evident from the above discussion, the ILE school tended toward the opposite approach and took an "externalist" perspective. They recognized the importance of good human relations and management practices but assigned these internal factors a distinctly secondary role. Instead, the ILE school located the major source of labour problems in forces and developments outside the firm. More important, for example, were the demand and supply conditions in labour markets, the seriousness of unemployment and business cycles, the legal regime regulating the employment relationship, the degree of class stratification and social mobility, and the history of employer–employee relations. Correspondingly, their search for solutions to labour problems tended to focus on corrections to these problems, such as trade unionism, labour legislation, social insurance programmes, free public education, and full employment monetary policy. As previously stressed, the ILE writers did not neglect management, but they did tend to take a wider perspective and neglect the operational details. Also, while the PM school portrayed the firm's industrial relations strategy and practices as largely a choice variable of management, the ILE school considered management's room for independent choice to be highly constrained by and contingent on external factors. For these reasons, the theories and ideas of the ILE school were first and foremost from the discipline of economics (broadly defined), followed by other "external" disciplines such as law, history, political science, and the macro side of sociology.

A composite model

The PM and ILE schools represented distinct and partially rivalrous approaches to improved industrial relations in the United States. Over the course of the 1920s, however, Commons and colleagues of the ILE school gradually incorporated more of the PM approach into their problem-solving agenda and modified or softened portions of the early ILE approach (Kaufman, 2003c). The result was a synthesis of the two problem-solving perspectives, in effect accomplished by a melding of "American shoemakers", *Principles of labor legislation*, *Industrial goodwill*, and the monetary and business-cycle theory in *Institutional economics*. This composite industrial relations model, described below as a stylized generalization, is the best representation of the distinctly American approach to problem solving and improved industrial relations. The unique feature of this composite model is that it incorporates both the unitarist and pluralist components of the two schools of thought and relates them in a contingent way to the macroeconomic environment.

In this composite model, the leading edge of best-practice employment relations is established by progressive employers using a unitarist, welfare capitalist model. These firms offer high wages and superior employment conditions, provide some method of employee involvement or representation to give workers a measure of voice and influence, and endeavour to treat workers with fairness and respect. As a result, these workers are typically satisfied with their terms and conditions of employment, often feel loyalty to the employer, and the majority have little desire for independent union representation. These firms, therefore, will typically be non-union, and with standards considerably above the minimum set out in most protective labour legislation. Although these firms are also likely to provide workers with various welfare and insurance plans, a government-provided safety net of social insurance programmes is still necessary to provide full protection and reduce potential employer monopsony power.

The role of the pluralist industrial relations model comes in the lower and middle reaches of the labour market, per Commons' (1921a: 15) statement "[l]abor [i.e., the trade union] has not come into existence at all to deal with that first class of employers [welfare capitalist firms]. ... It has come in solely in order to use coercion with ... those who need it because they will not or cannot meet new conditions." Descending from the top level of firms, labour problems start to grow and intensify. Wages are lower, benefits fewer, personnel practices less professional and equitable, and management more authoritarian and arbitrary. It is here that trade unionism and protective labour law are most needed and best suited for improving industrial relations. Employees in these firms are much more likely to want union representation, and unions fulfil a valuable role by giving these workers negotiating power to obtain reasonable wages and a measure of industrial democracy. Another consideration is that workers at the lower end of the labour market are more likely to be unskilled, less educated, from disadvantaged gender, religious, ethnic and racial groups, and to suffer unemployment. Unions can thus compensate for their lack of individual bargaining power. In the composite model, unions also need to be complemented by a web of protective labour legislation and social insurance programmes. Minimum wage and other protective labour laws fill in the gaps where unions are absent, and national social insurance programmes extend protection to a large portion of the workforce that would otherwise have little or none.

Thus the early composite model of American industrial relations is a dual model, containing both a unitarist and pluralist component. The pluralist component of trade unionism and labour law covers the portion of the workforce having significant labour problems. Here the employment relationship is likely to be adversarial, while wages, working conditions and management treatment are often below reasonable levels. Unions and legislation play an important social role by establishing a floor of labour standards and gradually raising over time what the ILE group called the plane of competition. At the top end, progressive employers using a welfare capitalism type of employment strategy establish the upper limit of wages and labour conditions, and gradually improve the level of best practice over time.

The dividing line between pluralist and unitarist models in the labour market is determined by several factors. The most important is the state of the macroeconomy and level of unemployment in the labour market. The closer the economy operates to full employment, the greater is the ability and incentive of employers to voluntarily provide reasonable conditions and treatment of their employees, while collective bargaining runs the risk of generating monopoly wage premiums and cost-push inflation. Correspondingly, the countervailing power of collective bargaining and government legislation is in greater need when extensive unemployment puts workers in a weak and vulnerable position.

A second factor determining the dividing line is the trade-off that exists between high labour costs and fewer jobs. The purpose of the pluralist combination of trade unions and legislation is to raise wages and conditions above the level the labour market otherwise yields. But doing so, at least if done quickly and by a large amount, makes firms less competitive and reduces their demand for labour. The institutional economists accept the possibility of some job loss as the necessary price to pay for reasonable and just standards of employment at low-road employers, for otherwise all efforts at social advance through institutions (e.g., workplace safety and child labour laws) are blocked and laissez-faire rules by default. In doing so they follow Adam Smith and take the optimistic view that economies in the long run perform better with higher labour standards than lower, and assign to government the responsibility for successfully managing the short-run problem of re-employment (if any exists) through retraining programmes, expansionary monetary policy and other such measures. Importantly, however, Commons (1934a: 526) also points out that profit is the life force of capitalism and the wellspring of new jobs. Society must balance, therefore, the desire to advance the conditions of labour in the short run through trade unionism and labour legislation with the need to create new jobs in the long run through profit and the innovation and capital investment it makes possible. This was the challenge of industrial relations then, and remains the central challenge today.

American industrial relations in international context

Before moving to the next chapter and the United Kingdom, it is useful to step back and put early American industrial relations in an international context. Indeed, the subsequent development of the field cannot be adequately appreciated without this larger perspective. Americans and Europeans (and the European transplants in Australasia) were not on the same social and political wavelength in the early part of the twentieth century. Americans were inward looking and uninterested in (if not disdainful of) foreign developments and ideas. Europe was the Old World, with its feudal remnants, class-divided societies, monarchies and aristocratic elites, socialist revolutionary movements and constant national rivalries and wars. The United States, on the other hand, was the New World. Seeing much to lose and little to gain, the United States ended the First World War with a national urge to leave Europe and return to North America where in splendid isolation the country could develop its national destiny. Symbolic of this urge was the decision not to join the League of Nations and the ILO, and President Coolidge's dictum that "America's business is business". Most emblematic of the new era, however, were Henry Ford and the Model T. Ford's new production system and business model, quickly labelled Fordism, had a revolutionary impact by making possible mass consumption, huge industrial facilities with thousands of blue-collar workers, and much-expanded social and geographic mobility. Suddenly it appeared that the wedding of Tayloristic scientific management and Fordist mass production could achieve the best of all worlds – a gushing of material prosperity for all classes and an ending of class conflict through rational (and equitable) design of the industrial apparatus. As the Roaring Twenties proceeded, Americans became convinced they had discovered the door to the "new era" and thus had little to learn from the Europeans. Rather, the trade should be in the other direction (Rodgers, 1998).

Europeans, on the other hand, looked at the United States through quite different eyes. All but the most jaundiced and critical of European observers were impressed by the tremendous economic dynamism and material prosperity of the country. As the United States vaulted to the world's leading industrial power after 1900, many Europeans came to the United States to see for themselves this new powerhouse – reminiscent of the trek of Americans to Japan during the miracle economy of the 1980s. Many returned home, however, with a feeling of ambivalence and varying proportions of love and hate. On the positive side was not only American prosperity but also greater social exuberance, openness and equality. In the United States, people of all social classes were addressed as "you", while in Germany people were separated by "Sie" and "du". But there was also a downside. The Webbs came to the United States and vowed never to return, with Beatrice (1948: 185) writing in her diary "we loathe of what we saw of Pittsburgh". Another British visitor described Chicago (Rodgers, 1998: 42) as "like a demented creature, harum, scarum, filthy from top to toe". Their criticism of the United States was much deeper, however, than dirty cities and unkempt people. H.G. Wells (1906: 61) got closer to the core issue when he observed, "There is no order, no provision, no common and universal plan." For the Europeans, the United States was at once a land of unparalleled plenty and a descent into social atomism and economic anarchy where the social Darwinist idea of "everyone for himself and the Devil take the hindmost" seemed to be embraced as a national creed. To these visitors, Europe was harmonious and organic, with governments that promoted a thriving civic society and sense of social solidarity, and a culture that exalted more than money making and materialism. Many thus returned to Europe feeling that the United States was materially prosperous but socially backward, culturally impoverished and yoked to an industrial machine that used up working people in the name of serving them.

Early American industrial relations was a piece in this larger picture and its character, development and slow spread outward from North America can only be fully understood against this backdrop (themes which are further developed in Chapters 3 and 9). To the average American in the 1920s, and probably to many Americans today, the development of the industrial relations problem-solving agenda described in this chapter looks like another example of the United States "leading the way" in crafting a better world. After all, the industrial relations programme combined in one synergistic package a four-pronged strategy to solve the Labour Problem through trade unions, progressive management, labour policy (law and social insurance) and macroeconomic stabilization. And, in the 1920s, it appeared to work.

Standing outside the United States, things again looked quite different. What most Europeans saw was the problem-solving face of American industrial relations. From an external viewpoint, this aspect of industrial relations appeared to be a relatively belated, managerialist, narrowly structured and idiosyncratic programme that left many Europeans as unimpressed as by Pittsburgh or Chicago. The United States had a reputation for industrial violence and lack of social order (Adams, 1966), so the Europeans could well imagine that the United States – but not Europe – might need this new industrial relations. From their perspective, however, there seemed little that was new or interesting in most parts of its problem-solving agenda. Indeed, for two of the core areas the Europeans could rightfully claim that the direction of trade was all from Europe to the United States, while a third was equally well known on both sides of the Atlantic and, in any event, too embryonic and untested to merit serious attention. Only the fourth area was a new and uniquely American development, but many Europeans were not attracted to it.

One of the four elements of industrial relations, for example, was protective labour law and social insurance. The United States in the 1920s was the most backward country in the industrialized world in this area of social policy (Rodgers, 1998). Even the most basic aspects, such as national-level laws governing child labour and accident insurance, were not to be found. The United Kingdom, on the other hand, had pioneered factory act legislation throughout the nineteenth century, while Germany had pioneered social insurance programmes in the 1880s. A number of countries, such as New Zealand, put these diverse elements together in a social labour policy that in the early part of the twentieth century was far ahead of what the United States had until the New Deal of the 1930s. Emblematic of the American position, hanging from the walls of Commons' seminar room at Wisconsin were large sheets of paper listing all the labour laws of other countries.

Americans also had little to teach the rest of the world about trade unionism and collective bargaining. The American model was largely transplanted from the United Kingdom but with an even stronger emphasis on craft unionism, business unionism and voluntarism. To many Europeans, the American labour movement and collective bargaining system was not one that inspired emulation. The European unions were part of a broad-based social movement that sought to represent and lift up the entire working class through a combination of collective bargaining and broad-based political action. The mainline AFL unions, on the other hand, eschewed organizing the unskilled and semi-skilled, stoutly resisted nearly all forms of labour improvement through legal enactment, and limited their social programme to a monopoly-like extraction of "more" from business firms. The ire of European progressives was particularly aroused by Samuel Gompers' insistence at the Versailles Peace Treaty that the mission of the ILO be limited to promoting American-style collective bargaining. Then, in the 1920s, the AFL veered further to the right and openly adopted a strategy of cooperation with employers and suppression of leftists, reaching a point where the most progressive American union of the 1920s (the non-AFL Amalgamated Clothing Workers) was hiring its own efficiency engineers to help employers rationalize production.

Nor did Europeans see much to take note of regarding the third element of industrial relations: macroeconomic stabilization. Even in the United States this part of industrial relations policy was by far the least developed and discussed, so it could well have gone unnoticed by most Europeans. Using experience rating in unemployment insurance to stabilize unemployment was just a theoretical proposal in the 1920s that no American state government had tried, while stabilizing the business cycle through monetary policy was also a largely untried and foreign idea to most labour reformers. Countercyclical public works spending, on the other hand, was a well-known idea across the world, but also one little implemented.

Only with regard to the subject of labour management did the United States really have something new to present to the world. Before the First World War,

German employers were the leaders in employee welfare programmes and shop committees (Spencer, 1984). After the war, however, American employers caught the attention of the world with their innovative programme of welfare capitalism. The pioneering aspect was not so much any one piece of welfare capitalism but rather that it was developed as an integrated set of employment practices, was deliberately constructed to achieve competitive advantage through socially engineered mutual gain, and was less the product of overt paternalism (the German case) than professional, scientific management (Balderston, 1935). Today these ideas are generally considered part of strategic human resource management, participative management, and organizational development, and are implemented in their highest form in the high-performance workplace. In the 1920s, however, these ideas were the special province of industrial relations and reached their highest form in the corporate practitioners of industrial relations (Kaufman, 2001b; 2004e). When Europeans looked at American industrial relations, it was the progressive management dimension – and particularly the application of science and expert administration to all phases of the employment problem – that most caught their attention and which defined in their eyes the unique aspect of industrial relations. This new model of industrial relations was, in turn, heavily identified in Europe with the new Fordist non-union mass production model and was typically seen as its labour policy component (Nolan, 1994).

Evidence on these matters can be found in several places. Delegations from Australia, Germany and the United Kingdom, for example, came to the United States in the last part of the 1920s to learn about the new practice of industrial relations. A summary of the British delegation's report states (*Monthly Labor Review*, 1928: 1199):

> Management and the attitude of labour are two matters singled out for special comment. The technique of management has been greatly advanced, and particularly notable is the manner in which the benefits of experience in production, marketing, organization and industrial relations are shared, even in 'competitive industries'. As to the workers, it is noted that they accept experiments toward reduced cost of production, as they have found that the result of lower costs has been increased consumption, and consequently more employment. Their morale is increased by high wages for high output, by grading according to skill, and by promotion for those who show ability to executive and administrative posts. On both sides there has been an increased recognition, during late years, of the importance of industrial relations.

Also illuminating are the observations about American unions made by one of the Australian delegates (quoted in *Monthly Labor Review*, 1928: 905–6):

The American unions are organized on a craft, not an industrial, basis. Each is formed strictly for the benefit of those engaged in the particular trade, and does not consider it any part of its work to worry about the workers outside that trade. The unskilled worker who belongs to no trade is nobody's business. From that it is easy to arrive at the reason for the failure of unionism to gain a hold in the mass-production industries.

He then describes American employers and their labour policies:

An essential condition of mass production is that each individual worker shall place himself unreservedly in the hands of management. The circumstance that made mass production possible and that must be recognized if its prosperity is to continue, is that unskilled labor is unorganized. The controllers of these great industries recognize the proposition. They are aware that when once unskilled labor becomes organized and can be directed by union leaders, their day of trouble begins. Their continued prosperity depends upon the subservience of their workers. So they have deliberately gone out of their way to do part of the work of the unions. I give them all the credit for their strategy. They have asked themselves what material advantages has the union won for the workers in industries that have fallen victim to unionism? With good grace they have given these advantages to their workers and also others that are new. But note the difference: It is they who are giving them out of generosity, and not the workers who are winning them as a right. Unions are formed through grievances and thrive on disaffection. The mass-production corporations of America spend much thought and large sums of money to make it difficult for their workers to think that they have grievances. Labor leaders frankly admit that they cannot organize these workers. Each man had been bought in an individual bargain, and his neighbour's case stands in no relation to his own.

Although modern-day American industrial relations scholars tend to identify the early years of industrial relations with famous ILE books and articles, such as the Webbs' *Industrial democracy* and Commons and associates' *History of labor in the United States*, these works did not represent industrial relations as seen by foreign observers of the 1920s. Rather, in their eyes industrial relations meant the industrial relations model of Rockefeller, Ford and the PM school, represented by large non-union corporations practising welfare capitalism ("corporate social policy") and employee representation, with American-style collective bargaining largely omitted as irrelevant to the new age of Fordism, and labour law and social insurance in a very backward and undeveloped state.

Were the international observers attracted to the new model of industrial relations? On certain counts they definitely were. Many foreign visitors went home impressed that the new Fordist model had apparently solved the Labour Problem by achieving higher wages, lower prices, material abundance, and all without exploiting labour. The industrial relations model itself, though, was regarded as culture bound and freighted with drawbacks. Nolan (1994: 106) states, for example:

> For German industrialists, engineers, and industrial sociologists welfare capitalism was interesting but incidental to the essence of Americanism ... [It] was embedded in a completely different set of institutional arrangements and power relationships. Labour law, collective bargaining, the state, and trade unions bore so little resemblance to their German counterparts that the American model seemed inapplicable.

On their part, both the British and Australian visitors were not convinced that the benefits to the workers outweighed the costs. The British concluded that wages were definitely higher in the United States, but that workers had less voice, protection and security than in the United Kingdom. Presciently, the British also noted that "[i]t is perhaps too soon to express a definite opinion as to the permanence of the machinery which has been set up in the event of the United States suffering from a severe trade depression such as has been experienced in Great Britain during the last few years." Australians took a similar view (summarized in the U.S. Department of Labor's *Monthly Labor Review*: 907):

> To sum up, the author [the Australian delegate] feels that mass production in the United States is so closely connected with conditions not prevailing in Australia that it is neither possible nor desirable to introduce its methods there. He is rather doubtful how long these methods will be successful even in this country; they have flourished in the time of our prosperity, but as they have not been tested by a period of industrial depression, nor is it certain how they will meet the growth of a spirit of real unionism among the workers. Certain specific features of industry in the United States might well be adopted by Australia, but only with the safeguard of unionism as it is there understood. In terms of human value, the Australian worker is better off than the American, and he will be wise to scrutinize carefully any changes it may be proposed to introduce.

Notes

[1] Given the almost complete omission of Rockefeller in other contemporary accounts of the history of industrial relations, to list him here as a co-founder may strike some readers as exaggerated or exceptionally revisionist. I wrestled with this issue more than any other in the volume, but concluded that his contribution to the birth and early development of industrial relations as an institution was both fundamental and strategic, as the facts cited in this and succeeding chapters indicate. For additional evidence, see Derber (1961), Harvey (1982), Domhoff (1990; 1996), Richardson and Fisher (1999), Magat (1999) and Kaufman, Beaumont and Helfgott (2003).

[2] A closed shop is where the employer agrees to hire only union members in good standing, effectively giving the union control over the supply of labour and who is hired. Workers who are not union members cannot be hired, and workers who lose their membership must be discharged.

[3] The Wertheim family stipulated that the money be used to promote research in "industrial cooperation" (Walker, 1956: vii), but the title of the book series was changed to industrial relations.

[4] The posthumously published *Economics of collective action* (1950) provides a reworked synthesis of ideas in *Institutional economics*, while his earlier book *Legal foundations of capitalism* (1924) anticipates many of the arguments. The summary of Commons presented in this section is elaborated in Kaufman (2003d, 2004a).

[5] Budd (2004) argues that the trilogy of goals is efficiency, equity and voice, but I subsume voice under what I consider is the more fundamental construct – development of the self. The institutionalists advocated both concepts and the theoretical implications are largely the same.

[6] Although rarely recognized today, Commons in the 1920s was one of the nation's foremost monetary experts (Whalen, 1991) and in the 1940s and 1950s, Slichter was an internationally recognized business cycle analyst (Dunlop, 1961).

[7] Fitch went on to become a professor and associate editor of *The Survey* magazine and helped to author the petition to President Taft for the creation of the Commission on Industrial Relations.

[8] Locke, Piore and Kochan (1995: xiii) state, for example, "Industrial relations emerged as a distinct field of study and a locus of public policy in the aftermath of the Great Depression and the Second World War. Its focus was upon the organization of workers through trade unions." A notable exception is Denker (1981: 11), who says, "Industrial relations had first gained a foothold on the campus as part of a foundation-sponsored effort to modernize the personnel function of large corporations."

[9] Detailed case studies of the early personnel programmes in these leading companies are described in Balderston's valuable but much-neglected book *Executive guidance of industrial relations* (1935).

[10] An important implication is that Keynesian economics and institutional economics, and thus industrial relations, are close intellectual kin, because both deny the neoclassical proposition that flexible wages and prices can self-coordinate labour markets and the macroeconomy. This close kinship is also suggested by the statements Keynes made to Commons in a personal letter (Skidelsky, 1992: 229): "There seems to be no other economist with whose general way of thinking I feel myself in such general accord." Another part of the concept of a managed equilibrium is that wages are typically an administered price (rather than purely market determined) and, thus, microeconomic theories of imperfect competition, such as by Edward Chamberlin and Joan Robinson, are also close intellectual kin with institutional economics.

EARLY INDUSTRIAL RELATIONS IN EUROPE: THE UNITED KINGDOM, THE ILO AND THE IRI

3

This chapter describes the first appearance and early development of the industrial relations field outside North America. The beginning point is the United Kingdom. Although industrial relations was already institutionalized in the United States in the early 1920s, it did not gain a foothold in British universities until a decade later and remained in a quite marginal position until after the Second World War. After recounting these events, I offer some explanations for this disparate pattern.

Outside of North America and the United Kingdom, industrial relations appeared in a substantive form in only two other places prior to the Second World War. The most important was the International Labour Organization (ILO). The birth of the ILO in 1919 coincided with the birth of the industrial relations field and the philosophies and objectives of the two were tightly linked. Also, the ILO played an important role in disseminating the idea and philosophy of industrial relations around the world through its publications and activities on behalf of improved labour standards. The other place industrial relations appeared in the interwar period was in the name and programmes of a Europe-based professional association of industrial welfare and personnel workers, the Industrial Relations Institute (IRI). Founded in 1925, the IRI sought to promote improved industrial efficiency and human welfare through a combined programme of scientific management, social work and economic planning. The IRI came to an end with the start of the Second World War.

Industrial relations in the United Kingdom

The previous chapter noted an interesting paradox. Given that the United Kingdom was the home of the Industrial Revolution and the two most influential early academic writers on trade unions and collective bargaining, a reasonable supposition is that the United Kingdom, not the United States, would be the birthplace of industrial relations and that the field would have first sunk deep roots there. It turns out, however, that the opposite is closer to the truth.

Looking back on the development of the industrial relations field in the United Kingdom, Berridge and Goodman (1988: 156) remark, "Prior to the 1960s, the process of acceptance of industrial relations was slow and problematic." This conclusion seems surprising on the face of it, for reasons just cited, but is nonetheless an accurate statement.

Pre-history

Research and writing on what is now called industrial relations has a long history in the United Kingdom, as has been touched upon in the preceding chapters. As noted in Chapter 1, in 1854 Charles Morrison published *An essay on the relations between labour and capital*. Both title and content are remarkable harbingers of the future field of industrial relations. In the opening pages Morrison raises two of the central concerns of industrial relations – fostering greater efficiency and cooperation in industry, stating (1854: 2): "The incessant and energetic cooperation of labour and capital in productive industry is the condition, on which the dense populations of civilized communities live: and the degree of energy and efficiency, to which their joint action attains, is the measure of the degree of progress of these populations." He then states in one sentence the *problématique* of industrial relations from the workers' perspective (p. 3):

> A very general disposition prevails among them [the working classes] to believe, that the relations between themselves and the capitalists are less advantageous to themselves, than is either just or necessary, and that by some regulation of these, for which the power to exact and enforce only is wanting, a great and permanent improvement might be effected in their condition.

Although Morrison stands out for his early and direct treatment of the relations of capital and labour, numerous other authors in the United Kingdom also wrote on subjects directly related to labour and industrial relations during the last half of the nineteenth century. The plight of workers was highlighted, for example, in Friedrich Engels' *The condition of the working class in England in 1844*, while Charles Williams published in 1859 *The great social problem: Four lectures on labour, capital, and wages*. Historical works on trade unions and the labour movement also began to appear. In 1869, for example, the Comte de Paris published *The trades unions of England* and one year later German historical economist Lujo Brentano published *On the history and development of gilds, and the origins of trade-unions*, a study of English unions. An insightful case study of work and trade unionism among miners, *The miners of Northumberland and Durham*, was published in 1873 by Richard Fynes, and in 1878 George Howell published *Conflicts of labour and capital historically and economically considered*.

Further movement toward a distinctive field of labour studies in the United Kingdom came from the work of two other well-recognized scholars. The first was Charles Booth. Booth conducted a painstaking survey and participant-observer study of labour and living conditions in the city of London, eventually published as a 17-volume series *Life and labour of the people in London*. Booth was aided by research assistant Beatrice Webb. Volume 5, "Industry" (1902, 2nd series), provides copious documentation of the low standard of living, long hours and intermittent employment suffered by many manual workers and their families.

The second person is Alfred Marshall, the doyen of British economists and a leader of the neoclassical school. Marshall served as a member of the Royal Commission on Labour between 1891 and 1894 and co-authored the majority report (the minority report was unofficially written by Sidney Webb). The commission heard testimony from hundreds of witnesses about the real-life nature of work, trade unions and employer–employee relations and amassed over 16,000 pages of testimony and evidence. Marshall's experiences and observations from the commission found expression in the second edition of *Elements of economics of industry* (1896), in which he added a new chapter: Chapter 13, "Trade unions". This chapter is far more in the inductive, historical and institutional style than is his text *Principles of economics* and provides a cautiously positive assessment of unions. Both Marshall and his fellow members on the Royal Commission hoped that extensive organization of industry through employers' associations and trade unions would provide stability and peace and end the sweating of labour. Also noteworthy is Marshall's early use of the term industrial relations (Rimmer, 2003). He states on p. 409, "The system of piece-work is seldom found in the finest and best of industrial relations."

The Webbs

These works are suggestive of industrial relations, but the real beginning point for what became the industrial relations field in the United Kingdom (and, to a large degree, the rest of the world) is the two volumes by Sidney and Beatrice Webb, *The history of trade unionism* (1894) and *Industrial democracy* (1897). These books are by common agreement landmarks and remain today unparalleled accomplishments. States one of their biographers (Harrison, 2000: 218):

There has been no want of able successors, many of whom the Webbs inspired and encouraged. Yet after fully a century, no one has attempted to supplant their general *History of trade unionism*, nor has anyone succeeded in producing a work which could compare in point of originality and comprehensiveness with *Industrial democracy*, which has been described by a distinguished authority as 'the best single book ever written on the British Trades Unions'.

Of these two books, *Industrial democracy* is the one that had the most significant and enduring influence on the field of industrial relations. The particular significance of *Industrial democracy* arises from Part III of the volume: "Trade union theory". Here the Webbs pass from historical narrative to the task of science building and problem solving and it is here that the field of industrial relations – particularly its ILE branch – has its original statement.

Before examining the contents of *Industrial democracy,* it is useful to locate the position of the Webbs in the stream of social and economic thought of their day. The most important point to be made is that regarding method and theory the Webbs were very close to the American institutionalists and likewise had strong ties to the German historical–social economists.

Regarding method, their approach was solidly in the tradition of English and German historical economics. In his book *English historical economics*, Gerard Koot (1987: 178–9) states:

Sidney and Beatrice Webb, who have often been viewed as historians and sociologists, can also be seen as historical economists. ... The joint historical and economic work of the Webbs, and especially that of the 1890s, bore such trademarks of historical economics as a vigorous opposition to the method and many of the conclusions of orthodox economics, a pessimistic interpretation of the social effects of the Industrial Revolution, an embrace of a state-regulated economy of trusts and labor unions, an appeal for a measure of national social reform that they termed evolutionary socialism, and a healthy respect for a British imperial mission.

Looking more closely at the labour research of the Webbs, one sees confirmation of Koot's assertion. For example, key to the method of historical and institutional economics is an inductive approach to theorizing, coupled with rejection of the "armchair" deductive theorizing of the classical and neoclassical schools. The Webbs were strong, life-long advocates of the former. Thus they chose to start the Preface of *Industrial democracy* with this statement:

We have attempted in these volumes to give a scientific analysis of Trade Unionism in the United Kingdom. To this task we have devoted six years' investigation, in the course of which we have examined, inside and out, the constitution of practically every Trade Union organisation, together with the methods and regulations which it uses to attain its ends.

Clearly stated here is the inductive (or "adductive") approach to theorizing in which the scholar first uses "go and see" field research and fact-gathering to both develop a rounded understanding of the institution and fix the main points of behaviour and, only then, passes on to the task of using these facts and observations to adduce a theory. With regard to the deductive method of the neoclassical school, they state on the same page of the Preface (emphasis added):

Nor can any useful conclusions, theoretical or practical, be arrived at by arguing from 'common notions' about Trade Unionism; nor even by refining these into a definition of some imaginary form of combination in the abstract. Sociology, like all other sciences, can advance only upon the basis of a *precise observation of actual facts*.

Several pages later (p. x) they add, "What is dangerous is to have only a single hypothesis, for this inevitably biases the selection of facts; or nothing but far-reaching theories as to ultimate causes and general results, for these cannot be tested by any facts that a single student can unravel."

Also uniting the Webbs, the American institutionalists and the German economists was a focus on the role of institutions in economic affairs, the use of a historical and evolutionary approach to economic theorizing, and an effort to marry sociology, political science and economics in pursuit of a holistic understanding of economic behaviour. On the role of institutions, Harrison (p. 68) states, "What most distinguished them [the Webbs] ... was their preoccupation with institutional relationships [and] their rejection of historical materialism and the class struggle, in favour of an institutional interpretation of history." Regarding the historical dimension, the Webbs were greatly influenced by the work of the great British historian Arnold Toynbee (Kadish, 1993). With this in mind, Koot (1987: 179) states, "Their research programme had been Toynbean. They claimed to have used their historical research to determine the direction of social evolution; having determined its path through the history of trade unionism, the cooperative movement, the Poor Laws and local government, they hoped to guide society peacefully along its natural path of evolution." Later Koot describes their research as (p. 182, emphasis added) "a partnership of historical research that criticized the ideal of free competition and chronicled the rise of *alternative models of social organization* (i.e., "varieties of economic systems")".

Regarding the multidisciplinary approach, one of the above-cited quotations makes clear that the Webbs portrayed *Industrial democracy* as a work in sociology. But sociology was broadly constructed, in their view, to be the "science of society" and thus included in its broad domain political economy. In fact, the last one-third of *Industrial democracy* is largely a work in economics, per chapter titles such as "The verdict of the economists" and "The economic characteristics of Trade Unionism". Furthermore, their effort in these chapters was not only to offer a new theory of trade unions – a "political" model of the trade union opposed to the "monopoly" view of the neoclassical economists – but to lay the groundwork for an entirely different approach to political economy.

Following on this line of thought, the Webbs were well schooled in orthodox economics. Beatrice undertook a self-study of political economy in 1886. Although she (1926: 290) considered the subject "a most hateful drudgery", she nevertheless persevered and later published two articles: "The rise and growth of English economics" and "The economic theory of Karl Marx". Sidney Webb also had a deep interest in economics. He read the books of all the great economists of the period, including John Stuart Mill, Henry George, Karl Marx and the German historical economists (Webb read German), and was admitted as one of the founding members of the British Economic Association. Both of the Webbs also followed the developments in the new marginalist economics pioneered by Jevons and Marshall and gave Marshall's work a large measure of respect (Harrison, 2000). The Webbs faulted both Marx and the British classical economists for pursuing an overly abstract, deductive approach to economic theorizing that elevated self-interest, profit making and competition to all-powerful forces. They were also critical of Marshall and other neoclassical economists for this same tendency, although their criticism of Marshall was tempered by his sympathetic treatment of unions in *Elements of economics of industry* and efforts to introduce historical and ethical elements into *Principles of economics*.

Broadly viewed, what they found most objectionable in economics was, first, the proclivity of economists to engage in theorizing divorced from social reality and knowledge of the facts and, second, to propound an economic doctrine – "laissez-faire" – that obviated all possibilities for social reform, placed the blame for poverty on the shoulders of the poor, and treated society as nothing more than a mass of competing individuals. In an interesting characterization of competitive economic theory and the doctrine of laissez-faire, Sidney Webb (quoted in Dahrendorf, 1995: 41) observed with some acerbity that the idea that "absolute freedom in the sense of individual and 'manly' independence, plus a criminal code, would bring about a good society had clearly been refuted". Also illustrative of his attitude on these matters is his contention that the orthodox economists are "a compound of text-book theory and ignorance of fact" and his statement that "we must have regard not only to the development of the individual, but also to that of the Social Organism" (quoted in Harrison, 2000: 283, 36). A more detailed critique is provided by Beatrice (1948: 87–8), who points to

> our common dislike of the so-called Manchester School, of its unverified inductive reasoning and abstract generalizations, and its apotheosis of the 'economic man', exclusively inspired by the motive of pecuniary self-interest and the passionate defence of the rights of property as against the need of humanity. And, secondly, our common faith in the practicability and urgent necessity of a concrete science of society implemented through historical research, personal observation and statistical verification.

Industrial democracy was, therefore, partly a historical study of British trade unions. However, the Webbs had loftier ambitions for the book and used it to lay the groundwork for an alternative political economy. The grand nature of their aspirations is suggested by Harrison (2000: 220) when he states, "they aspired to write a work for their own time that would be as influential and definitive as *The wealth of nations* – to create a new political economy, to draw anew the map of learning." In this effort, they did not – just as the American institutionalists did not – completely reject orthodox theory. Their view, rather, was that Marshall and colleagues had put forward a useful apparatus (models of supply and demand and perfect competition) for considering certain issues but that these were apt to be misleading and incomplete for most real-life situations. When a historical perspective and more realistic and complete set of assumptions are added, however, quite possibly the predictions and implications yielded by standard theory may be reversed.

The central objective of Part III of *Industrial democracy* is to outline such an expanded (or "complete") model and apply it to the case of trade unionism. The Webbs open Part III by outlining the position of the classical economists on trade unions, noting in the first sentence (p. 603): "Down to within the last thirty years it would have been taken for granted, by every educated man, that Trade Unionism, as a means of bettering the condition of the workman, was 'against Political Economy'." After a lengthy review of this work, in the next chapter "The higgling of the market" they turn to the development of their own theory.

It is instructive to note that they start the analysis from a neoclassical baseline, saying (p. 655), "To reveal these characteristics [the economic effects of trade unions], we must assume a market in a state of perfect equilibrium, where the supply is exactly equal in quantity to the demand." Over the next two chapters, they then modify this model to take into account various real-life features. For example, the first tack is to argue that labour markets are fundamentally different from commodity markets and that these differences, on net, tip wage determination in favour of employers, creating an inequality of bargaining power. In this regard, the Webbs note that the individual worker, even in an otherwise competitive market, is at a disadvantage relative to the employer because the worker has fewer market alternatives, fewer financial resources, poorer information, less negotiating skill, and is selling a perishable good.

Then the Webbs note three additional realistic features of labour markets that further tip the wage determination process in favour of employers. The first (p. 648) is that labour markets are not, in fact, competitive but highly imperfect ("competition between individual producers and consumers, laborers and capitalists is ... in actual life very far from perfect"); the second (p. 658) is that labour contracts are incomplete and this gives the employer a greater opportunity than the worker to shift *ex post* the terms of the wage bargain in its favour (a "far more fruitful source of personal hardship [to the worker], against which he has no practicable remedy"); and the third is the existence in normal times of considerable excess labour supply in the form of workers involuntarily unemployed.

As noted in the previous chapter, the American institutionalists believed unemployment to be the most serious defect of capitalism and that this factor substantially obviates many of the predictions of neoclassical competitive theory (which presumes free labour markets will be in a demand/supply equilibrium of full employment, or have an automatic tendency toward this position). In the real-life labour markets of the late nineteenth century, state the Webbs, substantial long-lasting unemployment is the normal case. They are thus aligned with the institutionalists on this matter. The effect on wage determination, in turn, is to turn competition from a beneficial force to a destructive force that leads to exploitation and oppression of labour. They describe the process in these words (p. 660):

> When the unemployed are crowding round the factory gates every morning, it is plain to each man that, unless he can induce the foreman to select him rather than another, his chance of subsistence for weeks to come may be irretrievably lost. Under these circumstances bargaining, in the case of the isolated individual workman, becomes absolutely impossible. The foreman has only to pick his man, and tell him the terms. Once inside the gates, the lucky workman knows that if he grumbles at any of the surroundings, however intolerable; if he demurs to any speeding-up, lengthening of the hours, or deductions; or if he hesitates to obey any order, however unreasonable, he condemns himself once more to the semi-starvation and misery of unemployment.

The Webbs conclude, therefore, that the actual state of affairs in labour markets is quite different from that pictured in orthodox competitive theory. Their amended version has two important features. The first is a general tendency for wage determination to be tipped against the individual employee. Rather than a competitive labour market where workers and employers face each other on a level playing field and wages adjust to maintain full employment and compensate workers for risks of injury and other hazards of employment, the Webbs conclude that actual labour markets have many serious imperfections and considerable unemployment that, on net, give employers a marked superiority in bargaining power. This inequality of bargaining power leads, in turn, to poverty-level wages, long hours and sweatshop conditions as workers are coerced by the twin forces of lack of jobs and the threat of starvation to put their labour on the market in a "forced sale". The second aspect is that the presence of imperfections and factor immobility create pockets of economic rent that open up extra opportunities for appropriation through bargaining. Firms, for example, typically generate quasi-rents in the short run (revenues above average variable cost) that can be bargained away, albeit at the risk of eventually driving the firm out of business, while some firms earn super-normal profits and these "monopoly rents" form a "debatable land" that trade unions can redistribute from capital to labour without harm to long-term employment. And while most manual workers suffer from an inequality of bargaining power, the minority of "brain workers" and craft workers also may earn a large rent due to the "strategic position" their education and skills give them in the labour market.

This picture tends to throw a bad light on most employers because their superior power in the market puts them in the position of grinding down the wages and conditions of the bulk of their workers in a system of individual bargaining, leading on the face of things to larger profits (rents) at the expense of lower wages for labour. But the Webbs note that employers are not entirely to blame, and indeed some are as much victims of the market as are the workers. In the latter part of the chapter "The higgling of the market", the Webbs broaden the analysis and place the employer and worker in a larger chain of bargains. At the top of the chain of bargains is the consumer who "higgles" with the retailers for the best terms of sale. The retailers, in order to offer the lowest price and win the sale, exert pressure on the wholesalers at the next lower step of the chain of bargains to reduce their prices. The wholesalers, in turn, pass the pressure for lower prices to the manufacturers who in turn bargain with their suppliers for lower prices. The last step in the chain of bargains, according to the Webbs, is when the pressure for lower prices initiated by consumers in product markets reaches the labour market, and manufacturers and other suppliers exert pressure on their workers to accept lower wages and conditions lest they "lose the business" and workers lose their jobs.

Thus, in the larger picture it is the consumers who rule the capitalist market system and pit company against company in a competitive struggle for survival. To avoid this pressure, the companies individually and collectively pursue three strategies: (1) to erect barriers ("dykes and bulwarks") to competition in the product market through a variety of stratagems such as monopolies, cartels, government regulation and product differentiation; (2) lower cost through technological innovation, new capital investment and managerial efficiency; and (3) gain lower input prices from suppliers, particularly lower labour cost since labour is often the largest cost of production. Where companies are successful in pursuing one or both of the first two options, they earn above normal profits (rents) and face less pressure to pursue option three ("the low road" in modern terminology) and are not as likely to cut wages and working conditions.[1] Indeed, say the Webbs, most employers know that it is in their self-interest to pursue what Commons (1919b) later called a "goodwill" labour policy of fair wages, good working conditions and respectful treatment. They state (pp. 661–2) in this regard, with implicit reference to the concept of *cooperation*:

> A capitalist employer who looks forward, not to one but to many years' production, and who regards his business as a valuable property to be handed down from one generation to another, will, if only for his own sake, bear in mind the probable effect of any reduction [of wages and working conditions] upon the permanent efficiency of the establishment. He will know that he cannot subject his workpeople to bad conditions of employment without causing them imperceptibly to deteriorate in the quantity and quality of the service that they render. As an organizer of men, he will readily appreciate to how great an extent the smooth and expeditious working of a complicated industrial concern depends on each man feeling that he is being treated with consideration, and that he is receiving at least as much as he might be earning elsewhere.

The Webbs stop far short of Commons, however, on how much cooperation is ideal between the employer and employees and, indeed, it appears that they repudiate the desirability of creating a unity of interest even if such is possible (p. 552):

> To the Trade Unionist, it seems a very doubtful kindness for an employer to indulge his feelings of philanthropy in such a way as to weaken the capacity of the workmen for that corporate self-help on which their defence against unscrupulous employers depends. ... an employer who desired permanently to benefit the workmen in his

trade would seek in every way to promote the men's own organization, and would therefore make his own establishment a pattern to the rest in respect of the strictest possible maintenance of the Standard Rates of wages, hours of work, and other conditions of employment.

Cooperation, therefore, is desirable in the sense that the employer should treat the workers with respect and always pay the Standard Rate or even higher, but cooperation does the workers a disservice if it leads to a "blurring of the line" and a weakening of the trade union as an organization.

Even this level of cooperation is difficult for many employers to maintain, however, because their competition to win the consumers' business – absent some protective barrier in the product market – exerts continual downward pressure on prices and thus on wages and labour conditions. On this phenomenon the Webbs state (p. 62):

> Unfortunately, the intelligent, far-sighted, and public-spirited employer is not master of the situation. Unless he is protected by one or other of the dykes and bulwarks presently to be described, he is constantly finding himself as powerless as the workman to withstand the pressure of competitive industry [and forced] in sheer self-defence, to take as much advantage of his workpeople as the most grasping and short-sighted of his rivals.

The implication of the foregoing is that a certain degree of protection in both product and labour markets can create economic rents that may be used to elevate the conditions of employment and create a more cooperative and productive long-term industrial partnership between capital and labour.

The final element in the Webbs' theory of the chain of bargains is the proposition that of all the sellers in the various markets it is the individual worker who is in the most vulnerable and powerless position to ward off the downward pressure from the higgling of the market. The reasons are several. Employers, for example, have many more options to erect effective barriers to competition through monopoly, collusion and product differentiation and, as Adam Smith noted in *The wealth of nations*, the law tends to take a far more hostile stance toward workers' combinations than combinations among capitalists. Also, capital can hold out longer for a better return than can labour. Labour is perishable and the sale of labour is typically the worker's only source of income. These facts, combined with a frequent scarcity of jobs and the pressure of ongoing fixed costs of survival (food, shelter, etc.), make it impossible for the worker to keep their product off the market and wait for a better price. Indeed, while neoclassical theory pictures the person who is supplying labour as making a choice between labour and leisure, in reality individual workers in nineteenth-century labour markets – without savings, unemployment insurance, the extra income of a dual-earner spouse and other such income supports – faced a far different and grimmer choice: labour or starvation. Thus part of the dysfunctional aspect of competitive labour markets, as seen by the Webbs and the institutionalists, is that in periods of recession and depression the labour supply expands (the "added worker" effect) as wives, children and the aged enter the labour force in a desperate search for work to make up for the lost income of the unemployed male breadwinner – leading to a further imbalance between labour supply and demand, and even greater downward pressure on wages and working conditions.

With all of these considerations in mind, the Webbs reach this conclusion about the worker's position in a capitalist system of free, unregulated labour markets (pp. 671, 672–3):

> We thus arrive at the consumer as the ultimate source of that persistent pressure on sellers, which, transmitted through the long chain of bargains, finally crushes the isolated workman at the base of the pyramid. Yet, paradoxical as it may seem, the consumer is, of all the parties to the transaction, the last personally responsible for the result. ... All he does – and it is enough to keep the whole machine in motion – is to demur to paying half a crown for an article, when someone else is offering him the same thing for two shillings. ... Such, then, is the general form of the industrial organization which, in so far as it is not tampered with by monopoly or collective regulation, grows up under 'the system of natural liberty.' The idea of mutual exchange of services by free and independent producers in a state of economic equality results, not in a simple, but in a highly complex industrial structure which, whether or not consistent with any real Liberty, is strikingly lacking in either Equality or Fraternity. ... At each link in the chain of bargainings, the superiority in 'freedom' is so overwhelmingly on the side of the buyer, that the seller feels only constraint. This freedom of the purchaser increases with every stage away from the actual production, until it culminates in the anarchic irresponsibility of the private customer, 'free' alike from all moral considerations as to the conditions of employment, and from any intelligent appreciation of the quality of the product. On the other hand, the impulse for cheapness, of which the consumer is the unconscious source, grows in strength as it is transmitted from one stage of bargaining to another, until at last, with all its accumulated weight, it settles like an incubus on the isolated workman's means of subsistence.

Having rendered this portrait of the worker in capitalist industry, the Webbs turn in the next chapter of *Industrial democracy* ("The economic characteristics of Trade Unionism") to erect a positive case for trade unions, at least within limits. Their argument is in one sense more general, however, in that it also provides justification for protective labour legislation, such as a minimum wage law.

To begin, the Webbs again return to a neoclassical baseline. They open the chapter with this statement (p. 703, emphasis added): "The economist and the statesman will judge Trade Unionism, not by its results in improving the position of a particular section of the workmen at a particular time, but by its effects on the permanent *efficiency* of the nation." What they seek to demonstrate in this chapter, therefore, is that even on the strictest of economic grounds trade unionism deserves social support and encouragement. When other welfare goals are introduced, claim the Webbs, the case becomes even more compelling.

The Webbs note that the purpose of trade unions is to improve the economic position of workers, and they do this through various means, including the method of mutual insurance (acting as a "friendly society" that provides insurance and other forms of assistance to members), the method of collective bargaining, and the method of legal enactment (lobbying Parliament for favourable legislation for workers). In their economic analysis they devote the preponderant attention to the method of collective bargaining. They claim (p. 704) that collective bargaining can be used to win more favourable wages and conditions through two distinct approaches: the device of restriction of numbers and the device of the common rule.

The device of the restriction of numbers, as its name implies, endeavours to raise wages, reduce hours of work and gain other such benefits for workers through various types of restrictions and limitations upon the employer. Examples include limiting the labour supply to the firm through the closed shop, limitations on the number of apprentices, work rules that restrict the available work to certain crafts or trades, and requiring the employer to promote and lay off only by seniority. They claim (p. 710) that all of these actions are monopolistic in effect and, like monopoly in the product market, labour market monopoly in an otherwise competitive situation "appears wholly injurious to industrial efficiency". They quickly note, however, that most labour market situations are not competitive, so some degree of protective monopoly may be socially beneficial as a means to offset the evil results of unequal bargaining power and destructive competition.

The second way in which collective bargaining can be used by trade unions to improve wages and conditions is the device of the common rule. The common rule, as the name implies, is a common standard that applies to all firms in a labour market and sets a minimum level for wages, hours and work conditions. According to the Webbs, the great virtue of the common rule is that it only sets a floor under competition but in no other way restricts the employers or the operation of demand and supply. Thus a trade union may set a minimum rate of pay that all firms have to follow, but individual employers are free to pay more if they wish to attract a higher grade of worker. The Webbs further suggest (p. 715) that the trade unions should aim to set the common rule, not at the highest level their bargaining power can obtain (the monopoly outcome), but at a level roughly corresponding to the average or "fair" rate of wages existing in the market. They go on to say (p. 738), "The Trade Unionist has a rough and ready barometer to guide him in this difficult navigation. ... So long ... as a Trade Union, without in any way restricting the numbers entering the occupation, finds its members are fully employed, it can scarcely be wrong in maintaining its Common Rules at their existing levels."

Translated into a neoclassical framework, the Webbs are presuming that the wage rate is depressed below the competitive, full employment level by labour's inequality of bargaining power, and the goal of the trade union should be to use the common rule (or restriction of numbers) to raise wages and conditions up to the competitive level, or modestly beyond if there are monopoly rents to share. The Webbs oppose, on the other hand, using collective bargaining simply to protect a long-established vested interest if the economic basis of the claim is outmoded, and using a trade union's favourable strategic position to extract the maximum of monopoly rents. Their position thus favours using collective bargaining to restore and maintain a *balance* in wage determination (Budd, 2004). The goal of restoring balance in wage determination can be represented with the standard neoclassical monopsony model. In this model the union can raise the wage, ending the exploitation of labour, but as long as the wage is not increased much above the competitive level employment may increase or at least not decline (Manning, 2003; Kaufman, 2004a). In neoclassical terms, one might say that trade unions in this context are "monopsony reducing" rather than "monopoly creating". The Webbs and neoclassical economists, therefore, both agree that unions raise wages but in the view of the former this improves economic efficiency (within limits) while the latter – starting from the premise of competitive markets and rational behaviour – conclude that the union wage gain reduces efficiency. Unemployment, more than pure monopsony, was viewed by the Webbs and other union supporters as the more important source of unequal bargaining power, and here too holding the line on wages or a modest boost in wages could be either benign or helpful (as later argued by Keynes).

From the Webbs' perspective, the use of the common rule to eliminate substandard or "sweated" labour conditions is a clear plus for economic efficiency because it improves the quality of the workforce and eliminates employers' "parasitism" – i.e., making profit by paying workers less than the full social cost of labour. But the efficiency gains from the common rule go beyond this, say the Webbs (p. 733). The other positive effect is to transfer the forces of competition among employers from cutting wages and lowering conditions to finding improvements in other areas of the business, such as better management methods, workforce development and training, more capital investment and greater technological innovation. In modern terms, the common rule forecloses seeking competitive advantage through a "low-road" strategy of cutting wages and lowering conditions and encourages firms to seek competitive advantage through "high-road" strategies, including a "goodwill", high-performance employment system. Thus they state (p. 734):

> In short, whether with regard to Labor or Capital, invention or organizing ability, the mere existence of a uniform Common Rule in any industry promotes alike the selection of the most efficient factors of production, their progressive functional adaptation to a higher level, and their combination in the most advanced type of industrial organization.

The Webbs then further generalize the concept and application of the common rule. They argue that certain labour conditions, such as a minimum level of income (called by the Webbs the "Doctrine of the Living Wage"), child labour, excessive hours of work, and the use of phosphorous in industry (the cause of a disfiguring disease), are clearly detrimental to all workers and an affront to an advancing society. While trade unions may set different levels of the common rule in particular industries, a *national minimum* should be established for certain "core" labour standards as a nationwide common rule. In their words (p. 767), "The remedy is to extend the conception of the common rule from the trade to the whole community, and by prescribing a national minimum, absolutely to prevent any industry being carried on under conditions detrimental to the public welfare." Of course, by setting a national minimum, or any common rule, labour costs may be raised and some jobs lost. The Webbs maintain this cost is worth paying on three counts: first, the national minimum improves the efficiency and quality of labour; second, it improves resource allocation by forcing employers to bear the full social cost of labour; and third, not eliminating these jobs means that *all* workers are forced to labour under these substandard conditions, in effect penalizing the many to help the few.

To this point the Webbs have argued the case for trade unionism purely on efficiency grounds, in effect meeting the neoclassical economists on their own territory. However, like the institutional economists, the Webbs argued that trade unions also have a political function that is equally important. The political function is to replace industrial autocracy with *industrial democracy*. They note (p. 841):

> Even at the present day, after a century of revolution, the great mass of middle and upper-class "Liberals" all over the world see no more inconsistency between democracy and unrestrained capitalist enterprise, than Washington or Jefferson did between democracy and slave-owning. ... The agitation for freedom of combination and factory legislation has been, in reality, a demand for a 'constitution' in the industrial realm. The tardy recognition of Collective Bargaining and the gradual elaboration of a Labor Code signifies that this Magna Carta will, as democracy triumphs, inevitably be conceded to the wage-earning class.

The industrial democracy function of trade unions occurs at two levels, according to the Webbs. The first is at the level of the industry and workplace. Here the trade union provides the worker voice and influence on the terms of the employment contract and the administration of the rules of the workplace. Only then, say the Webbs (p. 842), is there really "freedom of contract". The second tier of industrial democracy is at the level of the state. Here trade unions participate in the national political process and, in particular, advise and counsel government in the setting of the national minima.

As the reader approaches the end of *Industrial democracy* a surprising shift in the argument emerges. Until the last chapter, the endeavour of the Webbs is to demonstrate that the trade union generally promotes, rather than harms, economic efficiency and social well-being. In this regard, they are ploughing the same ground as the American institutionalists. Both are making the case that, first, a measure of social control through collective action will improve the operation of firms and markets and, second, the solution to the labour problems generated in unregulated markets is the introduction of a new institution – the trade union. Having laid out the argument for trade unions, they then consider whether there is an institutional device that is superior to the trade union. And, somewhat surprisingly, the answer the Webbs give is a qualified "yes". This alternative institutional device is what they call the method of legal enactment.

The method of legal enactment is the use of labour law to establish the common rules and national minima. Relative to the space devoted to trade unions, legal enactment is touched upon only lightly in *Industrial democracy*. Given this, one reads with some surprise the conclusion (p. 803): "the Method of Legal Enactment has, where it can be employed, a considerable balance of economic advantages over the Method of Collective Bargaining". The Webbs support this contention with two lines of argument.

The first argument concerns defects and shortcomings of trade unions. The Webbs note, for example, that trade unions (p. 816) "show no backwardness in exacting the highest money wages that they know how to obtain", thus leading them to raise the common rule of wages and conditions to a "monopolistic" level. Furthermore, the Webbs hold that the use of the device of restriction of numbers is in principle to be condemned (p. ix), yet many trade unions nonetheless continue to make extensive use of restrictive practices. Another problem with trade unionism is its reliance on strikes and other methods of "industrial warfare" to win their demands. Finally, trade unions are prone to take a narrow, sectional view of their interests, in which they pursue the maximum gains for their members without due regard to other parts of the workforce and community.

The second line of argument advanced by the Webbs concerns the positive advantages of legal enactment. The most important, they state (pp. 800–803), is that legal enactment is in a number of situations the more effective method for establishing a common rule. In many industries, trade unions are able to organize only a portion of the employees, so their ability to establish and enforce a common rule is compromised. This problem is particularly acute for common rules that take the form of a national minimum. Also, they say, trade unions are more likely to set the common rule in light of their strategic bargaining position, while government is better able to make this determination on the social merits of the case. Finally, the enactment and enforcement of labour laws often engenders less adversarialism and conflict than does trade unionism.

As painted by the Webbs, unregulated labour markets are prone to numerous labour problems and have no a priori claim to virtue on account of efficiency or social welfare. Through most of *Industrial democracy* they set as their task building and elaborating an expanded, more complete picture of the economy and trade union, always basing their theoretical argument on the empirical evidence discovered through field investigation. Like the American institutionalists, they emphasize that the solution to labour problems is use of collective action – and always *democratic* collective action – to invent and develop new institutions that can balance and redirect competitive market forces so that they are socially constructive rather than destructive. In their analysis, trade unions provide a powerful stabilizing, balancing and democratizing role by establishing common rules in the labour market and introducing industrial democracy in the workplace and polity.

As democratic, industrial societies evolve, however, the Webbs see the baton of collective action and institutional regulation of labour markets and firms slowly passing from trade unions to government and the method of legal enactment. Some evidence indicates that the American institutionalists also came to this conclusion, at least in the 1920s before the Great Depression hit (Kaufman, 2003c). Trade unions do not disappear in their vision of the future but gradually shed their sectional bargaining function and evolve into consultative, administrative and educational bodies working to set common rules and represent the interests of workers to the leaders of the democratic states. Thus the Webbs state on this matter (pp. 825–6):

> as industry passes more and more into public control, Trade Unionism must still remain a necessary element in the democratic state, [but] it would, we conceive, in such a development undergo certain changes. ... The Trade Union function of constantly maintaining an armed resistance to attempts to lower the Standard of Life of its members may be accordingly expected to engage a diminishing share of its attention. ... We may therefore expect that, with the progressive nationalisation or municipalisation of public services, on the one hand, and the spread of the Co-operative movement on the other, the Trade Unions of the workers thus taken directly into the employment of the citizen-consumers will more and more assume the character of professional associations. ... each Trade Union will find itself, like the National Union of Teachers, more and more concerned with raising the standard of competency of its occupation, improving the professional equipment of its members, 'educating their masters' as to the best way of carrying on the craft, and endeavoring by every means possible to increase its status in public estimation.

The London School of Economics

Given the Webbs' pioneering and classic statement of the theory of industrial democracy, one would expect that their work would have led directly to the field of industrial relations. This supposition is reinforced by the fact that the Webbs took the leading role in the founding of a new educational institution, the London School of Economics and Political Science (LSE). Surely at the LSE labour problems and industrial relations would be central topics of teaching and research. But, surprisingly, such was not the case.

In the mid-1880s, while in his mid-twenties and still unmarried, Sidney Webb shifted position from a middle-class reformer (an "ameliorationist") to a proponent of socialism, albeit at this time a non-radical or "soft" social democratic version. Beatrice had already made this shift. His entry point and lifelong association with socialism was through a small group of intellectuals called the Fabian Society. The Fabian Society promoted a peaceful, evolutionary transition to a democratic socialist state.[2] The basic point of view was that the prevailing unequal system of property ownership – coupled with large elements of industrial monopoly, backward and self-aggrandizing economic management by an aristocratic elite, and the government's abdication of social responsibility in the name of laissez-faire – contributed to a range of economic and social woes including retarded economic growth, large income inequality, great urban poverty and a growing labour problem. Unlike the Marxists and anarchists, however, the Fabians believed in neither inexorable economic laws nor the necessity of class struggle and revolution. Their point of view was that socialism is demonstrably superior on *both* economic and moral grounds. The mass of ordinary people, once educated and equipped with the facts (and empowered by extension of the suffrage), will make the intelligent choice and vote in legislators who will use the power of the state to gradually replace competitive capitalism with a democratic planned socialism.

In 1894, Sidney Webb attended a meeting at Oxford University on the state of economics in England. He came away depressed and disturbed by the discipline's low status, few university positions, and continued allegiance to the deductive method, individualism and laissez-faire. Webb believed that economic education and research were crucial to the programme of the Fabian Society for two reasons. First, the case for socialism would be greatly advanced if a sound body of economic theory could be developed that supported it and, second, a good programme of "applied economics" was crucial in order to provide the well-trained technical experts and administrators that a socialist economy requires. Yet at the time, England had very few universities offering any kind of economics. Moreover, Oxford and Cambridge, the two most prestigious universities, were in the eyes of Webb (Harrison, p. 264) "centres for social prestige rather than learning", "preparatory schools for the ruling class", and socially retrograde because they "shut out strenuous effort in favour of indolence" and "suffered from the cardinal sin of traditional university life – the separation of thought and action".

At exactly this time a wealthy gentleman and member of the Fabian Society committed suicide and left a modest-sized estate to be administered by Sidney Webb, with the directions it be used to promote the causes championed by the Society. Beatrice Webb recorded in her diary (quoted in Caine, 1963: 2, emphasis in original):

> Now the question is how to spend the money. It might be placed on the credit of the Fabian Society and spent in the ordinary work of propaganda. [But] mere propaganda of the Shibboleths of Collectivism is going on at a rapid rate ... [and] it looks as if the great bulk of the working men will be collectivists before the end of the century. But Reform will not be brought about by shouting. What is needed is *hard thinking*. ... So Sidney has been planning to persuade the trustees to devote the greater part of the money to encouraging *Research and Economic Study*. ... Above all, we want the ordinary citizen to feel that reforming society is no light matter and must be undertaken by experts especially trained for the purpose.

Later, she is quoted as saying about the LSE (Koot, 1987: 169): "We have turned our hopes from propaganda to education, from the working class to the middle class."

Also instructive are Sidney Webb's first recorded thoughts on the subject (Caine, p. 36, emphasis in original):

The greatest needs of the Collectivist movement in England appear to me

(a) An increase in the number of *educated* and able lecturers and writers, as apart from propagandist speakers;

(b) The further investigation of problems of municipal and national administration from a Collectivist standpoint. This implies original research, and the training of additional persons competent to do such work;

(c) The diffusion of economic and political knowledge of a real kind – as apart from Collectivist shibboleths, and the cant and claptrap of political campaigning.

With these thoughts in mind, Sidney Webb set off to found a new educational institution, to be called the London School of Economics and Political Science. It was a monumental undertaking, considering the huge amounts of additional money that had to be raised, the opposition encountered from conservatives and other vested interests, and the daunting task of recruiting a high-calibre faculty with the appropriate training and outlook.

A significant clue to the direction the new school was to take in economic research and education was the person the Webbs chose to be the director of the LSE. He was W.A.S. Hewins. Hewins graduated from Oxford with a degree in mathematics. He became interested in social problems, however, and gradually fell under the sway of the historical/heterodox economics of Carlyle, Ruskin and the German historical school. Although advised that his career prospects in economics were dim given his heterodox views, he persisted, noting (quoted in Koot, 1987: 161):

I set myself as my object to substitute for, or at any rate, to supplement, the theoretical system based upon an analysis of motives and the philosophy underlying orthodox economics, a political economy based upon the study of society and pursued in accordance with the modern historical and scientific method.

Unlike the Webbs, Hewins was not a socialist, although he had earlier flirted with Christian Socialism, trade unions and the cooperative movement. According to Koot (p. 164)

He [Hewins] remained firmly committed to capitalism. His suggestions for state intervention were designed to prevent its violent overthrow and to preserve the empire. ... he still believed in the possibility of educating the workers to accept their role as partners in an enlightened capitalism. This education required that they be taught a historical economics that was free of dangerous socialist theory and the useless abstractions of economic orthodoxy. This goal lay behind much of his intellectual justification of the extension movement and other schemes for worker education. At the same time, he urged the middle and upper classes to abandon their individualistic economics of laissez-faire and assume their rightful social responsibilities.

Under the direction of the Webbs and Hewins, the LSE was built from the ground up and soon became a world-recognized institution of higher education. In 1898 it became a part of the University of London. Several features of the early LSE deserve mention.

First, according to Dahrendorf (1995: 33–46), the LSE under the Webbs and Hewin stressed "the Five Es": Economics, Education, Efficiency, Equality and Empire. The first four of these, it will be recalled from the previous chapter, were also pillars of the American institutional economics and the new field of industrial relations. The fifth (colonialism/imperialism) was a strong element in English and German historical economics but not the American branch (a measure of statism and collectivism, yes, but largely not imperialism).

A second characteristic is that it was expressly established as a "dissenter's alternative" to Oxford, Cambridge and orthodox economics. Hewins' prospectus for the new school declared (Koot, p. 171): "The special aim of the School will be, from the first, the study and investigation of the concrete facts of industrial life and the actual working of economic and political relations as they exist, or have existed, in the United Kingdom and foreign countries." In his history of the LSE, Dahrendorf (p. 33) also quotes Koot, noting that the Webbs and Hewins "sought to mould economic history and applied economics into an alternative economics to Marshall's more theoretical vision of the subject". Toward this end, the LSE recruited a number of faculty members committed to the historical method, such as Edwin Cannan, Herbert Foxwell, Arthur Bowley and William Cunningham, and invited other "economic heretics", such as John Hobson, to lecture.

A third feature of the LSE was an emphasis on making college education more relevant, applied and useful to persons entering the worlds of business, government and administration. By construction, this charge also meant catering to a non-elite student body drawn from the middle class and often working at a job. Thus the LSE offered night classes and more professional/vocational courses in subjects such as public administration, public finance, insurance and transport economics, and law. More surprisingly, the LSE also began to offer courses in 1899 on "commercial education" – surprising because any kind of commercial (business) course was regarded at the time as hopelessly vocational and unsuited for university instruction, and because one might think the Webbs and Hewins would be unreceptive to business education on political/ideological grounds.[3] On the contrary, however, they saw the development of management and administrative skills as a crucial area of need in both the present-day capitalist economy and future socialist economy.

Given the dedication of the Webbs and Hewins to a historical/institutional type of economics, the Webbs' world-famous scholarship on labour and trade unions, and the establishment of the LSE with its applied educational mission, one would seem on safe ground to believe that all conditions were ripe for the introduction of industrial relations – perhaps differently titled or packaged – as a subject area for research and teaching. Such a surmise would be further strengthened by an examination of Sidney Webb's first written proposal outlining the work of the new school. In it he states (quoted in Caine, 1963: 37):

> The subjects I thought about as such as we could take up at once and get good work done are the following: The History of the Regulation of Wages by Law, and its results; Growth and Development of the English Working Class Movement (Chartism, etc.); The Working of Democratic Machinery (home and foreign); Arbitration and Conciliation, and Sliding Scales, etc.; Railway Economics; Factory Act experiments.

It will be noted that five of these six subjects fall in the area of labour and industrial relations.

When the new school started up, however, no labour subjects were offered. Indeed, the subject of industrial relations was not taught at the LSE for another three decades. The reason, in turn, does not appear to be happenstance or benign neglect but a deliberate choice of policy. In this vein, Sidney Webb cautioned Hewins in a personal letter to steer away from labour courses, saying (quoted in Dahrendorf, 1995: 66, emphasis in original): "we ought not to let it be imagined that the School is especially for study of *Labour questions*".

The reason why labour dropped out of sight at the LSE appears to have four connected explanations: status, money, educational function and a dedication to value-free research. On the last item, the Webbs (most particularly Sidney) scrupulously put aside their political and ideological beliefs when it came to designing the curriculum and making faculty appointments. Beatrice Webb wrote in her diary (quoted in Dahrendorf, p. 38), "We believe in a school of administrative, political, and economic science as a way of increasing national efficiency, but we have kept the London School honestly nonpartisan in its theories", while Dahrendorf (p. 18) states, "[Sidney] Webb in fact placed much emphasis on value-free social science, more than any of his associates including his wife". One possible explanation for the omission of labour and capital–labour relations is thus that they saw it as inevitably introducing an undesirable "partisan" element.

But this cannot be the entire story, for surely railway studies and commercial education also risk introducing a partisan element into the university. We then come to money and status. The Webbs and Hewins were repeatedly accused of establishing the LSE as a propaganda vehicle to promote the Fabian Society and socialism. This suspicion threatened both fund-raising and the school's academic credibility, given that both "goods" were largely supplied by social conservatives: industrialists, wealthy benefactors, government officials and upper-class university administrators and faculty members. Thus Dahrendorf states (p. 64), "[Sidney] Webb went on to lean over backwards in denying a Fabian bias, almost to the point of admitting an opposite inclination". Harrison (p. 289) also notes in this regard that Webb told Hewins on his way to solicit funds from the Chamber of Commerce that he should give the businessmen the assurance "the School would not deal with political matters and nothing of a socialist tendency would be introduced". One can reasonably infer that as Webb was "leaning over backwards" to avoid any hint of a "socialist tendency" at the LSE he would quickly realize that dropping labour and labour–capital relations from the programme of the school was the first and most obvious place to start.

Finally, a fourth factor that may also have come into play was that the subject of labour did not fit in with the professional school programme that the Webbs and Hewins were building. According to Harrison (pp. 293, 291), the Webbs envisioned the LSE as a "technical school for all brain-working professions" and never "as a workers' educational institution". Since at this time the business function of personnel management (or labour relations) had not been invented, no "brain-working profession" for labour existed for the university to provide technical training in.

The emergence of industrial relations in the United Kingdom

The Webbs laid the intellectual foundation for industrial relations but did not actually "birth" the subject. As described in the previous chapter, industrial relations as a formal entity instead arose in the United States during the 1910s. Only later did it then appear in the United Kingdom. This section recounts this process, taking the story up to the late 1930s.

A precursor to the subject of industrial relations in the United Kingdom was the derivative concept of *industrial peace*. Books on industrial peace date to the 1880s, but the most prominent example is by Marshall's star student and protégé A.C. Pigou, entitled *Principles and methods of industrial peace* (1905). Pigou's theme in the book is that industrial conflict is the most serious repercussion of the Labour Question and thus the most pressing issue is to find methods to facilitate peaceful settlement of disputes. His treatment of this subject presupposes organization among workers and is principally concerned with the theory and practice of mediation and arbitration.

Although the term industrial relations began to appear with growing frequency in the United States in the mid-1910s and was widespread by the early 1920s, this was not the case in the United Kingdom.

At the end of the First World War, the United Kingdom, like the United States and Canada, appointed a blue-ribbon commission to study the causes of labour unrest and make recommendations. The British commission was called the Committee of Relations between Employers and Employed, or more popularly the Whitley Committee in honour of its chairperson. Evidently from its title, the commission's prime subject area is what the Americans and Canadians were at that time calling industrial relations. The British chose not to use this term, however, and instead emphasized throughout the reports of the committee the term *industrial reconstruction*, indicating the overarching concern of the government and public in getting the British industrial system back on a sound footing. The conclusion of the committee (quoted in United Kingdom Committee on Industry and Trade, 1926: 260) followed along an oft-stated theme of the labour reformers of this period:

> We are convinced, moreover, that a permanent improvement in the relations between employers and employed must be founded upon more than a cash basis. What is wanted is, that the workpeople should have a greater opportunity of participating in the discussion about, and adjustment of, those parts of industry by which they are most affected.

The form of participation advocated by the committee was collective bargaining by independent trade unions, but with a new system of joint industrial councils – popularly known as Whitley councils – grafted on to the existing labour relations system in order to provide another forum for joint consultation by employers and unions.

According to Morris (1987: 535), the first official usage of the industrial relations term was in 1924 when an Industrial Relations Department was established in the Ministry of Labour, while Hyman gives a date of 1926, citing a report from the Board of Trade entitled *Survey of industrial relations*.[4] Whatever the precise date, a survey of the literature reveals scant usage of the term through the 1920s. The best evidence on this matter comes from Bain and Woolven's (1979) massive bibliography of research in British industrial relations. In it, only two citations in the "general works" section contain the term industrial relations up to and including the year 1926 – a speech in 1919 entitled "A new spirit of industrial relations" by William Hichens (an employer) and the previously mentioned report from the Board of Trade.

Thereafter, the term industrial relations starts to appear with modestly greater frequency, but up to 1930 only one book written by a British academic used industrial relations in the title. This book is Henry Clay's (1929) *The problem of industrial relations, and other lectures.* Clay does not provide an explicit definition of industrial relations but suggests a relatively narrow perspective roughly equivalent to Pigou's use of the term industrial peace. Thus Clay states (p. 2), "The problem of industrial relations does not lend itself to ... easy diagnosis. ... I follow common practice in taking the number of working days lost as a measure of the problem."

We then come to the work of G.D.H. Cole of Oxford University. Chronologically, Cole was in the generation after the Webbs. In terms of scholarship and political orientation, he was also their unquestioned successor in British academia (McCarthy, 1994). Cole was an indefatigable author and a polymath intellectual. He published a great number of books on British trade unions, unemployment and British working-class history, as well as more general works on social and economic policy. Like Commons, Cole considered unemployment the greatest defect of capitalism. But while Commons thought capitalism could be stabilized near to full employment through institutional interventions such as monetary and fiscal stabilization policies, Cole (1929: 114) believed that capitalism was caught in an inherent contradiction of under-consumption, caused by growing imbalance between capacity to produce and ability to buy (due to productivity growth leading to less employment and purchasing power). The way out was thus a socialist planned economy. However, Cole was also an ardent critic of the Webbs' version of "bureaucratic socialism", seeing it as merely replacing the capitalist's domination of workers with domination by state managers and technical experts. Cole thus promoted an alternative form of socialism, called guild socialism, that placed the control of industry in trade unions and other producers' organizations, in effect initiating workers' industrial self government. He was also sceptical that capitalism would in the near future self-destruct, or that workers would on their own push toward socialism, so Cole became an activist in the Labour Party (formed in 1906) and sought to put the party in power and then move to socialism by legally disappropriating the capitalists. Illustrative of his position on employer–employee relations, Cole espoused the principle of "sensible extremism" and viewed class struggle as a "monstrous and irrefutable fact" (quoted in Wright, 1979: 2, 27), while he saw collective bargaining as "acceptable in the context of war between two sides, as a truce on the way to workers' control" (Charles, 1973: 26). Cole's research strategy on labour, and his views on the cause of labour problems and their solution, were thus not compatible with American-style industrial relations and, indeed, were hostile to it.

Industrial relations did not fare much better in the wider world of British academia and industry. In the academic world, as far as I can determine, no British university in the 1920s offered coursework in industrial relations. The first mention of such a course is by Ben Roberts (1972: 254), who observes that economist (and later Nobel laureate) John Hicks offered a course of lectures "Economic Problems of Industrial Relations" at the LSE in 1931. Likewise, no professional association in industry or the universities with the term industrial relations in its title was created during the 1920s, nor had the term industrial relations caught on as a designation for the employment management function in industry. Perhaps most indicative of industrial relations' marginal position in the United Kingdom is evidence from *Pitman's Dictionary of Industrial Administration* (Lee, ed., 1928), a widely cited reference work of the period. It does not even contain a listing for the term industrial relations.

When industrial relations first entered British universities, it did so in much the same way as it gained an institutional presence in American universities – through the philanthropy of a wealthy and socially minded businessman. Roberts (1972: 252–3) explains:

> The General Strike, the failure of the Mond–Turner talks, followed by the great depression, made the labour question a matter which deeply troubled the social conscience of some industrialists and it stirred Montague Burton, the well-known clothing manufacturer, to press his own solution. In the mind of Burton the dangers were clear and present. He saw the conflicts between labour and capital as not totally dissimilar to the conflicts between states. Industrial conflicts and international conflicts had their roots in social injustice and they could only be solved by the adoption of an appropriate code of international and industrial ethics. ... [Burton] was concerned to find that international and industrial relations were relatively little developed as subjects of academic study in the universities. This led him to decide in the early 1930s to found a number of chairs in international and industrial relations. ... Burton found that not every university he approached was ready to accept his ideas or his money. In the event it was Cambridge, Cardiff and Leeds, where Burton had his factory, which agreed to establish his chairs in industrial relations. ... Although universities inspire radical ideas, they tend to be conservative institutions and established faculties are generally reluctant to admit new areas of study to academic grace. Burton's beneficence had been accepted under the pressure of events outside the universities, but the new chairs did not arouse great enthusiasm from the established disciplines.

As the Roberts' quote indicates, Burton was in the men's clothing business and had very large manufacturing facilities in and around Leeds. He was also a very progressive employer and provided numerous welfare benefits to the workforce (Sigsworth, 1990).

According to Elvander (2002: 8), Burton initially proposed that these three chairs be given the title "Industrial Peace" rather than "Industrial Relations", but was persuaded by J.M. Keynes of Cambridge to adopt the latter.[5] The purpose of the chairs, as stated by Burton (quoted in Lyddon, 2003: 95), was to "study and give instruction upon the conditions of employment and the relations between employers and employed, with special reference to the causes of industrial disputes and the methods of promoting industrial peace". Early holders of the Burton chairs included John Hilton, J. Henry Richardson, Hilary Marquand, Arthur Beacham, Harold Kirkaldy and Michael Fogarty. Hilton, who Lyddon (p. 95) states was the most famous of the early chair holders, offered this definition of industrial relations, made in a BBC radio address in 1933 (ibid.): "Industrial relations ... [is] how people who draw wages and the people who pay the wages get on together."

Although the Burton chairs helped institutionalize industrial relations in the United Kingdom, they did not materially move the field forward as an academic subject. According to Bain and Clegg (1974: 98), the chairs generated little visibility or forward momentum for the field over the next two decades. Lyddon (2003) attributes this lack of momentum, in part, to the fact that the chair holders eschewed scholarly publication for the nitty-gritty of arbitration, serving on trade boards and consulting with the ILO and other government agencies. This general picture is also affirmed by Bugler (1968: 222), who states (with reference to the 1940s): "On other university fronts, matters were relatively dormant. The Montague Burton chairs at Cambridge, Cardiff and Leeds were occupied by men who were interested primarily in economics or by a series of professors who, although often able, have not generally stayed on long enough to build a real department." Other British universities continued to neglect industrial relations through the 1940s, and only in 1949 were academic appointments in industrial relations made at the LSE, Oxford and Manchester (Bain and Clegg, 1974). Regarding research in industrial relations, Bain and Clegg conclude (p. 98), "few works of note were published during those fifty years [following the Webbs' *Industrial democracy*]".

The divergent American–British pattern: Explanatory factors

Some explanation has already been offered for the industrial relations field's divergent pattern of development in the United States and the United Kingdom. A comparative perspective offers yet other insights.

Intellectuals and labour reform

The fact that industrial relations emerged first in the United States is partially explained by differences in characteristics of the intellectuals who were leaders of labour research in the two countries. In this early period (up to the Second World War) one may distinguish a first and second generation of labour scholars.

Among the first generation of labour researchers, Commons in the United States and the Webbs in the United Kingdom were the undisputed intellectual leaders. They shared many similarities, as the previous pages have demonstrated. They also had several significant differences.

Commons, for example, became more conservative as he grew older, while the Webbs became more radical. When the industrial relations movement appeared in the late 1910s, it was a mid-career point for both sets of people. Thereafter, Commons maintained interest in trade unions and supported the principle of collective bargaining to the end of his life, yet at the same time he scaled back the role of the labour movement in solving labour problems and increasingly looked to management for innovation and leadership in industrial relations. Illustrative of his position late in life, for example, he declares in *Institutional economics* (p. 875), "If the profit-motive, in the field of economics, can be enlisted in the programme of social welfare, then a dynamic factor, more constructive than all others, is enlisted." Also revealing is the fact that Commons' writings were cited more frequently in the early American literature of personnel management than those of any other academic author (Rossi and Rossi, 1925; Kaufman, 1998a). The Webbs, on the other hand, largely ceased active research work on unions in the early 1900s and moved on to other topics, such as municipal ownership and public administration. The subject of labour management, however, was not one that the Webbs ever devoted much attention to, with the single exception of Sidney Webb's modest-sized book *The works manager to-day* (1917). Of equal importance, the Webbs drifted towards a more pessimistic and critical position on capitalism, advocacy of a more thoroughgoing version of socialist society, and in their late years a measure of sympathy and apology for the Soviet experiment under Stalin. Illustrative of this trend is the title of two of their books written in the early 1920s: *Decay of capitalist civilization* (1923) and *A constitution for the socialist commonwealth of Great Britain* (1920). Unlike Commons, therefore, they were well positioned neither intellectually nor ideologically to take a leadership role in establishing and developing a new field of industrial relations.

These differences appear in even starker form among the second generation of labour scholars in the two countries. As described in the previous chapter, people such as Leiserson and Slichter had a keen interest and close personal involvement in the practical aspects of employer–employee relations. Furthermore, they took a relatively pragmatic perspective on the virtues and vices of both trade unions and employers and were politically conservative in the sense of desiring to promote greater labour–management cooperation within the context of the existing socio-economic system. For them industrial relations was a natural fit. In the United Kingdom, by way of contrast, Cole was the major labour scholar of the second generation. Cole was an intellectual and had little interest in the practical aspects of workplace management and organization. Furthermore, as earlier noted, Cole was an ardent advocate of guild socialism and was known in the United Kingdom as "one of the greatest of Red professors", albeit of a non-Marxist (Fabian) variety (Wright, 1979: 9). Industrial relations was thus not only an unattractive field of study for Cole but one towards which he was politically and ideologically hostile.

Universities

A second strategic factor that influenced the divergent patterns of development in industrial relations between the United States and the United Kingdom is the characteristics of the two countries' university systems.

For example, in the early twentieth century the United States had the largest university system in the world, as measured both by number of universities and enrolments relative to adult population. England, on the other hand, had one of the smallest (Trow, 1993).[6] From a purely practical point of view, a new field of study such as industrial relations had more opportunity to become established in the United States than the United Kingdom.

Another consideration is that British higher education was dominated by the two elite universities of Oxford and Cambridge (or "Oxbridge"). In a review of British universities, Annan (1975: 20–21) relates, "Only 10 per cent of university students go to Oxford and Cambridge. But, just as a dominant social class imposes its style of life upon the rest of society, so the ancient universities have imposed a style upon all British universities."[7] And, as earlier noted, Oxbridge was a bastion of classical liberal education where Greek, Latin and philosophy were foundation subjects and the purpose of university education was to train "gentlemen, clergy and teachers" (Kearney, 1973). Flexner (1930) called Oxbridge "finishing schools". Starting in the nineteenth century, the United Kingdom also established urban ("redbrick") universities and polytechnics. But these universities were forced to follow traditional curriculums in order to demonstrate they were "academically respectable", with the result, according to Annan (p. 24), that "It was only after the First

World War, with the foundation of [the University of] Keele, that a new university could work out its own curriculum and way of life." Besides traditionalism and organizational rigidity, Annan notes yet a third feature of the Oxbridge heritage that worked against the introduction of a new problem solving field such as industrial relations – an aversion to teaching the applied, vocational aspects of academic subjects. He states (p. 19): "Despite the fact that many of the civic universities founded in Victorian times were firmly turned towards vocational subjects – to the study of textiles at Leeds and of metallurgy at Sheffield – the British universities have never seen themselves in the role of the American land-grant colleges. The dons do not picture themselves as vocational teachers."

The situation in the United States in the early twentieth century was quite different. The American university system was not only quite large but also highly decentralized and variegated. The United States also had its elite institutions of higher education, such as Harvard, Princeton and Yale, but most of the fifty states also had large public "land-grant" universities (e.g., the University of Wisconsin) that were under individual state control and a myriad of private secular colleges, Church-affiliated colleges, and specialized engineering and teachers' institutions. Looking at the American system, Grant (1973: 34) was led to conclude: "All that the American higher institutions have in common is that they are postsecondary, they vary in practically every other respect." The decentralized and heterogeneous nature of the American university system was favourable to new fields such as industrial relations because it promoted competition among universities in new curricular ideas and reduced barriers to innovation. Equally important, the American universities forsook the medieval traditions and classical education model of Oxbridge and instead took a "modernist" approach that emphasized the development of practical knowledge through research, drawing in particular on the Scottish tradition that "education is a sober, practical business" (Wilcox, 1975: 34) and the German tradition of encouraging academic research in order to promote national economic development (Wittrock, 1993). Symbolic of the difference between England and the United States in this regard is the fact that Harvard – the most elite of American universities – was one of the first to have a business school. And, if elite institutions could teach business administration, then it was only a short step to teaching the management of employer–employee relations.

Next in consideration is the development of the social sciences in the two countries, given that industrial relations is part of the social sciences and is thus influenced by broader trends in the latter. German universities in the late nineteenth century were widely regarded as the best in the world, while universities in the United States and the United Kingdom lagged behind (Wittrock, 1993). Hundreds of American students travelled to Germany, obtained advanced university degrees and then returned to the States and sought to integrate the German system into the American. No similar migration, however, from the United Kingdom to Germany took place. One of the key aspects of German higher education was the development of science to promote industrial and economic development, or as Manicas (1987: 200) frames it, "the industrializing of science". The Germans, however, emphasized the promotion of the physical and engineering sciences, such as chemistry, physics and electrical engineering, while they gave much less emphasis to the "human" or social sciences. The reason, in turn, was that the ruling class in Germany saw development of the physical sciences as promoting their interests and the interests of the nation (by fostering economic advance), while promotion of the social sciences threatened their interests and the nation's social stability by introducing potentially revolutionary questions about the existing social and political structure. Further, most German intellectuals and professors were from the upper class [called by Ringer (1969) "social Mandarins"] and were a conservative, inward-looking group more focused on history and philosophy than current social problems.

For these reasons, Germany shied away from attacking its Social Question through scientific investigation and, accordingly, the social sciences in the universities lagged behind. In 1900 it had only seven social science "Lehrpersonen" in the entire country and the first department of sociology was not created until after the Second World War (Hardin: 1977: 52). Sociology's lack of institutionalization prior to the Second World War arose from a twofold critique: it lacked any organizing theory or core subject and thus was a "borrower" field with no claim to independent status; and it was at heart a project of "political opportunism" used by partisans to push their ideological and policy agenda in the universities (ibid.).

The United States chose the opposite course of action. In the late nineteenth century American elites faced a wide range of social problems stemming from large-scale immigration, the development of big cities, the proliferation of crime, and – of course – the Labour Problem. The Americans were able, however, to take a more proactive and pragmatic approach to solving these problems because of their bourgeois, middle-class culture and national ethos that celebrated "Yankee ingenuity" and democracy. Less restrained by class lines and divisions inherited from the past, and imbued with a "can do" attitude, American universities became leaders in the late nineteenth century in a new-found drive to apply principles of rationalism, science and technology to the solution of social problems – or the new field of "social engineering". The first American sociology department appeared in 1893 at the University of Chicago and by the 1920s were a common fixture in large American universities, while American professors of sociology got out in the field and through the Hawthorne experiments and similar applied research projects founded the subfield of industrial sociology in the 1930s (Wren, 1994).

Sociologists, political scientists and economists were thus transformed from moral philosophers into *scientists*, and their disciplines were transformed from areas of moral instruction and sterile scholasticism into bodies of knowledge derived from the professional application of the scientific method. Regarded as instruments of social advance, the social sciences in the United States became rapidly and deeply institutionalized by the early twentieth century (Ross, 1991). Among the manifestations were the creation of separate social science disciplines and departments in American universities, such as in economics, sociology and political science; a rapid expansion of social science faculty members, and the creation of separate professional journals and associations – for example, the American Economics Association (1886), the American Psychological Association (1892), the American Political Science Association (1903) and the American Sociological Society (1903). All of these conditions were, in turn, conducive to the development of the industrial relations field, given the widespread viewpoint that it was the scientific approach to resolving labour problems.

British universities lagged behind both the German and American universities in the early twentieth century and did relatively little to promote either the physical or social sciences. Naturally, the new field of industrial relations was thus less likely to sprout in this relatively infertile intellectual soil. Seear (1967: 175) states of the situation in the United Kingdom:

> The tradition of British universities was not favourable to the development of the human sciences, which until the Second World War did not begin to compete with the older academic disciplines in status, in financial resources, or in the career opportunities available to their students. Psychology departments were established in most universities during the interwar period, but were mainly small in scale; while sociology, as understood today, was not studied at all in the majority of British universities.

Seear attributes part of the slow progress in the development of the social sciences in the United Kingdom to (p. 184) "the traditional suspicion of applied studies useful in the solution of practical problems", while Burns (1967: 198) notes that industrial sociology was retarded because of the "ideological bias against business and against internal studies of business undertakings".

Moving on, also entering into the picture are differences between the United States and the United Kingdom in the social and academic acceptability of labour studies. In both countries prejudices existed against the study of labour subjects, partly because they were tinged with radicalism and partisanship, and partly because they were seen as applied or vocational and thus lacking academic standing. This bias worked against industrial relations in both the United States and the United Kingdom, but probably more so in the latter.

In the United Kingdom, for example, society was more class-stratified and British higher education was largely the province of the upper classes and elites. Likewise, the British labour movement had little interest in promoting industrial relations instruction in British universities, not only because its members had scant chance of attending a university but also because British labour was more class conscious and committed to some form of socialism and/or nationalization of industry. Reflective of these considerations, Allen (1972: 16) observes, "The examination of the structure of activities of organized labour was eschewed in academic circles because of its political implications", while McCarthy (1994: 210) remarks, "until the late 1950s the mandarins of St. James Square did not regard industrial relations proper as a respectable field of study in its own right – more an uneasy mix of labour market theory and industrial sociology, biased towards its roots in union history". To fill the gap in labour education, the British labour movement established labour colleges around the nation, leading to the creation of the National Council of Labour Colleges in 1922 (Yeo, 1996). These colleges typically had a significant socialist/Marxist orientation and were expressly chartered to teach social science subjects from a working-class perspective, in the belief that "impartiality in such subjects is impossible, that the mere attempt to realize it betokens a failure to grasp the root facts of social development" (ibid., p. 282). The traditional universities also made some effort to reach working-class students through extension courses. Upon the instigation of an American socialist millionaire, Oxford also established a semi-autonomous unit called Ruskin College that provided college instruction to working students and union staff (Chester, 1986).

The situation regarding labour studies was considerably different in the United States. Prior to the First World War the study of labour in American universities was also inhibited by concerns over its partisan and radical overtones. As Derber (1967) notes, for example, much of the labour writing in this period was largely "agitational" and expressly sympathetic to the cause of labour and critical of capitalism and employers. After the war, the ethos of "professionalism" in American universities moved labour research towards a more objective, scientific mode that increased its acceptability. Also, the rise of personnel management in industry made the study of labour far more acceptable to even the most conservative business leaders. Equally important, the American labour movement in the 1920s moved in a direction that facilitated labour studies in universities. The labour movement did not directly lobby for industrial relations programmes or provide funds for such in this period, given their significant degree of management orientation in this early period and the trade unions' general distrust of universities as "defenders of capitalistic ideas" and "centers of reaction" (quoted in Cummins and DeVyver, 1947: 284, 291). Unions did lobby for workers' education programmes in public universities, however, and achieved success at several, such as the School for Workers at the University of Wisconsin (established in 1928). Unlike the British labour movement, the AFL did not actively promote independent labour colleges, fearing they would become a centre for more radical ideas than the conservative leadership favoured.[8] Also illustrative of the AFL's more accommodationist stance was its formal membership and participation in business groups, such as the Taylor Society and Personnel Research Federation, and support for scientific methods of labour management and programmes of labour–management cooperation. Thus, while organized labour in the United States did not directly promote the study of industrial relations in universities, it indirectly did so by giving its seal of approval to the subject's general method and philosophy towards labour problems and labour–management relations (Denker, 1981).

Yet an additional difference of considerable importance between the university systems of the two countries is the professional school of business. A common denominator across all countries at the turn of the twentieth century was widespread scepticism among educators that business methods and commercial activities were appropriate subjects for a university. The idea of business schools thus faced widespread opposition, described by one American critic (quoted in Daniel, 1998: 48) as "glorified schools of typing and secretarial science". This scepticism notwithstanding, the United States was the first nation to establish professional schools of business, starting with the Wharton School at the University of Pennsylvania in 1881. As noted in the previous chapter, a number of the early industrial relations units in the United States were located in business schools. Most other business schools offered labour courses in personnel management, industrial relations and labour problems. While only 20 universities had a freestanding business school in 1911, a decade later the number had mushroomed to 147.

In the United Kingdom, university business education appeared later than in the United States and did not really establish a significant presence until the 1970s (Keeble, 1992). Several universities in the early part of the 1900s, such as Birmingham and Liverpool, established undergraduate degrees in commerce, and advanced courses in management and administration were offered at technical schools, such as the Cranfield Institute of Technology (established in 1946). But an American-style professional graduate school of business was unknown in the United Kingdom until the 1960s when upon the instigation of the influential Robbins Report on British management education, two such programmes were started at the University of Manchester and University of London. Soon thereafter, master's in business administration (MBA) programmes began to multiply rapidly. Not surprisingly, since management education in general was sparsely offered in British universities the subject of personnel management was even scarcer.[9] Barry (1989: 56, 59) explains the slow uptake of management education in the United Kingdom with the observation that "The general mores of British society have favoured the amateur tradition; ... lack of social recognition [has] resulted in careers in management being perceived as less attractive, ... [and also] the hostility shown by businessmen to the concept of formal training in management."

A final trend is that the historical/institutional school of economics was more rapidly displaced in the United Kingdom after the First World War than in the United States. Even at the LSE the historical approach withered as new faculty members, such as Lionel Robbins and Friedrich von Hayek, were hired into the Department of Economics (Dahrendorf, 1995). In the United States, the institutional tradition in labour economics maintained a relatively strong presence into the 1950s.

Management thought and practice

Industrial relations developed quickly in the United States, in significant measure because an influential wing of the employer class promoted it as a new and more effective strategy of labour management. Not only did they adopt the language of industrial relations; the progressive wing of American employers also articulated at a relatively early date a concrete, coordinated programme of industrial relations, supported a scientific research programme in industrial relations, and formed a network of professional associations and meetings to promote the field. The same did not occur in the United Kingdom.

The antecedent of labour management in both countries was the development of industrial welfare work, or "industrial betterment". As in the United States, prior to the First World War a small group of progressive and humanitarian employers in the United Kingdom started to introduce improvements and amenities for their employees, such as lunchrooms, libraries, drinking fountains, a company doctor and so on. In the United Kingdom, well-known examples include Edward Cadbury, Seebohm Rowntree and Montague Burton (Fitzgerald, 1988). And, like the United States, a number of these companies hired women to direct their welfare programmes, some of whom then moved into the new field of personnel management (Guillén, 1994: 230).

Welfare work was more extensive in the United States prior to the First World War, but formal programmes of labour management (e.g., an organized personnel function) were almost completely absent in both countries. In the next fifteen years, however, developments in labour management greatly diverged in the two countries.

The concept of a specialized management function dealing with labour took hold in the United States in the First World War years, and quickly spread and deepened. By the early 1920s, several hundred firms had personnel and industrial relations departments and the universities were starting to train students in these new vocations (Jacoby, 1985). American firms were motivated to establish these departments for three reasons that were not prevalent in the United Kingdom: the growth of the large multi-plant corporation and the need to professionally manage labour relations; prosperous economic conditions in the 1920s that helped require and support a "goodwill" welfare capitalist approach to labour management, and the larger opportunity to avoid unionization through effective industrial relations practices.

In the United Kingdom, by way of contrast, the concept and practice of a specialized management function devoted to labour developed much more slowly and no significant wing of progressive welfare capitalist employers appeared to promote a strategic, coordinated approach along the lines of industrial relations (McGivering, Matthews and Scott, 1960: 91–101; Clegg, 1972: 161–8). Further, British employers were indifferent-to-sceptical to the scientific management movement and preferred to stay with traditional, largely informal and unsystematic procedures – an approach Hyman (2003: 41–3) calls "unscientific management" and others have called "muddling through". Many British firms also remained smaller sized and managed by family members, while the depressed economy of the 1920s made rationalization and cost cutting – not investment in positive industrial relations practices – the order of the day. British employers were also much more inclined to accept trade union organization of their employees and practise "live and let live" labour relations rather than try to use industrial relations and personnel programmes to remain union-free. Thus, even up to the eve of the Second World War relatively few

British employers had established a formal personnel department or programme (McGivering, Matthews and Scott, 1960: 98; Gospel, 1992). Likewise, the United Kingdom had a dearth of academic scholars interested in labour management. The most prominent British scholar in the area of management was Lyndall Urwick, but he largely wrote on issues of general management.

National labour movements

Industrial relations is centred on fostering efficiency, cooperation, stability, peace and positive-sum outcomes between labour and management. A lesson of history is that *both* labour and management, or at least significant elements of the two groups, have to want these goals and be willing to work with the other party to gain them if industrial relations as a field and movement is to emerge and grow. On the management side, as just noted, conditions were much more propitious for industrial relations in the United States than in the United Kingdom. The same is true on the labour side.

During the 1920s the American labour movement turned more conservative and conciliatory, forsaking militancy and class advancement for business unionism and labour–management cooperation. In part the trade unions were adjusting to the pronounced rightward shift in the national mood after the war and Red Scare, as well as a sharp decline in membership and challenge from employers' more sophisticated union avoidance programme contained in welfare capitalism. More fundamental, however, was the unions' apparent loss of mission and strategy. The 1920s in the United States was seen as something of a "Second Industrial Revolution", marked by the rise of mass production, a professional managerial class, scientific management, welfare labour practices and a consumer society (Millis and Montgomery, 1945). Henry Ford became a national icon and symbolic representation of this new age (a "miracle maker" according to Commons). The system of Fordism, built on mass production and associated economies of scale, high-volume production of standardized goods, falling unit prices and stimulation of mass consumption, ushered in a new vision of steadily rising material prosperity and middle-class position for the average person (Piore and Sabel, 1984). The working-class ideology and rhetoric of organized labour, the theme of protecting workers from capitalist exploitation, and the traditional union programme of organizing workers by craft all seemed increasingly irrelevant and out of touch. Working-class consciousness and loyalty to labour as a social/ideological cause were steadily being replaced by the ethos of individualism, consumerism and upward social mobility (Cooper, 1932; Helfgott, 2003). Likewise, in the new industrial heartland of mass production, the traditional business model of entrepreneurial, rough and tumble capitalism symbolized by Rockefeller, Sr., and Carnegie was rapidly being replaced by the modern, rationalized and legitimatized corporation envisioned by Max Weber. In the leading-edge firms, such as General Motors, DuPont and Standard Oil, ownership was separated from control, management was taken over by a salaried cadre of more professional, educated and socially enlightened executives, and principles of science and administration were systematically applied to the problems of organization, production and industrial relations. These compromises created a mini internal welfare state for employees, based on an implicit contract promising good-faith job security and fair treatment for employees in return for their loyalty and hard work.

Organized labour thus found itself confronted with a new and far more sophisticated foe. After Gompers died in 1924, the AFL quickly began to grapple with its declining strategic position under new president William Green. The result, announced in 1925, was a new mission statement and strategy for trade unionism called "the modern wage policy". Unable to win new members through the traditional methods of organizing, strikes and class rhetoric, the AFL sought to gain recognition by convincing employers that unions could be good for profits and were prepared to work with management as a responsible junior partner. In the words of Millis and Montgomery (1945: 173), "Its [the AFL's] task became convincing management that only the trade unions. ... were able to provide the labour cooperation necessary in achieving greater efficiency and higher quality of workmanship, in reducing personnel turnover, in attaining regularity of operation and employment, and in improving production methods in general." Reflective of this new spirit is this statement made by Green to the Taylor Society (quoted in Richardson, 1929: 75): "Labor is understanding more and more that high wages and tolerable conditions of employment can be brought about through excellency in service, the promotion of efficiency and the elimination of waste." These sentiments of cooperation and partnership largely disappeared in the 1930s, particularly when prospects for organizing during the New Deal turned favourable, but again resurfaced in the 1990s in another era of union weakness.

As noted previously, the AFL did not actively lobby universities to establish industrial relations programmes and, indeed, the trade unions were generally suspicious and distrustful of universities and intellectuals.[10] But the fact that the AFL tacitly endorsed the programme of industrial relations was very helpful, for it effectively "de-radicalized" (or de-politicized) the study of capital–labour relations and gave the new field legitimacy and support (or at least lack of opposition) from not only corporate leaders such as Rockefeller but also labour leaders such as Green.

A different situation prevailed in the United Kingdom after the war. The American and British trade union movements were similar in that the strategy of both emphasized economic gains through collective bargaining and a high degree of autonomy from state regulation (voluntarism). The British labour movement, however, entered the 1920s far larger, stronger and more militant than its American cousin. The unions enjoyed spectacular growth during the war and by 1920 represented nearly one-half of the British workforce – almost three times the American level (Clegg, 1985: 304). Ideologically, the British labour movement was also considerably to the left. For example, according to Jacques (1976) the four defining ideological principles of the British labour movement in the early 1920s were: (1) industrial conflict and capitalism's decline are inevitable; (2) labour is a distinct class with opposed interests to capital; (3) capitalism should be replaced by socialism (nationalization of industry); and (4) strikes and other forms of industrial action can be used to pursue both economic and political ends. Emblematic of these positions is the statement by Albert Purcell in his 1924 presidential address to the TUC (quoted in Jacques, p. 380) that the trade union movement should be an "instrument of solidarity capable of changing the existing structure of capitalism and bringing into being a Workers' State". This objective was not far-fetched since in early 1924 the union-dominated Labour Party successfully formed its first government, with Ramsay MacDonald as prime minister and Sidney Webb as a member of Parliament. Even more revealing, while the AFL was advocating scientific management and labour–management cooperation programmes, the British Trades Union Congress (TUC) called a nine-day General Strike in 1926 that turned out to be the largest and most militant display of labour solidarity in the country during the twentieth century (Fox, 1985). Thus not only were British employers not attuned to the agenda of industrial relations, but neither were the British trade unions. After their defeat in the General Strike and in reaction to the growing joblessness and the passage of repressive labour legislation (the Trades Disputes Act, 1927), the British labour movement subsequently shifted towards a more conservative position. But active efforts at labour–management cooperation on American lines never proceeded beyond high-level discussion (the Mond–Turner talks).

Foundation funding

The early birth and steady spread of industrial relations in America, and the field's slow and anaemic start in the United Kingdom, also owe much to one other strategic factor: *money*. By the 1880s the American industrial sector had surpassed the British in value of output and by the First World War American industry out-produced all other European countries combined. One result was the creation of many fantastically large family fortunes. A number of wealthy industrialists used their fortunes to endow charitable foundations. The two richest industrialists, Andrew Carnegie and John D. Rockefeller, Sr. (and son Jr.), gave away over $850 million to charitable causes (Magat, 1999). Most of the philanthropy was channelled through private foundations controlled by these men and their heirs and advisers, such as the Carnegie Corporation and the Rockefeller Foundation. The Carnegie and Rockefeller foundations, while the largest, were hardly the only ones. Also established in the early 1900s were the Russell Sage Foundation (railways), the Elizabeth McCormick Memorial fund (farm equipment), and somewhat later the Twentieth Century Fund (department store owner Edward Filene and manufacturer Henry Dennison). Later yet was the Ford Foundation (automobiles).

These foundations funded a wide range of community, public service, educational and social reform projects. Labour reform was a major focal point. The motivations were diverse and, depending on the particular industrialist and viewpoint of the observer, somewhere between socially progressive at one end and cynically manipulative at the other (Richardson and Fisher, 1999). Men such as Carnegie and Rockefeller were, in part, moved by the Social Gospel and the desire to improve society. Carnegie, for example, spelled out his philosophy in *The gospel of wealth* (1884: 279), stating that the wealthy industrialist "should consider all surplus revenues ... as trust funds ... to administer in the manner best calculated to produce the most beneficial results for the community". But they also gave away large parts of their fortunes for more strategic and worldly reasons. Certainly one was a calculated decision that the "Haves" were ahead in the long run by improving the lot of the "Have-Nots" rather than face the potential of class war and disappropriation. Carnegie thus justified his expenditures on churches, schools, libraries and other such projects "as an antidote for radical proposals for redistributing property and a method of reconciling rich and poor". Also, say many observers, the rich and powerful use foundations for ideological purposes – to shape intellectual discourse, policy debates and belief in a direction that justifies free market capitalism and bestows legitimacy on their social position (Domhoff, 1996). Fones-Wolf (1994: 1) states, for example, "business sought to construct a vision of Americanism that emphasized social harmony, free enterprise, individual rights, and abundance". Finally, a basic tenet of faith among the Progressive Era reformers was that social problems can be solved by a combination of objective investigation and fact gathering, the development of new social science theory, the rational design and administration of organizations and policy, and the replacement of passion and ignorance with reason and understanding. The foundations were the key source of "social investment capital" to set this process in motion.

These new foundations were crucial to the development of the industrial relations field in America. One channel of influence was funding groups and activities aimed at improving capital–labour relations. Carnegie and Rockefeller, for example, helped set up the National Civic Federation – an early 1900s non-profit group of progressive industrialists, moderate trade unionists and academics (such as Commons) dedicated to promoting industrial reconciliation and peace – while Rockefeller helped fund the AALL. Revealingly, the motto of the AALL (quoted in Magat, p. 26) was "Social justice is the best insurance against labor unrest". Rockefeller and/or Carnegie money also helped fund the National Bureau of Economic Research (NBER) and the Brookings Institution, both of which took a liberal line on labour matters. Rockefeller went further and provided the capital to start the University of Chicago in 1892, which grew to be one of the nation's leading universities and, in the early twentieth century, a centre for the new discipline of sociology (Harvey, 1982; Richardson and Fisher, 1999).

The foundations' second channel of influence was the direct funding of labour and industrial relations research. Commons, for example, received funding from the Russell Sage Foundation to do the Pittsburgh Survey and cover the publishing cost of the associated six volumes (e.g., Fitch's *The steelworkers*), while the Carnegie Institution of Washington funded the eleven volumes of Commons' *A documentary history of American industrial society* (1910–11) and the first two volumes of *History of labor in the United States* (1918).[11] Another influential industrial relations researcher of the 1920s was Australian Elton Mayo, whose emigration to the United States and subsequent research at the Harvard Business School was financed with Rockefeller money. The Russell Sage Foundation established an Industrial Studies Department, directed by liberal social reformer Mary van Kleeck, and funded numerous influential studies on industrial relations, including a quasi-critical evaluation of the Rockefeller employee representation plan at CF&I (Selekman and van Kleeck, 1924). Finally, as noted in the previous chapter, the first six university industrial relations centres in the United States and Canada were funded with Rockefeller-connected foundation money.

The United Kingdom had no similar network of foundations and industrial philanthropists. To be sure, the United Kingdom had families with great wealth, but a much larger share of this wealth was in the hands of hereditary landowners and aristocratic elites who had a much smaller incentive and interest in funding new social science research. Similarly, the United Kingdom's industrial power peaked in the 1880s and by the 1920s was well into decline, sapping the industrial class of the financial wherewithal to fund applied research in industry. Certainly examples stand out of private philanthropy that moved forward research on labour and industrial relations in the United Kingdom, such as the Montague Burton chairs. Another example, although not focused on labour *per se*, was the creation of the Rhodes scholarships in 1902 at Oxford University by Cecil Rhodes, founder of De Beer's Mining Company in South Africa. But the size and scope of the money devoted to development of the social sciences and labour research in the United States dwarfed what the United Kingdom could muster.

Illustratively, Dahrendorf states of the situation at the LSE in the early 1920s (1995: 159):

> The School was established now as a teaching institution in the social sciences but its research facilities were rudimentary. The Library needed expansion. Teachers needed time and space to do their research, as well as research assistance. Graduates had to have a perspective of research scholarships and junior fellowships. Funds for all of this, the other half of a modern university as it were, could not be found in the City of London or even in the University Grants Committee. They probably could not be found in the United Kingdom at all, where the Oxbridge type of collegiate university was still the dominant model.

Then, in the next sentence, he reveals this irony (emphasis added): "The only hope lay abroad, in America, and contrary to the illusory hopes of the 'cargo cult' of anthropologists' islanders, the ship did come over the horizon and bring the wares; its name was *Rockefeller*." As he explains, (Lord) William Beveridge, the new director of the LSE, convinced the director of the Laura Spelman Rockefeller Memorial Fund, Beardsley Ruml, that the cause of international social progress would be materially advanced by a large investment of funds to upgrade the British social sciences. Thus, between 1923 and 1937 the Rockefeller foundation gave the LSE two million dollars – an amount equivalent to one-fourth of its entire income over this fourteen-year period. Thus, through this financial largesse the school founded by the socialists Sidney and Beatrice Webb became known in the inner circles as "Rockefeller's baby" (ibid., p. 162).

The Rockefeller money was not used to fund research or faculty positions in labour or industrial relations, but a portion was used to fund a new Chair in Political Economy for Allyn Young. Young was an institutionally sympathetic American economist whose recent publications on increasing returns to scale (along with those of Piero Sraffa) had seriously wounded, if not wrecked, Marshall's model of short-run competitive price determination. Unfortunately for institutional/historical economics in the United Kingdom, Young soon died and was replaced with Lionel Robbins in 1929. Robbins, in turn, led a purge of institutional/historical economics at the LSE and went on to become one of the most influential early figures in the resurgence and triumph of neoclassical economics (Robbins, 1932; Yonay, 1998; Kaufman, 2004c).

The International Labour Organization

After the United States and the United Kingdom, the third major line of development of industrial relations in the period before the Second World War took place through the creation of the International Labour Organization (ILO) in 1919.

As described in an earlier chapter, during the nineteenth century a number of social reformers, trade unionists and humanitarian employers had lobbied for adoption of international labour standards. Their motivation was partly a humanistic desire to improve the conditions of labour, and partly recognition that a coordinated effort across countries to raise labour standards is necessary if one country's forward movement is not to be undercut by the threat of lower cost competition from others.

Starting in the 1890s, the government of Switzerland took a leading role in the push for international labour standards and hosted several conferences. The core group of participants and activists was largely made up of middle-class reformers and intellectuals, while governments, national labour movements and employer groups took a largely indifferent-to-hostile attitude. One visible outcome was the creation of the International Association for Labor Legislation in Basel in 1901, and the establishment of an International Labour Office to serve as secretariat (Follows, 1951: 156).

Without government support and involvement, the accomplishments of the Association were necessarily limited. The events of the First World War and the wave of labour unrest it set off quickly brought a shift of attitude and engagement of all major parties with a stake in the Labour Question. A historical review of the first ten years of the ILO says of this period of transformation (ILO, 1931: 25–6):

> The War, by the change it wrought in men's minds and the tremendous increase in the power of the trade unions which followed, brought within the workers' grasp possibilities which a few years earlier seemed unattainable. The appeal which was made by Governments in every country to the working class not only developed in it a consciousness of its solidarity, but also turned the attention of the whole nation to that class and to the necessity for raising it to a higher material and moral standard of life. ... The sufferings of the War had developed in every stratum of society a feeling that peace must mean something more than a return to the conditions of 1914. A new order must be created which would guarantee the peace of the world and give to everyone the just reward of his labour. This vague idealism, sustained by the promises of statesmen who were indeed not a little troubled by the agitation among the workers, ensured the triumph of these claims.

For a brief time in 1918–19 it appeared that the revolutionary moment predicted by the Marxists and anarchists might finally be at hand (Lorwin, 1929). When the delegates convened at the Paris Peace Conference in early 1919, their task was to restore order in the world and bring about peace. But order and peace seemed threatened at two levels of world society – political war waged by one block of countries against another and industrial war waged by the working class against the capitalist class. It appeared to many delegates that securing a lasting political peace could not be done without also securing industrial peace, so they came to Paris in effect to craft two peace treaties. The first peace treaty was to end the military war, the second was to seek a peaceful resolution to the class (industrial) war.

Toward this end, on 25 January 1919 the delegates to the Peace Conference at Versailles appointed a Commission on International Labor Legislation to formulate special labour clauses for the Treaty of Peace. The chair was Samuel Gompers, president of the American Federation of Labor. The commission was split by deep disagreements (ILO, 1931). Gompers wanted to create an international organization to strengthen workers' rights to organize and collective bargain, believing that unions were the workingman's salvation. He strongly opposed, on the other hand, any international organization that would get involved in politics, fearing that governments and employers would combine against labour or that the organization would be captured by the socialists and used to advance the class struggle. On the other side, many trade unionists and social democrats from Continental Europe were angered by the Americans' narrow approach to social reconstruction and argued that the ILO should pursue an extensive programme of political and economic reform on behalf of the working class.

A host of other thorny issues also arose that threatened to scuttle the nascent organization. Advanced industrial countries, for example, wanted a uniform set of labour standards that applied to everyone, but less-developed countries wanted a graduated set of standards so they would not be placed at a competitive disadvantage. Also, should international labour standards and declarations of workers' rights apply only to sovereign nation-states, or also to their colonial territories and dependencies? Also ticklish was the issue of racial equality. Japan refused to join any organization that did not adopt this principle, but doing so was resisted by other countries that had *de facto* or *de jure* systems of racial segregation, such as the United States in its southern states and the United Kingdom in a number of its territories.

A compromise was reached on all of these issues, following in broad outline a plan proposed by the British. As specified in Part XIII of the Versailles Treaty, a new international body, called the International Labour Organization, was created. Its headquarters were to be in Geneva, Switzerland. The Organization was set up under the aegis of the League of Nations, and all nation-states belonging to the League automatically became members of the ILO. In a short time, nearly forty countries were members of the ILO – the most conspicuous omissions in the first decade being the United States and the Soviet Union.

In grand design, the ILO was conceived by its creators as an international "House of Parliament" and world "Department of Labour" for the working classes (Thomas, 1921), with its members to be not only appointed government representatives from each country (two per country) but also appointed representatives from workers and employers (one each per country). This form of tripartite representation was unique and intended to give the parties to the employment relationship – particularly labour – an explicit voice in the operation and policies of the Organization. Stated one ILO report on the tripartite principle (ILO, 1965: 39),

> Anyone who is familiar with the events lying behind the Labour Part of the Peace Treaties concluded at the end of the First World War must be aware that there was a strong desire on the part of labour in many countries that its voice should be heard in international discussions upon industrial conditions. In order to ensure a just equilibrium, it was necessary that the employers should likewise be represented.

In a concrete and visible way, the major governments of the world, by adopting the tripartite principle, pledged themselves to change the status of labour from "outsider" to "insider" in the polity.

The principal activity of the ILO was to be the enactment of international Conventions and Recommendations pertaining to the status and conditions of labour. Conventions are submitted directly to members for ratification and become binding upon ratification; Recommendations are suggested labour provisions submitted to members for legislative consideration in some form. Conventions and Recommendations are adopted by a two-thirds vote of the delegates, meeting once a year as a general Conference. To coordinate and organize the work of the ILO, and to conduct research, education and public communication, an International Labour Office was created, headed by a Director-General. This secretariat was also to be responsible for publishing research and new developments in labour in a monthly journal, the *International Labour Review (ILR)*, as well as in longer research studies and monographs.

With respect to the development of industrial relations, six aspects of the newly created ILO deserve emphasis.

First, the creation of the ILO represented at significant move away from a laissez-faire and commodity approach to labour and shift toward a more humanistic and social approach (ILO, 1931). Commenting on the events that led to the formation of the ILO, John E. Solano (1920: xli) states, "Yet the main obstacle to industrial reforms before the war was a selfish and narrow social spirit, which caused men to consider vital questions of public welfare almost entirely from the standpoint of their private or class interests." He goes on to say (p. lvii),

> The tardy declaration of Civilization at Paris in the year 1919 that workers must no longer be regarded merely as 'articles of commerce,' and the subsequent declaration of Civilization at the Washington Conference concerning the extent to which the mothers and children of workers, regarded as industrial assets, might at least be protected against serious evils, are in fact accusations against cultured man for his lack of humanity and his complacent disregard of his social obligations in the past. Thoughtful men of all classes in civilized countries are now awake to the need of prompt and generous reform.

Second, like the new field of industrial relations, the ILO was established to pursue both "science building" and "problem solving" in the field of labour. The ILO's tenth-anniversary volume (ILO, 1931: 26) states, for example, that the Organization had a "double origin: what may be called the 'scientific' movement for the legal protection of the workers and the great urge towards social reform". Part of the ILO's mission was to advance the state of knowledge on labour problems and their solution through sponsored research, conferences and educational programmes, and communication and information dissemination. But the ILO was also explicitly established to improve labour conditions and employer–employee relations through a wide-ranging programme of reform, accomplished by publicity and education, adoption of international Conventions and Recommendations, training and technical programmes, and political lobbying.

Third, in joining the ILO the major nations of the world committed themselves to protect and advance human rights in the workplace and provide equitable conditions of employment. Nine principles from the Peace Treaty of 1919 (reproduced in Solano, 1920: 273–4) were written into the ILO's Constitution:

- labour should not be regarded as a commodity or article of commerce;

- the right of association;

- payment of a reasonable wage to maintain a reasonable standard of living;

- a eight-hour day or forty-eight-hour week;

- a weekly rest of at least twenty-four hours;

- abolition of child labour;

- equal pay for equal work;

- equitable treatment of all workers in a country (e.g., immigrants and citizens);

- enforcement of laws for worker protection.

These principles were also basic planks of the ideological programme espoused by the early pioneers of the industrial relations field.

Fourth, the ILO's Constitution explicitly made "social justice" an end-goal of national labour policy. Contained in another ILO history is this observation (ILO, 1965: 38): "It became clear during the First World War (1914–18) that the coming peace would have to take account of the strivings of the worlds' workers. There were many factors which brought the Organization into being, but the need to base peace firmly on a foundation of social justice was undoubtedly the most important." In this spirit, the ILO's Constitution begins with this declaration:

> Whereas universal and lasting peace can be established only if it is based upon social justice;
>
> And whereas conditions of labour exist involving such injustice, hardship and privation to large numbers of people as to produce unrest so great that the peace and harmony of the world are imperilled ...

A half-century later, ILO Director-General David Morse (1969: 9) reaffirmed these principles when he described the ILO's mandate as "Lasting Peace Through Social Justice".

Fifth, quite apart from ethical/humanistic concerns, the establishment of the ILO and the promulgation of international labour standards was justified on economic grounds as a necessary device to take wages out of international competition and create a minimum acceptable level of labour conditions across countries. The ILO was, in effect, an international application of the Webbs' concept of the device of the "common rule" and, in the words of Valticos (1969, reprinted in *ILR*, 1996: 397), a "kind of code of fair competition between employers and countries". The labour standards promulgated by the ILO did not seek to end competition for labour, but only to impose limits preventing nations from gaining economic advantage at the cost of labour. Over time, the ILO then sought to raise the plane of competition in labour markets, as advocated by the American institutionalists, by a gradual upward advance in minimum international labour standards.

Thus the ILO history (1931: 31) states:

> Whether well founded or not, the fear of foreign competition has alarmed industrialists and has paralysed or hindered social progress. ... The remedy which suggested itself to the authors of the Treaty as likely to lead to a reasonable and systematic improvement in working conditions ... is ... to induce a parallel improvement in working conditions in every country and fix the minimum standard which every country would undertake to maintain.

As the ILO report acknowledges, however, an ever-present hurdle in the Organization's quest to strengthen workers' rights and raise the conditions of labour is the fear on the part of individual industries and countries that they will be put at a competitive disadvantage or suffer a decline in jobs. This fear is acknowledged in these words, written one year after the ILO's founding (Barnes, 1920: 4):

> Nations are deterred from carrying out reforms because they fear that the added cost of production consequent on these reforms will handicap them, as regards competition in international trade, just as individual employers in a country fear reform – even when they sympathise with the demands of their workers for better conditions – because they think that the cost of these reforms may handicap them in competition with their trade rivals at home and abroad.

Lastly, the purpose of the ILO was explicitly seen by its leaders as promoting class accommodation and liberal/progressive labour reform with the purpose of preserving basic capitalist and democratic institutions and blocking more radical and revolutionary solutions to the Labour Question. Director-General Thomas states in this regard (quoted in Fine, 1972: 87):

> Far from representing a means of developing and promoting international socialism, or to speak plainly, Bolshevism, the ILO by establishing a system of sound and advanced labour legislation, by multiplying the relations between employers and workers, and by inducing the governments to introduce better conditions of labour, tends on the contrary to bar the way to all movements of disorder and to all Bolshevist propaganda.

These six principles of the ILO, along with that of tripartite representation and negotiation, were also guiding positive and normative principles of the new field of industrial relations. But, despite their common features, they were also distinguished by subtle yet real differences.

The common link between the ILO and industrial relations field is perhaps most vividly indicated by the first issue of the *International Labour Review* (January 1921). Six "special articles" are featured. Four deal with various aspects of the founding and activities of the ILO. The remaining articles are by the two "fathers" of the field of industrial relations. The first is "The process of amalgamation in British trade unionism" by Sidney Webb, the second is "Industrial government" by John R. Commons. Also of interest, Volume II of the *International Labour Review* carries an article by John D. Rockefeller, Jr., "Cooperation in industry": one of a very small number of articles written by an employer.

Equally interesting are the differences between the ILO and industrial relations. Industrial relations, for example, was more committed to the intellectual and academic side of science building, given that many of its members were academics whose professional mission was, in part, to push forward the frontiers of knowledge through pure research. The ILO also had a research mission but since it was an international agency and not a university, the type of research performed and the nature of the staff hired to do it were distinctly more applied and problem solving in orientation.

The field of industrial relations also took a broader approach and perspective on problem solving than did the ILO. As described in the previous chapter, in its problem-solving dimension the early field of industrial relations had a four-pronged programme: trade unionism and collective bargaining, personnel management and methods of welfare capitalism, protective labour law and social insurance, and countercyclical monetary and fiscal policies (the first three being more prominent than the fourth).

The ILO in its first decade concentrated most attention on the area of labour law and social insurance, such as the Conventions and Recommendations adopted on hours of work, working conditions for seamen, unemployment insurance and child labour. This focus is to be expected given that the ILO's principal mission is promulgating international labour standards. The ILO certainly supported trade unionism and collective bargaining but its efforts were more indirect and limited on this front, largely taking the form of pressure on member States to observe the principle of freedom of association contained in the Organization's Constitution and publicizing through books and articles in the *International Labour Review* new developments and accomplishments in collective bargaining.

During the 1920s the ILO published a number of studies on unemployment and promoted methods to reduce unemployment, such as labour exchanges and unemployment insurance. The ILO also participated in the World Economic Conference, sponsored in 1927 by the League of Nations (ILO, 1931). A central topic on the agenda of the conference was economic stabilization. Beyond these modest steps the ILO did not go in the 1920s. In the early mid-1930s, however, several ILO staff economists published widely read articles in the *International Labour Review* that talked about macroeconomic solutions to the Depression (Endres and Fleming, 1996).

The problem-solving area that received the least attention in the ILO's programme was the "employer's solution", including the methods of personnel management, human relations and the other accoutrements of welfare capitalism. A careful distinction must be made, however. The ILO maintained an active interest in the topic of scientific management, more often called "rationalization" in Europe. A financial gift from the American foundation the Twentieth Century Fund (principally connected with progressive business leaders Edward Filene and Henry Dennison) allowed the ILO to establish in 1928 a semi-autonomous unit called the International Institute of Management, directed by the noted British management expert Lyndall Urwick (ILO, 1938). The Institute survived ten years and then was closed for lack of additional funding, having sponsored two conferences on scientific management and a number of publications. Apart from interest in the general topic of rationalization, the ILO and the Institute did not delve deep into particular aspects or practices of personnel management. The *International Labour Review* featured very few articles over the first decade that in any respect dealt with the personnel-management side of industrial relations. Likewise, the book published by the ILO (1931) to provide a tenth-anniversary retrospective on its activities and accomplishments devotes over 150 pages to the following topics: conditions of work, social insurance, labour statistics and wages, employment, special classes of workers, workers' living conditions, workers' general rights, and the ILO and economic problems. No separate section, or even brief account, is devoted to the management side of industrial relations.

As is often the case, the exception to this rule may be the most interesting. From its founding days, the ILO published reports and studies under the titles "Series A", "Series B", and so on. In 1927, however, Series A began a new category of reports under the heading "Industrial Relations". Why the appearance of the industrial relations name? The Foreword to Series A, No. 36 (*Industrial relations in Great Britain*, by J. Henry Richardson, Montague Burton Professor of Industrial Relations at Leeds University and a recent visitor to the United States and Canada to research employee representation plans for the ILO) explains that the International Labour Conference adopted a resolution in 1928 offered by a Canadian employers' delegate. It read (emphasis added):

> Whereas it is contended that a policy of *active collaboration between employers and employed*, such as exists in certain countries, has resulted both in an improvement in the level of real wages and working conditions, and also in greater and more economical production, ... [it is requested] that the International Labour Office follow with due attention the progress of the spirit of collaboration between employers and employed and to report on the subject from time to time.

Consequently, a series of in-depth studies on industrial relations was carried out, including case studies on the organization and administration of industrial relations (terminology used at that time to connote the management side of employee relations) at several individual companies, including at least one (The Zeiss Works) that was largely non-union. Not only were these studies a marked departure from previous ILO work; they required a large amount of funding. The pieces of the puzzle start to come together when the reader observes that the author (or co-author) of several of the reports is Thomas Spates. A further clue comes from the last sentence of the Foreword of the Richardson report: "It is a pleasure to the Office to place on record its large debt of gratitude to Industrial Relations Counselors, Inc., of New York City, for the generous assistance which has made it possible to carry through this programme of studies on industrial relations." As indicated in the previous chapter, Rockefeller provided funds for the IRC to establish a mission at the ILO between 1927 and 1932, so the sudden appearance of a broader interpretation of industrial relations and greater attention to management and employer–employee collaboration arose from this source. However, the Depression forced even the world's richest capitalist to curtail expenses. By 1944, these studies on industrial relations had come to an end.

With due cognizance given to this "exception", one may nonetheless state as a reasonable generalization that while the ILO and field of industrial relations were tightly linked in these early years, the ILO was, by the nature of its mission, structure and philosophy, the more narrowly constructed of the two and had a problem-solving approach and ideology that was much more ILE centred. This latter fact is not surprising if one considers that the long-term core constituency and base of support for the ILO was the trade union movements of the member States, while the American field of industrial relations gained much of its funding and institutional infrastructure from Rockefeller, the Rockefeller-connected foundations, and business schools.

A further examination reveals that not only did the ILO have a more labour-focused approach to problem solving but it also took a narrower perspective on the intellectual and topical domain of industrial relations itself. The standard definition of industrial relations in the United States in the 1920s was a broad one and included within the field topics such labour legislation, social insurance, personnel management and so on. At least until Rockefeller entered the scene, the ILO defined industrial relations narrowly to include only dealings between employers and trade unions (labour–management relations). This fact is illustrated in the early issues of the *International Labour Review*, where the table of contents for each annual volume lists the articles by subject. Among the 10 to 12 subject areas is "industrial relations", which includes only articles related to unions and collective bargaining, while social insurance, labour conditions and other such topics are separately listed.

One contribution of the ILO to the development of the industrial relations field has still to be pointed out. As succeeding chapters will elaborate, the spread of the industrial relations field to the developing countries of Africa, Asia and South America would have taken far longer without the ILO first paving the way. In many poor and less-developed nations, whether earlier in the century or in the present day, labour rights and labour conditions are often low-priority items for governments and the social elites who control them. Indeed, in a number of countries workers' rights and trade unions are actively suppressed. The historical record reveals that the field of industrial relations has great difficulty in establishing a foothold in those countries where labour is suppressed or marginalized.

Since its founding in 1919, the ILO has been the single most active and influential force in the world community pressuring these governments to take a more humane, progressive stance on labour. In a real sense, therefore, the work of the ILO and, in particular, the passage of the many Conventions and Recommendations on child labour, freedom of association, equal opportunity and other such labour rights has been the opening wedge that allows industrial relations to successfully follow. In this vein, Kassalow (1968: 95) remarked in the late 1960s: "the International Labour Organization has rendered powerful support over nearly five decades, to the spread of knowledge and concern about the entire world labour field. From both an operational and scholarly viewpoint, its contributions have been enormous." The same is equally true today.

The Industrial Relations Institute

The third place industrial relations appeared in Europe in the years before the Second World War is a remarkable but scarcely known organization called the Industrial Relations Institute (IRI), founded in 1925 and headquartered in The Hague, Holland.[12]

The story of the IRI is not only interesting but illustrates several important themes about the early development of the industrial relations field. As noted in the previous chapter, to a degree not well appreciated today the early industrial relations field had a substantial managerialist orientation and was heavily influenced by the socialized version of Taylor's philosophy of scientific management (Maier, 1970). Also noted there, a number of people involved in the early industrial relations movement were women who came to the field largely through social work and social reform channels. They formed a discrete community in the industrial relations world, gaining access to an otherwise male-dominated field through industrial welfare work and promoting what Rodgers (1998) refers to as a model of "social maternalism". And, finally, as we have seen in this chapter, foundation funding played a significant role in starting and directing the new field. Each of the same elements came into play with the IRI.

The IRI was largely the creation of two pioneering women in industrial relations, Mary van Kleeck of the United States and Mary Fleddérus of Holland. Fleddérus was the personnel manager of the Leerdam Glassworks outside Rotterdam (Alchon, 1992). Van Kleeck, also of Dutch origin, was the director of the Industrial Studies Department of the Russell Sage Foundation. Under her leadership, the department produced a steady stream of research studies on industrial relations throughout the interwar years that were widely cited and praised, including a number for which she was a principal author.[13] Van Kleeck was heavily influenced by Taylorism, became an officer and activist in the Taylor Society in the 1920s, and was on the leading edge of efforts to fuse scientific management and social work into a mutual gain model of industrial relations. As happened with many other industrial reformers of the 1920s, when the mutual gain/welfare capitalist experiment was shattered by the Great Depression she moved leftward in her politics and solution to labour problems, taking up the cause of national and international social/economic planning (realizing that economic stability and full employment are the preconditions for successful industrial relations) with an increasingly sympathetic position toward Russian central planning.

The genesis of the IRI was in 1922. A small group of mainly women welfare and personnel workers organized the First International Welfare Conference, held at a chateau in Normandy in 1922 with representatives from eleven countries (Alchon, 1991, 1992). The group appointed Fleddérus to organize a more permanent organization, leading to another conference in 1925 in Holland, the International Industrial Welfare (Personnel) Congress, attended by 50 delegates from 21 countries.

The delegates decided to form a permanent organization and hold triennial conferences. They selected its name, and its charter was determined to be "the study and promotion of satisfactory human relations and conditions in industry". A later publication of the IRI (1935: 25) offers this definition of industrial relations: "Industrial relations refers to the associating of groups and individuals whose working together constitutes economic life. These relations may be regarded as satisfactory when they permit all groups concerned to function effectively toward a socially desirable end."

The first president of the IRI was Sweden's chief inspector of factories, Kersten Hesselgren, while van Kleeck was elected to serve on the governing council. Also attending the conference were Louise Odencrantz (personnel manager and Russell Sage Foundation member) and Lillian Gilbreth (consultant and writer on scientific management, with her husband Frank) from the United States, Dorothy Cadbury from the United Kingdom (a managing director of the famous Cadbury chocolate company), and Frieda Wunderlich from Germany (a researcher with the Bureau für Sozialpolitik in Berlin). The mutual gain philosophy underlying the approach of the IRI is spoken to by van Kleeck (1928: 56–7), stating that the goal of industrial reform is

> the establishment of a new functional relationship of labor to managerial policy, whereby separate and limited aims, such as the forcing of a wage reduction by management, or the attainment of an increase in rates by labor, are merged in a larger purpose, such as to make goods well with satisfaction for labor in works and wages, with effective service at the lowest possible price to the public and with a fair return for capital.

The pragmatic, problem-solving approach taken by the IRI towards industrial relations is reflected in the statement of one participant at an IRI event: "The conference [the IRI 1929 regional conference in Germany] definitely aimed at being practical. The proverb 'An ounce of practice is better than a ton of theory' was quoted with approval" (quoted in Johnston, 1929: 626).

The first triennial conference was in 1928 at Cambridge University on the theme of the Fundamental Relationships between All Sectors of the Industrial Community. In attendance were people such as Paul Devinat of the ILO, British management doyen Lyndall Urwick, *Survey* magazine editor Paul Kellogg, Taylor Society president Harlow Person, and Mary Gilson of IRC (formerly industrial relations director for Joseph & Feiss Co., a pioneering company in the scientific management movement). At this time a decision was also made to adopt the name International Industrial Relations Association which thereafter started to appear on IRI publications (e.g., Fleddérus, 1930; IRI, 1935: 13). Also at this time Fleddérus and van Kleeck became vice-presidents of the IRI and effectively ran the organization for the rest of its life, the two of them spending half of each year in New York City and the other half in Holland. Funding came from the Russell Sage Foundation and other contributors.

Several regional IRI conferences were held in Europe, including Italy, Germany and Switzerland, which helped spread the concept of industrial relations to an area of the world where the term was virtually unknown. Then the next triennial conference was the Amsterdam World Social Economic Congress in 1931. The high-water mark of the IRI, this conference made social and economic planning the focus of attention. Although the personnel managers and welfare workers who formed the IRI had started out with a largely "internalist" perspective on labour problems, the events of the Great Depression made it plain that the goals of "satisfactory human relationships" could not be achieved unless the national economies were stabilized. The group thus started to shift toward an "externalist" perspective. Illustratively, at a planning meeting IRI participants concluded (quoted in IRI, 1935: 14, emphasis in original), "We intended to centre our discussions chiefly around the industrial establishment, but time and again our attention was drawn back to underlying principles, to Industry's economic foundation *as conditioning* these human relations. [Thus] we are being forced to an international consciousness of the distant influences affecting the success of an industrial enterprise." In one respect, however, the topic of social–economic planning was in keeping with the IRI's philosophical heritage, for it was simply an application of rational organization and scientific management to the coordination of national and international economies.

The next triennial conference of the IRI was in 1935 in The Hague, again on the subject of social–economic planning. By this time, however, Europe was in increasing political turmoil with the rise of fascism in Germany, Italy, Portugal and Spain, while the continued Depression sapped the IRI of funds and organizational support. When war broke out in 1939, the organization ceased. During its relatively short life, however, it had been, in van Kleeck's words, an innovative "factory of ideas" (quoted in Alchon, 1992: 115).

Notes

[1] Note, however, that even here workers suffer an inequality of bargaining power for reasons already explained.

[2] The group's name came from Roman general Quintus Fabius, who defeated the enemy through patient, well-timed battles. Under the Webbs, this strategy was called *permeation* – the "inevitability of gradualness" (Dahrendorf, 1995: 39).

[3] Beatrice Webb (1948: 185) in her diary called industrialist and philanthropist Andrew Carnegie, whom she and Sidney met on a trip to the United States in 1899, "a reptile".

[4] The latter is noteworthy because the term industrial relations is used only one other time in the 500-page report and then only in the generic sense of "industrial relationships".

[5] Burton became interested in industrial peace partly through his participation in the ill-fated Mond–Turner talks after the General Strike of 1926.

[6] Although of considerably smaller population and wealth, Scotland had more major universities in the nineteenth century than did England.

[7] The term "ancient universities" connotes the medieval roots of Oxbridge.

[8] The AFL thus exerted considerable pressure to close the Brookwood Labor College, the most influential labour school in American in the inter-war years (Howlett, 1993).

[9] The major supplier of vocational-oriented training in personnel at the time was the Institute of Personnel Management, the main practitioner professional association in the United Kingdom, founded in 1913.

[10] Gompers is quoted as saying (Magat, 1999: 35), "God save us from our intellectual friends. All I ask is that they get off our backs."

[11] Wisconsin industrialists funded *Industrial government* (1921). Commons states in his autobiography (1934b: 189), "What my paper manufacturers said they earned for their money, when I reported to them, was that the best way to beat the unions was 'to beat them to it'." As this quotation suggests, welfare capitalism was partly a union avoidance strategy, as well as a new high-performance mutual-gain employment system.

[12] Several years later the organization amended its name to International Industrial Relations Association (not to be confused with the modern-day association of the same name, discussed in detail in Chapter 6). This new title was translated as *Association Internationale des Relations Industrielles* in French and *Internationale Vereinigung für Bestgestaltung der Arbeit in Betrieben* in German (Fleddérus, 1929). Literally translated, the German title in English is International Association for the Best Shaping (Arrangement) of Work in Enterprises.

[13] Van Kleeck's association with the Russell Sage Foundation started with field investigation for the Pittsburgh Survey (the first social science survey of an American city), sponsored by the foundation in 1907, for which Commons and students conducted the labour research.

AMERICAN INDUSTRIAL RELATIONS IN THE GOLDEN AGE   4

This chapter carries forward the development of the industrial relations field in the United States from 1933 to the end of the 1950s. During these years industrial relations experienced tremendous growth. It became firmly institutionalized, with its own centres and degree programmes, scholarly journals and professional associations. It also experienced a golden age of research and influence on policy and practice, and witnessed a marked evolution and growing incompatibility in the theory and ideology of the PM and ILE schools. The end product was a marked transformation in the industrial relations field relative to the original model of the 1920s.

The United States: Re-emergence of the Labour Problem

During the decade of the 1920s, the employer-oriented PM wing of industrial relations was ascendant in the United States. Even the more ardent proponents of the ILE approach in industrial relations gradually shifted support over the 1920s from the cause of organized labour to the cause of welfare capitalism (Slichter, 1929; Perlman, 1928; Kaufman, 2003c). Illustrative is the evolution in the position of William Leiserson. In the late 1910s, Leiserson expressed considerable scepticism about the staying power and success of personnel management and employee representation, and maintained that collective bargaining was the preferred method of wage determination and workforce governance (Eisner, 1967). Ten years later he had substantially modified his position. Writing in 1929, he surveyed the state of industrial relations in American industry and reached this positive assessment of the PM approach (p. 141):

> The trade unions may pooh-pooh the idea that there can be any other labor leaders
> than those who are officials of bona fide labor organizations, and they heap derision
> on welfare workers and organizers of company unions. But the facts are there for all

who view them disinterestedly: that the Personnel Managers are leading the great masses of unskilled, semiskilled, and clerical workers away from the official labor movement, and attaching them with various devices more or less loyally to the management of the corporations. These personnel workers ... know as well as the union leaders that injustice, exploitation, low wages, unfair discharges, overspeeding, and overwork cause resentment, discontent, strikes, and unionization. They know also that it is bad for business, leads to low productivity and high costs. They therefore make the prevention of such conditions their main task, and they try to impress on the managers of industry their responsibilities in this respect.

Leiserson then goes on to offer this pessimistic assessment of the state of the labour movement (pp. 146–7):

The weakening of trade unionism that has resulted is an undesirable consequence, but who will say then that we should go back to the days when management neglected its social responsibilities toward its employees. ... The labor movement must have a mission beyond the program which personnel management has shown itself willing to adopt. If it is weakened by the activities of personnel management, it needs to look to its larger program.

Shortly after these words were written, the United States and the rest of the industrial world started down the steep descent of the Great Depression. For the next ten years wrenching poverty, insecurity and hard times was the lot of workers and their families. Also unleashed by the Great Depression was a series of political events that no one could foresee. These political events started with the election of Franklin Roosevelt to the Presidency in 1932 and the inauguration of the New Deal in domestic policy. In the international arena, a series of transforming political events unfolded – the rise of fascist Germany, Italy and Japan; the outbreak and devastation of the Second World War; the communist takeover of much of Central and Eastern Europe and threat to Western Europe; and the ensuing Cold War struggle between the totalitarian East and democratic West. All of these developments – both economic and political – rocked American industrial relations to its core.

Out of this jumble emerged a substantially reconfigured industrial relations system that only modestly resembled the one Leiserson extolled in 1929. Not unexpectedly, the field of industrial relations in American universities was transformed with it. A hint of the new direction American industrial relations took in the 1930s is given by the shift in Leiserson's position on unions versus employers. Even before the introduction of the New Deal, Leiserson began to turn noticeably more critical of employers, castigating them for maintaining dividend payments to stockholders while cutting the wages of their employees and throwing their labour out on the street while continuing to maintain their capital (Kaufman, 2003c). Later, in testimony before Congress, he strongly advocated enactment of Senator Wagner's proposed National Labor Relations Act – legislation intended both to protect and encourage trade unionism and collective bargaining and eliminate the employee representation plans Leiserson had earlier touted as the "crown jewel" of welfare capitalism. The turnaround in his philosophy is complete when, in 1938, he states without qualification (p. 40), "Popular judgment now favors collective bargaining" and (p. 43), "the organization of labor and collective bargaining [are] necessary and inevitable."

Leiserson's thoughts became the conventional wisdom in American industrial relations and guided policy and academic study for several decades. Illustrative of the newfound consensus in support of collective bargaining is this statement by George Taylor, professor of industrial relations at the Wharton School of the University of Pennsylvania and renowned labour arbitrator and mediator. He states (1948: 1), "A rare unanimity of opinion exists about the soundness of collective bargaining as the most appropriate means for establishing the conditions of employment."

What caused Leiserson, Taylor and much of the rest of the industrial relations community to abandon welfare capitalism and embrace trade unionism? The key events have already been mentioned, but deserve modest elaboration.

The Depression

During the 1920s the Labour Problem seemed to be retreating into history as economic prosperity, welfare capitalism and a new consumer society reduced labour's sense of class solidarity and grievance, at least outside a few "sick" (depressed) industries such as the needle trades and coal mining. But the Great Depression made all industries sick with excess capacity and surplus workers, and the ensuing struggle of the employers and workers to survive the catastrophe inevitably created the clash of interests and sense of injustice necessary to bring back the Labour Problem in full force. By the winter of 1932 unemployment reached 25 per cent, while those who were working had their hours reduced, suffered repeated wage cuts, and experienced speed-ups and the constant threat of dismissal. Personnel programmes were curtailed or disbanded, representation plans fell into disuse, and foremen and supervisors developed a hard-bitten attitude and allowed favouritism and harsh treatment to become common practice in the shop. Robert and Helen Lynd (1937: 41) in their famous *Middletown* study conducted in-depth interviews with working families in the early 1930s and found an overwhelming sense of "fear, resentment, insecurity, and disillusionment".

The New Deal

The Depression put the welfare capitalist employers on the defensive and undermined their credibility and legitimacy. They had struck an implicit "mutual gain" contract with their employees – in return for cooperation, loyalty and saying no to unions the employers promised fair wages, job security and a measure of voice. As the Depression deepened, however, the progressive employers began to bleed red ink and found it increasingly difficult to live up to their end of the bargain, particularly as "traditionalist" rivals did not hesitate to cut wages and lengthen hours. The 1920s had also impressed on everyone's minds the importance of purchasing power in keeping the economy at full employment. The wonder of the era was the Fordist mass production model, and the man on the street knew that Henry Ford had been able to reduce the price of his automobiles only through volume sales and economies of scale. For employers now to cut wages was seen as undercutting aggregate demand and the virtuous circle of high wages, volume production and falling prices that had fuelled the prosperity of the 1920s. But, in the autumn of 1931, the dam broke when the steel industry initiated the first round of wage cuts among the big industrialists, leading to a quickening disinflationary spiral of more wage cuts, lay-offs and speed-ups. As tens of thousands of the unemployed marched on Washington in 1932, suddenly it appeared that the Marxian crisis of capitalism might be on the horizon.

The stage was set for a near revolution in industrial relations policy when Franklin Roosevelt was elected president in late 1932 and soon thereafter launched the New Deal. Roosevelt thought the cause of the Depression was the worsening distribution of income in the 1920s as the growth of profits outstripped wages, leading to a shortfall of aggregate demand and an eventual collapse in the stock market, industrial production and employment (Fusfeld, 1956; Kaufman, 1996). The Depression was then made worse, in his view, by the deflationary cycle of price and wage cuts caused by cutthroat competition in product and labour markets. To stop the downward spiral of the economy and to jump-start recovery, Roosevelt and his Senate ally Robert Wagner worked with business and labour groups to craft an economic programme that would stabilize the price/wage structure and augment purchasing power. Their approach was based on a combination of elements drawn from German cartel theory, Italian-inspired economic corporatism (i.e., management of the economy by organized interest groups), a heterodox economic theory of under-consumption popularized by Americans Waddill Cathings and William Foster and Englishman John Hobson, and the ideas of the Webbs and the early American institutionalists regarding the role of trade unions in taking wages out of competition. The hastily constructed end product, the National Industrial Recovery Act, was enacted in 1933 amidst great fanfare. It allowed business firms to work together in industry associations to set production quotas and prices in negotiated "codes of fair competition", while it sought to stabilize labour markets and wages by establishing minimum wage levels and expanded collective bargaining. Expanded collective bargaining was also intended to redistribute income from profits to wages, thus boosting household purchasing power and aggregate demand. If employers could not maintain high wages on their own, then unions would help them do it.

To foster greater unionism, Section 7a of the National Industrial Recovery Act expressly forbade employers, for the first time in American history, from interfering with workers' rights to join unions and bargain collectively. Both organized labour and major parts of the business community supported the Act since both had a community of interest in stabilizing markets and stopping destructive competition. With respect to the collective bargaining part of the scheme, however, opinion was sharply divided. Conservative segments of the business community, such as represented by the Chamber of Commerce and National Association of Manufacturers, were dead set against any extension of trade unionism. The progressive companies associated with industrial relations, however, took a generally supportive line as long as unionism was not forced on employers. In this respect, they followed the position enunciated by Rockefeller in 1919 at Wilson's Industrial Conference: namely, that workers should have the right to representation but should be free to choose the form of representation (if any). Thus, in a radio address broadcast across the nation in mid-1933, Rockefeller told listeners he supported the National Industrial Recovery Act, stating (quoted in Kaufman, 2003a: 96–7),

> A further and fundamentally important advantage growing out of the National Recovery Act is the hastening of the day when labor shall have proper and adequate representation in industry. ... Whether the workers shall have a voice in industry through some such representation plan or through some kind of trade unionism is a question which the workers in each plant should be free to determine. The National Recovery Act makes this choice possible, and is all the stronger in that it refrains from specifying the adoption of any particular form of collective bargaining.

The National Industrial Recovery Act was declared unconstitutional in early 1935. The Roosevelt administration acted quickly to replace it with three new pieces of legislation. The first measure was the National Labor Relations Act (the "Wagner Act"), the second was the Social Security Act, and the third was the Fair Labor Standards Act. The Wagner Act represented a much-strengthened version of the National Industrial Recovery Act's Section 7a and its object was to encourage and protect the practice of collective bargaining. The Social Security Act established a nationwide old-age social insurance programme and unemployment insurance programme, such as had been established in Germany four decades earlier. The Fair Labor Standards Act established the first national system of minimum wages and maximum hours and prohibited child labour.

These measures had long been advocated by Commons and the Wisconsin school of institutional labour economists as a way to stabilize labour markets, equalize bargaining power and bring constitutional government to industry. For this reason the enactment of this legislation was considered by many to be a crowning achievement and fulfilment of the ILE policy programme. Illustrative are newspaper headlines at the time that proclaimed Commons "Prophet of the New Deal" and "Father of brain-trusting" (quoted in Kaufman, 2003c), while economist Kenneth Boulding remarked two decades later (Boulding, 1957: 7), "Commons was the intellectual origin of the New Deal, of labour legislation, of social security, of the whole movement in the country toward a welfare state." Although Commons was by this time too old to take an active part in the New Deal, many of his students were recruited to Washington and played key policy roles, as were numerous other institutionalists from the Mitchell and Veblen wings of the field.

Due to several ironic and unexpected twists and turns, the final package of New Deal labour reforms irreparably split the industrial relations community and helped contribute to a gradual divorce between the PM school of progressive employers and the ILE school of institutional labour economists. The corporate liberals actively supported one part of the New Deal labour policy, the Social Security Act, and worked closely with the Wisconsin group to draft and enact the legislation. Bryce Stewart and Murray Latimer from IRC, for example, worked under Edwin Witte from Wisconsin to prepare the Social Security Act (Witte, 1963). Likewise, corporate liberals such as Edward Filene and Henry Dennison had long advocated minimum wages and an end to child labour, putting them in the same camp as the Wisconsinites on the Fair Labor Standards Act (Bruce, 2004).

Even with respect to the Wagner Act – the most controversial and divisive piece of New Deal labour legislation – common ground existed on which the two industrial relations groups could meet to fashion a compromise. The common ground was the ideological commitment of both sides to guaranteeing the right to collective voice in the workplace. The employers were more hesitant to actually put this guarantee in writing and back it up with meaningful enforcement, but when push came to shove in 1934–35 they were prepared to accept legislation broadly along the lines of the new act (Domhoff, 1990). This acceptance was subject to two conditions, however. The first – as stated by Rockefeller in his radio address – was the principle of free choice: that employees be able to choose the form of representation, meaning a company-created representation plan or an independent trade union. The second was the employers' adamant resistance to the closed shop, believing it was both an infringement of employees' rights and gave unions control of the employers' business (Young, 1935).

Despite intense behind-the-scenes lobbying on the part of employers, the version of the National Labor Relations Act that was passed went in the opposite direction on both principles. Wagner included in the bill provisions (Sections 2(5) and 8(a)(2)) that effectively created a blanket prohibition of all employer-created forms of employee representation, such as the Rockefeller/Hicks type of representation plan at CF&I, Standard Oil and other welfare capitalist firms. The choice of representation was thus narrowed to no representation or union representation, with the clear preference given by Wagner and supporters to the option of union representation. Union representation and collective bargaining were thus not only protected and encouraged by law but also popularly interpreted as the *preferred* option. Illustratively, Kochan, Katz and McKersie (1986: 24, emphasis added) state that the Wagner Act enshrined collective bargaining as the "preferred institutional mechanism", while the quotes from Leiserson and Taylor cited above as to the preferred and inevitable status of collective bargaining are also relevant. Similarly, the Wagner Act outlawed a variety of unfair employer labour practices (e.g., various forms of anti-union discrimination) but imposed no similar restriction on union conduct, thus allowing unions to use weapons such as the closed shop, secondary boycott, and discrimination in dues, discipline and membership.

Both the proponents and opponents of the Wagner Act agreed it was one sided. The proponents claimed that it had to be one sided because the existing industrial system was so tilted in favour of employers (Keyserling, 1945). The aim was thus to promote union memberhip and power with the idea that unionism and collective bargaining would restore balance in external labour markets (eliminating labour's inequality of bargaining power), internal firm governance (replacing employer autocracy with industrial democracy) and the national political process (provide bipartite and tripartite interest representation). Further, the proponents believed the one-sided push the Act gave to unionism and collective bargaining was, on net, beneficial for economic efficiency, social justice, and human development in the workplace. At a macroeconomic level, efficiency is promoted, in this view, because union wage gains keep aggregate demand growing in line with supply (the underconsumption/income redistribution argument) and prevent deflationary destructive competition (the taking wages out of competition argument); at the firm level, collective bargaining forces managers to eliminate slack, improve operations, standardize and professionalize personnel practices, and invest in new capital and technology. Likewise, the proponents held that more extensive unionism promotes equity and justice by enforcing "equal pay for equal work", eliminating discriminatory and arbitrary management treatment and giving workers the protection of due process and outside representation in the resolution of disputes (the constitutional government in industry argument). Human self-development is also promoted by making the worker, in Wagner's words, "a free man". Illustrative of this position on unions is the Congressional testimony of Harry Millis, student of Commons and professor of labour economics at the University of Chicago. He states (Millis, 1935: 1553–7, condensed from original):

> The great majority of wage-earners are employed under such conditions that they must act in concert with reference to wage scales, hours, and working conditions if they are to have a reasonably effective voice as to the terms on which they shall work. Without organization there is in most modern industry unequal bargaining power. ... He [the individual worker] fears to push a claim vigorously lest he be discriminated against or lose his job; he is likely to reason that it is better to accept or to retain employment on adverse terms than to lose working time while waiting for another job; ... the terms of his contract, like the railway timetable, [are] 'subject to change without notice.' Informed labor leaders and observers recognize that most employers really wish to do what is fair but that competition frequently prevents them from doing what they would like to do in labor matters. Nowadays we [have] the need for standardization and control, of placing all firms in a market on pretty much the same plane of labor costs, and having competitive success depend largely upon managerial ability, sound organization and the like. ... One is thus driven to the conclusion that hours of work and conditions of work – things that intimately concern workmen – are best decided collectively. ... The case for collective bargaining is only less strong with respect to wages. ... Pressure group must be balanced by pressure group under democratic society.

While proponents of the National Labor Relations Act justified its one-sided nature as a necessary offset to the employers' domination of industry, the opponents believed it went too far in the other direction. As noted above, the large block of employers in the "traditionalist" camp were unalterably opposed to the extension of trade unionism and blasted Wagner's bill in vitriolic language. To them, the bill was a basic assault on employers' property rights and an attempt to foist labour union monopoly on industry. Illustratively,

Mr. James Donnelly (1935: 1895) of the Illinois Manufacturers' Association states in Congressional testimony on the Act:

> They [the employer members] regard this bill as the most amazing attack upon the rights of employers and the great mass of workers that has thus far been devised. ... The proposal should be entitled 'A measure to promote strife and increase unemployment.' It is clearly designed to discourage the friendly settlement of industrial relations problems, to encourage strife and dislocation, and to delegate to labor union agents ... a dictatorial power over American industry.

The employers in the progressive liberal wing also objected to the Wagner Act as unbalanced and unfair but sought to work with Wagner to amend it rather than scrap the entire project. Their principal objection was not to collective bargaining per se, which they supported with significant caveats in order to protect and raise labour standards at low-road employers. (Hicks, for example, wrote several private letters to Wagner in which he unreservedly expressed support for legislation that enshrined Section 7a's protection of the right to collective bargaining.) Their objection was to the idea that collective bargaining should be the preferred mode of wage determination and should as far as practical replace individual bargaining and employee representation. As they saw it, the Act violated the principle of free choice by making it impossible for workers to choose an alternative form of voice other than collective bargaining and by failing to restrain union practices that coerce workers in the choice of representation. Furthermore, they argued, collective bargaining is not the best-suited method of employee relations and wage determination at high-road employers and will actually reduce efficiency and worker well-being. The reason is that collective bargaining is a "fighting model" based on the adversarial principle and is thus antithetical to and destructive of the unitarist welfare capitalist strategy of fostering cooperation through a mutual gain/goodwill approach. In addition, these employers felt that as a class they were being unfairly blamed for labour troubles caused by events outside their control (the Depression) and largely perpetrated by the grasping and short sighted among them. Illustrative of this perspective is the Congressional testimony of progressive employer Henry Dennison (1935: 436–7):

> I am against one big union, the growth of which is surely here invited, because no single system of labor or other organization can be sufficient to cope with the complexities of a modern industrial civilization. May I remind you that, usually unwisely, but, nevertheless actually, millions of working men and women in the United States are as much or more afraid of the A.F. of L. than are thousands of employers. Such deep-rooted fears are no basis upon which we can force the growth

of a single form of unionism and hope to have the slightest hope of success. As to the attitude of and practices of many employers, I have no illusions. I have fought these practices too long for that. I can understand and appreciate Senator Wagner's natural desire, arising out of his inestimable service on the Labor Board [created by Roosevelt to solve disputes arising from Section 7a of the National Industrial Recovery Act], to use a scalpel on them. But by virtue of its task, that Board saw chiefly the bad and some of the worst of cases. There are hundreds of companies in which a sound system of joint and mutual participation in management has developed or is developing. ... Even if few, these companies who have established a basis for wholesome mutual business relationships between management and workers should be cultivated as seeding ground or laboratories from which we may learn. ... You are acting here not for the short but for the long pull, and in your eagerness to cure immediate ills cannot take too much risk of building up our industrial system into two armed camps.

Roosevelt and a large Congressional majority sided with Wagner and allies and the National Labor Relations Act became law in 1935. The passage of the Act, according to Dunlop (quoted in Kaufman, 2002), probably would not have happened (at least in the form it took) "if we had conditions of full employment during the thirties" and was made possible by the fact "Mr. Roosevelt needed something to keep the political support of the labor movement", while legal scholar Janice Bellace (1994: 36) calls the Act an "aberration" and historian Daniel Nelson (2000: 71) observes, "It [the National Labor Relations Act] probably could not have passed before 1935 or after 1937." In hindsight, the passage of the National Labor Relations Act can be seen as the turning point for the American field of industrial relations. Before the Act, the field was composed of a coalition of progressive employers, intellectuals, policy-makers and social reformers who marched together under the banner of industrial relations to solve labour problems and improve the work world. Although divided into PM and ILE schools on particulars, these people were nonetheless united on broad goals and strategy. The goal was to increase efficiency, equity and self-development through labour reform, and the strategy was the balanced "composite model" described in Chapter 2: the use of the "employers' solution" of personnel management and welfare capitalism to push forward the envelope of best practice in industrial relations; the use of the "workers' solution" of trade unionism and "community's solution" of protective labour legislation and social insurance to set and gradually raise a floor of minimum standards and offset market imperfections; and a "macro solution" of monetary and fiscal policy to maintain full employment and price stability.

Due to the events of the Depression and New Deal, the commitment to the consensus strategy unravelled and fell apart. In particular, it appeared to many in the ILE camp that two of the four legs of the policy stool had failed – monetary policy had failed to stabilize the economy and maintain full employment, and personnel management and welfare capitalism had failed to deliver reasonable wages, employment security and fair treatment. Left adrift in a sea of unemployment and wage cuts, they abandoned these two policy instruments and cast their lot with a much-expanded programme of trade unionism and labour law – in effect abandoning the composite model of the 1920s and reverting to the more "primitive" ILE model of the 1910s (the model implicit in Commons' "American shoemakers" and *Principles of labor legislation* but without *Industrial goodwill* and the business cycle theory in *Institutional economics*). Desperate to stop the deflationary spiral of wage and price cuts caused by destructive competition, eager to augment purchasing power and aggregate demand through higher wages, and appalled by the worsening of labour conditions and more draconian and unjust treatment of workers, the ILE group looked to their theory of labour markets for guidance and latched on to the one principle that above all others seemed to offer a hopeful way out – the Webbs' *device of the common rule*.

As they came to see it in the mid-1930s, the central task was to stabilize labour markets, equalize bargaining power and introduce industrial democracy. This could be achieved by using collective bargaining and labour law to take wages and labour standards out of competition at a point, gradually raising wages and thus augmenting purchasing power, and by replacing employer autocracy with a constitutional form of industrial government. For the device of the common rule to be effective, however, it needed to bring under the umbrella of collective bargaining and labour law *all firms* in the labour market. Thus, while the Preamble of the National Labor Relations Act only speaks of "protecting and encouraging" collective bargaining, to Wagner and allies collective bargaining was more than this – it was "preferred", because it was seen as the best way to simultaneously promote macroeconomic recovery and bring industrial democracy to the workplace (Mitchell, 1986; Kaufman, 1996). Correspondingly, if unions and collective bargaining are preferred, then it is only a short step to conclude that non-union employers and the system of individual bargaining – no matter whether traditionalist or progressive – are inferior and second-best options and, indeed, a threat to a wage-led macroeconomic recovery and the spread of genuine industrial democracy.

The exemplar of this line of reasoning is the National Labor Relations Act's ban on non-union employee representation plans. Although many of the thousands of plans created in the New Deal period were hastily thrown together, largely ineffective, and frequently a union-avoidance scheme, practically every person who looked at the plans operated by the leading welfare capitalist firms in the 1920s concluded that they not only accomplished worthwhile objectives but in some cases were preferred by the employees to independent unions (Leiserson, 1929; Kaufman and Taras, 2000; Kaufman, 2000c). Yet the National Labor Relations Act banned all representation plans in order that unionism might be spread as widely as possible so as to take wages out of competition and redistribute income from profits to wages. Clear evidence on this matter is provided in this statement by Wagner (1935: 22):

> The company union has improved personal relations, group-welfare activities, discipline, and other matters that may be handled on a local basis. But it has failed dismally to standardize or improve wage levels, for the wage question is a general one whose sweep embraces whole industries, or States, or even the Nation. Without wider areas of cooperation among employees there can be no protection against the nibbling tactics of the unfair employer or of the worker who is willing to degrade standards by serving for a pittance.

By elevating the role of trade unionism to a "preferred" status and taking active steps to dismantle and obstruct the welfare capitalist model, the National Labor Relations Act split the industrial relations community and alienated the PM school of progressive employers. Whereas in the composite model of the 1920s the employers' solution of personnel management and welfare capitalism and the unitarist model of mutual gain and cooperation were regarded in industrial relations as complements to trade unionism and the pluralist model of adversarial, arm's-length bargaining, after the National Labor Relations Act they became transformed into substitutes and, thus, rivals. The inevitable effect was to drive a wedge between the two schools in industrial relations – a wedge that deepened and widened over the next two decades until the PM school finally abandoned industrial relations and created a separate, rival home in personnel/human resource management and organizational behaviour. What was left in industrial relations was a narrower and truncated version of the ILE school – and one that in its collective memory had all but forgotten the PM school. Were this not so, how could one leading scholar (Somers, 1975: 1) state in the 1970s that the core values of industrial relations are "the uniqueness and value of the free collective bargaining system, voluntarism, liberal pluralism, [and] consent", or another maintain that (Barbash, 1979: 453) "two leading principles govern the American ideology of American industrial relations: the adversarial principle and the principle of voluntarism"?

Ironically, this modern and more narrow vision of industrial relations is often attributed to Commons, yet the academic father of the American field did not hold this view. He did not, for example, reject the progressive non-union employment model or advocate making collective bargaining the preferred model across industry.[1] Further, the task of industrial relations, Commons states in *Institutional economics* (p. 6, emphasis in original), is "the necessity of *creating a new harmony* of interests – or at least order, if harmony is impossible – out of the conflict of interests among the hoped-for cooperators". In terms of problem solving, what this statement leads to is the composite model: that is, trying to use working rules in industrial relations to create a unitarist, goodwill employment model, since this maximizes cooperation and the joint surplus, but where this is impossible then falling back on a pluralist model to at least ensure order and justice (or "mutual survival", to use a phrase later coined by Bakke, 1946). In this composite model, employers and personnel management and trade unions and collective bargain-ing have valuable, complementary roles to play in solving labour problems and each has its appropriate role and place in the industrial relations system. The composite model, however, is *not* the New Deal model that the American industrial relations field came to rest on after the Second World War.[2]

Mass unionism

One stimulus to the field of industrial relations in the United States in the 1930s was the emergence of unprecedented labour problems because of the economic depression; a second was the equally unprecedented and near-revolutionary shift in national labour policy under the New Deal. Yet a third impetus came from the meteoric rise of trade unionism unleashed by the New Deal. Together they represented, in the words of Saposs (1956: 26, emphasis added), a "*transformation* [from] the good old days".

When the United States entered the Great Depression in late 1929, only slightly more than 10 per cent of American workers were members of a trade union – a substantial decline from the high of 18 per cent reached a decade earlier in the immediate aftermath of the First World War. Union membership then plunged in the next three years as companies made round after round of lay-offs. In his presidential address to the AEA in December 1932, labour economist George Barnett (1933: 6) held out little hope for a rejuvenation of the labour movement, stating "We may take it as probable that trade unionism is likely to be a declining influence in determining conditions of labor."

To nearly everyone's surprise, six months later a wave of union organizing broke out and within a year union membership had grown by over one million. By the end of the decade union membership had grown by five million and density had climbed to 28 per cent. This upward trend continued until a high-water mark was reached in 1953, with a density level of 35 per cent. Unionism was now widespread across the manufacturing, mining, transportation and construction industries, and only a handful of the welfare capitalist firms of the 1920s made it to the 1950s without being organized (Bernstein, 1970; Jacoby, 1997).

The surge of unionism in the 1930s and 1940s arose from a complex interplay of motives and events that are still debated today (Freeman, 1998; Bennett and Kaufman, 2002). Certainly, the deprivation and insecurity experienced by the mass of workers in the 1930s is one factor, as is disillusionment and resentment toward employers (Williams in Kaufman, 2001c). Also important was the belief of many people that under the National Industrial Recovery Act the government wanted workers to join unions as a way to raise wages and jump-start economic recovery. Unionism in American industry was given yet another big boost in 1935 when John L. Lewis, president of the miners' union, led a breakaway group of industrial unions and established the Congress of Industrial Organizations (CIO). The AFL had stoutly clung to a craft model of union structure to this point, even though it appeared to be an ineffective device for organizing the mass production industries. Under Lewis' leadership, the CIO chartered a number of new industrial unions and within several years scored major victories, including the unionization of the key firms in the auto and steel industries (Zieger, 1995).

Second World War

Over the decade of the 1940s union density continued to expand, reaching slightly over one-third of the workforce in the early 1950s. The continued expansion of collective bargaining after 1940 owed much to the Second World War (Brody, 1980). The government was desperate for all-out production of war material and could ill afford widespread strikes and labour unrest. To secure labour peace, the Roosevelt administration pressured highly visible anti-union firms, such as Ford Motor and Bethlehem Steel, to recognize unions and agree to dues check-off and union shop (or closed shop) membership provisions. Until they were banned by the Taft–Hartley amendments to the National Labor Relations Act in 1947, a number of unions (particularly the Teamsters) used secondary boycotts quite successfully to extend unionization across their industries.

Industrial conflict

A concomitant of collective bargaining is strikes and the threat of strikes. The rapid increase in union density, the desire of employers to contain and roll back the union advance, and the problem of inflation and loss of real income combined to cause mounting strikes and labour unrest from the late 1930s until the early 1950s. The late 1930s witnessed a number of large and sometimes violent strikes, including the famous sit-down strikes that helped unionize the auto industry. During the war an elaborate system of wage–price controls and dispute resolution procedures was inaugurated, creating a mushroom growth in labour mediation and arbitration. Then, when unions and employers were freed in 1946 from government controls, a strike wave of unparalleled proportion swept over all the major industries of the United States (Nelson, 1997). So serious was the problem of industrial conflict that President Truman in 1952 declared a national emergency and seized the steel mills to prevent an industry strike from curtailing production for the Korean War. Also noteworthy of the unsettled and contested nature of collective bargaining at that time is the fact that nearly one-quarter of strikes occurred during the term of a negotiated contract, often in the form of a "wildcat" action led by the rank and file to pressure settlement of a grievance or obtain a demand through a plant-level form of direct action.

The communist threat

Another stimulus to industrial relations was the threat of communism. As earlier noted, a major impetus to the founding of the field of industrial relations in the years immediately following the First World War was the Red Scare. The Bolshevik Revolution in Russia, combined with communist movements and uprisings in most of the industrial countries, created a wave of fear in the United States that labour radicalism was going to fuse with communism and lead to the country's overthrow. A similar Red Scare swept over the United States in the years after the Second World War, set off by the Russian occupation of central and eastern Europe, the fall of China to the communist forces of Mao Tse-tung, and the advent of the Cold War. As happened three decades earlier, the spectre of communism – coupled with an aggressive union movement and a wave of strikes – suddenly elevated improved industrial relations to a national priority. Besides motivating employers, universities and government to give more attention to industrial relations, the Red Scare also shifted the entire spectrum of discussion and policy in the United States about labour in a distinctly more conservative, less open direction. Many leftist/communist union leaders and activists were purged or muffled, a number of communist-dominated unions were expelled from the CIO, and progressive/leftist intellectuals were intimidated and harassed during the communist witch-hunt of Senator Joseph McCarthy in the early 1950s (Zieger, 1995; Kelly, 1999). The attack on the left, according to Adams (1989: 62), "left the labour movement bereft of idealism and passion".

Combined effect on industrial relations

The combined effect of all of the events discussed above created conditions ideal for the growth of the field of industrial relations. The Great Depression and wartime crisis of the Second World War created immense labour problems that demanded immediate and effective resolution. These labour problems brought with them a wave of union organizing and strikes, and a threefold increase in union membership. Suddenly, in the decade after the Second World War, most of the major industrial sectors of the American economy were unionized. Not only did the nation need scholars to study these new phenomena, but it also needed thousands of practitioners to fill new labour relations jobs in industry, the labour movement and government regulatory agencies. Finally, the 20-year period commencing with the New Deal saw the effective repudiation in theory and practice of a laissez-faire, free market economy. The Depression was taken as confirming evidence that a capitalist economy needed considerable institutional regulation and control, and that full employment was facilitated by a policy of social Keynesianism – stabilization through activist fiscal/monetary policy and longer-term economic growth through a steady increase in wages and purchasing power achieved by income redistribution through collective bargaining, protective labour laws and social insurance programmes (Zieger, 1995). Finally, the widespread fear of communism reinforced the perceived importance of using effective industrial relations practices to integrate the labour movement into the American social order and staunch radicalism.

The human relations movement

The development of industrial relations in the 1935–60 period in the United States was also significantly influenced by the rise of the human relations movement.

As described earlier, for the first decade and a half of the twentieth century the management wing of American industrial relations was heavily concentrated among practitioners and consultants and had only modest academic representation. Although many universities set up business schools in the 1920s, the field of management was not yet well established as an integrated subject. Likewise, while the behavioural science disciplines of psychology, sociology and anthropology had formed in the early 1900s, they too were relatively underdeveloped and had very little contact with work-related subjects. The most significant exception to this rule was a modest amount of academic research by industrial psychologists such as Walter Dill Scott, Arthur Kornhauser and Morris Viteles. Just as economists tended to view industrial relations and personnel management as "applied labour economics", so the psychologists viewed these fields as "applied psychology". But the psychologists had much less influence on the early development of the field than did the economists. An important reason was that they primarily focused on measurement issues and a narrow range of "technical personnel procedures" (quoting Kornhauser, 1948: 172), such as selection tests and job analysis, causing them to have only a "narrow technician's role" (quoting Leavitt, 1961: 25). Illustrative are the titles of articles in the first issue of the journal *Personnel Psychology*, established in 1948: "Vision tests for precision workers at RCA", "Interest tests reduce factory turnover", "Testing programs draw better applicants", and "An attitude survey in a typical manufacturing plant".

The situation on the PM side changed dramatically, however, with the development of the human relations movement. The term "human relations" was widely used in the American literature beginning in the late 1910s and connoted the basic idea that labour is embodied in human beings and thus effective work relations require attention to human relations (Guillén, 1994). The human relations concept was given scientific and academic legitimacy and substance only in the 1930s, however, through the Hawthorne experiments and the writings of Elton Mayo and colleagues from the Harvard Business School. This work also spawned in the early 1940s the new field of industrial sociology in the United States which, in turn, was an important influence in the late 1950s in the development of the new field of organizational behaviour (Wren, 1994).

The Hawthorne experiments took place at the Hawthorne, Illinois, plant of the Western Electric Co., starting in 1927. Large-scale funding for the Harvard group came from Rockefeller-connected foundations (Harvey, 1982). According to Mayo (1933: 99), Western Electric was by all accounts a model employer and morale at the plant was high. Yet the research team from Harvard found widespread evidence of deliberate restriction of output on the part of employees, as well as other negative behaviours such as frequent absenteeism and non-attention to work tasks. Mayo and colleagues set out to discover the source of these problems. (See Gillespie, 1991, for a detailed account of the Hawthorne experiments, a critical evaluation of the findings, and a review of Mayo's controversial role in shaping and publicizing the conclusions.)

Mayo frames the problem this way (1945: 9):

> Every social group ... must face and clearly state two perpetual and recurrent problems of administration. It must secure for its individual and group membership: (1) The satisfaction of material and economic needs (2) The maintenance of spontaneous cooperation throughout the organization. Our administrative methods are all pointed at the materially effective; none, at the maintenance of cooperation. ... Problems of absenteeism, labor turnover, 'wildcat' strikes, show that we do not know how to ensure spontaneity of cooperation; that is, teamwork.

The welfare capitalist employers sought to achieve cooperation and unity of interest through employee representation, job security and a "square deal". Earlier, Frederick Taylor had advanced the theory of scientific management as a way to create teamwork and unity of interest, giving emphasis to gain-sharing forms of compensation and impartial rule making by experts. Mayo was attracted to neither of these approaches. Instead, he drew inspiration from the theories of French sociologist Emile Durkheim and Italian sociologist Vilfredo Pareto, as well as French psychopathologist Pierre Janet. Mayo concluded that cooperation depends first and foremost on a sense of social identity among group members and feelings that they are integrated into and have a stable place within the group. These feelings, in turn, are to a significant extent non-logical in nature.

Mayo's diagnosis of labour problems was thus fourfold: industrialism has unleashed major forces of change that disrupt social groupings both external to and within work units; the disruption of social groups creates a psychological condition of *anomie* (rootlessness and disorientation); *anomie* undercuts spontaneous collaboration and leads to a variety of work and social pathologies (turnover, etc.); and management efforts to impose a technological, rational order to production further fragments social cohesion and exacerbates *anomie*. Thus, he states (1933: 120):

> Human collaboration at work ... has always depended for its perpetuation upon the evolution of a non-logical social code which regulates the relations between persons and their attitudes to one another. Insistence upon a merely economic logic of production – especially if the logic is frequently changed – interferes with the development of such a code and consequently gives rise in the group to a sense of human defeat.

The lesson for management theory, according to Mayo, is that the factory is not only a technological/economic system but also a social system and that effective cooperation can only be gained when an equilibrium or *modus vivendi* is worked out between the logic of efficiency and the non-logic of worker sentiments. With respect to management practice, Mayo's research pointed to the importance of interpersonal relations, socio-psychological skills training for leaders, recognition of informal work groups and their norms, interviewing and counselling so that workers have an opportunity to "vent" and release emotions, and the importance of social over economic determinants of work effort.

Mayo's writings on the Hawthorne experiments, along with the companion books *Leadership in a free society* by Thomas Whitehead (1936) and *Management and the worker* (1939) by Roethlisberger and Dickson, precipitated great interest in both academia and industry in the new subject of human relations. Interest was further fuelled by the largely independent work of Kurt Lewin, a German-trained psychologist at MIT, on leadership and group dynamics. The more general subjects of management and organization theory were likewise coming alive at this time, fuelled by the influential book *The functions of the executive* (1938) by Chester Barnard, the lectures of Mary Follett in the United Kingdom and the United States, and the translation into English of the works of Henri Fayol and Max Weber.

Paradoxically, therefore, even as the welfare capitalism experiment fell into disrepute and trade unionism swept over most of American industry, in the academic world new ideas about management and the practice of employee relations began to percolate and draw attention. In the 1940s several centres or institutes, such as at Yale and Chicago, were established to promote human relations research, and scholars such as William Foote Whyte (sociologist) and E. Wight Bakke (economist) developed national reputations in the area (Kaufman, 1993). While much of this activity was labelled "human relations" and took place in the new sub-field of industrial sociology, most people at the time nonetheless perceived it as a component of industrial relations. Illustratively, anthropologist Conrad Arensberg considered three names for this line of research – human relations, industrial sociology and industrial psychology – and rejected all three as unduly narrow in perspective. He concluded (1951: 330), "The best common description of the field, then, is the historical one: scientific study of the sources of unrest in labor and management relations, that is, the study of the problems of industrial relations."

While human relations fell within the domain of industrial relations, in certain respects it represented a new paradigm and significant departure from the PM school of the 1920s. The model of welfare capitalism was largely developed by leading employers in industry and the contribution of intellectuals was for the most part a secondary one of commentary, critique and analysis. Likewise, improved human relations was only one part of the welfare capitalism project and, broadly viewed, a relatively small part. Much more important in welfare capitalism were new organizational-level programmes, such as personnel management, employee benefits and employee representation. The Harvard School human relations movement, on the other hand, was for the most part popularized and shaped by academics with a strong research interest in the disciplines of psychology, sociology and anthropology. These people had scant interest in the applied field of personnel management, viewing it as largely administrative and reactive, and a number (e.g., Mayo) were indifferent to or sceptical of trade unions, seeing collective bargaining as an institutionalized form of conflict and thus a threat to the teamwork and organizational integration they sought to promote (Whyte, 1944; Bendix and Fisher, 1949). Human relations, therefore, approached workplace study and reform with a much greater *micro* emphasis on individuals and small groups. It also had core principles and interests that were more orthogonal or opposed to collective bargaining and a pluralist philosophy of labour–management relations and put forward new management and organizational methods (e.g., a non-authoritarian leadership style, an integrative organizational culture, and non-pecuniary reward and social status systems) that were grounded in new and sometimes controversial theories of human psychology. All of these features created a larger gap between the PM and ILE schools, particularly when public policy and current events in the United States were shifting intellectual interests and ideological sympathies toward unions and collective/institutional aspects of employment relations.

Labour economics: From labour problems to labour markets

The emergence of the human relations movement considerably strengthened and energized the management side of the industrial relations field in American universities. A contemporaneous transformation in the field of labour economics had equally far-reaching consequences for the ILE school in industrial relations.

The study of labour in the United States in the 1920s and 1930s was dominated by the economists broadly affiliated with the institutional school. Following in the German and English historical tradition, their approach emphasized inductive, empirical and historical research; a holistic, multidisciplinary approach to theory building; a critical attitude toward unregulated markets and employment relations; a focus on improved economic performance and labour conditions through institutional reform; and a predilection to favour greater trade unionism and government regulation. Commons and colleagues of the Wisconsin school were the epitome of this approach, but even the foremost analytical labour economist of this period, Paul Douglas of the University of Chicago, was considered by his colleagues to be an institutionalist (Reder, 1982). (This interpretation reflected both Douglas' empirical approach to developing economic theory and his favourable attitude toward trade unionism and labour law.) Viewed as a whole, therefore, the field of labour economics was much less centred on economic theory per se and the study of markets and much more oriented to the historical and institutional study of the causes of and solutions to labour problems. Thus the very term "labour economics" was not born until the mid-1920s, did not become the generic label for the field until the 1950s, and in the 1920s and 1930s was not clearly delineated from industrial relations (Kaufman, 1993, 1994).

Over the years, however, labour economics and industrial relations not only developed a clearer line of demarcation but also gradually grew apart in intellectual and normative perspective. This trend is intimately associated with the rise of the neoclassical school in the discipline of economics and its gradual spread into labour economics.

Neoclassical economics originated in the late 1800s in Great Britain and Europe, as described in an earlier chapter. However, four decades passed before the neoclassical school entered the field of labour. If the neoclassical tradition in labour economics has a birth year, it is probably 1932, when British economist John Hicks published the *The theory of wages*. Illustrative of the neoclassical approach to labour markets, Hicks declares in the first sentence of the book, "The theory of the determination of wages in a free market is simply a special case of the general theory of value." Hicks notes that labour markets are in some respects different from commodity markets, but concludes that (p. 4), "the general working of supply and demand is a great deal more important than the differences between markets". In building his model of wage determination, Hicks follows neoclassical tradition by making a number of simplifying assumptions, such as the stipulation that workers' effort level is a "given" and involuntary unemployment does not exist. He justifies these departures from reality with this statement (p. 7): "It is true that we only achieve this isolation [of pure market forces] at the expense of a series of highly artificial assumptions; but in economics, as in other sciences, abstraction is usually the condition for clear thinking."

The neoclassical approach to the study of labour was anathema to most of the institutionalists and had next to no presence in American labour economics in the 1930s and early 1940s. An attempted rapprochement and melding of the two perspectives was begun in the 1940s and continued into the 1950s, however, under the leadership of a new generation of labour economists.

Important names among this group are E. Wight Bakke, Neil Chamberlain, John Dunlop, Clark Kerr, Richard Lester, Charles Myers, Lloyd Reynolds, Arthur Ross and Lloyd Ulman. Although their effort at theoretical integration ultimately failed and has almost no influence in contemporary labour economics, their work nonetheless had a huge effect on industrial relations.

In their own eyes, this new generation of labour economists sought to chart a middle course between the neoclassical and institutional schools (Dunlop, 1988; Kerr, 1988). For this reason, in an earlier work I coined the neutral term "postwar labour economists" to describe them (Kaufman, 1988). However, in the eyes of many other economists both then and now the commitment of Dunlop, Kerr and colleagues to an interdisciplinary approach, the pursuit of realism in theory building, rejection of competitive market theory and attempt to create a "social economics of labour" inexorably placed the post-war economists in the institutional camp (Segal, 1986; Kaufman, 1993; Boyer and Smith, 2001). Cain (1976), for example, labels them *neo-institutionalists*. I earlier avoided this term since Dunlop and Kerr strongly denied its applicability, but now after their passing I can say that the "neo-institutional" label is, in my view, a reasonably accurate label.[3]

Like their neoclassical brethren, the new group of "revisionist" or neo-institutional labour economists sought to focus labour economics more squarely on the operation of labour markets, rather than the older concept of labour problems, and utilize basic theoretical concepts such as demand and supply as the conceptual scaffolding for the study of labour. Thus their central research subject was wage determination and, in particular, the influence of market versus institutional forces on wage levels and wage changes. But they also thought the neoclassical approach of Hicks was far too simplified and unrealistic. Thus, like the earlier generation of institutionalists, the neo-institutional labour economists continued to practise inductive, historically informed and case-study research methods, and to take a multidisciplinary social-science approach to theory building. Like the institutionalists, they also stressed the imperfect nature of labour markets and the importance of rigidities, involuntary unemployment and deficient aggregate demand. In developing new labour market theory, therefore, this younger generation of labour economists looked to models of bargaining; behavioural and social representations of the human agent; theories of imperfect competition as earlier pioneered by Edwin Chamberlin and Joan Robinson; and the macroeconomic model of income determination advanced by J.M. Keynes.

A flavour of their approach is given in this passage written by Kerr (1994: 73–6, emphasis in original):

In wage stabilization, we looked for the 'going wage' and found 'going wages,' often with two or more modal clusters when there should be, we had been told, only one. In dispute settlement, we found many factors at work in addition to the dispassionate calculus of economic costs and benefits, as we saw internal divisions within labor and capital that made a mockery of concepts of *the* union and *the* employer. ... We saw [in labor markets] not equilibrium but disequilibria. We saw not determinate solutions but indeterminate ranges of solutions. We saw not a market for labor but many markets with distinguishing characteristics. We saw collective action as well as atomistic decision making. We saw systems of beliefs, including justice and benevolence, affecting people, as well as self-love. We were highly conscious of social change as well as timeless truths. We were more concerned with what was barely workable than with what was optimal under optimal conditions. ... Our goal was to understand reality, and one result was to propose revisions of received doctrines. If the younger revisionists can be said to have had a personal guru, it was Sumner H. Slichter. ... If the young revisionists can be said to have had a call to action, it was made by John Dunlop ... [who] wanted to see an effort 'to bring theory and observation closer together.' If the young revisionists can be said to have had a mantra, it was 'theory and practice,' said and written over and over again.

Another perspective is provided by the remark of Lester (quoted by Levine, 1978: 55) that "some of us preferred to be roughly correct rather than precisely wrong".

Coming to the subject of labour economics with this rather eclectic and heterodox theoretical view, the post-war labour economists were able at an intellectual level not only to easily accommodate collective bargaining and labour law within labour economics but to take a generally sympathetic or favourable position on them. Their intellectual inclinations were then buttressed and reinforced by considerable real-world experience gained during the wage–price controls programme of the Second World War and subsequent careers as arbitrators and mediators (Dunlop, 1988; Kerr, 1988; Kaufman, 2002). In these experiences, they saw first hand that market forces are often attenuated and frequently tipped in favour of employers, leading them to conclude that in the absence of collective bargaining and labour law many workers lack adequate protection, power and voice. Their experiences also led them to become advocates of negotiation and consensus building, tripartism and pluralism in social and economic life (Kerr, 1955).

From 1940 to 1960, the post-war labour economists became increasingly involved with and interested in industrial relations. At the start of their careers in the 1930s, several of the most prominent men in this group (e.g., Dunlop, Lester, Reynolds) had little contact with the field; two decades later they were writing the most important works and serving in the most prominent positions in industrial relations (Lester, 1988; Reynolds, 1988; Kaufman, 1993). In part, this shift reflects a pragmatic repositioning in their research interests in light of the rise of mass unionism, national concern with securing industrial peace, growing government regulation of labour markets, their high-level participation in labour arbitration and national labour policy, and generous financial support received from the Social Science Research Council (SSRC) for labour market studies. (J. Douglas Brown of Princeton's Industrial Relations Section was president of the SSRC.) This shift also reflected, in part, their growing dissatisfaction with the larger discipline of economics and, in particular, the growing power and influence exercised by neoclassical-oriented price theorists. The "young revisionists" initially sought to remain members in good standing in the economics discipline and work from within to promote labour theory that is more realistic and grounded in the social sciences and theories of imperfect competition. This effort received a cool reception, however, and was aggressively attacked by several price theorists, such as Milton Friedman, Fritz Machlup and George Stigler. As a result, the post-war labour economists came to feel increasingly estranged from their mother discipline and gravitated toward industrial relations as a new home for their more multidisciplinary, heterodox type of economics (Kerr, 1983).

Evidently, numerous parallels exist between the development of labour economics and human relations. Both fields had intellectual antecedents in the 1920s and 1930s but emerged in the early 1940s as distinct subject areas, with articulated theoretical frameworks and intellectual boundaries. Both fields also developed a strong affiliation with industrial relations, with human relations becoming the intellectual centre of the PM wing of the field and labour economics becoming the intellectual centre of the now solidly pluralist ILE wing. The major difference is that the labour economists had been more actively involved and more widely represented in the academic arena of industrial relations before the Second World War than the behavioural science and management researchers. Coupled with the surge in unions and labour–management relations in the 1935–55 period and the greater relevance of economics to issues of public labour policy, this placed the labour economists in the dominant, most influential position in the industrial relations field.

Institutionalizing industrial relations in American universities

Through the years of the Second World War the industrial relations field had a small but discernible institutional presence in American universities and social-science scholarship. As noted in Chapter 2, Clarence Hicks and Rockefeller had established industrial relations sections at six American and Canadian universities by the late 1930s. These units were, however, small and largely devoted to sponsoring research, collecting library materials, and offering short management education seminars and programmes. They had no faculty members of their own, however, and offered no "for credit" courses or degree programmes. Likewise, at the time no national industrial relations association existed for either practitioners or academics, nor was there any academic journal catering specifically to industrial relations.

Academic programmes

The situation changed dramatically at the end of the Second World War (Adams, 1993; Kaufman, 1993). Starting in 1945, over two dozen independent schools, institutes and centres of industrial relations were established in American universities. The first, largest, best-known and most influential was the New York State School of Industrial and Labor Relations (NYSSILR) at Cornell University in Ithaca, New York. The Cornell ILR programme was followed by industrial relations units at numerous other universities, such as Chicago, Yale, Illinois, Wisconsin, Rutgers and Minnesota, and the two University of California campuses at Los Angeles (UCLA) and Berkeley. A number of smaller Catholic colleges and universities also established units, such as Loyola University in Chicago and Seton Hall University in New Jersey.

The Cornell industrial relations programme was in many respects the exemplar for those that followed. For example, the ILR school was established as a separate unit within the university, equivalent to a school of law or engineering. It was not housed within the business school or economics department for two reasons: first, to help ensure its neutrality with respect to the divergent interests and needs of labour and management and, second, in recognition that industrial relations is inherently multidisciplinary and needs to draw faculty members from across the numerous disciplines and departments within the university. Unlike the earlier industrial relations sections, the Cornell programme also had its own appointed and tenured professors and offered its own degree programmes (undergraduate and graduate). The intellectual jurisdiction of the school was broadly conceived to include all aspects of work and employment, per the historic meaning of the term "industrial relations", but inclusion of the qualifier "and labour relations" in its name also indicates an emphasis on the ILE tradition and, in particular, the institutions and practices of collective bargaining. The broad conception of industrial relations in the school's name and representation of the PM and ILE traditions in its academic programme is well illustrated by the major areas of study available to its students (Kaufman, 1993). Graduate students, for example, could choose a major (area of concentration) in seven different subjects: collective bargaining, mediation and arbitration; human relations in industry; industrial and labour legislation and social security; labour market economics and analysis; labour history, organization and management; personnel management; and industrial education. The ILR school also established an extension division and provided considerable continuing education (off-campus) classes for practitioners, particularly in the area of labour education/labour studies.

Other industrial relations programmes were on a smaller scale, some only had joint-appointed faculty members (professors with a tenure home in another academic department), and some were freestanding units while some were housed in business schools. Their orientation also differed, as some leaned more heavily toward the ILE side (e.g., Wisconsin, Illinois, Michigan State, Berkeley) while a smaller number leaned toward the PM side (e.g., Minnesota, Yale). Some universities also created separate labour studies departments outside the industrial relations centres and institutes, while others kept them inside. Most of the new industrial relations centres and institutes had an ILE emphasis and many of the faculty subscribed to the idea that collective bargaining was now the preferred method of wage determination and workforce governance. Many of the new programmes also made a deliberate attempt to include union leaders in programmes and on boards of advisers. Because of this, they were viewed suspiciously by many employers as "pro-union" and by some as covert agents of socialism.

A particularly significant development was the decision of the Wisconsin faculty to create in 1956 the nation's first Ph.D. programme in industrial relations (followed shortly thereafter by Cornell and, later, by a number of others). The programme was justified as a vehicle to promote interdisciplinary research and teaching on labour (Fried, 1987). Other departments at the university found this argument cogent for the creation of a master's programme. American industry had a large demand for personnel and labour relations practitioners and, for these jobs, students clearly needed training in the various subject areas related to industrial relations, such as law, economics, sociology and business. The interdisciplinary argument encountered considerable opposition, however, as a justification for creating a doctoral degree in industrial relations. The worry was expressed that Ph.D. students would emerge as a "jack of all trades but master of none" in the area of research. The supporters of industrial relations successfully overcame this opposition and won approval for the programme. In practice, however, the fears of the opponents had considerable merit, leading to pressure on professors and doctoral students to differentiate industrial relations from other subject areas so that they could claim an area of expertise and comparative advantage in research and teaching. The one area that was most in demand at the time, and which other departments had not yet established a clear claim to, was collective bargaining and labour–management relations. For this reason, the decision of Wisconsin and other industrial relations programmes to establish doctoral degrees in industrial relations proved to be a double-edged sword for the field. It helped create a stronger institutional identity and academic community of interest for industrial relations but also contributed to a narrowing of the subject. What had been a PM and ILE version of the field, encompassing both personnel management/human relations and trade unions/labour–management relations, became an increasingly ILE-dominated version centred only on the latter part.

The Industrial Relations Research Association

The second major event that helped firmly institutionalize the industrial relations field in the United States was the founding of the Industrial Relations Research Association (IRRA). The IRRA was established in late 1947. The person who took the lead in this effort was Richard Lester (Kaufman, 1993). Lester was a heterodox, neo-institutional labour economist at Princeton and a member of the university's Industrial Relations Section. Edwin Witte, an institutional labour economist and student of Commons, served as the IRRA's first president. Within a year, membership passed the 1,000 mark.

The meteoric increase in IRRA membership in the first year reveals the tremendous amount of interest existing in the post-Second World War period in industrial relations. According to Witte (1947), industrial relations was one of the three most popular fields of study (in addition to engineering and accounting) among people returning from military duty after the war, while research in industrial relations received great impetus from the sudden spread of collective bargaining, the need to settle disputes and restore industrial peace, and the pressing issues associated with national labour policy. Although the precise growth of the field is impossible to determine, clearly it was rapid. Kerr (1994: 71) estimates, for example, that in the early 1930s no more than 100 people in American universities were doing specialized research on labour markets and institutions, but that this figure grew to more than 1,000 by the end of the 1950s. All of these new recruits to industrial relations needed an organizational home in which to meet, develop a community of interest, present research work, talk about teaching programmes, recruit new faculty members and place graduate students. No such organization then existed, however, so the IRRA filled a notable void.

The very fact that the field now had a professional association spoke to the coming of age of industrial relations.

The IRRA rode the wave of growth of industrial relations in the late 1940s and 1950s and helped, in turn, to propel it forward. Membership in the IRRA tripled by the early 1960s and numerous local chapters for practitioners were started. The organization also held an annual winter meeting that attracted hundreds of people. Papers from the annual meeting were then published in a proceedings which, at that time, was one of only two publications in the United States dedicated to industrial relations research. The IRRA also began to publish in the 1950s a series of well-regarded research volumes on leading industrial relations topics that featured chapters by the top scholars in the field. Moreover, the people elected to serve as president of the IRRA represented the leading names in the field among academics and practitioners. The list of IRRA presidents reads like a "who's who" for industrial relations of the 1950s: Edwin Witte (1948), Sumner Slichter (1949), George Taylor (1950), William Leiserson (1951), J. Douglas Brown (1952), Ewan Clague (1953), Clark Kerr (1954), Lloyd Reynolds (1955), Richard Lester (1956), Dale Yoder (1957), E. Wight Bakke (1958), William Haber (1959) and John Dunlop (1960).

In hindsight, one can see that the formation of the IRRA, while bringing many benefits to the field, also brought costs. These contradictory outcomes reflect the conflicted purposes and ideology of the IRRA. On one hand, the IRRA was meant to conform to the broad "all aspects of work" conception of industrial relations that prevailed up to that time. The constitution adopted by the IRRA, for example, states that one of its purposes is "the encouragement of research in all aspects of the field of labor – social, political, economic, legal, and psychological – including employer and employee organizations, labor relations, personnel administration, social security and labor legislation". The IRRA also sought to stake out a neutral position vis-à-vis management and labour, stating in its constitution that "the Association will take no partisan attitude on questions of policy of labor, nor will it commit its members to any position of such question".

Thus, at least in word the IRRA was committed to including both the ILE and PM schools and to taking a neutral position regarding employers, unions, and the desirability of individual versus collective bargaining. However, the IRRA did not fully practise these principles.

The bulk of the people involved in establishing the IRRA were institutional-oriented labour economists and most of the early presidents also came from this group. Thus the ILE school in industrial relations effectively controlled the organization. Although the IRRA was established to promote the field of industrial relations, other motives were also present. One motive was related to science building. The ILE group set up the IRRA, in part, to serve as an alternative home to the AEA for labour economists interested in pursuing a more heterodox social/neo-institutional form of research (Kerr, 1983). Thus, while the IRRA was nominally oriented to all aspects of work and welcomed people from all scholarly disciplines and fields of study, in fact its centre of gravity was clearly in economics and the study of labour markets. Compounding the problem, some of the more prominent and influential ILE labour economists also took a sceptical and sometimes even hostile attitude toward the PM school and, in particular, human relations. This stance further cemented the IRRA's position as a *de facto* organization for heterodox labour economics. Trade unionist and IRRA president Solomon Barkin noted this characteristic of the association when he stated (quoted in Cochrane, 1979: 128),

> The great misfortune in the development of the Association was that it was dominated by the academics who adapted themselves to the presence of other groups but who provided no strong guidance toward broadening its membership or in offering new scope. Repeatedly gestures were made to extend the subject matter by inviting academics from other disciplines to speak. But these intermittent efforts proved insufficient. The permanent leadership of the organization never strove to devise a workable formula.

Then, the ethical/ideological face of industrial relations also entered. Most of the ILE labour economists were strong supporters of the principle of collective bargaining and industrial pluralism. A number also made significant second incomes from labour arbitration and thus had a vested interest in maintaining the labour–management system, while several had earlier worker in union staff positions (e.g., Barbash, Kassalow, Stern at Wisconsin). While in principle, therefore, the IRRA took an even-handed attitude toward employers and unions, in practice an ideological streak ran through the organization that favoured collective bargaining, took a more sympathetic stance toward unions than employers, viewed practices of personnel management and human relations as suspiciously tainted with anti-unionism, and effectively made non-union employers *personae non gratae*. Although not a serious problem in the 1950s, these positions became increasingly problematic for industrial relations in later decades.

Industrial and Labor Relations Review

The third significant event in the late 1940s that signalled a much deeper institutionalization of the field was the founding in 1947 of the academic journal *Industrial and Labor Relations Review*. The journal was sponsored by Cornell's

245

ILR. The journal also adopted a broad interpretation of the term industrial relations, per its decision to include in the book review section of each issue a selection of publications spanning all work-related disciplines and topics pertinent to both employers and organized labour. The actual mix of articles published in the journal was heavily weighted, however, toward the ILE perspective, such as unions, collective bargaining and labour legislation. Twenty of the 26 articles ILE the first four issues, for example, dealt with these topics.

Research in the golden age

Following these three seminal developments in the mid–late 1940s, the industrial relations field in the United States grew rapidly and established what appeared to be a secure place in leading universities and the social sciences. I have elsewhere called this period, dating roughly from 1948 to 1960, the field's "golden age" in the United States (Kaufman, 1993).

One aspect of industrial relations that made it a golden age was the remarkable multidisciplinary group of scholars attracted to the field and the breadth, depth and quality of research they published. As noted above, the institutional labour economists were the core group in industrial relations of this period. Their research, while certainly oriented toward labour markets and wage determination more than any other subject, was nonetheless remarkably diverse and eclectic and spanned nearly all the major areas of industrial relations. In turn, this diversity reflected the fact that labour economics in the 1940s and 1950s was still heavily influenced by the institutional tradition and many people who graduated with economics degrees in this period (e.g., Herbert Heneman, Herbert Northrup, George Strauss) were as conversant with organizations and management as with markets. Thus the institutional labour economists of the 1950s wrote some of the most influential works on labour markets of this period (e.g., Reynolds, 1951; Lester, 1952). Then they moved into collective bargaining, analysing not only the union impact on labour markets but also the process and mechanics of collective bargaining, the theory of bargaining power and the evolutionary development of unions as organizations (Ross, 1948; Chamberlain, 1951; Reynolds and Taft, 1956; Lester, 1958). From there it was a short step to research on all aspects of labour law, including social security, minimum wages and government regulation of unions (e.g., Summers, 1958). Moving yet further afield, it turns out that most of the best-known textbook authors in personnel management in the 1950s were economists, such as Myers and Pigors (1951), Yoder (1959), and Strauss and Sayles (1960). Finally, we come to the other end of the spectrum from markets and find ILE economists doing pathbreaking work on management and organizations. Examples include Chamberlain (1948), Bakke (1950), Slichter, Healy and Livernash (1960).

Although the bulk of labour economists were affiliated with the ILE school, not all were. In the mid-1950s the Chicago school of economics was starting to emerge and Chicago was the home to what Kerr (1988) has called the "neoclassical restorationists" in labour economics. Notable names include Gary Becker, Greg Lewis, Melvin Reder and Albert Rees. All of these men wrote articles on industrial relations in the 1950s and most participated in IRRA meetings and published in the IRRA proceedings. Lewis' article on "Hours of work and hours of leisure", for example, arguably marks the beginning of the neoclassical restoration in labour economics (Kaufman, 1988) and it was published in the 1956 IRRA proceedings.

Industrial relations also attracted a large number of researchers from other fields. Many were associated with the human relations movement and the budding field of management. Among the important names were anthropologists, such as Conrad Arensberg, Eliot Chapple and Lloyd Warner; psychologists, such as Chris Argyris Fredrick Herzberg, Daniel Katz, Arthur Kornhauser and Douglas McGregor; and sociologists, such as George Homans, Wilbert Moore, William Foote Whyte and Harold Wilensky. McGregor was a member of the Industrial Relations Section at MIT and went on to achieve fame for his "theory x and theory y" models of work motivation (McGregor, 1960); Whyte was a member of the Cornell School of Industrial and Labor Relations and went on to become a founder of the new field of organizational behaviour (OB) (Whyte, 1965); while Argyris was affiliated with the Yale Human Relations Center and later became one of the most influential OB theorists (e.g., Argyris, 1957). A wide group of other non-economists, with no connection to human relations (indeed, some were hostile to it), were also attracted to the field, including sociologists, such as Reinhard Bendix, Robert Dubin and C. Wright Mills; law, such as Benjamin Aaron and Clyde Summers; political science, such as Lloyd Fischer; history, such as Irving Bernstein; and management, such as Herbert Simon.[4]

Women were not well represented in post-Second World War American industrial relations. The recitation of authors on the last several pages contains the names of practically no women and, indeed, very few were in the field. The paucity of woman is also revealed by looking at the list of authors and presenters at annual IRRA meetings. In several years (e.g., 1954) not a single woman is on the programme (revealed by the table of contents of the annual proceedings), while in others (1953, 1960) one woman is included – compared to 30 to 40 men. Not until 1988 was the first woman (and African-American), Phyllis Wallace, elected to be an IRRA president. In the 1920s a significant-sized cadre of women were part of industrial relations, albeit not as professors but as leaders of foundations, social reform groups, government agencies, and personnel and welfare departments. The area of the field where women had the least representation, however, was in the "manly" practice of collective bargaining and labour relations. (Even the governing board of the International Ladies' Garment Workers' Union was for many years all men.) With the rise of unionism and collective bargaining in the 1935–55 period, the number of women in industrial relations shrank to a very small number and the field became quite literally a "boys' club". Only in the 1980s did the representation of women in industrial relations begin to substantially increase (and the boys' club become an "old boys' club").

For a brief period in the 1950s, a remarkable constellation of scholars from all the diverse fields affiliated with the ILE and PM schools conducted labour-oriented research and engaged in dialogue and joint research under the intellectual umbrella of industrial relations. Several examples provide evidence. One is the book *Industrial sociology* by Miller and Form (1951). They present a comprehensive bibliography of industrial relations research, divided into eleven distinct disciplinary or theoretical points of view. Among the branches of industrial relations are: institutional, industrial and labour economics; industrial sociology; human relations; industrial management; personnel management; and industrial psychology.

A second example is a massive bibliography of the industrial relations field compiled a few years later by Wilensky (1954), entitled *Syllabus of industrial relations*. He divides the subject matter of the field into five principal areas: the characteristics and direction of development of urban industrial society; the organization of work in industrial society (including labour markets and the management of human resources), trade union history, organization, administration and impact; collective bargaining systems, processes and issues; and public policy. Listed for each section is a cross-section of academic journals that span a wide swathe of the social sciences (e.g., *Journal of Applied Psychology, Harvard Business Review, American Economic Review*). Of relevance for later discussion, Wilensky (p. 6) also notes that "few students identified with the field confine it only to union–management or employee relations".

A third example of the intellectual breadth and multidisciplinary nature of industrial relations research of this period is the book *Industrial conflict* (1954), edited by Arthur Kornhauser (psychology), Arthur Ross (economics) and Robert Dubin (sociology). It contained contributions from over thirty scholars, including many of the most prominent names in industrial relations from economics, psychology, sociology, law and history.

A further example is the IRRA's 1960 research volume, entitled *Employment relations research* (Heneman et al., 1960). Among the editors and authors were George Shultz and Arnold Weber, later United States Secretary of State and president of Northwestern University, respectively. Individual chapters covered a wide and diverse set of topics spanning both the PM and ILE perspectives: "The labor force and labor markets", "Selection and placement – The past ten years", "Employee and executive compensation", Public policy and dispute resolution", "History and theory of the labor movement", and "Technological change and industrial relations".

The battle over human relations

No other time in the history of American industrial relations witnessed such a broad, interdisciplinary coalition of scholars working together in the field. Unfortunately, centrifugal forces were also at work weakening and pulling this coalition apart. The most visible was the "spectacular academic battle" (Landsberger, 1958: 1), which developed during the 1940s and 1950s between the proponents and critics of the human relations approach to industrial relations – a division that corresponded closely to the historic division of the field into the PM and ILE schools.

The battle lines over human relations tended to form around the "externalist" versus "internalist" distinction earlier made. Scholars who took an external perspective on the cause of labour problems were generally in the camp of the critics, although it may be said that a number were not so much critical as indifferent. Included in this group were most of the ILE labour economists, including Dunlop and Kerr, who took a strong and relatively uncompromising stance against human relations (Dunlop, 1950; Kerr and Fisher, 1957). Sociologists were deeply split about human relations, with one group from the macro/external side of sociology lining up with the critics and the other from the micro/internal side lining up with the proponents. Psychologists and anthropologists also tended to side with the proponents. And, of course, some scholars from both camps took an ecumenical view and endeavoured to integrate the best of both perspectives.

The critics attacked the human relations school on a variety of counts (Landsberger, 1958; Arensberg et al., 1957). Some argued, for example, that human relations research neglected the influence on industrial relations outcomes of external economic, social, political and technological conditions and overemphasized the influence of internal and individual social and psychological factors. Others claimed that the psychological and sociological variables focused upon in human relations research were not independent causal forces but were themselves intervening variables, and that human relationists overemphasized non-rational sentiments and non-pecuniary motives. Probably more important in motivating the critics was their perception that human relations either by design or effect was a manipulative managerial strategy to strengthen employer control over labour and keep the workplace union-free.

The proponents of human relations felt their position was frequently misinterpreted or caricatured by the critics and that at least some of their opponents were motivated by their own partisan ideological and disciplinary agendas. For example, to the proponents it appeared that the ILE leaders were simply dishing out to the human relations school the same imperialistic, dismissive treatment their own heterodox research had received at the hands of the neoclassical price theorists. To a degree the proponents tried to answer their critics (e.g., Arensberg and Tootle, 1957). They argued, for example, that they were not ignoring external forces but were simply taking them as a "given" in order to focus on the internal factors associated with small group dynamics, managerial leadership styles and individual psychological differences. They also accused the ILE group of treating organizations as a "black box". Towards the end of the 1950s, seeing that they were outgunned and the other side was not always interested in dialogue and compromise, the proponents of human relations quietly adopted a different strategy – instead of fighting they withdrew from industrial relations, with some returning to their home disciplines and others migrating to the new field of organizational behaviour.

By 1960, the academic guns largely fell silent in the battle over human relations with the ILE side firmly in control of the industrial relations field. The ILE victory was won at a significant price, however, for it helped push the management/internalist group out of industrial relations and, thus, destroy the coalition of PM and ILE schools that had existed since the field's founding in 1920.

Dunlop's *Industrial relations systems*

The zenith in the prestige and intellectual power of the American industrial relations field was reached in the late 1950s. Two books mark the summit. The first is the publication in 1958 of John Dunlop's *Industrial relations systems*. The book is widely viewed as one of the most influential pieces of scholarship ever written in the field and many would say the seminal work in industrial relations theory. Illustrative of this sentiment is Roberts' (1972: 263) claim that Dunlop's book is "without doubt the most important study in the field since the Second World War", Bellace's (1994: 20) statement that *Industrial relations systems* "is perhaps the most influential work of the last fifty years", and Cochrane's (1979: 97, emphasis in original) conclusion that:

> This book [Dunlop's] continues to be the basis for a large portion of industrial relations research around the world. It is impossible to emphasize too strongly how important this book has been for teaching of industrial relations in countries such as India. It is impossible to overemphasize the number of situations which have been *directly* shaped to conform with Dunlop's perception of a country's industrial relations system.

Dunlop sets out in the book to give industrial relations a new identity and definition. The traditional model of industrial relations, he claims, is largely defined by its problem-solving face and, in particular, its (p. 380) "preoccupation if not obsession with labor peace and warfare". This orientation is wanting, according to Dunlop, because it unduly restricts the subject matter of the field and focuses on subjects that are not amenable to analytical theory building. Dunlop's goal is to reorient industrial relations so that it rests on a foundation of theory, in the process changing it from a "meeting place of ideas" to a unique discipline.

Dunlop starts the book by bemoaning that industrial relations scholars have unduly focused on fact-gathering, descriptive studies and the faddish problems of the day at the expense of developing a generic theoretical structure for the field. In this regard, he states (pp. vi–vii):

> The field of industrial relations today may be described in the words of Julian Huxley: "Mountains of facts have been piled up on the plains of human ignorance. ... The result is a glut of raw material. Great piles of facts are lying around unutilized, or utilized only in an occasional manner." ... This volume reflects the judgement that far too much of the writing concerned with industrial relations ... has lacked intellectual rigor and discipline. The need has been for theoretical structure and orientation.

Highlighting the need for a theoretical structure, Dunlop proceeds to outline his version. He first offers a definition of industrial relations as (p. v) "the complex of interrelations among managers, workers, and agencies of government". Dunlop then introduces the core analytic concept: the *industrial relations system*. He states of this concept (p. 5), "An industrial relations system is to be viewed as an analytical subsystem of an industrial society on the same logical plane as an economic system. ... [It] is not coterminous with the economic system; in some respects the two overlap and in other respects both have different scopes." Dunlop further states that the central object (dependent variable) to be explained by the theory of an industrial relations system is (p. ix) "why particular rules are established in particular industrial relations systems and how and why they change in response to changes affecting the system". This task leads, in turn, to consideration of the *process* of rule making, called by Dunlop (pp. 26–27) the "common denominator" for comparative analysis of different industrial relations systems.

Dunlop then proceeds to flesh out the structure of the industrial relations system concept and the process that determines the *web of rules*. The web of rules concept was earlier developed by Kerr and Siegel (1955) who, it may be noted, are seldom given due credit by later authors (and only minimal credit by Dunlop). Dunlop argues that every industrial relations system is composed of three groups of actors: workers and their organizations, managers and their organizations, and government agencies concerned with the workplace. These three actors individually and jointly determine the web of rules that structures the industrial relations system. Although the process by which the rules are determined would appear to be at the core of his theory, Dunlop does not elaborate this component. He only notes (p. 13) that their determination may come about by management fiat in a non-union environment, joint deter-mination through collective bargaining, union fiat in syndicalist system, or fiat by government. Whatever the case, their choice of rules is constrained and shaped by three exogenous environmental constraints: technology, markets, and power/status relations. As one or more of these exogenous constraints change, so do elements in the web of rules. The last component of Dunlop's theory is ideology: the set of shared values and beliefs that help bind the system together and give it stability.

A large literature has developed over the years, analysing and critiquing Dunlop's model (e.g., Heneman, 1969; Wood et al., 1975; Meltz, 1993; Kaufman, 2004d). Without going into great detail, the most important points to make about it are the following.

First, the majority opinion is that Dunlop did not succeed in developing a genuine theory of industrial relations, where the sine qua non of a theory is ability to yield falsifiable hypotheses and predictions. What he provided is instead a taxonomy, conceptual framework and checklist. Nonetheless, one can state without fear of exaggeration that Dunlop's industrial relations system model has been by far the single most cited and influential conceptual construct ever published in industrial relations, not only in the United States but around the world. The basic framework developed by Dunlop soon became paradigmatic: an autonomous sphere of activity devoted to industrial relations; the union, employer and government actors; the economic, legal and techno-logical environment; the web of rules as the dependent variable; and a shared ideology. These elements, and the general concept of an industrial relations system, became the basic organizing framework for numerous textbooks, survey chapters and government reports.

Second, the most significant aspect of Dunlop's book is his attempt to reorient the subject matter and focus of industrial relations. Up to the time of his book, the emphasis in industrial relations was on the tenor of the relations between employers and employees – were they good, bad, peaceful or conflictual? Given this emphasis, strikes and other forms of conflict were the central dependent variable (implicitly if not explicitly) of industrial relations, and finding ways to promote harmony, cooperation and industrial peace was its central mission (recalling the origins of the field as a response to labour conflict and search for labour peace). But, claims Dunlop, this preoccupation with industrial peace and warfare, and the tenor of relations in general, turns the field into an applied art of problem solving and provides scant basis for the development of an analytical theory and, hence, science of industrial relations.

Dunlop in effect rotates the field on its conceptual axes. He argues that the focus of the field should be on the rules that structure the relations between employers and employees, such as labour laws, the rulings of arbitrators, compensation schedules and seniority provisions, since these rules in significant measure determine the industrial relations outcomes and behaviours. These rules thus become the dependent variable in industrial relations, the purpose of theory and research is to explain why different rules emerge, and each unique constellation of rules defines a different industrial relations system. The advantage of his conceptualization, Dunlop argues, is that it makes the dependent variable of industrial relations an observable construct that can be compared across industries, nations and time periods (as opposed to the unmeasurable "quality" of employer–employee relations). Moreover, it allows for the identification of a more compact and observable set of independent variables (e.g., financial resources of the rule makers as opposed to psychological determinants of cooperation versus conflict), and leads to the concept of an industrial relations system as a unique regime of rules. As others have noted (e.g., Kassalow, 1968), an equally important feature of Dunlop's model is that the concept of an industrial relations system is generic (if nonetheless descriptive) and thus provides an organizing framework for the field that is independent of particular national institutions and practices. In addition, a focus on "relations" almost inevitably introduces a normative element into the subject (are relations good or bad? What and whose criteria determine this judgement?), while an analysis of rules and institutions can proceed on a purely factual basis.

Third, given these (alleged) merits, Dunlop's proposed theory also has its problems and shortcomings. He does not, for example, include in the theory a model of the human agent, a model of the different processes that determine the rules, or an explanation for why one rule-making process is chosen over another. Nor is it clear that the rules of the workplace are the appropriate dependent variable in industrial relations research, as opposed to outcome variables such as wage rates, strikes and employee selection. Dunlop appears to assume that the rules more or less mechanically determine these outcomes (such as pay rates being determined by compensation schedules), but economists would claim that market forces of demand and supply, not institutionally determined rules, are the major influence on work outcomes, while behavioural scientists would look to psychological and sociological factors such as motivation and social class.

Fourth, although Dunlop (1988) consistently denied that his work had an intellectual link to institutional economics, the links are nonetheless plain to see in *Industrial relations systems*. Dunlop's industrial relations system can easily be thought of as a governance structure composed of a hierarchy of institutions, all bound together by what Dunlop calls the web of rules and Commons called the system of working rules of collective action. Within Dunlop's industrial relations system are markets, organizations (firms, unions, etc.) and units of government, and they yield outcomes, such as wage rates, employment levels, labour laws and strikes, through bargaining, rationing and managerial transactions. Also of note, Dunlop acknowledges that his theoretical model is based on earlier work by sociologist Talcott Parsons and that, as pointed out in Chapter 2, institutional economics is often considered to be a branch of economic sociology.

Fifth, although in principle the notion of an industrial relations system is generic and covers all forms of employment relations, in Dunlop's exposition the idea is largely coterminous with organized, collective forms of employment relations (i.e., systems of labour–management relations). Non-union employment situations are almost totally absent from the book, even though they are governed by their own web of rules, while separate chapters are devoted to rule making in unionized industries such as construction and coal mining. This omission, I conjecture, reflects both positive and normative commitments on Dunlop's part. In terms of a positive body of knowledge, Dunlop was prone to define industrial relations narrowly to largely include only the organized (collective) part of the employment relations system, per his statement in an earlier work (Dunlop, 1954: 92) that "the locus of industrial relations [is] ... union and management organizations and interactions at all levels". In terms of normative values, Dunlop was a lifelong believer in the value of collective bargaining and frequently expressed a sceptical attitude toward the field of human resource management ("descriptive and normative, without significant abstractions or analytical concepts") and employers' use of human relations practices (Dunlop, 1993: 5–6; Strauss, 1993).

Sixth, Dunlop largely excluded the PM school and the behavioural/administrative sciences from his theory of industrial relations systems. The organizational structure of firms, principles of management and practice of human resource management were all conspicuously absent. Also absent, as noted above, were most psychological or sociological aspects of industrial relations behaviour. In this respect the book was similar in orientation to mainstream economics.

Seventh, Dunlop's formulation also tends to make the industrial relations system relatively autonomous and self-contained vis-à-vis the larger economy, society and polity. As a consequence, scant attention is given to the role of the state in determining the web of rules and resource endowments of the actors. Larger political economy issues of class, power and control are also slighted. In addition, the model posits a shared ideology when in many countries the ideologies of labour and management are sharply opposed. His theory also focuses most attention on the intermediate (meso) level of the industrial relations system, where firms and unions engage in collective bargaining, thus neglecting industrial relations developments at the level of the shopfloor/labour process (micro) and at the level of the nation state (macro).

Eighth, and finally, the systems model is largely static in nature and has difficulty explaining in a substantively revealing way either evolutionary change or sudden transformations. It also leaves unanswered a range of important questions, such as the origin, structure and performance of institutions (trade unions, firms, etc.) and the shape and content of national ideologies.

Whatever its faults and shortcomings, there can be no gainsaying that Dunlop's *Industrial relations systems* made a tremendous impact on industrial relations. As Geare (1977: 276) observes, the book "has often been criticized but rarely ignored". In the American context, *Industrial relations systems* had a marked effect because it seemed to lay out another distinct crossroads for the field. One option was to remain on the traditional path, characterized by a multidisciplinary approach to the applied study of labour problems and industrial conflict. The other option was to follow Dunlop and turn industrial relations into a more narrowly constituted but theoretically informed discipline centred on the rules of the workplace, with a substantial orientation toward economics and collective bargaining and little direct contact with the management and the behavioural science parts of the PM school. As events developed over the next two decades, it is clear that the field chose to follow broadly the path laid out by Dunlop.

Industrialism and industrial man

The second book that marks the zenith of the American field is *Industrialism and industrial man* (1960) by Clark Kerr, John Dunlop, Fred Harbison and Charles

255

Myers. This book represents the largest and grandest attempt at theorizing in American industrial relations and, arguably, in the global history of the field.

Something of a boom in international and comparative industrial relations research occurred in the 1950s, particularly cross-national comparisons of industrial relations institutions and practices. In part, this newfound interest in the international dimension was spurred by the emigration to the United States of labour scholars from war-ravaged Europe. Prominent examples are Adolf Sturmthal from Austria and Reinhard Bendix from Germany.[5] Also operating at the time was a surge in scholarly interest in the role of labour in economic development, particularly in the newly independent countries of Asia and Africa. But more important was the fact the United States suddenly found itself after the end of the Second World War enmeshed in large-scale nation rebuilding in Europe and Japan and the Cold War battle to prevent communist takeover of these countries (Cochrane, 1979; Cox and Sinclair, 1996). Central to both tasks was reconstructing the industrial relations systems in countries such as Germany and Japan and keeping their labour movements from turning communistic. Americans were ethnocentric, however, and knew little about industrial relations in Europe and Asia. The result was to create an immediate need for greater knowledge and expertise on international industrial relations, and also to open up for the nation's new generation of industrial relations scholars a large research opportunity with the potential for generous government and foundation funding.

Into this opening walked four of the nation's most able and prominent labour economists and industrial relations scholars: Clark Kerr (Berkeley), John Dunlop (Harvard), Frederick Harbison (Chicago and later Princeton) and Charles Myers (MIT). Kerr took the initiative in 1951 and proposed to the Ford Foundation a multi-year research project initially titled "Labor relations and democratic policy" (Cochrane, 1979). The first paragraph of the proposal states (ibid., p. 61):

> It is the premise of this proposal that the condition, character, and beliefs of the working classes will be among the decisive influences upon the political structure of modern nations and therefore upon the prospects for domestic tranquillity and world peace. It follows that the United States in seeking the conditions of harmony among and within nations must be concerned with the economic, intellectual and psychological status of the working classes. The development of an effective American worldwide strategy demands a profound understanding of the position of the working class in a variety of societies.

Although the initial request was rejected, Kerr resubmitted a modified proposal, called Utilization of Human Resources, A Comparative Analysis, and it was accepted in 1952 with an initial grant of $80,000, with the clear recognition that this amount was seed money for a larger proposed project. Stated one Ford Foundation official in an internal memorandum recommending acceptance of the proposal (ibid., p. 59):

> The project would involve not only research in the sense of fact-gathering and appraisal but also consideration of possible action by the U.S. government for the purpose of influencing the development of the labour movement in other parts of the world and of encouraging the development of free rather than communist-controlled labour unions. I am convinced that this type of intellectual inquiry would be of very great practical importance to policy-makers in the government, in addition to its inherent intellectual value.

A year later Kerr submitted a proposal for a multi-year project called the Inter-University Study of Labor Problems in Economic Development. This proposal, while building on the first, represented a clear shift in orientation. De-emphasized was the labour movement and decisive role of the working class. In their place Kerr, Dunlop, Harbison and Myers proposed to focus on the process of industrialism and certain key labour problems that are crucial to the evolution and success of industrialism. They proposed to study initially five countries at various stages of development and then broaden the research to other countries. After much internal debate about the scale and feasibility of the project, the Ford Foundation awarded Kerr et al. a three-year grant of $475,000.

All told, the Inter-University Study project stretched over more than two decades, involved more than ninety scholars and investigators from more than a dozen countries, and received more than $1 million of funding from the Ford Foundation and, later, the Carnegie Corporation. In the context of the early 1950s, the money given to Kerr et al. was a huge amount and, to the dismay of some other labour researchers, effectively foreclosed funding for other projects for a number of years. Without question, the most influential publication to emerge from this gargantuan effort was Kerr et al.'s book *Industrialism and industrial man*. But many other publications were generated, including twelve books and more than twenty articles published during the 1950s. Over its entire life, the project produced ten conferences, about 40 books and over 50 published papers, ending with the Final report authored by the four principal investigators in 1975 (Dunlop, Harbison, Kerr and Myers, 1975; Cochrane, 1979).

Kerr et al. used the ILO as a hub for their international activities, published their first article of the project in the *International Labour Review* (Kerr et al., 1955), and Dunlop wrote *Industrial relations systems* while in residence in Geneva. As recounted in a later chapter, Kerr et al. had a significant effect in shaping ILO labour strategy and operational policy in the late 1950s and 1960s.

Kerr et al. were also highly influential in spreading the industrial relations field outside its narrow Anglo-American base. Many of the project's conferences were held in the countries under study, such as Egypt, India and Japan, and were the first time that many of the scholars in those countries had personal contact with the subject of industrial relations. Kerr et al. also formed contacts with a number of highly placed government officials in these countries, particularly in labour ministries, which also helped establish a foothold for industrial relations. Also of great significance, Kerr et al. recruited indigenous scholars from these countries to work with them (and other American academics) as field investigators and co-authors of books and articles. Representative books include Frederick Harbison and Ibrahim A. Ibrahim (1958), *Human resources for Egyptian enterprises*, Charles Myers and Subbiah Kannappan (1970), *Industrial relations in India*, and Solomon Levine and Hisashi Kawada (1980), *Human resources in Japanese industrial development*. Kerr et al. spent a good part of several years criss-crossing the globe in slow-moving propeller airplanes to reach then remote countries, earning them the sobriquet "the four horsemen".

In the Introduction to *Industrialism and industrial man*, Kerr et al. candidly state (p. 6): "we failed to find some things we expected to find, but we found some other things instead. ... The major point we 'unlearned' [was that labour] protest was not such a dominant aspect of industrialization, and it did not have such an effect on the course of society as we once thought." They go on to say (pp. 7–8):

> Instead of concentrating so much on protest, we turned to the really universal phenomenon affecting workers – the inevitable structuring of the managers and the managed in the course of industrialization. Everywhere there develops a complex web of rules binding the worker into the industrial process, to his job, to his community, to patterns of behaviour. ... Not the handling of protest but the structuring of the labor force is *the* labor problem in economic development. So we turned from concentration on protest to the problem of providing a structure for the managers and the managed.

Then, at the end of the Introduction, they state (p. 12):

> We offer here an approach to understanding of industrial relations which seeks to draw on the experience of several countries rather than of one or a few; and a way of looking at the problem which seeks to place labor–management–state relations in the context of the imperatives of industrialism, the desires of the controlling elites

and the demands of the particular environment. ... This approach runs against tradition; against Marx, the Webbs, Commons and Perlman, and Mayo, alike. We have redefined the labor problem as the structuring of the managers and the managed under industrialization rather than as the response of unions to capitalism.

Probably the best known and most discussed proposition that emerged from *Industrialism and industrial man* is the "convergence hypothesis" (Cochrane, 1979). In a nutshell, the convergence hypothesis maintains that the process of industrialization causes nations to move toward a common form of social/economic order they call "industrial pluralism", characterized by an open and mobile society, an educated and technocratic workforce, a pluralistic set of organized interest groups, a reduced level of industrial conflict, and increasing government regulation of the labour market. Also noteworthy are several other propositions or perspectives. One, for example, is Kerr et al.'s contention that labour economists and industrial relations scholars had too narrowly concentrated on labour problems in capitalist societies when the industrial-ization process is really the generic phenomenon needing study. Given this perspective, they also expressed considerable dissatisfaction with existing theories of the labour movement, viewing them as too ethnocentric and narrowly linked to particular forms of capitalism. A second proposition that subsequently received relatively little notice and commentary is their contention that the prime mover in shaping the course of industrialism is not the labour movement and class conflict but the strategies and values of the managers and other "modernizing elites". A third proposition is that the working class becomes increasingly integrated into society as industrialism progresses, unions evolve from class-based protest organizations to occupational interest groups to professional associations, and overt conflict in the form of strikes, protests and other disturbances gradually diminishes. The last proposition was also put forward by Ross and Hartman (1960) who framed it in terms of the "withering of the strike". No one at the time went on to consider whether the field of industrial relations would survive the conversion of trade unions into professional associations and the withering of the strike, but given recent trends and the advantage of hindsight one can quickly appreciate the virtue of Dunlop's attempt to shift the field from a focus on industrial conflict to a web of rules.

As is true of Dunlop's *Industrial relations systems* book, Kerr et al.'s *Industrialism and industrial man* has been the subject of considerable debate and criticism over the years. Without reviewing all of the arguments for and against, a few salient points nonetheless deserve mention.

First, like Dunlop's book, *Industrialism and industrial man* has a number of links to the institutional tradition in labour economics. On a theory level, the parallel between Commons' concept of working rules and Kerr et al.'s web of rules has already been noted. Critics also pointed to a second link with institutionalism. In his review of the book, for example, Chamberlain (1961: 476) states,

A framework of analysis and an approach to a denationalized understanding of industrial relationships is here, but I have searched in vain for the theory. The book is long on categories and classifications and impressionistic observations, but it is short on analysis. It is perhaps best described as a latter-day descendant of the 19th century German school of economic history; whose hallmark was a literary exposition of the transition from one idealized state of economic development to another.

Economist Gary Becker (quoted in Cochrane, 1979: 137) voices the same complaint, saying that the research in *Industrialism and industrial man* is "individualistic" (idiosyncratic and incapable of being generalized, like the findings of case studies) and not "programmatic" (yielding theoretical constructs of broad applicability), like the notions of human capital and of demand and supply in neoclassical economics.

A second point is that Kerr et al. wrote *Industrialism and industrial man* with the intent of fundamentally reshaping the domain and character of discourse in the field of industrial relations. As they saw it, the field was too preoccupied with American conditions and narrow issues of collective bargaining and labour policy. Although one can argue that this view of the field reflected their own preconceptions, the fact remains that Kerr et al. made a great effort to broaden the field by introducing the comparative, international dimension and expanding the nature of the labour problem to include the processes of industrialization and economic development. An example of this goal in action is illustrated by the subtitle chosen for the second American scholarly industrial relations journal, *Industrial Relations*, headquartered at the University of California, Berkeley. Reflecting Kerr's influence and intellectual agenda, it is expansively framed *A Journal of Economy and Society*. As described in a later chapter, this effort at broadening and internationalizing the American industrial relations field was for the next two decades largely unsuccessful and, indeed, events went in the opposite direction.

Third, one must also note certain ironic aspects of *Industrialism and industrial man*. Kerr et al., for example, end up downgrading the role of the labour movement and giving pride of place in their new theory of industrial relations to managers and other elites. Their emphasis on the role of elites is also paradoxical given Kerr's stinging attack on the human relations school for (allegedly) elevating managers to a paternalistic elite charged with leading the malleable worker "aborigines" (Kerr and Fisher, 1957). Finally, although Dunlop in *Industrial relations systems* appears to dismiss the utility of the "labour problems" concept for industrial relations theorizing and attacks the penchant of earlier industrial relations scholars to "grub for facts", in *Industrialism and industrial man* the labour problem reappears as a central construct while Dunlop and his colleagues circled the globe grubbing for their own facts in order to inductively generate the theory in the book. In general, an odd and never explained disjunction exists between the theoretical frameworks developed by Dunlop in *Industrial relations systems* and Kerr et al. in *Industrialism and industrial man*.

Fourth, despite the massive amount of time, effort and creativity that went into *Industrialism and industrial man*, one must conclude that in the long run the book has had a surprisingly modest influence on the intellectual (science-building) side of the industrial relations field. The book is rarely cited in the modern literature and, except for occasional references to the convergence hypothesis, has generated little in the way of ideas or concepts that are used in other research work. Also surprising, rather than generating a wave of follow-up research and dialogue, the publication of *Industrialism and industrial man* seemed to be followed by a noticeable "thud" and then silence, as if the definitive word on the subject had just been spoken and nothing was left to say or add.

Notes

[1] While Commons had earlier in his career also believed in the income redistribution and underconsumption theory of business cycles and depressions (what he called the 'profit share' theory) professed by Roosevelt, Wagner and many ILE supporters, in the 1920s he shifted to a monetary theory of cycles and never abandoned it (Kaufman 2003c). Writing in 1934, for example, Commons states (1934b: 189), "I had learned in my Syracuse days [in the 1890s] to look upon the money question as the most important of all labor problems". Thus while Commons most certainly advocated greater collective bargaining and supported the Wagner Act in broad principle, he believed that the crucial factor causing the Depression was a lack of adequate money and credit in the world economy and that the path to macroeconomic recovery was monetary expansion by the world's central banks. For this reason, Commons did not become as disillusioned with non-union welfare capitalist employers as did other ILE proponents because he saw that the collapse of the economy made it impossible for them to maintain progressive industrial relations practices. In this vein, he states (1934b: 192), "I could not blame the capitalists. They too were victims." Likewise, Commons did not swing as far in support of mass unionization of industry as did Wagner and Leiserson; Commons thought the Federal Reserve was the key to recovery, while the latter promoted a union-led wage recovery programme (complemented by income redistribution and higher wages to be generated by a national minimum wage, shorter working hours and old-age pension laws). The genesis and role of the Wagner Act as an economic recovery measure, and the perspective of Roosevelt and Wagner on the cause and solution of the Depression, is discussed in Kaufman (1996).

[2] A second important irony should also be noted. While the New Deal tilt toward collective bargaining and labour law tended to drive away one part of the industrial relations' community within the United States (the PM school), globally viewed this tilt made the field considerably more attractive and compatible in Europe and Australasia (with much stronger union movements and/or regimes of legal regulation) and thus facilitated the spread of industrial relations to these parts of the world after the Second World War.

[3] Part of the problem in fixing the intellectual place of this new generation of labour economists is that they shifted emphasis depending on the issue at hand. The clearest case is Dunlop, who in certain places would criticize economists for not considering informal work groups and the political nature of unions but then in other circumstances would dismiss human relations as inconsequential and a political model of unions as misconceived.

[4] C. Wright Mills is very rarely mentioned by modern American industrial relations scholars yet, interestingly, Richard Hyman (1994b: 158) claims that he was "the most important theorist in the last half century to write on industrial relations in North America".

[5] The brain drain from Europe was large. For example, according to Müller-Jentsch (2002: 228) two-thirds of German academic sociologists emigrated during the Nazi period.

THE INSTITUTIONALIZATION OF INDUSTRIAL RELATIONS IN AUSTRALASIA, CANADA AND THE UNITED KINGDOM

5

This chapter carries forward the development of the industrial relations field in other countries of the world from the end of the Second World War to the mid-1960s. During this period, the field is still almost entirely limited to North America, the United Kingdom and a handful of former British colonies. The last chapter examined the United States; this chapter turns to these other countries and regions. Included are Australasia (Australia and New Zealand), Canada and the United Kingdom. Developments in India and South Africa are reserved for a later chapter.

Although the industrial relations field had a toehold in the United Kingdom before the Second World War, only after the war did the field really become established and develop a presence in the academic world. The most important development in British industrial relations of this period is the emergence and rise to international prominence of the Oxford school. Also appearing in this time period were other signs of the field's institutionalization in British academia, including a growing network of well-known industrial relations scholars, the first master's programme in industrial relations, the first industrial relations journal, and the country's first professional association for industrial relations academics.

Attention then shifts to Australasia and Canada. Not coincidentally, Australia, Canada and New Zealand are not only Anglophone countries but also have close intellectual and cultural connections with the United States and the United Kingdom. Although relatively small, the field of industrial relations in these countries became firmly established and began to develop a community of scholars, with the supporting infrastructure of teaching programmes, journals and professional associations.

Developments in the United Kingdom

The field of industrial relations began to coalesce and take on an institutional presence in the United Kingdom after the Second World War. It did so, however, on a much smaller scale and without the broad disciplinary representation found in the United States. The golden age of the field in the United Kingdom actually came later – roughly 1965–79, a period covered by a later chapter. Nonetheless, the two decades from 1945 to 1965 effectively laid the foundation for what is now the British field of industrial relations.

As described in an earlier chapter, the industrial relations field's only visible institutionalization during the 1930s was in the form of the three Montague Burton chairs in industrial relations. But, according to Bain and Clegg (1974: 98), "they [the chairs] did not contribute much to the development of the subject until the 1960s". Marsh (1968: 66) states more generally of this period in the United Kingdom:

> During the 1930s the study in the industrial relations field languished. The depth of the economic crisis, the plight of the unemployed, the weakness of the unions, and the overwhelming importance of the economic policy debate overlaid all other considerations. Looking back to the 1930s produces an impression of stagnation.

But immediately after the Second World War the vital signs of the industrial relations field started to quicken.

The institutionalization of British industrial relations

The first visible evidence of industrial relations' institutionalization in the 1940s was the establishment of a one-year course in trade union studies at the LSE in 1945. Roberts (1972) relates that the idea of the course originated with R.H. Tawney, who had been assigned by the Ministry of Labour to spend the war in the United States reporting back on the attitudes of the American trade unions which, the British believed, had a good deal of influence over Roosevelt.

The trade union studies course was a precursor to industrial relations, but according to Bain and Clegg (1974: 98), "No other academic posts in industrial relations were established [after the three Burton chairs] until 1949 when appointments were made at Oxford, the London School of Economics, and Manchester."

Without question, the most important of these appointments for the future development of British industrial relations took place at Oxford. Allan Flanders was appointed senior lecturer in industrial relations in October 1949, and, coincidentally, Hugh Clegg was in the same month appointed a fellow of one of Oxford's graduate colleges, Nuffield. Clegg and Flanders formed the nucleus for what later developed into the Oxford school of industrial relations – universally agreed to be the pre-eminent group in British industrial relations through the mid-1960s. According to Clegg (1990), no degree programme or diploma was established in industrial relations at Oxford, but Clegg, Flanders and Kenneth Knowles (hired at Oxford to conduct a statistical study of strikes) joined forces to teach a weekly class in industrial relations. Illustrative of the subject's tenuous academic standing at the time, Clegg relates that it was mainly attended by students of Ruskin College – an adult education college affiliated with Oxford that catered to working-class students and staff of trade unions.

The next step in the institutionalization of the field was the establishment of the British Universities Industrial Relations Association (BUIRA). Its history has been detailed by Berridge and Goodman (1988). The genesis of the association was a meeting held in 1950 at the University of Manchester by a group of fourteen academics, coming from Oxford (3), Manchester (3), Glasgow (2), London (2), Leeds (2), Cardiff (1), and Cambridge (1). Professors H.A. Turner and Arthur Lewis played a leading role in convening the meeting (Roberts, 1972: 260). The outcome was the decision to form an association of academics interested in industrial relations and sponsor an annual conference. Unlike the American IRRA, the BUIRA was set up to include only academics. The original name for the group was the Inter-University Study Group in Industrial Relations, changed to BUIRA in 1967. Perhaps reflective of the tradition of informalism in British industrial relations, the group had no written rules or by-laws for the first 17 years of its life.

BUIRA started out with 18 members and grew slowly but steadily until by 1960 membership stood at 88. (By way of contrast, in the American IRRA academic membership in 1960 was nearly 600.) The largest disciplinary representation was economics. The association did not attempt to put down in black and white a definition of the industrial relations field, but Berridge and Goodman (1988) relate that it was the subject of considerable debate among the founders. Perhaps the greatest agreement was reached on what industrial relations was not, such as the statement that industrial relations was "not a branch of economics merely" and was "wider than the 'Trade Union' Studies".

The next step in the institutionalization of industrial relations in the United Kingdom was the publication in 1954 of two books that represented the first textbooks of the post-Second World War period. The first was J. Henry Richardson's *An introduction to the study of industrial relations* and the second the edited volume by Allan Flanders and Hugh Clegg, *The system of industrial relations in Great Britain*. The latter proved particularly influential and, according to Lord William McCarthy (quoted by Brown, 1997: 146), is the point where "the systematic study of industrial relations began". The two books exhibit an interesting contrast, as will be described shortly.

Although industrial relations was sprinkled across a number of British universities in the 1950s, the field developed the greatest institutional presence at Oxford. Starting with Clegg and Flanders, Oxford added a number of other new faculty members with interests in industrial relations in the 1950s and 1960s, in the process forming the most prominent and productive group of industrial relations scholars in the country. Several, such as famed labour law scholar Otto Kahn-Freund, came to Oxford from other universities.[1] But most new industrial relations faculty staff at Oxford were "home grown". Among this group were Alan Fox, Arthur Marsh, William McCarthy and Derek Robinson. Fox and McCarthy, for example, obtained diplomas at Ruskin, gained admittance at Oxford to do graduate work and later obtained appointments as Oxford faculty members. Fox started at Oxford in various research posts, became a lecturer in industrial sociology, and became one of the leading intellects in British industrial relations in the 1970s. As the reputation of the Oxford industrial relations programme spread, it also started to attract graduate students from other countries, some of whom also took positions at Oxford or other English universities; a prominent example is George Bain (from Canada).

Next in the evolution of British industrial relations is the establishment of that country's first academic journal devoted to the field, the *British Journal of Industrial Relations*. The BUIRA had early on considered establishment of a journal, but decided that the small readership base meant that such an endeavour would not be financially viable. In 1962, the idea was taken up again, spear-headed by Ben Roberts (Gennard, 1986). He secured a charitable grant to support the journal and the commitment of the LSE to provide institutional support. The first issue appeared in 1963 and continues to be published today, widely recognized as one of the leading industrial relations journals in the world. Roberts remained editor until 1984; the current chief editor is Stephen Wood.

It was only in 1964, at the LSE, that the first master's degree programme in industrial relations in the United Kingdom was established (Gennard, 1986). Contemporaneously, a separate Department of Industrial Relations was created. Thus industrial relations at LSE had a remarkably long gestation period before it emerged as a bona fide teaching and research area, given that Sidney Webb founded LSE in the last years of the nineteenth century and he and Beatrice published one of the landmark books in the field (*Industrial democracy*, 1897) at practically the same time. For the first few years at the LSE, industrial relations and personnel management were kept separate, but later the Personnel Management Course in the Department of Social Administration was merged into the Industrial Relations Department. Reflecting on the creation of the department, Roberts (1972: 259) relates, "By the early 1960s it was apparent that interest in industrial relations was growing considerably and the number of graduate students was steadily increasing. I became convinced that we needed a department to coordinate our interdisciplinary activities."

Next to the formation of the Oxford school, the most significant event moving British industrial relations to the take-off stage came in 1965 with the government's creation of the Royal Commission on Trade Unions and Employers' Associations, popularly referred to as the Donovan Commission in honour of its chair (Clegg, 1990). The Commission was formed by the new Labour government headed by Harold Wilson amidst a backdrop of mounting economic and industrial difficulties, including lagging productivity and competitiveness, chronic inflation pressure and balance of payments problems, and increasingly chaotic shopfloor relations in unionized industries and mounting numbers of unofficial strikes. The United Kingdom was developing the unenviable reputation as the "sick man of Europe" and many people inside and outside the country were coming to the conclusion that part of the explanation lay with the nature of the British industrial relations system. Appointed to the twelve-person Commission were Clegg and Kahn-Freund from Oxford, while McCarthy was appointed as Research Director. Contemporaneously, Flanders was appointed to a position on the Prices and Incomes Board (charged with administering national wage–price guidelines).

The Donovan Commission greatly accelerated the acceptance and spread of the industrial relations field in the United Kingdom. Indeed, Martin (1998: 91) refers to the Donovan Commission as "the summit of the influence of the British industrial relations community". Previous government commissions had been appointed to investigate capital–labour relations and had sporadically used the term industrial relations, but the term had never been "canonized" in the public consciousness, as had happened in the United States with the Commission on Industrial Relations. Although the official name of the Donovan Commission omitted the term, the proceedings of the Commission, its final report and the dozens of studies it spawned were all framed in terms of the question of industrial relations. In a tangible, way, therefore, the Commission put industrial relations on the public stage in a way it had never before enjoyed and gave it the government's official imprimatur. Equally important, the Commission's work, and the central role played by the Oxford school, paved the way for the introduction of industrial relations courses and programmes into a number of new universities. And, finally, the Commission and its substantial research budget made possible the funding of dozens of reports and studies on industrial relations, significantly enhancing the knowledge base of the field and attracting top-flight academic talent to the subject. Alan Fox's several well-regarded books on industrial relations published in the 1970s, for example, have roots in the work he did for the Donovan Commission (Fox, 1966, 1974).

The subject matter and method of British industrial relations

Knowing the institutional developments, we now need to ask how British scholars in this period approached industrial relations in terms of subject area and research method.

To start, one needs to ask: why did industrial relations in the United Kingdom begin to show more activity after the Second World War? One answer, according to McCarthy (1994: 210), was the emergence of three societal problems related to industrial relations: wage drift, the inadequate utilization of labour, and the rise in unofficial strikes. He also notes that another major stimulus was the growth of various tripartite government boards, agencies and commissions, all of which created a demand for academic industrial relations experts. A more detailed perspective is provided by Allen (1972: 17). He states:

> In 1945 the economists, constructing even more complicated models, were preoccupied with repairing the breach caused by Keynes; sociologists were still social pathologists; and economic historians were continuing to read the Webbs for their lectures. The collective or individual activities of labour played virtually no part in their university curricula, and no part at all in their researches. Then quite suddenly the situation changed [with the incoming of the third Labour government and the crisis of British competitiveness in the world economy]. Labour in all its aspects became nationally important. The level of wages influenced the level of prices, which influenced the level of exports. What determined the level of wages? Strikes reduced the national product. What caused strikes? Workers' attitudes were influenced by long-established traditions. What was their history? Full employment had removed the 'economic whip'. What was the substitute? These and other questions became of vital national importance. Various members of the social science faculties rushed to the colours and gave answers. ... The emphasis shifted from regarding trade unions purely as vehicles for social change to looking at them as productive agents. Individual workers were brought prominently into the picture. What could make them work harder? Here was an opening for the psychiatrist. Coloured machines? Work time music? How did they work best? In groups or individually? What was the principal incentive? Money? Here was an opening for everybody.

The next interesting issue is how the field of industrial relations was conceived in the United Kingdom. In the United States, the term industrial relations in the 1950s was generally defined broadly to include all types of employment relationships, although as noted in the previous chapter some tendency existed among the ILE segment to take a narrower view. This trend was even more evident in the United Kingdom, reflecting in part the almost total absence of a self-identified management-oriented PM wing to the field.

The dual (broad/narrow) vision of industrial relations in the United Kingdom is acknowledged by Behrend (1963: 383), noting: "The term industrial relations is used in two different senses: it is sometimes used as an all-inclusive term and sometimes as a term restricted to collective relations."

One of the few industrial relations publications of the period that prominently featured the all-inclusive perspective is Richardson's industrial relations text (cited earlier). Richardson was Montague Burton Professor of Industrial Relations at the University of Leeds and in the early 1930s had written a lengthy report, *Industrial relations in Great Britain*, for the ILO. As mentioned in the previous chapter, Richardson's research was partially funded by Rockefeller-affiliated Industrial Relations Counselors, Inc., and Richardson had visited the United States and Canada in the late 1920s to study systems of labour–management cooperation and employee representation. Only with this background knowledge is it possible to appreciate Richardson's unique (for the United Kingdom) approach to developing the subject of industrial relations.

Speaking of industrialist Montague Burton, but also reflective of the position earlier taken by Rockefeller, Richardson (1954: 5) states in the Introduction: "He [Burton] believed that such conflicts were frequently based on misunderstandings, and that the universities could make a contribution to improvements in industrial relations by systematic and impartial studies and investigations, and by the training of students who would later undertake responsibilities for dealing with human problems in industry." Richardson goes on to state that industrial relations as a subject is (p. 12)

> concerned with relations between the parties in industry, particularly with the determination of working conditions. No advantage would be gained in attempting a more precise definition of the boundaries, as there are considerable areas of 'no man's land' with other subjects. The emphasis, however, is upon 'relations,' human relations in the processes of production.

Several pages later he tells the reader (p. 18), "Industrial relations can conveniently be divided into four parts: (1) Relations within the undertaking, (2) Collective relations, (3) The function of the State, (4) International aspects." The inclusion of the first part (relations within the undertaking) is the province of the PM school and, practically unique to a British text, Richardson features it first in his book and devotes eight chapters to the subject (e.g., personnel management, selection, training, etc.). Collective relations come next but get only six chapters. Partially justifying this greater weight to PM topics, Richardson says (p. 20), "In the U.S.A. before the New Deal ... the central features [of industrial relations] were personnel management, labour incentives, time studies, and other aspects of relations within the undertaking."

More often, however, British academics adopted the narrow conceptualization of industrial relations. Phelps Brown (1959: 114) opens his chapter on the "Development of industrial relations" with the declaration that "The story of modern British industrial relations begins with the beginnings of the unions." A focus on trade unions, and largely the institutional aspects of that subject, remained the defining feature of British industrial relations for most of the remainder of the twentieth century. For example, sociologist Tom Burns wrote in 1967 that labour problems grow out of two key aspects of the employment relationship: the dominated nature of the relationship in which some people (managers) wield power over others (workers), and the constraining and stultifying effect of division of labour. He argues that the social scientist's primary interest is in understanding the responses to these conditions, which he categorizes into institutional responses (e.g., forming a trade union) and individual responses (e.g., resigning). He then states (p. 195), "It is the first of these subdivisions to which the title 'industrial relations' has been appropriated for text-books and, indeed, government publications. Normally, it is reserved for all aspects of collective bargaining between employers and labour, whether the issues are national or local."

The major figures in British industrial relations in this period also took this perspective. Flanders and Clegg (1954), for example, exclude personnel management and human relations from the field of study and instead concentrate (p. v) "on the formal institutions of industrial relations". Reflective of the roots of the institutional approach in early English and German historical economics, they go on to say, "Most of the chapters include a substantial historical section. ... Institutions are not separable from their history." In a later essay, Flanders (1965: 10) again took the position that industrial relations covered only collective aspects of employment relations, stating "the subject [industrial relations] deals with certain regulated or institutionalized relationships in industry. Personal, or in the language of sociology 'unstructured', relationships have their importance for management and workers, but they lie outside the scope of a system of industrial relations." Influenced by Dunlop, Clegg (1972: 1) later says of the question "what is industrial relations?" that "[t]he answer which is now generally given is that they deal with the rules which govern employment. Sometimes these are described as the rules which regulate jobs, so that industrial relations could be briefly defined as the study of job-regulation."

As is evident from these quotations, British academics such as Clegg and Flanders were not particularly receptive to or interested in the PM side of the employment relationship and took a less inclusive view of the subject than did Richardson (Lyddon, 2003). During the period considered in this chapter, they were instead well within what in the American context I have called the ILE school, albeit a truncated version. After the Donovan Commission investigations, they broadened their perspective and management began to take on a larger if still somewhat critically viewed presence.

Regarding the ILE link, it is interesting to note that Flanders, Clegg and like-minded colleagues of the 1950s were explicitly called members of the institutional school of industrial relations (Fogarty, 1955). The appellation "institutional" connoted many of the same features as did the term in America, but not all. As applied to Flanders and Clegg, the term meant a focus on formal institutions and collective relations in the work world, a penchant for a historical and descriptive treatment of the subject, an effort to be interdisciplinary (only modestly practised and realized), and an open sympathy for the main object of study (trade unions). It is also, according to Marsh (1968: 70), "a denial of the validity of economic determinism". Where the British institutional tradition differed from the American was in having less direct linkage to the discipline of economics in general and practically none to institutional economics per se (outside the ideas coming from the Webbs), while giving more attention to sociologists such as Durkheim. Broadly viewed, it seems fair to say that problem solving far overshadowed science building among both the British and American industrial relations institutionalists, but particularly among the former.

But the ILE version of British industrial relations was also narrower than the American version. As noted in an earlier chapter, the American problem-solving version of industrial relations focused on, respectively, the employers' solution, the workers' solution and the community's solution to labour problems. American ILE scholars, though they gave considerable emphasis to trade unions and collective bargaining, nonetheless wrote extensively from the 1920s through the 1950s on aspects of management, labour law and social insurance. British industrial relations academics, on the other hand, focused much more exclusively on trade unions and wrote relatively little on these other approaches to problem solving. Management is discussed below, so attention here is given to labour law and social insurance.

Part of the distinctive character of the industrial relations field in each nation is shaped by strengths, weaknesses and special attributes of the neighbouring disciplines and fields it draws on. British industrial relations is a good case in point. The field of labour law in the United Kingdom was not well developed in this period, in large part because the British industrial relations system remained largely unstructured by law and public regulation. No British version of the American National Labor Relations Act existed, with its myriad rules governing union recognition, unfair labour practices, mandatory subjects of bargaining and prohibited weapons such as secondary boycotts. Nor was there any attempt to regulate internal union affairs as there had been in the United States with the Landrum–Griffin (1959) amendment to the National Labor Relations Act. The United Kingdom did not even enact a national minimum wage law until the late 1990s. The determined adherence to voluntarism and what Kahn-Freund famously labelled "collective laissez-faire" thus made labour law a peripheral subject in British industrial relations – despite the fact that Kahn-Freund was considered one of the world's leading labour law scholars (Clegg, 1983). Wedderburn (1983) relates that only two British universities offered a labour law course in the late 1940s and the subject was widely regarded as a "trade school" subject.

More surprising is the situation concerning social insurance. The entire corpus of social insurance was an integral part of American industrial relations through the 1950s. Further, many of the prime architects of American social insurance programmes were explicitly identified with the field of industrial relations; indeed, as noted in the previous chapter, Boulding went so far as to claim Commons to be the intellectual father of the American welfare state.

Paradoxically, however, the literature of British industrial relations – both in the 1950s and today – is marked by an almost complete absence of or even reference to social insurance and, more generally, the development of the modern welfare state. I use the word "paradoxically" for several reasons. One is that the Webbs devoted considerable attention to the insurance and benefit function of trade unions in the United Kingdom, calling it the "method of mutual insurance". The second is that the United Kingdom adopted programmes of social insurance (e.g, unemployment insurance, old-age pensions) two decades before the United States and, after the Second World War, moved to a far more integrated and extensive version of the welfare state (e.g., with nationalized health care). These initiatives were, in turn, intimately concerned with improving the conditions of labour and promoting improved employer– employee relations. The third is that the academic person most identified with and responsible for the adoption of social insurance programmes and the development of the welfare state in the United Kingdom was an institutional-oriented labour economist closely associated with the Webbs and the LSE (Harris, 1977). I refer to Lord William Beveridge, who served as Director of the LSE from 1919 to 1937, wrote numerous publications on labour and authored the intellectual blueprint for the modern British welfare state in his internationally influential book *Full employment in a free society* (1945). Yet Beveridge's name rarely gets more than passing mention in British industrial relations.[2] One possible explanation is provided by Arthur Marsh (1968), who notes that British industrial relations after the Second World War had its principal roots in trade union education – a foundation more narrow and focused on collective bargaining than was the case with American industrial relations.

Returning to the issue of the PM school in British industrial relations, it is instructive to look deeper and inquire about the subject of human relations and, more generally, management. Both, after all, were prominent parts (albeit perhaps junior partners) of American industrial relations of the 1950s.

Regarding management, Howard Gospel and Gill Palmer (1993: 2) state, "For many years academics in the United Kingdom also saw the subject [of industrial relations] as being about the study of trade unions and only later did they come to focus much on management." In a similar vein, John Gennard (1986: 11) states, "Relative to the time they spent on analysing trade unions Roberts and his major contemporaries did not devote much time to exploring management." As previously discussed in Chapter 3, a variety of reasons can be cited for this neglect of management in British industrial relations. Included among them are a normative bias against employers on the part of many British labour scholars of that era, the tradition of "unscientific management" in British industry, the underdeveloped and low-level administrative character of British personnel management, and the larger role played at the time of employers' associations and centralized labour negotiations. Going further, if industrial relations scholars neglected management it was at least in part a reflection of the lack of substantive research and new ideas on management coming from British universities and industry. Looking at the situation as it existed in the late 1960s, for example, John Child (1969: 206) was led to conclude, "Overall, British management thought today is disorganized and in decline."

The general neglect of management in British industrial relations during this time period was also mirrored in the treatment of what in the United States was a major boom area of research – human relations. The subject of human relations came to the United Kingdom in the late 1930s, principally through the favourable reception that leading management journals and spokespersons gave to Thomas Whitehead's book *Leadership in a free society* (Child, 1969: 93). It was only during and after the war, however, that it gained significant attention in British management circles, spurred on by the much-publicized productivity and morale problems afflicting British industry and the penchant of British manual workers to stretch out the work and restrict output (Guillén, 1994).[3] The rejuvenation of the union movement in the 1940s, and the subsequent struggle of British management to preserve control over and loyalty of the workforce also stimulated interest.

As noted in the previous chapter, several university-connected institutes and centres devoted to human relations were established in the United States in the 1940s. In the United Kingdom, the most notable development along this line was the creation of the Tavistock Institute of Human Relations in 1946 (Trist

273

and Murray, 1990). Based in London and made possible through a large grant from the Rockefeller Foundation, the Institute operated as an independent non-profit consulting and research organization. Most of its staff were trained in the behavioural sciences, with psychologists and psychiatrists forming the largest group (the Institute was an off-shoot of the Tavistock Clinic, a medical and psychiatric consulting organization that gained recognition through its work with the British military on methods to improve organizational control and morale). The Tavistock Institute undertook a number of pioneering studies of work performance and relations, such as by Eric Trist and Fred Emery, which led in the 1960s to the development of the socio-technical theory of work systems (Trist, 1981). Socio-technical theory subsequently provided one of the major intellectual pillars for the pioneering work on industrial democracy and humanization of work life in Scandinavian countries in the 1960s and 1970s and, later, the development of high-performance work systems in the United States (Cole, 1989; van Otter, 2002). Because existing academic journals were reluctant to publish the research being done at the Institute, it partnered with Kurt Lewin and the University of Michigan and launched a new journal in 1947 titled *Human Relations*. Interdisciplinary or "integrative" research was in vogue at this time, illustrated by the journal's subtitle: *A Quarterly Journal Towards the Integration of the Social Sciences*. Although this grand vision was not accomplished, the journal is a well-recognized and prestigious publication for behavioural science research on workplace issues.

In the United States, human relations was generally viewed as part of the field of industrial relations, even if the ILE majority in academia had serious reservations about it. During the 1950s, the two fields in the United Kingdom were typically regarded as largely independent and to some significant degree opposed. Illustratively, J.H. Smith (1955) observes in an article titled "The scope of industrial relations" that (p. 84), "Oddly enough, the field of human behaviour in industry is still regarded as being divided between 'industrial' and 'human' relations – the first of these being generally accepted as the study of formal structures, the second as the detailed examination of 'situations' or informal processes." He goes on to say that industrial relations and human relations (p. 85) "seem to be regarded at present as two distinct fields of study". Balfour (1955: 89) goes further and states "a state of ideological cold war seems to exist between [the] schools". Although part of the divide between them was ideological, another arose from a difference in "external versus internal" perspectives on workplace research and the location of labour problems. Marsh (1968, p. 68) states, for example, "The 'industrial relations' school preference was to emphasize external factors in workplace regulation; the industrial sociologists preferred to emphasize the factors internal to the workplace."

In an interesting twist, however, the two fields gradually grew apart in the United States from the late 1950s onward, while in the United Kingdom they gradually came closer together. In a review article on British industrial relations, for example, Bain and Clegg (1974) note that most British industrial relations participants in the 1950s were from "external" disciplines such as economics, law and history. They go on to note (pp. 99–100):

> Then, from the middle of the 1950s, industrial sociologists and psychologists began to show that they could contribute to industrial relations. 'Human relations' had a considerable following among British practitioners of industrial relations, but academics were initially sceptical. For especially as expounded by such writers as Elton Mayo, human relations concentrated on the primary work group and labour–management cooperation, ignoring or belittling most of the topics in which students of industrial relations were interested. It was only when such British students as Joan Woodward, E.L. Trist, and Tom Lupton took the theories and methods developed in the United States and reworked them in such studies as *The dock worker* (1954), *Organizational choice* (1963), and *On the shop-floor* (1963), thereby throwing light upon such issues as strike proneness, pay systems, and union attitudes, that the contribution of their disciplines to industrial relations came to be understood and recognized. Indeed, their analysis of work group behaviour was gradually taken over during the 1960s by more traditional students of industrial relations as they sought for concepts to use in analysing the material coming in from the studies of shop stewards then being undertaken.

This last sentence captures a significant feature of British industrial relations quite the opposite to its American counterpart. While sociology and plant-level studies of work relations were dropping out of American industrial relations in the 1960s, they were becoming more important in British industrial relations, albeit shorn of a good deal of the unitarist and managerial perspective contained in American human relations.

If human relations was not part of British industrial relations circa the 1950s, then what did define the field's central core of research? In terms of underlying principles, Roderick Martin (1998: 95, emphasis in original) describes the position of major figures in the field in the 1950s and 1960s as

> based on a set of political concerns ultimately grounded in political pluralism, with a high value placed on collective laissez-faire, the role of collective bargaining and independent trade union representation. ... The priority in industrial relations is not to create a more efficient labour force, nor to further the interests of the working class through class struggle in the enterprise. Instead, the priority is to provide the institutions and processes for 'industrial citizenship' or more narrowly equitable job regulation.

Another approach to answering this question is to examine the distinctive features of the Oxford school, given that it dominated the field at this time. One perspective on the Oxford school is provided by Jeremy Bugler (1968) (see also Robinson, 1981; Clegg, 1990; Ackers and Wilkinson, 2003), who states:

> Its real distinguishing characteristic is a rabid, and thoroughgoing, concern to get the facts about plant and union organization right – an 'institutional bias' as one of them puts it. ... For this reason, a term of abuse applied to the Oxford man is 'fact grubber'. ... For this reason, there are no extremists in the group; their ideology is tempered with a thorough knowledge of the possible. They own to ideals rather than ideologies. Furthermore, their theorising is largely theorising to clarify the nature of problems, theorising in so far as it can be useful. They have other characteristics: a belief that you can't do much without an incomes policy. ... They hold that though there is a conflict of interests between management and men, these interests can be adjusted so that a common course can be agreed which will satisfy both interests, different though they may be. The outstanding example of this tenet is productivity bargaining, on which Alan Flanders is the major academic authority. ... Finally, they all lay great stress on the responsibility (moral too) of management. One of Flanders' particular messages is that 'management must manage'. In saying this they do not absolve the unions, but they point out that the first responsibility for innovation rests with management.

In America, the heart of industrial relations in the 1950s was defined by the research agenda of the neo-institutional social science labour economists who founded and led the IRRA, such as Kerr and Dunlop. Thus, while the field in America included a heterogeneous mix of subjects and participants, the core of industrial relations was centred on the discipline of economics (broadly defined) and took a relatively analytical approach (for that time period) to the study of labour markets, trade unions and the practice/impact of collective bargaining. While these American industrial relations leaders were strong advocates of pluralism and collective bargaining, they were typically of middle-class or professional backgrounds and promoted a relatively moderate political and social agenda (Schatz, 1998). One telltale sign was the notable absence of any quasi-radical or socialist ("leftie") participants at IRRA programmes.

The situation in the United Kingdom was different and gave a different cast to this period in British industrial relations. Certainly there were British heterodox economists interested in labour, such as William Beveridge, Maurice Dobb (a Marxist), Henry Phelps Brown, J.F. Rowe and Barbara Wootton, but they did not form a cohesive group, nor were they (Phelps Brown excepted) at the centre of the new field of industrial relations. Rather, the line of research of the core British group of early industrial relations academics followed a largely empirical, descriptive, fact-based account of labour history and institutions, with only modest reference to underlying disciplinary theories or constructs (Brown and Wright, 1994). Bain and Clegg (1974: 98, 99) describe the industrial relations research of the 1950s this way: "Research thrived, leading to what might be described as a brisk business in guide books. ... Almost without exception the main intention of these works was to describe and classify what was available or what came to light with a little searching or digging. In most instances material was organized in the categories which were at hand."

Also noticeably different from the American industrial relations mainstream was the political and ideological orientation of the key British industrial relations academics. Although certainly a significant majority of the American industrial relationists were ideologically predisposed to favour collective bargaining, in the overall spectrum of opinion the American position exhibited greater dispersion of ideological commitments, much smaller representation in the left-hand tail, and a more moderate (or less progressive) overall stance. Illustrative of the near-uniformity of ideological positions in the United Kingdom, Fox (1990: 229) states:

> Trade unions themselves were seen, by most of us, as fully legitimate associations to be encouraged, though there were one or two dissentients. I recall, at one of the early academic conferences, a moment in discussion when a participant asked sharply, 'We seem to be assuming that trade unionism and collective bargaining are desirable. Surely we shouldn't be doing so?' After a brief embarrassed silence discussion continued as if he had not spoken.

British opinion was also more to the left of that among American academics. According to Bugler, for example, all but one member (Clegg) of the Oxford school came from a working-class background and several had worked on the factory floor. (Fox, for example, worked in a factory making camera film.) He states (1968: 222), "They share a general political attitude: ... all confess to a commitment to the Labour movement. Politically, I'd guess, they range leftwards from mainstream Labour." Indeed, Clegg was a student of G.D.H. Cole and a member of the Communist Party until the end of the Second World War (Bugler, 1968), while Flanders had been an activist in various non-Marxist socialist organizations since his youth (Kelly, 2003a). After witnessing the horrors associated with fascist and communist dictatorships, however, both Clegg and Flanders became committed pluralists, albeit along left-of-centre, British-style social democratic lines. At this time, for example, Fox (1990: 193) characterized himself as a "democratic socialist". Also, unlike the American industrial relations leaders of the 1950s (e.g., exemplified by the presidents of the IRRA), a number of the industrial relations academics in the United Kingdom had earlier worked in various staff and research positions with the labour movement and continued in their academic jobs to have strong organizational links with the unions (Gennard, 1986).

Canada

The second country outside the United States where industrial relations established a solid institutional presence in the years before the mid-1960s is Canada. This section relates the main developments and actors.

The story of industrial relations in Canada starts, as in the United States, with the Labour Question (Giles and Murray, 1988: 781). The Labour Question first emerged in Canada as a serious social issue in the 1880s, called to attention by the mounting labour unrest and deplorable working conditions associated with the early stages of industrialization. The roots of industrial relations in Canada can be traced back to at least 1886 with the appointment of the Royal Commission on the Relations of Labour and Capital (Woods and Goldenberg, 1981). As already noted in a previous chapter, similar to most other industrial countries, Canada also experienced a wave of labour unrest in the late years of the First World War, culminating in the Winnipeg General Strike. The tumultuous state of labour relations, combined with fears of Bolshevism, led to the appointment in 1919 of, respectively, a National Industrial Conference and Royal Commission on Industrial Relations. Two years later, another industrial relations conference was held in Ottawa.

The report of the Royal Commission (1919: 5) testifies to the crisis situation then affecting all industrial countries when it states, "The upheaval taking place throughout the world, and the state of men's minds during this critical period, make this the time for drastic changes of the industrial and social systems of Canada." In the next paragraph, the report then states the essence of the problem-solving face of industrial relations. It notes that the Commission is "charged with the duty of considering and making suggestions for establishing permanent improvement in the relations between employers and employees, whereby, through close contact and joint action, they can improve existing industrial conditions and devise means for their continual review and betterment."

Three other notable aspects of the report deserve mention. First, of the ten conditions identified as causing poor industrial relations, unemployment is selected as the most important. Second, echoing a worldwide feeling at the time, the report states (p. 9, emphasis added):

> To a considerable extent in the past labour has been regarded as a commodity to be bought and sold in the open market, the price to be paid being determined by the supply and demand. We believe that labour should no longer be so regarded, but that

greater recognition should be given to human rights and human aspirations, and that the chief consideration in industry should be the health, happiness, and prosperity of the workers and service to the community.

Third, the Commission affirmed the need to provide workers with means of collective voice but divided into majority and minority reports regarding whether collective voice should take the form of collective bargaining with independent unions (the majority) or should also include employer-created representation plans (the minority).

In broad outline, since 1919 the development and perspective of Canadian industrial relations mirrors in many respects the development of American industrial relations (Thompson and Taras, 2003). This correspondence is to be expected, given the common border shared by the two countries and their many points of economic, political and social overlap and linkage. But there are also some interesting divergences.

Although the labour question surfaced in Canada at approximately the same time as in the United States, the development of an academic field of industrial relations lagged behind that in the United States by 15 to 20 years. In this respect the Canadian experience more closely resembled the British pattern.

Relative to the United States, the study of labour in Canada received only modest attention from academics before 1960. H.D. Woods and Shirley Goldenberg (1981: 23), for example, cite two "classics" in early Canadian industrial relations: Logan's (1948) history of trade unions in Canada and the case study of a Canadian asbestos strike by Pierre Trudeau (1956). (Trudeau later became prime minister of Canada.) According to Anthony Giles and Jacques Bélanger (2002: 47), a smattering of research by sociologists was done on labour-related subjects prior to the 1970s, but it "would have made very quick reading indeed". Likewise, in her review of Canadian industrial relations Louise-Marie Tremblay (1968: 27) states, "Trade union research in Canada is little developed as yet."

Similarly, while the first academic industrial relations unit in the United States was at Princeton in 1922, the first industrial relations unit in Canada did not appear until 1937 at Queen's University in Kingston, Ontario. As noted in the previous chapter, the founding of the Queen's industrial relations programme owed much to Clarence Hicks of the Standard Oil Company and Industrial Relations Counselors, Inc. In the next decade, the industrial relations field made major institutional progress in Quebec (the predominantly French-speaking part of Canada) with the founding of the industrial relations programmes at Laval University, the University of Montreal and McGill University (the first two are French-speaking institutions, the last is English-speaking). In the remainder of

English-speaking Canada, however, the industrial relations field made little institutional progress during the 1940s and 1950s. Industrial relations programmes were started at the University of Toronto and Dalhousie University immediatcly after the war, but they did not survive (Woods, 1949: i). Another unit was started about 1960 at the University of British Columbia but no longer exists. The first book offering a general overview of industrial relations in Canada, *Industrial relations in Canada* by Stuart Jamieson, was not published until 1957. Likewise, while the IRRA was founded in the United States in 1947, the Canadian Industrial Relations Association (CIRA) was not established until 1963. It was only in 1965 that the second major, long-lasting centre for industrial relations was established outside of Quebec, with the creation of the Industrial Relations Centre at the University of Toronto.

The real take-off phase for the industrial relations field in English-speaking Canada, according to Woods and Goldenberg (1981), did not occur until 1968. In response to worsening inflationary wage settlements and strikes in the unionized sector of the economy, the federal government of Canada appointed a blue-ribbon Task Force on Labour Relations. The Task Force was popularly known as the Woods Commission in honour of its chair H.D. Woods, director of the industrial relations unit at McGill University. Since the work of the Woods Commission falls outside the time period under consideration here, additional discussion of its work and influence is reserved for a later chapter.

The slow development of industrial relations in Canada arose from a variety of national characteristics, in addition to the ones just identified. Canada up to the time of the Second World War was an immense country geographically but had a very small population base. Likewise, the country's economy was more rural, centred in primary resource and extraction industries, and with a smaller and less capitalized manufacturing sector. These conditions inhibited the emergence of an urban-based, wage-earning labour force of substantial size – in many respects crucial conditions required for the emergence of industrial relations as an active area of academic and social concern.

Also important was the slower development of a sizeable labour movement. According to Jamieson (1957: 29), "As a social movement of nationwide proportions, trade unionism has had a shorter history and a much smaller scope in Canada than in the United States." At the turn of the twentieth century, union membership in Canada was probably no more than one hundred thousand, scattered largely among American-chartered craft unions in railroads, printing, the building trades and other traditional industries (Craig, 1983: 80). Unlike the situation in the United States, the union movement did not experience the same dramatic growth during the First World War nor during the latter part of the Depression years. While the New Deal period saw an explosion of union growth in the United States, in Canada union density was the same in 1940 as it was in 1933 (16 per cent of non-agricultural employment). And, unlike the British case, no union-supported Labour Party arose in Canada in these early years.

Not only was the Canadian labour movement smaller, more fragmented, and slower to develop than in the United Kingdom or the United States; it did not receive a sympathetic, in-depth scholarly treatment as in these other countries. Giles and Murray (1988: 789–90) state, for example,

> There was not yet, however, the same legitimation of certain types of collective worker action which was already evident in the work of the American institutionalists (such as Commons and Perlman) let alone the vision of trade unionism as a vehicle to the new industrial citizenship of the twentieth century associated with the British pluralists (such as the Webbs, G.D.H. Cole, Milne-Bailey, and Laski). ... It was only during and after World War Two that a more positive vision of the role of organized labour became widely propagated.

The slower growth of unionism in Canada, and the emergence of academic industrial relations in that country, cannot be fully explained without giving attention to the influential role of William Lyons Mackenzie King. As described in Chapter 2, King played a central role in the early development of industrial relations in the United States, particularly in the Rockefeller/PM branch of the field. But his influence was also directly felt in Canada. Not only did King's philosophy of industrial relations reflect important dimensions of the Canadian world view, but he was in a direct position to influence Canadian industrial relations policy: first through his stint as deputy minister of the Department of Labour and, later, in his 22-year service as prime minister of Canada. Perspectives differ, however, on King's record. Taras (1997: 297), for example, states that while Canada was a decade later than the United States in enacting legislation protecting union recognition, "in other respects the Canadian state acted earlier and more aggressively in regulating labor relations". Among the laws she cites is the Industrial Disputes Investigation Act (1907), which King had a hand in crafting. The act requires compulsory investigation of labour disputes by third-party neutrals, publication of the investigatory reports to bring pressure on the parties to compromise, and the prohibition of work stoppages pending investigation. Other scholars reach a more negative verdict on King's labour record, however, noting that during King's 22 years in office as prime minister he moved to provide legal protection of the right to organize only under the crisis situation generated by the Second World War. Thus Lipset (1986: 434) concludes, "Prior to World War II, ... the Canadian legal environment was extremely hostile to unions, more so than the American."

Amplifying on Canadian–American differences, Taras (1997) notes that Canada has always put greater emphasis on preserving industrial peace than the United States. An important reason, she concludes, is the greater vulnerability of the Canadian economy to the disruptive effects of strikes and labour conflict, given its greater reliance on a few key industries, such as transportation, mining and forest products. Also important are differences in the national psyche of Canadians versus Americans, with the former placing more emphasis on conciliation and compromise, having greater aversion to violence and confrontation, and holding values more communitarian and statist.

These considerations, she claims, were evident in King's approach to industrial relations and clearly separated him from the chief political architect of the new American industrial relations system of the 1930s, Senator Robert Wagner. Wagner sought to promote greater unionism as part of a larger political strategy to create a quasi-corporatist form of industrial self-government and to stimulate macroeconomic recovery from the Depression by boosting wages and purchasing power.[4] King, on the other hand, took a much more ambivalent stance toward unions. On one hand, he saw unions as necessary to protect workers from exploitation and unjust treatment and to bring some element of equilibrium in the power relations between capital and labour. On the other hand, he was repelled by the adversarialism and conflict that often accompanies trade unionism and collective bargaining, and thought that efficiency in production and peace in labour relations was better promoted by fostering cooperation and unity of interest between employers and employees. Thus the American New Deal adversarial model of industrial relations did not appeal to King, nor did it resonate as broadly among the Canadian electorate. Further, according to Jamieson (1957), Canadian employers were even more hostile to unions than the American employers and thus used political pressure to avoid Wagner-type legislation. For these reasons, King did not promote legislation in this vein during the 1930s, preferring instead to follow a mixed strategy combining British voluntarism in union recognition, promotion of American-style welfare capitalism and company unionism, and government-mandated mediation and fact finding in labour disputes along faintly Australasian lines (absent the latter's binding arbitration and wage setting through government-appointed tribunals).

For these reasons, Canadian labour policy in the 1930s did not swing to support organized labour as it did in the United States. When legislation similar to the Wagner Act was adopted at the national level (PC 1003 in 1944), it included legal protection of the right to organize and collective bargaining but, unlike the American approach, also continued to permit non-union companies to operate employee representation plans – the creation of King and Rockefeller in the 1910s

(MacDowell, 2000; Taras, 2000). Thus the union movement in Canada remained smaller and employer–employee relations remained a less pressing issue. Illustrative of King's influence on Canadian industrial relations, and the slower rise to influence of the labour movement, are the events surrounding the establishment of Canada's first academic industrial relations centre.

As previously noted, Canada's first industrial relations centre was established at Queen's University in Kingston, Ontario. The prime movers in its establishment were Clarence Hicks and Bryce Stewart. Stewart was a graduate of Queen's, worked as a staff member for the clothing workers' union in the United States, later became director of research for Industrial Relations Counselors, Inc., and according to Commons (1934b: 200) was "the leading authority in the country on unemployment insurance" (Kaufman, 2003a). The Queen's Industrial Relations Section, not surprisingly, had a heavy PM orientation. To lay the groundwork for the section and develop external sources of financial support, Queen's sponsored the first university industrial relations conference in Canada in 1936. Tellingly, it was co-sponsored with the Toronto and Montreal Personnel Associations and, according to Kelly (1987: 479), the attendees were "mainly senior industrial relations and personnel managers from large companies in Canada and the United States though there was more than a sprinkling of representatives from government, universities, and other educational institutions". Kelly makes no mention of attendees from organized labour.

The new Industrial Relations Section was located in the School of Commerce and Administration and its first director was James Cameron, a practitioner from industry. It did not offer classes in industrial relations or a degree programme, but served as a clearinghouse for information, a provider of special research reports on industrial relations topics, and a source for conferences and short training courses. In this respect, it resembled the other industrial relations sections created by Hicks at Princeton, MIT and Michigan. In his detailed history of the Queen's section, Lawrence Kelly (1987: 483) states,

> The term 'industrial relations' was not defined in any of the Section's documents but it is obvious from the range of topics covered in the conferences and publications that it was construed in the same broad way as it was by Hicks. As Hicks defined it, 'industrial relations' included the development and administration of policy on all matters concerned with or growing out of the employment relationship which concern employees and the various levels of management.

In 1944 the Industrial Relations Section was upgraded to a Department of Industrial Relations and a one-year diploma course was offered. Cameron remained as director until 1960, when he retired and was replaced by

W. Donald Wood. Wood obtained a Ph.D. in economics from Princeton under the supervision of J. Douglas Brown, director of Princeton's Industrial Relations Section. Later he served as head of the employee relations research division for the Imperial Oil Company, Ltd., a Rockefeller-connected company and operator of the most extensive employee representation plan in Canada (Taras, 2000). Wood went on to become one of the most prominent industrial relations academics in Canada.

After the founding of the Queen's Industrial Relations Section in 1937, the next significant industrial relations programme in the English-speaking part of Canada was not established for nearly thirty years. This unit was the Industrial Relations Centre at the University of Toronto, created in 1965 as an independent body with joint-appointed faculty.[5] The person taking the lead in establishment of the centre was John Crispo, who also served as the unit's first director. Crispo was later succeeded by Noah Meltz. The original mission of the Toronto Industrial Relations Centre was to serve as a source of information collection and distribution and to provide practitioner-oriented conferences and seminars. Unlike the industrial relations units in Quebec or the United States, the Toronto Industrial Relations Centre did not offer academic coursework or degrees in industrial relations (these were added later), and unlike the Queen's unit, which was oriented more towards management, the Toronto Industrial Relations Centre had more of a labour–management relations focus.

Developments in French-speaking Canada offer a remarkable contrast in the early development of Canadian industrial relations. During the early to mid-1940s three formal industrial relations programmes were established in universities in Quebec, as was Canada's first and only scholarly industrial relations journal. In terms of size and scope, the industrial relations programmes at Laval University and the University of Montreal have to be ranked as the Canadian equivalent of the industrial relations programme at Cornell University, the leading industrial relations centre in the United States. What makes these developments particularly noteworthy is the incongruity they demonstrate not only with English-speaking Canada but also with France. For France is the country with which Quebec in many respects has the closest social, cultural and linguistic ties, and which has exhibited little historical or social affinity for the Anglo-American concept of industrial relations.

The three industrial relations programmes established in Quebec are at Laval University, the University of Montreal and McGill University. All three industrial relations programmes were set up as independent centres or departments. At the present time, Laval and Montreal comprise the largest industrial relations programmes in Canada, each having approximately twenty-five faculty members and graduate and undergraduate enrolment of many hundreds. The McGill programme, once quite prominent in Canada, has been phased out.

Of these programmes, Laval was the first and for many years the largest. Laval University is the oldest university in North America, established in 1683. From its inception until 1971, it was a Church-affiliated ("clerical") institution, administered and operated under the aegis of the Catholic Church. Similar to most of its European counterparts, the social sciences at Laval were poorly developed and institutionalized in the early part of the twentieth century. Although this situation did not significantly change across much of Europe until the 1960s and after, at Laval (and Montreal) the progressive and politically liberal clerical leaders began to institute a wide-ranging academic reform programme much earlier. In 1938, a separate Faulty of Social Sciences was created, and in 1943 it was split into five departments. One of these five departments was a newly created Department of Industrial Relations (Faucher, 1988). At Laval, George Henri Levesque was a leader in this movement, and Father Emile Bouvier played a similar role at Montreal.

The Dean of the new industrial relations department at Laval was Gerard Tremblay. Tremblay was also Deputy Minister of the Department of Labour in the Quebec government, so responsibility for running the department largely devolved to Abbé Gérard Dion. Dion was a cleric and scholar and became acquainted with the Anglo-American field of industrial relations while doing graduate work at McGill University. Later, he became director of the Laval industrial relations programme and one of the most influential people in the early Canadian industrial relations academic community. To recognize Dion, the CIRA created an annual Gérard Dion award. The academic recipients since 1990 are: W. Donald Wood, A.W.R. Carrothers, Alton Craig, Gérard Hébert, Roy Adams, Noah Meltz, Tony Smith, Shirley Goldenberg, Mark Thompson and Morley Gunderson.

Like the NYSSILR at Cornell University, the Laval industrial relations programme offers courses and degrees at both the undergraduate and graduate levels. It also takes an expansive view of the intellectual domain of industrial relations. Included within the original curriculum were courses spanning diverse disciplines and fields, including management, economics, sociology, psychology, law and history. To the present time, both labour relations and personnel/human resource management are housed within the Laval industrial relations programme. Also noteworthy are two other developments. The first is that in 1946 the Laval industrial relations department started publication of Canada's first industrial relations scholarly journal, the *Bulletin of Industrial Relations* (*Bulletin des Relations Industrielles*), later renamed *Relations Industrielles/Industrial Relations* (a quarterly bilingual publication).

The second is that in 1945 the Laval industrial relations department began to host an annual industrial relations conference that brings together practitioners from around the province. The conference continues to the present year.

Given this institutional overview of industrial relations programmes in Quebec, the interesting question is: why did Quebec take the lead in establishing industrial relations programmes in the 1940s in Canada? The answer has several parts (Murray, 2001; Boivin, 2003).

The first concerns national-level trends in unionization and strikes. As earlier observed, Canada did not have the same meteoric growth in union membership that the United States did during the 1930s. After the stability of the 1930s, however, unionization and labour conflict increased dramatically during the Second World War years. A wartime economy created many new industrial jobs, as well as strains and dislocations that fostered labour– management conflict. Like the United States, Canada also saw the emergence of industrial unionism in the late 1930s and the creation of two rival federations, a craft-union-based Trades and Labour Congress (TLC) and an industrial-union-based Canadian Congress of Labour (CCL), which vied with each other for new members during the war. Unions also seized the leverage given them by the demands for all-out production, and used this to pressure employers and governments for recognition and bargaining rights.

These wartime events thus created labour market developments that brought labour conflict and the state of employer–employee relations to the top of public and policy attention. In response, all the provincial governments in the war years enacted some form of Wagner Act legislation, as did the federal government in the last year in which King was prime minister. Among the provinces, the decision to follow the American model in legal treatment of unions and collective bargaining was most problematic in Quebec, given the provinces' tradition of stronger political and cultural autonomy in the Canadian confederation, the history of pluralist workplace unionism along French lines, and the relatively repressive stance toward unions taken by the conservative provincial premier Duplessis. The political foes of Duplessis promoted a more constructive course on industrial relations and an expansion of the labour movement. This group of liberals and "modernizers", although dominated by Catholic clerics, was nonetheless progressive in outlook and sought not only to liberalize Quebec society but also to introduce a more scientific approach to resolving labour conflict. They were motivated by a number of considerations: the creed of social Catholicism and support of labour expressed in several Papal encyclicals (e.g., *Reum Novarum*, 1891); the desire to keep labour conflict from becoming more radicalized and workers from defecting from the "tame" Catholic unions to more aggressive (but secular) American-based international unions; and a commitment to promote a more liberal, open society. During Duplessis' term out of office (1940–44), the modernizers passed Wagner Act legislation in Quebec and established the industrial relations programme at Laval.

The Laval and Montreal industrial relations programmes were thus born out of a larger political struggle over the stance of public policy toward labour. After the Duplessis era came to an end, Quebec in the early 1950s embarked on its "quiet revolution". The quiet revolution was marked by a strong assertion of Quebec separatism and nationalism. The Quebec labour movement became a leader in this cause and steadily gained members and political influence. As a result, industrial relations in Quebec continued to remain a vital force throughout the post-Second World War period, as did the industrial relations programmes in Quebec universities.

Australia

The third area of the world where industrial relations emerged as a recognized field of study in the years prior to the mid-1960s is Australasia and, in particular, the countries of Australia and New Zealand. I examine Australia first and then turn to New Zealand.

The nation of Australia examined in this section and the nation of Canada examined in the last share a number of characteristics despite being located on opposite sides of the globe. Both had a long history of British colonial rule and drew the dominant part of their culture, political institutions and legal system from the British. Both are also immensely large but sparsely settled countries with people concentrated in a modest number of urban areas separated from other parts of the nation by vast distances. Also common among them is an economy heavily dependent on agriculture, natural resources and exports. And, finally, both are also lands of immigrants, drawing waves of settlers from many different countries.

If one compares Australia with the English-speaking part of Canada, certain broad similarities also appear in the development of the field of industrial relations. As in Canada, the roots of industrial relations in Australia go back to the last two decades of the nineteenth century and, in particular, the emergence of a wage-earning labour force, trade unions and the labour question (D. Kelly, 1999). Similarly, the initial period of expansion for the industrial relations field in both English-speaking Canada and Australia began after the Second World War, although at a somewhat earlier date in the latter. Between these two end points, however, is a good deal of diversity in the development of industrial relations in the two countries.

One point of diversity concerns what Diana Kelly (1999) classifies as the pre-history stage of industrial relations, i.e., the period before the industrial relations field takes on a self-conscious identity and institutional form. In nearly every one of the industrialized countries, the roots of labour scholarship go back to early studies of trade unions, usually in the form of a historical narrative of the national labour movement. In the United States, Ely (1886) and Commons et al. (1910) define this as the beginning point, while in the United Kingdom the beginning point is marked by the Webbs' two books (1894, 1897). The same is true of Canada and Australia: in the former case the early union histories by Latham (1930) and Logan (1948) and in the latter case the histories of Coghlan (1918) and Sutcliffe (1921).

There are two main distinctions between the pre-historical scholarship in Australia and that in Canada, however: industrial relations scholarship began earlier and was produced in more breadth and depth in Australia, and it embraced a wider range of disciplines and academic perspectives.

Speaking of pre-Second World War Canada, for example, Giles and Murray (1988: 790) state that "with only a few exceptions ... trade unionism and collective bargaining did not figure largely in the research agenda of the day". In Australia, on the other hand, a steady stream of labour-oriented research was produced, beginning before the turn of the century and proceeding through the Second World War. Particularly noteworthy was the work of Orwell de R. Foenander (University of Melbourne), starting with an article in the prestigious American periodical *Quarterly Journal of Economics* (1928) and proceeding to numerous books (e.g., *Towards industrial peace in Australia*, 1937; *Better employment relations and other essays in labour*, 1954).

Early Australian labour research also covered a broader range of topics, with particular emphasis on wage determination and dispute resolution (McCawley, 1924), and involved not only historians but also scholars from economics and law. More so than in Canada, an early literature on personnel management and the employer's role in labour relations also developed in Australia, although it did not coalesce into a formal PM branch of industrial relations as in the United States. One early academic contributor to this Australian literature was Elton Mayo, who then immigrated to the United States in the early 1920s. The Australian system of industrial relations also generated more international interest than that of Canada. In their text *Principles of labor legislation* (1916), for example, Commons and Andrews give extensive coverage of the Australian system, as did the publications of the ILO, while the work of H.B. Higgins, the founding father of compulsory arbitration in Australia, came to prominence through his 1915 article in the *Harvard Law Review*.

The second area of diversity relates to the circumstances behind the establishment of industrial relations' first formal presence in a university. Common to Canada, the United Kingdom and the United States was the establishment of the first industrial relations centres or chairs through the financial contributions and influence of socially progressive businessmen and associates. In all three countries, the result was the initial institutionalization of industrial relations in universities, beginning in the 1930s or earlier. No similar event occurred in Australia. As a result, the emergence of industrial relations in the form of separate degree programmes and centres waited another two decades in Australia. Kelly (1999: 127) states, for example, "In the early 1950s there were no subjects in Australia which dealt solely with industrial relations. There were, however, courses and subjects in labour studies and personnel management, as well as labour law, employment law and labour economics."

The formal institutionalization of the industrial relations field in Australia began in the mid-1950s. And rather than starting at one university, industrial relations emerged roughly simultaneously at several.

The industrial relations programme that was in subsequent years to become the largest and best known in Australia was at the University of Sydney. It originated in 1953 with a single course in the Economics Department taught by Kingsley Laffer (Kelly, 1999: 144). The industrial relations course was described by the university as a "branch of applied Economics". Laffer was an indefatigable promoter of industrial relations and had a major impact on the development of the field in Australia (Isaac, 1993). At Sydney, he overcame considerable institutional inertia and resistance to transform industrial relations from a single course to, twenty years later, a stand-alone department with full undergraduate and graduate programmes. He also founded in 1959 the flagship industrial relations academic journal in Australia, the *Journal of Industrial Relations*, serving as its editor until 1975, and he took a leading role in the founding of the Industrial Relations Society of Australia (a predominantly practitioner group) in 1965.

Industrial relations also emerged in the late 1950s to early 1960s at three other Australian universities: the University of Western Australia, the University of Melbourne and the University of New South Wales.

At Western Australia, the introduction of industrial relations was largely the accomplishment of Kenneth Walker. Walker had a long-time interest in labour problems and was an ardent proponent of an interdisciplinary approach to the subject. In this spirit, Walker served as both a professor of economics and professor of psychology. In the early 1950s Walker wrote his Ph.D. under Dunlop at Harvard and thereafter returned to a faculty position at Western Australia. His dissertation was published in revised form in 1956 as the book

Industrial relations in Australia. In the book, Walker sought to adapt Dunlop's model (at that time still unpublished) to analyse the Australian system of labour relations. More than any other academic of this period, Walker brought the American conception and practice of the industrial relations field to Australia.

Melbourne also introduced industrial relations into the curriculum in the 1950s. After the break-up of the Faculty of Commerce in 1950 into separate departments of commerce and economics, Foenander joined the latter and soon thereafter introduced a new course on industrial relations. In 1955, a Department of Industrial Relations was created, with Foenander as chair (Isaac, 2003). Later, Joe Isaac, who obtained his Ph.D. from the LSE but also studied at Harvard with Dunlop, succeeded Foenander as department chair and went on to become a major figure in Australian industrial relations (Hancock, 1998). In the early 1960s, the Department of Industrial Relations was again merged into that of Economics and did not reappear as a separate department until 1990.

The University of New South Wales introduced a degree programme in industrial relations in 1959 within the Faculty of Economics. In the early years, students took a standard repertoire of economics courses, followed by an industrial relations seminar in the last year. Throughout the 1960s the industrial relations programme was expanded and strengthened with new courses and faculty under the auspices of Bill Hotchkiss and Bill Ford. Eventually industrial relations was split from economics and became an independent department. The first chair in industrial relations in Australia was established at New South Wales and was held by John Niland. Niland also succeeded Laffer as editor of the *Journal of Industrial Relations* and later served as president of the IIRA (see Howard, 1991).

Given this overview of the early institutionalization of the industrial relations field in Australia, several points about the Australian experience deserve brief discussion. One must ask, for example: why did the study of labour develop earlier and more broadly in Australia than similar countries, such as Canada? The primary answer rests with the compulsory conciliation and arbitration system introduced in 1904 by the federal and state governments to regularize employer–employee relations and maintain industrial peace (Lansbury and Michelson, 2003). The system, maintained through most of the twentieth century, gave legal protection to collective bargaining but required as the quid pro quo that trade unions and employer associations register with the government and submit disputed contract terms to a state tribunal for conciliation and, if need be, binding arbitration. This legal framework encouraged organization on both the employer and employee sides and a relatively centralized and highly regulated system of industrial relations.

Given the Anglo-American penchant for voluntarism in industrial relations, the Australian system is a remarkable movement in the opposite direction. The primary impetus came from two sources – first, fear that strikes and labour unrest were growing out of control and that bargaining and dispute resolution needed to be regularized and, second, a growing feeling that the labour market needed regulation to prevent destructive competition and sweated labour (this period being one of both depressed economic conditions and widespread union organizing). Braham Dabscheck (1994) also attributes the adoption of the awards system to the Australian legislature's greater receptivity to North American progressivism, Catholic social thought and the Fabian socialism of the Webbs (who visited Australia at the turn of the century). Whatever the case, with extensive unionism, collective bargaining and state intervention in the wage determination process, the Australian situation provided both greater need and opportunity for academic research on labour. Remarkably, however, it nonetheless still took nearly a half-century for conditions to evolve to the point that a field of industrial relations emerged in academia and industry.

A second aspect of Australian industrial relations deserving consideration is the conceptualization of the field's domain. As it developed in Australia, industrial relations was primarily located in three disciplines: foremost was economics, followed by law and history (Lansbury and Michelson, 2003). The subject also exhibited a science-building and problem-solving duality, but was most oriented toward the latter. Illustratively, for example, Walker (1956: xvi) promoted Dunlop's systems model as a basis for industrial relations research but nonetheless concluded that "my experience of both practical industrial relations and research has left me with the firm conviction that progress in this area will come mainly from problem-centred interdisciplinary research". According to Hancock (1998: 484), early industrial relations scholars shared the assumption that the object of industrial relations should be "fruit-bearing rather than light-bearing". Reflective of industrial relations' largely applied and non-theoretical nature, one of the arguments most often used by academics opposed to granting industrial relations independent status as a major field of study or department was that it lacked intellectual substance and was overly descriptive, institutional and vocational (Kelly, 1999).

Also of interest is the Australian perspective on the definition of the field. In the 1950s a broad and eclectic definition was common. In 1957, for example, Laffer (quoted in Kelly, 1999: 162) states that the industrial relations field includes

the functions, policies and problems of trade unions and employer organizations; informal groups and their significance; the role of the State in industrial relations; the determination of wages and conditions under arbitration and collective bargaining; industrial morale, labour turnover, absenteeism, industrial disputes; welfare, personnel and human relations policies and their effects; incentive plans; joint consultation and other forms of worker participation; the effects of industrial relations on administrative structure and technological organization; influence on industrial relations arising from the social organization of the community; [and] legal aspects of industrial relations.

Other scholars, however, took a more narrow perspective, emphasizing collective relations and institutions and downgrading or omitting aspects related to management, work organization and individual employment relationships. Over time, the narrower perspective dominated, as Kelly observes (p. 169) that "in the mid-1970s, most industrial relations study had become narrowed to the collective institutions and formal institutional processes. Organizational and management factors had been all but eliminated." Laffer exemplifies this paradigm shift, as a decade after making the above-quoted statement he (1968: 13) defines industrial relations as "an interdisciplinary subject having as a central theme the bargaining relations between employers and employees".

A final aspect of Australian industrial relations deserving mention is the balance between "domestic" and "imported" contributions to the field. As in Canada, a considerable amount of early labour scholarship was home grown. Over time, however, possession of a doctoral degree became more important for an academic position, and Australian universities provided few opportunities to acquire one. Increasingly, therefore, Australians pursued graduate study abroad. In the 1950s, the only choices in the labour area were the United States and the United Kingdom, so these two countries came to have a dominant influence on the Australian industrial relations field. Because of the close political and cultural links between Australia and the United Kingdom, the majority of Australians with advanced educational degrees in the 1950s obtained them from British institutions. Also of significance, the Australian system of higher education was largely based on the British model with thesis-only doctoral programmes and emphasis on qualitative over statistical research methods (Lansbury and Michelson, 2003). Thus, in the 1950–70 period Australian industrial relations had a substantially British flavour, tending to shift it more toward institutional and historical case studies, fact-finding, and relative neglect of management and the behavioural sciences. While American industrial relations also exhibited many of these features, it nonetheless took (in relative terms) a more analytical science-building approach and made greater effort to link research to useful applications in industry. Thus one Australian academic commented upon visiting the two countries (quoted in Kelly, 1999: 146):

> While overseas in 1956 I made a point of looking at what was done in the same field in Britain and North America. The British approach is sufficiently similar to our own to call for little comment. In the United States, however, development of the field is both far more extensive and takes more varied lines. ... [in part because] Americans are more ready to believe that they have much to learn in the field, a belief which is strongest amongst business executives and trade union leaders.

The two research traditions coexisted in Australia, although the American approach became steadily more influential over the years (Kelly, 2004). By the 1970s, however, some Australians also began to question the country's heavy dependence on ideas, theories and literature imported from abroad, leading to greater efforts to develop a uniquely Australian version of industrial relations (Dabscheck, 1980).

New Zealand

The history of industrial relations in New Zealand shares a number of features with Australia, as might be expected from the many similarities in the two countries' geographic location in the southern Pacific region. The population base of both countries was derived largely from emigration from the United Kingdom and, secondarily, from other European countries, and they have a shared early political history as British colonies and, later, independent nations in the British Commonwealth. There are economic similarities, too, with both countries oriented toward agriculture, natural resources and export trade. Differences exist nevertheless, arising in part from New Zealand's much smaller population size and small-scale and late-developing industrial sector.

Like Australia, New Zealand saw the emergence of the first trade unions, strikes and public concern with labour problems in the late nineteenth century. New Zealand also adopted a similar approach to bringing order to industrial relations and improving labour conditions and, in fact, acted a decade earlier in this matter. In landmark and then-radical legislation, New Zealand adopted in 1894 the Industrial Conciliation and Arbitration Act. According to an early participant in the system (Findlay, 1921), the purpose of the legislation was twofold. It was to end "sweating" of labour and other anti-social employment conditions by creating a floor of minimum labour standards in the labour market (an application of the Webbs' device of the common rule three years before they published the idea), and it would also provide an institutional mechanism for resolving industrial disputes without resort to costly and sometimes disruptive strikes. The act created an Industrial Conciliation Council and an Industrial Arbitration Court. Any registered trade union could bring a dispute with an employer before the courts. Although only one employer might be directly involved in the dispute, all employers in the relevant district or industry automatically became respondents. The first step of the procedure was to present the facts of the dispute before the Conciliation Court and endeavour to secure a voluntary settlement. Failing this, the dispute would be passed on to the Arbitration Court, where a binding settlement would be issued, again applicable to all employers and workers in the relevant market area. Substantial penalties were then imposed on unions or employers who breached the agreement through strike action or non-compliance.

According to Margaret Wilson (1978), the pre-history of industrial relations research in New Zealand effectively commenced with enactment of the 1894 statute. Over the next 10 to 15 years a number of books and articles were published by both New Zealanders and visiting writers from North America and Europe on the Conciliation and Arbitration Act. Typically, this literature focused on the features of the legislation, the advantages and disadvantages of state conciliation and arbitration of labour disputes, and the effects on the trade unions and workers.[6] Wilson notes, however, that once the novelty of the act wore off and procedures became regularized, the literature on labour by New Zealand scholars greatly slackened, being confined largely to the occasional thesis or short piece on a specific labour problem, and did not pick up again in a substantive way until the 1960s. Kevin Hince also reaches this conclusion, stating (1991: 73), "It can be asserted that industrial relations education in New Zealand generally, and in New Zealand universities particularly, dates from the late 1960s, with the 1970s as the key take-off date."

Since the late 1960s and the 1970s fall outside the period considered in this chapter, further discussion of the development of the industrial relations field in New Zealand is postponed until Chapter 8. However, between the early twentieth-century literature on the Conciliation and Arbitration Act and the institutional-ization of the field in the 1970s, one notable work on industrial relations in New Zealand stands out in splendid isolation. In 1946, A.E.C. Hare published a lengthy monograph entitled *Industrial relations in New Zealand* (updated in 1958).[7] Hare held a Ph.D. from the University of London and was at the time Research Fellow in Social Relations in Industry at Victoria College in Wellington, New Zealand. He relates in the Preface that the research was made possible by a generous endowment from Mr. H. Valder, a progressive employer who instituted profit sharing and employee stock-ownership in his company. The purpose of the grant was to investigate "relations of capital and labour in industry with a view to discovering means that will make for harmony in those relations".

Hare's book is noteworthy, in part, because it represents the first time the term industrial relations is prominently featured in the New Zealand labour literature. More important, however, is that Hare also provides in the first two chapters of the book one of the clearest expositions of the pluralist industrial relations perspective on the cause of and solutions to labour problems available in the English language. I quote from it at length, since it summarizes many of the points and conclusions reached in earlier chapters about the philosophy and strategy of early industrial relations.

Illustrative of the problem-solving face of early industrial relations, Hare devotes Chapter 1 to "The causes of industrial unrest" and Chapter 2 to "The remedies". Hare begins the first chapter with an analysis of the origins of worker dissatisfaction and unrest. To do so he looks inside the workplace at the labour process. He notes, for example, that industrial production entails considerable division of labour and specialization of tasks, leading to jobs that are monotonous, repetitive and alienating. Further, the more thorough is division of labour and specialization of jobs, the more crucial and demanding becomes management's task of coordinating the production process. Management, therefore, endeavours to exert tight control and discipline over workers. Hare (pp. 17, 18) states,

> The power of control thus exercised by the employer extends to every aspect of the worker's life whilst he is at work. It is used to control the times at which he starts and stops work, has his meals and rests from work, ... and many other details of daily life. It is seldom that the purpose of such rules is explained to those who must obey them, and so they often appear as an unnecessary and arbitrary interference with freedom. ... In the employer's power to exercise arbitrary control over his workers lies one of the chief sources of industrial unrest, because few men are given the power by nature or upbringing to exercise control in detail over the life and work of others without causing irritation and resentment among them.

Discontent is then further aggravated, according to Hare, by the worker's continual state of insecurity, fuelled by the employer's ability to dismiss the employee at any time for any reason and the existence in most periods of a surplus of job seekers.

Hare then considers the worker's position in external labour markets. After a lengthy discussion he concludes (p. 27),

> The economic position of the industrial wage earner may be summed up as one of great weakness in bargaining with the individual employer and of considerable insecurity in livelihood. In those matters which it is possible to include in a contract for the sale of labour, the worker is at a severe disadvantage; whilst there are many other matters which greatly affect the physical effort and the subjective cost of labour, but cannot be included in any contract and are thus left entirely at the discretion of the employer.

Later (p. 28), he adds,

The term 'wage slavery', familiar to all who come into contact with the organization of workers, expresses more tersely than any other phrase could do the workers' view of the factors we have been studying. The term 'wage' indicates all that complex of factors which make the economic circumstances of the worker so uncertain, and 'slavery' the way in which this economic weakness is used to enforce discipline upon an unwilling worker.

Finally, Hare turns to the subject of injustice. He notes (pp. 41–2),

At every point of contact between the employer and the worker, the relationship tends to be vitiated by a consciousness on both sides that the relation is one in which one party is making a gain out of the personal exertions of the other. It is, of course, the characteristic of all economic transactions that they bring a gain to both sides, otherwise they would not take place. Two things, however, make the contract for sale of labour different. ... The first is the extreme inequality in the respective strength of the parties and the second the fact that it is labour which is bought and sold and that this involves the subjection of the personality of one person to the will of another. ... Even if the employer pays more than a fair wage, ... the dissatisfaction caused by the feeling of being sold for profit will come into accentuate discontent. [Further], this sense of injustice will be heightened by the feeling that the worker's relative poverty is due to his labour being used to increase the gain of others who have more than he has himself.

Hare then declares (p. 40), "[T]he sense of injustice which this situation begets becomes the basis for a common bond between all grades of workers against an organization of society which perpetuates inequality. This revolt against social injustice is the moral basis of socialism."

In Chapter 2, Hare then turns to remedies for industrial unrest. He opens the chapter with this declaration (p. 49): "Neither compulsory works councils, nor compulsory arbitration of disputes can, by themselves, produce either industrial peace or goodwill in industry. Without goodwill all else must fail, and it is, therefore, primarily to methods of encouraging the development of goodwill that we must look in securing a remedy for industrial ills." A few pages later (p. 58), he states, "The primary aim of industrial relations must be to modify the competitive struggle over the proceeds of industry, in which each side seeks to increase its share at the expense of the other, by substituting for it cooperation which will increase the income of both parties."

In the body of the chapter, Hare notes that efforts to solve labour unrest can come from three principal agents: employers, trade unions and the state. He starts with the state and says (pp. 50–51), "The fundamental problem to be solved in this connection is how to maintain full employment. As long as unemployment exists and the worker cannot be sure of a market for his labour, whilst the employer can dismiss the worker with the certainty of being able to obtain another, the worker's economic problem is incapable of solution." He then goes on to say (p. 51), "Of secondary importance to the problem of how to maintain full employment, but complementary to it, is the problem of how to provide the worker with complete economic security against the risks of ill health, accident, old age and temporary unemployment." He then next turns to a third avenue for state action (p. 52): "The state can ... also intervene directly to regulate the actual terms of the bargain by which the workman is employed." Also discussed is a fourth state action: a progressive system of taxation to reduce income inequality.

Regarding trade unions, Hare concludes they are an essential part of the solution to industrial unrest. He states (pp. 55–6), "The economic disabilities of the wage earner and the inability of the State to give him complete protection are the social justification for the development of strong trade unions." Then he goes on to say, "But there is a further reason for believing that unions promote social progress. In industry the forces of competition always tend to take the line of least resistance. ... The constant pressure of trade unions to make labour dear is in fact one of the greatest forces contributing to the search for efficiency." Finally, Hare (p. 57) notes that trade unions are also vital because "union organization enables the rank and file of the workers to participate in self-government and to have a consultative voice in the working of industry". He also introduces two caveats about unions, however. The first is that union wage bargaining will probably become inflationary in a full-employment economy and require state regulation; the second is that methods (e.g., a sliding wage scale, profit sharing) must be devised to shift the focus of unions from "bargaining and trials of strength" to active cooperation.

Hare then turns to employers. He states (p. 68),

There are two primary aims which should form the basis of management policy in all its aspects. The first is to obtain economic cooperation through the development common interests. The second is to reduce the burden of discipline by substituting self-discipline for an arbitrarily imposed discipline and, where that is not possible, by making discipline impinge upon the individual as lightly as may be.

He goes on to state (p. 69),

Modern management policy does not regard the management of labour as a matter of secondary importance to be handled by a manager who is burdened by many other duties, but aims at substituting for him a specialist trained in methods of labour management. Every firm of any size should employ a Personnel Officer or Labour Manager. ... The function of the labour manager is therefore to stand between the worker and the manager and to see that the search for efficiency which is the manager's duty is not made at the worker's expense.

Finally, Hare observes (p. 70), "Unless steps are taken by the management to ensure permanency of employment and thus to build up a permanent staff of workers, all efforts to establish cooperation will fail. ... A stable workforce is a prerequisite for good industrial relations."

Hare devotes the next eleven chapters of the book to a detailed examination of specific aspects of industrial relations in New Zealand. The last chapter is then on "Recommendations". Particularly noteworthy is the last recommendation, for it presages and justifies the academic study of industrial relations. The title of the last recommendation is "School of Social Studies". Hare then states (p. 341),

The importance of training as an aid towards solving the problem of social discord has been emphasized in each section of these recommendations. Training is needed by those who manage industrial labour, whether as foremen, personnel officers or managers. Training is also needed by negotiators, whether employers or trade union officials. Again, officials of the Department of Labour, factory inspectors, ... and administrative officers need training for their tasks.

Regarding the type of education needed, Hare states (pp. 341–2),

All need as a basis for their special technique a broad understanding of the nature of the social problem facing them. Without a knowledge of the causes of industrial unrest, of the methods employed in other countries in attempting to overcome it and of their relative success or failure, the social worker will tend to have a parochial outlook ... his actions may be ill-judged and even harmful in the long run apart from the immediate case.

Hare ends the book with this declaration (p. 342): "In the long run, no other step could contribute more to industrial peace and to social progress than the establishment of a good School of Social Studies." Here, contained in a book that lies in obscurity, from a country not traditionally looked to for early contributions to industrial relations, is as good a statement of the original rationale for the academic field as can be found anywhere.

Notes

[1] Kahn-Freund escaped Nazi Germany and taught at the LSE before going to Oxford.

[2] Charles' (1973) book *The development of industrial relations in Britain 1911–1939*, for example, contains no reference to Beveridge in its index, nor does Armstrong's (1969) textbook *Industrial relations: An introduction*.

[3] These issues had, however, received some earlier attention, such as through the work of the Industrial Fatigue Research Board during the First World War.

[4] Wagner, it may be noted, emigrated to the United States with his family from Germany and his economic and political ideas reflect this national heritage.

[5] Twenty years earlier a PM-oriented Institute of Industrial Relations was founded at the University of Toronto but was folded into the business administration programme in 1949 (Bladen, 1978).

[6] The effect on trade unions was paradoxical – the act greatly stimulated union growth since only workers organized into trade unions could bring a dispute to the court, but strong unions also found that the court and the arbitration process limited their exercise of bargaining power.

[7] Extensive reference is made to Hare's book in this chapter. Unfortunately attempts at tracing the copyright holder have proved unsuccessful.

THE IIRA: TAKING THE INDUSTRIAL RELATIONS FIELD GLOBAL

6

This chapter represents a pivotal point in the history of the field of industrial relations. Up to the mid-1960s industrial relations was effectively confined to the English-speaking part of the world. This situation changed quickly, however, upon the founding of the International Industrial Relations Association (IIRA) in 1966. Within a decade the industrial relations field had spread to numerous other countries around the world, witnessed by the proliferation of new industrial relations programmes in universities, professional associations, academic journals and books, and conferences. In this chapter, I tell the story of the IIRA's founding and, over the next decade, the role it played in globalizing the field of industrial relations. To do so, however, first requires bringing the ILO back into the picture, for the IIRA and ILO are tightly linked.

Antecedent events: The ILO

The IIRA was officially established on 30 June 1966, at a meeting in London. The founding members were the BUIRA, the Industrial Relations Research Association (United States), the Japan Institute of Labor (JIL) and the International Institute for Labour Studies (IILS) of the ILO. The ILO agreed to serve as the sponsor of the IIRA and the group's headquarters, and administrative staff were located at the ILO in Geneva, Switzerland. This choice was not accidental, for the ILO served as a catalyst and focal point for the formation of the IIRA. The trail of events goes back two decades, however, to the end of the Second World War.

When the Second World War began, the ILO's continued existence was in doubt. The war spelled the end of the League of Nations and the ILO was an official body of the League. Furthermore, the ILO had fled Switzerland and, on the invitation of Canadian Prime Minister Mackenzie King, taken up temporary residence at McGill University in Montreal, Canada.

As victory by the Allied powers began to appear more certain, Western political leaders started to plan for the new post-war international order. The Treaty of Versailles was widely viewed as fundamentally flawed and a major cause of the interwar political and economic breakdown. Roosevelt, Churchill and their advisers thus wanted to avoid a repeat of this outcome. Their viewpoint was that the League of Nations had been a worthy endeavour but had failed because ruinous economic competition among nations had fuelled radical nationalism and war. The greatest culprit was the Great Depression and the collapse of the major world economies. But the Depression had roots, in turn, in the Treaty of Versailles that ended the First World War and the overly punitive and unbalanced schedule of reparations it forced upon Germany and the other defeated nations.

Against this backdrop, the Allied powers sought to build a new international economic order based on a stronger foundation of economic growth and shared international prosperity. Also crucial was the development of new democratic institutions in the defeated Axis countries, which would serve as a bulwark against the re-emergence of authoritarianism. The groundwork was laid at two major Allied socio-economic conferences held in 1944 (Lorenz, 2001: 123).

The first conference was in Bretton Woods, in the United States. The Bretton Woods conference paved the way for the creation of the International Monetary Fund (IMF) and World Bank, as well as the post-war system of fixed exchange rates and tariff reductions. The purpose of the IMF was to provide short-term liquidity for countries experiencing balance of payments crises; the World Bank was to provide long-term investment funds for economic development.

The second conference was also in the United States, in Philadelphia, PA, and marked the XXVI Annual Conference of the ILO. Although the ILO's fate had earlier been in doubt, by 1944 Allied leaders had decided that economic and political issues concerning capital–labour relations were crucial for the post-war international order and the ILO was the best-equipped body to push forward a new labour programme. Thus the conference was attended by leading political figures from the Allied nations (excepting the Soviet Union) and the ILO's mission received strong endorsement from President Roosevelt.

The importance attached to the conference derived from four premises on the part of Allied leaders. The first was that the preservation of liberal democracy and the maintenance of world peace depend on achieving economic prosperity, growth and rising living standards. The second was that protection of basic human rights is a bulwark against the re-emergence of totalitarian regimes, such as the fascist governments of the Axis powers. The third was that political democracy and economic stability are promoted by further integration of the working-class and labour movements into the national and international polity. The fourth was that progress in these areas of economic and political reform requires multilateral, coordinated action among nations.

In some respects, these premises were a re-play of the economic and political forces that led to the creation of the ILO in 1919. Nevertheless, there were also fundamental differences. Most notable was the greater attention given in Philadelphia to basic human rights and the macroeconomic challenge of promoting economic growth and full employment, together with a de-emphasis on worker protection per se and the role of legislated labour standards as the ILO's chief policy instrument. This shift was most evident in the famous declaration adopted at the conference and incorporated into the ILO Constitution. The Declaration of Philadelphia reaffirmed the basic mission of the ILO but established a revised agenda and set of priorities.

The mix of old and new priorities is evident in the various sections of the Declaration. The Declaration begins in Section I with a statement of fundamental principles: (a) labour is not a commodity, (b) freedom of expression and association is essential to sustained social progress, (c) poverty anywhere constitutes a danger to prosperity everywhere, and (d) solving labour problems requires concerted tripartite national and international dialogue and decision making among representatives of workers, employers and government. While the first and last of these principles are express carry-overs from the labour sections of the Treaty of Versailles, the others are significant generalizations and extensions in the areas of human rights and economic growth.

Section II then reaffirms another fundamental principle from the Treaty of Versailles, stating that "experience has fully demonstrated the truth ... that lasting peace can be established only if it is based on social justice". The Declaration then lists five principles that are central to the attainment of social justice. These principles also represent a significant expansion in philosophical scope and policy programme of the ILO. Illustrative, for example, are these three statements (Section II, (a), (c) and (d)):

all human beings, irrespective of race, creed, or sex, have the right to pursue both their material well-being and their spiritual development in conditions of freedom and dignity, or economic security and equal opportunity.

all national and international policies and measures, in particular, those of an economic and financial character, should be judged in this light [achievement of conditions in (a) above] ...

it is the responsibility of the International Labour Organization to examine and consider all international economic and financial policies and measures in the light of this fundamental objective.

Section III of the Declaration then outlines ten specific goals that the ILO is committed to achieve. Several are quite close to the ten objectives listed in the Treaty of Versailles (see the list in Chapter 3), but a number are new or substantially revised. The ten are (paraphrased in some cases):

- full employment and the raising of standards of living;
- employment of workers in the most productive and satisfying occupations;
- facilitating training and migration of labour;
- equitable sharing of the fruits of economic progress and a minimum living wage;
- recognition of the right of collective bargaining and promotion of labour–management cooperation for productive efficiency;
- extension of social security measures to provide a basic income, medical services, and other protections to those in need;
- adequate protection of workers' health and safety;
- provision for child welfare and maternity protection;
- adequate nutrition, housing and facilities for recreation and culture;
- equality of educational and vocational opportunity.

Section IV then contains this declaration:

> Confident that the fuller and broader utilization of the world's productive resources necessary for the achievement of the objectives set forth in this Declaration can be secured by effective international and national action, including measures to expand production and consumption, to avoid severe economic fluctuations, to promote the economic and social advancement of the less developed regions of the world, to assure greater stability in world prices of primary products, and to promote a high and steady volume of international trade, the Conference pledges the full cooperation of the International Labour Organization with such international bodies as may be entrusted with a share of responsibility with this great task for the promotion of the health, education and well-being of all peoples.

One cannot read the Declaration of Philadelphia without sensing that it represents a significant transformation of the focus and mission of the ILO (Lee, 1994). On one hand, the ILO was still firmly committed in broad outline to the same liberal, pluralist ideology that inspired its birth (Haas, 1964: 177). The Declaration reaffirms the fact that labour is not a commodity, commitment to the tripartite principle and the maintenance of minimum labour standards, as originally stated in the 1919 Constitution. Relative to the original Constitution, however, the Declaration gives far more emphasis to macroeconomic issues, such as economic development, preventing depressions and facilitating international trade. It also gives considerably more emphasis to the importance of basic human rights. Perhaps most significant, it represents a critical shift in the mission of the ILO. When first conceived, the ILO was expressly seen as "doing something for labour", which tended to be perceived as in opposition to employers and even governments. Toward this end, the major activity of the ILO was protecting and advancing the conditions of labour through legally promulgated Conventions and Recommendations. Twenty-five years later – reflecting the improved position of labour in the advanced industrial countries, the entrance into ILO membership of a growing number of newly independent and less-developed countries, and the devastation of the Great Depression and the Second World War – the policy programme of the ILO was broadened and given greater balance. That is, the policy programme was broadened to complement standard setting through Conventions and Recommendations with greater emphasis on promoting economic growth and development (a two-pronged approach to raising the plane of competition), while it was given greater balance by more fully recognizing that employers are not only a source of labour problems but also a potential instrument for raising living standards and providing well-paying, attractive jobs. The broadened scope and heightened ambitions of the ILO is illustrated by Valticos' (1969: 399) statement that the "Organization seemed on the way to becoming the chief co-ordinator of social policy throughout the world".

This shift in mission and activities of the ILO accelerated in 1948 with the appointment of David Morse as the Director-General. Morse was American and at the time serving as Under-Secretary of Labour in the Truman administration. He was a graduate of the Harvard Law School and began his career as a partner in a New York City labour law firm. Morse did extensive labour arbitration work in the garment industry, served in Washington, DC, as general counsel to the National Labor Relations Board, and organized the occupation labour relations programmes in Italy and Germany. Although Morse also served as an employer delegate to the ILO, when he assumed the position of Director-General he was from the point of view of the ILO bureaucracy an "outsider".

Under Morse, the ILO remained committed to the pursuit of social justice (Lorenz, 2001: 164–5). Morse also continued to press ahead with promulgation of new labour standards through Conventions and Recommendations, albeit with less emphasis and activity. But Morse's major initiative was to steer the ILO on to a new course of raising labour conditions through human resource development and employment growth (Haas, 1964; Cox, 1971a). The major instrument used for advancing these goals, in turn, was a wide array of training and technical assistance programmes, augmented by an expanded research and education capability. The idea was to assemble and bring to bear the best technical talent and know-how in the world to help nations spur growth through improvements in their labour input and supporting institutional infrastructure. Technical assistance was organized in three major areas: Development of Human Resources, Conditions of Life and Welfare, and Development of Social Institutions (Alcock, 1971: 217). As summarized by Alcock (ibid.):

> From being an organization devoted, before the Second World War, to protecting the worker in industrial life through labour legislation, it would now turn to preparing the worker for participation in industrial life. From working, before the Second World War, mainly with the highly developed countries, it would now give the wealth of its experience to the rest of the world.

Illustratively, between 1950 and 1959 more than 2,000 technical assistance teams were sent to various countries (Alcock, 1971: 243), while funding of human resource development programmes grew from one-fifth of the ILO budget in 1950 to 84 per cent in 1967 (Lorenz, 2001: 165).

Morse emphasized training and technical assistance partly out of the belief that an enduring improvement in human rights and labour conditions requires elimination of poverty and joblessness – conditions that cannot simply be legislated out of existence. In this respect, the ILO programme of economic development was a philosophical and policy extension of the Marshall Plan of economic reconstruction undertaken by the United States after the Second World War. However, Morse was also reacting to a variety of more specific environmental and political pressures. One source came from the United States, where employer representatives were strongly opposed to further labour standards. Another pressure was that the membership of the ILO was shifting from the developed countries to the less developed and the latter saw greater benefit to their economies from technical assistance programmes than from standard setting. Finally, the ILO was caught up in the politics of the Cold War and, in particular, the question of whether the Soviet Union and its satellite states should be admitted to the ILO. The American AFL–CIO, among other groups, vigorously lobbied against their inclusion on grounds that the employer and labour representatives were state agents and thus not an independent voice for employers and unions, thereby violating the ILO's cardinal principle of *tripartite interest representation*. But many other people maintained that to not admit the Eastern bloc countries violated another cardinal principle of the ILO – *universality* (all nation states qualify for membership). Morse successfully bridged these differences, gaining admission of the Soviet Union in 1954, in part by orienting the ILO toward technical assistance and training activities that were non-ideological and a potential "win" for all members (Cox, 1971a).

Key to the story being told here is yet another force that helped shift Morse and the ILO toward an expanded programme of human resource development.

As noted in an earlier chapter, in 1954 Kerr, Dunlop, Harbison and Myers formed the Inter-University Study of Labor Problems in Economic Development project. One of the motivations behind this was the conviction of Kerr et al. that American industrial relations was too insular and ethnocentric, and that the horizons of the field could be broadened through a cross-country comparison of labour in the industrialization process. The ILO quickly came to play a key role in the project. Most importantly, Kerr et al. were faced with the daunting task of gaining the cooperation of governments in countries as diverse as Egypt, India, Japan and Sweden, and enlisting the participation of the key actors in the government, employer, union and academic circles of each nation. No organization was better situated to help in this task than the ILO and, by good fortune, the Director-General was not only an American but also had a personal relationship with Dunlop and was interested and familiar with industrial relations studies. In short order, Kerr et al. formed a close working relationship with the ILO and used its facilities and contacts to help move their project forward. Thus Kerr et al. published the first joint article of the project in the ILO's *International Labour Review*, held a number of meetings and seminars at the ILO, briefed Morse and top officials on their ideas and findings, and worked through the ILO's country offices to help coordinate their visits and open doors to high-level officials.

The interchange between the ILO and Kerr et al. was not just one way, however. Morse was a forward-looking leader seeking to expand and strengthen the ILO's mission and role in the international community. Kerr et al. proved to be an important and influential conduit of ideas for Morse. When Kerr et al. initiated the project their focus was on industrial conflict and the impact of industrialization on workers and their unions. As the project progressed, however, the focus shifted to understanding the generic process of industrialization, the role of labour in economic growth and the impact of industrialization on labour. As their focus shifted, so did the emphasis in their research and theorizing. Industrial conflict and trade unions moved down to a supporting role, while human resource development and effective "structuring of the labour force" by political and managerial elites moved to the top of the agenda.

Although Morse and the ILO were already moving toward a greater emphasis on human resource development and economic growth before Kerr et al. arrived on the scene, the latter certainly provided further impetus by placing these activities in a larger and more compelling intellectual framework. But Kerr et al. and their expanded view of industrial relations also had other attractions. As already noted, for example, the idea of improving labour standards through the "pull" of economic development was an easier sell to ILO member States than was using the "push" of new Conventions and Recommendations to achieve this same effect. And, further, both the capitalist and socialist blocs in the ILO could find common meeting ground in the theory put forward by Kerr and his colleagues, since it broadened the subject of industrial relations from the study of capitalist economies to the generic process of industrialism and, in addition, made the success of industrialism hinge on "modernizing elites" that could just as well come from socialist as capitalist counties. And, finally, note must also be made that American-style industrial relations was also appealing to Morse for political reasons. Both the AFL–CIO and American employers were strongly committed to voluntarism and bilateral relations between employers and employees, and they brought considerable pressure upon Morse and the ILO to promote collective bargaining rather than legal enactment (i.e., Conventions and Recommendations) to raise labour standards and not to encourage the direct involvement of the government in labour markets through tripartite forms of market regulation.

For the reasons just outlined, as well as the fact that trade unions and collective bargaining in the mid-1950s were at their most successful in terms of membership, coverage and influence, Morse moved to make industrial relations a more central and strategic part of the ILO and its mission. This is not to say that industrial relations and collective bargaining were ever unimportant, for certainly they were not,[1] but it does suggest a greater priority and focus at the ILO on labour–management relations. Two pieces of evidence speak to this strategic shift, as well as the role of Kerr et al. in it.

The first piece of evidence is this observation from a highly placed ILO insider. He states (Cox and Sinclair, 1996: 442):

> From the late 1950s, a specifically American doctrine of industrial relations was given pride of place in the ILO as a rationale for its programmes. Two books expressing this tendency of thought, both products of this period, were John Dunlop's *Industrial Relations Systems* and the collaborative work, financed by the Ford Foundation, of Clark Kerr, John Dunlop, Frederick Harbison and Charles Myers, entitled *Industrialism and Industrial Man*. ... The American scholars provided a reformulation of operational ideology for the ILO.

The second piece of evidence involves the Cole Report, the shift of programme funding in the ILO toward labour–management relations and human resource development, and the creation in the ILO of the IILS. These parts of the story fit together in the following manner.

Morse devoted the major part of his Report to the 38th Session of the International Labour Conference to the subject of labour–management relations. The Report led to passage of a resolution asking the Director-General to "review the ILO's activities as a whole and to consider how these activities should be modified or supplemented so as to contribute effectively towards promoting labour–management cooperation and better human relations in industry throughout the world" (quoted in Cole, 1956). Morse then asked David Cole of the United States to prepare this review and offer a practical programme of action. Cole had formerly been director of the United States Federal Mediation and Conciliation Service and at the time was working closely with Dunlop in high-level arbitration and mediation cases (statement of Dunlop in Kaufman, 2002a). Cole's report, as summarized in the *International Labour Review* (Cole, 1956), was divided into two parts. The first part was titled "The Advantages of Collective Dealings" and made the case for using "collective dealings" as the major instrument for setting wages and labour standards. (Cole uses collective dealings instead of collective bargaining because, he says, the former connotes a more cooperative and less adversarial approach.) The second part then lays out a suggested programme of action for the ILO. The central idea he advances is that collective dealings work best when "less reliance is placed on threats and more on facts and reasoning" and that the mission of the ILO should be to "accelerate the transition to the rational approach to problems". To accomplish this goal, Cole recommends in turn that the ILO "set up a centre, preferably in Geneva", that conducts research and courses and seminars on principles and methods of labour–management cooperation.

Following the Cole Report, the ILO undertook a number of new initiatives starting in the last half of the 1950s that broadly reflected the "reformulation of operational ideology" coming from Kerr et al. and the American industrial relations model. According to Haas (1964: 185), for example, new educational programmes were established in management development, labour–management relations and worker education. And, as already cited, the proportion of the ILO's programmatic funding that went to human resource development activities increased sharply.

More important for this story, however, is the creation of the IILS, the "capstone", according to Ernst Haas (1964: 187), of Morse's educational and research programme. The institute was established in 1960 as an autonomous body within the ILO, with financing provided largely by contributions from France and several other member States. The IILS was an outgrowth of Morse's strategic design to move the ILO away from its traditional juridical emphasis on standard setting toward a more social science, industrial relations approach that emphasized human resource development and institution building. According to Dunlop (2003), Morse had discussed the idea of such an institute with him in the late 1950s and Dunlop had supported the concept. Robert Cox, then Chief of the Special Research and Reports Division and later

IILS director, also relates that he and Morse had conversations on the proposed institute and he likewise encouraged Morse in this direction.

Under its first two directors (Sir Douglas Copland and Hilary Marquand) the IILS served largely as a staff college by providing short, quasi-academic courses on various industrial relations-related subjects to students recruited from middle and middle-upper occupational positions in their respective countries. Over time, however, Morse and his supporters expanded their strategic vision of the role of the IILS to the point where it began to resemble in broad outline an American-style industrial relations institute. Courses were expanded in content and length and clearly differentiated from technical assistance and vocational courses; greater effort was made to move the student body "upstream" by recruiting students from the upper ranks of government management and unions; visiting university professors from around the world were recruited to teach institute courses; and discussion was given to offering some kind of official degree (never implemented).

Over time, Morse and Cox – the latter subsequently appointed by Morse to be the third director of the IILS – developed an expanded research vision for the IILS. Their desire was to make the ILO a larger and more influential player in economic development and world economic coordination and policy. To be successful, however, the ILO had to move beyond its specialization in labour law and, consistent with the broader vision contained in the Declaration of Philadelphia, develop expertise in subjects such as economics, manpower development, management, finance and public administration. It also needed a more proactive, forward-looking approach to policy development, in contrast to the largely reactive approach that had traditionally characterized ILO initiatives. Although the ILO already had a research department, it could not effectively take on this larger mission because of limited staff, the priority given to servicing the legal and technical assistance issues presented by member States, and the difficulty of taking on politically difficult topics within the ILO bureaucracy and constituency (Meyers, 1967: 23). Morse saw the IILS as a way to circumvent these constraints and develop a larger, more strategic and forward-looking research function. In effect, the IILS would become a social-science think tank on labour and employment with a network of affiliated research institutions around the world and enough independence to explore critical issues and politically sensitive topics.

Although some in-house ILO staff were given research positions in the IILS, most of the research talent was recruited in the form of visiting university professors. Examples of people spending time at the IILS include a large contingent of American industrial relations scholars, such as Everett Kassalow, Jack Stieber, Gerald Somers and George Shultz. Industrial relations scholars from other countries included Roger Blanpain (Belgium), Stuart Jamieson (Canada), Jean-Daniel Reynaud (France) and Ben Roberts (United Kingdom). The IILS also began publication of its own research journal, called the *Bulletin of the International Institute of Labour Studies* (later renamed *Labour and Society*).

According to Cox (2003), although the term industrial relations was not used in the official title of the institute, its programme and philosophy were most closely drawn from and modelled on the field of industrial relations, as the subject was broadly developed by Kerr et al. and practised at this time in the United States. Apparently, however, the exact boundaries of industrial relations remained ambiguous within the ILO. Cox endeavoured to promote a very broad "political economy" concept of industrial relations, in line with his definition of the field as the study of the "social relations of production" (Cox, 1971b). In other reports and memoranda of the ILO, however, industrial relations is defined more narrowly. The report of the meeting of experts convened pursuant to the recommendations of the Cole Report, for example, defines industrial relations as "group or collective relationships" at work, while human relations is defined as individual or "personal relationships" (ILO, 1956: 3). Also apropos, a later ILO report (1974: 12) states, "one might say that collective bargaining has become so firmly established in the past three to four decades that it is sometimes regarded as synonymous with, or as constituting the essence of, the prevailing system of industrial relations".

Founding of the International Industrial Relations Association

The establishment of the IILS set the stage for the birth of the IIRA. The people principally involved in the IIRA's formation were Cox, director of the IILS, and Roberts, professor of industrial relations at the LSE. Also playing a significant role were Gerald Somers, professor of economics and industrial relations at the University of Wisconsin, and Arthur Ross, professor of economics and industrial relations at the University of California, Berkeley, and at the time Commissioner of the United States Bureau of Labor Statistics.

Roberts had developed a wide range of international contacts in the industrial relations field. In the late 1950s, he was a visiting professor in the United States, in the early 1960s spent a sabbatical leave and several subsequent summers at the ILO, and travelled to Japan and a number of other countries (Roberts, 2002). Roberts was interested in institution building, having been a founding member of the BUIRA, the founder of the *British Journal of Industrial Relations*, and the prime mover in the founding of the

Department of Industrial Relations at the LSE. From his international travels, Roberts saw that no means existed to bring scholars interested in industrial relations topics together for collaborative discussion and research. He concluded, therefore, that an international organization along the lines of the IRRA in the United States and BUIRA in the United Kingdom could serve a valuable function. Roberts also noted that the subject of industrial relations was rapidly gaining recognition as a distinct area of university teaching and research in the world academic community – perhaps to the point of becoming a new discipline in the social sciences. Since other disciplines had an international association (e.g., the International Economics Association, the International Political Science Association) to promote cross-national dialogue and research, the time was propitious for industrial relations to establish a similar association.

Cox was a Canadian, who had become familiar with the ILO while working on his master's degree at McGill University and took a staff position with the ILO in 1947. In 1954, he became Morse's *chef de cabinet* (principal staff officer) and later was promoted to chief of the ILO's Planning and Programmes Division. Although Cox did not have a Ph.D., by all accounts he had a considerable intellect, interest in research and scholarly inquiry, and strong commitment to building the IILS. After leaving the ILO in 1972, Cox held professorships at several top-tier universities and developed an international reputation based on his writings in world politics and political economy (Cox and Sinclair, 1996: 3–38). Cox supported Morse's new strategy for the ILO and thought the IILS had a key role to play by serving as a social-science think tank. He realized, however, that the ILO did not have the critical mass of in-house research talent necessary to make the IILS a going concern, so he sought to recruit outside scholars for visiting positions at the IILS and form a network of relationships with prominent academics and research organizations in other countries. Not surprisingly, given the liberal/pluralist ideology of the ILO, its emphasis on labour law and tripartite systems of labour–management relations, and the social-science, institutional-oriented strategy being pursued by Morse, when Cox looked outward for allies and resources in the academic world his focus centred on the field of industrial relations. But industrial relations had little presence outside North America and the United Kingdom. Moreover, the Americans tended to be focused on domestic institutions and developments, and no interdisciplinary association or network existed to bring together social scientists in the world community conducting research in employment and labour. Well before becoming director of the IILS, therefore, Cox had started to think about creating some form of international association of industrial relations researchers and had broached the idea to Morse and several visiting scholars. As he was later to state in private correspondence (letter of 5 February 1966), "From the Institute's point of view, the new Association would be a useful means of contact with social scientists in countries throughout the world."

In the 1962–63 period, while Roberts was at the ILO, he and Cox discussed the need for an international industrial relations association. Both agreed this was an idea that should be carried forward and the planning for the new association began in earnest. In January 1963, the IILS sponsored a Meeting of Research Consultants that brought a number of prominent industrial relations researchers to Geneva. One of these people was Arthur Ross, another was Gerald Somers of the University of Wisconsin. Cox and Roberts discussed the idea of an international association with Ross and Somers, who took the idea back to the United States.

Work on an international association then proceeded in both Europe and the United States. In Europe, Roberts took the lead and wrote up a draft plan for an international organization in 1964. In the United States, Ross and Somers initiated discussion among colleagues about an international industrial relations association and put the issue before the IRRA. Somers, in his capacity as secretary of the organization and editor of its publications, became the person in charge of moving the idea forward and working with the Europeans. The draft plan for an international association was thus sent to Somers by Roberts in 1964 and circulated among the Americans. Fortuitously, in 1964 Ross was also nominated for the presidency of the IRRA and was thus in a strategic position to help move the discussion along in a favourable direction.

Roberts and Cox also initiated discussion with Otto Kahn-Freund and Alexandre Berenstein, president and secretary, respectively, of the International Society for Labour Law and Social Legislation (ISLLSL).[2] Since the ISLLSL had its administrative office at the ILO and had a focus on labour and employment conditions, Roberts and Cox wanted not only to promote cooperative relations between the two organizations but also head off possible feelings on the part of the ISLLSL that the new proposed industrial relations association was unduly encroaching on its territory.

Modest additional consideration of the ISLLSL is warranted here because it provides useful insight not only into the founding of the IIRA but also into the juxtaposition of the legal/statist approach to improving industrial relations favoured in continental Europe versus the social-science/voluntarist approach favoured in the Anglo-American countries.

The organizational roots of the ISLLSL are in 1951 with the First World Congress of Labour Law in Trieste, Italy. A second world congress was held in 1957 in Geneva, Switzerland, which the ILO co-organized and hosted. Wilfred Jenks, at the time Assistant Director-General of the ILO, played a central role in forging this cooperative relationship. An agreement was reached at this event to form an international association, and a year later (1958) the ISLLSL was formally launched. It was established as an independent association of scholars and researchers interested in labour law and social legislation, had its headquarters' office at the ILO in Geneva, and since 1974 has had an ILO official serve as secretary.

Regarding the respective roles and territories of the two organizations, Kahn-Freund (letter, 12 January 1966) wrote to Roberts with the following response:

> There is room for the two organizations, as long as we understand that a certain amount of overlap is not only inevitable but even desirable. You may not be able to cultivate your fields without paying attention to the law and if we look at the law divorced from its social, economics, political and cultural context we should be neglecting our duty.

Evident in this remark is the differentiation between the ISLLSL's focus on labour law and the future IIRA's focus on the social sciences (the "social, economics, political and cultural context"). This distinction is also highlighted in a letter Cox wrote to Roberts (28 September 1966) in which he notes that both the ISLLSL and the proposed IIRA include labour institutes as "institutional members", but that the institutes in the former are European "classical labour law institutes" and the latter are "the newer interdisciplinary institutes".

A similar perspective is provided by Alexandre Berenstein in his retrospective historical account of the development of the ISLLSL (1994). He states (p. 4), for example:

> A few years after the founding of the Society saw the creation of the International Industrial Relations Association (IIRA) which, while pursuing similar aims, focused on just one aspect of social policy, namely industrial relations and did this from different perspectives that went beyond a strictly legal approach of the subject. Hence, its membership included economists and sociologists in addition to jurists.

Perhaps of most interest in Berenstein's quote is his reference to "social policy" as the broad domain of the field of interest, with industrial relations being conceived as one particular approach to this subject.

Meanwhile, in the United States the matter of an international association was included for formal consideration on the agenda of the IRRA's Executive Board Meeting, held in conjunction with association's spring 1965 meeting in Buffalo, New York. A decision was made to direct Somers to publish in the IRRA's newsletter an announcement about the possible formation of an international industrial relations association and to solicit member comments and opinions. Somers also independently requested comments from a number of national and international scholars interested in industrial relations. Thirty written responses were received, with a significant number from researchers in other countries. While nearly everyone favoured the idea, they split into two groups with regard to how the new association should be organized. One group favoured creating an entirely new organization that was truly international in membership and outlook; the second favoured "internationalizing" the IRRA by creating foreign affiliate chapters. Surprisingly, a number of the foreign scholars favoured the latter option, including the three respondees from France and one from Japan. The most common reasons cited were the IRRA's ability to take on the administrative responsibilities for the new organization and the almost non-existent institutional infrastructure for industrial relations outside the United Kingdom and United States.

A series of meetings and exchange of letters ensued as the Americans and Europeans, centred around Roberts and Cox, sought to converge to a common plan. The Roberts' plan called for the new association to be based in Geneva at the ILO, sponsored by the IILS, and with administrative support provided by the ILO. The latter two respects went beyond the arrangement the ILO had with the ISLLSS, since the ISLLSS was neither formally housed in any unit of the ILO nor received any budgetary or staff support. Roberts further proposed that the organization be formed in parallel fashion to the BUIRA and include only researchers, unlike the American IRRA which included both academics and practitioners. The ISLLSS also included only scholars and researchers, but membership in the ISLLSS was not on an individual basis but through affiliated national labour law associations. Since the Americans were split on what to do, exploratory dialogue was held on a possible compromise. For example, discussion was given to having the international association located both in Geneva and Madison, Wisconsin (the IRRA's home at the University of Wisconsin). Roberts and Cox strongly argued, however, that the new association needed to be independent of the IRRA and the ILO was its natural home. Since a sizeable contingent of Americans had a similar view, within a short time the IRRA decided to formally endorse the Roberts–Cox plan.

At the IRRA's spring 1966 meeting the Executive Board approved American participation in the establishment of the new international association and instructed Somers to meet with Roberts and Cox to work out the remaining details. The Americans also indicated that it would be desirable to broaden the national representation of industrial relations associations on the organizing committee so it did not seem so completely an Anglo-American affair. At an earlier point Cox and Roberts had discussed bringing in the Australians and/or Canadians, since both countries had newly formed industrial relations associations that could provide institutional participation parallel with the IRRA and BUIRA, but then dropped the idea in order to keep the nucleus group small and manageable. The American suggestion brought the issue up again, however. Cox and Roberts agreed it was a worthy idea, but the practical difficulty was finding a suitable candidate.

Four options for non-Anglo-Saxon participation were considered: France, Germany, India and Japan. An inquiry was made to Professor Jean-Daniel Reynaud about French participation, but he indicated it would be impossible due to the lack of any industrial relations association in his country at the time. Likewise, an inquiry was made to the Germans but pursued no further upon Roberts' report to Cox (letter, 9 January 1966) that "it would be necessary to approach the Germans with some caution since there appears to be a certain degree of hostility [ideological and disciplinary] between them and it will not be easy to achieve a national committee". Roberts also made inquiries in India but received discouraging reports. In one letter (28 September 1966), for example, Subbiah Kannappan tells Roberts, "The problem in India is relatively simple. There is no national association which is an inclusive universal organization comparable to either the IRRA in the US or the British Universities Industrial Relations Association."

The best prospect was Japan, and it was this that Cox and Roberts explored most intensively. The Japanese government had established in the late 1950s an autonomous government-funded labour research institute, the Japan Institute of Labor (JIL). Although the JIL was not an independent private-sector association of academics like the IRRA and BUIRA, Cox and Roberts judged that it was sufficiently independent and research-oriented to qualify as an institutional member of the new IIRA. Furthermore, the JIL's director-general, Ichiro Nakayama, had earlier visited the ILO in Geneva, was known to Cox and Roberts, and was widely regarded in Japan as the nation's leading authority on labour–management issues. Accordingly, in early 1966 the JIL was officially invited to become a founding member of the IIRA and Nakayama accepted.

A meeting was set for 29–30 June 1966 in London to be attended by Roberts, Cox, Nakayama and Somers. Subsequently, Nakayama developed health problems and his place was taken by Shingo Kaite, managing director of the JIL. Arthur Ross (then president of the IRRA) had also planned to attend, but later cancelled. The four agreed upon the name for the new organization: the International Industrial Relations Association. No indication is contained in the archival records that the founders were aware that an organization of the same name had earlier existed (see Chapter 3). The group also approved the draft constitution; appointed Roberts as Chairman of the Provisional Executive Committee and Cox as Secretary; and Somers and Roberts agreed to submit the draft constitution for approval to their respective associations. The First World Congress was also set for 1967 in Geneva.

The IIRA's constitution is interesting in several respects. First, it proclaims the aim of the organization to be "of a purely scientific character" and stipulates that the association "does not endorse opinions on policy questions". Because it was thought that admitting employer and union representatives would inevitably introduce a partisan element, membership was restricted to researchers – a category defined broadly, however, to include not only academic researchers but also those from government, employers and unions.

Second, the constitution stipulates that the general purpose of the organization is "to promote the study of industrial relations throughout the world in the several academic disciplines". It then lists seven specific methods or activities the association will use to accomplish this broad purpose:

- encourage establishment and development of national industrial relations associations;
- facilitate the spread of information about significant developments in research and education in industrial relations;
- organize conferences and round-table discussions;
- promote internationally planned research in industrial relations;
- convene an international congress every three years;
- convene specialized conferences and study groups on particular topics;
- encourage publication of papers and proceedings from sponsored meetings.

A third noteworthy feature is that the IIRA was established as an independent organization, but with sponsorship by the ILO. Thus, the constitutions states, "The seat of the association is at Geneva, Switzerland. It may be transferred to another place by decision of the Executive Committee." The Executive Committee, composed of eleven association members from different countries, is thus the governing body of the organization and has ultimate decision-making power on matters of policy.

A fourth point is that nowhere does the IIRA's constitution define what is "industrial relations" or the topics or academic disciplines that constitute the field. According to Roberts, this omission was deliberate on the grounds that industrial relations needs to be construed with considerable elasticity given the subject's broad domain and different articulations among countries. The archival records are almost entirely free of any discussion of the definition of the field among the founders of the association, although in his original draft proposal for the IIRA Roberts suggests that industrial relations is concerned with "the social problems arising out of employment" and is "recognized as a legitimate field of academic study, research and teaching". Certainly the desire was to frame the field broadly and in a generic way, given Cox's (1971c: 277) opinion that "in order that the concept of industrial relations be valid for a global study, it must be shorn of any ideological affiliation with the particular historical development which gave rise to the term itself".

Fifth, the founders agreed to adopt the universality principle of the ILO. Thus the constitution states, "Membership in the Association is without national limitation." This stipulation meant that researchers from the Soviet Union and Central and Eastern bloc countries were welcome and that challenges to members from countries such as Israel, South Africa and Taiwan, China, would not be considered. The Association also created several levels of membership: full membership for national or regional industrial relations associations; institutional associate membership for universities, colleges and industrial relations research institutes; and individual associate membership for all individual persons engaged in industrial relations research.

Sixth, and finally, the constitution also established the governing and administrative organs of the IIRA. The Association is led by an elected president, the governing body is the Executive Committee, and ongoing administration of the Association is overseen by the secretary. All officers normally serve for three-year terms, with the possibility of re-appointment. The Executive Committee nominates a member to stand for election for president. It also nominates a person to serve as secretary. By tradition this person is a senior official in the ILO.

Although not written in the constitution, two other important considerations received attention at the founding meeting. The first was the decision that all programmes and publications should be bilingual. The two languages selected were English and French (Spanish, the third official language of the ILO, was added later).

The second topic was future publications, such as a newsletter, journal and congress proceedings. All three were deemed desirable but out of reach for the new Association because of lack of staff and financial resources. With regard to the newsletter, a partial solution was obtained by including new items about the IIRA in the IILS's *Bulletin* and distributing a free copy to all association members. Discussion was also given to forming a partnership with existing academic journals in lieu of establishing a new one. For example, one proposal was to publish articles written in English in the *British Journal of Industrial Relations* and articles written in French in *Sociologie du travail*. This proposal was also deferred and the *Bulletin* was again utilized on an ad hoc basis to publish research articles and notes related to industrial relations. Publication of the Proceedings of the World Congress was also deemed prohibitively expensive for the newly formed IIRA and authors were to be encouraged to find publication outlets on their own.

The First World Congress was held in Geneva from 4 to 8 September 1967. Initially, expectations were that perhaps one hundred people would attend but, in fact, 204 scholars registered from 39 countries.

The four themes of the Congress were:

* Bargaining and conflict
* Resistance and response to change
* Incomes policy
* Teaching and research in industrial relations.

Twenty-three invited papers were presented. Many of these were later published in a volume edited by Roberts (1968a), entitled *Industrial relations: Contemporary issues*.

Until the First World Congress, the IIRA was governed by the Provisional Executive Committee. They held their second meeting on 4 September at the beginning of the First World Congress. Three industrial relations associations were admitted to membership: the Austria Industrial Relations Research Association, the Belgium Institute for Industrial Relations, and the Industrial Relations Research Association of Israel. The minutes also note that several other countries were in progress of setting up industrial relations associations and agreed to invite representatives from each country to attend the Executive Board Meeting. Those invited were Henning Friis (Denmark), Rudolf Meidner (Sweden), Jean-Daniel Reynaud (France), Z. Rybicki (Poland) and E. Stafforini (Argentina). Also attending were Roger Blanpain (Belgium), John Crispo (Canada) and Kingsley Laffer (Australia).

At this meeting the issue of electing a slate of officers was also considered. Roberts and Cox had earlier approached Japan's Nakayama with the suggestion that he serve as the IIRA's first president, but Nakayama declined for reasons of poor health. The Committee then agreed to propose Roberts as the first president, with Cox serving as secretary.

The first meeting of the Executive Board of the IIRA was convened, the slate of officers was elected and Roberts assumed the duties of president. Approval was also given to organizing a Second World Congress in 1970.

Early progress and challenges

Once launched, the fate of the new IIRA was now to be determined. Would it be financially viable? Would it attract a large and growing membership? Would it succeed in fostering the growth and transplantation of the industrial relations field outside the Anglo-Saxon countries? And would it stimulate expanded international, comparative dialogue and research on labour and employment issues?

Although uncertain at the time, in hindsight the answer turned out to be 'yes' to all of these questions. But the first decade of life for the IIRA also had its share of difficulties.

Certainly the IIRA proved quite successful as a catalyst for the introduction of the industrial relations field into new countries. Prior to its founding in 1966, national industrial relations associations and university industrial relations degree programmes existed in Australia, Canada, the United Kingdom and the United States. Due to the contacts and initiatives started by Cox and Roberts, and the visibility generated by the First World Congress, the number of national industrial relations associations and university programmes grew quickly.

The best indication is provided by statistics on IIRA membership cited by Roberts (1970, 1973) in his two presidential addresses to the Second and Third World Congresses, respectively. The numbers are reproduced below.

1967
- Full members   10
- Institutional members   11
- Individual members   160

1973
- Full members   19
- Institutional members   36
- Individual members   341

On the reasonable assumption that the number of "Full members" captures the universe of national industrial relations associations at this date, we see that the original four national associations more than doubled to ten in number by the time of the First World Congress in 1967. Then, between 1970 and 1973 the number of national industrial relations associations had nearly doubled again.

Provided below is a complete list of the nineteen Full members. Evidently, the founding of the IIRA contributed greatly to the spread of industrial relations to numerous countries around the world.

Argentina	Industrial Relations Association of Argentina
Australia	Industrial Relations Society of Australia
Austria	Austrian Industrial Relations Research Association
Belgium	Belgium Institute for Industrial Relations
Canada	Canadian Industrial Relations Association
Chile	Chilean Industrial Relations Association
Denmark	Danish Group on Labour Market Studies

Ethiopia	Ethiopian Industrial Relations Research Association
France	French Industrial Relations Association
Federal Republic of Germany	German Industrial Relations Association
Ireland	Irish Association for Industrial Relations
Israel	Industrial Relations Research Association of Israel
Italy	Italian Industrial Relations Research Association
Japan	Japan Industrial Relations Research Association
Netherlands	Netherlands Industrial Relations Research Association
Poland	Polish Industrial Relations Section
Sweden	Swedish Industrial Relations Association
United Kingdom	British Universities Industrial Relations Association
United States	Industrial Relations Research Association

These associations were typically small and often the work of one or two energetic and influential scholars. In a few cases, as Cox states in an internal memorandum, they were little more than "paper organizations". But they nonetheless represented a valuable beachhead for introducing industrial relations to other parts of the world. The German Industrial Relations Association, for example, began with ten people and depended heavily on the organizing work of Professor Neuloh. The same situation was true in other countries where academics such as Blanpain (Belgium), Fürstenberg (Austria), Giugni (Italy), Nakayama (Japan), Reynaud (France) and Stafforini (Argentina) played key roles in starting and nurturing industrial relations associations.

A similar pattern is found with respect to industrial relations university programmes and institutes. One of the central goals of the founders of the IIRA was to promote research and teaching in industrial relations, particularly from an interdisciplinary perspective and in new countries where the study of labour and employment problems was largely absent. Outside of the Anglophone countries, university industrial relations programmes and institutes were nearly completely missing. After the founding of the IIRA, however, institutes and programmes devoted to labour and employment began to appear in increasing numbers in other countries. In 1973, for example, among the "institutional members" of the IIRA were these university institutes and programmes:

Argentina	Universidad Católica de Córdoba, Departamento Organización y Personal
Belgium	Université Catholique de Louvain, Institut Supérieur du Travail
Chile	Universidad de Chile, Departamento de Relaciones del Trabajo y Desarrollo Organizacional
India	Tata Institute of Social Sciences, Department of Personnel and Industrial Relations
Israel	Israel Institute of Industrial and Labour Relations
Republic of Korea	Korea University, Labour Education and Research Institute
Taiwan, China	College of Chinese Culture, Institute of Labour Studies
Venezuela	Universidad de Carabobo, Escuela de Relaciones Industriales

Although difficult to determine with certainty, it is highly likely that the activities of the IIRA were a principal factor behind the emergence of these new industrial relations and labour programmes. Not only did the IIRA include a full session in its First World Congress programme on industrial relations teaching and research, but the role of industrial relations centres and institutes was then singled out for in-depth treatment in later programmes. Shortly after the First World Congress, the Executive Board approved a proposal to establish Regional Meetings of the IIRA (forerunners to the Regional Congresses). The first one was held in Chicago in the United States in May 1968. Somers was the lead organizer. The main topic of the conference was The Role of Industrial Relations Centers and a proceedings with four papers was published. The first Asian and European Regional Meetings were then held, respectively, in 1969 in Tokyo, Japan, and Linz, Austria, with Nakayama and Fürstenberg the lead organizers. Both conferences also included a session on the role of industrial relations centres in teaching and research. The topic was then again highlighted at the Second World Congress.

The Second World Congress of the IIRA was held in September 1970. Given that the IIRA's home was with the ILO in Geneva, and the ability of the latter to provide administrative and financial support, a decision was made to again hold the event in Geneva. The programme included five sessions:

- Evolution of manpower policies
- Workers' participation in management
- Industrial relations and industrial change
- Political systems and industrial relations
- The role and function of industrial relations centres

Ben Roberts gave the presidential address to the 351 attendees. The following passage merits quotation for it speaks to the core identity and intellectual raison d'être of the field (Roberts, 1970: 2–3, emphasis in original).

> During the past few years the importance of industrial relations to the welfare of mankind has become increasingly evident, and the significance to employers and workers and to society at large of the way in which industrial relations systems function is now generally recognized as a matter of immense public concern. As a legitimate field of academic interest, industrial relations has been established in the major educational institutions in some countries for a long time. In many others it has only recently been accepted as a branch of learning important in its own right as, say, the study of international relations or the governmental systems of states.

> It is perhaps not surprising that recognition of industrial relations as a distinct branch of scientific inquiry has been slow, since academics are notoriously conservative, especially those who profess the most revolutionary ideas about the nature of man and society. There are, of course, important problems of definition, since to some the term industrial relations suggests concern only with the problems of employer–employee relations in industrial establishments. However, I think that it is now generally recognized that *industrial relations* as a description of our field of interest embraces the whole gamut of relationships in the context of the total work environment. Wherever there are employers and employees, whatever economic or social activity they may be involved in carrying out, there are 'industrial relations' and these are within our field of interest.

> Research in the social sciences is inevitably greatly influenced by the predominant problems of the time. ... They [present-day problems] cannot be solved by the application of any single economic doctrine, whether it be out of Cambridge or Chicago. A multidisciplinary approach is essential. In this respect, the industrial relations specialist has much to contribute since he is concerned with the behaviour of men and their institutions as they are influenced by the full range of social forces, whether they be economic, political, legal, sociological or psychological.

At the Second World Congress, Roberts and Cox were again nominated and elected to serve as president and secretary, respectively, of the Association. It is here that some early bumps and challenges enter the story. Luckily, none posed insurmountable problems for the organization.

The plan was to have Roberts serve one term as president and then put forward another candidate for election at the Second World Congress. But events kept taking unexpected twists and turns. Roberts and Cox initially proposed to the Executive Board that Nakayama of Japan be invited to serve as the next president. It will be recalled that he had been considered for the position in 1967 but had demurred for health reasons. He did express willingness, however, to consider taking the presidency for the 1970–73 term if his health (a heart condition) improved. During 1968 and 1969 Nakayama appeared to gain a full recovery and Cox and Roberts made a formal invitation to him to be the nominee. Unexpectedly, in late 1969 they received word from Nakayama that his heart condition had become more serious and he would have to decline the nomination. With the World Congress barely nine months away, Cox and Roberts had to start a fresh search for a candidate.

After consultation with the Executive Board, they decided that the nominee should come from the United States. For procedural reasons, Cox and Roberts decided to ask the American IRRA to propose the candidate. The IRRA considered a number of people but decided on Frederick Harbison, director of the Industrial Relations Section at Princeton and IIRA president in 1969. This proposal was received and agreed to by Cox and Roberts when a letter was received from Harbison in January 1970, stating he too had to decline for health reasons. So the search began again. Several names were considered, including George Hildebrand, George Shultz and J. Douglas Brown, but a decision was made to offer the position to Clark Kerr. Kerr had earlier indicated interest but, to Cox and Robert's surprise, he now said he was also unable to accept the nomination due to work conflicts.

One would have thought that John Dunlop's name would have been at the very front of the list of American candidates, but to this point his name had not appeared in the discussion, at least as represented in the archival records. According to Roberts (2002) and Cox (2003), the reason is that by the time Nakayama declined the nomination Dunlop was already heavily involved in administering the American wage–price controls programme started by President Nixon (in the construction industry in 1969 and extended to the entire economy in 1970) and was unavailable to serve as IIRA president. As a fallback position, Roberts agreed to serve a second term if Dunlop would agree to be the IIRA's presidential nominee at the Third World Congress in 1973. Dunlop agreed, so Roberts accepted the nomination for a second term.

As it turned out, having Dunlop in the wings as the presidential nominee was fortuitous. The reason has to do with unexpected events affecting Cox and the IILS.

In 1969, Morse unexpectedly resigned as Director-General of the ILO. His successor was Wilfred Jenks, a British national and a long-time ILO official. Jenks sought to move the ILO back towards the more traditional and European-oriented juridical strategy grounded in standard setting through Conventions and Recommendations. He also sought to reduce the autonomy of the IILS, seeing it as a potentially "loose cannon" within the ILO. These actions led to growing conflict between Jenks and Cox and ultimately the latter's resignation in 1972. The situation at the IILS remained troublesome for Jenks, however. Cox was succeeded by Kenneth Walker of Australia, but Walker also encountered internal political difficulties in the ILO and resigned in 1974. (Walker served, however, as IIRA secretary from 1970 to 1976.) At this time, Jenks unexpectedly died and was succeeded by Francis Blanchard of France. Blanchard appointed Albert Tévoedjrè of Benin to succeed Walker. Unlike Walker, who was a well-known industrial relations scholar and active participant in the IIRA, Tévoedjrè was a career ILO official with little industrial relations experience or research interests. Blanchard and Tévoedjrè were also political rivals in the ILO, given that Tévoedjrè had run against Blanchard to succeed Jenks as Director-General.

For these and other reasons, both Jenks and Blanchard sought to impose tighter control on the IILS and reduce its independence. Unfortunately, the IIRA could not entirely escape negative repercussions, particularly since Cox had played such an important role in starting the organization and using IILS staff and resources to provide organizational and administrative support. Questions were raised about the amount of staff and money devoted to the IIRA, the independence of the organization relative to the ILO, and the appropriate place of the IIRA within the ILO. Given his stature in the world policy-making community and long-time involvement with the ILO, Roberts concluded that Dunlop was the best person to mediate a resolution of these issues. Dunlop accepted Roberts' invitation, flew to Geneva several times (both as president-elect and president) to meet with Jenks and Blanchard and was able to successfully gain agreement on all outstanding points. The result was a written memorandum of understanding between the ILO and IIRA. The IIRA remained an autonomous organization, the ILO pledged to continue staff and financial support, but the secretariat of the IIRA was to be eventually transferred from the IILS to the Labour Law and Labour Relations division of the ILO. Blanchard subsequently initiated the transfer in 1976.

With these matters taken care of, the IIRA was free to continue to grow and develop. A decision had been made in 1970s henceforth to hold the World

Congress in the country of the retiring president, so the Third World Congress was held in London in early September 1973. Over 300 people registered. Papers and discussion were organized around six themes:

- Theoretical frameworks for the study of industrial relations
- Industrial relations and inflation
- The structure of power in trade union movements
- The multinational corporation and industrial relations
- Labour relations in the public sector
- Workers' participation in management

In his presidential address, Roberts (1973) reviewed the numerous other activities undertaken by the IIRA. He states (p. 2):

> Since the last Congress our affiliated associations and institutions have been extremely active. Apart from national activities, a number of international meetings have been organized by national associations under the auspices of the IIRA. A Nordic regional meeting with forty participants from the Scandinavian countries was organized by the Swedish Industrial Relations Association in 1972. And also in 1972, the member associations in Belgium, Germany and the Netherlands organized an extremely successful joint conference on worker participation. In March this year, a conference of twenty-five European university specialists in industrial relations was organized by the German Industrial Relations Association and, in the same month, the Japanese Industrial Relations Association, in cooperation with the Japan Institute of Labour, held an Asian Regional Conference on Industrial Relations in Tokyo. The Industrial Relations Research Association of the United States organized a Pan-American regional meeting in Jamaica last April. The national activities of the affiliated associations and institutes have now become too numerous to mention.

Tenth anniversary: Progress and prospects

The Fourth World Congress in 1976 marked the tenth anniversary of the IIRA. The event was again held in Geneva, a fitting decision since Geneva was the IIRA's birthplace but also one made necessary by Dunlop's indication that he was too committed to a range of other activities to undertake organizing the event in the United States. Dunlop ended his three-year term as president at this congress and gave a presidential address entitled "Industrial relations, labour economics, and policy decisions". During his term as IIRA president Dunlop also served as Secretary of Labor in the Ford administration, and his address and subsequent published paper reflected and was informed by this experience. An expanded version was published by Dunlop (1977) the next year in an American industrial relations journal and set off a lively debate – given

Dunlop's rather pointed dismissal of much academic research as irrelevant for policy making. Reynaud succeeded Dunlop as president and Nakayama was president-elect. Nakayama, however, died before taking office and the new director-general of the JIL, Mikio Sumiya, stepped in to serve as the fourth IIRA president in 1979.

The World Congress attracted nearly 400 registrants. The six themes of the conference were:

- A review of labour problems in selected countries
- Manpower, employment and foreign workers
- Industrial relations and social policy in developed countries
- Industrial relations and labour markets in developing countries
- Methods of work organization
- Labour studies

The expense of the congress is listed as 102,000 Swiss francs or 41,000 US dollars.

What had the IIRA accomplished in the ten years since its founding? To begin to answer this question it is helpful to know the objectives of the association. On this matter, Roberts states in his first presidential address (p. 1):

> The aim of the founders of the Association was to create a body that would foster the objective study of industrial relations throughout the world without regard to political philosophies or other ideological limitations. ... The immediate practical purpose of this Association has been to encourage the establishment of national associations of industrial relations specialists, to facilitate the spread of information about significant developments in research and education in the field of industrial relations and to promote the organization and regional and world-wide conferences.

In his second presidential address, Roberts (1973: 3) boils the matter down to this one sentence: "The main purpose of the IIRA is to promote the study of industrial relations through research and teaching."

With these statements as a benchmark, one must conclude that in the relatively brief time span of ten years the IIRA had accomplished a great deal and made very impressive progress.

To start this evaluation, the first important point to note is that in its activities and programmes the IIRA marked out a broad, relatively inclusive conception of the intellectual territory comprising industrial relations. Although a broad definition was never formally stated in the constitution or other written records of the Association, such can be inferred from the programme themes of the four World Congresses. Certain themes were evidently viewed as relatively important and were repeated in two or more sessions. Examples include manpower policy, industrial relations and inflation, workers' participation in management, and research and teaching in industrial relations. But a variety of other themes was also included, spanning both unionized and non-union employment relationships (albeit with emphasis given to the former), public and private industrial sectors, developed and less-developed countries, and issues of concern to management, trade unions and public policy. Although a common denominator does not immediately stand out, arguably the congress themes cluster around and inform the interests of the ILO at this time in education, economic development and human resource development set in a pluralistic context of tripartite interest representation. Alternatively, one can equally well argue that they fit the "social problems of employment" definition proffered by Roberts in his original draft plan for the IIRA or the themes set out by Kerr et. al in *Industrialism and industrial man.*

Whatever the case, equally noteworthy are the topics and perspectives that are conspicuously missing. No session was devoted to private sector collective bargaining and labour–management relations per se (arguably the centre of gravity in American and British industrial relations of this period), nor to the practice of personnel management/human relations. Likewise, the subject of strikes (and its obverse, industrial peace) – also at the centre of Anglo-American industrial relations – was featured only at the First World Congress and in somewhat tangential form ("bargaining and conflict"). Also conspicuously missing was an explicit behavioural-science perspective, while an economic and institutional approach predominated. In this regard, the IIRA clearly leaned towards an institutional and political economy "externalist" perspective on labour and employment issues and de-emphasized a psychological and management "internalist" perspective.

Proceeding, we can now look more closely at the objectives discussed by Roberts. One goal of the Association was to spread the field of industrial relations around the world. Certainly, the IIRA enjoyed considerable success in this regard. Starting from zero in 1966, by 1976 the IIRA had 394 individual members. More instructive is the fact that these members came from 51 countries. As noted earlier, prior to the founding of the IIRA the industrial relations field was almost completely confined to Australia, North America and the United Kingdom. In the next ten years industrial relations truly spread across the world. Illustratively, in 1976 the Anglo-American countries accounted for only slightly more than one-half of IIRA individual membership (55 per cent), while 45 per cent came from countries such as Argentina, Belgium, Egypt, Finland, Ghana, Italy, Nigeria, Norway, Philippines, Singapore, Turkey and Venezuela.

Another goal set forth by Roberts was the spread and development of national industrial relations associations and industrial relations institutes and university programmes. Here too the IIRA saw great progress over a ten-year period. At the time of the IIRA's founding in 1966, national industrial relations associations existed in Australia, Canada, the United Kingdom and the United States. Ten years later, 20 national industrial relations associations belonged to the IIRA, including new associations in the following countries: Argentina, Austria, Belgium, Denmark, Ethiopia, Finland, France, Germany, Ireland, Israel, Italy, Netherlands, Poland and Sweden. A similar development is evident with respect to industrial relations institutes and university programmes. In 1976, 44 industrial relations institutes and university programmes were institutional members of the IIRA, with only nine (19 per cent) coming from the Anglo-Saxon countries. The IIRA thus materially facilitated the extension of such organizations and degree programmes to the countries of Africa, Asia, continental Europe and Latin America.

Oftentimes only one or a handful of IIRA members were from any one of the new "non-traditional" countries, while the national associations and university programmes were likewise small and scattered. They nonetheless formed an important entry point for the introduction of industrial relations to key universities and government ministries. Indeed, the formation of the IIRA was typically far more important for promoting the industrial relations field in these new countries than in places such as the United Kingdom and the United States. In the former, the concept was already developed, a network of scholars existed, and one or more journals were available as a conduit for research. The main contribution of the IIRA in these countries was to promote a greater comparative and international perspective in teaching and research, but even without the IIRA the industrial relations field in these countries would largely proceed apace (if perhaps in a more ethnocentric direction). In the countries of Africa, Asia, Europe and Latin America, on the other hand, the establishment of the IIRA was crucial for the industrial relations field to germinate and take root. The organization's association with the ILO gave the industrial relations field intellectual and political legitimacy in countries where ruling elites might have otherwise suppressed it. Likewise, the IIRA provided a forum to introduce teaching and research in labour and employment issues to academics and government researchers from countries with no such experience or tradition. Also important, these academics and government researchers gained a central meeting place to exchange ideas and experiences, form a network of international contacts, and present papers and research findings, that otherwise was not available in their home countries and, perhaps, home continents.

Another goal for the IIRA, as stated by Roberts, was to develop industrial relations conferences around the world. Here too the founders had good reason to be satisfied. In its first ten years, the IIRA had organized four World Congresses, bringing people from nearly forty countries to discuss teaching and research in industrial relations. Quickly the IIRA also spawned a series of regional meetings. By 1976, one or more regional meetings had been held in Asia, North America, South America and Europe; the first regional conference in Africa was 1988, while the Middle East has had no regional conference to date. The conferences proved to be a very useful device to form a denser network of industrial relations scholars and researchers at the regional level and to further deepen the field of industrial relations in new and non-traditional countries.

A final goal listed by Roberts was to spread the industrial relations field to countries regardless of ideology and form of government. At the time this position was highly controversial, given that the Cold War was at its height and political controversies associated with the Arab–Israeli conflict, China–Taiwan conflict and South African policy of apartheid were in full force. But the Association remained steadfast to this position throughout. Although few scholars or researchers from the Soviet Union and most Eastern bloc countries chose to participate in the IIRA, the doors were open and, indeed, Poland was a participant from the beginning. The officers of the IIRA also refused to expel Israel or South Africa, despite political pressure to do so. The officers of the IIRA were also mindful that the organization, while dominated by members from Western developed countries, had to welcome members from non-Western and developing countries and make the programmes and discussion groups relevant to these people. A review of the session themes listed above for the four World Congresses suggests discernible progress in this area, although the significant share of attention remained on the Western industrial countries. As described in a later chapter, however, this issue became more pressing in the 1980s and 1990s with the growth of membership from less-developed countries, leading to additional efforts to open up and "internationalize" the officer ranks and programmes of the IIRA.

Notes

[1] Industrial relations, as pointed out in an earlier chapter, was dealt with by the ILO from its earliest days, while the Declaration of Philadelphia affirmed as a core principle the right to collective bargaining and three years later the ILO adopted the Freedom of Association and Protection of the Right to Organise Convention, 1948 (No. 87).

[2] In 1974, the ISLLSL substituted the term "Social Security" for "Social Legislation", so now its official title is International Society for Labour Law and Social Security (ISLLSS).

INDUSTRIAL RELATIONS IN THE UNITED STATES: CHALLENGES AND DECLINING FORTUNES

7

Paradoxically, just as the industrial relations field was spreading to the far corners of the world it entered into a long period of slow but cumulatively significant decline in the country of its birth, the United States of America. This chapter describes these events and proffers explanations for their occurrence. Central to the story are the rise of neoclassical economics and of the field of human resource management; the long-term decline of the American labour movement; a narrowing conceptualization of the domain of industrial relations and a shift toward unidisciplinary science building in research; and the field's normative tilt in favour of collectivist solutions to labour problems and its distrust or neglect of management and non-union employers.

Decline of American industrial relations

Viewed over the long term, American industrial relations crested in influence and vitality around 1960 and then went into a period of slow but noticeable decline. The decline was marked by a narrowing of the intellectual domain of industrial relations and a reduction in active participants and associated disciplines, leaving a palpable sense that the field was becoming increasingly stale and marginalized. Historian David Brody (1989: 9) captures well the main drift:

> There was, at once, a retreat from the interdisciplinary scope and the methodological eclecticism that had for so long characterized labor scholarship. Sociologists, political scientists, and anthropologists lost interest in labor topics, while labor economics took up neoclassical analysis with a vengeance, applying it first to the study of human capital, then to whatever else could be subjected to deductive, individual-level microanalysis. The academic high ground was meanwhile seized by the new discipline of organizational behavior, which had sprung from the human relations strain within the post-war industrial relations field and now pronounced

itself a behavioral science capable of conducting rigorous quantitative and theoretically grounded analysis. Industrial relations itself shrank down into a kind of mini-discipline, confined as before to the union sector, but striving belatedly to assert its own credentials as a rigorous social science.

In hindsight, these developments are easy enough to see, but at the time were neither obvious nor anticipated. Observers did note that starting in the early 1960s and extending into the 1970s the field seemed to lose momentum and excitement, while at conferences and IRRA meetings a certain amount of hand wringing and negative introspection took place about industrial relations' lack of a theoretical base and secure disciplinary status. George Strauss and Peter Feuille (1981: 77) note the loss of momentum in the field when they refer to this period as the "Doldrums".

Most outward signs, however, suggested that the industrial relations field's future remained relatively bright. The number of industrial relations programmes in American universities, for example, continued to increase so that by 1965 more than 40 had been established (Derber, 1967: 8). Additional industrial relations units appeared in the early 1970s (Kaufman, 1993). Encouragingly, or so it seemed at the time, a number of these new industrial relations programmes were established in business schools, thus further consolidating the presence of the field in this fast-growing part of American higher education.

Progress was also evident on other fronts. One important sign was the establishment in 1961 of the second American academic industrial relations research journal, *Industrial Relations*. The journal was published under the auspices of the Institute of Industrial Relations at the University of California, Berkeley, and the first editor was Arthur Ross. Ross introduces the first issue with this statement (Ross, 1961: 7):

> *Industrial Relations* will deal with all aspects of the employment relationship in modern industrial society. The research program of the Institute of Industrial Relations will serve as an analogy. When the Institute was established 15 years ago, we concentrated initially on problems of union–management relations and wages. But as our first Director, Clark Kerr, recognized at the outset, a restrictive definition of the field would have been stultifying. Therefore, the scope of our research has been broadened gradually to include studies of social movements, political processes, economic development, economic security, managerial organization, and other subjects. The scope of *Industrial Relations* will be equally broad.

In 1980, another industrial relations-oriented journal, the *Journal of Labor Research*, was created under the editorship of James Bennett at George Mason

University. The focus of the journal was more directly on labour–management relations but with a greater willingness to publish pieces with critical or controversial implications regarding unions. Then, in 1983, yet another research outlet appeared with the annual research volume *Advances in Industrial and Labor Relations*, edited by David Lewin, David Lipsky and Donna Sockell (now Lewin and Kaufman). The field's first and most highly ranked journal, the *Industrial and Labor Relations Review*, also experienced sustained growth in professional visibility and readership under long-time editor Donald Cullen and, succeeding him, Tove Hammer and Harry Katz. *Industrial Relations* is now under the editorship of David Levine and Daniel Mitchell.

In addition to new journals, another propitious sign for the industrial relations field was the fact that academic membership in the IRRA nearly tripled between 1960 and 1979. And, finally, the field was also animated by a conviction among a number of scholars that a theoretical foundation, if not yet fully formed, was nonetheless in sight and would provide industrial relations with the intellectual moorings needed to establish itself as a separate discipline in the social sciences. Indicative of the optimistic, upbeat spirit in American industrial relations at the time, Herbert Heneman (1968: 49) enthusiastically declared, "The two most important disciplines of the first half of this century were mathematics and physics; beyond reasonable doubt industrial relations is the most important discipline of the second half." Striking a more guarded but nonetheless distinctly positive note, Strauss and Feuille (1981: 77) were moved to declare after their detailed review of the industrial relations field, "Perhaps, however, we are entering a fourth period which we venture to call a renaissance."

Despite the talk of a renaissance, underneath the surface the foundations of academic industrial relations in the United States were steadily weakening and eroding. Although not starkly evident in the 1970s, the deteriorating state of industrial relations came into full view in the 1980s and worsened in the 1990s. Suddenly optimism turned to pessimism and then a palpable sense of crisis. Illustrative of the turn of events and attitudes, for example, is the question posed by Arnold Weber (1987: 9) in the late 1980s – "Will industrial relations institutes and the study of industrial relations go the way of home economics?" Also illustrative of the sea change that hit industrial relations in the 1980s is this pessimistic statement by Strauss (1989: 257): "Short of an unexpected resurgence of union victories academic industrial relations will have to make major readjustments. Otherwise, it may follow the example of the Cigarmakers and Sleeping Car Porters, both leaders of their times." By the late 1990s, the gloomy prognostications of Weber and Strauss seemed to be distressingly prescient, per Thomas Kochan's (1998: 31) acknowledgement that "the field of industrial relations is in a state of profound crisis".

Behind these negative assessments of the future of industrial relations were a number of concrete trends and developments. The growth of industrial relations academic programmes came to a halt in the latter part of the 1970s and then sharply reversed course in the 1980s and 1990s. Numerous universities (e.g., Columbia, Iowa, Purdue) closed their industrial relations centres and institutes, cut their budgets and staff, or sought to reposition them by dropping the term industrial relations from the name in favour of "employment relations", "human resources", "work and employment research" and various other permutations. The Industrial Relations Section at MIT, for example, became the Institute for Work and Employment Research, while the Institute of Industrial Relations at Georgia State became the Institute of Personnel and Employment Relations. Student enrolments in industrial relations courses and programmes also dropped sharply, while enrolments in the rival field of human resource management (HRM) grew rapidly. Business schools either dropped or renamed their industrial relations courses en masse. New Ph.D.s in industrial relations also slowed to a trickle as the job market for assistant professors of industrial relations steadily deteriorated.

Among established scholars, many people who had once attended IRRA meetings and participated in industrial relations research left the field and went back to their home disciplines, associations and journals. Illustratively, by the 1990s relatively few of the labour economists in the prestigious National Bureau of Economic Research actively participated in industrial relations, while sociologists interested in work and employment issues largely left industrial relations for new groups, such as the Society for Socio-Economics. As these scholars departed, the interdisciplinary coalition that once defined industrial relations became increasingly bare.

Further adding to the problem, as the inflow of new scholars dwindled in the 1980s and 1990s and the generation of industrial relations scholars from the 1950s aged, the field took on an increasingly dated and grey look. Much the same process afflicted the intellectual side of the field as the mainstay of industrial relations research after the Second World War – trade unions and collective bargaining – became passé and little-followed in the news while research in competing areas of the work world, such as labour markets and HRM, entered a boom period. Caught in the middle, industrial relations was not only squeezed from both sides but also increasingly lost its unique identity and rationale for existence (Cappelli, 1991).

The pernicious effect of these trends is evident in the American industrial relations journals. The field's leading journal, *Industrial and Labor Relations Review*, has gradually shifted toward applied neoclassical-oriented labour economics, while periodic calls from its editors for more "institutional" research go unanswered. The editor of the *Journal of Labor Research*, meanwhile, was forced by the long-term decline of the industrial relations field to recently reposition the journal so that it caters more to labour market and human resource topics. Also illustrative are the findings of a recent empirical study of publishing activity in the field (Jarley, Chandler and Faulk, 2001). The authors conclude that the bulk of industrial relations research now emanates from a relatively small network of scholars, perhaps no more than fifty in number, with doctoral degrees largely from three universities. They also find that a growing proportion of articles published in the industrial relations journals are not from people in this group but from outsiders (e.g., labour economists), who use the industrial relations journals as a convenient publishing outlet for their research. They are thus led to conclude (pp. 342–3) that

> [c]ombined with the well-documented declines in IR programs ... these numbers cause us to question whether IR can sustain a unique scholarly community. ... We suspect that as IR programs and the IRRA wane, casual authorship in IR journals will rise, and the research in IR journals will lack coherence. Atrophy in IR programs and the IIRA will breed atrophy in published IR research and erode our scholarly community.

The hollowing out and decline of the industrial relations field is captured in membership statistics of the IRRA, as alluded to in the above quotation. Academic membership shrunk by nearly one-half between 1980 and 2000 (from 2,046 to 1,144) at the same time as membership of the Human Resource Division of the Academy of Management (the main academic rival to the IRRA) more than doubled and more than 700 labour economists chose to form and participate in a new association, the Society of Labor Economists. The IRRA also manifests other signs of the decline of the field, such as an ageing membership, slowly shrinking attendance and participation at the annual winter meetings, and the gradual loss of people of high national academic and political stature able and willing to serve as the Association's president. Other professional associations closely connected to the industrial relations field, such as the National Academy of Arbitrators, have experienced the same problems (Gruenberg, Najita and Nolan, 1997; Kaufman, 1999a).

Amidst this overall pattern of doom and gloom were several bright spots. American industrial relations academics continued to be involved, for example, in high-level policy-making. The most notable example was the Commission on the Future of Management–Worker Relations, formed under President Clinton in 1993. Several prominent industrial relations academics served on this commission, including John Dunlop (chair), Ray Marshall, Thomas Kochan, Richard Freeman and Paula Voos (commissioners), and Paul Weiler (legal counsel). Also on the commission were prominent industrial relations practitioners and policy-makers, such as William Usery, former United States Secretary of Labor and Director of the Federal Mediation and Conciliation Service (FMCS). The commission (more commonly known as the Dunlop Commission) put the issues of employer–employee relations, worker voice and national labour policy on the front burner for national debate, in the process precipitating a good deal of useful and insightful research from the commission members and other colleagues in the industrial relations academic community. Perhaps the most notable and influential publication coming directly from the commission's activities was Richard Freeman and Joel Rogers' book *What workers want* (1999), publicizing the existence of a large "representation gap" in the American system of industrial relations.

The subject of research raises the second bright spot for American industrial relations in the 1980s and 1990s. Paradoxically, even as the field contracted and lost membership and momentum over these two decades, the breadth and depth of industrial relations research advanced in several notable directions. In terms of depth, research on traditional industrial relations topics of unions, collective bargaining and strikes exhibited considerable progress over these two decades in theory development, use of modern research methods and statistical tools, and analysis of previously neglected topics. A prime illustration is Freeman's book with James Medoff, *What do unions do?* (1984) – a volume that examined a well-worn subject but brought to it a new theoretical perspective (the exit–voice model), an impressive set of new data sources and advanced statistical techniques, and a host of outcomes largely neglected in past research (e.g., the union effect on benefits, profits and turnover).

Perhaps even more significant was the expansion of industrial relations research into new subject areas that had long been neglected (the "breadth" dimension). First and foremost in this regard was the subject of management. Although earlier generations of industrial relations scholars had written extensively on the management side of industrial relations, after the mid-1950s management increasingly moved to the sidelines in the field, acknowledged as an important actor in the field but no longer the focus of study per se. As unions declined in importance both quantitatively and strategically, however, this lacuna became an increasingly glaring omission in the field. The first significant work in the post-1980 period to attempt to bring management back into the purview of the field was Kochan, Katz and McKersie's (1986) *The transformation of American industrial relations*. In the book, they acknowledged that the strategic influence in employment relations had passed from unions to management and that the locus of leading-edge employment practices was increasingly found in progressive non-union firms pioneering a new high-performance work system (HPWS). Their book and subsequent work in this area precipitated a wave of research in American industrial relations on the HPWS and, more generally, the influence of alternative human resource practices on firm performance and worker well-being (see Ichniowski et al., 1996; Appelbaum et al., 2000).

Although these developments provided some relief to the otherwise palpable decline of the American industrial relations field, they were not able to stem the tide. Indeed, the severity of the crisis was put into stark relief by a seemingly unimaginable event. In 2003, the University of Wisconsin – the academic birthplace of the industrial relations field, the home of Commons and four generations of famous industrial relations scholars, the long-time organizational home of the IRRA (recently transferred to the University of Illinois), and the location for many years of one of the highest-ranking industrial relations programmes in the nation – announced the closing of the Industrial Relations Research Institute and its degree programmes. With these events in mind, one must thus ask the hard question: how could the industrial relations field in the span of several decades go from a golden age to a state of crisis where not even the Wisconsin programme can survive?

The answer turns on the synergistic, cumulated effect of a number of adverse developments relating to the problem-solving, science-building and ethical/ideological faces of industrial relations. Six of the most important of these developments are described below.

The narrowing of industrial relations to labour– management relations

Although industrial relations over the years has made efforts to establish itself as a self-contained academic discipline with a distinct core of theory and methods, this effort has to date largely failed (Müller-Jentsch, 2004; Kaufman, 2004d). Hence, the academic and social justification for the field continues to rest where it always has – on the field's ability to address and help solve practical, real-world problems. In this regard, the position of industrial relations is no different from other applied fields in American universities, such as international relations, urban affairs and public administration. Each has to earn its keep by attracting a paying audience of students, raising research funds from foundations and government agencies, and conducting research on issues that other people find useful. Success in these matters hinges, in turn, on having a significant set of problems to address and useful tools and insights for solving them.

A root cause of the decline of industrial relations in the United States is that neither of these conditions is well met any longer. The problem area upon which the industrial relations field originally staked its claim is *labour and employment*. In an earlier chapter I suggested that at least in the American context these boiled down to four major issues: promoting economic efficiency, cooperation between capital and labour in production, the peaceful resolution of conflict (industrial peace), and justice, voice and due process in workforce governance (industrial democracy). A myriad of more specific problems is then contained within each of these categories, such as employee turnover, strikes and wage determination.

For a field that continues to claim jurisdiction over "all aspects of work" and the various problems just enumerated, the seeming descent into crisis and academic marginalization would appear to be one of the great academic ironies. After all, who would say that events in the work world today are *less* important than they were one, two or eight decades ago? So, how did industrial relations fall into its present predicament?

The place to start, and the common point around which the rest of this chapter revolves, is to note that American industrial relations has always had multiple definitions or "selves". Most broadly defined, industrial relations has claimed to be "all aspects of work" or "the study of labour". Not only is this conception of the field quite encompassing; it also suggests that the field of industrial relations is generic and thus not contingent on a particular label or set of institutions. The term "industrial relations" could disappear, as could all the industrial relations programmes or even the trade unions, and the field of industrial relations (defined as the multidisciplinary study of labour by scholars with certain theoretical frameworks and normative principles) could continue and, indeed, possibly prosper. This is one scenario and it captures a portion of the truth. But there are other portions of truth, reflecting the fact that industrial relations has also over the years taken on a succession of more narrowly defined self-identities.

As noted in Chapter 2, for example, the very term "relations" in the name of the field immediately emphasizes one feature of "all aspects of work" over the others – the *relations* between employers and employees. The emphasis on employer–employee relations, in turn, grew out of the central work-related issue that gave birth to the field: the market commodification of labour accompanying the "Great Transformation" (Polanyi, 1944) and the Labour Problem that grew out of it. The Labour Problem had numerous dimensions, but the heart of it was the antagonistic, sometimes violent relation developing between the two classes of labour and capital in the late nineteenth and early twentieth centuries. Reconciling labour and capital, and preserving industrial peace, thus formed the core *problématique* of industrial relations at the time of its birth.

This fact immediately points to one important reason for the field's long-term decline in fortunes. The subject of industrial relations gains saliency and social value when relations between capital and labour become contested and problematic and thus a threat to economic progress and social order. In such historical moments, such as the late nineteenth century, the First World War period and the New Deal/Second World War period in America, industrial relations experiences a surge of interest and vitality – just as does the field of international relations when conflict and war break out among nation states. Fortunately for the country, but unfortunately for the field, America in the last half of the twentieth century did not experience any significant flare-up in capital–labour relations. Indeed, the grand project of the industrial relations reformers of the early twentieth century – the inclusion of the working class into the polity, the humanization of the workplace, a full employment economy and the erection of a modern welfare state – appears to have made tremendous if still incomplete progress.

Of course, at the same time one must acknowledge that numerous labour problems remain and some are growing in seriousness. For the most part, however, these problems do not seem (yet) to manifest in the public conscious-ness as ones of *industrial relations* – that is, capital versus labour. Rather, most involve other aspects of economic and social policy, such as the outsourcing of jobs to other countries, illegal immigration and work–family balance, that arise from other sources (markets, lack of opportunity in poor and developing countries). While the interests of capital and labour remain divergent with regard to many of these issues, they nonetheless do not seem to suggest that the root cause of these problems lies with maladjusted or inflamed employer–employee relations per se. Indeed, in an interesting way the globalization of markets is leading to a fundamental realignment in the divergence of interests within society, with consumers and globally mobile capital on one side and labour and immobile domestic capital on the other. Thus one must ask: does a field that locates its raison d'être in the contested nature of employer–employee relations, and has taking wages out of competition through the device of the common rule as perhaps its central policy tool, still have something important to contribute as we head into the second "Great Transformation"? The answer may well be yes (recalling that the first age of globalization was in the late nineteenth century and helped spawn the Labour Problem through the extension of markets), but from today's vantage point it is certainly less obvious and immediate. Accordingly, relative to a field defined as "all aspects of employment", a field defined as "capital–labour relations" faces more problematic prospects.

The problem-solving dilemma of industrial relations goes deeper than this, however. Once must note, for example, that industrial relations in the early

1920s had moved beyond the study of the singular Labour Problem to the study of the plural concept of *labour problems*. In attacking these labour problems, industrial relations in turn developed a multiplicity of approaches, including personnel management, collective bargaining, legal enactment and macro-economic policy. Thus, even though capital–labour relations were likewise receding in salience over the course of the 1920s, the field nonetheless prospered as it sought to apply these diverse methods to solving the numerous labour problems of the day.

Unfortunately, the same multi-pronged approach to solving labour problems was no longer a viable strategy for industrial relations after the 1960s, because the concept of industrial relations narrowed even further from a preoccupation with *relations* to a preoccupation with one particular category of relations – collective or labour–management relations.

In the 1920s, the field of industrial relations did not give precedence to one approach to problem solving over the other, at least not as a formal feature of its self-definition and ideology. Thus personnel management and collective bargaining were *complements* in that both were viewed as equally valid and valued methods to solving labour problems, depending on the time and situation. Events of the 1930s, as described in an earlier chapter, changed this situation. Of these four approaches, one of them – trade unionism and collective bargaining – became endorsed as the field's *preferred* method for regulating and improving employer–employee relations, transforming the other methods into either substitutes or second-best complements. Slowly, the other approaches to solving labour problems moved to the periphery of the field and, eventually, were no longer included as core subjects. By the 1980s, industrial relations in the United States was firmly associated in both the public and academic minds as the study of unions, collective bargaining and labour–management relations. Dropping out of the field as active, core research topics were not only management (the heart of the PM school) but also two branches of the 1920s ILE school – social insurance and, to a lesser degree, protective labour legislation.

Evidence on the narrowing of the field to a labour–management domain is readily available. As a base line, it is useful to repeat Harold Wilensky's (1954: 6) caution from the mid-1950s, that "few students identified with the field confine it to union–management or employee relations". Thirty years later industrial relations and union–management relations had become largely synonymous terms. Roy Adams (1993b: 8) noted this trend when he observed that "industrial relationists, while paying lip service to the goal of achieving understanding, prediction, and control of all aspects of employment, in practice tend to focus most of their attention on unions, collective bargaining, and miscellaneous labour market issues". Whitfield and Strauss (1998: 6) make a similar observation: "In the United States, the Industrial Relations Research Association claims jurisdiction over 'all aspects of labour, employment, and the workplace.' In practice, however, most of what has been called industrial relations research has focused on union–management relations and their impact."

Industrial relations textbooks offer a particularly clear example of this trend at work. Through the 1950s, American labour textbooks provided multiple chapters on the function and practice of management, protective labour laws and social insurance programmes. Three decades later, textbooks in industrial relations courses had dropped much of this material and took a much more focused look at labour–management relations. The most heralded textbook of the 1980s, for example, was Kochan's *Collective bargaining and industrial relations*. The second edition (1988), co-authored with Katz, provides a particularly clear illustration of the transition from the broad definition of the term industrial relations to the narrow. In the first sentence of the text they define industrial relations as "a broad, interdisciplinary field of study and practice that encompasses all aspects of the employment relationship". In the third sentence, however, they introduce a qualifier that permits them to move swiftly to the narrow "labour–management" conception of industrial relations: "Within this broad field industrial relations professionals have historically given special attention to relations between labour and management." The remainder of the text is then devoted to the theory and practice of union–management relations.

As Adams suggests, American industrial relations research in the post-1960 period is not focused *solely* on labour–management relations. As the field lost the PM school and many scholars from sociology, management and related disciplines, it became more heavily dominated by labour economists and industrial relations research increasingly resembled a relatively low-tech, applied version of labour economics. Big topics in industrial relations in the 1960s and 1970s, for example, were manpower and training programmes, internal labour markets, and poverty and discrimination. Particularly in the 1960s and early 1970s this research still in many cases had an identifiable industrial relations orientation that distinguished it from the orthodox (neoclassical) research going on in labour economics proper – that is, it had an ILE emphasis on a social-science, imperfect competition theory of labour markets and tended to rely on a case-study, qualitative methodology. Alternatively stated, this research still had some contact with the theory and methods of institutional economics. However, as time went on and the ILE labour economists faded from the scene, even this differentiation was largely lost.[1] In the 1980s and 1990s, the major industrial relations journals increasingly became just one more publishing outlet for labour economists, albeit featuring lower requirements of theoretical and methodological rigour (compared to the flagship *Journal of Labor Economics*, for example, a new field journal started in 1980 at the University of Chicago) and with a greater receptivity to non-standard topics and departures from orthodoxy.

Together, collective bargaining and applied labour economics effectively came to define the core of American industrial relations. Thus articles in these two areas comprised roughly 90 per cent of the papers published in the two major American industrial relations journals in the late 1970s. Ten years later, the published articles revealed the same concentration. This worrisome trend led the editorial board of the *Industrial and Labor Relations Review* to include this statement in the October 1989 issue (emphasis in original): "Members of the Editorial Board are concerned that many scholars believe the journal welcomes only papers on labour economics and collective bargaining. ... We should like to assure potential contributors that we welcome papers from *all* the specialties of our field." This appeal notwithstanding, the journal continued its drift toward becoming an applied labour economics journal, only with a relative decline in union-related topics and increase in standard labour market topics (e.g., wage differentials, human capital).

The narrower labour–management focus of American industrial relations led to several problems for the field. First, it created an identity problem for the industrial relations institutes and degree programmes. More so than industrial relations research, the industrial relations degree programmes have remained to this day broadly focused on all aspects of the employment relationship and, in particular, offer a wide mix of courses that span various disciplines, topics and the PM and ILE schools. As industrial relations narrowed to a labour–management focus, the titles of the degree programmes and institutes no longer adequately communicate their broad coverage. Thus, by the 1980s a programme name, such as Cornell's School of Industrial and Labor Relations, seemed increasingly narrow, for to most people "industrial relations" now meant roughly the same things as the modifier "labour relations" and, thus, the two terms in the title stood for roughly the same thing – the study of unionized employment relationships. Not only were the Cornell programme and other similar industrial relations programmes much more broadly constructed than the name might imply, but as student and employer demand swung toward HRM in the 1980s and 1990s this misalignment became increasingly problematic from a marketing and competitive advantage point of view. Indeed, so strongly had industrial relations become associated with the "U word" at both a positive and normative level that some employers decided to no longer recruit or interview students at the industrial relations programmes – even if the students were majoring in HRM. Accordingly, as noted earlier, a number of universities and degree programmes either dropped the industrial relations label or added some HRM-type term to it to signify their inclusive and "neutral" orientation.

Of course, this trend solved one problem but led to another. As industrial relations centres and degree programmes added the HRM term to the programme's name and augmented the number of business and management courses in the curriculum, the programmes increasingly lost their interdisciplinary, social-science character and differentiation from business-school offerings. Not unexpectedly, a number of universities, particularly under the pressure of budget cuts and orders to reduce costs, decided to amalgamate the free-standing industrial relations programmes into their business schools and, in so doing, abolish the industrial relations term and most of the inter-disciplinary nature of the programme. In effect, industrial relations was merged into management departments. In the short run, the outcome was not a complete elimination of industrial relations since industrial relations-oriented faculty members and courses were often retained. Over time, however, these courses were dropped and industrial relations staff not replaced when they retired, moved or died. Over a five-to-ten-year period, therefore, the industrial relations component is gradually downsized until it is finally eliminated, except possibly for an elective collective bargaining course (Kaufman, 1993).

A second problem was created by the long-term decline of the American labour movement and the shrinking role of collective bargaining in American social policy. Even if the PM school broke away from industrial relations and the focus narrowed to only labour–management relations, the field would still have a solid base and bright future were collective bargaining to cover a sizeable proportion of the workforce and remain the nation's preferred method of wage determination and workforce governance. In the 1950s this condition was largely met, since unions had organized over one-half of the workforce in the goods-producing industries and collective bargaining dominated both labour law and market forces as the major workplace regulatory mechanism in the core part of the economy. Beginning in the mid-1960s, however, these conditions started to weaken and, after 1980, imploded.

From 1935 to 1964, the United States largely relied on collective bargaining as the active form of labour market regulation. After the enactment of the Social Security Act in 1935 and Fair Labor Standards Act in 1938, very little additional labour legislation was passed for the next 25 years. This period was, in effect, the trial period for collective bargaining. Unfortunately for unions and industrial relations, public opinion slowly concluded that collective bargaining brought too many social costs and not enough social benefits.

The Depression and the urgent need to give workers protection against wage cuts and tyrannous employers provided the social rationale for mass unionism in the 1930s, and the social Keynesian idea of expanding aggregate demand through union-led wage increases provided further support in the 1940s and into the 1950s. But once Keynesian fiscal and monetary policies proved able to stabilize the economy and keep it close to full employment, widespread collective bargaining lost its macroeconomic rationale and, in the process, the monopoly union wage effect went from being a social virtue (offsetting labour's inequality of bargaining power) to a social vice (wage-push inflation). Keynes (or Keynesian policies) may have saved capitalism, but it was at the long-run cost of seriously reducing the social appeal and raison d'être of trade unions. Added to the equation, the promise of industrial democracy had also begun to look seriously tarnished. During the late 1950s, Congressional investigations revealed shocking corruption and racketeering in a number of unions and widespread denial of democratic rights in others. A number of unions, particularly in the AFL, also had a long history of discrimination against women and minorities. And, finally, the defiant "public be damned" attitude of several highly visible union leaders, such as John L. Lewis of the Mineworkers, and repeated industry shutdowns from strikes spread a message that unions were perhaps too intent on gaining "more" at the public expense.

These events led to a slow but cumulatively significant shift in American social policy. Viewed from 1960 to 2000, social regulation of the labour sector expanded significantly. The idea that the American employment relations system underwent *de*-regulation during this period is inaccurate; rather, it substantially changed the *form* and *type* of regulation. Good labour conditions can be provided by some combination of full-employment labour markets, trade unions and legislation. From the early 1960s onward, collective bargaining was effectively downgraded, while legal enactment and markets were upgraded. The shift toward legal enactment started in earnest with the Civil Rights Act of 1964. It then continued on an upward trend through both Democratic and Republican administrations. By the year 2000, the original troika of labour laws (National Labor Relations Act, Social Security Act and Fair Labor Standards Act) had been joined by over 150 other pieces of labour and employment regulation. To a large degree, the plaintiff attorney and the regulatory agency replaced the union organizer and the trade union (Bennett and Taylor, 2002).

The shift away from collective bargaining toward legal enactment was, on net, harmful to industrial relations. The extent of the threat was mitigated, however, because legal enactment and industrial relations are complementary in objective if not in method. A far more mortal threat came, however, from the ascendancy of neo-liberalism and a shift toward greater reliance on market forces. The movement toward greater legal enactment started in the mid-1960s; the movement toward greater reliance on markets only began in earnest with the election of Ronald Reagan to the presidency in 1980. Reagan's election coincided with Thatcher's (1979) in the United Kingdom and the two jointly ushered in a sweeping neo-liberal reorientation of social policy. High on the agenda were market deregulation, a rollback of the welfare state, supply-side economics and a more assertive foreign policy. Trade unionism was particularly disliked and both Reagan and Thatcher sought to weaken and dislodge it (though paradoxically Reagan is the only American president to have also been an officer in a trade union, the Screen Actors' Guild). Reagan did so partly by a direct attack on union power, such as the firing and replacing of the striking air traffic controllers and pro-management changes in regulatory policy. Far more effective in undermining the unions, however, were his trade and macroeconomic policies that opened American markets to far greater international competition. As chronicled by John Hoerr (1988) in his book *And the wolf finally came*, within a space of two years the mighty Steelworkers' Union was rocked by an onslaught of cheap foreign steel, a wave of plant closings, and the loss of hundreds of thousands of high-wage jobs. A similar process occurred across industrial America, with the result that ten years after Reagan's election the American labour movement had haemorrhaged over two million members.

Although a more labour-friendly president, Bill Clinton, was in the White House from 1992 to 2000, the fortunes of the labour movement continued to wane. Economic trends – particularly intensified global competition and heightened pressure from financial markets for higher corporate earnings – led to continued downsizings and lay-offs in the unionized sector of the economy (Farber and Western, 2002). The nation also enjoyed nearly a decade of prosperity, and with labour markets at full employment the need for trade union protection waned further. Political lobbying by organized labour and liberal allies to erect protections against the competitive onslaught were largely defeated by business and conservative forces; this was exemplified by labour's inability to stop the passage of the North American Free Trade Agreement (NAFTA), secure a legislative ban on striker replacement, or gain enactment of the measures proposed by the Dunlop Commission to strengthen legal protections of the right to organize (Logan, 2004). Efforts of organized labour, particularly under the AFL–CIO's new president John Sweeney, to improve its public image, forge a broader alliance with other progressive social groups and substantially boost organizing success also yielded only modest gains. By the end of the 1990s, therefore, organized labour's economic and political position had further deteriorated. Most emblematic of labour's fall from power was the decline in private-sector union density. By 2000, private-sector density dropped to 9 per cent – a level nearly the same as a century earlier when the organized labour movement was just emerging as a visible national force. Although over 7 million American workers in the private sector were covered under collective bargaining contracts, the shrinking union perimeter was evident to everyone. Certainly the picture for unions was considerably more positive in the public sector (a density rate of 40 per cent), but slowing growth in government jobs and heightened budget pressures provided little room for further union expansion.

The long-term decline of the American labour movement, the near disappearance in the 1990s of strikes and other manifestations of serious, systemic labour–capital conflict, and the rise of the neo-liberal movement left the industrial relations field in a much shrunken state in terms of both numbers of participants and intellectual energy and momentum. Job regulation was now being done by the market, management and the state, while the role of collective bargaining steadily shrank. While numerous labour problems remained, and some grew in seriousness, collective bargaining was often not the obvious best way to deal with them. During the 1990s, job opportunities for holders of MBAs and lawyers boomed but positions for labour relations specialists shrivelled. Not only did industrial relations programmes have a problem with a stodgy and out-of-date image; they faced the much larger problem of sharply falling enrolments in the labour relations part of the curriculum. Fewer students and courses translated, in turn, into less hiring of academic staff in industrial relations. Likewise, the decline of labour–management relations meant that the industrial relations field was no longer attractive to researchers. External grant money became much more difficult to obtain, the field had fewer exciting topics, fewer publishers were willing to take on industrial relations books, and the audience for industrial relations research steadily shrank. To survive and prosper, a number of industrial relations scholars – particularly those in business schools – tacked with the winds and took up new topics outside the traditional labour–management domain, such as the high-performance workplace. Illustrative of the impact these events had on the field, at a doctoral student consortium in the mid-1990s sponsored by the Human Resources Division of the Academy of Management I asked the 60 plus people in attendance how many were listing industrial relations as the primary field of interest on their curriculum vita. Not a single person raised their hand.

The events described above also worked to undermine academic and public support for the problem-solving programme of industrial relations. The heart of the New Deal labour programme is workplace-centred adversarial collective bargaining. The two pillars of this model as a problem-solving programme are to take wages out of competition by setting a common rule through industry-wide collective bargaining and to bring industrial democracy to workforce governance. None of these features of the traditional model resonates well, however, in the economy and heterogeneous workforce of contemporary America. With globalization and the migration of jobs overseas, adversarial collective bargaining seems incompatible with supply-side concerns of growth and industrial competitiveness. Likewise, as markets become more open and competitive both domestically and internationally, labour unions face ever-greater difficulties in taking wages out of competition and protecting wages and labour standards at organized companies. Nor is it evident to many people that the workers that unions still bargain for, such as airline pilots, auto workers and electricians, are among society's downtrodden and exploited. And, finally, while workers continue to express a strong demand for some form of voice at work, the majority want some alternative besides a trade union, which they see as too political, adversarial and bureaucratic (Freeman and Rogers, 1999). The wild card is full employment, for extensive joblessness changes the entire picture for trade unionism, but from 1980 to 2000 the American economy did well on this score – certainly compared to the countries of Europe.

Amidst all of these developments, to many outside observers it appeared that thinking in American industrial relations had become badly frozen in time and place. Emblematically, in the early 1980s two dozen of the field's leading scholars met at a special conference at Berkeley on "The Future of American Industrial Relations". The summary report of the conference proceedings states (*Industrial Relations*, Winter 1983: 131):

> To the extent the conference had a theme, it was that of continuing faith in the efficacy of collective bargaining as the cornerstone of the American industrial relations system. Few participants saw any serious alternatives to it on the horizon. Collective bargaining may have to adjust, but it is too entrenched and too useful to society for it to collapse. ... The conference closed with what came close to a consensus: our economic and social problems can best be resolved through tripartite union–management–government discussion and collaboration. No better model was presented.

One would have to judge this statement as strong evidence that the American industrial relations community remained committed to the tripartite, collective-bargaining-centred model that came out of the New Deal of the 1930s and, also, an open admission that the field had no other alternative model to present to policy-makers and fellow academics.

The situation did not appear to change measurably a decade later when the Dunlop Commission issued its final report. As early noted, the commission was appointed in 1993 and its membership had a large representation of influential industrial relations academics. Reflecting the new era's concern with competitiveness, the commission's charge was to recommend changes in the nation's labour law that would promote workplace productivity and cooperation through increased employee involvement and participation, greater cooperation and productivity in labour–management relations, and the private settlement of employment disputes outside the court and government regulatory systems. The commission's final report, guided with a firm hand by its chairman, did not depart far from the vision statement reached a decade earlier at the Berkeley conference. The central thrust of the recommendations was to meet the three objectives cited above by reforming the nation's labour law to make it easier for workers to organize and gain collective bargaining rights, reasoning that greater unionization would promote more employee voice, deeper participation and greater self-governance in industry (Mitchell and Zaidi, 1997). While favouring greater participation through unions, the report recommended only a minor change in the NLRA's Depression-era Section 8(a)(2) that imposes significant limitations on the types of participation programmes non-union companies can operate, known as the company union ban (Kaufman, 2000c; Kaufman and Taras, eds., 2000).

At least as seen by many outside observers, the Dunlop Commission and its industrial relations academic members had visibly leaned in favour of the organized labour movement and collective bargaining (see the symposium in the Winter 1996 *Journal of Labor Research*). A significant intellectual justification for this position came, in turn, from the work of Freeman and Medoff (1984), who argued in their "exit–voice" theory that unions on net improve efficiency by reducing costly employee quits and improving voice and productivity. Based on both theory and empirical evidence, Freeman (1992) concluded that the "optimal" level of union density in the United States was closer to the level prevailing in the American public sector (40 per cent) and somewhere between the overall density level in the United States (20 per cent) and the level in Scandinavia (80–90 per cent), or roughly 35–40 per cent by both calculations. Although only a rough estimate and not necessarily representative of the views of other commission members, this conclusion nonetheless seems broadly in the spirit of their recommendations, certainly is in keeping with the Berkeley conference report, and starkly indicates the gulf that was opening up between the policy programme of industrial relations and the steadily advancing neo-liberal agenda of free labour markets.

Faced with a rapidly changing world and a static policy programme from the New Deal, American industrial relations academics have struggled since the Dunlop Commission report to fashion a new policy vision and programme that is at once attuned with modern realities but also consistent with past principles. The most visible and influential work along this line has come from the industrial relations groups at MIT, including Thomas Kochan, Paul Osterman, Robert McKersie, Michael Piore, Richard Locke and a network of associated industrial relations scholars at other universities. The common denominator of their work is giving greater emphasis to management as a strategic player and innovative force, strengthening and updating where possible collective bargaining, devising new labour market institutions to deal with emergent labour problems related to training, work–family balance and so on, and searching for ways to replace zero-sum employment outcomes with positive-sum outcomes.

One snapshot of their approach is given by Kochan (2000) in his presidential address to the IRRA. There he laid out a four-part plan for achieving a "new social contract at work": a multiple stakeholder view of firms, next-generation unions and professional associations, new labour market intermediaries and community organizations, and expanded government involvement. Evident here is a continued commitment to ILE principles – the use of institutions to regulate and structure employment relations in order to promote efficiency, equity and voice – but broadened beyond traditional collective bargaining and protective labour law.

Another, more in-depth presentation is provided in the book *Working in America: A blueprint for the new labor market* (Osterman et al., 2001). The book in method and theory is a twenty-first-century version of the classic Wisconsin school approach of institutional labour economics. The Preface opens with a long list of labour problems confronting the nation. The authors also state that to write the book they spent several years fact gathering from their own field studies and reports of 259 people given at 17 workshops. Also noted is that the Ford and Rockefeller Foundations are again the principal source of external funding. Then, in Chapter 1, Osterman et al. state that the intellectual framework they use to guide them is the "institutional perspective". They describe this perspective in these words (p. 3):

> The institutional perspective recognizes a set of moral values, which individuals seek to realize through work. These values are distinct from economic efficiency and are not necessarily promoted by the market. They include equity and due process in the management of the workplace, equal employment opportunity, work as a creative and dignifying activity, and the right of workers to a voice in the organization and governance of the workplace. An institutional perspective understands the economy as embedded in the social structure and as depending on

that structure for its capacity to operate effectively. It sees a need for the active cooperation of workers in the work process, and it emphasizes the difficulty of achieving that cooperation if the non-market values are not respected. And, as the name implies, it recognizes the role of institutions and the role they play in creating a framework in which a market operates, in mediating the relationship between the economy and society, and in reconciling economic efficiency with other social goals.

The first chapter also states the fundamental problem to be solved (p. 5): "a basic mismatch between the institutional structure and reality of today's world of work". Then, reminiscent of the 1920s labour problems texts, the second chapter presents a review of recent changes in labour markets, providing greater evidence on the abovementioned labour problems (work–family imbalance, growing contingent work, lack of health insurance, etc.). This review of problems is then followed by four chapters that lay out the institutional solutions (following the same topics as in Kochan's IRRA address). Chapter 3 is devoted to employers, Chapter 4 to unions, Chapter 5 to new labour market institutions and Chapter 6 to the role of government – thus broadly following the employers', workers' and community solutions from the 1920s.

Theory and method aside, the interesting question is whether this book, and other recent policy research from American industrial relations academics, has succeeded in repositioning the field such that it has greater relevance and influence in both the scholarly world and the world of practice and policy. One can say that this literature has, with a good deal of success, attempted to move the field away from its narrow labour–management orientation and back toward a broader conceptualization of industrial relations. Also noteworthy and valuable, Osterman et al. have likewise attempted to more visibly and directly connect their policy programme to the underlying paradigm of institutional economics, thus establishing both a stronger theoretical and historical linkage to the earlier industrial relations tradition. And, finally, relative to the position staked out at the Berkeley conference two decades earlier it is apparent that the policy programme of industrial relations, at least as represented in the work of these leading scholars, has been considerably broadened.

The jury is still out on whether these new initiatives by American industrial relations scholars will be able to reverse the long-term slide in the field. And, being realistic, one must note that all such institutionalist labour market programmes face formidable challenges. In a review symposium on Osterman et al.'s book (*Industrial and Labor Relations Review*, July 2002), these arguments quickly came to the surface. Neumark, for example, raises a fundamental objection to Osterman et al.'s "institutional perspective" – that the conclusions are tainted by the mixing of normative values and objective analysis. This objection harks back to the *Methodenstreit* and German historical economics. Likewise, Peter Cappelli notes that Osterman et al. seek to strengthen institutional structure and regulation of labour markets when public and academic opinion seems to be going in the opposite direction, while Rebecca Blank predicts that union density will continue to shrink and trade unions will not adopt new innovative structures and practices as the authors envision. Most fundamentally, as Sanford Jacoby asks, how can the new institutional infrastructure proposed by the authors avoid being undermined by the same competitive forces and pressures for more flexibility and lower labour cost that undermined the old industrial relations system? These are fundamental issues that continue to challenge industrial relations, not only in America but across the globe, and for which effective answers are difficult to construct.

Rise of the rival fields of human resource management and organizational behaviour

A second event that contributed to a narrowing and hollowing out of the industrial relations field in the post-1960 period was the divorce of the PM and ILE schools and the emergence of the former as two rival fields of study in the guise of HRM and organizational behaviour.

As argued in an earlier chapter, through the 1950s the American field of industrial relations comprised two schools of thought, the PM and ILE schools. The former had its intellectual centre of gravity in business schools, the organizational and behavioural sciences, and the subjects of personnel management and human relations; the centre of gravity of the latter was in colleges of arts and sciences, the social-science disciplines of economics, law, history, political science and the macro part of sociology. The PM school also tended to focus on the employer's solution to labour problems, examined labour problems from an "internal" perspective and tended to look more favourably on management than unions. The ILE school, by way of contrast, tended to focus on the workers' and community's solution to labour problems, took an "external" perspective on labour problems, and tended to take a relatively favourable attitude toward unions.

Although the confederation of PM and ILE schools under the intellectual umbrella of industrial relations was sometimes uneasy, American scholars in both camps recognized they were part of a common enterprise. At its most prosaic level, in the university world this meant that teachers and researchers in personnel management and labour–management relations both conceived themselves to be members of the field of industrial relations. That industrial relations in the 1950s had this broad, inclusive coverage in the United States is clearly indicated in this statement by Yoder et al. (1958: I-22):

> In current practice, careful usage employs the terms personnel management or personnel administration to refer to the management of manpower within a plant or agency, and the terms emphasize employer relations with individual employees, in such activities as selection, rating, promotion, transfer, etc. In contrast, the term labor relations is generally used to describe employer relations with groups of employees, especially collective bargaining – contract negotiation and administration. Industrial relations, or employment relations, in recent years, has come to be used as the broadest of these terms, including the areas of both personnel management and labor relations. "Industrial relations" or "employment relations" thus describes all types of activities designed to secure the efficient cooperation of manpower resources.

After 1960, however, the confederation between the PM and ILE schools started to dissolve and by the 1980s the two had largely broken apart (Mahoney and Deckop, 1986). As a result, the field of personnel or HRM and that of organizational behaviour were increasingly regarded in American academia as separate and largely independent from industrial relations. Industrial relations, in turn, became increasingly identified with the ILE portion of the field and, in particular, the topic of labour–management relations.

Although the breakaway of the PM school was not viewed with much alarm at the time by industrial relations scholars, in hindsight this development proved to be a serious blow to industrial relations in the United States. A brief recounting of events suggests why.

One factor American industrial relations scholars in the 1960s could not foresee was the rebirth of the fusty and lowly regarded field of personnel management into the more highly esteemed and intellectually interesting field of HRM. To a degree this re-labelling of the field of personnel was simply an adroit marketing move, aimed at shifting its image and status from a relatively old-fashioned, low-level, vocational and administrative function in the academic and business worlds to one that was broader, more strategic and modern sounding, and intellectually appealing. But behind the cosmetic changes were also some changes of substance that made HRM an increasingly strong challenger to industrial relations.

The name change from personnel management (or personnel administration) to HRM unfolded from the mid-1960s to the early 1990s. In actuality, the terms "human resources" and "management of human resources" can be found scattered in various writings well before this period. Indeed, Commons (1919b: 130) had used the term a half century earlier. But until the 1960s, the human resource label never achieved widespread currency nor was used as a substitute term to describe the field of personnel management. According to Strauss (2001), the terms human resources and, equivalently, HRM were first used in this substitute sense in the mainstream literature in 1964 when Myers, Pigors and Malm renamed their personnel readings text to *Management of human resources: Readings in personnel administration* and, in the same year, Wendell French published the first edition of his book *The personnel management process: Human resources administration*. As far as I can determine, their inspiration for using the term human resources came from two identifiable sources (Kaufman, 2004e). The first is a published lecture (cited by French, p. 5) given in 1958 by economist E. Wight Bakke titled *The human resources function*. In it, Bakke clearly defines the HRM function in terms of the management of people in organizations and articulates many of the main themes of contemporary HRM. For this reason, Bakke appears to deserve the honour of coining and popularizing the human resources term. The second source, as described in an earlier chapter, is that Myers, Harbison and other industrial relations scholars were doing research in the late 1950s on the role of labour as a factor in economic growth and in that context used the human resource term in various publications. An example is Harbison and Ibrahim's book *Human resources for Egyptian enterprises* (1958).

For the next ten years or so, the "personnel" and "human resources" terms were largely used interchangeably. Then, beginning in the early 1980s, sentiment started to shift rapidly in favour of the latter. In 1989, for example, the major professional association for personnel managers in the United States changed its name from the American Society for Personnel Administration to the Society for Human Resource Management. This shift was mirrored in industry, where titles such as Vice President of Personnel and Vice President of Industrial Relations, the most common titles through most of the 1960s, were replaced by Vice President of Human Resources. Likewise, in academia nearly all business schools by the mid-1990s had renamed their majors and courses from "personnel" to "human resources management" and almost all textbooks had dropped the personnel term in favour of HRM (Strauss, 2001).

Accompanying the name change was also a gradual shift in outlook in the United States about both the philosophy and conceptualization of the field. The new outlook is well captured by Dulebohn, Ferris and Stodd (1995: 30). They state:

> The connotation of the term HRM is distinct from PM in the following ways. First, whereas PM implies human resources are expenses, HRM indicates an organizational emphasis on human resources as organizational assets. ... Second, PM signifies a group of discrete human resource administrative subfunctions and

maintenance activities that are reactive, passive, and secondary to the other significant business functions. HRM on the other hand indicates a proactive approach, an integration of human resource subfunctions, and an enhancement and expansion of the function, position, and strategic importance of HRM within the organization.

This view is widely repeated in textbooks and professional publications, has spawned a new and rapidly growing subfield called strategic HRM and in the eyes of most participants has contributed to a major strengthening of the field. Less often remarked upon, this conceptualization of HRM also leads to two problems (Kaufman, 2001a; 2004e). If taken seriously, this definition limits HRM to only the subset of firms using an investment or human capital approach to labour, which by most accounts is far less than a majority of employers. If this is the case, then what are the other firms using? Personnel management? Industrial relations? And doesn't the concept of strategic HRM become an empty box if HRM only contains one approach? The popular definition of HRM also leads to a potentially troublesome conflation of positive and normative analysis, in that HRM scholars are at once asked to examine objectively "what is" in the world of work while maintaining a commitment to "what should be".

At the same time as personnel was metamorphosing into HRM, the latter was also moving away from industrial relations. In the early 1960s, for example, the journal *Personnel Management Quarterly* was published under the auspices of the Bureau of Industrial Relations at the University of Michigan and the editor, George Odiorne, held the title "Professor of Personnel and Industrial Relations", which suggests as earlier argued that personnel was subsumed as part of industrial relations. Two decades later, the journal had been renamed *Human Resource Management*, the Bureau of Industrial Relations no longer existed, the journal was under the auspices of the Management Department in the business school, and the editor was Noel Tichy, who had a national reputation in the fields of management and organizational behaviour (Kaufman, 2001a).

Numerous other examples indicate that, by the 1980s, HRM and industrial relations were conceived as largely separate fields. Illustratively, the organization for university programmes in labour and employment in the United States changed its name in the late 1980s from the Industrial Relations Center's Directors Group to the University Council of Industrial Relations and Human Resource Programs (UCIRHRP). Many industrial relations centres and institutes have also changed their names, or the titles of their degree programmes, to include both the labels human resources and industrial relations. At Loyola University in Chicago, for example, the Institute of Industrial Relations became the Institute of Human Resources and Industrial Relations, while the University of Minnesota changed its master's degree from master's in industrial relations to master's in human resources and industrial relations. Also illustrative of the bifurcation in the field is the title adopted by Kochan and Barocci (1985) for their textbook – *Human resources management and industrial relations*. While the conventional view is that HRM and industrial relations are now separate fields (albeit with some overlap), the shift in interpretation has proceeded sufficiently far that some American scholars now view HRM as encompassing the broad field of labour and employment while industrial relations (i.e., "labour relations") becomes a subsidiary subject thereof. Consider, for example, this definition of HRM recently offered by Ferris et al. (1995: 1): "Human resource management is the science and practice that deals with the nature of the employment relationship and all of the decisions, actions, and issues that relate to that relationship." They have effectively turned the tables on industrial relations – HRM is now defined to cover the entire employment relationship and all aspects therein, while a half-century earlier this had been industrial relations' broad mandate.

Simply changing the name of the field from personnel to HRM was not by itself sufficient to cause the PM and ILE schools to break apart. Other factors were also in operation. One such factor was a growing divergence of research interests; another was a clash of ideologies. Both are discussed in later sections. A third, described here, is the rise of business schools and the massive shift of student enrolments from industrial relations to human resources courses in the United States.

One important reason for industrial relations academics' initial lack of early concern about the breakaway of the PM school is that at the time business schools were regarded by many as something of an academic backwater, with personnel management held in particularly low regard. During the next 40 years, however, American business schools experienced dramatic growth in student enrolments and intellectual prestige, pulling the field of personnel or HRM with it and leaving the industrial relations field behind.

The low status of business education in American universities in the early part of the twentieth century has already been remarked upon in an earlier chapter. But this situation persisted through the 1950s. Arnold Weber, an industrial relations centre director and later president of Northwestern University, states in this regard (1987: 19), "When I received my Ph.D. in economics from MIT in 1958 and went to teach at a business school, it was something like running away with a bareback rider at the circus. ... Business schools had courses in window display design and turret lathe set ups, and all those pragmatic things." And within business schools, few courses had lower status than personnel management. In their influential report on business education in the late 1950s, Gordon and Howell (1959) remark that (p. 189), "next to the course in production, perhaps more educational sins have been committed in the name of personnel management than in any other required course in the business curriculum". Also illustrative are these comments by Weber (p. 15):

> When I studied labor relations at Illinois in 1950–1951, there were a few students at the institute who were taking personnel; they were déclassé by definition. I would approach these fellows and quizzically ask why they were going into personnel. ... They always gave one of two answers which were descriptive of the field: (1) 'I did it in the Army,' or (2) 'I like people.'

Personnel's low reputation was a product of long-standing problems – its dearth of intellectual substance, the fragmentation of the subject area into a congeries of functional specializations (e.g., selection, compensation, training) with little theoretical or conceptual connection one to the other, and the non-strategic, primarily administrative role it played in most (but not all) business organizations. In this vein, management expert Peter Drucker commented (1954: 274–5) that

> everything we know today about personnel administration was known by the early twenties, everything we practice now was practiced then. ... Personnel administration is largely a collection of incidental techniques without much internal cohesion. ... [I]t is partly a file clerk's job, partly a housekeeping job, partly a social worker's job and partly "fire-fighting" to head off union trouble or to settle it.

These shortcomings were much in evidence two decades later. Examining the state of the personnel function, for example, Fred Foulkes (1975: 71) comes to this conclusion:

> In many companies, the responsibilities of personnel departments have been confined to insignificant kinds of activities. The staffs of these departments have rarely been consulted on matters of corporate policy. They have only implemented rather than participated in the development of strategy. They have developed and implemented too many personnel programs not closely enough related to the objectives of the company.

Foulkes goes on to note that as of the mid-1970s only 150 of the Harvard Business School's 39,000 graduates were employed in either a personnel or industrial relations position, explaining (p. 74), "Many of them [the graduates] feel that the personnel field is 'low status' and 'bad news'."

Gradually, personnel's fortunes began to pick up. A variety of factors account for this trend. One, as already described, is the change in the name of the field from personnel to HRM. A second is the dramatic increase in American workplace regulation and legislation (e.g., anti-discrimination, affirmative action, pension administration) that most companies delegated to personnel/HR to handle. A third is the decline in power and membership of the organized labour movement that allowed personnel/HRM to shift from a defensive focus on labour relations and union avoidance to a more proactive, strategic emphasis on organizational change and competitive advantage through people (Jacoby, 2003). Job opportunities also shifted to the non-union sector, leading students to see an HRM major as a far better option in the job market. And, finally, HRM's potential to create competitive advantage and superior employment relations was demonstrated by a small group of companies in the United States that bucked conventional practice in the 1950s and 1960s and implemented it in a strategic, thorough-going manner (Meyer, 1976; Foulkes, 1980; Jacoby, 1997).

Of most importance to the improved fortunes of personnel/HRM, however, were two other developments – the successful application of behavioural-science research to issues of management and organizational design, and the development and implementation of the strategic management concept.

Regarding the former, Dunnette and Bass (1963: 116) state:

> many of the leading schools of business and industrial administration have shifted from the descriptive study of current personnel practices to the application of principles of the social sciences to the analysis of organizational problems. ... The behavioural sciences are making rapid strides and are moving to a central position in the study of industrial behaviour.

The focal point of this activity was the new field of organizational behaviour (OB) and its close intellectual cousin organizational development (OD). The OB field emerged in American universities in the early 1960s, largely as a fusion of two branches of research in management that had earlier proceeded largely independent of each other: human relations and business organization and administration (Whyte, 1965; Strauss, 1993). While personnel/HRM remained an intellectual backwater in the 1960s and most of the 1970s, the new field of OB took off and experienced dramatic growth and influence. Many of the "big names" among management writers of this period were associated with OB, such as Douglas McGregor, Chris Argyris, Rensis Likert, Albert Maslow and Frederick Herzberg, while most business schools (prodded by curriculum and accreditation standards established by the American Association of Collegiate Schools of Business, AACSB) made an OB course a required part of the curriculum.

The development of the OB field proved to be a major boon for personnel/HRM. Martin (1975: 150) states, for example, "Personnel administration and management as taught in collegiate schools of business changed drastically during the 1960s. This change stemmed in large part from two 1959 foundation-sponsored studies of business schools, which argued persuasively that business school curricula should incorporate more of the behavioural sciences." The "drastic change" that Martin refers to is that OB helped bring intellectual substance and theory to personnel/HRM, changing it from a largely descriptive, administrative and vocational field of study to one that had at least a modicum of intellectual content, theory and application to substantive issues in business. In the process, personnel/HRM drifted away from industrial relations, shifting from a field that had several decades earlier been viewed as "applied economics" and taught by industrial relations professors to one increasingly taught as "applied OB" and staffed by industrial or organizational psychologists hired in business school management departments (Kaufman, 2000b).

While OB had its home base in business schools and the behavioural sciences, at least through the early 1970s it still had a connection to industrial relations and was loosely subsumed within it. The forerunner of OB, human relations, was the subject of the 1957 IRRA research volume, *Research in industrial human relations* (Arensberg et al.) and one of the leading scholars of human relations, William Foote Whyte of Cornell University, was elected IRRA president in 1963. Then, in the 1970 IRRA research volume, *A review of industrial relations research*, George Strauss authored a chapter on "Organizational behavior and personnel relations". The link between OB and industrial relations is, apparently, already tenuous, given his comment (p. 201), "I must predict this may be the last review which deals with OB as a part of industrial relations. ... Though industrial relations claims to be multi-disciplinary, it is in fact heavily dominated by labour economists and for many in the field the terms industrial relations and labour economics are inter-changeable." Strauss was too pessimistic, however, for the IRRA decided to devote the entire 1974 research volume to the subject of *Organizational behavior: Research and issues* (Strauss et al.). The fractured state of the relationship between industrial relations and OB is attested to in the Preface, however, where the editors state, "The question of whether to publish a book devoted to Organizational Behavior (OB) caused strenuous debate within the Executive Board. There was one group which felt that OB did not really belong within Industrial Relations. The other group was willing to provide an opportunity to test OB's relevance." From this date forward industrial relations had little formal contact with OB.

Looking beyond the academic world, the rise of OB and the application of the behavioural sciences to management and organizational design also had significant repercussions in the real world of business. Through the 1950s most large American corporations were unionized and the conventional wisdom of the period held that this was the normal and expected condition. Not only were employers' efforts to remain non-unionized often regarded with opprobrium as regressive and anti-social; many companies simply did not have the ability to manage their workforces effectively without a union. In this context, industrial relations was viewed as a necessary and important branch of study in universities and an area of vocational practice in industry.

By the mid-1960s, however, leading management writers were starting to produce theoretical and empirical studies that pointed the way to significantly different models of organizational design and management. Examples include the socio-technical model developed by Trist and colleagues in the United Kingdom (Trist, 1981) and the "high-commitment" or "high-performance" model developed by Louis Davis, Richard Walton and others in the United States (Davis, 1966; Walton, 1985; Nadler, Gerstein and Shaw, 1992).[2] These new models feature a flattened organizational hierarchy, employee participation, gain-sharing, extensive communication, formal dispute resolution, and an egalitarian culture and promised higher organizational performance through a strategy emphasizing mutual gain and effective utilization of human capital for competitive advantage.

This new model was a boon to the personnel/HRM field on three counts (Beer and Spector, 1984): its emphasis on competitive advantage through people was a natural fit with the new "human resource" perspective sweeping the field; successful implementation of the new model rested on effective HRM policies and practices and thus heightened the perceived importance of personnel/HRM as an academic and practitioner subject; and the model's apparent success in generating both improved financial performance and worker job satisfaction gave it and personnel/HRM an aura of progressivism and "wave of the future". The new high-performance model also threatened industrial relations in two ways: it emphasized a unitarist approach of goal alignment and integration of interests rather than the traditional, pluralist industrial relations approach centred on power balancing and negotiated compromise, and by creating much improved work conditions and management systems it also reduced workers' demand for union representation and thus contributed to the de-unionization of American industry (Troy, 1999; Delaney and Godard, 2001; Kaufman, 1997b).

Personnel/HRM was also dramatically affected by the development and popularization of the strategic management concept. Apart from leading welfare capitalist firms of the 1920s and a few progressive firms of the 1950s and 1960s, most American employers practised a relatively reactive, non-strategic approach to personnel/HRM. The situation changed dramatically, however, in the early 1980s (Jacoby, 2003; Beaumont, Bccker and Robertson, 2003). Strategic management – earlier called strategic planning and earlier still "policy" – originated out of work by Michael Porter, H. Igor Ansoff and others. It was soon thereafter imported into personnel/HRM. In one of the earliest contributions, for example, Devanna et al. (1982: 11) say of the traditional personnel function, "The recent popularity of human resources management is causing major problems for traditional personnel departments. For years they have been explaining their mediocre status by bewailing their lack of support and attention from the CEO." They then go on to outline a new approach, saying:

> Whether the human resources component survives as a valuable and essential contribution to effective management will largely depend on the degree to which it is integrated as a vital part of the planning system in organizations. In large part, the management of human resources must become an indispensable consideration in both strategy formulation and strategy implementation.

The next two decades in the United States witnessed a veritable explosion of writing and research on strategic HRM in the academic world and a major reorganization and reorientation of the HRM function in many companies. To some degree, this burst of research was a faddish development and one that generated more printed words by academics than concrete innovations in the actual practice of HRM. Indeed, one of the nation's leading HRM academics and consultants concluded in an article in the *Harvard Business Review* (Ulrich, 1998) that the HRM function – despite all the talk of becoming a proactive, integrated, strategic business partner – continued to be practised in many firms in a largely reactive, administrative and value-sapping way. Given this dose of reality, it remains the case that the development and integration of the strategy concept into the field of HRM has noticeably strengthened and broadened its intellectual content and value added in the business world. While industrial relations academics have also introduced the strategy concept into industrial relations (e.g., Kochan, Katz and McKersie, 1986), the gains are not so clear cut. Part of the reason has to do with various conceptual and methodological weaknesses (Lewin, 1987), while another is that gaining competitive advantage is a less obvious and compelling goal for industrial relations.

The rise of HRM, while certainly threatening "classic" industrial relations and the people who practise it, has also brought benefits and, in important ways, actually enriched and strengthened the American industrial relations field writ large. Just as economists and industrial relations experts were among the leading scholars and textbook authors on personnel/HRM in the 1920s and the 1950s (Kaufman, 2002b), they began to establish themselves in the same role in the 1990s. HRM textbooks remained woefully descriptive into the 1990s while much of the research was heavily micro and psychological in orientation, reflecting the dominance of the behavioural sciences in management departments and industrial-organizational psychologists in the OB field. Industrial relations scholars, having a more externalist orientation and familiarity with economic theory and econometrics, quickly entered the HRM field and established a significant presence (Mitchell, 2001). Economists, for example, have carved out an entirely new subfield called the economics of personnel, and this literature is highly theoretical and sophisticated (Lazear, 1999; Gunderson, 2001). Much like industrial relations, HRM has never had a theoretical base but economics may well succeed in providing it (Kaufman, 2004e). Also, a large empirical literature has developed on the link between human relations/industrial relations practices and firm performance, which has been predominantly authored by economists and industrial relations scholars (Kleiner et al., 1987; Delaney and Godard, 2001; Lewin, 2004). Also of note are new HRM textbooks by industrial relations scholars (e.g., Lewin and Mitchell, 1995) and handbooks (Lewin, Mitchell and Zaidi, 1997).

These positive developments notwithstanding, a widespread feeling pervades the American industrial relations field that its future is imperilled by the ascendancy of HRM. This situation is, historically viewed, paradoxical. As earlier described, the field of personnel/HRM originated from industrial relations and its earliest and most influential academic writers came from industrial relations. Indeed, I have argued here and elsewhere (Kaufman, 1998a) that Commons deserves the title "co-father of personnel/HRM" (along with the duo of Tead and Metcalf), while the evidence reveals that industrial relations scholars such as Douglas, Leiserson, Lescohier and Slichter were the most authoritative experts on personnel/HRM in the 1920s. Furthermore, Commons in *Industrial goodwill* not only developed a fivefold model of strategic HRM but also laid out most of the core tenets for the high-performance workplace system (HPWS). Also, both the theory and practice of strategic HRM and participative management were fully grasped by the early practitioners of welfare capitalism and were implemented at Standard Oil and other leading firms in the 1920s as part of their industrial relations programmes (Balderston, 1935; Kaufman, 2001b).[3]

The irony in industrial relations' current situation is thus fourfold. First, the HRM field that now seems to dominate industrial relations was actually born out of industrial relations and was once a subsidiary component of it. Second, the emergence of the HPWS in the 1980s was heralded as the "new industrial relations" paradigm *(Business Week*, 11 May 1981; Kochan and Barocci, 1985) when, in fact, the basic ideas for this paradigm were in large measure "new" sixty years earlier.[4] Third, the HPWS that is now the focus of so much favourable attention in industrial relations was delayed and frustrated for three to four decades by the Great Depression and New Deal labour policies – policies long touted, paradoxically, as the epitome of the field's positive and normative agenda. And fourth, a number of modern-day industrial relations scholars criticize and reject the unitarist/HRM model when in fact it was early industrial relations scholars and practitioners who helped invent, popularize and implement key parts of it. The last point is made *not* to imply that HRM and the HPWS should be accepted without judgement, for clearly both deserve critical scrutiny and have their own contradictions and shortcomings. What it does suggest is that where the unitarist/HRM model can contribute to a positive-sum outcome it should be welcomed and not spurned – at least if one follows the example of the founders of the field.

The rise of neoclassical labour economics

The position of American industrial relations was further undermined by the rise to dominance of the neoclassical school in labour economics. During the 1950s, the core group in American industrial relations was the neo-institutional labour economists, such as Dunlop, Kerr, Lester and Reynolds (Kaufman, 1988). Although the fact that they were economists gave the industrial relations field even in that period a tilt toward the discipline of economics, their social-science, heterodox research orientation and real-world participation in industrial relations nevertheless allowed them not only to straddle successfully the divide between the two fields but also to remain committed to the underlying pluralist ILE model of industrial relations. Beginning in the late 1950s, however, the position of the neo-institutionalists was challenged by a new group of labour economists committed to neoclassical economics. The centre of this group was composed of price theorists and labour economists from the University of Chicago. Kerr (1988) called this group the "neoclassical restorationists". Included in this group were Gary Becker, Milton Friedman, H. Gregg Lewis, Jacob Mincer, Melvin Reder, Albert Rees, Sherwin Rosen, George Stigler and a number of others.

The events of the Great Depression had seemingly discredited competitive neoclassical price theory: a point of view exemplified by the antagonistic attitude of the ILE-oriented labour economists toward it. Stigler and Friedman launched a major counterattack on several fronts (Kaufman, 1994; 2004c). In the first, Friedman sought to show, with respect to macroeconomic theory, that the Depression was not the inherent fault of the price system but resulted instead from erroneous policies of government, thus negating the ILE (and Keynesian) belief that the price system at the aggregate level is often dysfunctional. The second was the rigorous development of the theory of price determination in competitive markets, thereby providing an analytical framework that the ILE critics lacked. The third was the application of the competitive model to a host of new labour market issues, such as hours of work, discrimination, education and family size. This line of attack was started by Lewis (1956) (in the *Proceedings* of the IRRA!) but was pursued most strenuously by Becker (1957, 1976).

The fourth line of attack was the methodological assault on realism in theory. A foundation stone of historical/institutional economics is that theory should be built on realistic premises and assumptions which have been formed through inductive empirical investigation. Following in this methodological tradition, the ILE economists attacked neoclassical theory for its unrealistic assumptions and concluded that it provided an often inaccurate representation of how labour markets really work.[5] But Stigler and Friedman counterattacked, arguing that the true test of a theory is its predictive ability, not the realism of its assumptions, and that in most cases neoclassical theory gives the right answer (Friedman, 1953). This argument proved persuasive to many economists then and now (e.g., Boyer and Smith, 2001).

Finally, the restorationists also pioneered the application of statistical methods to the analysis and testing of labour market hypotheses (Lewis, 1963). The indeterminacy and non-quantitative factors in economic relationships emphasized by the ILE economists became lost in the error term of the regression equation, while a statistically significant coefficient of the right sign on a key economic variable of interest – no matter how small its quantitative size – was taken as support of the validity of neoclassical theory.

These developments had a markedly adverse impact on industrial relations. The rise of neoclassical theory, for example, struck at both the intellectual and ideological foundations of ILE-style industrial relations. The focus of industrial relations is the study of labour problems in the employment relationship and methods to resolve them. The fundamental assumption underlying the ILE (and Keynesian) perspective is that wage rates are not able to coordinate and equilibrate labour markets due to a wide variety of market imperfections and failures. As a consequence, no presumption exists that labour market outcomes are optimal and, indeed, the presence of restricted labour mobility, lack of compensating wage differentials and a surplus of jobseekers is certain to create many labour problems, such as substandard wages, excessive hours and unhealthy working conditions. Hence, in institutional theory the imperfect nature of markets (and the human beings in them) creates not only an intellectual rationale but also a social mandate for the "visible hand" of institutional intervention in labour markets to make them work more effectively and fairly.

In contrast, the fundamental premise of neoclassical labour economics is the "invisible hand" story of Adam Smith – that wage rates in competitive labour markets are able to equilibrate demand and supply and thereby lead to full employment with a welfare-maximizing structure of relative wages, employment and working conditions. In a recent article, for example, Boyer and Smith (2001: 210) state, "One characteristic of the neoclassical labor economists – and one that sharply distinguished them from the neo-institutionalists – was their dogged determination to find maximizing behavior and equilibrium outcomes throughout the labor market." Because the theory predicts that labour market outcomes are efficient and welfare maximizing, the concept of labour problems so central to industrial relations is rendered moot, while the case for institutional intervention through trade unions, minimum wage laws and other such methods is obviated.

At one level of neoclassical theory, the existence of labour problems is simply denied by the nature of the assumptions. In the simple competitive "price theory" version of neoclassical economics, for example, labour problems such as involuntary unemployment, excessive work-hours and wage exploitation rarely exist, except as a short-run disequilibrium phenomenon or isolated occurrence of monopsony. Likewise, this theory predicts that introducing minimum wage law or collective bargaining into such a market will quite likely lead to inefficiency and loss of jobs.

At another, more sophisticated level of neoclassical theory, market imperfections and deviant labour outcomes are recognized as occurring in real life but then are explained away as optimal outcomes (Kaufman, 2004c). For example, using the more general "choice theory" (rational behaviour) version pioneered by Becker (1976), neoclassical economists demonstrate that unemployment arises as an optimizing outcome from job search, implicit contracts, inter-temporal substitution of work and leisure, an efficiency wage argument, or some other such phenomenon. Likewise, the fact that women are paid lower wages than men is also an efficient outcome because they choose to accumulate less human capital in light of their prospective time out of the market to raise children. Because these outcomes are the product of rational behaviour and exploit all gains from trade, they are deemed optimal adaptations to constraints of life and, thus, are no more a labour problem in a substantive sense than is the fact that workers have to buy food to eat or wear clothes to stay warm in winter. Nor, then, is institutional intervention warranted or likely to make labour markets operate more efficiently and effectively. Reflective of this perspective, after reviewing implicit contract theory Boyer and Smith effectively minimize the intellectual challenge of unemployment by concluding (p. 211), "In sum, it is the view of neoclassical labour economists that layoff unemployment is not inconsistent with economic theory."

Quite apart from issues of theory and policy, one must also note that the neoclassical school has triumphed in part because of the perceived superiority of its method. The name of the game in modern economics is model building and the derivation and empirical testing of hypotheses (Solow, 1997). The neoclassical tools of constrained maximization and equilibrium have allowed economists to develop highly mathematized and formalized models of economic behaviour and institutions. The historical and interdisciplinary nature of institutional economics, on the other hand, makes it far more difficult to formalize into an analytic model, thus severely limiting its appeal in modern-day labour economics. Indeed, many labour economists believe that institutional economics is largely synonymous with "descriptive economics" and thus is incapable of generating either theory or models (Addison and Siebert, 1979). Another attribute of the neoclassical method that has conquered modern labour economics is the insistence on methodological individualism – that all group behaviour must be explained in terms of the behaviour of the constituent individuals. This position has also significantly undermined the attractiveness of institutional economics, given its focus on the independent importance of collective forms of behaviour in labour markets, and tends in the minds of most economists to place institutional economics in the realm of sociology.

Neoclassical labour economics grew rapidly in the 1960s, and by the 1980s had largely displaced the institutional, industrial relations version. By the late 1990s, hardly a trace of the institutional tradition was left in mainstream labour economics, while even in industrial relations few self-identified and practising institutional economists remain (as old institutionalists retire and die, new neoclassically trained assistant professors take their place). So scarce, for example, has institutional labour research become that the editorial board of the *Industrial and Labor Relations Review* ran a "Notice to Contributors" (October 1989: 4) stating, "We wish to receive more 'institutional' papers." The response, as revealed in subsequent published articles, was nil and led the editors to run the same statement several years later, with no greater effect.

Given that institutional economics has provided the core of theory and method for American industrial relations over the years, the decline and near disappearance of institutionalism in labour economics is surely one of the most mortal threats to the continued survival of the field. Viewing the matter from the opposite angle, one may also say that the decline of industrial relations has an inverse relationship with the rise of neoclassical economics and the triumph of the latter more than likely spells the effective demise of the former. If American industrial relations is to avoid this fate, it desperately needs a stronger theoretical base of institutional economics – or some other body of theory along heterodox lines (Cappelli, 1985; Adams, 1988; Kaufman, 2004d).

The future in this matter has to be rated as highly uncertain and, if history is a guide, relatively gloomy. But rays of hope exist nonetheless. Within American labour economics and industrial relations remains a small contingent of scholars who are committed to an institutional research agenda. Names such as Appelbaum, Brown, Budd, Katz, Kochan, Levine, Osterman, Piore and Voos immediately come to mind. A shining example of the power of the institutional method in empirical research is provided by Truman Bewley's (1999) recent book, *Why wages don't fall during a recession*. Also deserving note is another group of labour economists, more closely associated with the Association for Evolutionary Economics, who are trying to rebuild the "old" institutional tradition coming from Commons and the Wisconsin school (Champlin and Knoedler, 2004). Yet another source of theory for industrial relations comes from the "new" institutional economics built on the work of Coase and Williamson (Dow, 1997), while the heterodox work of general theorists such as Akerlof, Simon and Stiglitz provides yet another source of theoretical ideas. Also promising is the considerable activity in other heterodox areas of the discipline, such as behavioural economics and economic sociology (Kaufman, 1999b; Smelser and Swedberg, 1994; the new journal *Socio-Economic Review*). And, finally, Europe provides a fertile source of new theory for industrial relations, such as the work of the French regulation school (Boyer and Saillard, eds., 2001), the literature on "varieties of capitalism" (Hall and Soskice, 2001), labour process theory (Thompson and Newsome, 2004) and European versions of new institutional economics (Kasper and Streit, 1998).

Viewed in this manner, the issue is not whether an alternative theoretical base to neoclassical economics can be built for industrial relations but, rather, whether American researchers in the field will grasp the opportunity and meet the challenge. As noted later in this chapter, the record to date is not terribly encouraging, although progress is being made.

Neglect of the left or heterodox alternative

The defection of personnel/HRM and the rise of neoclassical economics can both be viewed as eroding the industrial relations field from the right, while the centre was hollowed out by the decline of unions and collective bargaining. Looking to bolster membership and seek new intellectual ideas and allies, one obvious option for American industrial relations would have been to look to the left in the American academic community – where "left" connotes a more radical and heterodox intellectual and policy approach. Or, if new ideas aren't available in America, industrial relations scholars could have looked to Europe or elsewhere. But these options were not pursued with any vigour or commitment and, indeed, were met with considerable indifference and even resistance in a large part of the American industrial relations community.

In the 1960s, the older generation of heterodox neo-institutional labour economists who had centred so prominently in the golden age period of the 1950s were gradually ceasing active involvement in the industrial relations field and, thus, opportunities for a new generation to take control appeared. Coincidentally, the late 1960s was also a period of social and political activism and radicalism on college campuses, fuelled by opposition to the Viet Nam War and social and economic inequalities in American society. Emblematic of the leftward drift of the social sciences during this time period, a group of young economists founded in 1968 the Union for Radical Political Economy (URPE). A number of the founders, such as Barry Bluestone, Samuel Bowles, Herbert Gintis, David Gordon and Howard Wachtel, wrote extensively on labour and employment issues. Although their writings are diverse, Marxist concepts such as class, exploitation and managerial power and control figure prominently. Positioned somewhere between radical political economy and orthodox economics was another group of young labour economists, such as Peter Doeringer, Michael Piore and Lester Thurow, who also took a heterodox approach to labour market issues. Their research developed institutionalist-based theories on dual and segmented labour markets (e.g., Doeringer and Piore, 1971) and job-competition labour markets (Thurow, 1975), and critiques of neoclassical economics (Thurow, 1983; Piore, 1995). Piore and Sabel's book *The second industrial divide* (1984) also set off a small boom of research on the demise of the Fordist production model and the rise of flexible specialization, although more of this research was located overseas than in America.

In the 1970s, another leftist, heterodox opportunity opened up. In 1974, Harry Braverman, a sheet-metal worker turned self-educated Marxist intellectual, published *Labor and monopoly capital: The degradation of work in the twentieth century*. The thesis of the book was that employers use a strategy of Taylorism (subdividing and routinizing jobs) to de-skill jobs in order to lower wages, reduce worker bargaining power and extend management control of the workplace. Braverman's book precipitated a wave of interest among heterodox and left-wing academics, particularly in sociology, on management control systems, the interface between technology and workplace organization, and worker resistance through individual and collective means.

The model they developed became known as the labour process. Two influential American contributions to this literature are Richard Edwards' *Contested terrain: The transformation of work in the twentieth century* (1979) and Michael Burawoy's *Manufacturing consent: Changes in the labor process under monopoly capitalism* (1979).

In the 1970s, yet a third opportunity for intellectual exchange opened up on the left side of the intellectual spectrum. During the 1970s the industrial relations field in the United Kingdom was in the midst of its own golden age. Much of the leading research was coming from an insurgent group of British sociologists and historians of varying radical and Marxist orientations who were challenging the pluralist–institutional model of industrial relations, typified by the work of Clegg and Flanders in the United Kingdom and Dunlop in the United States. The senior figure in the group was Alan Fox, newly converted to a more radical perspective on industrial relations, while the younger generation included Victor Allen, Paul Edwards, John Goldthorpe and Richard Hyman.

The pluralist–institutional model posits a fundamental but limited conflict of interests in the employment relationship and seeks to balance and humanize the system through selected reforms, such as encouragement of collective bargaining. Attention is focused on the institutional actors (firms, unions, government labour-regulatory bodies) and outcomes at the firm and industry level (wage settlements, strikes, etc.), while actors and developments at the lower shop-floor level (shop stewards, informal bargaining) and higher nation-state level (the working and capitalist classes, systems of power and control) are typically omitted or given cursory treatment. Strauss (1982: 97, 98) characterized the conventional American industrial relations model of the 1970s and 1980s as a "narrow closed system approach", "largely ahistoric", and having "almost no interest in international comparisons". He goes on to say (p. 98), "Like the air we breathe, the major premises of our industrial relations system can be ignored just as long as they remain unchanged."

Hyman (1982) offers an even more critical view on the state of American industrial relations scholarship. He concludes (p. 113):

> The 'new generation' of scholarly work ... proclaimed by Strauss and Feuille as heralding a renaissance in American industrial relations, can be regarded as such only in the narrowest of terms. These scholars are remarkable for their unconcern with the larger context which gives current American collective bargaining its historical specificity; or with comparative 'industrial relations systems' which fail to match their own behavioral science models; or with notions of a labor movement which cannot be forced within their fetishistic matrix of quantification; or with

writers whose orientations do not merely reinforce their own. The well-nigh unprecedented parochialism of such scholars involves an antiseptic retreat from the broader sensibilities of such students of American labor as Commons, Hoxie, Perlman, or Mills.

With regard to the penchant of American industrial relations scholars to ignore the literature on the left, Hyman remarks (p. 108), "[they] may shudder at the idea of consulting such periodicals as the *Insurgent Sociologist*, *Kapitalistate*, *Labor History*, *Monthly Review*, *Politics and Society*, *Radical America*, *Review of Radical Political Economics*, and *Socialist Revolution*".

One may of course question whether authors in *Insurgent Sociologist* and *Kapitalistate* are any more catholic in the range of journals they cite (*Harvard Business Review*? *Academy of Management Journal*?), but Hyman nonetheless makes a valid point. Not only had American industrial relations largely divorced itself from any contact with the left (noting that "left" in an American context is often "mainstream" in a European context), but it was also drifting toward a narrow empiricism and ethnocentric insularity. But this leads to the next subject.

The rise of science building

In addition to the factors cited above, yet another cause of the declining fortunes of American industrial relations is found in the rise of science building in the academic world. Science building – the pursuit of knowledge for its own sake through the application of the scientific method – promotes more rigorous, high-quality research in industrial relations, but at a considerable cost. The specialization and division of labour that go with science building undercut the interdisciplinary approach to research that was a principal rationale for the field, while the scientific method tended to cut off industrial relations researchers from the worlds of practice and employment reform.

When industrial relations was born in the late 1910s, no other academic field existed in universities that encompassed labour and employment. Industrial relations thus took on a broad "all aspects" definition for two reasons: first, a large intellectual void existed and industrial relations could step in and claim sovereignty over this broad subject area of work and, second, the heavy emphasis on problem solving in the early industrial relations field also encouraged an expansive viewpoint, given that labour problems span a highly diverse range of phenomena and touch upon many academic disciplines.

In hindsight, the transition of industrial relations from a broadly constructed to more narrowly constructed field in the social sciences was to some degree inevitable and unsurprising. As knowledge production proceeds, efficiency and productivity in teaching and research are facilitated by growing specialization and division of labour. Thus, at the time of Adam Smith, economics, political science and sociology were all subsumed within moral philosophy; one hundred years later they broke away to become separate disciplines when their respective *problématiques* and supporting bodies of knowledge became sufficiently dense and differentiated to support separate academic "production units" (e.g., disciplines, university departments, specialized research journals and conferences). The same process was bound to happen with industrial relations, the only question being when rather than if.

In the 1920s, industrial relations was in the same position as moral philosophy in the early 1800s – it subsumed the ILE and PM schools and, in particular, the subjects of labour law, labour history, personnel management, labour relations, trade unionism and applied labour economics. As science building and knowledge production proceeded, each area of industrial relations developed increasingly well-identified and distinct bodies of literature, theoretical perspectives and sense of professional identity among their academic practitioners (i.e., craft consciousness). Thus, by the 1950s the intellectual centrifugal forces activated by specialization and division of labour began to dissolve or break apart the broad "all aspects" configuration of the industrial relations field and cause various parts to be spun off into new and separate fields. In the early 1950s, for example, industrial sociology was considered part of industrial relations, as were human relations and personnel management; fifteen years later these fields had become autonomous academic specialty areas with slowly weakening affiliations with industrial relations. What was left was the largely applied aspects of trade unionism and labour–management relations – the subjects that were arguably at the centre of post-Second World War industrial relations and that were not (as yet) readily absorbed into another existing field or discipline (e.g., labour economics).

While a narrowing of intellectual domain was probably inevitable, industrial relations had the ill fortune to adopt as its residual core topic a subject area that after 1960 went into a pronounced decline as an interesting and important area of research. Collective bargaining coverage gradually shrunk, the problems of labour–management relations became routinized, and federal-level developments in labour policy were largely outside the labour–management area. Thus Strauss and Feuille (1978: 265) were led to conclude, "as many industrial relations problems became less urgent, the field's reason for existence became less clear".

Without new or urgent problems to solve and with the growing emphasis in American universities on scholarly research published in refereed journals ("publish or perish"), the incentives and peer pressure were to move toward pure research and publication. Older professors of industrial relations, having tenure and unwilling or unable to learn calculus and multiple regression, continued to do traditional case studies and field research, augmented in many cases by substantial outside labour arbitration practices. Other members of the field moved into university administration and government service. Indeed, a number of the field's most prominent scholars went on to hold very prominent and prestigious university and government appointments. Dunlop, for example, was United States Secretary of Labor, administrator of several wage–price controls programmes, and held a long list of other public service and university positions (Kaufman, 2002a). Similarly, Clark Kerr was president of the University of California system (Kerr, 2003); George Schultz was United States Secretary of State and Secretary of the Treasury; and Arnold Weber and Edwin Young were presidents, respectively, of Northwestern University and the University of Wisconsin, Madison.

The remaining group of industrial relations academics in the 1970s, including a large crop of new assistant professors from the baby-boom generation, shifted into science building. Particularly the new generation of industrial relations academics, with doctoral degrees in the late 1960s and 1970s, took a markedly different approach to industrial relations research. Their training emphasized research skills, quantitative methods and scholarly publication. Unlike the previous generations, they were not social reformers nor problem solvers but, first and foremost, *social scientists*.

As they pursued science building, however, the entire complexion of industrial relations began to change. Cappelli (1991: 5) observes, for example:

> IR found itself in competition with the rest of the social sciences in its efforts to understand employment issues. And it began to change in order to be competitive according to the social science rules. There was a general movement toward using theories from the mainstream of the social sciences to explain IR phenomena and within that trend, a dramatic shift toward economics and psychology and away from sociology and political science. ... As industrial relations scholars moved toward the application of existing social science theories, IR began to disappear first as an independent discipline and then as a unique topic area. If, for example, one's theory comes from labor economics, then the uniqueness of IR lies in the choice of topics. And the uniqueness of IR as a topic area began to erode in the 1980s as other disciplines also began to investigate union–management issues. This was particularly true in labor economics.

As Cappelli indicates, science building puts an applied, problem-solving field such as industrial relations into a competitive game for which it is ill suited and has little advantage. When industrial relations was a problem-solving field and research and publications were less emphasized and sophisticated, a new scholar could take an interdisciplinary industrial relations degree and still survive and even prosper. Illustratively, Frederick Harbison once remarked (quoted in Walker, 1968: 115), "I'm a lousy economist. I'm a lousy sociologist. I'm just an industrial relations man." He nonetheless held faculty positions at Chicago and Princeton and achieved national and international prominence. Today, a young aspiring scholar who repeated Harbison's words would be lucky to get a job and luckier still to get tenure.

Larry Cummings (1982: 79) states of industrial relations, "Industrial Relations traditionally has staked its claim for a place in the intellectual sphere of employment relations as an integrating and integrative discipline." He goes on to note, however, that the field typically honoured the interdisciplinary goal more in word than deed, leaving it as "a disparate and largely insulated collection of subfields". As science building proceeds, each subfield becomes prey for researchers from the traditional disciplines who can bring stronger theory and methods to the research issues contained within. Hence, industrial relations gets picked apart and becomes a hollow shell, defined perhaps by the topic of unions and labour–management relations but otherwise lacking substantive content or unique methods.

As grasped by several generations of industrial relations scholars, one solution to this problem – indeed, perceived by many to be the holy grail for the field – is the development of a unique body of theory that industrial relations can call its own, thus carving out a secure position in the social sciences as a unique discipline (Kaufman, 2004d). Heneman (1969: 5–6) states well this point of view, saying:

> A discipline requires a general theory or general conceptual system and framework. Industrial relations can become a discipline if it deals with and prevents employment problems more effectively than does any other discipline. To do so, industrial relations must improve its theories. Since industrial relations has the advantage of concentrating on employment, whereas this is not of central interest to other disciplines, we have a possible and probable advantage. If industrial relations fails to be more effective, it does not deserve to be a discipline and will deservedly disappear.

The effort to develop industrial relations theory started with Dunlop's industrial relations systems model and has progressed with fits and starts to the present time. A variety of models, frameworks and concepts has been advanced, but none has provided a general theory that explains in a causal sense the workings of the industrial relations system. An early and much-cited work is Walton and McKersie's *A behavioral theory of labor negotiations* (1965). Also in this genre, but published two decades later, is the strategic choice model and "transformation thesis" of Kochan, Katz and McKersie (1986). Also prominent is Jack Barbash's juxtaposition of efficiency and equity in his book *The elements of industrial relations* (1984). Another interesting effort is Stephen Hills' (1995) model of alternative regimes of control, while John Budd in *Employment with a human face: Balancing efficiency, equity, and voice* (2004) provides the most comprehensive and insightful development of the traditional multidisciplinary industrial relations model available. The most recent attempt to advance industrial relations theory is the 2004 IRRA research volume, *Theoretical perspectives on work and the employment relationship* (Kaufman, 2004f). However, perhaps indicative of the current intellectual malaise in American industrial relations, most of the authors in this volume are from outside the United States. Also reflective of the slow progress made in this area of research, in the opinion of several scholars (Cappelli, 1991; Kochan, 1993), the most enduring theoretical generalization of American industrial relations remains Commons' thesis about the extension of markets.

The uneven record in advancing industrial relations theory in the United States has several roots. One, no doubt, is that most people who are in the field are oriented to empirical work and applied problem solving and thus have neither skills nor particular interest in theory development per se. Also, industrial relations scholars tend to value theory, not for its own sake, but as a useful tool and thus put less effort into abstraction and formalization. Illustrative of this pragmatic slant, Commons (1934a: 723) says theory is "only a tool for investigating practice, like a spade for digging up facts and converting them into an understandable system", while Dunlop (1958: viii) in the same vein says his motive for building theory is "to make one world of direct experience in industrial relations". One must also note that American scholars have by and large shown a lamentable parochialism with respect to theoretical work from other disciplines, paradigms and countries. Finally, the multidisciplinary nature of industrial relations makes the subject so sprawling and complex that large-scale theorizing becomes daunting if not impossible. Derber (1982: 88), for example, states that the field must develop "a theoretical framework integrating institutionalism, labour economics, and behavioural science". One can agree with Derber but note with some apprehension that this is a very tall order. Some scholars (Kochan, 1993) thus counsel a less grandiose strategy centred on developing "middle range" theory. The record even at this level is quite spotty.

Values and ideology

A final factor that has contributed to the narrowing and hollowing out of American industrial relations is a more restricted set of normative values that has come to define the boundaries of the field. Absent a core of theory and given the encroachment of other fields and disciplines into the area of work and employment, scholars in industrial relations have been forced to define the field partly on the basis of distinguishing normative commitments. Barbash (1989: 3) states in this regard, "If we are not bound by one theory it is just possible that common values inform our work." Unfortunately for the fortunes of American industrial relations, the value set chosen in the post-1960 period was not only a narrower version than earlier years but has increasingly lost appeal in the academic community and polity.

As described in an earlier chapter, from the earliest days of the field American industrial relations had an ethical/ideological face. Core components of the ethical/ideological face were rejection of the "labour as a commodity" and "autocratic employer" principles. Stated in the positive, the ideology of early industrial relations placed emphasis on humanizing the employment relationship, providing some form of collective voice for employees, and balancing the quest for efficiency with the pursuit of fairness and opportunities for self-development. These goals, in turn, were believed to require a multi-pronged programme of institution building and adaptation, including improved management, collective bargaining, labour law, and full-employment fiscal and monetary policies.

Stated as a criterion for membership in a field of study, any explicit set of normative values is necessarily delimiting. Those for early American industrial relations were delimiting in that they excluded from the field people espousing any of three extreme positions – unregulated laissez-faire capitalism, authoritarian regimes of workforce governance, and economic systems of socialism, syndicalism and communism. Beyond this, the value set and ideology of early industrial relations was relatively broad in that it allowed space for both the PM and ILE schools and a unitarist and pluralist approach to work organization and improved employment relations. Illustratively, the value set of early industrial relations was broad enough to encompass both John Commons and Elton Mayo.

Looking at the matter a half-century later, one can ask: would the values and ideology of American industrial relations post-1960 continue to provide room for both John Commons and Elton Mayo as members in good standing? The answer is a clear 'no'. Commons and the ILE school would continue to fit within the normative boundaries of contemporary industrial relations, but Mayo and the PM school would not. Extrapolated forward to the present time, the result of ideological exclusiveness is a further limiting of the field.

What is the ideology and value orientation of modern American industrial relations? As with the definition of the field, one can find both broad and narrow statements on this subject. A broad statement is by Barbash (1991: 91), who says, "Industrial relations' underlying value ... is the human essence of labor as a commodity or factor of production and, in consequence, labor's right to equity in the employment relationship." He goes on to say (p. 108),

> The duality between labor as a factor of production and labor's human condition ...
> becomes the moral premise which justifies (a) why the labor factor is entitled to
> equity, (b) why the market, left to its own devices, falls short of equity, (c) how trade
> unions and collective bargaining, public policy and management 'human relations'
> can variously compensate for the market's equity deficiencies, (d) why equity is
> indispensable to the stability of an industrial order and (e) why industrial relations
> came into being as a field of study and practice primarily concerned with equity in
> the employment relationship.

But many American industrial relations scholars, including Barbash, soon pass on to a more narrow perspective. For example, Somers (1975: 1) describes the ideology of American industrial relations as "the uniqueness and value of the free collective bargaining system, voluntarism, liberal pluralism [and] consent", while Barbash (1979: 453) elsewhere states, "As I see it, two leading principles govern the American ideology of American industrial relations: the adversarial principle and the principle of voluntarism." A further comment is offered by Franke (1987: 479): "It is probably fair to say that the distinctive character of many [industrial relations] programmes has been the study of trade unionism and collective bargaining and the value system that supported these institutions."

These statements seem to focus on three "isms" as the central normative premises of American industrial relations: pluralism, voluntarism and collectivism in employment relationships. These statements may also be regarded by many researchers as positive premises of industrial relations (statements of fact), but as normative statements they also describe subjective opinions about "ought" and "good and bad" in the work world.

Do these three "isms" accurately reflect the normative principles of leading industrial relations academics? The evidence seems affirmative. For example, the presidential address of Clark Kerr (1955) to the IRRA was entitled "Industrial relations and the liberal pluralist". In it he states (p. 6):

> Most of us are probably practicing, if not theoretical pluralists. We reject state
> absolutism as inimical to freedom and an atomistic approach as inimical to
> industrialization; and we accept the geographical decentralization of power in

governmental federalism and a functional distribution in a mixed system of public and private enterprise ... this power and this rule-making (although not ultimate sovereignty) are more safely and effectively distributed into many hands than into a few.

This statement clearly affirms both the principles of pluralism and voluntarism. Elsewhere in the article he also affirms the social desirability of trade unionism and collective bargaining, noting (p. 11), "It is probably only through effective self-government ... and responsible unionism ... that a pluralistic system can be indefinitely maintained. ... Management and unions need to accept fully each other's existence." And, finally, he rejects as inconsistent with the ideology of pluralism four alternative social systems: the atomism of neoclassical economics, the government control of state socialism, the "all embracing corporation of Mayo" and the all-embracing control of unions in the theory of syndicalism.

A second statement of the value set of industrial relations is contained in the IRRA presidential address of John Dunlop (1960). His talk, entitled "Consensus and national labor policy", makes the case for greater voluntarism in industrial relations, expanded collective bargaining, and formulation of national labour policy through tripartite involvement of labour, management and the public. He begins his article with this statement (p. 2): "The theme of these remarks is that our national industrial relations system suffers from excessive legislation, litigation, formal awards and public pronouncements." He then goes on to praise the performance of the collective bargaining system, stating (p. 2), "I do not agree that the country faces a crisis in collective bargaining. ... Rather, the overwhelming evidence is that on balance the relationships never were better." His major criticism of the American collective bargaining system, however, is that it had not spread far enough and, in particular, had not brought into the orbit of joint decision-making the management decision-makers at the industry and "confederation" level (e.g., the National Association of Manufacturers). Once high-level management is brought into the collective bargaining relationship, then labour policy can be developed through tripartite negotiation and consensus. Dunlop (p. 7) states, for example, "The legislative and administrative framework of collective bargaining should be changed only after extensive consultation and mediation through neutral or government experts with organized labor and management."

Do the three "isms" continue to reflect the ideology and normative premises of American industrial relations? As a broad generalization, the answer appears to be 'yes'. Consider, for example these remarks of the American field's leading contemporary scholar, Thomas Kochan (1998).

Following Barbash's position, Kochan states that the defining characteristic of the industrial relations field is its normative premises. Thus he says (p. 37, emphasis added), "I believe the primary feature that distinguishes the field from its counterparts lies in the *normative assumptions* and perspectives that underlie our conceptualization of the employment relationship." He goes on to note, however, that "Different schools of thought within the field vary ... in their assumptions about the sources of these conflicts, their scope (full or partial), and how they should be handled." He then distinguishes two alternative schools of thought within modern industrial relations – the pluralists and Marxists or neo-Marxists.[6] While Marxists and neo-Marxists fit within the ideological borders, Kochan states that the normative premises of neoclassical economics and OB/HRM are sufficiently different that they fall outside the field.

Kochan goes on to describe in more detail what he sees as the central normative premises of American industrial relations. He states (pp. 37–8), "Industrial relations theory starts from an assumption that an enduring conflict of interests exists between workers and employers in employment relationships." He further states, "Industrial relations researchers build on the views first clearly expressed by the Webbs and Commons that individual workers are generally at a bargaining disadvantage vis-à-vis employers." The one area where he revises the ideology of industrial relations is with respect to collectivism. Unions and collective bargaining remain fundamental institutions for balancing power and giving voice to workers, says Kochan, but are by themselves no longer adequate in light of the "new economy" and "new workforce". Thus he says (p. 44), "the New Deal labor relations system and its associated legal doctrines are no longer working" and therefore (p. 45) "we must think beyond the bounds of current institutions and broaden our focus beyond unions and collective bargaining as practiced today. Discovering and designing viable institutions for the workforce and economy of the future requires us to apply the enduring features of industrial relations outlined above to all aspects of the world of work." In Kochan's formulation, therefore, the industrial relations preference for collective voice in employment relationships is not abandoned but broadened to include a wider range of representational mechanisms.

A necessary although often unstated corollary of the industrial relations field's tacit or explicit preference for collective representation is a belief that the non-union system of individual representation is inferior and in some respect less desirable (Troy, 1999). Cappelli (1991: 7) states, for example,

Although it is hard to quantify, there is a clear sense among some faculty in industrial relations that the Second World War generation of scholars, who dominated both the field and the IRRA as an organization almost until the 1990s, saw the traditional union–management model of employment relations as the preferred form and resisted efforts to study alternative models. They saw non-union systems, for example, not as emerging approaches but as the old-fashion models (c.g., 'Welfare Capitalism' of the 1930s) that were tried and rejected once industrial unionism came along.

In a similar vein, Jacoby (1997: 8) describes the normative bias against non-union employers in the post-Second World War industrial relations field with the words: "liberal academics inevitably treated non-union companies as socially retrograde and thus undeserving of scrutiny", while Strauss (1994: 3) says of unions and collective bargaining, "Except for the extreme right and left, these hallowed institutions were not questioned for almost forty years."

The ascendancy of a narrow ILE ideology in the American industrial relations field from 1960 has had a number of consequences. The net effect has arguably been harmful to the long-run size and vitality of the field.

On the positive side, the ILE ideology defines a community of interest and scholarly identity for the industrial relations field. It also provides an intellectual lens giving a unique perspective on labour and employment issues and thus furnishes industrial relations scholars with a quasi-paradigm for guiding research and deriving hypotheses.In addition, the normative value set of the ILE tradition is still very attractive to portions of the polity and academic community, particularly those that believe workers' rights and interests continue to be systematically undervalued and/or abridged. They see the industrial relations field, and groups such as the IRRA, as a valuable mechanism for promoting workers' rights and collective bargaining and thus have strong incentive to join and participate.

But there are also a number of liabilities. First, when industrial relations' main claim to identity is a set of normative propositions, the field passes from being a community of scholars and scientific body of knowledge to a partisan advocacy group. Further, critics can easily dismiss industrial relations research and policy conclusions as normatively tainted or politically motivated. Also, defining the field in terms of commitment to particular normative principles automatically excludes all those scholars doing labour and employment research who do not hold these principles, even if their research is high quality and directly relevant to the field. Scholars who take a position critical on some aspects of unions, such as Herbert Northrup and Leo Troy, find themselves shunned, while others who study non-union firms, such as Fred Foulkes, are viewed with suspicion.[7] Dialogue and debate also become monochromatic and inbred since (by definition) only people subscribing to ILE principles are "in the room". One must also note that defining the field in terms of certain normative commitments puts organizations such as the IRRA in a difficult and perhaps contradictory position, given its constitutional commitment to neutrality in all policy matters. And, finally, the ILE bias in the field inhibits the objective, impartial study of new innovations and progressive employment practices in non-union firms. Many of the "100 best companies to work for" in the United States are largely or completely non-union, yet the ideological position of the field puts pressure on scholars and the IRRA to either ignore them or take a critical perspective. Such a position has its obvious contradictions and perils for long-term growth and, furthermore, is at odds with the ethical and ideological premises established by Commons, Rockefeller and other early founders of the field.

These issues have most recently been in play at the IRRA. The organization has experienced a significant long-term decline in membership and faces growing concern about its future survival. For over ten years various committees and study groups in the association have grappled with what to do to reverse these trends. One option is to change the name, dropping or modifying the industrial relations term for something more expansive and modern sounding. Despite considerable opinion in favour of such a name change, progress has been stalled by the lack of a good all-round substitute term for industrial relations in the English language and the politically sensitive connotations that go with alternative terms. As this book goes to press, the Executive Board of the IRRA has voted to change the organization's name to Labor and Employment Relations Association (LERA). The jury will be out for several years on whether the name change successfully brings in new members and holds old members. Relevant to the discussion in this chapter, however, is the implication of the new name for the way the subject matter and ideology of American industrial relations is popularly conceived in the academic and practitioner communities in the United States.

Certainly one plausible interpretation, although not the only one, is that LERA gives official sanction to what everyone has known for several decades – that the IRRA tilts toward the ILE and labour–management relations side of the field. Analogous to the point made earlier in this chapter about the name of the Cornell programme (and other similarly named industrial relations programmes), one can interpret the term "employment relations" in the new name as a modernized version of the original meaning of industrial relations used from 1920s into the 1950s – a subject field covering all aspects of work and employment in private and public and union and non-union situations, while the modifier "labour" in the new title connotes an emphasis on labour–management relations and collective bargaining. This combination of terms accurately, in my view, captures the intellectual and ideological centre of gravity in the organization. Whether it succeeds in revitalizing the organization is, of course, a matter to be determined in the years ahead. But the new name does also highlight the central theme of this chapter – the slow but inexorable narrowing of the field from the broad and inclusive "all aspects" conception of the 1920s–1950s period to a more narrowly construed "labour–management" version in recent decades.

Notes

[1] Jack Barbash served as president of both the IRRA and the Association for Evolutionary Economics (AFEE, the main professional home of institutional economics in the United States); among the younger generation of scholars, however, interchange between IRRA and AFEE is close to nil.

[2] Davis was a member of the Institute of Industrial Relations at UCLA, again pointing to the role of industrial relations scholars in developing the PM side of the field. On Davis' contributions to HPWS, see Kaufman (1997b).

[3] Of course, the field of HRM and the high-performance employment model of the 1990s were different from the PM version of industrial relations and the welfare capitalist employment model of the 1920s in certain important but largely tactical respects. The latter, for example, gave greater emphasis to union-inspired forms of collective voice and to workforce stabilization and maintenance, in contrast to modern employee-involvement programmes and organizational change and development (Beaumont, 2003; Tara, 2003).

[4] The concept of a "new industrial relations" was also advanced earlier than commonly recognized, illustrated by Arthur Ross' article in 1965 entitled "The new industrial relations". In it he states (p. 154), "Industrial relations theory must also recognize that the locus of initiative has shifted. Traditionally the unions have been regarded as the 'moving party'. By now it is plain that large corporations with professional managers must be regarded as the 'moving party'."

[5] Kerr (1994: 73) states, for example, "Neither Bakke nor I ever met an unemployed person who had voluntarily chosen the Great Depression as an excellent time to enjoy more leisure or to search for a better job", noting that the Chicago school held unemployment to be a largely voluntary choice.

[6] Marxist writers on labour and employment have traditionally been outside American industrial relations, but I believe Kochan is expanding the ideological boundaries to include the wing of radical and Marxist industrial relations scholars in Europe, such as Richard Hyman.

[7] On the case of Northrup, see Kaufman (1998b).

MODERN INDUSTRIAL RELATIONS IN AUSTRALASIA, CANADA AND THE UNITED KINGDOM   8

The last chapter carried forward the evolution of the industrial relations field in the United States over the last third of the twentieth century. This chapter does the same for the Anglo-American countries of Australia, Canada, New Zealand and the United Kingdom. This period saw the growth, consolidation and golden age of industrial relations in each country. The events, people and ideas that contributed to the field's ascendancy are described and analysed. After the golden age, the industrial relations field in all four countries started on a downward trend, albeit not nearly as steep as in the United States. The reasons for this decline are also described.

The United Kingdom

The course of industrial relations in the United Kingdom over the period 1965–2000 had distinct ups and downs. Three periods are distinguishable: a "golden age" from 1965 to 1979, followed by a "cold climate" from 1980 to 1996 (both terms come from Winchester, 1991), and a "new lease on life" from 1997 to 2000. These three periods closely track changes in governments, national labour policy and the fortunes of the British trade union movement, but with academic events – particularly the rise of HRM – also exerting influence. The effect of these events on the industrial relations field in the United Kingdom was on net negative, leading to a decline and overall weakening in the institutional and intellectual foundations of the field. The extent of decline in British industrial relations, however, was less severe than experienced by its American cousin and, as the two nations entered the new century, the prospects for British industrial relations in the short to medium run appeared more robust – or at least less threatening.

The golden age

By broad consensus, the field of industrial relations came of age in the United Kingdom with the formation of the Royal Commission on Trade Unions and

Employers' Associations or Donovan Commission in 1965. Indeed, into the 1990s it was common in the United Kingdom to discuss the history of the industrial relations field in terms of "pre-Donovan" and "post-Donovan" (Martin, 1998). Also by consensus, the golden age came to an abrupt end in 1979 with the election of a new Conservative government headed by Prime Minister Margaret Thatcher.

During the golden age, the industrial relations field enjoyed rising academic visibility and prestige, an expanding base of faculty and students, establishment of new industrial relations centres and journals, an aura of relevance and importance to events in industry, and strong links to and influence on national labour policy.

The formation and activities of the Donovan Commission were crucial for establishing the golden age on several counts. The formation of a royal commission, for example, was a clear signal to the academic community and nation that industrial relations was a subject of national importance. Inevitably, students and scholars were consequently drawn to the field and government funding for research started to flow. Likewise, the commission provided national visibility for several prominent members of the British industrial relations community, such as Hugh Clegg, Allan Flanders, Alan Fox and William McCarthy (Robinson, 1981).

Also important, through their collaborative research work and recommendations for the commission these scholars developed a more coherent, integrated perspective or "paradigm" that helped differentiate the industrial relations field from other academic subject areas related to work and employment and give it a more solid intellectual foundation. As noted in Chapter 5, this new paradigm – with roots in the work of Clegg and Flanders in the 1950s and drawing on Dunlop – became known as the "Oxford school". Ackers and Wilkinson (2003: 6) refer to the pre-Donovan period as the "older, more diffuse tradition of IR", while they say of the work of the Oxford school, "In effect, Flanders and Clegg had established a new paradigm that drew the new discipline away from Economics and Industrial Sociology, and back toward the sort of organizational analysis pioneered by the Webbs and Cole. At the same time, they distanced IR from Personnel Management." Ackers and Wilkinson identify five distinctive features of the new Oxford industrial relations paradigm:

- The research subject was defined as organized labour and the collective bargaining and other institutions associated with this.
- The interpretative framework was institutional rule-making.
- The practical policy orientation was towards third-party, state intervention in a primarily voluntarist system.

- The research methods were historical descriptions of institutions or case studies.
- The implicit epistemology and ontology was an unreflective pragmatism and realism, geared towards the discovery of "useful knowledge".

Ackers and Wilkinson (p. 7) quickly go on to note, however, that they use the term "paradigm" in a loose sense, since in the hands of Clegg and Flanders "the industrial relations literature became dominated by fact finding and description rather than theoretical generalization".

A further contribution of the Donovan Commission was to firmly associate the industrial relations field with a particular policy approach to improving British industrial relations. Up to 1979, this policy identification proved a boon for British industrial relations but quickly became a bane after the incoming of the Thatcher government. The formation of the Donovan Commission was largely the government's response to the United Kingdom's lagging economic performance, the worry that the nation was fast becoming "the sick man of Europe", and the growing belief that a root cause of the nation's difficulties was located in dysfunctional aspects of its industrial relations system. Of particular concern was the post-war record of anaemic productivity growth, worsening wage and price inflation, and mounting shop-steward militancy and unofficial (unauthorized) strikes (Towers, 2003b).

One stream of thought in the United Kingdom, associated with political conservatives and segments of the business community, pointed the finger of blame at the unions, alleging they were too powerful, too committed to restrictive practices and too unaccountable for the consequences of their bargaining claims and strikes. During the 1960s, however, the majority view in the nation, even extending well into parts of the Conservative Party, still favoured widespread collective bargaining and the nation's traditional approach of minimalist legal regulation of unions and bargaining. The report of the Donovan Commission fell solidly in this second camp and served to further identify the industrial relations field with the principles and practices of collective bargaining.

Regarding collective bargaining, for example, the commission's report states (quoted in Brown, 1993: 189):

> Properly conducted, collective bargaining is the most effective means of giving workers the right to representation in decisions affecting their working lives. ... While therefore the first task in the reform of British industrial relations is to bring greater order into collective bargaining in the company and plant, the second is to extend the coverage of collective bargaining and the organization of workers on which it depends.

Regarding the reform of British industrial relations, the Donovan report notes that (quoted in Gilbert, 1993: 236) "Britain has two systems of industrial relations. The one is the formal system embodied in the official institutions. The other is the informal system." The formal system was embodied in the industry-wide trade agreements negotiated by national unions and employers' associations. Formerly a source of stability and order in wage determination and employer–employee relations, the industry-wide system had deteriorated as bargaining and union–management relations became more decentralized. Hence the locus of wage determination, contract administration and conflict management was slowly shifting towards informality in the industrial relations system, comprising an ad hoc and relatively unstructured bargaining and negotiation process between local-level union leaders and shop stewards and their company- or plant-level management counterparts.

According to the Donovan Commission, the problems afflicting British industrial relations largely emanated from this informal sector of the industrial relations system and reflected a lack of well-developed institutions, rules and procedures at the local level. The result was a breakdown of orderly bargaining and relations, leading to problems with wage drift, inability to push forward productivity improvements, and growing numbers of strikes. Furthermore, the Donovan Commission, following the line of argument advanced by Flanders in his highly influential study *The Fawley productivity agreements* (1964), suggested that the nation's problems in collective bargaining were more the fault of management than of unions, for it was management's responsibility to take the lead and develop through joint governance with unions a rational, well-ordered system of workplace rules and institutions. Illustratively, the report states (Gilbert, 1993: 241), "If time-keeping (absenteeism) is bad, it is because management has been slack, not because unions have encouraged it." Thus the report concluded that the best approach to restore order in industrial relations was not abandonment of collective laissez-faire in favour of a highly structured regulatory framework as in the United States, but rather for individual employers to grasp hold and effectively structure and manage industrial relations. A more assertive and proactive management was always envisioned as taking place *within* the context of collective bargaining and joint regulation, however, and not in the form of a more unilateralist, American-inspired strategy of union minimization and avoidance. In the spirit of pluralism, Flanders' (1970: 172) dictum, "the paradox, whose truth management has found it so difficult to accept, is that they can only regain control by sharing it", was widely quoted.

The Oxford paradigm, the report of the Donovan Commission, and the unfolding economic situation in the United Kingdom set the tone for British industrial relations in the late 1960s. The field of industrial relations was heavily identified with pluralism, free collective bargaining and a largely descriptive, historical–institutional approach to research, all embedded in a national context of social democratic capitalism, Keynesian macroeconomics and a modern welfare state. Although putatively interdisciplinary, the Oxford version of British industrial relations was in this period relatively insular vis-à-vis economics, sociology and other allied fields of study, and hostile, or at least indifferent, to the non-union sector of employment and the practice of personnel management (Wood, 2000; Ackers and Wilkinson, 2003). To give the field a unique intellectual position among closely associated subject areas, the concept of "job regulation" was adopted as the organizing construct for carrying forward teaching and research. In terms of the normative or ideological face of the field, nearly all participants were committed to collective bargaining and predisposed to be "soft on unions" (McCarthy, 1994).

Over the next decade the British industrial relations field enjoyed considerable growth and further institutionalization, albeit not without challenge and controversy. Between the late 1960s and late 1970s several notable developments deserve brief mention.

First and foremost is the establishment in 1970 of the Industrial Relations Research Unit (IRRU) at Warwick University. The IRRU quickly became, in the words of one observer (Palmer, 1991: 67), "the academic symbol of Britain's golden age in industrial relations".

The 1960s was a growth period in British higher education, stimulated generally by the recommendations of the Robbins Report of 1963 and, within the social sciences in particular, the establishment in 1965 of the Social Science Research Council (SSRC). The SSRC was a government-created and -funded body charged with identifying and promoting areas of social science research important to the nation's development. Toward this end, it sponsored the establishment of large-scale research units attached to universities in four areas of the social sciences. One of these areas was industrial relations; the other three were ethnic (race) relations, demography, and socio-legal studies (Brown, 1998). The SSRC further promoted industrial relations research by funding individual and team studies on labour and employment subjects, soliciting research on national policy issues and providing stipends for master's and doctoral students.

After soliciting proposals for a new industrial relations unit from the seven leading centres in the field in the United Kingdom, the SSRC chose Warwick University (SSRC, 1980). A leading factor in this choice was that Clegg had moved to Warwick from Oxford and was giving considerable time to build up a graduate programme of industrial relations there. Also, Warwick is located in

Coventry and was thus strategically situated in the manufacturing heartland of the United Kingdom.

Originally, the IRRU was headquartered at the university but remained a separate research organization under the administration and funding of the SSRC. Later, in the early 1980s, control and funding of the IRRU was transferred to the university and today the IRRU is part of the Warwick Business School. The first director of the IRRU was Clegg, followed by George Bain, William Brown and Paul Edwards (Brown, 1998). During the 1970s, the IRRU employed approximately fifteen staff researchers drawn from a variety of academic disciplines. Economics was the most common subject area of the staff's undergraduate degrees, but postgraduate specialization tended to cluster in sociology, labour history and industrial relations. Many of the research staff hired in the 1970s, often as holders of newly minted Ph.D.s, went on to achieve national and international prominence in industrial relations. First in order would be Richard Hyman, who has become the leading modern-day theorist of industrial relations in the United Kingdom, followed closely by Paul Edwards and William Brown. Other well-recognized names from Warwick include Eric Batstone, Linda Dickens, Anthony Ferner, Stephen Frenkel, Paul Marginson, Keith Sisson and Michael Terry.

Warwick also hired Allan Flanders as a reader in industrial relations in 1971. Clegg was thus led to remark, "There is some truth in the quip 'The Oxford School has moved to Warwick'" (Clegg, 1990). He quickly notes, however, that Warwick was in certain respects different from Oxford. Certainly like Oxford, and reflective of the empirical, institutional orientation of British industrial relations, the research programme in the 1970s was heavily weighted toward applied problem solving and studies of collective bargaining. However, for reasons discussed in more detail shortly, the nature of the applied research done at Warwick was as a rule considerably different from that at Oxford, being more grounded in sociology and giving larger emphasis to in-depth case studies, field research and ethnographic investigations in individual plants and unions. Among the best-known studies of this genre are William Brown, *Piecework bargaining* (1973), Eric Batstone, Ian Boraston and Stephen Frenkel, *Shop stewards in action* (1977), and Paul Edwards and Hugh Scullion, *The social organization of industrial conflict* (1982).

In his reflections on the Oxford school, Clegg alludes to some of the differences separating Oxford and Warwick in these words (p. 15):

[T]here are considerable differences between the two. Industrial relations at Warwick
has been concerned mainly with relatively detailed topics; problems of trade union
organization and government, company employment policies, payment structures ...

Much less attention has been given to the philosophy of industrial relations reform which occupied such a major position among the Oxford School's interests. It is my impression that most of the members of the current industrial relations group at Warwick regard the central theme of the Royal Commission's report with a fair degree of scepticism; and some of them would definitely repudiate it.

Implicit in the last sentence of this quote is recognition by Clegg that another difference between Oxford and Warwick is the rejection by at least some of the Warwick research staff of the presumptive efficacy and value of traditional-style British industrial relations pluralism and voluntarism.

So far the discussion has centred on the industrial relations research programme at Warwick, but the university also became a leading teaching centre for industrial relations. The IRRU was solely a research organization, and the teaching and degree programmes in industrial relations were located within the business school of the university (called in the 1970s the School of Industry and Business Studies, later re-labelled the Warwick Business School). There was an industrial relations component to both the master's and doctoral business degree, and the latter attracted students from numerous countries outside the United Kingdom. In the late 1970s, the master's programme in industrial relations ran for twelve months, during which time the student took a core industrial relations course, selected a further course from two option areas comprising industrial sociology, labour economics, labour history, labour law and organizational psychology (personnel/HRM was not an option), and wrote a compulsory paper in industrial relations and a dissertation (SSRC, 1980).

The founding of the IRRU at Warwick is one indicator of industrial relations' forward momentum in the United Kingdom during this period but it is far from the only one. Existing industrial relations programmes, such as those at Cardiff, Leeds and the LSE, added students and lecturers, while new industrial relations courses and faculty positions in industrial relations were created at a number of others. Illustrative of the growth of British industrial relations is the trend in membership of BUIRA. In 1965, for example, BUIRA membership was 130, which then more than doubled to 268 in 1975 and crossed the 300 mark in 1981 (Berridge and Goodman, 1988). Another indicator of industrial relations' expansion was the establishment in 1971 of the second British field journal, *Industrial Relations Journal* (*IRJ*). Brian Towers served for many years as its editor.

Parallel to the experience of the United States, British industrial relations academics became extensively involved in national labour policy debates, government commissions and dispute resolution bodies during this time. On this subject, Brown (1978: 17) remarks of the 1960s and 1970s, "The best minds to enter the subject have tended to be sucked away down the twin drainholes of either lucrative consultancy or time-consuming public service." Regarding public service, McCarthy (1994: 205) observes, "This period was notable for the extent to which new government agencies and functions provided IR academics with opportunities for new forms of involvement." A major activity was serving on numerous wage–price control boards established during various Labour and Conservative governments. In nearly all cases these boards featured a tripartite structure, and industrial relations academics were often appointed to serve as one of the "public" members. Speaking of the national Board for Prices and Incomes, McCarthy (p. 206) remarks, "Sometimes it seemed as if half the BUIRA were 'doing something for the Board'." He also notes that during the 1965–79 period the amount of dispute resolution work roughly doubled, leading to numerous opportunities for industrial relations academics to do high-visibility arbitration and conciliation work. Henry Phelps Brown, for example, led three complex dispute inquiries in the bus, shipbuilding and engineering industries, while Donald Robertson chaired over a dozen similar committees. A third major area of public involvement for industrial relations academics was a steady stream of new advisory commissions and investigative committees, such as the Commission on Industrial Relations established in 1969 on the recommendation of the Donovan Commission (to promote best practice in industrial relations) and the Bullock Committee established in 1975 (to examine promoting greater industrial democracy through labour representation on boards of directors).

Although the golden age was a period of growth and consolidation for British industrial relations, several important challenges and conundrums nonetheless reared their heads. Among these was continuing uncertainty and debate over the definition of the field, its demarcation and core subject matter relative to contiguous social science disciplines, and the lack of a theoretical base for the field. Similar to the situation in the United States, British industrial relations academics defined the field both broadly and narrowly. The broad definition included practically every aspect of work and employment. Brown (1978: 2) declares, for example, "The subject matter of industrial relations is the employment relationship." Also illustrative is the declaration in the *British Journal of Industrial Relations* (March 1980) that it is a "Journal of Research and Analysis covering every aspect of Industrial Relations: Industrial Sociology, Industrial Psychology, Labour Economics, Labour Law, Manpower Planning, Personnel Policy, Systems of Remuneration, Collective Bargaining, Organizational Theory, Conflict Theory, Institutional Studies, Government Policies, Work Behaviour, [and] Industrial Relations Theory".

Bain and Woolven (1979), on the other hand, put forward a more focused definition in line with the perspective of Clegg, Flanders and Dunlop, stating in their book that (p. 2, emphasis in original) "the subject of industrial relations is defined as the study of *all* aspects of job regulation – the process of making and administering the rules which regulate and control employment relationships". They note that job regulation, while traditionally treated as largely coterminous with the union sector, can in concept be equally applied to the non-union sector. The narrow definition is then suggested by Marsden (1982: 232), who observes, "Everyone, instinctively it seems, knows what industrial relations is about, even those who have never studied the subject. It is 'about' trade unions, managers, and collective bargaining." An examination of the articles published in the *BJIR* and *IRJ* during the 1965–79 period provides support for all three definitions, although the large bulk of articles fit the narrow definition best.

Substantial debate also emerged over the central object of study in the field. I noted in the last chapter that Dunlop sought to shift the focus of industrial relations from the relations between capital and labour (or employers and employees) – and the emphasis this orientation inevitably gives to matters of workplace conflict and peace – to the study of the web of rules that structures and regulates the employment relation. Part of his rationale for doing so was that industrial relations (in his opinion) needs a theoretical base and the web of rules provides an object of study far more amenable to theoretical development than the tenor of employer–employee relations. This argument was quite influential but also met resistance at two levels. The first was the counter-claim that industrial relations is inherently a multidisciplinary problem-solving field and an integrative theory is impossible to construct (Chamberlain, 1960). The second was that even if a theory of industrial relations is possible, Dunlop mis-specified the dependent variable; rules are better considered an independent or mediating variable, while the dependent variable should be the outcomes of the system, such as job satisfaction, wage differentials, strikes and so on (Heneman, 1969).

These same issues also emerged in British industrial relations and, in fact, generated a larger stir than in the United States. Prior to Dunlop, British authors generally defined industrial relations in terms of employer–employee relations and framed the object of the field as devising procedures to foster cooperation and diminish conflict (see Chapter 3). Illustratively, Kirkaldy (1947: 5) states:

> The problems of industrial relations arise with and from the divorce of the worker from the ownership of the instruments and materials of production. … Obvious elements of a conflict of interest exist between the employer who wishes to buy

labour cheaply and the worker who wishes to sell it dearly. The whole problem of industrial relations can be very shortly stated as the devising of means to reconcile that conflict of interest. ... Until the spirit of partnership becomes the spirit of industrial relations, conflict as to the division of the existing product of industry obscures the need for cooperation towards greater productivity out of which alone can come any real advance in material prosperity.

By the mid-1960s, however, a shift in opinion was evident. Like Dunlop, some leading British scholars began to decry the lack of theory. Flanders was in this camp. *In industrial relations: What is wrong with the system?* (1965), he writes (p. 9), "theory is needed to pose the right questions. ... An indiscriminate accumulation of facts leads not to conclusions but to confusions. Some framework of theoretical analysis, however rudimentary and provisional, is always needed." He then discusses Dunlop's theory, commenting (p. 10), "The subject [of industrial relations] deals with certain regulated or institutionalized relationships in industry ... [and] 'rules' is the only generic description that can be given to these various instruments of regulation." He then concludes, "The study of industrial relations may therefore be described as a study of the institutions of job regulation."

Over the next 15 years a good deal of ink was devoted to discussing various facets of this subject. Could industrial relations be a discipline? Was it possible to build a theory of industrial relations? Are the rules of the workplace a productive analytical construct? A fair conclusion is that no conclusion was reached. Brown (1978) represents one point of view. He states (pp. 3, 10):

The driving force behind the subject [industrial relations] has been the need to cope with real live problems. Generally academics have become involved in the subject ... because they have been dragged out of universities to arbitrate, advise and analyse. The employment relationship is at so complex a confluence of different forces that any simple modelling of it is a forlorn activity.

On the other side, Bain and Clegg (1974) argued that Dunlop and Flanders had pointed the field in the right direction. They conclude (p. 92), "The emphasis which Dunlop and Flanders place on the rules and institutions of job regulation as the central core of industrial relations is a significant insight which provides the subject with a certain analytical unity" and (p. 97) "this definition with its emphasis on job regulation may well point to the direction in which general theory in industrial relations is likely to develop".

As the British industrial relations field moved into the 1970s, the debate over the pros and cons of the Dunlop/Flanders model was soon overshadowed by a far more radical challenge to the conceptual and theoretical orientation of the field. Whatever the disagreements in detail, until the late 1960s the core of British industrial relations was unified around a pluralist and institutionalist framework and ideology. This consensus was challenged and then torn apart, however, by the emergence of what one author (Hill, 1976) labelled "the new industrial relations". The "new industrial relations" was not the unitarist challenge of the 1990s but the radical/Marxist challenge of the 1970s.

The late 1960s were a time of radicalism and social criticism on college campuses. Opposition to the Viet Nam War was the unifying element and out of it grew the American New Left movement among students and academics. Although the movement became quite large and stridently anti-establishment, it had only a small ripple effect within American industrial relations. Given industrial relations' earlier life in the United States as a progressive social reform movement with moderately radical overtones, one would think the industrial relations field in the 1960s would have been a receptive home for New Left attacks on social injustice, corporate power, the hegemony of the military–industrial complex and all the "isms" of the period – racism, sexism, militarism, environmentalism, consumerism, etc. But none of this happened in the United States. The swirl of the New Left bypassed the labour movement and industrial relations as a field, like a river flowing around a well-entrenched rock. By the 1960s the labour movement had long since lost most of its crusading zeal and social reformism of the 1930s and was now part of the establishment that the New Left set out to attack. If the "long hairs" of the New Left had an archetypal opponent, it was blue-collar "hard hats" at a unionized construction site. And, if there was one academic field in America where organized labour had considerable clout, it was industrial relations. The AFL - CIO's staunch support for the Viet Nam War and antipathy to the New Left, led by the conservative and fervently anti-communist George Meany, thus effectively quashed radicalism in American industrial relations.

The situation was considerably different in the United Kingdom and the rest of Europe. Substantial elements in the British Labour Party and the trade unions were in the radical or Marxist camp and the official programme of the Labour Party called for British disarmament, withdrawal from the North Atlantic Treaty Organization (NATO), and abandonment of nuclear weapons. Disenchantment with American involvement in Viet Nam was widespread and grew in size and strength during the late 1960s. Also pervasive was a strong sense of alienation, social exclusion and idealism among substantial segments of the young and working class. Across continental Europe, these elements fused together and boiled over in the "days of May 1968", when social order seemed to dissolve in large-scale riots, strikes and near-insurrections (Crouch and Pizzorno, 1978).

As described in Chapter 9, these events – and the general feeling of anti-Americanism and anti-capitalism they precipitated – were important reasons why the industrial relations field (being an American product and self-avowedly seeking to accommodate capital and labour and bring about an "end of ideology" and workplace politicization) had a very difficult time taking root in continental Europe during the 1960s and 1970s. In the United Kingdom, on the other hand, the field was already well established by the mid-1960s – if small in size – and so anti-Americanism and anti-capitalism, rather than blocking the formation of the field, led scholars instead to try to take it over and remake it along radical or Marxist lines. Illustrative is this statement by Richard Hyman, the most influential industrial relations scholar in the British New Left group. He states in the Preface to his book *Industrial relations: A Marxist introduction* (1975: x, emphasis in original): "May this book soon become redundant: first, by stimulating more and better Marxist scholarship in industrial relations; second, and far more important, by the *abolition* of 'industrial relations' as it exists today through working class struggle."

The New Left group in British industrial relations were diverse. Some, like Hyman, subscribed to Marxism, while others, like Paul Edwards and John Goldthorpe, were radicals but non-Marxists. Hyman was thus prone to cast industrial relations theory in class terms. He (1975: 23, 26) states, for example, "Between these two classes [labour and capital] there exists a radical conflict of interests, which underlies everything that occurs in industrial relations. ... An unceasing power struggle is therefore a central feature of industrial relations." The non-Marxists, on the other hand, tended to give more emphasis to the labour process and the shop-floor struggle over control and work effort. Edwards (1995) thus looked at the employment relationship as one of "structured antagonism". Whatever the case, a key reason why the United Kingdom had a much stronger base of radical and Marxist industrial relations scholarship was that sociology and history were the dominant disciplinary bases for the field, while in America economics served this role. Sociology, far more than economics, seems to be an accommodative intellectual environment for radicalism.

British sociology spawned radicalism from an unexpected source. In the mid-1960s the best-known British industrial relations scholar in sociology was Alan Fox. Fox at this time was a pluralist and institutionalist. In an influential paper prepared for the Donovan Commission, Fox (1966) argued there were two theoretical "frames of reference" in industrial relations: the unitarist and pluralist models of the employment relationship. As depicted by Fox, the unitarist view draws theoretical inspiration from fields such as human relations and envisions the business organization as a team led by management and united by a common purpose, while the pluralist view draws inspiration from political science and envisions the firm as a coalition of interests kept in equilibrium through joint governance. Having developed the unitarist model, Fox (p. 4) proceeds to negate its significance and relevance to industrial relations with the observation that "this unitary emphasis has long since been abandoned by most social scientists as incongruent with reality and useless for purposes of analysis".

The New Left insurgency quickly suggested that Fox had omitted an important third perspective – the radical frame of reference. Like Fox, the radicals had no use for the unitarist model and dismissed it out of hand as a fatally flawed intellectual construct and approach to problem solving. But they also attacked the pluralist/institutional school for a variety of intellectual sins and omissions – for example, ignoring the role of class in the employment relationship, the exploitative nature of the labour process, the systemic power imbalance between employers and individual workers, and the co-optation of unions by employers and the state for the sake of preserving order over the advancement of workers' collective interests.

To the consternation of his Oxford school colleagues, Fox was persuaded by these arguments and moved toward the radical camp in his later writings (e.g., Fox, 1974). In an illuminating passage in his autobiography, Fox provides a snapshot characterization of the premises and perspective of the Oxford school to which he originally belonged and the radical school to which he later shifted. Of the former he states (1990: 228–9):

> Most of us held, explicitly or implicitly, a 'reformist' view of society and the desirable type of change to be sought within it. This was often little more than an extrapolation of Britain's social development over the past century. While there was no assumption of automatic social 'progress', it was supposed that the incremental concession of political rights and social welfare in the past gave rise to a reasonable assumption of its continuation into the future. Some of us hoped and believed that this long-term historical process would eventually produce a less unequal, democratic-socialist society. In the meantime it made sense to help the reform process along in any reasonable way one could. As applied to industrial relations this meant furthering and enlarging, through teaching, research, and practical involvement in industry, that long-growing system by which trade union representatives ... negotiated settlements of terms and conditions of employment with management, and participated in a range of economic, social and political decision-making or advisory bodies covering wider areas of the national life. The aim was the extension of a rational order regulating industrial relations which was fairly negotiated between independent associations of both sides.

Then Fox offers this description of the radical critique (p. 233):

[T]he entire reformist approach of the Oxford school and those who thought like them was guilty of helping to buttress the existing capitalist system and its exploitative class relations of profit-seeking and wage labour. This it did in two principal ways. It supported, practically and theoretically, the process of collective bargaining, which by producing relatively modest concessions reconciled employees to their lot when they might otherwise have mobilized to throw off this unjust system. And secondly, the reformist approach pursued research or theoretical analysis which, like collective bargaining, personnel 'management', and similar strategies, helped an essentially exploitative system to operate more smoothly. Worst of all, in their eyes, was that this help and support were presented, in our writing, lecturing, and tutorial work, without any attempt to make explicit the political implications of what we were doing and the values and choices it embodied.

While Fox shifted to the radical camp, he remained in the non-Marxist wing and, indeed, pointed out the limitations and dangers that accompany Marxism. In this regard, he observes (p. 235):

I was forced to decide that an analysis of social power recognizable by Marxists was more convincing. ... But the same readings also confirmed a long-standing belief that the generality of Marxists also offered no convincing procedures of defence against abuses of power and no convincing institutions of political accountability. ... Where many Marxists fell short was in emphasizing the exploitative power that derived from ownership of economic resources but failing to show the same concern for the abuses and non-accountability of power that derived from position in a bureaucratic hierarchy.

A second influential stream of thought, also Marxist in orientation, came out of the labour process literature that sprang to life in the mid-1970s with the publication of Harry Braverman's book *Labor and monopoly capital* (1974). Although centred in sociology and considered distinct from industrial relations (broadly speaking, the former's scope of analysis is considered to be at the shop-floor level, the latter's at the level of the business enterprise and collective institutions), the labour process movement nonetheless had a significant linkage to industrial relations and influence on it (Thompson and Newsome, 2004). Also important from a left perspective, it should be noted, was the influential radical/Marxist labour history of Thompson and Hobsbawm.

The radical challenge to mainstream industrial relations had pluses and minuses for the field. On the plus side, it brought more scholars to the field, stimulated a considerable amount of research and debate on fundamental aspects of the employment relation, and led to insightful critiques of prevailing workplace institutions and practices. Also salutary was the broader "political economy" perspective taken by the radicals which helped keep British industrial relations from becoming as narrow and parochial as its American cousin. But there were also minuses. The work of the radicals tended to push British industrial relations outside the political mainstream, associating it with the more leftist elements of the Labour Party and trade unions. After Thatcher came to power, this association became a major liability. Also not clear was what the radicals had to offer besides criticism of the present social order and dire portraits of growing class conflict and alienation. Even sympathetic members of the Labour Party and trade unions could wonder what the radicals had to offer from a practical policy perspective, short of revolution and workers' control. And, finally, in the words of Ackers and Wilkinson (2003: 10), "there emerged a narrow obsession with strikes and 'shop stewards in factories', coupled with a tendency to idealize conflict and disorder".

The confluence of the Donovan Commission report and the development of the Marxian and labour process research programme led to a further reorientation of British industrial relations worth noting. The authors of the Donovan report suddenly "discovered" the existence of a complementary informal sector in the industrial relations system where shop stewards and plant-level managers struggled over the "contested terrain" of shop-floor control and local working conditions. This discovery had an interesting parallel with the "discovery" of the ubiquitous role of informal work groups in regulating shop-floor practices by Elton Mayo and colleagues in the United States in the Hawthorne experiments of the early 1930s. Just as the Hawthorne experiments ushered in a period of extensive involvement in American industrial relations research by what Kerr and Fisher (1957) called "plant sociologists", much the same process happened in British industrial relations in the late 1960s and 1970s.

The outcomes for the industrial relations field in the two nations were quite different, however. By the early 1960s the workplace sociologists had largely disengaged from American industrial relations and the focus of the field became more tightly identified with the institutions and processes of collective bargaining. After 1980, few vestiges of this tradition could be found. In the United Kingdom, on the other hand, the workplace studies of sociologists represented part of the defining core of the field in the 1970s and continue to be an influential (if attenuated) and frequently cited part of the British industrial relations literature today. As noted shortly, the case study, ethnographic and "hands-on" quality of the sociological style of research imparted to British industrial relations a distinctly different character from that of its American counterpart, for which deductive model building, econometric regression analysis, and hypothesis testing with secondary data sets became "best practice" after 1980.

Challenges of a cold climate

In 1979, the Callaghan Labour government went down in a crushing defeat and into office came a new Conservative (Tory) government headed by Margaret Thatcher. For the next 18 years, the Tories (Thatcher and her Conservative Party successor John Major) were firmly in control of the United Kingdom, while the Labour Party roamed in the political wilderness. Labour faced the daunting task of re-tooling its image and programme to simultaneously appeal to the broad middle of the electorate, remain true to the party's core social democratic values, and provide effective answers to the United Kingdom's pressing economic and social problems in an increasingly competitive and globally integrated world. The field of industrial relations found itself in an uncomfortably similar situation.

The Tories had periodically taken over the reins of power from Labour governments in other post-Second World War elections and nothing earth-shaking had happened (Brown, 1997). But the election of Thatcher in 1979 represented a true turning point in British history. The reasons for Thatcher's victory were themselves closely related to developments in industrial relations.

In the decade after the Second World War, the United Kingdom transformed its economy and social policy through a multi-pronged programme featuring nationalization of key industries, Keynesian full-employment fiscal policies and establishment of a broad-based welfare state. An integral part of this social democratic system was widespread unionism, in order to achieve a balance in wage determination, bring industrial democracy to the workplace and provide a neo-corporatist tripartite process of interest representation in political policy making. The post-war accord came under growing strain in the 1960s and 1970s. The rate of economic growth in the country was anaemic, productivity performance was poor, there was a gradual ratcheting upwards of wage and price inflation and recurring balance of payments crises. Earlier government efforts at legal reform of industrial relations had been an embarrassing failure, while in industry there were unofficial strikes and mounting shop-steward militancy, and the public services suffered a series of paralysing strikes (Fox, 1985). Paradoxically, as Winchester (1991) notes, the mounting labour problems and legislative failures of the 1970s only fuelled the demand for academic industrial relations specialists to advise Labour policy-makers and serve on boards and commissions.

One body of opinion pointed the finger of blame at organized labour. The problem, in this view, was that unions had become too powerful (abetted by the post-Second World War shift to a welfare state and Keynesian full employment) and unaccountable to the public interest. Moderates in this camp, such as Ben

Roberts (Gennard, 1986), urged reforms that would reduce the legal immunities of unions, put some restrictions on the right to strike, and increase protections to individual union members. Even proponents of collective bargaining, such as Flanders (1968), openly questioned whether extensive unregulated collective bargaining was compatible with wage–price stability in a transformed labour market of near full employment. More hard-line elements urged tougher measures to break the grip of the unions, such as an American-inspired set of restrictions on unions like that contained in the 1947 Taft–Hartley amendments to the NLRA (e.g., banning the closed shop and secondary boycott, allowing the government to take out court injunctions to stop strikes). The Conservative Heath government of the early 1970s endeavoured to implement in legislation (the Industrial Relations Act) some of the moderate reform agenda, but the unions successfully boycotted the procedures and the legislation was later repealed. The Labour Party, on the other hand, moved further toward a neo-corporatist strategy. As articulated by the Donovan Commission, the goal of improved economic performance and more orderly and productive industrial relations was better achieved by strengthening and cooperating with organized labour rather than attempting to weaken and oppose it. Thus, as enshrined in a formally articulated "Social Contract" in the Callaghan Labour government, the government enacted legislation that gave new rights and power to trade unions but with the understanding that organized labour would work with the government and employers in a tripartite framework to curb strikes and rein in wage inflation (Fox, 1985; Ewing, 2003).

This strategy slowly frayed and unravelled during the late 1970s amidst mounting strikes, inflation and economic stagnation brought on by oil shocks and other maladies, finally collapsing in the "winter of discontent" in 1978–79. To an increasing number of people, collective bargaining seemed to be out of control as the United Kingdom lurched into what one observer (Dunn, 1993) called a system of "anarcho-pluralism" and "mindless power bargaining". Rather than promoting macroeconomic stability and coordination along social democratic, Scandinavian lines, the combination of widespread unionism and collective laissez-faire seemed to degenerate into a disorderly power struggle as individual organized workgroups battled to promote their sectional interests with scant concern for the disruption and privation caused to others. At this point, the pluralist ideology and policy recommendations of the Donovan Commission and mainstream industrial relations community appeared increasingly discredited. Clegg (1983), for example, could only ruefully note the great paradox of British industrial relations – the system that gave shop-floor workers greater control and involvement than any other in the world was also pushing the nation down the slope of long-term economic stagnation – and then follow up with the not too hopeful observation that finding a solution would be a (p. 28) "superhuman task". Nor were the industrial relations radicals in the United Kingdom any better positioned to offer constructive solutions, partly because they took the breakdown of capitalist industrial relations as an inevitable and perhaps desirable fact, and partly because they were predisposed to recommend more of what already appeared to ail the system – more worker control and state regulation of the economy.

Against this backdrop of events, the Thatcher government was elected. The industrial relations strategy pursued by Thatcher took the nation in the opposite direction promoted by Labour governments and the academic industrial relations community. Fox (1985: 425) summarized the Tory view thus:

> In a very real sense, the current argument goes, the working classes have got in on the act. They are no longer a separate estate, contained ghetto-like, within the old-fashioned communities, their own culture, their all-inclusive organizations, beliefs and institutions. They have become fully paid-up members of the competitive, acquisitive society, and a good thing too. Their trade unionism is no longer a total 'way of life', but merely an instrumentality that has got beyond itself and must be cut down to size. Since it is invested with no moral purpose there is no occasion to feel guilt at reducing its status and powers. Moreover, since it speaks only for a segmental aspect of the employed person's interests there is no occasion for it, or its central organization the TUC, to be accorded privileged treatment with respect to consultation, discussion and participation on public bodies generally.

Some Conservative Party leaders spoke in less measured terms about organized labour. One, for example, referred to organized labour as "the enemy within", while another declared the government's policy was "a war on unions" (Brown, 1998). For a field that was "a virtual synonym for collective bargaining" (Towers, 2003a: xiii, quotation modestly rearranged), this shift in policy clearly bode ill for the future.

Thatcher and her American counterpart Ronald Reagan implemented a sweeping shift in economic and labour policy in their respective countries that has since been labelled *neo-liberalism.* Neo-liberalism emphasizes individualism, private ordering over public ordering, and free markets rather than social democracy's tilt toward collectivism, tripartism and market regulation. Toward this end, the Thatcher government vigorously sought to curb the power of unions by rolling back traditional union immunities, passing a series of more restrictive laws regulating unions, and taking a hard negotiating position with unions even if it meant a major strike. The classic example of the latter was the twelve-month battle with the militant National Union of Mineworkers in 1984–85 that ultimately led to the rout of the union.

The Thatcher government also attacked other pillars of the post-war Labour programme of social democracy. The Keynesian programme of deficit spending and activist aggregate demand management was jettisoned in favour of monetarism and minimalist government intervention. Likewise, the Thatcher government scaled back the welfare state by cutting social spending on a wide range of public services, while a number of government-owned industries were privatized. Thatcher also encouraged free markets and pro-competition policies, pushing market deregulation in the domestic economy and free trade in the international economy. The theme was to move the United Kingdom from an ideology of collectivism and entitlement to individualism and personal initiative – often referred to as "the enterprise culture".

Not surprisingly, the Thatcher revolution posed a major challenge to the pluralist and radical academic industrial relations community, for it took British social policy in a direction antithetical to its intellectual, problem-solving and ideological positions. In this regard, Ackers and Wilkinson (2003: 11) state:

> Thatcherism and the economic and social changes in its train dissolved the 'labour problem', marginalized trade unions and manufacturing industry, undermined the voluntarist system of collective bargaining and removed opportunities for public policy interventions by industrial relations academics. ... This 'shock to the system' marked the end of an era and undermined the intellectual confidence of the discipline [of industrial relations], which limped on without really attempting to rethink its paradigm until the mid-1990s, ... fighting what seemed like a desperate rearguard action. ... In the 1980s, radicals and pluralists sank together, and neither offered a new vision for industrial relations research and teaching.

As pluralists and radicals sank together, a sense of crisis and marginalization inevitably permeated the industrial relations field in the 1980s. Given industrial relations' continued inability to develop a compelling theoretical framework, the field's continued survival and raison d'être for inclusion in university research and teaching programmes rested primarily on its contribution to problem solving in the worlds of industry and policy. Both suffered serious setbacks.

In the world of policy, industrial relations academics – earlier welcomed in the corridors of power in Labour governments – were suddenly pariahs in the Thatcher government. Brown (1998: 272) states, for example, "So radical was the shift in policy that those developing it sought little guidance from industrial relations research. At best, its findings were too detailed to guide broad strategy; at worst, it was a source of political embarrassment." The result, according to Towers (2003b: 12), was that:

> Industrial relations ... largely retreated into academe because it has had no options. In 1970s there were very few professors of industrial relations though there were large numbers of academics, working at all levels from FE colleges to funded research institutes – who were involved as advisers, consultants, arbitrators and serving on agencies and commissions – reflecting the extent and significance of industrial relations in the workplace. ... But within a decade it had all largely vanished, ... swept away in 1980 [leaving] Clegg [to return] to Warwick to complete his three volume history of trade unions.

Speaking of the "precipitate decline in involvement since 1979" of industrial relations academics in policy-making, McCarthy (1994: 211) attributes the phenomenon to "the consequences of collapsing demand: the flight from 'corporatism', the advance of 'legalism' and the determination to do away with 'collectivism'". Meanwhile, in industry the "mighty and apparently indestructible system" of collective bargaining celebrated by the Oxford school in the 1950s became "no more than a colossal wreck" (Brown, 1997: 135).

The "cold climate" followed industrial relations academics back to the universities, however, and forced sometimes wrenching and often unwelcome changes. In this regard, industrial relations was threatened on three fronts – from events in British industry, from new developments in American business education and from (in McCarthy's words) the "advancement of legalism".

The first prong of attack on industrial relations came from the substantial decline in the size and power of the British labour movement. When Thatcher entered office, union density in the United Kingdom was at its highest post-war level – 50 per cent – while effective coverage was 70 per cent or more. Two decades later, union density and coverage had fallen sharply to around 30 per cent for density and 50 per cent or less for coverage: the decline of unionism was largely in the private sector, however, as density in the public sector remained around 75 per cent. Part of this decline was directly attributable to anti-union legislation brought in by the Thatcher government, such as the Employment Acts of 1980 and 1982, but a significant portion had roots in structural economic change (such as the decline in manufacturing employment), more restrictive macroeconomic policies, and other such factors. The manufacturing sector, for example, was hit hard by global competition in the 1980s and early 1990s and numerous companies made major redundancies or closed their doors. Other industries, such as mining and shipbuilding, contracted sharply due to loss of traditional markets or structural economic changes, while lightly organized service and financial industries expanded. New investment in the United Kingdom by foreign companies, particularly American and Japanese, partially offset these employment losses, but often these companies refused to extend union recognition.[1] Finally, employers in some industries, such as newspapers, waged a hard-fought battle to dislodge their unions, while evidence shows that unions had a difficult time gaining recognition in new "greenfield" plants (Machin, 2000).

The collapse of collective bargaining into a minority system of employment relations in the United Kingdom was not wholly negative. It generated a boomlet of industrial relations research on the causes and consequences of union decline, leading *IRJ* editor Towers (2003b: 10) to quip, "the *IRJ* was in clear and present danger of becoming the journal of union decline" – a market position with some upside potential in the short run but obvious liabilities in the long run. However, the decline of the union sector also shrank student demand for industrial relations courses and degree programmes. Given significant reductions in educational funding mandated by the Thatcher government, British universities were forced to merge departments and programmes, downsize academic and non-academic staff and reduce financial aid and faculty research support.

Faced with a loss of government support and a declining constituent base in industry, academic industrial relations was in a particularly vulnerable situation. Nowhere was this threat more evident than in industrial relations' flagship programme at Warwick. The Thatcher government initiated a wide-ranging review of the SSRC in 1981, with a view to eliminating it (Brown, 1998). The report by Lord Rothschild recommended maintaining the SSRC, but within the body of the report was noted a complaint by a member of the House of Lords that the research projects done at Warwick's IRRU are (ibid.: 274) "unfairly biased in favour of the unions". This complaint precipitated a year-long investigation and much fear at Warwick that the charge would be used as a pretext for shutting the IRRU. The committee's report exonerated the IRRU on all but minor aspects of the charge and industrial relations' premier academic programme in the United Kingdom thus "dodged the bullet".

Related to this last element is the second line of attack on industrial relations. States Winchester (1991: 56), "The single most important change in the institutional context of industrial relations teaching in the 1980s has been the growth of business schools and the development of MBA programmes." Closely related to the rise of business education, he notes (p. 53), "has been a phenomenal recent interest in human resource management (HRM) in the United Kingdom".

As described in an earlier chapter, business education in the United Kingdom was for many years regarded as largely a vocational subject best taught in polytechnics and night schools. Only in the 1960s were the first university business schools established and only in the 1980s were they widely adopted. Based on the American model, business programmes saw a rapid growth in enrolments, particularly in the Thatcher years of emphasis on market competition and business enterprise. And, as in the United States, the MBA degree became very popular and represented both a visible image of the United Kingdom's new enterprise culture and a passport to a challenging, well-rewarded career in management, finance or consulting. By 1990, over a hundred MBA programmes had sprouted in British universities and many more followed over the rest of the decade.

Although industrial relations, at least in the early years, was frequently included in the curriculum as a required or (more often) elective course in MBA programmes, the subject's union-heavy focus, critical perspective on management, and pluralist underpinnings in bargaining and conflict considerably reduced its popularity among students and fit awkwardly with other managerial-oriented courses. As Winchester (1991: 57) notes, "the contest between industrial relations, organizational behaviour, and human resource management is rarely a close one – a third-term Industrial Relations 'elective' typically attracts 15 per cent of the students". He goes on to observe that this trend is also true at the undergraduate level (p. 58):

> [T]he number of undergraduate [business study] degrees with Industrial Relations in the title – always quite small – has declined, and formally-recognized 'programmes of study' or 'majors' in the subject are relatively rare [and] relatively few undergraduates on business studies and management science degrees choose to specialize in the Industrial Relations/HRM areas, in comparison with marketing, accounting, and other subjects.

The position of industrial relations within business schools ranks as a major influence on the field, in part because – more so than in the United States – the great bulk of industrial relations faculties are housed in business schools (Ackers and Wilkinson, 2003: 15). The development reflects, in turn, the fact that British industrial relations never achieved the same level of independent institutionalization in British universities as occurred in the United States. As described in an earlier chapter, the core of industrial relations in America was established in the 1945–55 period with the founding of the several dozen industrial relations schools, institutes and centres – for the most part positioned outside business schools. Although many of these centres and institutes have disappeared or changed their name and focus, the survivors (e.g., Cornell, Rutgers, Illinois) continue to provide an institutional base for American industrial relations. Independent, free-standing industrial relations centres and programmes never gained the same presence in the United Kingdom and some that were created later disappeared. Winchester (1991: 58), for example, speaks of "the relatively weak – or fragmented – institutional identity of academic industrial relations in the United Kingdom" and goes on to say, "[t]here are very few explicitly-named Industrial Relations departments left after the mergers and reorganizations of the 1980s".

Compounding and exacerbating the peril posed to industrial relations by business schools is the correlative rise to prominence of HRM. HRM is almost always taught in a business school and is typically regarded as a substitute for industrial relations in terms of approach to employment relations, student course selection and teaching and research positions. For these reasons, the relatively sudden arrival and swift ascent of HRM in the United Kingdom in the mid–late 1980s caused considerable angst in the industrial relations community.

As discussed in an earlier chapter, HRM grew out of the field of personnel management, first appearing in American business schools in the mid–late 1960s and slowly spreading thereafter until in the 1980s HRM largely supplanted personnel. It is also worth stressing that into the 1950s personnel/ HRM was widely viewed as a subfield of industrial relations and thus one alternative approach to managing and structuring employer–employee relations. In this early version of the field, the rise of HRM and decline of collective bargaining would not unduly imperil industrial relations since the field included both. Unfortunately for the industrial relations field, after the early 1960s personnel/HRM gradually broke away from industrial relations, moved out of the intellectual orbit of applied labour economics and into the orbit of applied OB and thus developed an independent, largely rivalrous relationship to industrial relations. These versions of industrial relations and HRM are the ones that came to the United Kingdom and, indeed, Fox's unitarist–pluralist dichotomy had earlier established this line of thought. Viewed through this frame of reference, HRM connotes an individualistic approach to employment relations, a management-led and -controlled set of employment strategies and tactics, and a non-union system of wage determination and workforce governance; industrial relations, on the other hand, emphasizes collectivist, institutional aspects of the employment relationship, the setting of wages and conditions through collective bargaining and joint governance, and the presence of a trade union as the independent representative of the employees. An alternative perspective is provided by Dunn (1993), who argues that the "root metaphor" of "old industrial relations" is trench warfare and the root metaphor of the "new industrial relations" (the HRM version) is challenge and progress.

After incubating in America, HRM crossed the Atlantic and landed in the United Kingdom in the late 1980s, quickly appearing in business school curricula. As Ackers and Wilkinson (2003: 14) wryly observe, "the phantom conjured up by Fox [the unitarist model] has come alive", while Bach and Sisson (2000: xx) recall, "it is easy to forget in the current avalanche of literature that, as late as 1989, there was very little analysis of and information of personnel management in practice". What applied to personnel was even more true of HRM.

By and large, British industrial relations academics initially reacted with a mix of scepticism, alarm and hostility: scepticism because they saw HRM as promising far more than it could deliver; alarm because they perceived HRM to be an American import designed to undermine unions and establish a unitarist, management-dominated model of employment relations; and hostility because HRM was seen as a direct threat to the industrial relations field and the faculty positions within it. A left-of-centre industrial relations community thus experienced considerable discomfort and unease with HRM, worrying that behind the win–win façade of the new management movement, as extolled in *In search of excellence* (Peters and Waterman, 1982) and other such books, lay a darker and more sinister New Right agenda of increasing profits through greater employer control, work intensification on the shop floor, and de-unionization. Adding to the stew was that HRM had slowly developed in America from the late 1960s and thus represented incremental and more easily accommodated change, while in the United Kingdom it seemed to burst on the scene and represent a radical change in employment philosophy and practice. Illustrative of the shock wave that de-unionization and HRM unleashed on British industrial relations is the title of an article by John Purcell (1993): "The end of institutional industrial relations".

Fuelling the sense of radical change was the tendency of British authors to define HRM more narrowly and idiosyncratically than typically done by their American colleagues. In America, HRM was generally viewed as an updated, expanded version of personnel management, albeit with more emphasis on strategy, human capital and employee involvement (Strauss, 2001; Kaufman, 2004e). This distinction between personnel and HRM was taken further in the United Kingdom, to the point that personnel and HRM were often depicted as separate paradigms or subjects – sometimes with personnel and industrial relations lumped together and then contrasted with HRM (Storey, 1992). HRM, in this view, is one particular labour-management approach associated with a proactive strategic focus, employee commitment and involvement, and strong dedication to remaining union-free, while personnel and industrial relations jointly represent a reactive, cost-conscious strategy. An additional factor that contributed to HRM's "hard landing" in the United Kingdom was the much stronger and better-organized critical, radical tradition in industrial relations, sociology and management – a group well represented even in the business schools.

The result, reminiscent of the ILE attack in America on human relations in the 1950s, was a thicket of articles on HRM in the late 1980s to early 1990s by British industrial relations scholars that tended to take a highly critical, over-wrought and sometimes caricatured view of the subject. Strauss (2001: 876), for example, quotes one British author who called HRM "amoral, anti-social, unprofessional, reactive, uneconomic, and ecologically destructive", while others used terms such "Bleak House" and "black hole" to describe employment conditions at non-union firms.

After the dust settled, the effects of the HRM invasion into British industrial relations appeared to be mixed as the 1990s drew to a close. On one hand, HRM had clearly taken the lead and expanded its presence in both academia and industry at industrial relations' expense. In this vein, Guest (1991: 149) remarks, "New chairs in human resource management have been created in universities and polytechnics throughout the country, while industrial relations departments in many universities have altered their name to reflect the new interest in management. In industry, too, industrial relations departments are less common while departments of human resource management are emerging everywhere." As one marker of change, the label of the master's (M.Sc.) degree at the LSE was broadened from "Industrial Relations" to "Industrial Relations and Personnel Management", while the title of the undergraduate degree was shifted to "Human Resource Management and Employment Relations". As this is written, plans are also afoot to transfer the Industrial Relations Department at the LSE to the School of Management. Similarly, the administrative unit containing the industrial relations faculty at Warwick was broadened from "Industrial Relations" to "Industrial Relations and Organizational Behaviour" and, later, the title of the master's programme was broadened to "Industrial Relations and Personnel Management". Moreover, several new HRM journals, such as *Human Resource Management Journal* and *International Journal of Human Resource Management*, have been established in the United Kingdom and compete with the traditional industrial relations journals for research and readers.

It appears, nonetheless, that British industrial relations was able to accommodate and absorb the HRM challenge better than its American counterpart – at least in the short term. Several indicators suggest this outcome. For example, BUIRA has been able to successfully accommodate HRM scholars and, as a consequence, has not been threatened by the emergence of a rival academic HRM professional association. Likewise, the industrial relations journals (*BJIR* and *IRJ*) continue to serve as a publishing outlet for a significant share of HRM research in the United Kingdom. Further, as Ackers and Wilkinson (2003) note, leading industrial relations academics have moved into HRM chairs and journal editorships, unlike in the United States where these positions were mostly filled by management and OB faculty. For example, Keith Sisson was founding editor of *Human Resource Management Journal*, followed by John Storey and John Purcell, while Michael Poole edits the *International Journal of Human Resource Management*. Industrial relations academics have also authored or edited several popular HRM textbooks, while many others have with varying degrees of enthusiasm shifted from teaching industrial relations to HRM courses.

Several factors may account for industrial relations' greater success in the United Kingdom in surviving the HRM onslaught. One is that British industrial relations academics had already started to investigate the management side of the employment relationship before HRM arrived. The workplace case studies initiated at Warwick's IRRU during the 1970s and 1980s, by Sisson, Purcell, Marginson and Edwards, focused more attention on the role of management (Sisson being in the forefront of the study of management and HRM at Warwick), while several British industrial relations academics outside Warwick, such as Howard Gospel (1983), Stephen Wood (1982) and David Guest (1987), also did early and pioneering work on the management side of industrial relations. Thus when HRM arrived, the industrial relations side was not caught completely off guard and unprepared, and there was soon a realization that HRM could be embedded with industrial relations as one particular regime of employment regulation (Bélanger, Edwards and Haiven, 1994). It was also the case that the field of OB in the United Kingdom was relatively underdeveloped at that time and thus space existed in business schools for industrial relations academics to colonize this new area. Moreover, the less institutionalized structure of academic industrial relations (relative to the United States) proved, paradoxically, to be a benefit by making the walls separating HRM and industrial relations lower and more porous, thus facilitating industrial relations' ability to move into this new area and participate in it. In addition, British management had not implemented HRM in the breadth and depth done in the United States, nor did it successfully dispel the perception that in many cases it could not manage the workforce without a union (Sisson, 1993; Edwards, 2003b). Indeed, while union density declined a good deal during the 1980s, the unionized sector of the British economy nevertheless remained large and influential.

A further factor is that British industrial relations academics were led to give management more attention through the extensive work initiated on European Union (EU) developments, such as works councils, HRM practices at multinational corporations, and comparative studies of alternative employment systems (Marsden, 1999). Finally, the most important source of empirical data on HRM practices in the United Kingdom comes from the government-funded Workplace Industrial Relations Surveys, renamed in 1998 the Workplace Employment Relations Surveys (WERS). Carried out in 1980 and four additional times to date, the WERS are the oldest and most comprehensive survey of workplace practices in the world (Millward, Marginson and Callus, 1998; Marginson and Wood, 2000). The WERS are largely designed and administered by industrial relations academics, who have been the group most active in analysing and publishing research results on HRM practices from these surveys.

New lease on life

In 1997, British industrial relations appeared to get a new lease on life. Or, as Ackers and Wilkinson (2003: 12) put it, "the cavalry finally arrived". The key event was the election of a new Labour government headed by Prime Minister Tony Blair.

The new Blair government provided a much-needed boost to the industrial relations field on several counts. New openings and opportunities, for example, appeared for industrial relations academics to serve on high-level government boards and commissions, bringing them "out of the wilderness". As one example, the Blair government formed a Low Pay Commission and industrial relations academics George Bain, William Brown and David Metcalf were asked to serve as members (Metcalf, 1999).

The Blair government also passed new industrial relations legislation, the 1999 Employment Relations Act, which provided modest new support for the trade union movement (Brown, 2000). The principal addition was a legal process for union recognition, helping staunch the growing movement among employers to unilaterally withdraw recognition and bargaining rights.

The new Labour government also repositioned British economic and social policy more toward the middle of the political spectrum, moving away from some of the more hard-edged, American-inspired aspects of the Tory governments' neo-liberal agenda and toward a "soft" or "decaffeinated" version of European-inspired social democracy. The prime example is the Labour government's decision to end the United Kingdom's opt-out of what is popularly called the "Social Chapter" and what is officially known as the Protocol on Social Policy adopted by the members of the EU in the 1992 Treaty of Maastricht. The Social Chapter commits EU nations to implementing a wide range of employment standards, such as the 1994 Working Time Directive (limiting work-hours), 1998 Parental Leave Directive (providing both parents time off from work for child-rearing), and the 1994 Works Council Directive (mandating large multinational firms to create consultative employee committees) (Undy, 1999; Ewing, 2003).

Since the core of British industrial relations has traditionally been construed as revolving around the institutions and processes of job regulation, the new interest and emphasis on European developments is a logical extension. So too is the perceptible shift in the centre of gravity of research and dialogue in the British industrial relations community away from America, where neo-liberalism and de-institutionalization are most advanced, and toward western Europe where collectivism is still in favour and social policy remains a strong regulative force. The net outcome has been to broaden British industrial relations from its traditional focus on labour collectivism to a wider range of social policy issues, and to introduce a more pragmatic, social democratic dialogue on the left side of the field in place of the radical/Marxist theoretical critique that had predominated in earlier years. British industrial relations has also benefited greatly from generous research funding by the EU, a fact that also explains part of the field's re-direction toward Europe.

Amidst this more supportive political environment, and aided by other supporting developments (e.g., a stabilization of union membership, a substantial effort on the part of the unions to develop a more contemporary programme and collaborative posture with employers), the British industrial relations field appeared to end its long-term slide toward marginalization. Indeed, some observers (Edwards, 2003b) see grounds for guarded optimism for the future. Indicators, for example, are the continued expansion of BUIRA membership (from 346 in 1985 to 580 in 2003), the founding of two new industrial relations journals – *Historical Studies in Industrial Relations* and *European Journal of Industrial Relations* in 1995. There was also stable or growing demand for industrial relations courses, a new wave of industrial relations textbooks, the placement of a number of industrial relations academics in high-level university administrative positions (thus positioned to protect and grow the field) and considerable industrial relations research and publishing activity, with several new books aimed at developing a strengthened theoretical base for the field (e.g., Kelly's *Rethinking industrial relations*, 1998). The worryingly old-fashioned term "industrial relations" was substituted by the broader and more modern-sounding term "employment relations" (preserving the critical, pluralist substance of industrial relations but changing the external packaging). The growing links with Europe have also helped the field, by virtue of the EU's more friendly intellectual and policy environment. Industrial relations in the United Kingdom also has a reputation for high-quality research and bringing in external funding, attributes that help persuade university administrators to preserve and even add to industrial relations faculty positions. Relatedly, state funding is increasingly tied to research output, and industrial relations journals are in the class "A" list. Very few British management journals, however, so rate.

But other observers of British industrial relations take a more guarded or pessimistic view of the field's long-term prospects. State Ackers and Wilkinson (2003: 13), "For a moment, it might seem that IR can carry on regardless, as if the 18 year long New Right nightmare is over, and the discipline can return to something like the 1970s institutional approach. This would be an illusion, however." Arrayed on the negative side are several factors.

The election of the Blair government, for example, was not an unalloyed blessing for classic industrial relations. In introducing Labour's programme of industrial relations, for example, Blair did not sound very different from a Conservative prime minister when he announced (with pride), "even after the changes we propose, the United Kingdom will have the most lightly regulated labour market of any leading economy in the world" (quoted in Hyman, 2001b: 289). The Labour government's vision statement of the role of unions in British society was contained in the position paper *Fairness at work* (Brown, 2000). The report described a "third way" strategy that was friendly to workplace collective organization but only as long as unions acted in a socially responsible manner and contributed to the advancement of the national welfare. Thus the Labour government left in place many aspects of the Thatcher government's labour programme, declaring in *Fairness at work* (quoted in Smith and Morton, 2001: 121), "There will be no going back. The days of strikes without ballots, mass picketing, closed shops and secondary action are over." But, unlike the Tories, the Labour government also expressed a commitment to social justice and the protection of workers' right to organize and collective bargain. This commitment was significantly qualified, however, as indicated by this statement in the paper (ibid.: 122): "The extent of trade union growth and organization is dependent on trade unions being able to convince employers and employees of their value – how much they can help bring to the success of the enterprise, and how much active support they can offer employees."

Thus, in the third way, unions must earn their place in the polity, not by advancing the interests of the labour class against the owners of capital or protecting the employee underdogs from grasping employers, but by working in partnership with employers and creating greater economic value (Schmidtke, 2002). This new role for labour is a "grow the pie" function rather than the traditional "split the pie" role and is a natural adjunct of a supply-side economic programme. Although a laudable vision, a sceptic may ask whether unions are cut out for this role and, if not, what this implies for the future of both organized labour and the industrial relations field that studies them. A negative reply is sounded by Robert Taylor (2003: 7), who observes, "The sad truth is that trade unions in the United Kingdom have been virtually written out of New Labour's script for the country's modernization." One must then wonder whether British industrial relations will suffer the same fate, to the degree that its core assumption is that the employment relationship is one of "structured antagonism" and its key concepts are "contradiction, rules, conflict, and negotiation" (Edwards, 2003c). The third way these are not.

Caution is also warranted regarding another seemingly positive development initiated by the Blair government. In decades past, collective bargaining was the main instrument of social policy regulating the workplace. Starting in the 1970s and gathering speed during the Conservative governments, the protection of employees' rights through joint governance and collective contracts was gradually replaced by a juridical approach in which individual employee rights were protected through various statutory laws and regulations (Undy, 1999; Wood, 2000). One of the first examples is the 1975 Employment Protection Act, followed by several other pieces of legislation, that together prohibited or regulated subjects such as discrimination in pay and employment, unfair dismissal, and safety and health conditions. The pace of legal enactment continued under Blair, such as adoption of the nation's first minimum wage and the implementation of several EU directives on employment standards. Optimists see the spread of legal mandates, and the United Kingdom's opt-in to the EU's Social Chapter, as a positive development for the industrial relations field because they add subject matter and substance to the study of "job regulation". The optimists may be right, particularly if the phalanx of EU directives promotes greater union density. But another possibility is that in the long run, legal enactment and collective bargaining are substitutes, causing employees' (and society's) demand for unions and collective bargaining to decline as expanded legal enactment provides an alternative form of protection and representation. Since collective bargaining is at the heart of British industrial relations, this trend would on net lead to further decline in the field. In this regard, Keith Ewing (2003: 140) notes, "Gone are the days when it could be said that legislation regulating the employment relationship was ancillary to collective bargaining. ... For the majority of workers it is now the only external regulation of their working conditions." In such a world, lawyers replace shop stewards as the protectors of workers' rights and comparative advantage in teaching and research shifts from industrial relations faculty to law schools.

Finally, quite apart from the election of a new Labour government are other trends that raise questions for the long-term prospects of the industrial relations field in the United Kingdom. Most industrial relations academic staff and programmes, for example, are in business schools. This fit can easily become uncomfortable given the pluralist and often union-sympathetic perspective of industrial relations faculty. Although a critical management perspective has so far found considerable acceptance in British business schools, one can nonetheless wonder whether industrial relations will gradually be displaced by HRM and OB – particularly when the time comes to replace the large crop of industrial relations scholars who are approaching retirement age. Likewise, while industrial relations academics were able to successfully colonize HRM, writing HRM textbooks and editing HRM journals, one can equally well wonder if this event is a one-time happy occurrence never to be repeated. Also at issue is whether BUIRA can continue to keep the HRM wing in-house or whether the latter will break away and form a separate scholarly association. One person intimately knowledgeable of BUIRA stated that in his opinion this break-up is a matter of "when, not if". Among the reasons cited is a revitalization of the radical/Marxist wing in BUIRA, with the inevitable clash of intellectual cultures and perspectives this brings with the HRM group.

Also of note, Wood (2000) observes that the key disciplinary base for British industrial relations has in recent years shifted from sociology to economics. Since economics typically means neoclassical economics, and given the poisonous effect neoclassical economics has had on American industrial relations, this trend is worrisome. Wood (p. 3) also notes that despite the long-term decline of collective bargaining, "attention [in British industrial relations] has been slow to turn to the non-union sector, small-scale economic units or non-standard employment relations".

Another topic British industrial relations has been slow to turn to is gender issues at work. Wajcman (2000: 184) notes, for example, "That women are still marginal to the study of industrial relations is apparent from a survey of the major journals and textbooks over the last ten years." She goes on to observe, "Australian and Canadian industrial relations journals similarly maintain women's invisibility except in relation to a few recognized areas. ... Interestingly, the U.S. journals fare better." A potential growth area, therefore, for British industrial relations – and industrial relations in other countries – is consideration of the many dimensions by which gender structures and influences work relations and outcomes. Wajcman (op. cit.) and Greene (2003) also note that British industrial relations, as in other countries, has traditionally been a "boys' club" and to a significant degree remains so.

411

Finally, open to question is whether British industrial relations, like American industrial relations, will also suffer a gradual loss of intellectual vitality and distinctiveness from the cumulative effects of runaway science building in academic research. Industrial relations in the United Kingdom, as in the United States, remains under-theorized and thus weakly positioned to compete against other traditional disciplines (see, however, Kelly, 1998; Ackers, 2001; Edwards, 2003c). The science-building ethos in the United Kingdom, although still at a less developed stage than in the United States, is nonetheless also starting to undercut significantly the attractiveness and viability of the traditional industrial relations research model. Aided by new data sets such as WERS, and spurred by the incentives of tenure, professional recognition, and the British government's Research Assessment Exercise (a ranking of research productivity among departments and universities based on the quality of research publications), the British empirical tradition of inductive, case study, historical/institutional research is being displaced by a new American-inspired positivist research model utilizing large-scale secondary data sets, deductively derived hypotheses, and statistical analysis using regression and related methods. For a field that derives it energy and insights from hands-on, field-level experience with workplace problems, this shift in research methods in British industrial relations may have significant negative long-term consequences (Siegel, 1998; Ackers and Wilkinson, 2003).

Canada

The experience of the industrial relations field in Canada over the last third of the twentieth century reflects both similarities and differences with the United States and the United Kingdom. The chief similarity is the presence, albeit much less pronounced, of an inverted V pattern in the growth and academic fortunes of the field. Stretching roughly from the mid-1960s to the mid–late 1980s, the industrial relations field experienced modest expansion and consolidation among Canadian academics and universities, followed thereafter by some evidence of attrition and decline. The difference between Canada and the United Kingdom and the United States is that both the upswing and downswing were much less pronounced. Indeed, at century's end the industrial relations field in Canada appeared in major respects little different from two decades earlier and remained in a healthy condition, albeit on a relatively small scale.

As noted in Chapter 5, the industrial relations field in Canada as an institutionalized entity began with the founding of the Industrial Relations Section at Queen's University in 1937 and, immediately after the Second World War, with the founding of several additional industrial relations schools and institutes and the journal *Relations Industrielles/Industrial Relations*. Chief among the academic programmes were those at Laval, McGill, Montreal and Toronto. Emblematic of the overall stability in Canadian industrial relations, both the journal and the industrial relations programmes at these universities not only continued in operation over the next half-century but remained comparatively robust. The exception is the industrial relations programme at McGill, which gradually declined until being consolidated into OB in the management department.

Underneath the surface appearance of stability, however, the Canadian industrial relations field experienced some of the same ups and downs as the industrial relations field in other countries. Perhaps most central to the historical pattern of industrial relations' development in Canada is the trend in trade union density. Canadian union density, as in the United Kingdom and the United States, spurted upward after the Second World War, reached a peak, and then declined by the century's end. The significant aspects of this pattern for Canadian industrial relations are, first, that the peak of density in Canada occurred later (the mid-1980s in Canada, the mid-1950s in the United States and the late 1970s in the United Kingdom) and, second, the decline thereafter was slower and less precipitous. Thus, while in 1960 union density was *lower* in Canada than in the United States and the United Kingdom, by 2000 the ranking had reversed and density was *higher* in Canada than in these two other countries. Of particular significance for understanding the much healthier state of Canadian industrial relations relative to its southern neighbour is that density for the private and public sectors and overall economy in Canada in 2000 was double the American level.

The upward trend in union density facilitated the growth of the industrial relations field in Canada. At a social level, trade unionism enjoyed considerable intellectual and public support in the decades after the Second World War. Like the United Kingdom and United States, pluralism was in vogue and collective bargaining was seen as both a necessary and useful method for conducting employer–employee relations in large-scale enterprises. In this spirit, one Canadian observer (quoted in Giles and Murray, 1988: 792) called the collective bargaining contract "the peace treaty that binds capital and labour together". Also in vogue were Keynesian macroeconomics and an early North American version of the social democratic welfare state, and union-led wage gains were seen as a beneficial way to maintain aggregate demand and close income inequality. The spread of collective bargaining across Canadian industry also created a demand among companies for labour relations specialists, fuelling an expansion in student interest and enrolment on industrial relations courses. There were also the usual but then novel and challenging problems that accompany collective bargaining, such as training union and company personnel in grievance handling and arbitration, controlling wage-led inflation through incomes policies, negotiating the end of strikes and learning to cope with their disruptive effects, and settling controversies over union recognition and security provisions.

As the Canadian union movement grew in size and influence, universities saw a growing market opportunity to provide teaching and research service to the new industrial relations profession. The attraction of industrial relations was also heightened by the political pressure unions exerted on universities and politicians to carve out an independent place for the study of collective bargaining and the labour movement.

In the 1960s, the most visible indication of these trends was the decision of the University of Toronto in 1965 to re-establish and strengthen its industrial relations programme. As noted in an earlier chapter, the university had originally established an industrial relations centre in 1947 but had allowed it to lapse several years later. In 1965, it created a new and expanded industrial relations programme, housed in a free-standing unit called the Centre for Industrial Relations (CIR), in recognition of the rapid growth of labour–management relations in Ontario (the manufacturing centre of Canada). Several years after its founding, the CIR began to offer graduate degrees in industrial relations, first at the master's level and later at the doctoral level. The teaching programme also initially focused on union–management relations and gave little direct attention to personnel management – an emphasis that later shifted to include more HRM in the mid–late 1980s. Under the successive directorships of John Crispo, Morley Gunderson, Noah Meltz and Frank Reid, the Toronto programme grew to become nationally and internationally recognized.

The rise of collective bargaining in Canada, and the various problems and challenges that accompany it, also led to the creation of numerous government commissions and boards. These also facilitated the growth of the industrial relations field, at least in the short and medium run. The most visible and influential of these was the 1966 Federal Task Force on Labour Relations, popularly known as the Woods Commission (named after its chairperson, H.D. Woods).

The commission's final report strongly endorsed collective bargaining, much as did the Donovan Report. Mirroring the situation in the United Kingdom, however, the formation of the Woods Commission was also direct evidence that all was not well with the performance of collective bargaining. Indeed, the final report (Woods et al., 1968: 3) opens with this disquieting statement: "Periodically the conduct of labour–management relations in any country is subject to severe criticism. In Canada, as well as in many other western countries, the attack on collective bargaining has been mounting in recent years. The result verges on a crisis of confidence in the present industrial relations system."

Listed in the report as prime culprits for the state of crisis are the mounting number of strikes, too frequent outbreaks of violence in labour–management disputes, recent publicity given to undemocratic practices inside unions, and growing concerns that collective bargaining aggravates inflation. Picked out for particular concern are two items. Number one (p. 3) is the public's perception that "the protagonists seem to suffer less than the public" and "the parties are using the public as their whipping boy while they work out their differences"; number two (p. 5) is "the constant struggle to maintain an acceptable harmonizing of the competing goals of a high level of employment, a high rate of economic growth, reasonable stability of prices, a viable balance of payments and an equitable distribution of rising incomes".

After much analysis and discussion of these problems, the final report of the Woods Commission presents recommendations. The commission members conclude (p. 137), "We continue to endorse the present industrial relations system in Canada not only because of its virtues ... but also because we see no alternative that is compatible with the heritage of western values and institutions." The theme of "no alternative" is continued on the next page, where it is stated, "Collective bargaining is the mechanism through which labour and management seek to accommodate their differences, frequently without strife, sometimes through it, and occasionally without success. As imperfect an instrument as it may be, there is no viable alternative." The authors then make a bow to the Anglo-American commitment to voluntarism, stating, "We seek to minimize the role of the state in the collective bargaining process", but then follow the British and (particularly) American pattern and proceed to recommend the opposite. Thus the authors admit (p. 138) that "on balance we propose an increase in government involvement" and justify it on the grounds that "our objective is to facilitate more constructive relations between labour and management and protect the public interest".

The formation and report of the Woods Commission marked a distinct period of success for Canadian industrial relations, much as the Donovan Commission had done in the United Kingdom. Not only did the activities of the task force focus national attention on labour relations issues; they gave significant visibility to several prominent industrial relations academics and stimulated an outpouring of new research. According to Woods and Goldenberg (1981: 26), "The publication of many of the Task Force studies virtually doubled the serious Canadian literature (books) on industrial relations in less than a five year period." Also worthy of note, the report of the Woods Commission drew on the systems theory of Dunlop to provide an organizing and interpretative framework, giving emphasis to the rules of job regulation and their role in ordering and stabilizing industrial relations.

Continuing problems with inflation, strikes and unionization in the public sector led to a number other government-appointed industrial relations commissions and task forces, particularly at the provincial level (e.g., Ontario, Newfoundland). An important feature of the Canadian industrial relations legal system is that federal labour law covers only about 10 per cent of the workforce, while the remainder falls under provisions of the various provincial labour codes. This situation, coupled with the electoral rise and fall of a variety of provincial and national political parties, leads to more review and revision of labour law than in other countries, and opportunities for industrial relations scholars to provide research, consulting advice and service.

These trends provided the basis for a sustained growth in academic industrial relations programmes. One indicator comes from data on student enrolments and faculty positions at Laval's School of Industrial Relations. Between 1970 and 1986, the number of students enrolled in the undergraduate and graduate programmes increased from approximately 200 in 1970 to more than 1,000 in the mid-1980s. Not unexpectedly, faculty positions also grew at a similar pace – from eight in 1970 to 27 in 1986 (Faucher, 1988). Laval had at this point become the largest industrial relations programme in Canada and joined Cornell University in the United States as one of the two largest industrial relations programmes in the world. The number three position was occupied by the University of Montreal, which also had a very large faculty and full range of undergraduate, master's and doctoral industrial relations programmes.

Similar if less spectacular growth occurred at other Canadian industrial relations programmes. At Queen's University, for example, Kelly (1987: 496) notes that in the 1970s "[t]he result of this growth [in the importance of labour–management relations issues] was a substantial increase in the number of faculty teaching in various areas of the industrial relations field". In recognition of the growing importance of and interest in industrial relations, the university in 1983 upgraded the programme from a Centre of Industrial Relations to a School of Industrial Relations. The school was an interdisciplinary unit with a small number of its own faculty and a larger group of faculty drawn from the business school, law school and economics department. A new master's of industrial relations (MIR) degree was also created and, according to Kelly (p. 496),

It quickly became evident that there was indeed a demand for such a program. Reflective of the broad-based, interdisciplinary character of industrial relations, students were required to complete coursework in: Canadian industrial relations, labour law, human resources and human behaviour, labour market analysis and manpower policy, quantitative methods, and a research essay.

In addition to being interdisciplinary, the Queen's programme also reflected industrial relations' traditional emphasis on applied, problem-solving activities. Major activities of the School of Industrial Relations, for example, were practitioner-oriented conferences and continuing education programmes (ibid.). Research was also emphasized, but many of the publications were intended for practitioners and policy-makers. Illustrative, for example, was a new annual report *The Current Industrial Relations Scene in Canada*. In this respect, the problem-solving focus of the Queen's programme mirrored the applied nature of Canadian industrial relations in general. Woods and Goldenberg (1981: 55) note, for example, "In spite of a late start, there has been a marked increase in industrial relations research in Canada in recent years, a significant proportion of which has been problem-oriented and sponsored or inspired by government. There has been less research of a purely academic nature; certainly very few contributions to theory."

Two other indicators of industrial relations' growth in the years after the Woods Commission may be noted. The first is membership of the Canadian Industrial Relations Association (CIRA). Started in 1963 and headquartered at Laval, membership of the association grew slowly but steadily to approximately 90 people in 1979 and 160 in 1985. The second is the appearance of new industrial relations textbooks. The first industrial relations text written for a Canadian audience was Crispo's *The Canadian industrial relations system* in 1978, followed by texts by Alton Craig (1983) and Morley Gunderson, Allen Ponak and Daphne Taras (2001). The title of Crispo's book gives another indication of the influence that Dunlop's systems model had on efforts to frame and interpret Canadian industrial relations. Indeed, Crispo's colleague at Toronto, Noah Meltz, became one of the best-known advocates and expositors of the systems model in North America (see Meltz, 1993).

Although other supporting quantitative data are hard to come by, most observers of the Canadian industrial relations field believe that it crested in size and influence sometime in the last half of the 1980s. Although circumstantial in nature, one key indicator is trade union density, which peaked at about the same time. The link between the size and influence of the organized labour movement and the industrial relations field had become tighter with the passage of time, since Canadian industrial relations academics, like those in other countries, had increasingly shifted to the narrow labour–management conception of the subject. As earlier described, when the Queen's industrial relations programme was established in the late 1930s the founders explicitly conceived of the industrial relations term as subsuming personnel/HRM and oriented the activities of the centre to give precedence to these subjects. In the 1960s, however, industrial relations began to shed its association with the PM school and by the late 1970s the fields of industrial relations and HRM were largely separate. One piece of evidence is the bibliography of Canadian industrial relations literature by Fraser Isbester, Daniel Coates and Brian Williams (1965). In nearly 90 pages of citations, no section is given to management in general or personnel management in particular. A second piece of evidence comes from Crispo's (1978) pioneering industrial relations textbook. In the first paragraph he states:

> Industrial relations is a comprehensive term generally taken to embrace everything from individual employer–employee relations, through all forms of collective bargaining between labour and management, to the trade union movement and its many ancillary activities. Although the spectrum could be said to cover what has traditionally been termed personnel administration and what is today often referred to as organizational behaviour and development, these areas will only be dealt with briefly in this volume. Rather, the emphasis throughout will be placed on the relationships between employers and organized groups of their employees.

Perhaps labelling the mid–late 1980s a "golden age" for Canadian industrial relations is something of an overstatement but, nonetheless, by this time the field had become securely established and widely represented in Canadian universities. The best indication comes from a comprehensive survey of Canadian industrial relations programmes conducted in 1990 by Jean Boivin (1991).

According to Boivin, the anchor of the field comprised five free-standing programmes: Laval, Montreal, Quebec University at Hull, Queen's and Toronto. Together, these programmes had 28 faculty members with doctoral degrees in industrial relations or a closely related specialization, while over 100 academics taught a course related to industrial relations or HRM. As in earlier years, Quebec had the largest industrial relations programme in Canada and the greatest concentration of academics. These five programmes were broadly focused, in that they offered coursework on what Boivin considered to be the basic components of industrial relations as a field of study: labour–management relations, human resource management and public policy on labour.[2]

The other major locus of industrial relations teaching was in the business schools. Here were another 76 academics with industrial relations degrees and 298 faculty teaching an industrial relations or HRM course (based on data from returned questionnaires from 33 business schools out of a sample of 48). The largest concentration of industrial relations academics was at Western Ontario, followed by the École des Hautes Études Commerciales (HEC) Montreal, McMaster, Alberta and British Columbia. The most notable aspects of the industrial relations programmes at the business schools were the near absence of the "public policy" component of coursework, the greater emphasis given to HRM/OB and correlative downgrading of a broader social-science perspective, and the considerably greater weight given to promoting organizational efficiency vis-à-vis employees' interests and considerations of equity and social justice.

Boivin noted another interesting dichotomy between the two types of programmes (see also Chaykowski and Weber, 1993). In the free-standing industrial relations centres and schools, industrial relations was conceived as covering "all aspects of the employment relationship" and HRM was thus a component or subfield of industrial relations. In the business schools, by way of contrast, industrial relations and HRM were conceived as separate subjects, with industrial relations covering collective bargaining and HRM focused on the various aspects of personnel management. Furthermore, Boivin noted a growing trend in business schools to invert the relationship between HRM and industrial relations, with the former being treated as the broad subject area and the latter (labour–management relations) placed at the end of the HRM course or textbook and regarded as merely one of a number of different aspects of the employment management function.

Much more so than in the United Kingdom or United States, the industrial relations field in Canada managed to hold its own during the 1980s and 1990s, although with some modest signs of attrition as years went by. In the area of research, several Canadian industrial relations academics moved to the forefront of efforts to develop a stronger theoretical and comparative base for the field, as exemplified by Adams and Meltz's 1993 volume *Industrial relations theory*, Barbash and Meltz's (1997) follow-up volume *Theorizing in industrial relations: Approaches and applications*, John Godard's numerous articles (e.g., Godard, 1998) on industrial relations theory and his book *Industrial relations, the economy and society* (2000), Kaufman and Taras' edited volume on international comparisons of employee representation, *Nonunion employee representation: History, contemporary practice and policy* (2000), Anil Verma and Joel Cutcher-Gershenfeld's (1993) work on "Joint governance in the workplace", Anthony Giles and Gregor Murray's (1997) development of "Industrial relations theory and critical political economy", and Roy Adams' numerous publications on international/comparative industrial relations, such as *Industrial relations under liberal democracy* (1995). Canadian industrial relations research also became less inbred and narrowly quantitative than American industrial relations research, in part because some new Canadian industrial relations scholars chose to study for their doctorates in the United Kingdom rather than the United States.

In the area of teaching, the freestanding industrial relations programmes reported increasing student applications and enrolments from 1990 to 2003, albeit with a clear swing toward HRM and away from traditional labour–management relations. Equally noteworthy, Canada saw the establishment of a new industrial relations programme at Memorial University in Newfoundland in 2002 (a master's in employment relations in the business school). Similarly, while academic membership in the American IRRA fell by half, CIRA membership continued to grow – from 251 members in 1992 to 288 in 2002. Although hard data are unavailable, industrial relations textbook sales in Canada also appear to have held their own over time, suggesting stability in course offerings and student enrolments. On the other hand, the subscription count for *Relations Industrielles/Industrial Relations* declined in the 1990s. Inferences in this case are treacherous, however, given confounding events such as the growth of online readership.

Looking further, one finds yet other telltale signs of industrial relations' slippage. The greatest problem area is in Canadian business schools. Canada experienced the same rapid growth in business schools, MBA programmes and HRM courses as did other countries. At some universities, industrial relations held its own in the business schools despite these adverse trends. The University of Saskatchewan, for example, created a Department of Industrial Relations and Organizational Behaviour in the 1980s and the same department exists today. If in the United States, most surely the industrial relations part of the programme would have by now been dropped. At other universities, however, there does appear to have been a net displacement of industrial relations. At the University of British Columbia, for example, the business school decided to close the master's in commerce degree in industrial relations in order to concentrate on the MBA programme. Similar developments occurred at McGill University and McMaster University. Since the late 1980s, faculty positions in industrial relations at these schools have shrunk in both absolute and relative terms as new posts are allocated to service the growing student enrolments in HRM and OB and those vacancies created by the retirement of existing industrial relations staff members are shifted to other subjects. A development reinforcing this adverse trend is the evaluation procedure used to rank Canadian business schools – a process that relies in significant part on faculty publications in a list of top-rated journals. Unfortunately, while management journals such as *Academy of Management Review* and *Administrative Science Quarterly* are included in this list, even the best industrial relations journals are typically excluded. This omission provides a disincentive for deans to allocate money to hire and support industrial relations faculty members and for academics to specialize in this area of research and teaching.

Yet to be mentioned is one other outstanding fact of Canadian industrial relations that has posed a major challenge and obstacle. Canada as a society and polity is deeply split along a fundamental fault line – the division between French-speaking Quebec and the other English-speaking provinces. In many respects Canada is two nations (or "two solitudes"). The academic side of Canadian industrial relations both mirrors this divide and illustrates the continuing challenge Canadians confront in surmounting it. Two or three decades ago, industrial relations academics in the two parts of Canada were largely isolated from each other by language and cultural tradition. Since then, considerable efforts have been made to bridge this gap. Examples include bilingual articles in the journal *Relations Industrielles/Industrial Relations*, bilingual presentations at CIRA meetings, and greater mixing of the two communities of industrial relations faculty members through conferences and seminars. To a significant degree, however, the two wings of the Canadian industrial relations field still lead separate lives, with the English-speaking part of the field oriented toward American journals and conferences and the Quebec faculty oriented toward journals and conferences in France (but hardly exclusively). Illustrative of the latter linkage is the volume *L'état des relations professionnelles* (Murray, Morin and Da Costa, 1996), a collection of 41 French-language chapters on industrial relations jointly edited by faculty in France and Quebec and providing the only published source of information to date on the history of the industrial relations field in France. Also illustrative of the different axes of interaction, most American industrial relations scholars could easily name several of their English-speaking Canadian colleagues, but many would be hard pressed to name any industrial relations academics in Quebec and would probably be astounded to learn how large are the faculties and student bodies in the industrial relations programmes at Laval and Montreal.

These problems notwithstanding, broadly viewed, the salient fact of Canadian industrial relations is that the field weathered the 1980s and 1990s in considerably better shape than its North American neighbour. Why did this happen? Surely the leading factor is the more robust condition of the Canadian labour movement. Although union density in Canada has declined from its peak in the mid-1980s, density remains over 30 per cent in the entire economy, over 80 per cent in the public sector and twice the American level in the private sector. A larger union presence, in turn, creates larger interest in traditional industrial relations courses, provides more job opportunities for industrial relations graduates, makes union-related industrial relations research more compelling and relevant, and exerts political pressure on universities to maintain a balance between managerial and labour perspectives. Although both the United States and Canada have substantial public-sector union density, the topic is an active one only in Canada, while remaining largely invisible south of the border.

Also important are the political climate and management law regime in Canada, both of which have been more supportive of trade unions and industrial relations than found in the United Kingdom during the Conservative governments of the 1979–97 period or in the United States generally. Canada also experienced a rightward shift in political climate during the 1980s and 1990s. Although social welfare spending was curtailed and Canada opened its economy to free trade under the North American Free Trade Agreement (NAFTA), the shift in policy toward a neo-liberal agenda was never as sharp and intensely pursued as in either the United Kingdom or the United States. Likewise, labour law has on net remained much more supportive of unionism and collective bargaining in Canada than in the United States, reflecting the nation's stronger social democratic ethos, commitment to balance in industrial relations and abhorrence of social conflict (Taras, 1997).

Emblematic of these themes, and the positive climate that supports the industrial relations field, is the report issued in 1996 by the Federal Task Force (or Sims Commission) on Part I of the Canada Labour Code, which governs collective bargaining. The title of the report is *Seeking a balance* and it opens with this declaration (p. ix):

> Our approach has been to seek balance: between labour and management; between social and economic values; between the various instruments of labour policy; between rights and responsibilities; between individual and democratic group rights; and between the public interest and free collective bargaining. We seek a stable structure within which free collective bargaining will work.

After a comprehensive review of the Canadian industrial relations system, the commission concluded that the present legal regime is functioning reasonably well and recommended no major structural changes. The tenor of the report reflects the relative equilibrium in Canadian industrial relations of recent years and the reasons why the industrial relations field in Canada has itself experienced a considerable degree of stability.

Australia

Although different in many details, the broad outline of development of the industrial relations field in Australia mirrored in many respects that in Canada. Industrial relations in New Zealand, on the other hand, experienced greater turbulence in the 1990s.

Because of its much larger size, events in Australia form the dominant part of the story. Perhaps of most note, academic industrial relations in Australia enjoyed a slow but cumulatively significant period of growth into the 1990s, leading several observers to label this period Australia's "golden age of industrial relations" (e.g., Lansbury and Westcott, 1992). As in Canada, the field then came under stress in the 1990s from the rise of HRM and OB, the decline of the labour movement, and the shift in public policy toward neo-liberalism. Although challenged by these events, academic industrial relations nonetheless entered the twenty-first century in relatively sound condition. Illustrative, for example, is this assessment by Russell Lansbury and Grant Michelson (2003: 235): "the study of industrial relations in Australia remains relatively healthy ... [and] is continuing to evolve in a positive direction" and (p. 238) "perhaps this makes Australia something of an exception to notions of a 'crisis' in the discipline which have been advanced elsewhere".

As described in an earlier chapter, the field of industrial relations in Australia only emerged as a formal institutional entity in the 1950s. At this time, the intellectual roots of industrial relations were principally in economics and law. The dominance of these two disciplines reflected in part the influence on Australian industrial relations of the highly formalized and centralized state-centred system of labour conciliation and arbitration. Also a contributing factor was the marginal role of business schools in this period and the embryonic state of industrial psychology and sociology. Organizationally, the first industrial relations courses and programmes for the most part emerged in economics departments, such as at the University of Sydney under the leadership of Kingsley Laffer and at the University of Melbourne under Joe Isaac.

By the mid-1970s, the industrial relations field had spread to a wider range of universities and started to coalesce around a tighter self-conception in terms of problem area and body of knowledge. According to Diana Kelly (1999), there were undergraduate industrial relations degree majors at roughly one-third of Australia's principal universities. Examples included Melbourne, Monash, Newcastle, University of New South Wales, University of Sydney and University of Western Australia. Also, three professorships in industrial relations had been created by the late 1970s, the first of which was awarded to John Niland. In this position, Niland developed a national and international scholarly reputation in industrial relations and served as IIRA president from 1989 to 1992.

Despite the growing presence of industrial relations in Australian universities, the field's academic status was uncertain and subject to controversy. According to Kelly (1999), the industrial relations field into the 1970s was generally defined quite broadly to cover all aspects of the employ-ment relationship, leading her to call the field (p. 163) a "multidisciplinary smorgasbord". Although most of the teaching of industrial relations courses was done by economists, they were institutional in training and orientation and thus proponents of a multidisciplinary approach. Illustratively, students in

Laffer's introductory industrial relations course read chapters from Reynolds' *Labour economics and labor relations*, Brown's *Social psychology of industry*, and Argyris' *Personality and organization*.

But, as time passed, in the eyes of a growing number of people a significant explanation of industrial relations' "identity crisis" was its overly broad, inclusive conceptualization as "all aspects of employment". Certainly to the sceptics it appeared that industrial relations was "a mile wide and an inch deep", making it superficial from an intellectual point of view and largely descriptive in method. Reflective of this concern, Isaac (1980: vii) said of early Australian industrial relations, "The belief persists that the subject is a soft option, a 'descriptive appendage' to economics, from which it has generally been an offshoot, which anyone can easily 'pick up'" and (p. viii) "the question arises whether such a multidisciplinary area of study can ever be integrated into a field in its own right".

To overcome these problems, Australian industrial relations academics gradually narrowed the domain of the field in two respects. The first was to import from the United States Dunlop's industrial relations systems model, with its emphasis on the web of rules, and from the United Kingdom the Oxford school's concept of job regulation (Kelly, 2004). The second move was to concentrate teaching and research on the formal institutions of industrial relations – principally the tribunal system and the process of collective bargaining between trade unions and employers' associations. These two shifts complemented each other by making the subject of industrial relations largely coterminous with modes of regulation and rule making through formal institutions, with collectivist processes of legal enactment and collective bargaining at the core. Thus, Kelly states (p. 208), "by the mid-1980s there was a definable mainstream, an accepted domain with its allied methods, assumptions, and analytical etiquette". She goes on to describe this mainstream as (p. 225) "institutional industrial relations and in particular the study of unions".

Illustrative of this new and narrower conception of industrial relations is the content and perspective of one of the first industrial relations textbooks to come out of Australia: Plowman, Deery and Fisher's *Australian industrial relations* (1981). The first chapter develops a systems framework, based largely on the work of Dunlop and Flanders, while the remaining thirteen chapters focus on the federal tribunals; the employer, union and state actors; and the process and outcomes of collective bargaining. The authors also place the subject of industrial relations in a pluralist and radical frame of reference when they observe (p. 23), "Industrial relations are, largely, relations of conflict."

During the 1980s, the industrial relations field in Australia in both teaching and research dimensions continued to show substantial growth. One marker was the establishment of the Association of Industrial Relations Academics of Australia and New Zealand (AIRAANZ) in 1983 (Kelly, 2003b); Kevin Hince and Bill Ford were the lead founders. As noted in Chapter 5, the Industrial Relations Society of Australia had been established much earlier (1965) – but it was largely composed of practitioners and featured only a modest research component. It was only in the early 1980s that the academic body of industrial relations specialists achieved sufficient critical mass to make possible a scholarly professional association devoted primarily to industrial relations teaching and research.

Also noteworthy was the further extension of industrial relations majors and degree programmes in Australian universities. Lyndal Jenkins, Russell Lansbury and Mark Westcott (1991) provide a comprehensive overview of industrial relations teaching programmes in Australia in 1990. A survey of all institutions of higher education revealed there were 49 undergraduate industrial relations programmes (majors, concentrations, programmes of study and so forth) offered across Australia and 44 at the graduate level. Interestingly, at this time one-third more institutions offered an industrial relations programme of study than offered a similar programme in personnel/HRM. Many of these industrial relations programmes offered industrial relations only as a concentration, major or joint major, but not as a distinct, stand-alone degree programme. Thus, at the graduate level the most common delivery vehicle was an industrial relations major within an MBA (or master's of commerce) programme or within a master's of economics programme. Only two stand-alone master's of industrial relations degree programmes existed at this time: one at the University of Sydney and the other at the University of Western Australia. More numerous were organizational units (undergraduate and graduate) that had industrial relations, employment relations, or labour studies, in their title. Six such units were found: Philip Institute of Technology, University of Adelaide, University of New South Wales, University of Sydney, University of Western Australia and University of Western Sydney, Nepean.

The 1980s was also a period of expanding research activity. Both Nicholas Blain and David Plowman (1987) and Lansbury and Westcott (1992) published major surveys and evaluations of Australian industrial relations research in this period. The latter reach this upbeat conclusion (p. 412): "In comparison with the current situation in Britain, the United States, and New Zealand, industrial relations research in Australia appears to be flourishing."

Lansbury and Westcott cite a number of indicators of progress on the research front. One was the flow of government funding to support industrial relations research. Until the late 1980s, the only formal centre in Australia devoted to industrial relations research was the Industrial Relations Research Centre at the

University of New South Wales. In the late 1980s, however, the federal government strategically targeted funding to support critical areas of social science research, and industrial relations was one of the beneficiaries. As a result, two new centres for industrial relations research were established, the National Key Centre of Industrial Relations at Monash University and the Australian Centre for Industrial Relations Research and Training (ACIRRT) at the University of Sydney. The leading scholar at ACIRRT has been Russell Lansbury, elected to serve as IIRA president starting in 2006. A second indicator was the establishment of new journals in the industrial relations area, such as *Labour and Industry: A Journal of Social and Economic Relations at Work* (1987), the *Australian Journal of Labour Law* (1988) and the *Economic and Labour Relations Review* (1990). A third indicator was the sheer number of books and articles being published on industrial relations topics, including a number of new textbooks, comprehensive bibliographies and research monographs.

With increasing research momentum also came a more concrete sense of identity for the field. For example, in their review of industrial relations research Blain and Plowman (1987: 296) were able to offer this definition of the field: industrial relations is "the study of the interactions between and among employees and employers, their respective organizations and intermediaries, focusing on the regulation of work". This specificity stands in marked contrast to the situation only a few years earlier, when Plowman (with Stephen Deery and Christopher Fisher) was forced to begin Chapter 1 of their industrial relations textbook with this confession (p. 3): "There is little agreement about what the study of industrial relations should be."

As was true in other countries, the flowering of industrial relations research in Australia's golden age was not without its limitations and shortcomings, as duly noted by participants at the time. Lansbury and Westcott state (1992: 407), for example, "the criticism that the Australian industrial relations literature is parochial in character essentially remains valid". They also note (p. 396) that the research is "uneven in quality and predominantly descriptive rather than analytic". Another gap they cite is relative lack of attention given to issues of theory, the role of management in industrial relations, and shopfloor-level industrial relations practices.

If Australian industrial relations was enjoying a golden age in the 1980s, the question surfaces as to why. The answer Lansbury and Westcott (pp. 396 and 413) give is this:

> It [the golden age] has coincided with a period when the labour movement enjoyed almost unprecedented political power, having gained office in every state and at the federal level at some time between 1983 and 1990. The Accord between the

Australian Council of Trade Unions (ACTU) and the Australian Labour Party placed industrial relations at centre stage of the political and economic debate ... There have been major reports by the ACTU and the Business Council of Australia, as well as inquiries into the state systems of industrial relations in New South Wales and Queensland. Academics have been involved as contributors to most of these reports.

Modest further explanation will make these links clear. Australia, like the rest of the industrialized world, suffered growing macroeconomic problems in the mid–late 1970s, associated with rising inflation, rising unemployment and stagnating growth. Strike action in Australia was also relatively high by world standards (Dabscheck, 1995: 96). By the early 1980s, the situation was dire, with both inflation and unemployment over 10 per cent and the country's international balance of payments in a state of crisis. At the time, the Australian labour market was heavily unionized, with density in excess of 50 per cent and effective coverage of 80 per cent (Hancock and Rawson, 1993). Controlling wage growth was widely seen as a prerequisite to bringing inflation down, so in 1975 the Australian Conciliation and Arbitration Commission (ACAC) instituted an incomes policy based on a programme of wage indexation (Dabscheck, 1989). The programme's effectiveness was gradually eroded, however, by the refusal of growing numbers of unions and employers to keep wage increases within the prescribed limits. As described earlier in this chapter, the same situation arose in the United Kingdom in the late 1970s when the Labour government and the TUC entered into a neo-corporatist Social Contract in which unions gained a greater degree of "peak" influence in political decision-making in return for a pledge to pursue moderation in wage bargaining. In 1979, the Social Contract fell apart and the Conservative government came into power. Australia, in effect, followed the United Kingdom's example, but with a time lag and a less drastic switch in political regimes at the end.

Prior to the federal election of 1983, the head of the Australian Labour Party (ALP), Bob Hawke, and the leadership of the ACTU negotiated an "Accord" along the lines of the British Social Contract and both sides pledged to implement it if the ALP was elected. The ALP won the election, a corporatist-style National Economic Summit was organized at which the major trade unions, employers' associations and government officially endorsed the Accord, and the ACAC was delegated the job of establishing and monitoring appropriate wage norms. The Accord slowly unravelled, however. Unions grew disillusioned with it because they became party to holding down wages rather than raising wages, leading to membership apathy and restiveness. Employers, on the other hand, became increasingly convinced that the solution to Australia's economic problems required a substantial decentralization of industrial relations in order to address workplace incentive and productivity issues. For separate but mutually consistent reasons, therefore, both the unions and employers by the late 1980s were pushing for substantial change of the industrial relations system, moving in the direction of greater decentralization through enterprise bargaining. The result was a series of legislative acts at both the federal and state level (e.g., the Industrial Relations Act of 1988, the Industrial Relations Reform Act of 1993) that shifted power away from the centralized tribunals and downward to the enterprise bargainers. Stated Labour Prime Minister Paul Keating in 1992 to the attendees at the 9th World Congress of the IIRA (quoted in Dabscheck, 1995: 104), "The old system is finished ... bargaining is the new way."

This remark surely reveals why Australian industrial relations remained healthy in the 1990s, for in Australia "new industrial relations" meant a switch to decentralized collective bargaining while in the United States and the United Kingdom it meant replacing collective bargaining with HRM, markets and legal enactment. The most vigorous proponent among Australian industrial relations academics for the shift to decentralized collective bargaining was John Niland. Niland had earned his Ph.D. in industrial relations in the United States and, according to William Howard (1991: 436), some colleagues thought he was trying to "Americanize" the Australian industrial relations system. For obvious reasons, such a prospect would have its advantages and disadvantages.

Similar to the situation in the United Kingdom in the 1970s, therefore, the period of the Accord in Australia during the 1980s was a time of growth and influence for the industrial relations field. With the failure of the Social Contract in the United Kingdom, however, the national political regime shifted sharply to the right with the election of the Thatcher government and its neo-liberal, anti-union agenda, quickly creating a cold, inhospitable climate for industrial relations. Luckily for the industrial relations field in Australia, the shift toward neo-liberalism was more gradual and less directly aimed at eliminating trade union influence.

Neo-liberalism was not, of course, the only trend threatening the industrial relations field in the 1990s. As was true in other countries, the field in Australia was also challenged by the rise of business schools and HRM (Underhill and Rimmer, 1998). Australian higher education was modelled principally along British lines and, as in the United Kingdom, Australian universities had traditionally given short shrift to business education, seeing it as unduly vocational (Kelly, 1999: 328). Attitudes shifted markedly in the 1990s, however, with the rise of the business-enterprise-focused industrial relations system, the incoming of neo-liberal ideology, and national concern with international competitiveness. Suddenly, university after university was upgrading and expanding its business school, while MBA programmes proliferated.

Industrial relations programmes and academic staff were inevitably caught up in this swelling tide of change. It worked both to the benefit and detriment of the field. A number of industrial relations programmes were in schools of business or commerce and so the upswing in funding and enrolments made it possible to add new industrial relations courses and hire new teaching staff. A number of tertiary institutions of higher education (colleges of advanced education, similar to British polytechnics) also created business schools, and industrial relations was frequently included in them. On the downside, the orientation of traditional industrial relations toward pluralism and collectivism made it the odd man out in an otherwise managerialist-aligned curriculum. This problem of fit was then further accentuated with the rise of HRM.

According to Kelly (2000), the arrival of HRM in Australia was relatively sudden and pronounced, creating shock waves in the industrial relations community and causing (p. 152) "dismay, doubt, and deep concern", much as had happened in the United Kingdom. She notes that references to and warnings about HRM had been sprinkled in the pages of the *Journal of Industrial Relations* in the 1980s and explicitly addressed by several speakers at the 1989 AIRAANZ conference, including Plowman in his presidential address and Guille et al. (1989) in the provocatively entitled paper "Can industrial relations survive without unions?" But it was only at the 1990 AIRAANZ conference when seven sets of authors took up the cause of HRM (e.g., Boxall and Dowling, 1990) that the industrial relations academics woke up to the incipient invasion under way. According to Kelly, "debate followed on debate" and the bulk of the industrial relations scholars "rejected the foundations of HRM, the suggestions to integrate their field with HRM, and even notions that the emergent field of study should be taken seriously". As she notes, underlying the apprehension and hostility to HRM was a deeply felt sense that the industrial relations field had only recently achieved academic recognition and respectability (a "place in the sun") in the Australian academic community and now HRM threatened to wreck three decades of work. Also in play was a strong element of ideological antipathy to the managerialist slant of HRM, the seeming anti-union agenda of the new movement, the set of American cultural values HRM appeared to spring from and represent (e.g., unabashed individualism, "what's good for business is good for society", etc.), and its perceived "jingoism" (Kelly, 2000: 157).

Looking back on the HRM challenge from the vantage point of a decade later, both Kelly (1999, 2000) and Lansbury and Michelson (2003) conclude that Australian industrial relations, like British industrial relations, not only survived the storm but weathered it in reasonably good shape. Starting from an initial position of dismay and opposition, industrial relations academics gradually shifted ground and sought to bring HRM into industrial relations as an alternative regime of workplace regulation and/or to integrate industrial relations and HRM into some new hybrid field of study, most often called "employment relations". In making this transition, Australian industrial relations academics were fortunate to be still in a relatively strong position and have more institutional space to adjust than was true for industrial relations scholars in the United States in the same period. As in the United Kingdom, HRM and OB had a very small presence in Australian universities prior to the mid-1980s. When HRM landed in Australia in the late 1980s, industrial relations academics thus had a better chance to colonize and amalgamate this new subject. A common response was thus to broaden the title of the industrial relations degree programme to "Industrial Relations and Human Resource Management" or "Organizational Behaviour and Industrial Relations". Likewise, the main industrial relations academic professional association, AIRAANZ, broadened its meetings and programme to include HRM. Similarly, as student enrolments shifted heavily toward HRM, industrial relations academics re-tooled and moved into these courses. And, of course, the definition of industrial relations was broadened. Tom Keenoy and Diana Kelly (1998), for example, argue that industrial relations has two components: the first is represented by the term "industrial relation" in the singular, connoting the relationship between the employer and employee that is the core relation of the field, and then the plural term "industrial relations", which captures the network of additional relations of a social, economic and legal nature (interpretable, I note, as Commons' "working rules of collective action" and Kerr/Dunlop's "web of rules") that structures and regulates the employer–employee relation. The general definition of industrial relations is then given as (p. 77) "the administration and control of work and the employment relationship in industrial societies", which they claim allows full room for HRM.

Although Australian industrial relations made considerable progress in accommodating and absorbing HRM, the jury is still out on the field's long-run prospects. One positive development has been a boom in empirical research in the field, made possible by the wealth of new data available from the Australian Workplace Industrial Relations Survey (AWIRS). The AWIRS was modelled on the British WERS and the results of the first survey were reported in 1991 in *Industrial relations at work* (Callus et al.). What is significant about the AWIRS is not just the data but the fact that it represents recognition by policy-makers, unions and employers that much more needs to be learned about the "black box" of workplace practices (Callus, 1991). Obviously, industrial relations stands only to gain.

The future of Australian industrial relations is also clouded by several factors. For example, feeling that AIRAANZ was too dominated by academics from the "old" universities and convinced that industrial relations was too irretrievably pluralist, one group of Australian academics at "newer" universities (colleges of advanced education, CAE) created a new professional association, the International Employment Relations Association (IERA). Whether this evolves into a rival HRM organization is still to be determined. The future of Australian industrial relations is also clouded by the continued decline in trade union density – down to a level of 26 per cent by 2000. As trade unionism shrinks in importance, the experience of other countries indicates that student enrolments correspondingly shift away from industrial relations toward HRM, with deleterious consequences for industrial relations faculty positions and courses. Another factor clouding the picture is the ongoing process of renaming. The University of Sydney's industrial relations department is now called "Work and Organizational Studies". Is this industrial relations by another name, or a gradual shift toward management subjects, such as OB and organizational theory? Finally, Elsa Underhill and Malcolm Rimmer (1998: 152) question whether industrial relations will survive in the long term given "the vulnerability of the central core of the subject".

New Zealand

After publication of Hare's book *Industrial relations in New Zealand* in 1946, the field lay fallow for another quarter century. Kevin Hince (1991: 73) states that "prior to the 1970s, there was little discussion of modern industrial relations philosophy and practice". Given the high level of union density in New Zealand and the ubiquity of collective contracts (due to the centralized system of arbitration and conciliation and the mandatory nature of union membership), conditions would have seemed ripe for the field of industrial relations. Such was not the case, however, because the system was so regulated by law and court decisions and subject to little overt change or challenge. At the time, the New Zealand economy was protected by a steep wall of tariffs, while the system of state conciliation and arbitration was not subject to constitutional challenges as in Australia. Thus industrial relations in New Zealand was largely the province of lay people and was taught neither in law schools, business schools nor social science schools. Indeed, labour law was not even a recognized subfield until the 1960s and the first professor of business administration was not hired until 1962 (ibid.). States Rawson (1978: 107) of the situation as it existed up to the mid-1970s:

Industrial relations has continued for some 84 years to be the exclusive concern of the law, aided by facilities provided by the State. The community continues to identify industrial relations as a frequent confrontation situation seen in strikes, negotiations of terms and conditions of employment, aggressive demands on employers and grievances accompanied by threats. ... At least three generations of New Zealanders have known no alternative to legalistic constraints.

Two developments spawned the emergence of academic industrial relations in New Zealand. The first, in the late 1960s, was a move by several labour economists at the Victoria University of Wellington to broaden the labour economics course to include industrial relations. Their motivation was partly to expand the study of labour to bring in more institutions and cross-disciplinary perspectives. But they also chafed at the low status and marginal position that the study of labour then had in economics and saw industrial relations as an opportunity to break out on their own.

The second event was the convocation of a National Development Conference in 1969, called to address the need for better-trained managers, personnel officers and supervisors. Hare had recommended in his study in 1946 that a School of Social Studies be established to provide management training, but nothing had happened. The idea was resurrected at the conference, however, and the delegates passed a recommendation calling for "a special industrial relations conference, and the establishment of an industrial relations centre at a university".

Out of these two events was born the Industrial Relations Centre at Victoria University. Formed in 1970s, it was originally a semi-autonomous unit of the Department of Economics and had a teaching staff of three under the director-ship of John Young (Brosnan, 1978). Later it became an independent unit and grew to five people: a chair, a visiting fellow and three lecturers. The Centre did not offer its own stand-alone degree programmes but did provide an opportunity for students to develop a concentration in labour and industrial relations, and certificate programmes for practitioners were also provided.

At New Zealand's other six universities, industrial relations courses were also added, and later expanded to include various concentrations and majors. Initially, industrial relations was concentrated in the disciplines of economics and law. On this matter, Smith states (1978: 215), "one discovers that many [industrial relations academics] are based in departments of economics or of law. ... So far, it would be fair to say that there has been little involvement of behavioural scientists." Over time, however, the industrial relations programmes shifted toward business programmes. This shift was in reaction to the continuing need of New Zealand industry for improved training for personnel managers and supervisors. For example, at the University of Auckland, located in New Zealand's largest industrial area, the industrial relations programme was housed in the Faculty of Commerce. In 1985 the Industrial Relations Centre at Victoria was transferred to the Faculty of Commerce and Administration, while at the University of Otago industrial relations was split between economics and commerce.

Industrial relations in New Zealand enjoyed a modest golden age, stretching from the mid-1970s to the late 1980s. The field was always small – perhaps containing 15 faculty members who made industrial relations their central teaching and research area and another 15 or so for whom industrial relations was a secondary area of interest. But during this time the field nonetheless enjoyed continued expansion, buoyed by growth in the union movement and demand for personnel and labour relations specialists.

Two events signal the field's growing position and institutionalization in the academic community. The first is the founding in 1976 of the *New Zealand Journal of Industrial Relations*; the second is the holding of the first stand-alone conference for teachers and researchers in New Zealand and Australia, titled the Australian and New Zealand Conference of Teachers of Industrial Relations, held in Wellington in 1978. The journal continues to publish four times a year and has a circulation of approximately 300. The 1978 conference was so well received that it led directly to the formation of the AIRAANZ in 1983 (Kelly, 2003b). The AIRAANZ now sponsors an annual conference and publishes its proceedings. Meetings typically rotate among Australian universities for four years and then come to New Zealand every fifth year.

As in most other countries, the 1990s and early 2000s were difficult for the industrial relations field in New Zealand. Indeed, industrial relations in New Zealand suffered a much more severe shock and crisis than did the field in Australia. One source of the crisis came, as in the other Anglophone countries, from the appearance of HRM. Interestingly, until the late 1980s industrial relations fared well in New Zealand's commerce and business schools. Personnel management during this period remained largely technique-oriented and descriptive and was among the least favourite courses to teach – a situation true in the United States and other countries. Thus academics saw industrial relations as more intellectually expansive and substantive, and gravitated toward it as their area of teaching and research interest. Likewise, students often regarded industrial relations as the "macho" option, while personnel was for people who lacked motivation or ability to succeed in other areas. When HRM arrived in the late 1980s, however, the situation shifted rapidly. Although HRM remained heavily descriptive, it nonetheless had advantages not only over personnel but also industrial relations. The unitarist focus of HRM, for example, fit better with business courses and philosophy; the strategy component of HRM lifted it above technique (e.g., job performance reviews, selection tests); the

433

greater integration of principles from OB gave it at least a semblance of theory; and it had a more contemporary and modern aura than "smokestack" industrial relations. While in earlier years personnel management had been something of a poor cousin to industrial relations, during the 1990s the tables started to turn and industrial relations increasingly fell under HRM's shadow.

A second and more climactic effect was the government's decision to jettison the centralized system of labour conciliation and arbitration that had been in place since the 1890s. Criticism had been mounting, particularly from business groups, that the traditional system of industrial relations in New Zealand was increasingly non-competitive. New Zealand industry was gradually being exposed to greater international competition, but employers claimed to be hamstrung by inflexible labour contracts and wage rates, a collectivist mentality that prized the status quo and security over competition and change, and strikes and restrictive work rules that hampered productivity. In 1991, the government, under the neo-liberal National Party, passed the Employment Contracts Act. The Act banned compulsory unionism, dismantled the arbitration and conciliation courts, and encouraged individual bargaining (Hince and Vranken, 1991). Over the space of a decade, union density was cut by half (from about 55 to 22 per cent), leaving the New Zealand labour movement reeling and disoriented. As the union movement entered into crisis, industrial relations naturally felt the negative backwash and entered its own period of marked decline.

The situation for industrial relations appeared to bottom out by century's end. New legislation, the Employment Relations Act of 2000, reversed some of the more draconian features of the earlier legislation. After a sharp rate of descent, trade union density also began to hold its own. According to Geare (2004), however, the political and economic environment remains relatively austere for industrial relations and the field is now in a "stable slump". As in other countries, industrial relations academics in New Zealand are trying to adjust through a variety of stratagems. For example, courses are being broadened to include topics outside labour–management relations and industrial relations faculty are shifting over to teach HRM courses. Another tactic is to update the name of the field, increasingly viewed as old and stodgy by students and employers. Thus in 2004 the *New Zealand Journal of Industrial Relations* becomes the *New Zealand Journal of Employment Relations*.

Notes

[1] From 1980 until 1998, when the Blair Labour government reintroduced a statutory recognition procedure, union recognition was a voluntary decision for the employer.

[2] Note the correspondence to the 1920s typology of, respectively, the employers', workers' and community's solution to labour problems, or what might generically be called employment management, employment relations and employment policy. Ideally, however, the corpus of employment relations would cover employer–employee relations in both union and non-union situations, rather than just the former.

INDUSTRIAL RELATIONS IN CONTINENTAL EUROPE

9

Until the 1960s and the founding of the IIRA, the industrial relations field had a negligible presence outside its Anglo-American home base. From the early 1970s onward, however, the field spread across the world. In this chapter, I describe how this process unfolded in continental Europe. The first half of the chapter examines the broad outline of development, describing the key people, events and institutions that brought industrial relations to Europe and shaped its evolution. Given the large number and heterogeneous nature of individual countries in Europe, it is impossible to provide an account of the development of the industrial relations field in each. But, at the same time, the national experiences are so diverse that some indication of the different national patterns is required. To meet this challenge, in-depth case studies of the development of industrial relations in France and Germany are provided, with the thought that Germany represents the Rhineland model and France the Latin model.

Europe: Trends and developments

Europe includes over 500 million people, 40 countries and a highly diverse set of political systems, cultures and economies. For comparative purposes, Europe can be divided into four subregions: the British Isles (including Ireland), Germanic Europe (north and northwest), Latin Europe (south and southwest) and Slavic Europe (east and east-central). Of these four regions, most of the attention in this chapter is focused on the Germanic and Latin areas, given that the industrial relations field in the United Kingdom has already been examined in detail and in the former communist countries of Central and Eastern Europe it has only existed for little more than a decade. Hereafter in this chapter, I use the term "Europe" in the restricted sense of the continental countries (excluding Ireland and the United Kingdom).

I note at the beginning that making generalizations about "Europe" is a treacherous exercise because of the considerable diversity in national experiences and institutions (Crouch, 1993). Anthony Ferner and Richard Hyman (1992) pointedly allude to this problem in their overview chapter on industrial relations in the countries of the European Union (EU) by appending the subtitle: "Seventeen types of ambiguity". Since they wrote these words the number has increased substantially, as have the ambiguities. With this warning light in mind, I proceed.

Although industrial relations as a field of teaching and research appeared in North America in the early 1920s and the United Kingdom in the 1930s, it did not arrive in Europe until the second half of the 1960s. Even then, its presence remained quite marginal for nearly two decades, centred among a relatively small number of scholars who had visited or studied in North America or the United Kingdom or had otherwise developed contacts with the Anglo-American research community. This divergent pattern raises an interesting question: since both groups of countries experienced the same industrial relations *problems* during the late nineteenth century and first half of the twentieth century – i.e., the development of a large urban-based working class, national labour movements, bitter and sometimes violent strikes, and fears of socialist revolution – then why didn't they also develop a *field* of industrial relations in their universities to help solve these labour problems? Canada, the United Kingdom and the United States did, but France, Germany and Italy did not. Why?

The answer, although complex, can be usefully approached in terms of two factors. Hans Hetzler (1995), for example, in his historical review of the development of industrial relations in Germany notes that (pp. 313–14, translated from the German), "The history of industrial relations is as old as industrial society." Hetzler thus points to the same generic aspect of labour problems, as was just noted above. However, he then goes on to explain the field's late emergence in Germany with the observation that it "is not solely based on differences in scientific organization of the disciplines but also finds its explanation in a different understanding of the problem". In a comparative analysis of German and American industrial relations research, Carola Frege (2002) pinpoints the same two factors as the major explanatory variables for the different pattern of the field's development in the two countries. She describes them as (p. 868), "differences in the subject matter and its historical legacies", and "differences in national knowledge production in the social sciences".

Differences in understanding the problem

The cross-cultural variance in understanding the problem is a good place to begin the discussion. Americans, for example, have an instinctive sense for the meaning of the term industrial relations and its *problématique*. For Europeans, on the other hand, industrial relations has long been, and in some measure continues to be, a truly a *foreign* concept both literally and substantively.

Beginning at the literal level, the very term industrial relations is a confusing non-entity to many outside Anglophone countries. Walter Korpi (1981: 186) said of Sweden in the late 1970s, "no Swedish term exists corresponding to 'industrial relations'". Even when translated into the national language, such as the German phrase *Industrielle Beziehungen*, the term even today is a mystery to the average person. Usually, they will guess it deals with something about the economic relations between industries or business firms. The parallel situation would be if an English-speaking person were asked to describe what the German term "Sozialpartner" means, even if translated into its English equivalent "social partner". Most would assume it refers to a personal companion at a social event.

For this reason, in a number of European countries the term labour relations is instead used, such as *arbeidsverhoundingen* in the Netherlands and *arbejdsmarkedsorold* (labour market relations) in Denmark (Leisink, 1996; Ryberg and Bruun, 1996). The European meaning of labour relations is broader, however, than the Anglo-American and pertains to all types of employment relations. Another alternative construction is the Spanish term *relaciones de trabajo*, which means "work relations".

Going further, it should not be surprising that if the term industrial relations is not commensurate across national languages, other basic concepts and terms that form foundation stones of the field suffer the same fate. Kahn-Freund (1983: 2), for example, notes that the German concept of *Tarifautonomie* ("autonomous collective bargaining") "is virtually untranslatable into English and has in Britain no juridically construable meaning". Much the same could be said for the concept of *Wirstschaftsdemokratie* ("economic democracy"), while the American legal concept of *right to work* has no parallel concept in Europe. Another interesting example is the term "labour movement", which on one side of the Atlantic means a working-class-based social movement while on the other side it means people who are dues-paying members of labour unions (Sturmthal, 1972).

The disjunction between Anglo-American and continental European perspectives goes far deeper than just language, however. Also playing a key role are differences in *institutions* and *ideologies* and the *conceptualization* given to the subject matter of industrial relations.

As I will suggest at a later point, whatever its conceptual faults may be, the great virtue of Dunlop's formulation of an industrial relations system is that it gives the field a generic framework and object of study. Being generic, the field

437

then becomes independent of particular institutions and practices and takes on the attributes of a science (or at least a common language) that can be practised across all countries and cultures. If industrial relations remains purely a field of applied problem solving or an ethical value statement, on the other hand, it quickly loses identity and coherence as it moves across countries, given their huge diversity in national institutions, cultures and ideologies.

The industrial relations field came to Europe relatively late for a variety of reasons. But many of these are in one way or another tied to this distinction between industrial relations as a scientific field of inquiry and industrial relations as a field of problem solving and ideology (the "three faces" of industrial relations described in Chapter 2). For many years, and to a significant degree still today, the field has largely been defined in terms of the latter two faces. Inevitably, this made its passage from North America to Europe a slow and halting one. When industrial relations finally took root and started to grow in Europe, it was partly because a more generic way had been found to frame the subject and partly because differences in institutions and ideologies between Europe and the Anglo-American countries significantly narrowed.

As noted in an earlier chapter, industrial relations has been defined in many different ways. The traditional approach, however, has been to conceptualize it as dealing with the relations between employers and employees or, more broadly, between capital and labour. The central object of attention in this conceptualization of industrial relations is thus the degree of conflict between capital and labour, and the explicit or implicit goal of industrial relations is to find ways to promote more peaceful and cooperative relations. Illustrative of this perspective is this statement by Johannes Schregle, a German labour representative to the ILO. He (1981: 27) says:

> In every country, North and South, workers, employers and governments have both common and divergent interests, short term and long term. The divergent interests must be accommodated and reconciled. ... This principle applies to all countries. This way in which interests are expressed and reconciled is the subject of industrial relations.

Schregle provides a particularly expressive and well-crafted statement of the original *problématique* of industrial relations. But framing the field this way also leads to inevitable problems in trying to internationalize the subject.

One problem area regards the institutions and practices that each country uses to accommodate the divergent interests of employers and employees and promote peace. As described in Chapter 2, when Europeans came to the United States in the 1920s to look at the new experiments going on in employer–employee relations they saw not a generic body of knowledge (like economic theory) but a specific, largely culture-bound set of institutions and workplace practices. Unique to the rest of the world, the United States had a labour movement that accepted capitalism and openly preached the virtues of pragmatic business unionism and labour–management cooperation. But the centre of American industrial relations was not in the unionized sector, for it was small and located in traditional craft-dominated industries. Rather, when the Europeans came to see American industrial relations in action they went to see non-union companies such as Ford Motor, General Electric and Standard Oil, for it was here that the "new industrial relations" was on display. The core of the new industrial relations was the employment model of welfare capitalism and the Fordist regime of mass production, and its twin objectives were minimizing union and government involvement in the workplace and maximizing the productivity of mass production by winning employee cooperation and commitment. The philosophy of industrial relations was a combination of goodwill, unity of interest, enlightened paternalism and hard-headed business. Its practices were high wages, professional personnel practices, the internalization of employment through job security and promotion from within, human relations, employee representation through shop councils, and use of scientific management and industrial engineering to create a mass production work system.

When the Europeans returned home, they often had the same reaction Americans and Europeans had after a visit to see the Japanese miracle economy of the 1980s. That is, they could not help but be impressed by the material prosperity and smooth functioning of the industrial machine, but they also found a number of aspects they did not like or that could not easily be exported back to the home country. With regard to the 1920s industrial relations model, the Europeans saw many problems and incompatibilities: the fast pace of work; the replacement of skilled craft labour and small batch production with a mass production process using thousands of unskilled and semi-skilled workers; the commitment to keeping out unions; and the near-complete absence of social employment protection through labour laws and social insurance programmes. For all of these reasons, therefore, the American model of industrial relations was not exportable to Europe and, besides, the term "industrial relations" was confusing.

The situation did not change significantly after the Second World War. The field of industrial relations was still largely a North American product, although now having a toehold in the United Kingdom. On one hand, some convergence had taken place between Europe and North America – both had large labour movements, widespread collective bargaining, a strike problem, the early stages of a welfare state, and a large blue-collar workforce and factory system

– but many differences still made North American industrial relations a non-starter in Europe.

In particular, the institutional features of the American and European industrial relations systems remained very different. The United States had a decentralized collective bargaining system, business unions, a large non-union sector of employers and a relatively litigious and adversarial approach to bargaining and employee relations. A European reading an early issue of *Industrial and Labor Relations Review* or attending a meeting of the IRRA would have found the problems and institutions talked about in American industrial relations partially bewildering and partially irrelevant. The reason is that European countries in the decade after the war created an industrial relations system that in many respects went in an opposite direction. Centralized, corporatist bargaining structures emerged in the Germanic and Scandinavian countries, while unions and employers in the Latin countries continued to wage the class struggle (except in Spain and Portugal, which remained under fascist dictatorships). European trade unions were far more ideological and political, while the national governments went much further in regulating labour markets and building a cradle-to-grave welfare state (Slomp, 1990).

It is thus apparent that at one level all nations are practising industrial relations, as they are all seeking to find ways to reconcile the divergent interests of capital and labour and promote industrial peace – even if it means eliminating capitalists and a market economy to do so. Few people thought in terms of this disembodied notion of industrial relations, however. Rather, industrial relations was still "something from America" – a particular approach to solving labour problems. Not only was it a particular and idiosyncratic set of employment practices, it was also weighted down with political and ideological implications. These associations proved particularly problematic and, to a degree, remain so.

This issue may be approached by returning to look more deeply at Schregle's definition of industrial relations. The key assertions in his quotation are, first, that it is possible to reconcile the divergent interests of labour and capital and, second, that it is desirable to do so. Also implicit in his statement is social acceptance of a capitalist economic system and, particularly, capitalist employers hiring wage labour. To most Americans, his statement is completely conventional and would elicit no controversy. The same is not true in Europe, particularly in the first two to three decades following the Second World War. Many Europeans in this period did not accept these propositions, or at least had deep reservations about them (Sturmthal, 1983). A larger group accepted them as general social principles but only if implemented after a fundamental redistribution of wealth, political power and institutional access in favour of the working class. A yet larger group were in favour of some form of mixed capitalist economy and democratic parliamentary form of government, but only if developed by Europeans and congruent with European traditions and cultures and not as a clone of American society or an import foisted on Europe by American government or multinational corporations.

A key point developed in Chapter 1 is that all industrializing societies in the late nineteenth and early twentieth centuries saw the emergence of deep-seated and sometimes violent conflict between labour and capital. The process of working out a social compromise was easier in the United Kingdom and the United States, however, because democratic institutions were the most developed, feudal traditions less strongly felt and religious and political divisions less deep. For this reason, the Labour Problem could be more easily compartmentalized as a challenge to existing *employment relations* but not necessarily to the broader corpus of *social relations*. Similarly, solutions to the Labour Problem were easier to devise and implement because they could take the form of factory acts or trade unions rather than a fundamental change in social organization and form of government. In Europe, on the other hand, class divisions, religious and political schisms, the heritage of feudalism, and the reality of authoritarian governments weighed far more heavily. As a result, the labour–capital conflict and the Labour Problem could not be separated from the larger Social Question that haunted all of these nations and, thus, the issue of reconciling and accommodating labour and capital was more difficult, politically contentious and fraught with larger social implications.

Both the First and the Second World Wars had specific geopolitical and nationalist and imperialist origins. Viewed more broadly, these cataclysms also represented Europe's failure to reach a successful resolution to the Social Question through democratic means. Contained within this failure was also its inability to reach an acceptable and long-lasting solution to the Labour Problem. For this reason, after the Second World War large segments of European labour remained overtly class conscious and anti-capitalist, as did a large part of the intellectual elites. Adolf Sturmthal (1951: ix) explains the workers' outlook in these terms:

> European labor has grown up in a society in which the tradition of democratic compromise has been conspicuously lacking – moreover, in a society in which clear lines of demarcation separated class from class. The feudal tradition of a strictly hierarchial society allocated to everyone a distinct status. … The worker in industry did not need much education in class consciousness. It was impressed upon him by the powers that be and by his daily experience. It was this social and political disqualification, far more than his economic exploitation, which shaped the European worker's mind.

Post-war anti-capitalist feelings were heightened by the widespread perception that capitalism and imperialism (the two being commonly linked together) were partly responsible for the slide into conflict, compounded by the fact that major industrialists had collaborated with the fascist regimes, while the communists had played a leading role in the Resistance movement. The period of reconstruction also brought with it a general desire for a more planned and rational approach to economic organization. Illustrative of the constellation of forces and ideologies was the case of the Federal Republic of Germany, where 70 per cent of the working class voted for the Social Democratic Party (SPD) in the early years after the war and the SPD, in turn, made nationalization of industry and economic planning a major component of its official political programme (Berger, 2000: 182). In France, the governments gradually nationalized 40 per cent of major industry, adopted a system of five-year economic plans and the Communist Party routinely gained 25–30 per cent of the popular vote in political elections (Meyers, 1981).

In this milieu, industrial relations had a hard time taking root, for its ideology, problem-solving approach and American affiliation were all incongruent with European conditions. Industrial relations, for example, was affiliated with an ideology of voluntarism, individualism, business unionism and adversarial collective bargaining. None of these attributes resonated well in Europe. Many Europeans found the narrow, economistic approach of the American labour movement unappealing, while the fetish of individualism and competition coming from the United States was seen as excessive and dangerous. European trade unions deliberately assumed a wider political role and framed their mission as the social and economic representative of the working class. In the Latin countries, this role was to carry on class struggle and opposition to capitalist employers; in the Germanic and Scandinavian countries it was to work toward social and economic democracy in which capitalist industry was socialized and co-managed by labour. Out of this philosophy and the deep desire to promote social peace and stability (the heritage of the Social Question) grew the pervading emphasis on the social dimension of all aspects of labour and employment policy – social partners, the social contract, social dialogue, social justice, social exclusion and numerous other variants (Schwanholz, 2001). American industrial relations spoke to none of these ideological and policy goals and, indeed, its promotion of narrow-based individualism and adversarial collective bargaining seemed directly antithetical to the Europeans' desire for social peace and broad-based social advance and egalitarianism.

After the Second World War, the Cold War, Red Threat and McCarthy witch hunt for communist sympathizers quickly neutralized the political and intellectual left in the United States. In Europe, by way of contrast, the spectrum of political opinion was not only wider but had a far larger and more influential left wing, starting with the various mass-level social democratic parties and extending leftward to encompass a wide array of socialist and communist groups (Smith, 1994: 274). Within European universities, Marxism and other radical intellectual programmes were heavily represented and research and teaching had a far more ideological and politicized orientation.

The large position of the political, intellectual left in Europe was an important barrier to the successful transplantation of Anglo-American industrial relations on several counts. For scholars approaching capital–labour issues from a Marxist perspective – or even from the point of view of social democracy – the American-inspired concept and field of industrial relations cannot but be viewed with considerable scepticism and perhaps hostility. The entire programme of industrial relations is to accommodate labour into the existing socio-political structure, take politics and ideology out of capital–labour relations, minimize serious conflict and preserve social stability. From a radical perspective, industrial relations is simply one mode of repression and control, albeit a softened and pseudo-scientific, pseudo-democratic method, that hides under the mask of functionalism inequalities of power and social position. Also objectionable, industrial relations obfuscates and misrepresents the exploitative and subordinating nature of work under capitalism and serves to lock in and legitimize the hegemony of employers. Lastly, Europeans familiar with the American industrial relations field realized that it was explicitly anti-Marxist and anti-socialist. According to Gosta Esping-Andersen (1985: 14–15), for example, it is Selig Perlman who provided the "classical critique" of Lenin. He goes on to say, "Perlman's thesis has informed the more general hypothesis that pragmatic American unionism shows Europeans the wave of the future. It is not the absence of socialism in American that requires explanation but, rather, socialism's obstinacy in Europe."

The Marxist antipathy to industrial relations is well illustrated by the review of industrial relations practices in the American automobile industry by two French academics, Dominique Pignon and Jean Querzola (1976). They say (pp. 64–67):

> Absenteeism, labour turnover, botched work and even active sabotage have become the running sores of the American automotive industry. ... In the face of repression and revolt, the Taylorist school can respond only by repression, intimidation and physical violence. This terrorist regime is still the order of the day in big mass-production plants. ... But repressive methods are powerless against widespread and ever-present resistance. ... Some remedy had to be found, and American capitalists

443

were the first to pursue it. An initial policy was worked out in the United States in the late forties, at the instigation of a former steelworker and trade unionist, J.N. Scanlon. This policy [industrial relations and employee participation] ... starts from the observation that workers don't 'go all-out' or 'give their best' in their work because they are struggling against the boss. It follows that attempts should be made to eliminate this (class) struggle by means of a process of economic and ideological integration. ... But it is clear enough what the limits of such participation are. The economic class struggle is just pushed back a little. ... [T]he thing to do is not cover up this opposition, in the way that 'industrial relations' policies tend to do.

European academics who became involved with industrial relations were thus seen by their Marxist colleagues as enemies of the working class and collaborationists with capital. The ensuing conflict was not merely or even mainly intellectual but was highly political and ideological, given the Leninist viewpoint that it is the task of revolutionary intellectuals to lead the workers forward in the class struggle. As described shortly, the most important academic group in European universities doing research on capital–labour relations was sociologists, and no other field in European social sciences had a greater proportion of radicals and Marxists. Bourdieu and Passeron (1967: 150), for example, describe European sociology as "haunted by Marxism, the working class and the exploitation of labour". Evidently, the intellectual environment in the period of the 1950s–70s was not hospitable to the introduction of industrial relations. I interviewed many of the "first generation" of academics who started the field of industrial relations in Europe in the mid-1960s and early 1970s. They all described a polarized ideological atmosphere and a research style that eschewed "go and see" case studies and ethnographic studies of workplace condition for highly abstract theoretical debates and dogmatic arguments over Marxist doctrine. They also described the personal ostracism and criticism sometimes directed at them by Marxist and radical colleagues. Although the influence of Marxism has declined considerably since the mid-1980s, several younger European industrial relations scholars related in interviews that being involved in industrial relations still carries a negative stigma among some colleagues, but more out of nationalist than Marxist sentiments.

The political and ideological aversion to industrial relations in years past among large segments of the European left stems from more than just radical/Marxist doctrines. Geopolitical factors also count.

As perceived by a number of Europeans, the field of industrial relations and the American scholars involved in it were suspect because they served as overt or covert tools of American foreign policy, particularly in the Cold War battle against communism (Radosh, 1969). Industrial relations, from their perspective, was not simply a neutral academic field of study but was an explicit weapon wielded by the Americans to keep war-torn Europe (and Asia) and their socialist-leaning labour movements from drifting into the communist orbit (Cox and Sinclair, 1996).

The Marshall Plan after the Second World War funnelled a huge amount of money and American personnel into Europe, including many teams of managers and labour relations experts (Kipping and Bjarnar, 1998). A central objective was to transplant American management methods and industrial relations practices in Europe: partly to rebuild European industry but also in the desire to shift Europeans from class politics at the workplace to a non-ideological focus on productivity improvement and business unionism. Throughout the 1950s, the American government and private foundations, particularly the Ford Foundation, also devoted considerable funds to sending American industrial relations scholars and trade union leaders on extended visits to Europe (Gemelli, 1996). The Fulbright programme also brought a number of European academics to the United States for advanced training and doctoral degrees in industrial relations, with many spending time at the Cornell industrial relations programme. The Central Intelligence Agency (CIA) was also widely suspected of covertly supporting industrial relations missions and activities in Europe and overseas programmes of the AFL–CIO (Romero, 1992).

When the American scholars and trade unionists returned to the United States, they typically provided their government or foundation sponsors with reports and policy recommendations (Cochrane, 1979). The exemplar of this practice was the Inter-University Study led by Kerr, Dunlop, Harbison and Myers and funded by the Ford and Carnegie Foundations. As noted in an earlier chapter, the project leaders explicitly marketed the study as a valuable means to discover methods to contain labour radicalism and communism and were quite successful in helping spread American industrial relations ideas to Europe and beyond. While seen in the United States as a legitimate and worthy marriage of scholarship and national interest, in Europe this intermingling of scholarship and foreign policy caused the field of industrial relations to be viewed critically in some circles as a handmaiden of American geopolitical interests.

Negative feelings about the United States and the status quo in labour–capital relations then took a further nose dive in the latter half of the 1960s, associated with widespread opposition to the Viet Nam War and the rise of the New Left. As described in Chapter 8, all Western countries, but particularly European nations, experienced growing radicalism and rebellion among young people and large segments of the working class. Fuelled by discontent with social and political conditions at home, and serious disenchantment with American military involvement in Viet Nam, large-scale riots, strikes and clashes with police broke out across Western Europe, reaching a crescendo in May 1968 (Crouch and Pizzorno, 1978; Slomp, 1990). Since the American AFL–CIO was among the most outspoken proponents of American involvement in Viet Nam, the industrial relations field laboured under a particular handicap.

The Marxist condemnation of capitalism was now joined by New Left criticism. Although the two were closely linked, the New Left critique downplayed Marxian theory and gave greater emphasis to the (alleged) role of capitalism in promoting racism and sexism, a stultifying division of labour and alienation in the workplace, environmental degradation and meaningless consumerism. The Green parties in Europe have their origins in the New Left movement. Gerd Langguth (1995: 24) states that the New Left in Germany was a rebellion against pluralist democracy and a market economy and "supported an elitist ideology that made the intellectual into the political actor, the 'revolutionary subject'". Although not clear on what was to follow, the leaders of the New Left sought to steer society to class radicalization and social transformation. A prominent New Left intellectual who wrote on capital–labour relations and helped German and French unionists develop their political programmes in the early 1970s was André Gorz. He captures the tenor of New Left thought in this passage (1976: 60):

> Is it really possible to find meaning and take interest in assembling televisions when the programmes are idiotic; or in making fragmentation bombs, throw-away fabrics or individual cars built for obsolescence and rapid wear and destined to sit in traffic jams? What meaning does work have when its dominant aim (the accumulation of capital) is meaningless? Challenging the capitalist organization of work implies challenging the system as a whole. Reformist subjugation and co-optation of workers' resistance to factory despotism can be prevented only if this challenge is made explicit and autonomous.

As earlier noted, sociology in Europe was the major locus for academic research on the workplace and capital–labour relations, and Gorz's perspective was broadly representative of a wide swathe of opinion. The incongruity between American industrial relations and European social science was not just a case of Europe being to the left. Viewed from Europe, the United States was distinctly to the right.

To a degree often not appreciated by American industrial relations scholars, the field of industrial relations appears to Europeans to have a heavy component of managerialist content and ideology. Writing in 1981, for example, Wolfgang Conrad states (p. 209), "The concept of industrial relations is ambiguous in the Federal Republic of Germany; to many, it is synonymous with human relations and therefore burdened with ideological overtones." In a similar vein, Hyman (1995a: 26) notes, "In Italy the concept of *relazioni industriali* ... was originally closely linked to the growth of management education", and then quotes Gino Giugni (1981), who states, "it [industrial relations] was first introduced by managers – generally those with Anglo-Saxon training". The point is reinforced by the case of France, where Hyman (1995: 25) notes of the first two textbooks on industrial relations: "Their managerial orientation was clear: the former bracketed human relations and industrial relations as the object of study, the latter was published as one of a series of texts on business administration."

To Americans, to call industrial relations "managerialist" borders on the incomprehensible, since they associate the field with trade unions and collective bargaining. But they forget the close connection before 1945 between industrial relations and the PM programme of non-union welfare capitalism. Also forgotten is that through the 1960s industrial relations was home to the human relations movement; furthermore, some of the biggest names in the study of management and OB in the United States, such as Chris Argyris, William Foote Whyte and Douglas McGregor, were professors of industrial relations. It should also recalled that one of Kerr et al.'s major conclusions in *Industrialism and industrial man* was that the destiny of trade unions was to evolve into professional associations in a pluralistic state run by technocratic elites. Also illustrative is the fact that the single largest research topic in American industrial relations since the early 1980s is the high-performance workplace, that the epicentre of this research is the Sloan School of Management (MIT) and the lead research organizer, Thomas Kochan, is a professor of management (Kochan is also the only president of the IIRA to be a faculty member in a business school). Finally, to persons committed to replacing capitalism a research programme on trade unionism can nevertheless appear broadly managerialist, since an Anglo-American system of collective bargaining not only perpetuates management control of industry but also legitimates and protects management's rights by making them an integral part of the contract.

Given the left/right ideological mismatch between Europe and North America, lines of communication with Europe and areas of mutual interest were limited. An interesting illustration comes from Germany. The first time industrial relations was featured as a session topic at a meeting of the German Sociological Association was in 1979. According to a participant, few German sociologists were knowledgeable about industrial relations so the session organizers sought to include presenters from the Anglo-American countries who were familiar with its development and research programme. Whom did

447

they select? The first person was Richard Hyman, author of *Industrial relations: A Marxist introduction* (1975), and the second was Colin Crouch, well-known sociologist and past chair of the Fabian Society.

Of course, not all European sociologists were Marxists and New Left radicals, but the number in the non-leftist camp *and* interested in worker–employer relations was small. Illustratively, sociologists were the largest disciplinary contingent in the new German Industrial Relations Association (GIRA, established 1970), but it was only able to attract nine members and ten years later still had fewer then 20 (Hetzler, 1995). The GIRA, as noted later in this chapter, was run fewer as a professional association and more as a "members-only club" in the early years, with membership restricted to researchers from the non-leftist part of the ideological spectrum.

The political and ideological winds began to shift in Europe in a more rightward, neo-liberal direction in the 1980s, albeit with far less force than in the United States under Reagan and the United Kingdom with Thatcher. Nonetheless, this shift was a crucial step in opening the door wider for the industrial relations field in Europe. The most evident sign of change was the emergence of a European dialogue on the "crisis of social democracy" and the "crisis of the European social model". Accompanying themes were the first signs of erosion in union density and the centralized bargaining structures in several countries, and emergent concern about international competitiveness. The American founders of industrial relations were social liberals who sought to "save capitalism by making it good". Their model was a humanized market economy, political pluralism and a moderate infrastructure of welfare programmes that did not unduly impinge on the well-spring of growth – profits (see Chapter 2). The closest equivalent to this philosophy in post-Second World War Europe was among the various Christian Democrat parties and the German ordo-liberal theory of a social market economy (described in more detail later in the chapter).

Opposed to this vision were the various Social Democrat parties of Europe and their affiliated trade unions. The social democrats were self-consciously the party of the working class: they sought to slowly replace capitalism with some form of economic democracy or socialist economy and were committed to a large-scale welfare state financed through substantial wealth and income redistribution (Esping-Anderson, 1985; Scharpf, 1991; Berger, 2000). The German SPD opposed the social market economy concept until 1959, supported it with reservations and less than full commitment through the 1970s, and then only in the 1980s became an enthusiastic advocate and defender (Hardach, 1980; Tietmeyer, 1999). Behind this shift was, first, an erosion of the electoral base of the Social Democrat parties as the process of social integration, cultural differentiation and bourgeoisement cut into the ranks of the working class and, second, the growing doubts whether the advanced European welfare state was financially viable in light of rapidly rising costs and declining economic growth rates. Under these pressures, the social democratic parties gradually tacked to the right, in the process abandoning class politics and embracing a (social) market economy. All of these developments were propitious for industrial relations.

Another momentous political and ideological shift was unleashed by the fall of the Berlin Wall in 1989 and the collapse of the Soviet Union and its Central and Eastern European satellite states. Suddenly, the competition between economic systems was not between capitalism and socialism but different kinds of capitalism (Hall and Soskice, 2001). A scholarly growth industry developed, with numerous books written on alternative models of capitalism and their associated industrial relations systems – coordinated versus uncoordinated; liberal versus non-liberal; Anglo-Saxon versus Rhineland; Fordist versus post-Fordist (Albert, 1993; Streeck and Yamamura, 2001; Hollingsworth and Boyer, eds., 1997). Suddenly the industrial relations systems concept came into its own, not as a theory but at least a common frame of reference and descriptor for the object of study. With "really existing socialism" discredited, radical/Marxist politics and intellectual programmes further receded, while social democracy now travelled down a hybrid path of social neo-liberalism called the "third way" (Schmidtke, 2002). Not only had the constellation of political and ideological forces shifted in a direction markedly more favourable for industrial relations; similar developments were taking place in the world of practice and problem solving. Collective bargaining continued on a slow path of decentralization, thus giving greater salience to staple topics of industrial relations (contract negotiation, bargaining, workplace-level practices), while relations between employers and unions came to give more emphasis to economic and workplace issues and less to ideological posturing and class politics (Katz and Darbishire, 2000; Regini, 2003).

There is always the exception to the rule, and in this case tragically so. The ghost of the class war momentarily reared its head on 19 March 2002. On that day terrorists from the extreme left in Italy assassinated industrial relations scholar Professor Marco Biagi. Biagi had done graduate work at Johns Hopkins University in America and went on to become one of the founding fathers of Italian industrial relations (Tiraboschi, 2003). He was a noted scholar and editor of a well-recognized journal, the *International Journal of Comparative Labour Law and Industrial Relations*, a long-serving president of the Italian Industrial Relations Association and frequent consultant to government at the national and EU level. Biagi was selected for assassination because he had strongly endorsed and helped write a controversial report for the centre-right government, *White paper on the labour market in Italy: Proposals for an active society and quality employment.*

Differences in national knowledge production

We now come to the other factor described by Hetzler, differences in the structure and production of knowledge across countries. This requires a closer look at the unique characteristics of European university systems and intellectual traditions.

North American and European universities have traditionally been structured and operated quite differently (Frey and Eichenberger, 1992; Wittrock and Wagner, 1996). This gap is closing, however, as the academic and research marketplaces become increasingly internationalized. American universities resemble American society as a whole: relatively open and meritocratic, with considerable autonomy from direct state control, many competing institutions, an egalitarian, mass production philosophy and considerable emphasis on and monetary rewards to faculty research. European university systems, on the other hand, have traditionally been more closed, regulated, bureaucratic and elitist, with fewer institutions and less competition (small and thin academic markets). Political and status considerations play a larger role in faculty hiring, promotion and rewards; public service, government administration and policy work by faculty members receive greater emphasis while research and publication receive less; and the state exercises much greater control and supervision. In most European countries, university teaching and research staff are government civil servants, and curriculum and faculty appointments require approval of regional and national officials in the Ministry of Education.

These characteristics of European universities have influenced the development of the industrial relations field in several ways, on net acting to retard its development and spread. Academic entrepreneurship and innovation, for example, are stifled by the power of individual senior professors in control of research institutes to block change, by the time-consuming process needed to move proposals through the university, regional and national bureaucracies, and the weak link between financial reward and effort. Thus, starting up a new industrial relations programme in this context will not look like an attractive option. Likewise, interdisciplinary programmes are difficult to create because departments and faculties have traditionally maintained strong walls of separation between the disciplines and zealously protect their turf. Guy Caire (1996), for example, refers to a "disciplinary compartmentalization" of teaching in France. The culture of European universities, particularly in the Germanic countries, also emphasizes stability and order over risk and change. Industrial relations, being a newcomer on the scene, thus has great difficulty breaking into the formal university structure. The end result of these considerations is that it is very difficult for industrial relations to establish a formal institutional presence in European university systems, thus also inhibiting establishment of a self-identified community of industrial relations scholars and a network of industrial relations researchers.

Another difference among European and American universities concerns business schools. Business schools, in the American sense of a university-connected professional school, have been until recent years almost completely lacking. Even today in Germany these kinds of business schools are just in the early phase of development. Business schools in America were important to the development of industrial relations because they were for many years a major home for industrial relations centres and professors, reflecting the fact that the career goal of most students was to obtain a corporate management position in personnel or labour relations. European companies, of course, also need personnel and labour relations specialists, but in years past they obtained them through alternative channels. Law programmes, for example, were prominent, reflecting the strong juridical framework surrounding European employment and labour relations. Also important were business economics programmes, engineering programmes and training programmes financed by employers' associations and trade union federations.

In the last decade, American-style business schools have proliferated in many European countries, particularly in Scandinavia and the southern Latin region (Spain and Italy). But this development was too late in coming to be a boon to industrial relations. Reflecting American patterns, industrial relations courses have for the most part been displaced in the new curricula by HRM and OB.

Whether located in a business school or a school of arts and sciences, the disciplinary foundation of North American industrial relations programmes has been economics. Economics departments in Europe would have, at least until recently, appeared also to offer a friendly intellectual location for industrial relations. Until the mid-1980s and the growing dominance of the neoclassical approach, economics was frequently taught along more applied and institutional lines. In Germany, for example, the dominant approach was *Betriebswirtschaftlehre* – an expansive form of "industrial" or "business" economics with substantial emphasis on the business and administrative dimensions of economics, including applied subjects such as personnel management. In France, economics was for many years often housed in a faculty of law and was again relatively institutional. Other factors worked in the opposite direction, however, and kept economics a modest contributor. For example, economics for several decades after the Second World War was not as well supported in Europe as in the United States and thus remained somewhat underdeveloped. Also, the study of labour and trade unions was not popular or well accepted in economics for many years and, thus, relatively few scholars ventured into the area.

Certainly the same is not the case in sociology. If economics has traditionally been the social-science disciplinary locus of industrial relations in North America, sociology has played this role in Europe (Hyman, 1995a). Sociological research on work, trade unions, labour history and industry has a long and rich history in Europe. As noted in Chapter 1, three of the founding fathers of sociology came from Europe: Durkheim, Marx and Weber. By the early 1930s, the sociology of work began to coalesce as a separate subfield in Germany focusing explicitly on the *Betrieb* (enterprise, plant, etc.), with its own research institutes and literature (Müller-Jentsch, 2002). After the war, the sociology of work and industry experienced a boom in Germany and became a leading area of social science research. Much the same situation occurred in other countries. According to Michael Rose (1979), for example, the sociology of work was the most important branch of French sociology in the first two decades after the Second World War, while in Sweden sociologists were by far the dominant group studying work and employment into the 1980s (von Otter, 2002). A major impetus behind the expansion of work sociology in these countries was increased government research support, directed at areas such as quality of work life (particularly in Scandinavia) and the workplace effect of technological change. Given this substantial activity, when industrial relations did finally start to emerge in Europe it is not surprising that sociologists were one of the two leading groups of scholars to be involved. The case of sociologists Jean Daniel Reynaud in France and Friedrich Fürstenberg in Austria, both of whom helped start industrial relations in their counties, is illustrative.

Given this positive record, several aspects of European sociology have also inhibited or slowed the development of industrial relations. As already described, European sociology has had a particularly strong radical/Marxist component and has thus taken a critical view of industrial relations. Illustrative of this type of oppositional stance, Pierre Desmarez (2002) begins his historical review of work sociology in France with the statement, "The French-language sociology of work ... defines itself in opposition to the developments of mainstream industrial sociology in the United States that follow the line traced by the Hawthorne studies and *Management and the Worker*." Also apropos is the observation of Walther Müller-Jentsch (2002: 238):

As long as the neo-Marxist debate dominated German industrial sociology, there was no special interest in sociological research on management, because the so-called *Ableitungs-Marxismus* (deductive Marxism) was fully satisfied with the text-book tenets that capitalist management is only in existence for intensification and labor exploitation and maximization of profits.

After peaking in influence in the 1970s, the radical/Marxist tradition has declined in most areas of European sociology, thus opening the door wider for other sociologists to become involved in industrial relations. Unfortunately, also starting in the 1980s, the centre of gravity in the study of work and employment in many European countries began to shift from sociology to economics and business management, neither of which in their neo-liberal version are as hospitable to the field. With respect to Sweden, for example, Casten von Otter (2002) speaks of the "marginalization of sociology" and observes that research is guided "more by the business community, inspired by international consultants".

A second feature of European sociology that worked against the introduction of industrial relations was the expansive breadth and depth of sociology's research programme on work and employment. Part of the rationale for the industrial relations field in America was to promote an integrative, interdisciplinary approach that would surmount narrow departmental boundaries to the subject. One may also say it was an effort to broaden the orthodox economic treatment of labour with a dose of sociology and psychology. This project was less compelling in Europe, partly because orthodox economics was considerably less influential but also because sociology already covered so much of the territory. In France, the field of industrial sociology spawned a number of independent research institutes with different research programmes on work and employment. Hyman (1995a: 26) notes that "this has resulted in work closely parallel to the approach of Anglo-American industrial relations scholars". As another piece of evidence, Müller-Jentsch (2002: 222) states, "German industrial sociology includes a much broader field of study and research than in the Anglo-American countries (e.g., industrial relations, labour economics and labour law)." His point is then graphically demonstrated by the range of research topics covered in his review of German sociological research of the recent period (1980s to date): work in the service sector, small and medium-sized business, labour market segmentation and rise of contingent work, new technology and the structuring of workplaces, restructuring of organizations and the labour process, the sociology of management, industrial and labour relations, transformation of East Germany and the crisis of the "German model". One notes that in his review, industrial relations is presented as a special topic in industrial sociology identified as centred on "co-determination, trade unions and workplace representation". A final example comes from Sweden where, to promote a multidisciplinary perspective on work and employment, a new specialty field of *arbetsvetenskap* was created. The label for this new field is a direct literal translation of the French term *science du travail* (science of work), itself broadly associated with sociology (Hyman, 1995a).

Yet another factor behind the slow development of industrial relations as a significant area of teaching and research in European universities is the much greater role played by the discipline of law. Traditionally, teaching and research on labour, employment and collective bargaining took place in European law schools, reflecting the greater emphasis in these countries on political and juridical regulation of the employment relationship. Hyman (1995a) notes, for example, that sections on industrial relations and labour relations were established in a number of leading Italian law schools in the post-war period, because of the substantial corpus of employment law inherited from the fascist period and the enactment of subsequent legislation, such as the *Statuto dei Lavoratori* (Workers' Statute) of 1970, that further extended the legal structure. Illustrative of the importance of law is the fact that many of the best-known European scholars in industrial relations have legal backgrounds, such as Roger Blanpain, Manfred Weiss and Tiziano Treu, and law-oriented journals serve as a major publication outlet of industrial-relations-related research. With a substantial part of the study of labour and employment housed in law schools, establishing a social-science, interdisciplinary industrial relations programme becomes more difficult. Not only are the research traditions in the social sciences and law quite different; lawyers have also not been terribly keen on the interdisciplinary approach. Roger Blanpain (2002: 729–30) comments, for example, that academic legal scholars in Europe mostly pursue a "purely legal approach", while he combines labour law and industrial relations and thus concentrates "not only on the law, but also on the facts. ... But still I remain an exception." He goes on to recount how a research grant proposal he submitted to study how works councils operate in practice was turned down by the legal research committee because (p. 730) "this was not legal research, but food for social scientists and sociologists".

The European institutionalization of industrial relations

This long list of barriers and incompatibilities kept the industrial relations field as an institutionalized entity largely outside of continental Europe for many years. This situation persisted in Europe into the 1980s and only then started to change – to the point that by century's end, Europe had become the strongest area of new growth for the industrial relations field in the world. Although the depth and breadth of institutionalization of European industrial relations as an academic field remains on a considerably more modest scale than in North America and the United Kingdom, the field of industrial relations is nonetheless far more firmly embedded in Europe than in the 1980s. In terms of the actual practice of industrial relations, at least as conventionally defined in recent years, Europe may now be the the de facto centre of the field. In this spirit, Hyman (1995a: 13, emphasis added) observes, "In effect, the *realities* of industrial relations seem more firmly established elsewhere in western Europe today than in the United Kingdom itself." He goes on to note the opinion of many European labour scholars that they "have long been studying industrial relations without recognizing it!"

With regard to the Anglo-American model, no continental European university I am aware of has yet created a separate, stand-alone multi-disciplinary degree programme devoted to industrial relations. Nor in Europe do multidisciplinary research institutes or centres exist with the industrial relations name as found in North America, although Europe has a growing number of independent research institutes in the general area of work, employment and employment policy, as noted below.

Looking more broadly, however, reveals a number of indicators of industrial relations' growing presence in Europe. The number of European academics participating in and identifying themselves with the field is growing over time. Individual membership in the IIRA between 1986 and 2001 from 12 western and southern European countries, for example, increased by 70 per cent. At a national level, membership in the national industrial relations association in Germany was approximately twenty in the 1970s and is now more than 80. All together, 16 continental European countries have a national industrial relations association: Austria, Belgium, Cyprus, Denmark, Finland, France, Germany, Greece, Hungary, Italy, Netherlands, Norway, Poland, Portugal, Sweden and Turkey.

Also indicative of an upward trend is the creation of industrial relations textbooks and journals catering specifically to Europe and individual countries therein. Textbooks on industrial relations began to appear in the 1970s, such as Caire (1973) and Dmitri Weiss (1973) in France, Wil Albeda (1977) in the Netherlands, Gian Cella and Tiziano Treu (1982) in Italy, and Müller-Jentsch (1986) and Berndt Keller (1991) in Germany. Also appearing were a growing number of scholarly journals. Some of these journals reflect the traditional symbiosis between law and industrial relations in Europe, others are more social science oriented, and yet others are more nation specific. Several are also published in the United Kingdom but cover continental Europe. Examples include the *International Comparative Journal of Labour Law and Industrial*

Relations, *European Journal of Industrial Relations*, *European Industrial Relations Review*, *Industrielle Beziehungen – The German Journal of Industrial Relations*, and *Diritto delle Relazioni Industriali* (Italy). A number of journals in Europe also use the term "labour relations", such as *Bulletin of Comparative Labour Relations*. Although not containing the industrial relations term in the title, the journal *Economic and Industrial Democracy* (Sweden), edited for many years by Rudolf Meidner, is also an important outlet for industrial relations research.

Equally important as outlets for industrial relations research, if not more so, are a large variety of field journals. Some management journals are an outlet for industrial relations research, for example, such as the French HRM journal *Revue de gestion des ressources humaines*. Unlike in America, where labour economics has long been the dominant disciplinary influence on industrial relations, in most European countries sociology has played this role. Thus, in years past, and still to a significant degree today, specialized journals in the sociology of work are a major publication outlet for research on trade unions and other industrial-relations-related subjects in Europe. The best known is the internationally recognized French journal *Sociologie du travail*, but a number of others also exist (e.g., *Sociologia del Trabajo* in Spain).

The economics-oriented focus of North American industrial relations and the sociological (and political) focus of European industrial relations has given the two research streams a distinctly different hue. In North America, work and employment relations are most often modelled as a species of economic exchange with a central focus on the market context; in Europe work and employment relations are more frequently examined as social and political relationships. The situation is changing in Europe as the discipline of economics has become larger, more independent from law and commerce and more neoclassical in approach (Frey and Eichenberger, 1992). Labour economists are thus assuming an increasingly larger role in work and employment research in Europe and labour economics field journals, such as the *European Journal of Labor Economics* and *Labour Economics,* correspondingly become a more significant publishing outlet. To the degree that European experience parallels the American, this trend on net bodes ill for European industrial relations, given the incompatibility between neoclassical labour theory and the institutional labour theory that underlies industrial relations. Reasons for both hope and pessimism exist. Starting with pessimism, neoclassical economics is spreading widely in Europe and has become the lingua franca of European economists. One need only look at the research and publications of the current generation of labour economists in Germany, such as affiliated with the prestigious *Forschungsinstitut zur Zukunft der Arbeit*

(IZA, Institute for the Study of Labor) to see this trend face to face. It is nearly all in the neoclassical mould, relatively little focused on industrial relations issues, and generally promotes greater labour market deregulation and flexibility. But, on the hopeful side, heterodox economics remains alive and well in Europe, perhaps more so than in America. Of particular relevance to industrial relations, a resurgence in institutional economics has occurred in Europe, carrying forward some of the heritage of the early German political economy but for the most part taking a much more analytical approach inspired by the work of Coase, Williamson and other modern institutionalists in the United States (Kaspar and Streit, 1998; Mantzavinos, 2001). The German-based *Journal of Institutional and Theoretical Economics*, for example, has its roots in *Zeitschrift für die gesamte Staatswissenschaft*, a periodical started by the German political economists in 1844. The work of other heterodox economists, such as Robert Boyer of the French regulation school, also stands out as particularly useful for industrial relations.

In addition to journals, the growth of industrial relations in Europe is revealed by the expanding number of specialized institutes and centres devoted to labour and employment research. Many are university or government supported, but union federations and employers' associations in Europe also operate specialized research institutes and foundations, less commonly found in Anglo-American countries. Examples of such institutes and centres include:

Austria:	Betriebswirtschaftszentrum, Institut für Staatswissenschaft [Centre for Business Administration], University of Vienna
Belgium:	Institut des sciences du travail (IST) [Institute for Labour Relations], Catholic University of Louvain
Denmark:	Forskningscenter for Arbejdsmarkeds-og Organisationsstudier (FAOS), Sociologisk Institut [Employment Relations Research Centre], University of Copenhagen
Finland:	Löntagarnas forskningsinstitut [Labour Institute for Economic Research], Helsinki
France:	Institut de recherches économiques et sociales (IRES) [Economic and Social Research Institute], Paris
Germany:	Hans Böckler Foundation, Düsseldorf
Ireland:	Centre for Employment Relations and Organizational Performance (CEROP), Smurfit Graduate School of Business, University College Dublin
Italy:	Fondazione Istituto per il Lavoro (IPL) [Institute for Labour], Bologna

Netherlands: ELS/ISS, Employment & Labour Studies Programme,
              Institute of Social Studies, The Hague
Norway: Fafo, Senter for Studier av Fagbevegelse og Arbeidsliv
              [Institute for Applied Social Science], Oslo
Portugal: Dinâmia, Centro de Estudos sobre a Mudança
              Socioeconómica [Research Centre on Socio-economic
              Change], Lisbon
Spain: Fundación Centro de Iniciativas e Investigaciones Europeas
              en el Mediterráneo (CIREM) [Foundation Centre for
              European Initiatives and Research in the Mediterranean],
              Barcelona
Sweden: Arbetslivsinstitutet (NIWL) [National Institute for
              Working Life], Stockholm

At the EU level there are also several new research institutes related to industrial relations. The most noteworthy is the European Industrial Relations Observatory (EIRO). Created in 1997 and governed as a tripartite organization, EIRO is a project of the European Foundation for the Improvement of Living and Working Conditions, headquartered in Dublin, Ireland. Funded largely by the EU, EIRO sponsors research and disseminates books, reports and current news about industrial relations developments in all the Member States of the EU, as well as at the EU level itself. Its monthly digest is *EIRO Observer*.

The topics covered in EIRO publications provide one indication of how the subject boundaries of industrial relations are perceived in contemporary Europe. One representative publication is the booklet commemorating EIRO's fifth anniversary, entitled *Towards a qualitative dialogue in industrial relations*. It states (p. 3, emphasis added):

> Its [the booklet's] aim is to explore some of the recent new developments in industrial relations in Europe. The emphasis is on the processes and outcomes of *collective bargaining and dialogue between the social partners*, rather than on labour law or government initiatives. In the booklet we have chosen to focus on five main themes, illustrative of innovative developments in industrial relations: lifelong learning; equality, diversity and non-discrimination; health and safety at work; flexibility and the work–life balance; and social dialogue and worker involvement.

Three points from this quotation deserve mention. First, the focus of industrial relations is centred on trade unionism and collective bargaining, rather than the more expansive concept of the employment relationship. In this respect interpretation of the term industrial relations in Europe broadly corresponds to the popular "labour–management" meaning of the term in the

United Kingdom and the United States. Second, the phrase "dialogue between the social partners", typically referred to by the more compact term social dialogue, illustrates that industrial relations in Europe also covers a subject not typically found in the Anglo-American version of the field. To some degree, social dialogue is simply an alternative term for collective bargaining, or collective negotiations between employers and unions, and thus adds nothing new in a substantive sense. But social dialogue goes beyond collective bargaining in several respects. For example, social dialogue presumes a significant element of tripartism (or "concertation") in labour–management relations with unions, employers' associations and governments in mutual discussion and consultation at a strategic level, rather than the bilateral bargaining process with government as a detached observer in the United Kingdom and United States. It also assumes a more centralized form of negotiation between high-level (sectoral or even national) union and employers' association representatives – rather than the decentralized firm and plant-level bargaining more commonly found in the United States and the United Kingdom. Social dialogue also entails a societal-level commitment to cooperation and harmony between unions and employers – as indicated by the replacement of the terms "unions" and "employers" with the term "social partners", in contrast to the more overtly adversarial Anglo-American model of union–employer relations. The third point from the quote is that European industrial relations also covers a wide variety of workplace problems and practices, such as quality of work life, health and safety and other such topics, although typically these are discussed within the context of collective bargaining and social dialogue.

Another encouraging sign of growth for the industrial relations field in Europe is the surge in books and journal articles authored on the subject by European scholars. Writing in 1994, Hyman observed (p. 1), "A decade ago there was a dearth of literature on European industrial relations. Most of what was available was restricted to a small number of countries, and was often confined to the description of formal institutions." By the early 2000s, the situation is vastly improved.

From 1990 to the present time, several dozen books and many dozen journal articles have been authored by European scholars on aspects of industrial relations. A significant portion of these studies focus on individual countries, but a growing number are comparative (cross-national). Representative of this new genre of research, for example, are *Industrial relations in small and medium-sized enterprises* (Blanpain and Biagi, 1993), *Industrial relations between command and market* (Schienstock, Thompson and Traxler, 1997), *European Union – European industrial relations?* (Lecher and Platzer, 1998),

Employment and industrial relations in Europe (Gold and Weiss, 1999), *The Europeanization of industrial relations* (Eberwein, Tholen and Schuster, 2002); and *Industrial relations and European integration* (Keller and Platzer, 2003).

The title of *The Europeanization of industrial relations*, cited above, is meant to capture the integration of industrial relations systems across countries as the European Union project progresses. It also illustrates another trend – the adaptation or "Europeanization" of the Anglo-American subject of industrial relations so it better fits European institutions and traditions. In a theme to be explored in more detail below, part of this adaptation process involves reconstituting the industrial relations concept so it has a broader, more generic meaning that transcends particular institutional arrangements. Illustratively, the authors provide this relatively expansive description of the subject matter of industrial relations (p. 2):

> Our general interpretation of the term industrial relations in the first instance is that it covers:
> * economic exchange processes
> * the social relationships and conflict between capital and labour; and
> * the contracts, norms and institutions issuing from these social relationships.
>
> Specific areas of study include:
> * workplace and company organization;
> * collective bargaining;
> * trade unions and employers' associations; and
> * government regulations and legislative standardization.

They go on to say (p. 2), "we interpret the Europeanization of industrial relations as a socio-political process, that is: it is based on representation of different interests and therefore requires political regulation – and it is also socially based, and therefore presenting a specific interrelation of interaction".

Why is the field of industrial relations finally coming to Europe? Several parts of the answer have already been given. But there are others.

One is the role of the IIRA. The IIRA is discussed at length in Chapter 10 so only brief discussion of its contribution is provided here. However, the IIRA has undoubtedly been the most important institution behind the successful transference of the industrial relations field to Europe. Few scholars in Europe had even heard of the industrial relations field before the IIRA was created in 1966 and, as indicated previously, teaching and research in industrial relations did not exist. The IIRA effectively jump-started the field in Europe by substantially increasing the name recognition and visibility of the industrial relations concept, providing an opportunity for European scholars interested in labour and employment issues to meet their counterparts from other countries and learn about the Anglo-American industrial relations field, and actively encouraging the formation of industrial relations associations in individual countries across western Europe. The IIRA's effectiveness in these matters was greatly facilitated by the decision of the founders to locate the IIRA's headquarters in Europe (Geneva) and affiliate it with the ILO. The IIRA then contributed to a steady increase in interest and activity in industrial relations over the next three decades by helping develop a community of European scholars interested in industrial relations, providing opportunities for these scholars to meet and present research at a variety of regional conferences, regional congresses and world congresses, and promoting greater international contacts, exchanges of ideas and interest in comparative and international studies.

A second factor deserving note is the energetic efforts of several leading European academics to spread the industrial relations field to Europe. Certainly viewed over the long term, the Belgium labour lawyer and industrial relations expert Roger Blanpain deserves highlight. Blanpain has been a tireless promoter of industrial relations in Europe through a variety of venues: the activities of the Institute for Labour Relations at the Catholic University of Louvain, editorship (or co-editorship) of several journals and periodicals (e.g., *Bulletin of Labour Relations* and *International Encyclopedia of Labour Law and Industrial Relations*, with C. Engels), editorship of numerous books and conference proceedings on industrial relations, and presidency of the IIRA. Among the next generation, a second person deserving highlight is Richard Hyman, now at the London School of Economics and formerly at the United Kingdom's Warwick IRRU. Over the last decade Hyman has been a major influence in promoting the study of industrial relations in Europe and fostering greater integration of and interaction between Anglo-American and continental European research communities. He has done this partly through the founding and editorship of the *European Journal of Industrial Relations*, the editorship (or co-editorship) of several substantial books on European industrial relations (e.g., Ferner and Hyman, 1998), and his own research on European industrial relations (e.g., Hyman, 2001a, b). Thus, in this conceptualization the subject domain of industrial relations is not labour–management relations but alternative modes of political regulation of employment relations.

A third factor of considerable practical influence has been the emergence of English as the lingua franca of the worldwide academic community. Would industrial relations have spread across Europe and the rest of the world if some other language, such as German, French or Chinese, had instead become the lingua franca? The answer is doubtful, given the industrial relations field's origins and predominance in English-speaking countries. Today, nearly all presentations and papers at large scholarly meetings or in books with an international audience are done in English and thus the term industrial relations, and the constellation of ideas that it embodies, achieves growing universal recognition. Being conversant in English is also a key passport for European academics who want to achieve research recognition outside their home countries. Ironically, some researchers who are top figures in their home countries have little international recognition because they do not participate in events such as IIRA congresses or publish in English-language books and journals, while others may not be in the top tier of scholars domestically but are widely known internationally because they do use these access points.

A fourth factor that has helped spread the industrial relations field in Europe is the ongoing programme of greater European economic, political and social integration (Hoffman et al., 2003; Keller and Platzer, 2003). Integration has proceeded along several fronts. Two of these fronts are, respectively, greater integration of the markets for goods and services and greater integration of financial markets, including a common monetary regime. The integration of goods markets began in 1957 with the Treaty of Rome and has been substantially strengthened and broadened by the Single European Act (1987), the formation of the European Union in 1992 under the provisions of the Treaty of Maastricht, and the addition of many new Member States (from the original six members in 1957 to 25 in 2004). Financial market integration made a major step forward when in 1999 the countries of the EU agreed to eliminate national currencies and create a European Monetary Union (EMU) and one medium of exchange, the euro, under the control of a European central bank. The EMU was fully implemented in January 2002. Member States also agreed to give up a significant degree of discretion over fiscal policies, particular regarding the size of budget deficits.

The other area of European integration concerns labour markets and social policy. This area has proven the most controversial, unsettled and slow to take form. An initial but modest commitment to integrating social and labour market conditions was contained in the Single European Act. It expressed a commitment to a "social dimension" of integration. This was followed in 1989 by adoption of the Social Charter of Fundamental Social Rights of Workers (not signed by the United Kingdom until 1998). Although not legally binding, it carried considerable moral force as a "solemn declaration" of the countries' collective commitment to promote workers' rights of participation, representation and minimal social and workplace standards (Addison and Siebert, 1992). The Social Charter led to an Action Programme drawn up by the European Commission, proposing 50 measures to promote and realize the social dimension of the single European market. These initiatives were given new impetus with the signing of the Treaty of Maastricht in 1992. The Treaty contained a separate Protocol on Social Policy which authorized the 11 members of the EU (again, except the United Kingdom) to use the institutions and mechanisms of the Treaty to develop social policy in the Community (Lecher and Platzer, 1998). Under the Protocol, a qualified majority of Members are empowered to enact minimum social and labour requirements concerning health and safety, working conditions, representation and participation of employees, social protection (e.g., termination of workers), information and consultation, equality of treatment in employment between men and women, and integration of persons excluded from the labour market. The best example of such a requirement is European Works Council Directive (1994). The Protocol also pledged the Member States to promote and utilize the process of social dialogue for purposes of high-level communication, consultation and negotiation with the social partners (representatives of employers, workers and independent occupations). No legal basis has yet been provided, however, for supranational (EU-level) collective bargaining.

The formation of the EU and the pursuit of the social dimension has promoted the development and spread of the industrial relations field in Europe in several ways. Most prosaically, the EU through its various organs and commissions has been a generous source of funding for conferences, research projects and publications in industrial relations, in particular the establishment of EIRO, as earlier noted.

The social integration of labour markets and employment policy has also naturally focused attention on each country's set of institutions, laws and practices. The most commonly used concept for framing this discourse is an industrial relations system. As discussed more fully below, the industrial relations systems concept has proven to be particularly effective entrée for the field into Europe and is frequently encountered in discussions about the EU project.

A significant worry for proponents of EU social policy is whether the project for European integration will help protect or undermine existing social and labour standards in the high-wage countries (Streeck, 1994; Jacobi, 2001). If market integration proceeds ahead of social integration, market forces will lead to "social regime competition" as capital and jobs flow to lower-cost sites of production within the EU. At its worst, this process may lead to a race to the bottom and social dumping. Concern on these matters is also heightened by the very high and persistent unemployment levels in major European countries and the extra pressure this exerts on Member States to lower social standards. And, of course, solving this problem at the EU level still leaves the problem of global competition to be dealt with. No other field in the social sciences is more relevant to this issue than industrial relations, for the field was born out of concern to balance market competition with minimum acceptable social standards and has devoted nearly a century's worth of scholarship to solving this problem.

In addition, the formation of the EU and the social regulations it has created have brought to the forefront numerous issues for research and debate that are solidly in the area of industrial relations. Numerous books and articles written by European authors (e.g., Visser, 2001; Auer and Gazier, 2002), for example, have explored the consequences of EU integration for collective bargaining, the accomplishments and prospects of social dialogue, and the future of European corporatist employment relations. EU social directives, such as those on works councils, have also elicited considerable academic interest, again drawing scholars into the field of industrial relations.

Moving on, yet another positive development for European industrial relations is the new market economies and pluralist societies of Central and Eastern Europe. Under the communist regimes, industrial relations had no place in either theory or practice. Marxism seeks to solve the problem of industrial relations by eliminating capitalists and private property, thus eliminating exploitation and giving the working class control of the state. The project of industrial relations – achieving class accommodation and integration in a capitalist, pluralist economy – thus has no place or rationale. Further, the major institution of industrial relations, the trade union, changes from an autonomous bargaining agent to a "transmission belt" between the ruling party at the top and the workers at the bottom of the economic pyramid. Thus Gerd Schienstock and Franz Traxler (1997: 2–3) observe, "it is definitely a point of controversy whether industrial relations even exist at all in socialist countries". A prime example is the effort of the Polish government to suppress the independent Solidarity trade union (Morawski, 2001). Now all the nations of Central and Eastern Europe are struggling to put in place a new industrial relations system and find the right mix of markets, trade unions and government control. This development is a major opportunity for the industrial relations field because it opens up an entirely new "market" for teaching, research and problem solving, reflected in numerous books and articles on Central and Eastern European industrial relations (e.g., Hanke and Mense-Petermann, 2001; Stanojevic, 2003) and the growing number of scholars from those countries that participate in the field.

The final factor that has facilitated the entry of the industrial relations field into Europe is the adoption by European scholars of the industrial relations systems concept. As demonstrated above, trade unionism and collective bargaining form a core part of the subject of industrial relations in

Europe. However, if one looks through the European literature for the single most referenced industrial relations concept, the one that clearly dominates is an *industrial relations system* (Hoffman et al., 2003). Besides providing a common term of reference, the more important function of the industrial relations systems concept is that it provides the basis for a generic theoretical approach to industrial relations that frees the field from the limitations of being associated with one particular institution or institutional framework.

At one level, Europeans use the term industrial relations system as shorthand for the labour sector of the economy. In this guise, the industrial relations systems concept is entirely descriptive, albeit nonetheless of value to the extent that it solidifies industrial relations in European discourse. At another level, however, European scholars use the industrial relations system idea as a theoretical construct. Commonly, an industrial relations system is equated in European circles with a system of regulation or governance – the regime of rules and authority relations that structure the employment relationship and determines its key outcomes. In this sense, it is broadly consistent with Dunlop's original formulation and the idea of a web of rules.

Although not always labelled industrial relations, the most interesting and forward-moving research programme on theories of the employment relationship and regimes of employment regulation is now coming out of Europe (including the United Kingdom). Noteworthy books include Wolfgang Streeck's *Social institutions and economic performance: Studies of industrial relations in advanced capitalist economies* (1992), Crouch's *Industrial relations and European state traditions* (1993), Hollingsworth and Boyer's *Contemporary capitalism: The embeddedness of institutions* (eds., 1997), David Marsden's *A theory of employment relations systems* (1999), and Peter Hall and David Soskice's *Varieties of capitalism: The institutional foundations of comparative advantage* (2001). Some of these works are directly linked to institutional economics, while others (e.g., the French regulation school) have clear roots in that tradition (Basle, 2001). This type of European-based theory, together with related theorizing in the field of socio-economics, defines the leading edge in modern-day industrial relations.

Having surveyed the general situation for the industrial relations field in Europe, I now briefly examine the development of industrial relations in continental Europe's two largest economies, France and Germany. France represents in broad outline the Latin region of Europe, while Germany is an exemplar of the Germanic region.

France

The central fact about France is that of all the major countries of western Europe it is the one in which the field of industrial relations has the shallowest roots and least institutionalized presence. Christian Dufour and Adelheid Hege (1997: 338) make the following observation:

> In France there is no single field of study called 'industrial relations'. Economics, law and sociology have developed specialisms with a focus on 'labour' that relate primarily to the criteria and issues of the parent discipline. In so far as 'industrial relations' itself is a matter for discussion, it has to respond at the same time to the concerns within each discipline, reflect on the debate between disciplines, and respond to the 'social demands' from political discourse or the state. For this reason, it is particularly dangerous to attempt to assess the state of industrial relations research in France.

Part of the explanation for industrial relations' marginal status in France can probably be laid at the door of cultural differences and nationalistic rivalries, given the Anglo-Saxon origins of the industrial relations field, the chilly reception Anglo-Saxon institutions and ideas sometimes have in France (and vice versa), and the fact that in another Latin country – Italy – industrial relations has a much stronger presence. Other factors also enter, however, and probably play a substantially larger role. Prime candidates are the strong legacy of class conflict, anarcho-syndicalism and communism in the French labour movement; strong ideological opposition to power sharing on the part of French employers; the slow development of bilateral collective bargaining; the extensive legal regulation of employment relations; intellectual traditions that favour strong disciplinary boundaries and Marxist-oriented perspectives; and the intellectual imperialism felt by many French legal scholars toward the subject of law in the employment relationship.

To an outside observer unacquainted with the French employment relations system and national history, the marginal status of the industrial relations field in France is puzzling. The industrialism process started in the early part of the nineteenth century and soon thereafter the first craft unions emerged among printers, weavers and railway workers. Later in the century, the labour movement grew in size and power, and national union federations emerged, as did a definable and increasingly restive working class. With strikes and class conflict growing, France also confronted the Social Question at the turn of the century. After the First World War, France enacted the first collective bargaining legislation, and reformist leaders such as French trade unionist Léon Jouhaux and Minister of Armaments and first ILO Director-General Albert

Thomas sought to move the employers and socialist/syndicalist-dominated trade unions toward rapprochement. France also experienced a great leap in unionization and enactment of a broad programme of social and labour legislation during the Popular Front government of Léon Blum in the mid-1930s, parallel in revolutionary scope to the New Deal in the United States. After the Second World War, France emerged as a major economic power with large, technologically sophisticated companies, a substantial-sized labour movement and a well-established and extensive university system. At the present time, although union density is small (approximately 10 per cent), more than 90 per cent of French employees are covered by collective agreements. The background conditions thus seem conducive for a field of industrial relations, whether of this name or another.

The fact that neither the Anglo-Saxon variety of the field of industrial relations nor a French indigenous equivalent developed to any significant degree in the post-Second World War period could be viewed as a case of "French exceptionalism" (Sellier, 1978). An alternative perspective is that France simply mirrored larger European (and world) experience, but in more accentuated terms, and the development and growth of the field is more nearly a case of Anglo-Saxon exceptionalism (Rojot, 1989). A third view is that industrial relations is simply one of a variety of ways to structure or package teaching and research on work, labour and employment, and France chose one of the alternative approaches. On this third view, Caire (1996: 27) quips (in French), "one might have done industrial relations ... without knowing it".

The low presence and institutionalization of industrial relations in France appears to reflect all three perspectives. Thus, in the above discussion of Europe, practically every reason cited for why industrial relations only slowly came to Europe applies as well to France as to Germany, Italy or Scandinavia. On the other hand, most expert observers agree that the French system of employment relations is indeed unique in important ways. Frederick Meyers (1981: 171–2), for example, states that "What distinguished France from most of its European neighbours, as well as from the United States, was the strength and importance in union ideology gained by anarchosyndicalism, [leading to] a sort of French working-class cultural milieu of extreme distrust of government and employers, bitterness at the failure of 'revolution' after 'revolution' fundamentally to alter the class and power structure of French society in any way perceptively favourable to workers." In a similar vein, Jean-Francois Amadieu (1995: 345) states, "unquestionably, it is in France that the number of union organizations striving to represent the same worker is highest, the divisions are the deepest and the clashes the most violent", while Rose (1979: 132) describes a system caught between the employer "with a mania over his own personal authority" and trade unions more concerned with "preparing the labour force for a revolutionary effort, rather than that of securing a steady succession of higher or novel material benefits under the existing dispensation". Evidently, in such an environment the philosophy of accommodation, rationalist managerialism and pragmatic collective bargaining promoted by industrial relations will have difficulty taking root.

These unique aspects of French employment relations, along with the other factors earlier described for all of Europe, have over the years seriously retarded acceptance and development of the field of industrial relations in French universities and the business world. To some degree, this problem merely reflects the different way the French have organized and structured teaching and research on work, labour and employment within universities. In a fundamental respect, however, the fractionated and non-institutionalized condition of the industrial relations field in France mirrors the same underlying conditions in the social phenomenon (the industrial relations system) that it seeks to study.

In the United States, the history of the industrial relations field finds its intellectual roots in the development of institutional labour economics. In France, the roots of the field are in the field of sociology and, in particularly, *la sociologie du travail* – the sociology of work. The ancestral figure in French industrial relations is thus Emile Durkheim, whose studies at the turn of the century on the social consequences of division of labour and anomie laid the foundation for all future sociological research in industry.

The first emergence in France of the industrial relations concept did not occur, however, until the 1950s. But several anticipatory steps are noteworthy. Two early pioneers of what was to become industrial relations are Pierre Laroque and Paul Durand. Laroque taught a class on "social problems" at the Institut d'études politiques in Paris and in 1938 published *Les rapports entre patrons et ouvriers* (*The relations between employers and workers*). Durand is considered the pioneer of French scholarship on collective bargaining law (da Costa, 2003).

Also playing an important role in setting the stage of French industrial relations was sociologist George Friedmann. On this subject Rose (1979: 28) states:

> *Sociologie du travail* originated in a series of seminars on the nature and evolution of the labour process under modern conditions that was inaugurated in 1946 by George Friedmann and continued until the mid-fifties. Every investigator who by the early sixties had made a name for himself, and several of the figures who now dominate French Sociology as a whole, participated at some point or another in these meetings – or perhaps one could say these confrontations.

Friedmann introduced to the sociology of work several attributes that linked it closely to the Anglo-American field of industrial relations. He insisted, for example, that theorizing had to be based on field-level empirical investigation. He also sought to define the intellectual territory of the sociology of work quite broadly, per the observation of Desmarez (2002: 203) that "the new specialty was supposed to deal with all aspects of work, as well as the relationship between work and society". Friedmann was, on the other hand, a "fellow traveller" with the French Communist Party, at least into the 1950s when he grew disillusioned, and was a strong critic of certain philosophies of Elton Mayo and American human relations.

Of the many students inspired by Friedmann to pursue an academic career in the sociology of work, three went on to head their own *laboratoires*. Each established a major scholarly reputation and one is widely considered to be the founder of French industrial relations. The three men are Jean-Daniel Reynaud at the Conservatoire nationale des arts et métiers (holder of the George Friedmann chair of work sociology); Michel Crozier at the Centre de sociologie des organizations; and Alain Touraine at the Laboratoire de sociologie industrielle.

It is Reynaud whom most people in the field today consider to be the founding father of French industrial relations. On one level, this claim is not obvious. In 1956, for example, economist Robert Goetz-Girey is credited with teaching the first class in France with the name "industrial relations" (Caire, 1996). He then published the contents in book form under the title *Cours de relations industrielles*. Reynaud, on the other hand, did not publish his influential book, *Les syndicats en France*, until 1963 and it did not contain the term industrial relations in the title. Indeed, the first book by Reynaud to feature this term in the title did not appear until 1990: *Les systèmes de relations professionnelles: Examen critique d'une théorie* (with François Eyraud, Jean Saglio and Catherine Paradeise), a collection of essays commemorating the thirtieth anniversary of Dunlop's *Industrial relations systems*.

Instead, Reynaud's foundational influence came from another source. According to Rose (1979), Reynaud was the first person to introduce into French labour research the Dunlopian concept of an industrial relations system, the regulative function of the web of rules and Flander's corollary concept of job regulation. Earlier articles on these ideas had appeared in *Sociologie du travail* by Anglo-American authors. Reynaud was invited by the Club Jean Moulin (a political club of engineers, teachers, managers and civil servants that, according to Rose (p. 123), was "technocratic [in style] but compensated by a real concern with dialogue and participation") to explore these new ideas more fully. The title of Reynaud's book, according to Rose, could as well have been *Is there a French industrial relations system?* In the spirit of Dunlop's book, Reynaud developed the idea of an industrial relations system and then did extensive fieldwork to describe its empirical features. He related in an interview that the latter feature of the book was particularly noteworthy at the time because it represented a break with Marxist tradition in that he eschewed deductive arguments for visiting factories and determining "the facts" from personal investigation and interviews. In his work, Reynaud discovered that a large gap existed "between the affirmation of the class struggle and the necessity for revolution and the everyday practice of the unions ... A remote doctrine co-exists with an empiricism of deeds" (quoted in Rose, p. 138). This gap, he diagnosed, was caused by lack of supportive institutions and practices at the workplace and an ideology of "disassociation", leading to a dysfunctional system of work regulation that promoted strife, instability and emotionalism over pragmatism, order and cooperation. To solve this problem, Reynaud concludes (ibid.), "it is very necessary that intermediaries [e.g., trade unions with secure rights of recognition and negotiation] be set up between the solitary man and the state [to act] ... as an indispensable mediator". Translated into standard pluralist/institutionalist terms, Reynaud is arguing that the industrial relations system in France needed to be better instititionalized and the web of rules formalized and fleshed out, particularly in bridging between the macro (national) level and micro (shopfloor) level. This intermediate meso level, and the collective actors that fill it, has of course been the standard subject matter of industrial relations.

In addition to bringing the industrial relations system idea to France, Reynaud helped institutionalize the field of industrial relations in more tangible ways. He was, for example, a charter member in 1966 of the IIRA. In the same year, he took the lead in founding the French Industrial Relations Association, of which Laroque served as first president. In the early years, according to Reynaud, the Association had great difficulty surviving because representatives of employers and unions did not want to sit at the same table with each other, nor did even the representatives from different unions.

From 1976 to 1979, Reynaud served as president of the IIRA. In his presidential address (Reynaud, 1980: 2), he highlights one of the cornerstone ideas of post-Second World War industrial relations: "Industrial conflict in post-capitalist society has become less violent because its existence has been accepted and its form socially regularized. This refers to the development and growing experience of occupational organizations, particularly labor unions."

Several other people also deserve mention as significant figures in the birth and early development of industrial relations in France. The first is Yves Delamotte, whom Rose (1979: 137) refers to as one of the "two most influential figures in this emergent 'French school' of Industrial Relations" (the other being Reynaud). Delamotte's influence came largely from his position as director of the Institut des sciences sociales du travail (ISST), established in 1951. The ISST was a major sponsor of social science research projects and Delamotte used his position and interest in industrial relations to promote a wide range of studies on it.

Also important was François Sellier. Sellier was an economist but in the institutional tradition. Sellier wrote several influential books on industrial relations and founded an interdisciplinary research centre, Laboratoire d'économie et de sociologie du travail (LEST), in Aix en Provence. The centre established an international reputation for workplace studies and became known as the "Aix School". Janice McCormick (1986: vii) states of Sellier's book *Politiques d'education et organization industrielle en France et en Allemagne* (1982, with Maurice and Silvestre), "Similar to John Dunlop's theory of an industrial relations system, their societal analysis concretizes the links among the different levels of the social system."

A third name to mention is Jacques Delors. Delors was an economist who early in his career published studies in industrial relations. Later, he served in the French government as economics and finance minister and then for three terms as president of the European Commission (executive body of the European Community, now EU).

Since its founding in the mid-1960s, the industrial relations field in France has remained small and relatively marginal. In his historical review of French industrial relations, Caire (1996: 27) states (translated from the French), "What strikes the observer when comparing the French system of teaching industrial relations as compared to what exists in the U.S. is essentially three characteristics: its youth, its dispersion, and its lack of homogeneity." Industrial relations has never succeeded in establishing a presence in French universities as an officially recognized major or programme of study. A course on industrial relations might be offered in a scattered number of universities and several textbooks have been written. Among the first were Caire's *Les relations industrielles* (1973) and *Relations industrielles: Acteurs, auteurs, faits, tendances* by Dmitri Weiss (1973). Despite these forward steps, the very concept of industrial relations remains ill defined and problematic within France. Most often, the opening wedge for industrial relations in French universities in the 1980s was, somewhat paradoxically, the new schools of business and management, spurred in part by the labour unrest of the previous decade and belief that managers needed to be trained to deal with social conflict. Some industrial relations courses continue to be taught in these programmes, although HRM has displaced a significant share.

In the world of research, the state of industrial relations is only marginally better. Research on industrial relations in French sociology has substantially declined. At no time past or present has France had an academic journal devoted to industrial relations. A small group of French academics, such as Jacques Rojot, Isabel da Costa, Udo Rehfeldt, Jean Saglio, Alain Chouraqui and Antoine Lyon-Caen, have developed international visibility in industrial relations through English-language publications and extensive participation in international conferences and projects. Nevertheless, this has not translated equally well into higher visibility for the industrial relations field within France. Many French academics do not participate in international conferences or publish in English so their work remains largely unknown outside the Francophone countries.

In the 1980s some progress was made in establishing an internal network of industrial relations scholars in France and generating a self-sustaining research programme. France has a system of government-funded research centres, most of which are located in the Centre national de la recherche scientifique (CNRS). These centres are separate from universities (but with close ties) and have a large number of professional staff who work full time on individual and sponsored research. In 1982, the representative trade unions and government jointly founded a new centre, the IRES in Paris. The IRES set up four permanent research teams to pursue different streams of research on work and employment topics; one was devoted to industrial relations. Building on this, a network of a dozen research centres with an interest in industrial relations, including the LEST and IRES, came together in the 1980s under a CNRS umbrella structure called the Groupement de Recherche (GDR) "Relations professionnelles: Négociations et conflits". This network produced five books and a number of articles on industrial relations. A formal relationship was also established with the three industrial relations programmes in Quebec. In the mid-1990s, however, the CNRS withdrew funding and this GDR was forced to disband. Informal networking and collaboration continue but the net impact was to significantly undercut the perceptible, if modest, forward progress of the industrial relations field in France.

Germany

The Webbs' *Industrial democracy* was translated into German the year after it was published in England, but to this date has not been translated into French. If history is any guide, one would expect that the field of industrial relations would also have come to Germany well in advance of France. Surprisingly, however, the reverse is the case. The French Industrial Relations Association was founded in 1966 but its German counterpart was not launched until 1970 and began life with only nine members. Likewise, the first textbook in Germany devoted to industrial relations was not published until the mid-1980s. After a slow start, however, the industrial relations field in Germany in the last 20 years has registered modest but sustained growth, while at least in recent years the French industrial relations field has suffered some decline in vitality. The reasons for this disparate behaviour are interesting and are briefly described below.

Germany, like all western European countries, has an extensive pre-history of industrial relations. Indeed, perhaps the most influential theorist of all times in industrial relations came from Germany: Karl Marx. The roots of conventional industrial relations, however, find their location elsewhere.

Germany in the mid–late nineteenth century was preoccupied with the Social Question. Central to this was the conflict between capital and labour and the best strategy to solve it. Several options were advocated.

A small wing of German "Manchester" economists followed Adam Smith and took up the cause of classic liberalism. As the nineteenth century came to an end, however, they largely lost influence.

Most of the battle of ideas was over reform versus revolution (the *Strategiedebatte*, or "strategy debate"), with the industrialists and aristocracy looking on from the right with growing apprehension. On the side of revolution, Germany had the largest and best-organized socialist movement in the world in the late nineteenth century. It was, however, split into a variety of factions loosely organized around the Social Democratic Party (SPD) and offshoots. A group led by people such as Wilhelm Liebknecht, August Bebel and (later) Rosa Luxemburg followed a line broadly consistent with Marx and Engels; another followed Ferdinand Lassalle (founder of one branch of the SPD) with greater emphasis on socialism through electoral politics; yet another followed Eduard Bernstein (after his split with Marxism) and his theory of reform through evolutionary socialism (Günter and Leminsky, 1978; Berghahn and Karsten, 1987). Although the specifics differed, these groups were united by an anti-capitalist ideology and commitment to move toward socialism, either through electoral victory or revolution. Toward that end, the socialists were active in promoting trade unionism, with the idea that unions were the industrial arm of the Socialist Party: conceived of as being organized to secure short-run economic gains but with the higher goal of mobilizing the working class for political takeover of the state and the replacement (or substantial transformation) of the capitalist system.

Arrayed against the Marxists and socialists were a variety of reform groups. Most important for the development of capital–labour relations were the

German adherents of what became known (inaccurately) as "state socialism". As described in Chapter 1, the intellectual architects of state socialism were the German political economists associated with the historical–social school of economics and the Verein für Sozialpolitik, while the political architect of what is often called state socialism was Chancellor Otto von Bismarck. Also comprising an important constituency of state socialism were the Christian socialists and reformist Christian democratic trade unions.

The Social Question was widely acknowledged in Germany in the last three decades of the nineteenth century as the most pressing domestic problem. Gustav von Schmoller, a leader of the Verein economists, told readers in his article "The Social Question and the Prussian State" (1874, cited in Pyle, 1974) that class antagonisms had become so intense in Germany that unless drastic actions were taken by the government the country would soon come face to face with social revolution. In this respect, the *Verein* economists agreed that Marx and the socialists were mostly correct in their critique of laissez-faire capitalism, but they nonetheless strongly opposed Marxism and the allied political movement of social democracy. Their preferred approach was a state-guided market economy and state-led programme of social reform – a programme they called *Sozialpolitik*. As described by Gustav Schmoller (quoted in Pyle, 1974: 134), "They [the Verein economists] are sincerely for a constitutional system, but they do not want an alternative class rule by the various antagonistic economics classes; they want a strong state which legislates above egoistic class interests, administers with justice, protects the weak and elevates the lower classes." Another member of the Verein group was Max Weber. Weber, like Schmoller, agreed with a portion of the Marxian critique but sought to develop an alternative solution. Toward this end, he shifted attention from the labour process to the administrative process and sought to use rationalism and science to bring legitimacy, efficiency and fairness to the exercise of power and authority in the firm.

A number of pioneering studies that set the stage for more modern research on labour and employer–employee relations were published in Germany in the 1890–1910 period. An early work on trade unions was Wilhelm Kulemann (1890), *Die Gewerkschaftsbewegung*, while the labour question was explored in Heinrich Herkner's *Die Arbeiterfrage* (1895). Ferdinand Toennies (1897), founder of the German Sociological Association, published a detailed empirical analysis of the great strike of Hamburg dock workers, "Der Hamburger Streik von 1896/97". Also of note was the first empirical opinion survey on employer–employee relations: Adolf Levenstein's *Die Arbeiterfrage* (1912). And, of course, Weber contributed a number of significant works.

Without doubt, the policy programme of the Verein economists was directly in the tradition of what later became industrial relations. Müller-Jentsch (2002: 223) states that their goal was to "establish social fairness between capital and labor". To achieve social fairness, they advocated a broadened suffrage, public education for the working class and improvement of factory conditions. These economists favoured a market economy, but thought it needed a measure of collective organization and control to ensure stability and bring order out of the "anarchy of competition". Lacking any theory of macroeconomics, they looked favourably on cartels and trade unions as a neo-mercantilist mechanism for achieving these ends. Both trade unions and labour legislation were also favoured as a means to provide workers with greater social protection and social justice, thus stabilizing the social and political order. A portion of this programme was implemented by Chancellor Bismarck in the form of a set of social insurance programmes, revolutionary at the time, such as workplace accident and old-age insurance. As noted in Chapter 1, while the German government extended the "carrot" to the working class in the form of social insurance programmes, at the same time it used the stick of political suppression and police harassment, made possible by enactment of the Anti-Socialist Law in 1878, to restrain and harass left-wing trade unions.

A major turning point in the history of German capital–labour relations occurred with the First World War. As happened in other countries, under the pressure of war mobilization the German government shifted from a policy of suspicion to active consultation and cooperation with the trade unions. The labour movement thus gained for the first time "insider" status. German defeat in the First World War led to popular uprisings, abdication by the Kaiser and revolutionary takeovers of cities and factories by workers and left-wing political elements. The trade unions, however, formed an alliance with the industrialists, formalized in the Stinnes–Legien Agreement, 1918, to preserve representative democracy and the basic outlines of a market economy, despite their official political programme that called for a transition to socialism. This alliance formed the basis for what later became the principle of *social partnership* (Lehmbruch, 2001). The accord also opened the door for a continued programme of labour reform. The Constitution of the Weimar Republic, 1919, for example, guaranteed for the first time relatively unrestricted freedom of combination on the part of workers and proclaimed that labour unions have an equal position with employers in determining working conditions, while the Works Council Act of 1920 mandated the establishment of enterprise-level works councils.

A significant body of literature related to industrial relations appeared in Germany during the years preceding the rise of Hitler and the National Socialist

German Workers' Party (the Nazis) (Oberschall, 1965). Indeed, during the Weimar years a close parallel field to industrial relations developed in Germany, called *Arbeitswissenschaft* (the science of work). Mary Nolan (1994: 84) describes this new field as "a multifaceted interdisciplinary field devoted to analysing and improving all aspects of work". Centred in psychology and sociology, topics investigated included fatigue and job satisfaction, aptitude testing, vocational education and company social policy for workers. Job satisfaction or *Arbeitsfreude* (joy in work) received more research attention in Germany during this period than in any other country (Campbell, 1989).

With regard to capital–labour relations, Müller-Jentsch (2003) cites the work of several German scholars as foundational. One is Adolf Weber's (1910) *Der Kampf zwischen Kapital und Arbeit*, a book on the struggle between capital and labour that went through six editions. Also influential are the writings of sociologist Goetz Briefs, a Christian socialist who emigrated to the United States in 1934. According to Müller-Jentsch, Goetz Briefs' article "*Betriebssoziologie*" (1931) was a seminal publication that laid the theoretical foundation for analyses of the internal relations in business organizations and especially the role of labour in the hierarchically structured production process. Another noteworthy figure is Hugo Sinzheimer, whose writings formed the basis for the labour law policy of the Weimar government. Also to be mentioned are Emil Lederer and Jakob Marschak's work on the classes and the labour market, "Die Klassen auf dem Arbeitsmarkt und ihre Organisationen" (1927).

Another key intellectual included in this foundational group is German industrial sociologist Adolf Geck. Several of the authors cited above were among the first to write on *Tarifpolitik* (collective bargaining) and the institutional infrastructure of the industrial relations system. Geck, on the other hand, did pioneering work on work relations within the enterprise (plant sociology). With Briefs, Geck founded an Institute for Work Sociology (*Betriebssoziologie*) in 1928 at the Technical University of Berlin at Charlottenburg, and in 1931 published a book on work relations in changing times, *Die Sozialen Arbeitsverhältnisse im Wandel der Zeit*. More attuned to international developments in industrial relations than many of his contemporaries, Geck made note of the activities of the IRI at The Hague and wrote about the American personnel management and human relations movements and the research work of the Industrial Relations Section at Princeton University (Hetzler, 1995).

Müller-Jentsch (2002: 225), speaking of the sociologists in this group, summarizes their viewpoint this way: "If there was a common paradigm, ... it was the understanding that industrial production is the hub of modern capitalism, being organized in privately owned firms by vertical and horizontal division of labour and according to the principles of rationality and profitability." Hetzler (p. 314, translated from the German) provides an alternative assessment, stating that they attempted a "blending of industrial relations, human relations and personnel management" and "intended to take a social and political approach to examining the entire matter and proposed a 'Personnel Constitution' for the Works Enterprise in the spirit of co-determination".

The developments in labour research and industrial relations reform in Germany were aborted in 1933 with the coming to power of Hitler and the Nazis. Independent labour unions were abolished, union leaders were killed or imprisoned, ethnic minorities were sent to concentration camps and millions of other workers were conscripted to work in war industries with minimal rights and voice. As earlier noted, many German academics emigrated.

The modern German employment relations system that exists today was reconstructed from its Weimar roots after Germany's defeat in the Second World War. Central elements are as follows: the dual representation system, with workers represented at the enterprise level by works councils and at the sectoral or industry level by trade unions; a neo-corporatist bargaining structure with collective agreements negotiated at a medium–high level of centralization between sectoral or industry employers' associations and equivalent trade unions; treatment of labour unions as social representatives of workers rather than private bargaining agents; deeply institutionalized accommodation between unions and employers; and a system of co-determination (*Mitbestimmung*) in which workers have representation on corporate boards of directors. The institution of co-determination, originally limited to the coal and steel industries but extended in 1976 in modified form to other large companies, has long been a major object of scholarly attention in comparative industrial relations, followed closely by the German system of works councils (*Betriebsrat*). The German industrial relations system, in turn, is embedded in what has become known as the *social market economy* (*Soziale Marktwirtschaft*). Many of these elements had appeared in the Weimar period; the greatest change engineered with the support of the Allied occupation authorities was the unification of the socialist, liberal and Christian trade unions into the German Trade Union Confederation (DGB). This system is so distinctive and different from the Anglo-American version that later writers have called it *Modell Deutschland*, Rheinland capitalism, or coordinated capitalism (Albert, 1993; Streeck, 1992).

As alluded to above, a central component of the German industrial relations system is the social market economy. Parallel to early industrial relations in the United States, the important ideas and people behind the development of the social market economy in Germany were actually from the progressive centre of the intellectual and policy spectrum rather than from the socialist left. Indeed, had the German left won the intellectual and political struggle in the years immediately after the Second World War, the social market economy would have been stillborn. Also of interest in the development of the social market economy concept are the links to the earlier German school of historical–social economics, American institutional economics, the Kerr/Dunlop idea of a web of rules, and present-day theories that equate industrial relations with alternative systems of social regulation (Bélanger, Edwards and Haiven, 1994; Hollingsworth and Boyer, 1997).

Although the trade unions and the SPD entered into collaboration with employers and capitalism after the First World War, their official mission remained committed to replacing both. Moving away from Marxian notions of class struggle and revolutionary seizure of the state, however, the unions and SPD developed an alternative evolutionary strategy to attain socialism. This strategy was formulated in the late 1920s and became known as the model of economic democracy (*Wirtschaftsdemokratie*, also carrying the meaning in English of industrial democracy but more broadly conceived, with workers' control and participation at the national, sectoral and enterprise levels). The chief theoretician was Rudolf Hilferding of the SPD (labelled by Grebing, 1969: 95, as of the "moderate radical Left"), while an influential statement of the model was given in the book *Economic democracy: Its character, means and ends* (1928) edited by Fritz Naphtali and with contributions by Hilferding and Sinzheimer. Its most concrete development was in Sweden with the Meidner Plan (Abraham, 1982). The basic idea was to unite politically the working class behind the SPD and use the SPD to slowly legislate away the property rights and profits of the capitalists, ending in worker control of industry. This gradual "chipping away" starts with measures such as wage and lay-off guarantees, transferring administrative control of the unemployment insurance funds to the trade unions, giving trade unions co-determination rights on corporate boards of directors, and implementing equal worker representation on all economic policy-making bodies (e.g., the central bank). Workers control advances further when trade unions gain control over the distribution of profit and investment of capital and finally culminates in the socialization of industry.

The movement for *Wirtschaftsdemokratie* in the 1930s, it should be noted, did not go unchallenged in academic or industry circles. In opposition was a movement known as *Werksgemeinschaft*, or "enterprise community" (Campbell, 1989). The proponents of *Werksgemeinshaft* sought to foster greater collaboration and solidarity between capital and labour in the plant through shop committees, welfare programmes and other accoutrements of the welfare capitalist model. Thus German industry and academic circles had a similar division, in broad outline, to the PM and ILE schools of the United States.

After Germany's defeat in the Second World War, a struggle ensued regarding the restructuring and future direction of the German economy and industrial relations system. The programme pushed by the DGB and SPD was the model of economic democracy (Günter and Leminsky, 1978; Smith, 1994). The alternative model presented by the Christian Democratic Union Party (CDU) – and supported by the American occupation authorities – was the social market economy, a concept at first based largely on the twin policies of rapid price de-control and monetary stabilization. To the surprise of many observers, the CDU won the national elections in 1948 and the social market economy model was implemented by Minister of Economic Affairs (and later Chancellor) Ludwig Erhard. As described shortly, social democrats and trade unionists are today strong supporters of the social market economy and one now reads statements such as "one of the successes of the labour movement was to introduce the Social Market Economy in 1949" (Széll, 2001: 3). This is, however, a revisionist reading of history.

The ideas behind the social market economy came from a small group of German economists known as *ordo-liberals*. Key people were Walter Eucken, Alfred Müller-Armack and Wilhelm Röpke (Peacock and Willgerodt, 1989; Nicholls, 1994; Tribe, 1995). The ordo-liberals are an interesting blend of the Chicago school and the German historical–social school. They reflect the Chicago school in that they have a strong commitment to a competitive market economy; they reflect the historical–social school in insisting that economic theory and policy are historically contingent, must incorporate social and ethical concerns, and that the economy requires active management by the state. The ordo-liberals are thus close in a number of respects to American institutionalists and social liberals such as Commons and Coase (Grossekettler, 1989; Peukert, 2000).

The term "ordo" connotes "order", "system" and "framework". The central intellectual premise of the ordo-liberals is that all economic activity takes place within and is structured by the legal, social and ethical order. Thus Eucken states (quoted in Yamawaki, 2001: 190):

> Whether it is the economy of the ancient world or of Augustan Rome or of medieval France or modern Germany or anywhere else, every economic plan or economic action of every peasant, landlord, trader, or craftsman takes place within the framework of economic order, and it is only to be understood within this framework. The economic process goes on always and everywhere within the framework of historically given order. The order may be a bad one, but without order no economy is possible.

Evidently, "ordo" is closely equivalent to the concept of institution, governance structure, working rules of collective action, web of rules and social mode of regulation.

Unlike neoclassical economists, the ordo-liberals explicitly ground their theory of economics on an ethical value statement (Tietmeyer, 1999; Tezuka, 2001). The primary goal of economic policy, they state, should be to devise the ordo that maximizes individual freedom and personal development. The human condition, not the quantity of goods, is the object of economic science. As a general premise, they hold that a competitive market economy best promotes these values since it allows maximum scope for personal decision, initiative and responsibility. But they again depart from the neoclassical school in several respects. They do not believe, for example, that a competitive market economy is self-regulating, because of various types of embedded (or structural) market and human failures (e.g., externalities, bounded rationality). Thus they reject laissez-faire (the nightwatchman theory of government) and believe that government must actively manage the economy, albeit with a restrained hand and subject to the principle of subsidiarity (Nicholls, 1994). Also distinctive, the ordo-liberals believe that the economy evolves over time and thus the government must adjust the ordo to maintain balance and well-functioning markets. And, finally, the ordo-liberals do not believe that the functioning of a competitive market system can be divorced or isolated from social conditions and ethical considerations (Tietmeyer, 1999). A free market system, they hold, functions best and only survives in the long run when the people feel that the outcomes promote not only efficiency but human values of security, justice and self-actualization. Thus they favour certain institutional interventions in the market economy, such as protective labour laws, trade unions, progressive income tax systems and old-age pensions *as long* as these measures promote an ordo that is consistent with a well-functioning market economy and individual freedom. Whereas neoclassical economists generally reject the concept of social justice as a meaningless metaphysical concept or a thinly veiled excuse to redistribute income, ordo-liberals accept social justice: first, as an intellectual concept, because it effects economic behaviour and, second, as a policy goal, as long as it improves freedom and does not impair market competition (Yamawaki, 2001). The term "social market economy" thus reflects the idea that the market order has first priority but must be complemented by an appropriately structured social order to support the market order. Economic policy and social policy are thus linked rather than separated, as in much of neoclassical economics.

The model of social market economy was implemented by Erhard and was judged by most people to be highly successful, given Germany's rapid economic recovery and growth in the immediate post-war period. In 1959, the SPD modified its position and endorsed the social market economy, although with continued commitment to economic democracy as the long-term goal (Berger, 2000). Once in power (the Brandt and Schmidt governments), the SDP came to endorse fully the social market economy concept and used it to provide intellectual and political justification for further social legislation and market regulation. With some irony, the trade unions and the SDP are now the strongest proponents of the social market economy, albeit after having taken the concept much further in the "social" direction than the original founders probably ever envisioned (Tietmeyer, 1999).

Not unexpectedly, the re-creation of the German industrial relations system after the Second World War, and its many interesting innovations and features, sparked considerable academic research both in Germany and abroad. While American research on the German system was done by academics firmly associated with the industrial relations field, such as Adolf Sturmthal and Walter Galenson, German research continued to be done within the traditional disciplines. Indeed, industrial relations did not emerge in Germany for 25 years after the war.

The discipline most active in labour research was German sociology. Between 1947 and 1970, 69 chairs in sociology were established and a number of research institutes created. Müller-Jentsch cites three of particular importance in the labour area: the Frankfurt Institute for Social Research, the Sociological Research Institute in Göttingen and the Institute for Social Research in Munich. As noted earlier, one reason industrial relations was slow to take hold in Germany was the very expansive research programme in work and industry undertaken by sociologists. Topics receiving major attention included: technological change and the character of work; shop-floor cooperation among workers; co-determination; automation; industrial democracy; the class structure of the workforce; the structure of trade unions; strikes; works councils; managerial strategies; the organization of work and the labour process. Much of this research was fuelled by very generous government and trade union funding, stimulated in significant measure by that era's policy concerns with the humanization of work life, the impact of new technology and the democratization of industry. Also playing a part, according to Müller-Jentsch (2002: 232), was the desire of the SPD government to "substantiate its policies by social sciences".

Although the concept of industrial relations surfaced in Germany in the 1930s, it largely lay fallow until the GIRA was founded in 1970. Even then, it did not generate great interest. As was the case with France, the founding of the IIRA in Geneva in 1966 was the catalyst to the development of the field in Germany. The Executive Board of the IIRA made overtures to several German professors about founding a national branch of the Association in Austria and Germany. One of these, Friedrich Fürstenberg, then a professor of sociology at the University of Linz (Austria), took the lead and founded the Austrian Industrial Relations Research Association in 1967. The same year, Fürstenberg organized the first European Regional Conference on Industrial Relations at the University of Linz. This conference served as a forerunner and model for what later became the IIRA European Regional Congresses.

With these developments in mind, and with the encouragement of the German government, Professor Otto Neuloh sent letters to 30 German professors soliciting their interest in forming an industrial relations association. Hetzler (1995: 316) states that the call was greeted with "no overwhelming interest", illustrated by the fact that the initial organizing meeting of the GIRA was attended by nine people. One problem facing the group was that they were unclear about the definition and content of this new subject area.

To the Germans, the core idea of industrial relations was to promote cooperation and consensus between employers and employees, which to them seemed problematic as an academic study area since the post-Second World War legal regime in Germany – exemplified by the system of co-determination – had already established capital and labour as social partners. Thus industrial relations seemed perhaps culture-bound, in that it had application to countries with adversarial systems of labour relations but less evidently to countries with a cooperative system. Ideology also played a role, since at the time Marxist/radical theory had a large influence among German intellectuals and they viewed industrial relations as indelibly tainted with human relations (seen as the manipulation of workers), business unionism (interpreted as class collaboration), and American corporate foreign policy interests (Conrad, 1981; Hetzler, 1995). With this in mind, it will be recalled from Chapter 6, Roberts and Cox decided to drop Germany as a potential founding member of the IIRA because the scholarly labour community was deeply split and predominantly leftist.

Not knowing exactly what this Anglo-American field of industrial relations was, and needing to overcome lack of interest and scepticism in the academic community, the organizers of the GIRA made two decisions (Hetzler, 1995). One was to emphasize as a key distinguishing feature of industrial relations the field's interdisciplinary nature. This allowed the organizers to sidestep some of the definitional and ideological debates and promote industrial relations as an opportunity for scholars from various disciplines to learn from each other. The second, also to avoid definitional debates, was to forego attempts to translate the English term "industrial relations" into a German equivalent and simply incorporate the English term in the title of the new association.

In 1974, the GIRA nearly disbanded for lack of membership and clear sense of mission. Core members resolved, however, to try to move forward by bringing in non-university researchers as members and working to define better the unique intellectual content of industrial relations. Progress on the first front was quite slow because the group maintained into the late 1980s very selective membership procedures and qualifications. Applicants – even those relatively well known in national and international circles – were typically required to give a seminar or some form of demonstration of professional competence and then receive a formal vote of acceptance. In this regard, the rule-laden and formalistic procedures of GIRA provide an interesting contrast to the complete informality of the equivalent British association (the BUIRA had no written by-laws or membership procedures until the early 1980s) and seems to mirror larger national characteristics found in the industrial relations systems of the two countries.

To identify better the intellectual uniqueness of industrial relations, Hetzler states that core industrial relations members gave close examination to classic works in the Anglo-Saxon industrial relations literature, such as Dunlop (1958) and Hyman (1975), and attempted to find common elements with works of German authors, such as Ralph Dahrendorf's *Class and class conflict in industrial societies* (1959) and Weitbrecht's (1969) well-regarded study on collective bargaining in German industry (*Effektivität und Legitimität der Tarifautonomie*). The fruits of their efforts began to pay off as membership in the GIRA slowly increased to 21 by 1978. Independently, the first explicit research project on industrial relations was initiated by Otto Jacobi and Walther Müller-Jentsch in 1979 at the Institute for Social Research in Frankfurt, initiated in part through working relationships with Bain, Clegg, Crouch and Hyman in the United Kingdom. In the same year, the German Sociological Congress included industrial relations as an official topic in a programme track chaired by Gerhardt Brandt, a director of the Frankfurt Institute (Müller-Jentsch, 2003; Frege, 2002). Among the participants were three prominent names in today's German industrial relations: Keller, Müller-Jentsch and Streeck. According to Hetzler, the end of the development stage of industrial relations in German-speaking Europe was reached in 1985 with the publication of the first handbook of industrial relations as practised in Austria, German and Switzerland, *Handbuch der Arbeitsbeziehungen* (Endruweit et al., 1985).

Since 1985, the German field of industrial relations has become increasingly institutionalized and has continued to bring in new participants (Keller, 1996). It has also benefited from cross-fertilization of ideas with the Anglo-American industrial relations community through the work of German-speaking industrial relations scholars in America, such as Carola Frege, Wolfgang Streeck, Kathleen Thelen, Lowell Turner and Kirsten Wever.

A key event signalling German industrial relations' coming of age was the election of Fürstenberg as president of the IIRA and the holding of the IIRA World Congress in Hamburg in 1986. Fürstenberg was one of the earliest German scholars in the post-Second World War period to take an interest in industrial relations. He wrote his diploma thesis in 1951 on trade unions and distribution theory, was a visiting researcher at the Cornell University industrial relations programme in the United States in the mid-1950s, wrote one of the first articles in Germany describing the field of industrial relations (1969) and several years later published a book *Industrielle Arbeitsbeziehungen* (1975). As earlier indicated, he was for a number of years a professor of sociology in Austria, later returning to Germany. Although most contemporary German industrial relations scholars do not perceive that any one person qualifies for the title "father of German industrial relations", Fürstenberg is widely credited as a pioneer and one of the people who first put German industrial relations on the international stage.

Also appearing in 1986 was the first German-language textbook on industrial relations by Müller-Jentsch, called *Sociology of industrial relations*. Müller-Jentsch was a member of the Frankfurt school of critical sociology and, with Otto Jacobi and Joachim Bergmann, had earlier published pioneering research on German trade unions. Today he is recognized as one of the leading scholars in German industrial relations. In the book, Müller-Jentsch provides a substantial historical treatment of German industrial relations, casts the subject in a systems perspective, puts the collective actors and free collective bargaining at centre stage, and frames the subject as a study in "exchange relations" (*Austauschbeziehungen*) between labour and capital.

A second industrial relations text appeared in 1987, written by law professor Manfred Weiss. As Keller (1996: 203) notes, "The German system of industrial relations has long been noted for a degree of legal regulation which in international comparative terms is particularly high. For this reason, the work of academic lawyers has traditionally been of great importance, and provides an essential contribution to understanding how the system functions." However, despite the long-standing juridification (*Verrechtlichung*) of German industrial relations, most German legal scholars interested in labour and employment issues have traditionally pursued their research within the legal discipline and have largely eschewed an interdisciplinary exchange with the social and administrative sciences. Weiss is an exception in this regard and his book was an early effort to break down these walls. Since then, several other German law professors have been active in the industrial relations field, such as Wolfgang Däubler, Ulrich Mückenberger and Armin Höland.

The multidisciplinary perspective received another boost with a third text, *Introduction to the politics and policies of work*, authored by Berndt Keller in 1991. Keller is a political scientist and well-known author, particularly with respect to industrial relations and the EU project (e.g., Keller and Platzer, 2003). In his industrial relations text he developed the subject around the concept of *Arbeitspolitik* (politics and policies of work) in an effort to give more prominence to the role of the state in structuring the industrial relations system.

The German industrial relations field took another significant step forward in 1994 with the founding of the field's first German-language scholarly journal: *Industrielle Beziehungen – The German Journal of Industrial Relations*. The intent of the founders was to frame the intellectual domain of industrial relations broadly so the German subtitle of the journal is *Zeitschrift für Arbeit, Organization und Management* (work, organization and management). Although the founders of the GIRA in the early 1970s were unsure how to define the term industrial relations, two decades later the term had become definite enough that the founders of *Industrielle Beziehungen* could tell readers in the first issue ("Editorial", 1994, p. 9) that "the editors understand the concept to cover the historically developed systems of institutions for conflict resolution and consensus-building in the world of work. A key characteristic of these institutions is that they have emerged out of conflicts of interest, patterns of cooperation, and the political decision of individual and collective actors."

The one area of the German social sciences that is notably absent in industrial relations is economics. Few economists outside trade union research institutes and the area of business economics participate in the field. Noted one German scholar in private correspondence: "In general, no mainstream economist wants to be suspected to sympathize with trade unions."

Frege (2002) recently performed a content analysis of the articles published in the *Industrielle Beziehungen* in an effort to delineate the distinctive characteristics of German industrial relations research and differences with Anglo-American countries. The results indicate broad trends, although specific inferences are problematic since for promotion and tenure reasons many German scholars publish their more important industrial relations research in discipline-based journals. In terms of subjects, recent German industrial relations research clusters in four areas: reorganization of work (lean production, organizational change, works councils and so forth), transformation of industrial relations at the sectoral level (for example, industry-level collective bargaining), industrial relations transformation in former East Germany, and Europeanization. A second dimension Frege examined was "knowledge frame". She found two salient characteristics: a tendency of

German researchers to examine work and employment issues in a larger political and societal context and interpret industrial relations phenomena as part of socio-political processes; and an underlying assumption that social partnership is the ideal form of industrial relations. The third dimension Frege examined was research methods. Here distinct differences stood out with respect to Anglo-American countries and, most particularly, the United States. She identified four methodological characteristics of German industrial relations research: heavy reliance on qualitative and descriptive data and infrequent use of statistical techniques; less emphasis on positivist analysis and more emphasis on interpretative analysis (partially stemming, Frege states, from the tradition of historical–social economics); more frequent statement by authors of value and policy judgements and expressed effort to develop practice and policy in specific directions; and more reliance on broad socio-political theoretical frameworks and "grand theorizing" in the literary tradition and less emphasis on formal but narrowly constructed models and hypothesis derivation and testing.

Frege sums up her findings this way (p. 254):

> In a nutshell, German research is concerned with the institutionalization and functioning of collective actors, a topic which is neglected in current Anglo-American research, and also focuses on the 'black box' of industrial and workplace *relations* rather than in their outcomes (performance), a prime interest of Anglo-Saxon research in recent years.

She further adds, "What most Anglo-Saxon scholars take for granted is quite often what is regarded as most problematic by scholars in other countries." She then concludes with this observation (pp. 254–5):

> [T]he universal domination of the Anglo-Saxon research tradition would, in my view, only foster the ongoing decline of industrial relations research. ... Only by broadening rather than narrowing the research questions and methodologies, and in particular by (re)discovering the inherent political nature of industrial relations, can we save and develop industrial relations research as an independent discipline.

German industrial relations, as the narrative in this section suggests, has slowly but perceptibly grown and developed since first emerging in 1970, illustrated by the selection of German legal scholar Weiss to serve as president of the IIRA (2000–2003). In September 2003, over 800 industrial relations researchers attended the Thirteenth World Congress in Berlin, hosted by the GIRA. Also illustrative of the growing self-confidence of German industrial relations is the volume especially commissioned by the GIRA for the congress, *The changing contours of German industrial relations* (Müller-Jentsch and Weitbrecht, 2003).

The German industrial relations field remains relatively small, however, and suffers from the same angst over its long-term future as does the field in other countries. As Keller (1996: 202) notes, "Discussions of the future of industrial relations always tend to turn into a debate on the future of trade unions." Even in Germany, where union density is still comparatively high and collective bargaining is deeply institutionalized, one can reasonably worry about what the future holds on this score as globalization, EU market integration, and the forces of decentralization, union decline and individualization continue apace.

INDUSTRIAL RELATIONS IN ASIA, AFRICA AND LATIN AMERICA

10

Attention in this chapter is turned to the development of the industrial relations field in the three continents of Asia, Africa and Latin America. Parallel with previous chapters, I sketch the major ideas, people and events that led to the birth of industrial relations in these regions and then describe the main outline of development to the present time. Given the size and diversity of these three continents, the coverage is necessarily selective. The chapter also highlights at selective points the key roles played by the ILO and IIRA in the development of the field of industrial relations in these countries and regions, but a more in-depth analysis is postponed until the next chapter.

Asia

First considered is Asia. The continent of Asia extends from the eastern Mediterranean to Japan. Surveying developments in Asia is particularly challenging, given that the continent is the largest, most populous and most socially and ethnically diverse in the world. The cultures and traditions of Asian countries are also rooted in the East, while industrial relations as a field has its origins in the traditions and experiences of the West. Further complicating matters is that the difference between the languages of Asia and those of the West is most pronounced.

In a number of countries of Asia, the industrial relations field has practically no presence. Included are most of the countries of the Middle East and a number of the smaller countries of Southeast Asia. Principal reasons, in varying proportions across these countries, include a low level of industrialization, authoritarian political regimes, suppression of independent labour movements, religious and cultural attitudes at odds with social and political pluralism and lack of well-developed university systems. In several other Asian countries, such as China, Pakistan, the Philippines, Singapore and Turkey, industrial relations has successfully established roots, albeit on a small scale. Illustratively, Singapore hosted the First Asian IIRA Regional Congress (1987), the Philippines hosted the Second and Fourth (1990, 2001) and Taiwan, China, hosted the Third Regional Congress (1996). The Taiwanese congress was organized by the Association of Industrial Relations, Republic of China (AIRROC), founded in 1981. Also of note, the Philippines is home to the only free-standing School of Labour and Industrial Relations in an Asian university, located at the University of the Philippines. The School is also home of the Philippine Industrial Relations Society, founded in 1981. In the People's Republic of China, efforts are under way to establish industrial relations programmes or courses of study in several universities. The field has also recently established a presence in Micronesia, with the inauguration of a programme of study in industrial relations at the University of the South Pacific in Fiji (serving 12 countries, such as the Cook Islands, Fiji and the Marshall Islands).

The four Asian countries where the industrial relations field is best established are Israel, India, Japan and the Republic of Korea. Developments in each are reviewed briefly below.

Israel

The industrial relations field in Israel has been shaped by an interesting mix of ideas and traditions from continental Europe, the United Kingdom and the United States, including Zionism, socialism, corporatism, voluntarism and – more recently – neo-liberalism. If one looks at specific actors, however, one institution in Israel stands out from the rest as the most important influence on the historical development of industrial relations. This institution is the Histadrut, Israel's peak labour federation – described by Shalev (1996: 131) as "a formidable Hydra without peer in the postcommunist world".

The state of Israel was founded in 1948, but the Histadrut dates back to 1920. In 1880, only 20,000 Jews lived in Palestine, but over the next four decades several waves of immigrants arrived, coming in large part from Central and Eastern Europe. Living conditions were primitive, industry and social services were largely non-existent, and Jewish labour had to compete with a large, low-wage Arab workforce. Drawing, however, on strong Zionist and socialist ideologies, the settlers came to Israel with a vision of the society they wanted to create – an egalitarian, classless society based on hard work, equal sacrifice, democratic and cooperative principles, and commitment to the cultural and religious traditions of the Jewish faith (Galin, 1993). The agricultural cooperatives, known as the Kibbutzim, were one manifestation; the Histadrut was another.

The Histadrut's name is usually translated into English as the Israeli Federation of Labour, but it has never been a trade union, or union federation, in the traditional sense. The Histadrut was established, not simply to protect and bargain for workers, but to assist Jewish settlers with jobs, health, education and social welfare services. Toward that end, the Histadrut started business enterprises to provide jobs to Jewish workers, organized and operated banks to provide financial capital and credit, started a health insurance fund, provided primary medical care and established pension funds. A half-century later, the Histadrut was not only a federation of 40 trade unions but also owned the largest industrial conglomerate and largest bank in Israel and was the main source of medical care and health insurance, not only for union members but for Israelis of all occupations and walks of life. In an arrangement almost unprecedented in the non-communist world, the Histadrut often found itself formally or de facto on both sides of the bargaining table during labour negotiations. Further adding to the complexity, the Histadrut was tightly linked to the Labour Party, and government leaders, such as David Ben-Gurion, were often also highly placed leaders in the Histadrut. At one time, nearly 70 per cent of the Israeli population belonged to the Histadrut, making union density in Israel one of the highest in the world. In an interesting twist, people joined the Histadrut first and were later assigned to a specific union. The close relationship between the Histadrut and Labour Party is one factor, of a number, that contributed to the latter's uninterrupted control of the national government for the first 25 years of Israel's existence.

Given the high level of union density and the close relationship between the Histadrut and national government, it is not surprising that the Israeli industrial relations system quickly evolved into a relatively centralized, corporatist model. It was also operated on largely voluntarist lines, with a minimalist structure of legal regulation, reflecting the Histadrut's opposition to restrictions on its autonomy and activities and its ease of attracting and maintaining membership (many Israelis joined in order to have access to the health and pension funds). Along with voluntarism, however, went a relatively high strike rate in Israel, particularly in the large public sector of the economy.

It was against this background that the field of industrial relations came to Israel in the mid-1960s. Three events marked the start of the field.

The first of these events was the creation in 1968 of the first department or academic unit in an Israeli university devoted specifically to labour and industrial relations. This unit was called the Department of Labour Studies and was located in the School of Social Science at Tel Aviv University. Up to this time, individual courses on labour and labour relations topics were sprinkled across Israel's six main universities but nothing systematic existed. The idea and impetus for the new department came from people inside the Histadrut who believed that the role and problems of labour in society, as well as the more specific institutions and traditions of trade unionism, deserved a place in the teaching and research programme of the universities. To promote the research function on labour, in 1970 the Golda Meir Institute for Social and Labour Research was founded and made part of the Department of Labour Studies.

The second event was the founding in 1969 of the Industrial Relations Research Association of Israel (IRRAI). The person most centrally involved with the founding of the association was Professor J. Yanai Tabb, along with the active involvement of Professor Arie Globerson and a leading official in the Ministry of Labour. Tabb was an American with socialist political convictions who emigrated to Israel in the 1950s in reaction to the increasingly virulent anti-communist crusade led by Senator Joseph McCarthy. Tabb secured a faculty position in the School of Industrial Engineering at Technion, the Israeli Institute of Technology in Haifa, and introduced industrial relations into the curriculum. He also co-authored (with Ami and Shaal, 1961) *Labor relations in Israel*, the first Israeli textbook on industrial relations.

Meanwhile, in the mid-1960s plans were under way to launch the IIRA. As noted in Chapter 6, at the time of the IIRA's creation only a handful of industrial relations associations exited in the entire world. Thus Robert Cox, Ben Roberts and others associated with the IILS at the ILO worked actively through the labour ministries of various countries to promote the establishment of national industrial relations associations, with the idea that they would become a springboard for developing and recruiting new IIRA members. It was through this channel that Tabb got involved in organizing the Israeli association, aided by both the fact that he was personally interested in developing the field of industrial relations and that his American background gave him familiarity with and knowledge of the subject. Initially, membership in the IRRAI was restricted to academics (along the lines of the BUIRA) but later was broadened to include practitioners and policy-makers (like the American association). Today, approximately 80 per cent of the members come from outside academia.

A third significant event in the history of the industrial relations field in Israel was the creation in 1972 of the Institute of Industrial and Labour Relations (IILR). Unaffiliated with any university and having a staff of only six or seven people, the IILR was established and financed by government, employers and unions to provide a place where they could – in the words of its long-time managing director (Carmi, 2003) – "detach from the fighting between us and discuss what we have in common". Besides promoting labour–management cooperation and dialogue, the IILR also sponsored a series of training classes, generally for workers and lower-level union officers, published a series of books and manuals on Israeli labour laws and various practical aspects of labour–management relations, and offered consulting and dispute resolution services. In 1974, the IILR became the secretariat for the IRRAI.

Unlike some other countries, Israel never established an industrial relations academic journal. The reason is that most Israeli academics write their research articles in English, not Hebrew, and try to place them in the American or British journals in order to reach an international audience. It might also be noted that law journals, and the field of law in general, have never been significant for industrial relations in Israel, given the tradition of voluntarism and relatively low level of legal regulation of labour relations. At least in the early years of the industrial relations field in Israel, economics of a historical and institutional nature was the leading research influence, followed by sociology.

The field of industrial relations in Israel has evolved in several important ways since those early days, mirroring both larger world trends and developments specific to Israel. At a broad level of generalization, it may be said that the most fundamental trend has been a notable decline in academic interest and participation in the field of industrial relations since the mid-1980s. Several factors account for this development.

The first is the dramatic decline in influence and membership of the Histadrut and its member trade unions. The more conservative, right-wing Likud Party first came to power in 1977 and has since governed Israel for significant periods of time. The Likud Party had no fondness for the Histadrut and in 1995 the enactment of the National Health Insurance Law struck at its foundation by stripping it of a near monopoly of this vital service. Quickly, the Histadrut suffered a massive exodus of members and power, while trade union density dropped by 50 per cent in less than a decade. Inevitably, this sharp contraction in the central labour movement and union density had a strong negative repercussion on the field of industrial relations.

Israel has also experienced, like many other countries of the world, a social and economic shift toward a more conservative, market-oriented and individualist order. Fifty years ago the Histadrut and Kibbutz held a high place in public opinion as the embodiment of socialist and egalitarian ideals, while today many Israelis see these institutions as increasingly anachronistic and out of place in a global economy. These sentiments, coupled with large concerns over jobs and unemployment, inevitably work against the field of industrial relations and the standard setting, collective institutions, and concerns with equity that have animated it. The academic world has also seen changes. In the mid-1980s, there was a rapid emergence and growth of American-style business schools. Prior to this period, business and commerce were not significant areas of teaching and research in Israeli universities, and personnel management, in particular, had very little presence. Since then business schools have become a boom area and courses on HRM have proliferated. The end result is that industrial relations has frequently been demoted from a separate course to the last topic on the HRM course syllabus.

On net, these developments have led to a significant erosion in the status and prospects of the industrial relations field in Israel. The good news, for example, is that the Department of Labour Studies at Tel Aviv University is still alive and well; the bad news is that most of the faculty have shifted their teaching and research interests away from industrial relations and toward labour markets, organizational behaviour and other such topics. Likewise, the membership of the IRRAI continues to increase, but most members are not academics and the IILR was closed in 1997. Finally, the future for tripartism and collective bargaining in Israel – arguably the foundation stones of the field – remains relatively gloomy.

India

Industrial relations as a concept and field of study has a relatively long history in India, dating from the late 1940s. The roots of industrial relations extend back further to the beginnings of the industrialization process in the late nineteenth century and, more concretely, the first significant period of labour unrest during the First World War period.

The pre-history period of industrial relations in India was decisively shaped by the fact that the country was ruled by the British as a colonial possession of the crown. Although the first factories and mills appeared in India in the middle part of the nineteenth century, industrialization was slow to develop during the remainder of that century and only began to expand on a significant scale during the economic boom of the First World War years. At a relatively early time, however, the British began to introduce the first rudimentary labour laws to India, such as the Workmen's Breach of Contract Act (1859) and the Employers' and Workmen's (Disputes) Act (1860). According to an ILO report (1959, quoted in Doshi, 1992: 173), these laws were "aimed at protecting the social system against labour rather than protecting labour against the social system". More extensive legal regulation was not required, however, because union organization and labour conflict remained scattered and transitory, nor were the British inclined to go far down this road given their national philosophy of voluntarism in labour matters.

The First World War years gave rise to the first major period of union organization and strikes in India. The economy boomed with wartime production but wages badly lagged behind prices, leading to widespread discontent among workers. Also, political discontent with British colonial rule was pervasive, stoked by the demand of the Indian National Congress for immediate self-government. Added to this mix was the creation of the ILO in 1919, of which India was a founding member. The creation of the ILO gave visibility and legitimacy to the cause of workers' rights and led workers in India and around the world to take more determined efforts to gain them. The overall effect was considerable labour unrest, union formation and strikes.

One of the most famous of these strikes was in 1918 by textile workers in the city of Ahmedabad. Wedded to a commodity theory of labour, the employers in the dispute rejected a mediator's proposed wage increase, stating (quoted in Myers, 1958: 58), "Mills are privately owned, and are run with no other motive than to make profit. Workers are employed with this aim in view, and therefore employment of labour and conditions of employment are determined purely on the basis of supply and demand and from the point of view of their efficiency. This is as it should be ... ". To avert a strike, the workers and owners agreed to further mediation efforts by Mahatma Gandhi, already at this time a respected moral leader and spokesperson for Indian independence. Gandhi framed the dispute, not as a matter of economics, but as a "struggle for justice", and emphasized "truth and fairness" in the formulation of demands and avoidance of violence and bitterness during the dispute. When the mill owners refused to agree to Gandhi's proposed wage settlement, he went on a hunger strike until they eventually capitulated. His approach to settling this strike was the beginning of a "Gandhian" labour ideology in India (Bose, 1956). In spirit, one may say that the Gandhian approach is consonant with the strategy of negotiated compromise and social justice espoused in the industrial relations field, while it is at odds with strategies pursued by Marxists and militant nationalists based on class struggle, direct action and political agitation.

The labour movement and labour unrest continued to grow through the 1920s, fuelled partly by workplace dissatisfaction over wages and conditions. An equal or even more important provocation was the growing political radicalism over continued British colonial rule and the economic radicalism over the skewed distribution of wealth and British domination of the strategic parts of the Indian market economy. As occurred in other countries, when labour unrest became a threat to social order the government sought to contain matters by forming an investigative committee. Accordingly, in 1929 the British convened a Royal Commission on Labour in India. It recommended a variety of measures, such as a more liberal policy on recognition of unions, establishment of shop councils at the local workplace, and a tripartite labour–management committee at the national level. None of these provisions were implemented during the Depression years of the 1930s, however, and the militant nationalist–communist wing of the labour movement boycotted the entire proceedings. Illustrative of the non-institutionalized state of labour–management relations at this point in Indian history, the Royal Commission found that although the union movement was over 300,000 strong, the Ahmedabad Textile Agreement was the only instance of collective bargaining in the country (Malhorta, 1949: 88).

The period immediately following the end of the Second World War was a replay of the First World War years in India, except that union rebelliousness, labour unrest and civil disorder were on a far larger scale. It was in this environment that the British ceded independence to India and Prime Minster Nehru formed the first government. One of his first acts was to convene a conference of labour and management and obtain an Industrial Truce Resolution that pledged both sides to refrain from strikes and slow-downs for three years. The government also supported the formation in 1947 of an entirely new federation of trade unions, the Indian National Trade Union Congress (INTUC), which sought to follow the Gandhian labour ideology of seeking justice through negotiation and conciliation. Arrayed against it, however, were a number of rival union federations of various nationalist, socialist and communist stripes, often allied with a political party and led by political figures (Giri, 1959). Common to most of the important union groups, however, was a commitment to reduce social inequalities and private concentration of industry by moving to some form of a planned economy, albeit with considerable differences among them as to speed, extent and tactics.

It was in this economic and political environment that the Anglo-American concept of industrial relations came to India. It did so, originally, in three ways. One was in the form of legislation, such as the Bombay Industrial Relations Act (1946) – a measure providing different categories of legal recognition to trade unions. A second path was in the pages of newly published textbooks on labour problems. During the 1920s and 1930s in the United States, a number of labour problems textbooks were published by economists to be used for courses in labour economics. This same genre of text appeared in India after the Second World War (e.g., Agarwala's *Indian labour problems*, 1947). These texts, like their American counterparts, described a variety of labour problems and presented industrial relations as a portfolio of practices and strategies to solve these problems, though with emphasis on trade unionism and collective bargaining. The third entrée for industrial relations in India was through books on the Indian labour movement, such as Malhorta's *Indian labour movement* (1949). Here industrial relations is largely equated with labour–management relations and the prevention of industrial conflict.

In these ways the subject of industrial relations succeeded in establishing a toehold in Indian universities and policy-making circles. If Indian industrial relations had a launch point, it would certainly be in the early 1950s with the arrival of the "four horsemen" of Kerr, Dunlop, Harbison and Myers and their multi-year, multi-country project, the Inter-University Study of Labour Problems in Economic Development (described in detail in Chapter 4). As they travelled around the world, these scholars sowed the seeds of industrial relations outside the Anglo-Saxon group of countries and helped the field germinate and grow in these new areas. Certainly this process worked in India. The four horsemen visited India as a group, conducted interviews, gave seminars and met high-ranking government, employer, and trade union officials, all the time putting forward the concept of industrial relations and the role of positive industrial relations practices as a contributor to economic development.

Of the four, the one who played the most important role in promoting the industrial relations field in India was Charles Myers, professor at MIT's Industrial Relations Section. He began his work on India in 1952, hiring Subbiah Kannappan to serve as Research Associate. Kannappan was from India and had just completed his doctoral degree from Tufts University, with Myers serving as a member of the dissertation committee. Myers and Kannappan spent 18 months in the United States doing preparatory research and then travelled to India in 1954 for five months of interviews and field investigation. The end product was *Labor problems in the industrialization of India* (Myers, 1958), a revised edition of which was published in 1970 as *Industrial relations in India* (Myers and Kannappan). In addition, Myers and colleagues recruited several other Indian scholars to pursue other related lines of research under the auspices of the Inter-University project.

Dating from the early 1950s, industrial relations in India quickly developed an institutional presence. The field had several roots (Ratnam, 1997), one of which was social work. In the 1920s and 1930s, a small number of employers introduced various forms of welfare activities in the workplace, such as company housing and medical services. Typically, they hired a social worker to administer and coordinate these activities. These social workers were, like the welfare secretaries in early twentieth-century American firms, the forerunners of what later became the personnel and industrial relations function in large firms. In 1936, J.R.D. Tata, widely considered one of the most progressive employers in India, established the Tata Institute of Social Sciences in Bombay to train social workers for industry (Kannappan, 1959). In the 1950s, the Tata Institute broadened the curriculum to include courses on personnel management and industrial relations and, later, added a Department of Personnel Management and Industrial Relations (Bhowmik, 2002). It remains today one of the leading training institutions for personnel and industrial relations practitioners in India. Other social work institutes, modelled on the Tata example, were also established in the post-war period, with the result that by the late 1990s over 30 offered master's programmes covering labour welfare, industrial relations and personnel/HRM (Ratnam, 1997: 2).

Chronologically, another early contributor was economics. In India, economics has traditionally been the most important disciplinary home for industrial relations teaching and research. As indicated above, in the 1950s and 1960s the most frequent way industrial relations was introduced in university curricula was through a labour problems course, generally taught by a labour economist. As was true in the United States, these early labour problems courses were multidisciplinary and covered a diverse range of subjects spanning personnel management, labour relations and labour legislation. Hence, they were much more in the guise of an industrial relations course than a modern labour economics course, leading one scholar to remark (quoted in Ratnam, 1997: 1), "It is high time that Labour Economics ... be an independent subject not necessarily attached to Economics, but drawing on other allied Social Sciences or working in cooperation with Sociology, Psychology and Law. If for this purpose, the phrase 'Industrial and Human Relations' is used, it would perhaps be better."

As this quotation suggests, in the early post-war years the dividing line between labour economics and industrial relations was blurred and the two overlapped a good deal. The main academic association for scholars interested in industrial relations was thus the Indian Society of Labour Economics (ISLE). The Association was founded in 1957 by Shri V.V. Giri, an influential economist, author of a well-known labour problems text (Giri, 1959), and for several years the President of India. The ISLE's journal, the *Indian Journal of Labour Economics*, quickly became the main outlet for scholarly research on industrial relations (Papola, Ghosh and Sharma, 1993).

Also contributing to teaching and research in industrial relations are law schools, business schools and sociology departments. India has developed an extensive framework of labour law regulating the employment relationship, while trade unions and collective bargaining have historically been highly politicized. Labour lawyers have thus been important players in the industrial relations field in India, although they tend to practise teaching and research apart from their colleagues in the social-science wing of the field. Also of increasing importance in Indian industrial relations are schools of business and institutes of management. During the 1990s, however, these institutions increasingly changed the nomenclature of their courses from "personnel and industrial relations" to "HRM", or some variant thereof. Finally, a number of industrial sociologists have over the years contributed to the Indian field of industrial relations (Bhowmik, 2002).

India has few interdisciplinary teaching programmes on industrial relations. Of the academic programmes in industrial relations, two of the oldest and most highly rated are the Xavier Labour Relations Institute and the Sri Ram Centre of Industrial Relations and Human Resource Development. The Xavier programme was started in 1949 by Jesuit priest Father Quinn Enright. It has become over the years one of India's premier post-graduate programmes for personnel/HRM and industrial relations. The heads of personnel and labour relations at many large Indian corporations and multinational companies are graduates of the institute. The Sri Ram Centre of Industrial Relations was founded in the mid-1960s with a grant from the Ford Foundation. In the 1980s it added the term "human resource development" to its title. The centre is known for its research work and is the home of the *Indian Journal of Industrial Relations*.

India also has a number of other labour- and employment-related institutes. One of the most prominent is the V.V. Giri National Labour Institute, run by the Labour Ministry of the federal government. Also important are several regional labour institutes, such as the Mahatma Gandhi Labour Institute in Ahmedabad and a number of institutes of management, such as the International Management Institute in New Delhi.

Industrial relations in India had a "golden age" from approximately 1960 to the early 1980s, when a number of universities added industrial relations courses and majors and the number of academics teaching and doing research in industrial relations also grew apace. Signifying the advance of the field, the Indian Industrial Relations Association was established in 1994. Thomas Kochan, then serving as IIRA president, was invited to New Delhi to participate in a high-level conference organized by Professor C.S. Venkata Ratnam. The conference stimulated attendees to form the Indian association. The first president was C.P. Thakur of Delhi University and the association is currently headquartered at the Institute for Human Development (New Delhi).

The founding of the Indian Industrial Relations Association notwithstanding, since the early 1980s the field of industrial relations in India has suffered some loss of momentum. Active participation by researchers has declined, industrial relations courses and teaching programmes have been eliminated or downsized, and student enrolments have shifted from industrial relations to HRM. The reasons reflect a number of trends found in other countries, as well as factors unique to India. Included in the former is a decline in the size and influence of the labour movement, the transition of the trade unions from a popular-based social movement to a more sectional economic special interest group, the growth of a large service sector and increasing informal employment, the growth of student demand for business and management degrees, and the pressures exerted on labour standards and collective bargaining by global competition, neo-liberal ideology and International Monetary Fund (IMF) and World Bank policies. Among the last are India's movement away from a highly regulated and collectivist economic development strategy to a more open, market-oriented system, and falling public approval of the trade unions on account of their factionalism and politicization. One may say, therefore, that the status of industrial relations in India is mixed: positive because the field has a long tradition in India, is relatively well institutionalized, with an academic journal, professional association and university degree programmes; negative because external and internal developments are slowly eroding these foundations of the field (Thakur, 2003).

Japan

The pre-history of industrial relations dates from the early 1890s to the mid-1950s in Japan. In the pre-history period, labour research and policy were very influenced by the German approach of *Sozialpolitik*. After the Second World War, the United States replaced Germany as the most important foreign influence in Japanese academic thought and labour policy, and it was at this point that the field of industrial relations first appeared. As in many other countries, the industrial relations field in Japan experienced a golden age until the 1980s, followed by a period of decline.

The history of Japanese labour starts with the end of the feudal Tokugawa government in 1867 and the ascension of Emperor Meiji as the sovereign ruler of the nation. From this period forward, Japan embarked on a determined course of modernization and industrialization. Out of this drive grew the first factories and heavy industry, the emergence of an urban-based wage labour force, the problems of labour exploitation and mistreatment, and the stirrings of labour unrest and antagonism between employers and workers.

Although Japan was a latecomer to industrialization and thus lagged behind the economic development of the United States and Western Europe, this status also provided advantages. One of these was learning from the Western world both what to do and not to do for successful development. Toward this end, Japan sent many intellectuals, businessmen and government officials abroad to observe, study and work, and also opened its doors to the full range of influential Western writers and philosophers. Another important source of Western influence was Christian missionaries in Japan; a number of Japanese labour and social reformers in the early twentieth century were Christian converts. For example, Fusataro Takano lived in the United States for a period during the 1890s, converted to Christianity, learned the principles of trade unionism from Samuel Gompers, and returned to Japan and became the first trade union organizer.

Between the early 1890s and the First World War, a large number of Western schools of thought came to Japan and gained adherents. Political economy arrived first, including Smithian economic liberalism, the new marginalist economics of Alfred Marshall, and German historical economics and *Sozialpolitik*. Closer to the First World War, Marxism and anarchosyndicalism began to circulate, as did Taylor's new principles of scientific management.

Of these schools of thought, two had particular importance in shaping the early industrial relations experience of Japan. The first was the German school of *Sozialpolitik* (Morris-Suzuki, 1989; Kinzley, 1991); the second was the American school of scientific management (Tsutsui, 1998).

Japanese society and social values had far more in common with nineteenth-century Germany than with the United Kingdom or the United States (Lehmbruch, 2001). Neither Germany nor Japan were comfortable with the Anglo-American model of individualism, unrestrained competition and commercialism, and the laissez-faire approach of minimalist state control. Both German and Japanese societies featured strong hierarchial status relationships, an emphasis on maintaining social order and harmony, a communitarian or "organic" view of society (society is a living organism with its own will and destiny), a belief that successful economic development requires active state involvement and guidance, and a preference for governance exercised by an enlightened monarch and administered by a strong and capable bureaucracy (a model of "social monarchy"). After the Second World War these common features coalesced into the distinctive German–Japanese model of "coordinated" capitalism (Hollingsworth and Boyer, 1997; Streeck and Yamamura, 2001).

The Japanese who travelled to Europe and the United States reported back not only on the highly advanced state of industry and technology in the West but also on the grave social problems of unemployment, urban poverty and labour unrest that accompanied them. Of greatest concern to the Japanese were the apparent growing class lines, class conflict and portent of socialist revolution in the West – a development that if allowed to grow in Japan would tear apart the order and harmony of society and derail the drive for capital accumulation and economic growth. Beginning in about 1890, Japan was flooded with reports from Europe about the Social Problem. According to Kinzley (1991: 22), "From 1890 no issue so dominated intellectual discourse as the social problem [*shakai mondai*]. Following the Sino-Japanese War *shakai mondai* was one of the most fashionable phrases of the day." Kinzley goes on to say (p. 23),

> While the term 'social problem' was applied to an almost unlimited range of issues there was one that elicited the greatest and most persistent concern: the problem of labour. ... [T]he defining issue and the principal focus of the 'social problem' was discussion of the 'labour problem', namely the attempt to determine the proper place for industrial workers in the new society.

Academic writing on labour followed quickly. One early contributor was Touzo Fukuda. He studied under Brentano in Germany and in 1899 published an edited book of Brentano's articles, along with a lengthy introduction of his own, under the title *Labor economics* (Nishizawa, 2001). Fukuda went on to become one of Japan's most eminent economists, noted for his efforts to synthesize the German historical/institutional approach with the British neoclassical approach. One of his students was Ichiro Nakayama, who after the Second World War would become one of the leaders of Japanese industrial relations.

The person who did the most to popularize the German concept of social policy (*shakai seisaku*) in Japan was Noboru Kanai. Kanai spent four years studying economics in Germany (1886–90) and then returned to Japan and became "one of the most significant figures in the history of Japanese social thought" (Pyle, 1974: 140). Kanai became Japan's first major academic economist, a professor of law at the Imperial University (later, Tokyo University), and a founder of a new school of social theory. In 1896, Kanai and a small group of other scholars founded the Japanese Social Policy Association, an organization modelled on the German Verein. Alternative names considered by Kanai for the association included "Social Problem Research Association" and "Labour Problem Research Association". Until the mid-1920s the Association was the only professional organization for economists in Japan, included nearly every practising economist and professor of law in the nation, and had an influence that (p. 141) "pervaded the bureaucracy from the end of the 1890s down to the 1930s". Kanai also introduced a social policy course into the curriculum at Tokyo University (Hanami, 1971).

According to Kanai (quoted in Pyle, p. 144),

> Ultimately the highest object of social policy in modern times is to bring back together again the various social classes which are daily becoming more and more separated; and it must establish a socially cooperative life based on intimate relations of mutual help and interdependence. ... In this way we can establish the unity that national strength requires.

This philosophy is further elaborated in the Association's declaration of principles:

We oppose laissez-faire because it creates extreme profit consciousness and unbridled competition, and aggravates the differences between rich and poor. We also oppose socialism because it would destroy the present economic organization, obliterate capitalists, and therefore impede national progress. We support the principles of the present private enterprise system. Within this framework we seek to prevent friction between classes through the power of government and through individual exertions and thereby to preserve social harmony.

This declaration of principles, it might be noted, is quite similar in spirit to the declaration of principles American economist Richard Ely crafted for the American Economic Association he helped found in 1885 after returning from his graduate studies in Germany. Ely, of course, was an outspoken advocate of the historical/social approach to economics and was a major contributor to the development of American institutional economics – the most important intellectual root of American industrial relations. Interestingly, Ely's basic university textbook, *Outlines of political economy*, outsold all other English-language economics books in Japan in the early twentieth century (Rader, 1966).

The members of the Japanese Social Policy Association shared a common perspective and philosophy but differed significantly on specific aspects of dealing with the Social Question. Most supported some type of legislation to protect workers from excessive hours and unsafe conditions. Most also favoured encouraging employers to adopt a more benevolent approach to employer–employee relations and various welfare measures. The group split into factions, however, on the issue of trade unionism. Some members strongly favoured promoting trade unions and collective bargaining. A leader of this group was Iwasaburo Takano (brother of Fusataro Takano), a professor of law and the person who in 1927 translated the Webbs' *Industrial democracy* into Japanese. Another prominent Social Policy Association member, Kumazo Kuwata, played an important role in the development of the Yuaikai, which became the first major national labour organization in Japan and the genesis of the Japan Federation of Labour. Another sizeable group of association members were cool or outright opposed to trade unions, however. While recognizing that workers had legitimate grievances, they felt that the adversarial, sometimes militant and violent approach taken by unions undercut the spirit of cooperation, unity of interest and "warm family relationship" they desired to foster between employer and employee. Instead, they opted for other measures, such as employer welfare practices and educational campaigns (known as "thought guidance") among employers and workers to reaffirm Confucian values of harmony, loyalty, filial piety and reciprocal duty. People such as

Kanai tried to straddle these two positions. Said one such person (quoted in Kinzley, 1991: 61), "If unions are formed with no purpose other than to oppose capitalists they are not good. But, if unions are organized to improve the character of workers, elevate their status, or to meet special emergency situations, I am in no way opposed to them."

As actually practised, Japanese social policy from 1900 to 1930 strongly resembled the approach adopted in Germany. In 1900, a Peace Police Law was enacted that allowed police wide latitude to suppress labour unions and jail their leaders. Although only used when political authorities deemed necessary, the Peace Police Law remained a potent curb on union activity through the 1920s. While suppressing radicalism on one hand, the government sought to eliminate the grievances that promoted radicalism by enacting in 1911 a Factory Law and later a Health Insurance Law (1922) and strengthened version of the Factory Law (1926). Progressive industrialists also emerged from the ranks of Japanese businessmen and sought to encourage others to practise a more welfare-oriented style of labour management, thus maintaining the familial relationship at work that was thought to have characterized Japan in the earlier era of small-scale craft and artisanal production.

In 1919, the Japanese government sponsored a nominally independent group composed of industrialists, scholars and government officials to promote a progressive line in labour–management relations and mediation and reconciliation of labour disputes. Named the *Kyochokai* (Conciliation Society), its mission is described by Kinzley (1991: 84) as promoting social harmony and social justice through the "complete realization of social policy", while Dore (2000: 397) describes Kyochokai's mission as "concerned not only with promoting the new, firm-as-family ideology and all the welfare measures and systems which supported it, but also to the development of workers' councils and consultative committees as a means of co-opting the union movement". As Dore's quotation suggests, one visible outgrowth of this movement was the spread of employer-created shop committees and works councils among large Japanese firms in the 1920s (Totten, 1967). The final element of Japanese social policy during this period was continued emphasis on the necessity of harmony and cooperation among the social classes if Japan was to avoid foreign domination and take its place among the great powers. An oft-used exhortation was to "build a rich country and strong military" (Kinzley, 1991: 49).

A quest for harmony and efficiency also led to the popularization of another school of thought in Japan – scientific management. Although Japan and the United States were very dissimilar in many social and cultural dimensions, in certain areas there was a strong congruence. One of these was in the organization and management of industrial enterprise. The Japanese had a long tradition of emphasizing efficiency and harmony in industrial activities, for example. Japanese society was also less class divided and class conscious than many in continental Europe, and, like the Americans, the Japanese had a penchant for applying science and engineering to industrial operations. The gospel of Taylorism and its creed of harmony through the laws of science and shared fruits of productivity gain thus found a ready and eager audience in Japan.

Taylorism was introduced in Japan by Toshiro Ikeda, a visitor to the United States and employee of the Wrigley Chewing Gum's Japan branch (Tsutsui, 1998: 18). After returning to Japan in 1911, he wrote a series of articles explaining in popularized terms Taylor's principles, with one pamphlet selling more than 1.5 million copies. Two years later Taylor's *Principles of scientific management* was translated into Japanese and soon Japan was in the grip of an "efficiency craze". Hundreds of recruits were dispatched to the United States to learn about American production and management methods and a number of disciples of Taylor travelled to Japan to lecture and consult. Taylorism quickly evolved and broadened beyond its inventor's conception as early Japanese pioneers discovered the importance of the human factor and, in particular, the inability of stop watches and bonus systems to increase productivity without the active cooperation and trust of the workers. Tsutsui (1998: 27) thus notes that "harmony and cooperation became keywords of Japan's scientific management movement". Illustrative of this sentiment is this statement by Yoichi Ueno, the Japanese "father of scientific management", on the nature of the "Mental Revolution" required for industrial success (ibid.):

> Cooperation is absolutely necessary in all organizations. In business, success is doubtful without cooperation. If all, from the president down to the lowest functionary, can pool together their various personal abilities, work together for the common good of the company's prosperity and devote themselves as a group, then great increases in results are possible. If, however, capitalists live in fear of labor offensives, workers label capitalists as the enemy, and there is never anything but quarreling, then the company will decline day by day. Where there is no diligent cooperation there is no prosperity.

The First World War period introduced great strains into the Japanese economy. War-led prosperity created high inflation and tight labour markets, leading to great problems with employee turnover, spreading interest in unions, and a fivefold increase in strikes. Much as in Europe and North America, the Bolshevik Revolution in Russia – followed shortly by the large-scale Rice Riots across Japan – greatly stirred fears (or hopes, in some circles) of major social upheaval. According to Pyle (1974: 161), "Writers described the Bolshevik Revolution and the arrival of new radical thought as creating a shock in the intellectual world comparable to the coming of the black ships." Investigative books and articles on the harsh life of Japanese workers, such as Hajime Kawakami's (1917) *A story on poverty*, also stirred concern.

The fears of labour radicalism and the high costs of employee turnover, coupled with the emergence after the war of the first mass production industries and the need for labour peace, led to the appearance of a nascent welfare capitalist movement in Japan broadly similar to that in the United States. Indeed, the employment system developed among leading Japanese companies in the 1920s had greater similarity in structure and philosophy to the American PM-school version of industrial relations than that of any other country. The Japanese movement represented an intermingling of scientific management, *Sozialpolitik* and traditional welfarist paternalism. Illustrative of the intellectual linkages, Tsutsui (p. 27) states, "Ueno's ideas, and the Taylorite ideology from which they were derived, overlapped in many ways with the philosophy of the Kyochokai." Personnel departments were started, shop committees and works councils formed, welfare programmes expanded and internal labour markets developed (Totten, 1967; Gordon, 1987; Jacoby, 1991). The newly emergent Japanese employment system was not a carbon copy of the American, but the parallels were strong at the enterprise level. Indeed, this is not surprising, since leading American practitioners of welfare capitalism, such as General Electric and Westinghouse (both members of the SCC), had close ties to Japanese partner firms and transferred American management practices and ideas to them. Where the American and Japanese models diverged was that the latter adhered to a German approach at the industry and economy level. According to Tsutsui (p. 60),

> [T]he American and German models were considered related but distinct: the "American-style" rationalization was taken to concentrate on the firm and shop-floor reforms, while the German movement looked to the industry or national economy as its basis ... the U.S. experience contributing the micro-level approaches (scientific management and technologies of production), the German tradition providing the macro-level strategies of concentration, cartelization, and state intervention in industrial organization.

Other parallels to the American case also exist. The Japanese trade union movement, for example, was relatively weak and after a burst of militancy and organizing gains during the First World War was beaten back and largely driven out of the industrial core by a combination of employer resistance and government refusal to provide legal recognition. A modest advance in factory legislation was obtained, however, partly due to Japan's decision to join the ILO in 1919 and the evident concern of the nation's leaders that it not be seen as openly flouting the ILO's Conventions and Recommendations on workers' rights (Ayusawa, 1966). Also of interest, a wealthy businessman, Magasaburo Ohara, donated funds in the 1920s to promote more harmonious capital–labour relations through the establishment of the Ohara Institute for Social Research. Shortly thereafter, Ohara persuaded a physician–professor to establish a sister organization, the Labour Science Institute.

Dating from the end of the First World War, Japanese intellectual circles gradually became more polarized and factionalized, while government policy drifted toward a harder line dominated by militarists and nationalists. The ideological strains were such that the Social Policy Association disbanded in 1924 and the *Kyochokai* came under increasing internal stress.

Japan had a growing radical and socialist movement in both the trade unions and universities in this post-war period. By the early 1930s, a sizeable contingent of economists and other scholars in the social sciences were Marxists (but not necessarily communists). Among the governing elite, businessmen and more moderate intellectuals, the rise of social and labour radicalism was deeply alarming. The more centrist and progressive among these groups counselled that the best approach was further accommodation, such as the passage of laws protecting workers' rights to organize and mandating works councils, and strengthening protective labour legislation. The position of the moderates was greatly strengthened by Japan's earlier decision to join the ILO.

As Japan entered the 1930s, however, the position of the social policy moderates began to be undermined by the rightward shift in Japanese politics and public opinion (Garon, 1996). The Great Depression hit Japan hard and created large-scale unemployment and bankruptcies in the industrial sector. Japanese public opinion was also increasingly radicalized by the perceived imperialistic double standard of the Western powers as they sought to hold on to their colonies and spheres of influence but at the same time deny Japan the opportunity to expand in southern and eastern Asia. The rightward drift of Japan was then greatly accelerated by the armed conflict set off by the "Manchurian Incident" in 1931 and, later, the invasion of China in 1934. As the nation headed for war, right-wing Japanese politicians and military officers used the pretext of patriotism and national unity to suppress communists and radicals. A series of purges hit the universities and many professors with centrist or left-wing views were forced to resign (Marshall, 1978). Following the example of Germany and Italy, labour unions were outlawed in the late 1930s and a fascist-style government took over the reins of power. In 1941, Japan attacked Pearl Harbor and the ensuing war with the

United States and allies eventually led to Japan's surrender in 1945 and economic devastation.

The history of modern industrial relations in Japan begins with the post-Second World War reconfiguration of the Japanese government and economy under the direction of the Supreme Commander for the Allied Powers, General Douglas MacArthur (see Koshiro, 2000). Acting under orders from President Truman, MacArthur issued directives to the Japanese government in 1945 to enact legislation recognizing and encouraging trade unions and collective bargaining. Quickly, trade union membership mushroomed – from 420,000 before the war to over 5 million in 1946 (Gordon, 1985). To the consternation of the Americans, however, many of the new unions were radical and militant and espoused a socialist form of economy, while some practised a syndicalist form of direct action in which workers seized factories and ran them without the owners and salaried managers. As a result, new laws were passed restricting union activities and a "red purge" of radical unionists was instituted, while a post-war recession shifted bargaining power back to management, who took the opportunity to break industry-wide bargaining and re-establish the pre-war patter of bargaining at the enterprise level.

The creation of a national union movement more or less overnight, and the associated problems of recognition, bargaining and strikes, naturally created a need and opportunity for academics to move into this area. Hanami (1971: 5) states of this period:

> During the immediate post-war years, labour problems became one of the most popular dissertation subjects among young scholars. In most universities and colleges a chair on labour problems took on great importance. Almost all university departments of economics established lectures on 'social policy,' 'labour problems,' or 'labour economics' and every department of law set up 'labour law' courses, lectures on 'management' or 'labour management' were provided in departments of economics or in sociology courses in departments of literature.

Amidst this ferment, Kazuo Okochi, a professor of social policy at Tokyo University, took the lead. Before the war, Okochi had published *A history of thought on social policy in Germany* (1936) and, a few years later, S*mith and List: Economic ethics and economic theory* (1943). After the war, he re-established the Social Policy Association as the main professional organization for economists. In 1950, he and a research team published the first major research study on post-war unionism in Japan, *The actual conditions of the post-war labour unions*. Following this, Okochi received funding from the Ford Foundation to research and publish historical documents on the emergence of trade unions in Japan earning him recognition as the "J.R. Commons of Japan" (Koshiro, 2003).

A large component of the professors in the Social Policy Association were Marxists of various kinds, as was Okochi. Many were ideologically committed Marxists (reflecting the "hero's role" Marxists earned in resisting Japanese militarism, and capitalism's unsavoury connection with fascism, imperialism and industrial monopoly) while others, such as Okochi, were pragmatic or "theoretical" Marxists, in the sense that they used Marxist concepts and theories as a framework for research without necessarily being committed to Marxism as a political and social cause. This "opportunistic" use of Marxism reflected, in part, the relative paucity of theory in the German historical economics and social policy school, and that neoclassical economics was largely unknown at this time (Koshiro, 1980). With respect to his various early post-war studies of labour unions, Okochi's use of Marxist economics was minimal and these studies were instead largely "institutional" in the sense of emphasizing history, institutions and empirical facts.

Given the dominance of Marxists in the field of social policy in the 1950s, research in the field of labour – the work of Okochi and colleagues excepted – tended to follow along highly partisan and ideological lines, leading to polemical debates and much abstract argumentation (Hanami, 1971). Into this situation entered an American, Solomon Levine, who came to Japan in 1953 on a Fulbright grant. Levine, a professor at the University of Illinois' Institute of Labor and Industrial Relations, had learned Japanese in the military and came to Japan to write on post-war trade unionism and labour relations. He formed a close association with a small group of "moderates" in the economics and social policy field, including Okochi, Ichiro Nakayama and Keizo Fujibayashi. It was through Levine that the American concept and field of industrial relations sunk its first roots in Japanese universities.

A particularly important role in establishing industrial relations in Japan was played by Nakayama (see the translator's note in Nakayama, 1975), who was a well-respected economist, president of Hitotsubashi University, and public interest representative on Japan's Central Labour Relations Commission (Japan's federal-level tripartite agency responsible for labour–management matters). Nakayama's book *Industrialization of Japan and industrial relations* (1960) was influential in introducing and spreading the term industrial relations in Japan (Hanami, 2002). He also helped the industrial relations field to become known in Japan by helping to arrange travel to Japan by a variety of the American and British industrial relations scholars, including Kerr and colleagues. Nakayama then wrote the "Foreword" to the Japanese edition of *Industrialism and industrial man*.

Further, Nakayama became president of the Japan Institute of Labor (JIL) in the early 1960s and made it a centre for industrial relations research in Japan. The reader will recall from Chapter 6 that when Roberts and Cox formed the IIRA they invited the JIL to be one of the four founding associations and asked Nakayama to be the IIRA's first president (a request declined for reasons of health). The next year Nakayama, in cooperation with economists such as Okochi and Mikio Sumiya and a number of prominent legal scholars from the Japan Labour Law Association, founded the Japan Industrial Relations Association (JIRA).

The establishment and early development of the industrial relations field in Japan, as in continental European countries, stirred controversy. Although industrial relations has close kinship ties to German social policy, in Japan the two fields had important elements of rivalry. As already noted, the field of social policy in Japan had a large contingent of Marxists – as did the field of labour law at this time and its major academic association, the Association of Labour Law Studies. As in Europe, many Marxist scholars in Japan were hostile to industrial relations from both a theoretical and policy perspective. On the level of theory, Marxism uses class as a core concept and posits a deterministic evolutionary process in which capitalism eventually self-destructs. Industrial relations, on the other hand, eschews class and class struggle as organizing concepts in favour of a functional perspective of institutions (unions, employer associations, etc.) and the process of management, bargaining and negotiation. It was in order to encourage this more harmonious, cooperative approach to labour relations that the ruling Liberal-Democratic government endeavoured to encourage the spread of industrial relations in Japan by creating the JIL in 1958.

On the level of policy, Marxists are also typically committed to deep socialist transformation of the economy, while industrial relations academics desire to keep a pluralistic, mixed capitalist economy, but use selective reforms to increase its efficiency and equity. Illustrative of these different points of view, the term in Japanese for industrial relations is *roshi kankei*, which can be written in two different ways with two subtle differences in meaning. One way, giving it a Marxist emphasis, is to use characters that mean *labour–capital* relations, while a second is to use different characters that mean *labour–management* relations – the form favoured by pluralist industrial relations scholars. When Marxists such as Okochi, Nakayama and others "defected" from social policy to industrial relations (or, later, labour economics), this inevitably led to hostility and recriminations. The split should not be over-dramatized, however, since many industrial relations academics remained members of the Social Policy Association (and Association of Labour Law Studies) and, today, dual membership is common.

Marxists, it turns out, were not the only ones to find intellectual and ideological problems with industrial relations. Some economists also started to express reservations. Hanami (1971) notes that after the Second World War criticism began to be aimed at the field of social policy because its theories were perceived to be (p. 13) "superficial mixtures of theories of economics, jurisprudence, political science, etc. and ideology", causing scholars to ask "is social policy a science?" He goes on to to say:

> In particular, economists who had been engaging in research on labour problems attempted to establish the study of labour problems on a more scientific basis by applying economic theory. This effort shows that they regarded the theory of 'social policy' as a hodgepodge of various social sciences and ideology combined in an unsystematic form and hence they tried to establish a more sophisticated theory of labour economics.

Although this quotation is about social policy, industrial relations and social policy were quite close in their conception and practice and thus the criticisms and doubts raised by the economists against the latter carried over in almost all respects to the former. Only later, when neoclassical economics came to Japan in the 1970s and 1980s, did these alleged intellectual shortcomings really start to have serious effects.

The JIL and the JIRA did much to promote the industrial relations field in Japan and move it forward. The JIL published numerous books and research monographs on industrial relations. Its monthly publication, *The Japanese Journal of Labour Studies*, was for many years the major academic research outlet for article-length studies on industrial relations in Japan. The JIL was also a substantial source of funding and data for industrial relations research. The JIL and JIRA also sponsored numerous conferences, such as the first Regional Asian Conference on Industrial Relations in 1969 and two world congresses of the IIRA, the Sixth World Congress in Kyoto in 1983 and the Twelfth World Congress in Tokyo in 2000. Two presidents of the JIL and JIRA have also served as presidents of the IIRA: economist Mikio Sumiya and labour law scholar Tadashi Hanami.

Although the industrial relations field grew and prospered in Japan in the 1960s and 1970s, Japanese universities did not, in general, follow the American model and establish independent industrial relations institutes, centres or academic degree programmes. Several multidisciplinary research centres were established, however, but in some cases they covered more than just industrial relations (Hanami, 1971). Examples of important institutes include the Institute of Social

Science at Tokyo University, Institute of Management and Labour Studies at Keio University, Socio-Economic Institute at Sophia University, the Ohara Institute for Social Research at Hosei University, and the International Institute of Industrial Relations at Kansei University. The Sophia University institute, for example, published numerous industrial relations studies under the editorship of Robert Ballon, a Catholic priest and scholar. Some of these institutes and centres were established with financial support from American foundations (ibid.).

Hanami offers an interesting explanation for why multidisciplinary institutes and industrial relations research programmes had a difficult time getting started in Japan. One factor, he states, is a strong element of "disciplinary sectionalism" among faculty members, making them uninterested in collaborating with colleagues across disciplinary boundaries. A second factor is the divisive effect of ideology and political partisanship, for he notes that (p. 6) "each scholar and his group were regarded as belonging to, or at least committing themselves to, a certain cause". A third factor he cites is that scholars tended to get pulled either into the camp of labour or management because research funding and access would only be provided on condition that the results would promote the donor's interests.

In hindsight, the "golden age" of the industrial relations field in Japan extended from roughly 1965 to 1980. Exemplifying the golden age was the publication of *Workers and employers in Japan* by Okochi, Karsh and Levine (1973) – a product of a research team of nearly a dozen of the "who's who" in Japan's industrial relations community. Also noteworthy and insightful was Dore's (1973) comparative case study of industrial relations practices and competitive performance in British and Japanese factories.

A number of factors account for the golden age: union density was relatively high and organized labour played a major role in the economy; the post-war industrial relations system was a new phenomenon in Japan and many exciting and important research topics awaited investigation; Japanese and foreign scholars also created an expansion in comparative industrial relations research contrasting Japanese and Western industrial relations systems and highlighting the unique aspects of the former (e.g., enterprise unions, the dual system of employment, lifetime employment); unions and collective bargaining enjoyed considerable public and government support; and the weaknesses of the social policy and Marxist schools in the areas of theoretical and empirical labour research provided a major window of opportunity for industrial relations.

After 1980, conditions changed and the industrial relations field entered a period of slow but significant decline (Kume, 1998; Hanami, 2002b). By the end of the century, the industrial relations field in Japan was still active but at a noticeably reduced scale in terms of faculty participation, student enrolment and government funding. Perhaps most illustrative of industrial relations' fallen status is the decision of the Japanese government to merge the Ministry of Labour with the Ministry of Health and Welfare and, in 2002, to end the 45-year life of the JIL by merging it into another agency.

Many of the reasons for industrial relations' decline are mirror images of those that made the 1965–80 period a golden age: a substantial drop in the proportion of the workforce covered by collective bargaining; a sense that industrial relations practices and problems are no longer exciting or leading edge in the worlds of business and government; a waning of government and public support for unions and collective bargaining, with the rise of concerns over inflation, employment growth and international competitiveness; and the sharp fall-off in student demand for industrial relations courses. As in other countries, part of industrial relations' decline in Japan is also directly related to the growing popularity of business schools, the study of HRM and the rise of neoclassical economics. Also contributing is the decreasing attractiveness of interdisciplinary research and a retreat of academics to their home disciplines of economics, law, sociology and business administration.

Although all of these factors are important, Kuwahara (1989) in a study for the JIL points to a deeper and more fundamental reason. Just as the Depression and New Deal displaced the 1920s industrial relations model in the United States, the Second World War and the Allied Occupation Authorities displaced the similar industrial relations model that had arisen in Japan after 1920. The Americans in the 1930s and 1940s switched from a largely non-union welfare capitalism model to an industry-wide adversarial collective bargaining model. When the United States defeated Japan in the war, it sought to install the same model in Japan. Kuwahara suggests, however, that this model ultimately failed because it was contradictory to the key ingredient needed for growth and industrial competitive advantage – flexibility and cooperation. Between the mid-1950s and mid-1970s, Japan quietly introduced a "new" industrial relations model, though many of the basic ideas and practices were from the cooperative/family enterprise model widely used before the Second World War. Thus Kuwahara states (p. 7):

> Those seeking novel features [for Japan's economic success] eventually come to lifetime employment, seniority-based wages, enterprise unions, and the philosophy of cooperative management, all of which have been long regarded as characteristic of labor practices and industrial relations in Japan. Ironically, however, these are the features that were previously [in the immediate post-1945 period] regarded as anachronistic, and though the opinions of labor and management differed, attempts were made up until the beginning of the 1970s to abolish these "anachronisms".

In the 1940s–1950s, Japan, like the United States, adopted the collective bargaining model as the preferred employment relations system and sought to purge "anachronistic" elements. These elements were various features that underlay the cooperative unitarist/paternalist industrial relations model of the 1920s – such as employee representation plans in the United States and the enterprise-based lifetime employment model in Japan – and that were now viewed as backward or retrograde. More quickly than the United States, however, Japan moved away from the pluralist collective bargaining model and went back to an updated version of the cooperative PM model in the industrial sector of the Japanese dual employment relations system. This model proved highly successful, Japan enjoyed an economic miracle, and thousands of Americans travelled to Japan to discover the secrets of Japanese management. The Japanese had indeed developed a unique and high-performing industrial relations model, but if the Americans had looked below the surface they would have seen "Made in the USA" stamped on major components (Jacoby, 1991; Tsutsui, 1998).

Commenting on this matter, the leading historian of management thought in the United States, Daniel Wren (1994: 361), states, "the managerial revolution that occurred in Japan after the Second World War was made in the United States". Wren is referring to the ideas of Taylor (scientific management) and the writings of later management theorists, such as Deming (total quality management). The problem with this view is not that it is incorrect but that it is incomplete, for neither Taylor nor Deming either theorized or operationalized the employment part of what became the modern Japanese employment relations system. Rather, as pointed out in Chapter 2, the employment part of the mutual gains employment model was first articulated by the American founders of industrial relations, such as Commons, and first put into practice in a strategic way by industrial relations executives, such as Hicks. Visiting Japanese scholars and businessmen took this model back to Japan in the 1920s and developed and adapted it. After lying dormant for two decades after the Second World War, the Japanese resurrected and fine-tuned the cooperative/mutual gains model (including derivatives, such as the lean production model) and then turned it on the Americans to rout them from one market after another in the 1970s and 1980s. One may say, therefore, that the Japanese beat the Americans at their own game and that one of the tools they used was, paradoxically, first theorized and operationalized by people in industrial relations.

Unfortunately for modern American industrial relations, it has small opportunity to capitalize on its historical contribution because after the Second World War the field largely disowned the unitarist PM model in favour of pluralistic collective bargaining. The recent outpouring of research by American industrial relations scholars on the high-performance workplace can be seen as a belated effort to recapture this (largely unrecognized) legacy and school of thought, albeit constrained by certain ILE ideological commitments. Ironically, as the United States and other nations raced in the late 1980s and early 1990s to learn from and imitate the Japanese employment system, the economic pillars of this system were already starting to erode. Part of the explanation is unique to Japan, such as a stock market bubble and over-regulated financial sector, but another part stems from worldwide trends, such as globalization, market deregulation and excess industrial capacity. The result of these forces is that the Japanese lifetime employment system has gradually weakened and shrunk, accompanied by a shift to more open labour markets and market-driven HRM practices as found in the United States (Jacoby, Nason and Saguchi, 2004). These same trends are evident across nearly all industrial economies, suggesting that some convergence in employment systems is taking place. The employment model being converged on, however, may be neither the unitarist PM system nor pluralist ILE system of industrial relations but a variant of the neoclassical market model.

Republic of Korea

Similar to Japan, the origin of industrial relations in the Republic of Korea (henceforth Korea) is in the 1880s, with the opening up of the economy to foreign trade, the establishment of the first factories and the emergence of the modern employment relationship. The first strikes took place in the late 1880s and the first union was formed among longshoremen in 1898 (Lee, 1993).

The history of industrial relations in Korea in the twentieth century was heavily shaped by long periods of government repression of labour, particularly of leftist trade unions. The era of repression began in 1910 with Japan's military occupation of Korea and subsequent 35-year period of colonial rule. One part of the labour movement became a centre for nationalist and communist agitation against Japanese rule and was heavily suppressed, while other compliant unions were allowed to function but under tight control.

Korea was liberated from Japanese control in 1945 and soon divided into the Republic of Korea in the south and the communist-controlled Democratic People's Republic of Korea in the north. In the former, the American Military Government, with trusteeship of the country, sought to introduce democratic reforms, including independent unions. However, the military authorities quickly switched course and banned the leftist/communist-dominated General Council of Korean Trade Unions and replaced it with a more moderate rival, the General Federation of Korean Trade Unions (Park and Leggett, 1998). Protective labour laws were also passed but not effectively enforced. Over the next 40 years, a series of civilian and military governments ruled the country, generally with a high degree of authoritarian control. Although trade union membership grew steadily and density nearly tripled between 1960 and 1980, collective bargaining was tightly circumscribed both to limit political opposition and to promote greater industrialization and export-led growth. In this respect, Korea mirrored the practice of other East Asian countries and territories, such as Singapore and Taiwan, China. Quite specific to Korea, however, was the dominant role played in industrial relations by the *chaebol* – a small number of huge family-run firms that exercised great political and economic power.

Inevitably, the heavy hand of government and employer autocracy and lack of effective employee voice in either government or the workplace shifted the main body of Korean unions to a relatively militant, politicized and national-istic position. Matters came to a head in the Great Labour Offensive of 1987 in which workers staged thousands of strikes as part of a national movement for the end of authoritarianism and return of democratic government (Lee and Rhee, 1996). Since then, Korean industrial relations has been characterized by a high degree of confrontation and militancy in some industries and firms and growing accommodation in others, further limited attempts by the government to liberalize trade union law, an extension of unionism to white-collar workers and a modest decline in overall union density. Particularly noteworthy was Kim Young-sam's presidential address in 1996 in which he announced a New Conception of Industrial Relations, with the purpose of reforming Korean industrial relations through the deliberations of a tripartite Industrial Relations Reform Commission.

The emergence of the field of industrial relations as a recognized area of teaching and research in Korea did not take place until the end of military rule in 1987, although the Korean term for industrial relations (*nosa kwankye*, literally translated as labour–management relations) first appeared in the 1960s. Of course, professors in Korean universities had for many years written on labour and trade union subjects. Notable names from the 1950s through 1970s include Yoon-Whan Kim, Nak-Jung Kim, Chang-Wha Cho, Young-Ki Park and Chi-Seon Kim (Lee and Lee, 2004). Also setting the stage for the birth of industrial relations in Korea was the large number of Korean students who came to the United States and obtained doctoral degrees in industrial relations. Some remained in the United States but many returned to Korea to take academic, government and business positions.

With the return of democracy to Korea in 1987, events happened quickly. In 1988, the Korea Labour Institute (KLI) was created. Like the JIL in Japan, the KLI greatly promoted development of the industrial relations field in Korea through large-scale funding of labour research, data collection, and research and publication on labour policy. Many KLI researchers also served as professors in management, economics and law departments in universities.

Unlike Japan, Korea went one step further and established separate schools, institutes and graduate degree programmes in industrial relations. The first, established in 1988, was the Graduate School of Labor and Management Relations at Soongsil University in Seoul. Academic departments include industrial relations and human resources, labour law and industrial welfare policy. Between 1989 and 2002, the school produced over 300 graduates. The second programme is the Graduate School of Labor Studies at Korea University in Seoul, created in 1994. It includes departments in industrial relations and HRM, labour law, industrial welfare and policy, and labour economics, as well as an Executive Programme in Labor Studies. Over 700 students have graduated to date. A third example is the Institute of Industrial Relations, housed within the College of Business Administration of Seoul National University.

Other developments also signalled the growth of the industrial relations field in Korea. For example, in 1990 the Korean Industrial Relations Association was founded. Then, in 1991, the Association started publication of the *Korean Journal of Industrial Relations.* A year earlier another industrial relations journal, the *Journal of Industrial Relations*, had been started under the auspices of the Institute of Industrial Relations at Seoul National University. Also closely related to the industrial relations field is the *Journal of Industrial Labor* published by the Academy of Industrial Labor and the *Journal of Industrial Sociology* published by the Academy of Industrial Sociology.

Despite these encouraging signs of growth, recent years have seen a slackening of interest in industrial relations in Korea. Student enrolments in industrial relations courses have declined considerably, leading to the closing or merging of some industrial relations majors or programmes. Part of the explanation is that economic hard times have led Korean companies to substantially curtail hiring of new industrial relations and labour relations specialists; another part has to do with the increasing attractiveness of business schools and HRM. Industrial relations has also lost some of its glamour and excitement as trade unions turned from a crusading force for democracy and workers' rights to the more mundane aspects of collective bargaining. Public opinion of unions, for these reasons, has also slipped in recent years.

Africa

The first currents of economic development and industrialism appeared in Africa in the late nineteenth century but to date have spread and deepened relatively slowly. Large parts of the African workforce remain employed in agriculture, handicrafts and other activities in the informal economy, while a small formal employment base has developed in areas such as mining and petroleum production, manufacturing, transportation and government services. The low level of economic development, and the dual nature of the economy, has thus significantly affected the formation and development of the field of industrial relations in these countries.

Of equal importance in shaping the field of industrial relations in Africa is the experience of colonialism, imperialism and racism (Allen, 1972). Industrialism came to the continent in tandem with the colonialization of Africa by the various European powers. During the nineteenth century, Africa was carved up into a patchwork of colonies and protectorates by Belgium, France, Germany, Holland, Italy, Portugal, Spain and the United Kingdom. Colonial governments were established with a white-controlled admini-stration, police force and judiciary superimposed on a native population with few or no rights, resources or political voice. The purpose of the colonial governments, in turn, was to facilitate the economic exploitation of the African territories by European commercial and industrial interests. In effect, colonialism was the resource investment in political and institutional infrastructure that the Europeans had to make in order to reap the profits from its economic imperialism. The practice of imperialism took a variety of forms, such as dispossessing native Africans of their land and turning it into large white-run farms; opening up African natural resources, such as gold, diamonds, oil and timber, to exploitation by European corporations; and giving European companies a protected monopoly in manufacturing and commerce. Care was taken to keep the colonial economies in a satellite, supplementary position relative to the home market and not allow them to become a direct competitor. For the native workers, forced labour in primitive working conditions was not unusual.

Accompanying colonialism and imperialism was a third evil: deep and persistent racism and violation of basic human rights. Particularly in sub-Saharan Africa, racial segregation (apartheid) was widely and rigorously enforced in all spheres of life. In the work world, whites used law and coercion to gerrymander the job market so that they kept a monopoly on management and supervisory positions, skilled trades and other desirable, better-paying occupations. Native people, on the other hand, were either confined to the edges of paid employment (handicrafts, street selling, domestic help) or used for low-wage, physically arduous labour in mines, factories and construction. Trade unions were also frequently segregated, with the black unions denied the right to strike (Nel, 1997).

The story of industrial relations in Africa is complicated because, like Asia, it is a very heterogeneous continent in terms of people, cultures and political systems of government. The most fundamental division in this regard is between Saharan Africa in the north and sub-Saharan Africa in the south. Northern (Saharan) Africa is inhabited by Arab peoples who have more in common culturally and politically with countries of the Middle East. Southern (sub-Saharan) Africa, on the other hand, is inhabited largely by black Africans of many different ethnic groups and tribes. Several countries also have a significant minority population of East Indians (brought to Africa by the British to work on railway and other ventures).

The Saharan countries of Africa, such as Egypt, Algeria and Morocco, have a history of trade unionism and working-class movements that goes back to the late part of the nineteenth century. Historians of the Egyptian labour movement, for example, often date its emergence with a strike of cigarette rollers in 1899 (Lockman, 1994). Ten years later workers in Cairo formed the Manual Trades Workers' Union. The economies and political systems of the north African countries have not, however, developed over the intervening years in a direction that is conducive to the emergence and growth of the industrial relations field. The industrial sector, for example, remains relatively small, while the large bulk of the labour force is employed in agriculture, the informal economy or small-scale trade and service. Industrial workers, rather than being viewed as oppressed and exploited, are more likely to be seen as among the aristocracy of the workforce. Likewise, the trade unions that exist are largely state controlled and co-opted and, thus, autonomous collective bargaining and traditional problems of labour–management relations are for the most part absent (Beinin, 1994). Nor is industrial or social pluralism particularly encouraged or, often, tolerated, and university systems tend to be under fairly tight religious and political control. Finally, while these countries have very significant labour and social problems, such as massive unemployment and underemployment and large-scale urban poverty, these problems do not typically fall within the domain of industrial relations, at least as typically defined.

For these reasons, it is not surprising that the field of industrial relations, to the best of my knowledge, has no organized presence in the countries of north Africa. This absence, I note, is despite the fact that Egypt was one of the countries included in the Kerr, Dunlop, Harbison and Myers' Inter-University Project on Labour Problems in Economic Development. While the four horsemen helped bring industrial relations to other countries, their efforts did not bear fruit in north Africa.

In sub-Saharan Africa, on the other hand, industrial relations has established a small but significant presence. But even here there are significant differences that have to be accounted for. The most important with regard to industrial relations is the division between countries governed by the British and those under the rule of the other European powers, such as the French. Mirroring the traditions and histories of the home countries, the concept and practice of industrial relations was introduced into the African colonies of the United Kingdom, albeit unevenly and on a modest scale, while in the colonies of the French (and other powers) no such tradition emerged until the most recent times. Fashoyin (2003) reports, for example, that in Francophone Africa the first industrial relations association did not appear until 2001 (the Association Congolaise des Relations Professionelles), while in Anglophone Africa four industrial relations associations exist, with the first one being founded in 1982.

In French-controlled Africa the government administrators took a relatively repressive stance toward indigenous labour movements and trade unions through the 1930s (Martens, 1979). After the Second World War, the various union federations in France sought to develop a membership base in Africa, with some success. Reflecting French practices at home, the African trade unions in the French colonies were more political in orientation, and collective bargaining was less institutionalized (Damachi, 1985: 18). After national independence, most of these newly liberated countries developed into one-party political states and trade unions were integrated (or subordinated) into the party structures. According to Martens (pp. 38–9), the African political authorities endeavoured to exercise tight control over the trade unions, partly out of fear that they would become sources of political opposition and partly to channel their energies into "constructive" and "responsible" activities benefiting the cause of economic development. With little trade union autonomy or genuine collective bargaining, and a lack of any academic tradition of industrial relations, not surprisingly the field of industrial relations in the Francophone countries has so far failed to develop solid roots.

English-speaking Africa, not surprisingly, imported British industrial relations practices and thus developed along a different path. Trade unions in the United Kingdom were generally recognized as legitimate social actors and the British commitment to voluntarism gave them a fair degree of autonomy in the economic sphere. These same patterns were adopted in those African colonies controlled by the British, such as Ghana, Kenya, Nigeria, Rhodesia and Uganda. In Nigeria, for example, the first trade union appeared in 1912, while in South Africa the earliest trade unions appeared among black miners in the 1890s (Yesufu, 1962; Fashoyin, 1980; Nel, 1997). As long as these unions did not become overly militant or hotbeds for nationalist independence, the British tolerated them and even saw value in their activities, regarding the unions as a way to provide "indirect" control of the native workforce and useful vehicles to resolve problems before they festered to dangerous proportions (Matthews and Apthorpe, 1958: xiv).

In an interesting turn of history, the initial impetus for institutionalizing trade unions in Anglophone Africa came from Sidney Webb (then Lord Passfield). Acting in his capacity as Secretary of State for the Colonies, Webb in 1930 issued a colonial dispatch suggesting to the governors of the respective colonies that British interests would be furthered by enacting protective labour legislation, as well as legislation modelled on the British Trade Unions Act of 1871 to encourage the formation of trade unions (Yesufu, 1962: 29). He cautioned the governors, however, to proceed with care, noting that "without sympathetic supervision and guidance the unions ... might divert their activities to improper and mischievous ends" (quoted in Ojeli, 1976: 1). Slowly, such laws were passed in the British territories, such as the Trade Union Ordinance of 1938 in Nigeria and the Employment Act of 1938 in Kenya (Iwuji, 1979). A further impetus to these legal initiatives was the pressure the United Kingdom and other colonial powers felt to conform, or at least appear to conform, to the labour standards of the ILO, such as the Forced Labour Convention (No. 29), 1930.

The evolution of industrial relations in Africa falls into three phases. The first phase is represented by the development of trade unions, the promulgation of the first labour codes and early academic writings on labour. This phase started at the turn of the century and continued into the 1950s. In South Africa, for example, collective bargaining began to spread slowly after 1900 and with it came a series of labour laws, such as the Mines and Works Act (1911), the Industrial Relations Conciliation Act (1937) and the Black Labour Relations Act (1953). Sometimes the laws called into being the trade unions, while in other cases they were a response to the activities of the unions. In either case, the claimed object of these laws was to give workers new rights and freedoms, when in fact a major purpose was to preserve colonial control over the native workers and, in the case of South Africa, maintain apartheid. Routh (1959: 8) notes this paradox when he says, "Thus the two worlds of South Africa, the parliamentary democracy and the dictatorship, the industrial and the feudal, are reflected in the ... schemes of labour legislation."

In this early period, the first labour writings also began to appear. Examples include *The African factory worker* (University of Natal, Economics Department, 1950), *Trade unions in Natal* (Ringrose, 1951) and *The theory of collective bargaining* (Hutt, 1954). Also illustrative is the conference proceedings *Social relations in Central African industry*, edited by Matthews and Apthorpe from a conference sponsored by the Rhodes–Livingston Institute for Social Research in Northern Rhodesia (Zambia). Because the major thrust of activity in this period took the form of legal enactment, universities started to introduce the first training courses in labour law, sometimes as part of commercial or industrial law (Fashoyin, 2003).

The second phase of industrial relations activity in sub-Saharan Africa was associated with the development of personnel management. The interest in personnel management reflected several developments: the growing size of industrial establishments, doubts of colonial administrators and employers about the suitability of unions as partners in industry, and the publicity given to human relations as a new method to promote cooperation and productivity. Thus a number of colonial governments and universities started to introduce training courses in personnel and human relations. Nigeria, for example, started in the 1960s to actively promote personnel management through a Personnel Management Advisory Service, while Rhodes University in South Africa introduced a Diploma course in Personnel Management in the early 1970s. Some kind of personnel training course or programme was also created in Kenya, Swaziland and Uganda (Fashoyin, 2003). In the 1980s and 1990s, the interest in personnel grew again, fuelled in part by the introduction of HRM and in part by the pressure exerted on employers by market liberalization to find less conflictual and more cooperative ways to manage the workforce.

The third phase is the emergence and development of industrial relations itself. This movement is largely a product of the 1970s and afterwards, and is concentrated in two countries: Nigeria and South Africa, Each is considered below.

The growing popularity of industrial relations in the United Kingdom in the 1960s naturally had ripple effects on universities in the British Commonwealth. British industrial relations professors, such as Ben Roberts and Victor Allen, took an interest in labour developments in Africa and published studies on the subject (Roberts, 1968b; Allen, 1972). Graduate students from Africa also went to the United Kingdom to earn doctoral degrees in industrial relations, attracted in part by the publicity generated by the Donovan Commission and the debates between the pluralists and radicals in British industrial relations. The work of Kerr et al. and other the Americans on the role of industrial relations in economic development was another inducement, while the American AFL–CIO made Africa in the 1960s and 1970s a particular area of emphasis for training and education in trade unionism and collective bargaining (Radosh, 1969).

Nigeria

Nigeria has the longest industrial relations history of any African country. An industrial relations course was taught as far back as the 1950s in the

Extra-Mural Studies Department of Ibadan University, the premier university in Nigeria (Fashoyin, 2003). The presence of industrial relations in the universities as a formal entity had to wait until the 1960s, however. The pioneer was Tijani Yesufu, a lecturer in the Extra-Mural Studies Department, who enrolled at the LSE and did a doctoral thesis under the supervision of Roberts. Yesufu returned to Nigeria and taught industrial relations and economics at the University of Lagos and published his thesis as a book, *An introduction to industrial relations in Nigeria* (1962).

Later, in 1979/80, a full-fledged master's degree in labour and industrial relations was introduced at the University of Ibadan. Several years later a Department of Industrial Relations and Personnel Management was created in the Faculty of Business Administration at the University of Lagos, offering both undergraduate and master's degrees. The staff, mostly American- or British-trained, included well-known names in African industrial relations, such as Ukandi Damachi, Ekpo Ufot, Tayo Fashoyin and Eleanor Facohunda. Damachi published a number of books and articles on African industrial relations (e.g., Damachi, 1985) and went on to become dean of the business administration programme at the University of Lagos. Fashoyin has also developed national and international name recognition, partly through his several books and articles on African industrial relations (e.g., Fashoyin, 1980, 1992) and also because of his role as secretary of the IIRA.

The stimulus for the development of the industrial relations field in Nigeria arose from several factors. One was the need of the country to fashion its own labour laws and institutions after gaining independence from the British. The existing system was not only imported from the United Kingdom, where conditions and heritage differed greatly from Nigeria, but was also indelibly tainted by the ill effects of the three "isms" – colonialism, imperialism and racism. Nigerian leaders thus faced the task of crafting a new industrial relations system to take the place of the old. Also entering into the picture was growing public disenchantment in the first decade after independence with political influence in the wage determination process. Rival regional governments seeking electoral votes were accustomed to offering competing wage awards that frequently had little relationship to productivity and other economic fundamentals. These outsized awards then spilled over into the private sector and not only distorted wage determination in industry but also seriously disrupted the budding process of collective bargaining. As done by numerous other countries when faced with a national crisis in labour relations, the Nigerian government appointed a task force in 1963, called the Morgan Commission, to investigate and make recommendations. The commission proposed a far-reaching overhaul of the industrial relations system and recommended that collective bargaining be adopted as the primary means for regulating wages and labour conditions in both the private and public sectors.

The recommendations of the commission marked a significant turning point in the development of the industrial relations system in Nigeria (Fashoyin, 2003). Trade union organization and collective bargaining spread, as did strikes, creating a need for more personnel and labour relations staff in industry, trade unions and government agencies such as the Ministry of Labour. Several trade unions, such as the Trade Unions Congress of Nigeria, expanded their internal training programmes, while the Universities of Lagos, Obafemi Awolowo, Ahmadu Bello and the University of Nigeria introduced new courses on personnel management and industrial relations in the existing disciplines of law, sociology, public administration and economics. Then, in the early 1980s, the next step was taken and degree programmes in industrial relations were established at the University of Ibadan and University of Lagos (described above). With the addition of a new doctoral degree in industrial relations, Nigeria became the first country in Africa to have a full department of industrial relations extending from the undergraduate to doctoral level.

Also of note, a group of Nigerian academics, with encouragement from the IIRA, took the lead in founding the Nigerian Industrial Relations Association in 1982, the first such association in Africa. In 1988, it organized the First Regional African Congress of the IIRA in Lagos, the papers of which were subsequently published in book form as *Industrial relations and African development* (Fashoyin, 1992).

Looking back on these years, Fashoyin (1992: vi) observed:

> During the past ten years, many far-reaching and fundamental changes have taken place; the newly created industrial unions and [associations of] employers have taken collective bargaining initiatives in a manner unprecedented in the country's history of industrial relations. ... [M]onumental interest in industrial relations as a field of study has been generated in a decade. ... The Department of Industrial Relations and Personnel Management at the University of Lagos was established in 1982, to offer undergraduate and graduate degrees, while a master's degree programme commenced at the University of Ibadan about the same time. Also scores of specialized courses in both undergraduate and graduate programmes were introduced in other universities and colleges. All these show the importance of industrial relations in the institutions of higher learning as well as industries in Nigeria.

Industrial relations in Nigeria has continued to develop since the 1980s. Further progress for industrial relations has been hindered, however, by ongoing political instability, including several military dictatorships. The governments, while giving lip service to free collective bargaining, have in practice kept tight control of industrial relations, substantially politicizing the process. In the universities, industrial relations also remains a specialty area and subordinate to the mainstream disciplines. The growing popularity of business administration and HRM has, as in other countries, also led to some diminished interest in industrial relations.

South Africa

South Africa is the other country in Africa with a significant history of industrial relations. Trade union activity and strikes first appeared in the late 1800s in the mining and transport industries. The first legal regulation of industrial relations did not occur until 1924, however, with the introduction of the Industrial Conciliation Act (Bendix, 1989). This piece of legislation set a precedent that greatly shaped the character of South African industrial relations. The Act excluded black Africans from the definition of "employee" and thus debarred them from participating in the official industrial relations system. As a result, South Africa developed a dual union system, with one set of trade unions for whites in the official system and another for blacks that lacked legal standing. Reflecting this duality, the white unions bargained to promote the interests of white workers vis-à-vis the employer but also to keep out competition from lower-wage black workers.

The dual union system was strengthened after the Second World War when the Nationalist Party came to power and the social policy of apartheid was gradually extended and enforced with greater severity. In the late 1950s, the black trade unions became increasingly politicized and restive under these harsher policies. The government responded by banning the unions and the Resistance movement disintegrated. During the 1960s the labour relations scene was quiet and universities saw no need to do anything in the area of industrial relations. A small stream of labour research was published during the 1960s, largely in labour and trade union history.

The situation changed dramatically in the early 1970s with the outbreak of strikes and labour violence in Natal by angry black workers. The government faced a dilemma, trapped on one side by the policy of apartheid and white worker support for it and on the other by an increasingly radicalized black workers' movement demanding greater equality of treatment. In 1977, the Wiehahn Commission was appointed to recommend a way out of the impasse. In a controversial move, the commission proposed that freedom of association be granted to all black workers and that black trade unions be allowed to register, believing they could be better controlled from within the system than without. The government finally decided to adopt the commission's recommendations, which led to the Industrial Conciliation Amendment Act of 1979. This strategic ploy failed, however, and during the 1980s the black unions became increasingly militant and a leading force in the anti-apartheid movement. Radical politics and industrial relations were now linked together and the white government was faced with a growing challenge.

As is true in many other countries, when the labour relations scene in South Africa in the early 1970s shifted from peaceful to confrontational, interest in industrial relations suddenly started to bubble up. Up to this time industrial relations had no organized presence in South African universities. The first signs of life were labour courses offered as parts of sociology and economics programmes. These were followed by the establishment of a labour studies unit at the University of Witwatersrand in the early 1970s. The next step was the formation of the first formal industrial relations unit, which took place at the University of South Africa in 1976 with the creation of the Institute of Labour Relations. The director was Nic Wiehahn, considered by many to be the founder of South African industrial relations. The institute was a research organization and provider of continuing education courses (Bendix, 1978).

Soon afterward, other industrial relations units were established. For example, an Industrial Relations Research Unit was created at the University of Stellenbosch in the Graduate School of Business in the late 1970s, led by Willy Bendix and Blackie Swart. Bendix went on to become one of South Africa's best-recognized industrial relations scholars and chair of the IIRA's study group on industrial relations and societal transition. Gradually, other industrial relations programmes were also established, including the Centre of Industrial and Labour Studies at the University of Natal, the Industrial Democracy Programme at the University of Witwatersrand and the Industrial Relations Research Unit at the University of Port Elizabeth.

Two industrial relations journals were also established in South Africa, both initiated by Bendix: the *South African Journal of Labour Relations* and the *Industrial Relations Journal of South Africa*. Only the former journal still publishes. Along with journals came a number of industrial relations textbooks. A leader is *The South African Industrial Relations System in Societal and Historical Context*, first published in 1989 by Sonia Bendix.

A revolution came to South Africa in 1994, when Nelson Mandela was elected president and apartheid was swept out. The new constitution for South Africa was written with the technical and legal consultation of the ILO. As a result, most of the existing industrial relations law was maintained, though with all equal rights firmly established. Industrial relations has remained an active area in South Africa in the new era. The trade unions no longer have a revolutionary cause to back, but they remain militant and labour relations continues to draw attention.

The continued upward trend in industrial relations is evidenced by the founding in 1994 of the Industrial Relations Association of South Africa (IRASA). It now has units in several cities and is an active and growing organization. The Association hosted the 2002 meeting of the African IIRA Regional Congress.

Other developments

In addition to Nigeria and South Africa, the industrial relations field has begun to show a presence in several other African countries in recent years. National industrial relations associations have been founded, for example, in the United Republic of Tanzania (1990) and Zimbabwe (1992) and the University of Zimbabwe has introduced a post-graduate diploma in industrial relations (Fashoyin, 2003).

Latin America

The final region considered in this chapter is Latin America. Latin America is a tremendously large and diverse area. It includes four distinct subregions: North America (Mexico), the Caribbean, Central America and South America. Together Latin America comprises over 40 countries and a population in excess of 500 million.

The history of industrial relations in Latin America reflects and has been greatly influenced by its unique political and social development. Roughly a quarter of the Latin American population is fully or partially of indigenous origin, concentrated along the belt of countries straddling the Andes Mountains (e.g., Bolivia, Mexico, Nicaragua, Peru).

The term "Latin America" reflects its European colonial heritage, given that the Latin countries of Spain and Portugal occupied and for several hundred years ruled most of the region. Thus the major language is Spanish, with the notable exception of Brazil (the largest country in Latin America), where Portuguese is spoken; the dominant religion is Catholicism; and the legal code comes from Roman civil law. The Latin heritage of the region is also reinforced by large waves of immigration from Italy in the 1800s and early 1900s, particularly to Buenos Aires, São Paulo and several other major cities of the southern hemisphere, and the political and social influence exercised by France during the nineteenth century in Mexico and other countries.

The term "Latin America" also hides, however, a great deal of social and ethnic diversity. Over a 300-year period stretching into the late nineteenth century, over 10 million Africans were brought to work in Latin America, in most cases as slaves. The populations of some Latin countries are today primarily of African descent (e.g., Jamaica, Haiti), while several others (e.g., Brazil, Cuba) are one-quarter or more black or mulatto. The British, French and Dutch – and later the Americans – also occupied enclaves in Latin America, particularly in the Caribbean area, and brought with them their native people, languages and social institutions. Over a million Germans up to the First World War period also immigrated to Latin America, particularly to southern cone countries such as Argentina and Chile, while scattered throughout the region are a large number of people from Chinese, Japanese and East Indian ancestry.

The roots of industrial relations in Latin America go back to the late nineteenth century and the beginnings of large-scale wage labour, industrialization and labour unrest (Stavenhagen and Zapata, 1972; Berquist, 1986). At this time the first large urban areas were emerging alongside the first generation of mills, shipyards and other manufacturing operations. Also playing an important role were the building of railways outside the cities and the development of large-scale mining and petroleum operations, often in very remote areas.

Going hand in hand with these developments was the rise of the first trade unions, strikes and radical political movements. In Argentina, for example, the first unions formed in the 1860s and 1870s, the first strike was by printers in 1878 demanding a ten-hour day, the first trade union federation was formed in the 1890s and a series of general strikes immobilized Buenos Aires in the first decade of the 1900s (Alba, 1968). This pattern was repeated in broad outline in other countries. The first labour strikes occurred in Mexico in the 1860s among textile workers, in 1876 the first congress of labour organizations was held, and soon thereafter American trade unions, such as the Knights of Labor and unions affiliated with the AFL, began organizing. Similar labour developments occurred in other Latin American countries, but often pushed back in time by one or several decades because of their slower pace of industrialization. In Brazil and Peru, for example, the first significant stirrings of union activity and labour unrest did not begin until the first decade of the 1900s, and not until the 1920s in Venezuela (partly due in the latter case to considerable government repression of labour organization).

The first wave of union activity and labour unrest in Latin America before the First World War brought to public attention the issue of employer–employee relations. But it did not lead to the academic or vocational concept of industrial relations or a university field of study called industrial relations. Indeed, much as in the United States the initial impetus behind the early development of industrial relations in Latin America came not from the labour side but from the management side. In particular, this took the form of personnel and labour relations programmes introduced from the 1920s onward by American multinational corporations with Latin American subsidiaries and branch plants.

The late nineteenth-century and early twentieth-century Latin American labour movements were diverse and often fragmented along ideological, political and national/ethnic lines. The large majority, however, followed a philosophy and programme inspired by various European-based theories of anarchism, socialism, syndicalism and communism, albeit often adapted and interpreted to fit Latin American conditions (Romualdi, 1947; Carrière, Haworth and Roddick, 1989). Also present but in a distinct minority position were various Catholic-affiliated trade unions and, in Mexico, AFL-affiliated "business" unions.

The appeal of these radical labour ideologies derived from several sources. One was that a large portion of the newly emerging urban working class in Latin America comprised new immigrants from Europe and, in particular, Spain, Portugal, Italy and Germany. As described in earlier chapters, these radical theories enjoyed a wide following in Europe and not unexpectedly were transplanted to the New World by these immigrants.

A second consideration that heightened their appeal was the highly stratified, elitist and often repressive nature of the Latin American governments and societies. Well into the early twentieth century, agriculture and extractive industries were by far the largest sectors of the economy in Latin America. In both cases these sectors were dominated either by a relatively few wealthy families or foreign corporations. In the case of agriculture, large land holdings organized as *haciendas*, *fazendas*, *fincas* and *estancias* were the norm. In Mexico before the 1910 Revolution, 1 per cent of the population held 85 per cent of the land, in Argentina 2,000 families owned one-fifth of the land area, and in Chile 1 per cent of the population controlled 52 per cent of the land (Alba, 1968). Alongside these few wealthy families was a large mass of the population eking out a living in subsistence agriculture, as hired hands on these estates or as artisans and wage-earners in the newly emergent and rapidly growing urban areas. The lopsided nature of land holdings led to a similar lopsided distribution of income, political control and class stratification. In particular, the agricultural oligarchies and allied foreign business interests dominated the national governments, used their political control to promote their economic objectives over those of the urban-based working and middle classes, and passed repressive legislation and used the police/military to suppress trade unions and other groups that threatened their control. As a result, theories of anarchism, syndicalism, socialism and communism found a fertile breeding ground for it appeared quite obvious to many workers that only a revolutionary change in wealth holdings and political control promised significant hope for the future.

Also compounding the appeal of radical labour ideologies were attitudes and practices of Latin American employers (Derossi, 1971; Dávila and Miller, 1999). Similar to the situation in southern Europe of this period, agricultural, professional and clerical vocations were held in high social esteem, while making money through industry and commerce was looked down upon. Thus business and industry did not attract the highest calibre of talent, nor was the practice of management considered a profession as was the practice of law or medicine. Another attribute of Latin culture, reinforced by an unstable political environment, was the tendency of entrepreneurs and businessmen to take a short-run perspective, seeking to make a high and quick return rather than investing over the long term in either capital or labour. A final consideration is an attitude of social elitism and exercise of unquestioned authority among many traditional Latin employers – exemplified in early twentieth-century Europe by the French *patron*. Naturally, these factors aggravated conflict in the workplace, led to autocratic and haphazard work practices, and further heightened the appeal of workers' cooperatives, socialized industry and other revolutionary solutions.

As happened across the rest of the world, the economic and political shock waves unleashed by the First World War and the Bolshevik Revolution in Russia were strongly felt across Latin America. Prosperous economies, more buoyant job markets and rising inflation led to more union activity and strikes, while the communist takeover in Russia and newly completed revolution in Mexico stirred the hopes of Latin American radicals and struck fear into the hearts of the social elites and political oligarchs. Although the Social Question and Labour Problem were widely discussed and debated in Europe and the United States from the early 1880s, they were slower to receive the same attention in Latin America because the process of industrialisation, emergence of a large-scale capitalist market economy and rise of a large urban-based working class took longer to develop. The first writings began to appear in the 1890s, however, and were relatively numerous between 1900 and 1920 (Morris, 1966; Wiarda, 1976). Examples include *Cuestiones Sociales* by Sabas Carreras (1899) and *Problemas sociales* by Octavio Morató (1911).

Similar to other parts of the world, Latin American countries sought to develop and implement new institutions and practices to contain class conflict, preserve labour peace and keep the Social Question from erupting into revolution. Facing a different social and economic environment to those in either continental Europe or North America, and having different cultures and political traditions, they chose an alternative strategy and set of institutions and practices. Generically, this alternative was merely a different type of industrial relations system, as that concept was later defined by Dunlop (1958). In the

1920s–1940s, however, industrial relations was most widely viewed through a different lens – as a *particular approach to problem-solving* pioneered in the United States – and thus was very different from the problem-solving approach adopted in Latin America. Arturo Bronstein (1995), an ILO specialist in labour law and well-known expert on Latin America, summarizes the main lines of development of the early Latin American approach to industrial relations this way (pp. 163–4):

> The two most distinctive characteristics of Latin American industrial relations systems are the legal (heteronomous) regulation of employment and working conditions and the very high degree of state intervention in collective labour relations. Historical and cultural factors, such as the bureaucracy and legalism inherited from Spain and Portugal, the former colonial powers, have been the main outside influences, but the process of 'political modernization' has played an equally significant role. This process began in the 1920s and consisted of the transfer of political power from the traditional rural oligarchies to the urban bourgeoisie, which sought a tacit alliance with the emerging urban proletariat. In addition, protectionist doctrines were adopted from the 1930s onward, providing ideological support for a development strategy of import substitution. ... From the beginning, the combined effects of bureaucracy, legalism, modernization, and protectionism made workers' protection a state concern. ... In 1919 the creation of the ILO, of which most Latin American countries were founding members, provided further ideological justification for state intervention in labour market regulation. ... At the same time the social doctrine of the Catholic Church exercised an important influence.

Different labels have been used to describe the resulting industrial relations system, but Wiarda (1976) argues that it is best characterized as an Iberian–Latin American form of corporatism (a society of organized interest groups). Prior to the First World War the ruling elite used substantial overt repression against labour; after the First World War the elite used a carrot and stick approach to co-opting and controlling labour that drew inspiration from Bismarck, Franco and Mussolini. Following Bismarck, most Latin American countries sought to reduce labour's grievances and forestall the development of greater class conflict by enactment of an extensive set of protective labour laws (called "labour codes"), creating various social insurance programmes (old-age insurance, accident and unemployment insurance), and providing means for legal recognition of trade unions. As a package, the labour codes and social insurance programmes were of a breadth and depth surpassing those of many advanced countries, albeit often limited to the wage-earning minority of the still predominantly agricultural and artisanal labour force. At the same time, these countries also followed the example of fascist Latin dictators Franco and Mussolini by writing into the law a thicket of restrictions and sanctions, backed up by police action and threats of violence, that kept the unions and workers solidly under government control and gave authorities considerable power to disband or declare illegal any labour organization or activity not officially sanctioned (Epstein, 1989). Added to this package in the 1930s (as a result of the Great Depression and collapse of commodity prices and export markets) was a shift to a high-tariff, import substitution macroeconomic strategy for growth and, in the 1940s, emergence of a distinctive Latin American brand of political populism featuring military-backed strongman leadership, nationalization of foreign-owned industry, and a political programme aimed at forging unified support of the "producing classes" through various protective and income redistribution measures. An exemplar of the controlled, subservient type of trade union movement under corporatism is Mexico's Confederación de Trabajadores de México (CTM); an exemplar of populism was Argentina (1946–55) under President Juan Peron and his wife Evita (Alba, 1968; Zapata, 1981; Alexander, 2003).

These political and environmental conditions reduced the applicability and attractiveness of a North American-style programme of industrial relations, thus acting to retard and inhibit its appearance in Latin America. Other factors also worked in this direction in the academic world of Latin America. In North American universities, industrial relations appeared in the 1920s and onward as an academic field of specialization housed in economics departments and business schools, with a considerable emphasis on personnel management and collective bargaining. This intellectual format was not for many years a good fit in Latin American universities, however.

The first universities in the Western Hemisphere were in Latin America. The University of Santo Domingo, established in 1538 in what is now the Dominican Republic, and the University of San Marcos, established in modern-day Peru in 1551, pre-date by more than a century the first university in North America (Benjamin, 1965). By the early 1920s, when industrial relations as an academic field of study was established in the United States, nearly every independent Latin American country had a flagship national university and, typically, several other major universities in outlying provincial cities. Examples are the University of Chile, the University of Buenos Aires and the National Autonomous University of Mexico. These universities were, however, dissimilar in a number of respects to universities in English-speaking North America. They were, first of all, modelled on European universities and, in particular, the French system (Brock and Lawlor, 1985). As described in Chapters 3 and 9, the traditional European model of the university was not conducive to the adoption of industrial relations because it featured a much more centralized and bureaucratic structure (inhibiting curriculum innovation and cross-disciplinary programmes), a stunted set of social-science disciplines and absence of business schools, and tended to be more politicized and ideological with respect to issues surrounding capital labour relations. Latin American universities also shared these characteristics, as well as several others that further militated against the ready adoption of industrial relations.

For example, a unique characteristic of the traditional Latin American university was a predominant focus on training students for a small number of professions. The heart of these universities were faculties of law, engineering and medicine, supplemented by programmes in fields such as theology, dentistry and education (Economic Commission for Latin America, 1968). Often the law schools were of particular importance, reflecting the Roman law tradition of the region and the highly legalistic approach taken to regulating social and commercial relations. At the same time, the liberal arts and social sciences were not given much attention, typically included as lower-level survey courses for students pursuing one of the professional degrees. As a consequence, into the 1950s the economics and sociology professors were often housed within the law school (Davis, 1950). The subjects of business and commerce were even further down the intellectual and organizational ladder, typically being considered a subunit of economics and taught on a piecemeal basis as "applied economics". Alternatively, sometimes courses in industrial administration would be offered as part of the engineering programme.

Other factors may also be briefly cited. In years past, university education was largely the preserve of the upper strata of society and the study of labour problems and employer–employee relations was not therefore particularly attractive. Also, over the years most Latin American countries have had periods of military dictatorship and authoritarian regimes; hence controversial and possibly radical subjects such as industrial relations were thus dangerous and sometimes suppressed. Finally, for many decades Latin American universities did not give much emphasis to faculty research and, in particular, social-science empirical research; they also had relatively few professors with doctoral degrees, and paid such low salaries that most were forced to take second and third jobs (a condition still widespread).

With this background, we can now examine the process by which industrial relations came to Latin America. As a formalized field of study, industrial relations did not appear in Latin America until the 1950s and took another decade or two to become well recognized and established. Sometimes the field is called *relaciones industriales*, a direct translation of the English term. Often, however, two other terms are used more or less equivalently: *relaciones laborales* (labour relations) and *relaciones de trabajo* (work relations). The latter was promoted by the ILO as the term for the field. A person whose specialty area is industrial relations is often referred to as a "relacionista", meaning in English an "industrial relationist" (Zegarra Garnica, 1991). The term "industrial relationist" is rarely used in the English literature, however, although it is a directly parallel to terms such as "economist" and "sociologist".

In the universities, the study of labour was largely the preserve of law schools and law professors well into the post-Second World War period. The reason for the predominance of law in the field of labour was alluded to in the above-cited quotation from Bronstein, where he noted that the Latin countries (with certain exceptions such as Uruguay) adopted from 1920 onward a highly structured and detailed juridical framework for the regulation of the employment relationship and union–management relations (also see Aldao-Zapiola, 2000). In this regard, most of the Latin American countries were founding members of the ILO and over time had a strong record of adopting or otherwise incorporating ILO Conventions and Recommendations – sometimes going so far as to write them into the national constitution (Wiarda, 1976). The intersection between the study of labour, the juridical-based approach to labour regulation and the ILO is well illustrated by one of the interwar period's most noted Latin American labour experts, Moisés Poblete Troncoso. Troncoso was a Chilean labour reformer, a law professor and a regular contributor of articles on Latin American labour developments in the ILO's *ILR*. Also reflective of the important influence of labour law at the time was the book *Derecho del trabajo* (1939) by Rafael Caldera of Venezuela. Caldera later became president of Venezuela.

Although industrial relations in Latin America universities did not make its first appearance until the 1950s, the practice of industrial relations in industry emerged one to two decades earlier in several Latin American countries. The principal conduit was the American-based multinational corporations with subsidiary production facilities in the region. Similar to the situation in the United States, the business person most closely associated with the first appearance of industrial relations in Latin America was John D. Rockefeller, Jr., and, under him, Clarence Hicks of Standard Oil of New Jersey. Standard Oil acquired extensive drilling rights in Venezuela and Mexico and began oil production in the mid-1910s (Gibb and Knowlton, 1956; Lucena, 1980). Like the American petroleum firms of that era, the Latin American companies had no personnel function beyond the most elementary record-keeping activity and delegated to foremen and gang bosses most aspects of hiring, firing, training and compensation. As recounted in Chapter 2, Rockefeller and Hicks were the prime movers in North America in promoting the field of industrial relations in the form of a more scientific and progressive approach to labour management.

Under their guidance, Standard Oil gradually spread at least the rudiments of the new industrial relations system to subsidiary firms, and among these were Standard Oil's properties in Venezuela and Mexico. At the same time, the Rockefeller-connected consulting firm IRC spread the new industrial relations model to other the American petroleum and mining companies, and some of them also exported it to their properties in Latin America in the 1930s through the 1950s. Despite these efforts, many of the workers became increasingly dissatisfied with employer–employee relations, often fuelled by nationalist resentment over foreign economic control and the corrosive effects of extreme social and economic inequality. As a result, unionization spread, and strike and labour conflict worsened, contributing to the nationalization of the foreign oil properties in Mexico and a number of other countries (Brown and Knight, 1992).

Up to the First World War, the British were the largest foreign investors in Latin America. After the war, however, the American capital poured in and numerous well-known American corporations opened factories, mills, mines and other facilities all across the region, quickly displacing the British as the dominant foreign economic influence. With them came the industrial relations function. Thus, in Chile and Peru industrial relations first appeared when large American copper companies introduced it, as happened in Argentina and Brazil through the operations of the American auto companies (Ford and GM), agricultural implement manufacturers (John Deere, International Harvester), meat packing firms (Armour, Swift) and electrical equipment companies (General Electric, Westinghouse).

At these companies the function of industrial relations was broadly defined to include both the personnel and union-management functions. Most of the American companies tried to staff the industrial relations departments with managers and administrators from the local countries, but at the time no local-based training in industrial relations practices existed. Hence, a number of the American companies set up in-house training courses in industrial relations, while Standard Oil sent the most promising recruits to the United States to attend training courses provided by IRC and, later, Northwestern University (Lucena, 2003; Kaufman, 2001a). After the Second World War, a steady flow of industrial relations staff and managers from numerous other Latin American based companies came to the United States for executive education and master's degrees from the newly established industrial relations schools and institutes. The most frequent destination was Cornell University's School of Industrial and Labor Relations.

The next step on the road of development for the industrial relations field in Latin America was the establishment by employers of industrial relations associations. Early in the twentieth century, companies formed employers' associations to combat unions and promote their interests with local and national governments. By the 1930s, industrialization and economic development had proceeded far enough that the larger and more progressive companies began to broaden their focus from combating unions to also giving more consideration to the professional development of corporate personnel and labour relations practices. From this development grew the first employers' organizations that had some interest in modern labour management practices. An example is Mexico, where in 1929 a group of companies formed the Coparmex confederation. One of its objects was (Hicks, 2003: 3, translated from the Spanish) "the study for the benefit of the member companies of the social problems of the relations between employers and workers". Not until after the Second World War, however, did employers form professional associations expressly focused on personnel and labour relations practices and problems. And what name did they give to these new associations? The answer is: *industrial relations*.

In 1947, for example, Mexican employers formed the Association of Industrial Relations Executives. According to Hicks (op. cit., p. 9), "the fundamental objective was to bring together all the personnel managers from the different companies and keep them up to date on all the developments concerning the human element in industry". A second example is the employers' organization ADRIL (Asociación de Dirigentes de Relaciones Industriales del Litoral), established in Argentina in 1958. Also established in most Latin American countries were personnel associations, and in 1963 an inter-American federation of personnel management, FIDAP, was founded. Particularly in these earlier years, but still to some degree today, these personnel organizations also regarded themselves as part of the broader field of industrial relations (Aldao-Zapiola, 2000).

As industrial relations started to become a well-recognized functional area of business practice in Latin American companies, universities naturally also began to take notice and develop interest. The first university industrial relations programmes or courses of study I am aware of in Latin America were started in 1953. That year the University of San Agustín de Arequipa in Peru created an Institute of Industrial Relations and Productivity. The focus of the programme was on training engineers and managers in the human problems of industry.

The second industrial relations programme established that year was in Mexico at the Universidad Iberoamericana (Latin American University) in Mexico City. The university was a private Jesuit school and the professors, a number of whom had studied in the United States, sought to introduce new majors into the curriculum that would promote the economic development of Mexico. One of the new undergraduate majors was industrial relations, directed by Father Emile Bouvier (Hicks, 2003). Another founding professor of industrial relations at the university was Euquerio Guerrero. At this time the subject of industrial relations was given a broad definition and included both personnel management and labour relations. But the emphasis was on the employer's practice of industrial relations, reflected by the fact that the new major was part of the business studies programme. (Mexico had a relatively high union density rate but unions were largely under government control and contracts were determined by government officials and not through independent collective bargaining.) Professor Guerrero later became president of the Universidad de Guanajuato and at that school established in 1967 Mexico's second industrial relations programme, subsequently directed by Sebastian Sansberro.

The next development occurred in the late 1950s in Chile. As noted in Chapter 7, the American government and various scientific foundations (e.g., Ford Foundation) provided considerable financial support for academic research on labour problems and labour relations in other countries in the 1950s, spurred in part by the United States' Cold War fears of communist infiltration of foreign labour movements and desire to promote economic development along capitalist, free enterprise lines. With financial support from the United States government's Agency for International Development, Cornell University established a joint scholarly programme in industrial relations with the University of Chile in 1957/58. The programme was housed in the Institute of Business Administration (INSORA), itself part of the Faculty of Economics. James Morris of Cornell was the American co-director, Roberto Oyanever was the Chilean co-director; Henry Landsberger of Cornell was also actively involved. The programme did not offer a formal major or degree in industrial relations but did offer courses in industrial relations, sponsored research and external training classes for companies and unions, and promoted exchange programmes for faculty and graduate students between Chile and the United States (Morgado, 2004).

As we have seen, a significant impetus for the introduction of industrial relations in several other areas of the world in the late 1950s and early 1960s was the Inter-University Study of Kerr and colleagues. Latin America appears to be a significant exception, however, for none of the four authors published anything specifically related to a Latin American country, nor were any of the several dozen researchers affiliated with the project from Latin America. The only significant book on industrial relations in Latin America that came out of the programme over its twenty years was Robert Alexander's *Labor Relations in Argentina, Brazil, and Chile* (1962).

Although not affiliated with Kerr et al.'s project, several other American industrial relations professors travelled to Latin America in the 1950s and early

1960s to do research and to teach, thereby helping to introduce the subject and develop interest in it. Among them were Albert Blum, William Foote Whyte, William Form and Wilbert Moore and, somewhat later in the decade, Richard Miller and Mark Thompson. Whyte was the best known of these scholars in North America, being a leading researcher in human relations and one of the founders of the field of OB. In 1954–55, he spent a year in Venezuela studying industrial relations at a subsidiary of the Standard Oil Company. Then in 1960 he spent a year in Peru, returning several other times and publishing several books and articles based on his experiences (Whyte, 1994).

After Fidel Castro's successful revolution in Cuba in 1959 and subsequent embrace of communism, the American government became more concerned about the spread of revolutionary movements to other Latin America countries. Naturally, a high priority item was to contain communist and radical influence in the Latin American labour movements. During the Kennedy administration, the Alliance for Progress was enacted and it funnelled billions of dollars of development aid to Latin America, some of which went into promoting industrial relations programmes and activities (Belcher, 1965). In some cases, the American scholars were on the payroll of the State Department and the CIA (French, 2003). American foundations also invested a considerable amount of money in promoting academic research on Latin America. Also very active in promoting in the American-style industrial relations practices in the region was the AFL–CIO (Hawkins, 1965). During the 1960s and 1970s, the federation devoted considerable resources to promoting independent, non-communist unions in the region and ran an extensive education and training programme for Latin American union leaders and members.

Despite these developments, as of 1960 industrial relations remained virtually an unknown concept in the Latin American academic world. The best evidence comes from the voluminous (290 pp.) *Bibliography of industrial relations in Latin America*, published in 1967 by James Morris and Efrén Córdova. In the sections "General", "Management", "Unions and labor movements" and "Labor–management relations", the only citation to an article written by a person from Latin America with the term industrial relations in it published prior to 1960 is "La empresa y las relaciones de trabajo" by Mario Deveali (1953) in the law journal *Derecho del Trabajo*. Even by 1965, hardly any books or articles with industrial relations in the title had yet appeared in a Spanish- or Portuguese-language book or academic journal published in Latin America.

The founding of the IIRA in 1966 quickly changed the situation as it set about promoting the establishment of national industrial relations associations around the world. In Latin America, the first fruits of this effort appeared in

Argentina. Professor Eduardo Stafforini, assisted by several other people from industry and trade unions, took the lead in establishing in 1968 the Industrial Relations Association of Argentina. Stafforini was a well-known specialist in labour law and social security at the University of Buenos Aires and an official in the Labour Ministry. Following the organization of the association, an industrial relations programme was later started at the University of Buenos Aires. In the 1970s and 1980s, a number of other Latin American countries, such as Chile, Peru and Venezuela, followed suit and also established industrial relations associations.

Among the countries of Latin America, Venezuela has had one of the longest and strongest academic records in industrial relations, due in significant part to the guidance of Professor Héctor Lucena. The field first appeared in the academic world in 1964 when two universities simultaneously introduced the subject (Lucena, 2003). The first was the Universidad de Carabobo, a public university, and the second was Universidad Católica "Andres Béllo", a private university. The programmes covered both HRM and union–management relations. Then, in the 1970s the Industrial Relations Association of Venezuela was started, followed by the creation of two academic journals. In 1979, Lucena started the journal *Industrial and Labor Relations* at the Andres Béllo university; two years later the Venezuelan association started the *Journal of Labor Relations*. The former continues to publish; the latter ceased.

Peru offers another interesting case study of the development of industrial relations in Latin America. The first formal appearance of industrial relations in Peru came in 1953, as previously noted. In 1957, a "Club of Industrial Relations" was started by employers and officials from the Ministry of Labour (*Análisis Laboral*, November 1977, p. 9). In 1962, the organization changed its name to the Industrial Relations Association of Peru (ARI). Then, in 1963 the national government passed a law (El Servicio de las Relaciones Industriales, Labour Law No. 14371) mandating that every firm with 100 or more employees have an industrial relations department (op. cit., p. 6). In Peruvian universities, another early development was the founding in 1959 at the Universidad Nacional Mayor de San Marcos of an Institute of Human Relations under the directorship of Antonio Pinilla Sánchez-Concha. Subsequently, this programme evolved into the School of Industrial Relations and Productivity in 1966, also having a substantial orientation toward engineering. In 1964, a major in labour relations in industry and government was established at the Universidad Católica de Santa María and in 1968 the Universidad San Martín de Porres established a Faculty of Industrial Relations. The impetus for the latter programme came from Norman King, an industrial relations executive with an American copper company, who was in turn encouraged in this venture by a North American industrial relations professor, Maurius Trotta. Today the university offers a bachelor's degree with a major in industrial relations, directed by Professor Daniel Valera Loza.

The best-known and most influential academic person in Peruvian industrial relations is Luis Aparicio-Valdez. Aparicio-Valdez illustrates the close connection that exists in Latin America between labour law, social security and industrial relations. His graduate training was in law and in 1962 he became a professor of labour law and social security at the Universidad del Pacífico and from 1991–94 served as the vice-president of the International Society of Labour Law and Social Security (see Chapter 6). But relatively early in his career he also became interested in industrial relations, reflecting the industrial relations field's substantial juridical orientation in Latin America and the growing importance of industrial relations in Peruvian society. Thus, in 1977 he founded the journal *Análisis Laboral*, which has become one of Latin America's most prominent publications featuring news and developments on all aspects of labour. This publication is the only Latin American journal member of the International Labour Journal Club.

In 1982, Aparicio-Valdez took the lead in founding the Asociación Peruana de Trabajo (APERT) – a member organization of the International Industrial Relations Association. Serving on a number of government commissions and ministries, editor of *Análisis Laboral*, president of the Grupo AELE (a labour consulting organization and publisher of *Análisis Laboral* and several more recent labour publications, such as *Análisis Salarial* and *Análisis Tributario*), and lead organizer for the IIRA Third Regional Congress of the Americas in Lima in 1999, Aparicio-Valdez has had growing regional and international visibility in industrial relations. In 2003, he became the thirteenth president of the IIRA and the first person from Latin America to hold this position. Now he is preparing the XIV International Industrial Relations World Congress that will take place in Lima in September 2006.

Developments in Argentina, Brazil and Colombia also deserve mention. Industrial relations was first introduced to Argentina by foreign corporations, principally from the United States. Large Argentine corporations with progressive management, such as Fabrica Argentina de Alpargatas (owned by the Frazer family), soon followed suit. The Argentine Institute of Industrial Relations, founded in the 1950s, sponsored training classes and annual conferences and did much to publicize the new concept of industrial relations. The first appearance of industrial relations in the universities was in 1962 at the Universidad de la Empresa – a private business university sponsored by the Argentine Chamber of Corporations. In the late 1960s, under the direction of Professor Héctor Ruiz Moreno, the Law School at the University of Buenos

Aires created a course of study in industrial relations. Similar courses were established at a number of other universities in Argentina but gradually many of these have switched to the title human resources. Similarly, in industry the term "*relaciones industriales*" has increasingly been replaced by "*recursos humanos*" and the term "*relaciones laborales*" is now often used to describe the sub-function of labour–management (collective) relations.

The field of industrial relations also first came to Brazil through industry, principally the large auto companies around São Paulo. It then later spread to other domestic and foreign-owned firms in the 1960s and 1970s. Although Brazil is the largest country in Latin America in terms of area, population and economic output, the field of industrial relations has developed more slowly there than in most other countries of the region. A significant part of the explanation lies with the nation's strong juridical and centralized approach to labour regulation and collective bargaining, coupled with periods of severe political repression of labour unions and labour activism. The labour code adopted in 1943 covered almost every aspect of a worker's life and whenever a dispute arose it was referred to a labour court and adjudicated by judges and attorneys (Pastore and Skidmore, 1985). Also, unions and employers were organized along corporatist lines and collective agreements typically covered an entire industry or geographic area and were often effectively dictated by state authorities. In such an environment, industrial relations in the North American sense had a very difficult time becoming established and is still today underdeveloped.

Reflecting this situation, industrial relations in the universities of Brazil has never become firmly established as a field of study. But several academics have become known in the area of industrial relations, several universities have labour programmes of various types, and unions and labour problems are active research topics. The person who pioneered the industrial relations field in Brazil is José Pastore. He studied the sociology of labour at the University of Wisconsin and started to teach and research industrial relations at the University of São Paulo in the early 1980s. Interestingly, however, his faculty position was in the Economics Department because his pluralist perspective on labour–management relations was not well accepted by fellow sociologists of a radical left/Marxist orientation. Pastore started a cooperative exchange programme with Wisconsin and groups of union and management people from Brazil went there for short courses, as did several people for Ph.D.s in industrial relations. An example is Hélio Zylberstajn, also in the Economics Department at São Paulo. Pastore and Zylberstajn co-authored the first academic book on Brazilian industrial relations, *A administração do conflito trabalhista no Brasil* (1987). In recent years, industrial relations has remained a fringe field occupied mostly by lawyers and sociologists (Araujo Guimarães and de Paula Leite, 2002). Labour economics is a strong area of research in Brazilian universities but little attention is given to unions and labour–management relations. These subjects are, however, given considerable attention by sociologists, although not from what would be considered a traditional industrial relations perspective. An interdisciplinary group, called the Brazilian Association of Labour Studies (ABET), is active, however. Also present is a Labour Relations Group at the Catholic University of Minas Gerais and the Center of Studies on Unions and Labour (CESIT) at the University of Campinas. Finally, note should also be made that Brazil's current president, Luis Inácio Lula da Silva, was earlier a well-known and highly influential union activist.

Industrial relations also has a modest but discernible presence in Colombia. The entry point for the field was in 1967 with the founding of the ADP, an association composed of corporate personal directors. Its first president was Carlos Triana of the General Electric Company. In 1975, under the leadership of Professors Clemente del Valle and Martha Monsalve of the University of Bogotá, the organization was reconstituted as the ACRIP, the Colombian Personnel and Industrial Relations Association. Recently, the Association again changed its name, as have many other industrial relations associations across the world. The new name is Asociación de Gestión Humana – the Association for the Management of People. The term "human resources" was deliberately avoided because of a belief that human labour should not be regarded as another "resource" on the same plane as capital or land. No Colombian university has a major in industrial relations. However, in 1984 the ACRIP collaborated with the Universidad la Gran Colombia to establish a graduate specialization in industrial relations with a number of specific options in HRM and labour relations. Also, La Universidad Externado de Colombia initiated in the early 1990s a specialized course of study in labour law and industrial relations.

After 1980, the industrial relations field in Latin America was caught in a strong cross-current of events and ideas that both helped and hurt it. On the positive side were several developments.

Foremost among these factors was the return of democracy and end of military dictatorships in a number of Latin American countries. The history of Latin America in the twentieth century has been one of periodic political crises and upheavals, in numerous cases leading to military coups and dictatorships. A cycle of political instability and military coups started in the 1960s and continued into the 1970s, beginning with Honduras (1963), moving next to Bolivia and Brazil (1964), Argentina (1966), Peru and Panama (1968), Ecuador (1972), Chile and Uruguay (1973) and Argentina again (1976). At the end of the 1970s, a cycle of democratization began, beginning in Ecuador (1979), spreading to numerous other countries (such as Uruguay, Paraguay, Argentina, Peru) and culminating in the return of democratic government to Chile (1990). The military regimes were often brutally repressive, including the banning of trade unions and imprisonment of union leaders, widespread violation of human rights, and the murder or disappearance of thousands of suspected political opponents (Bronstein, 1995). Not unexpectedly, this environment was not at all conducive to the development of industrial relations in universities; conversely, when democracy returned across Latin America the study of labour gained a new freedom to grow and develop.

Also exerting a positive influence was the decline in the intellectual appeal of Marxism and other anti-capitalist ideologies. As described in an earlier chapter, a large segment of the European intellectual community through the 1970s subscribed to some version of Marxism, socialism, or New Left radicalism. Frequently these viewpoints made them uninterested in or hostile to industrial relations, since they sought to use the trade union movement to promote fundamental social and economic transformation while the American-inspired programme of industrial relations expressly aimed to defuse class conflict and promote an accommodation between employers and workers. The same situation existed in Latin America, albeit with a unique orientation reflecting the region's different position in the world economic order.

Classical Marxism in Latin America (with the exception of Cuba and perhaps Chile) had a smaller following, since it seemed to speak more directly to the economic conditions of advanced industrial countries. More powerful were various theories of imperialism, colonialism, dependency and structural underdevelopment. All four were closely intertwined and proved particularly influential in the 1960s and 1970s. Dependency theory was founded by neo-Marxist Fernando Henrique Cardoso; the structuralist theory of under-development was popularized by economists such as Raúl Prebisch with the Economic Commission for Latin America (Fishlow, 1988; Love, 1990; French, 2000). Intellectuals subscribing to these theories were, like their European counterparts, frequently not friendly toward or interested in industrial relations, since in Latin American countries it frequently had a managerialist orientation toward personnel/HRM, was associated with American multinational corpor-ations that were seen as the leading edge of American imperialism and Latin American dependency, and sought to de-radicalize the labour movement and shift it toward an AFL–CIO style of reformist accommodation with the existing social order (a social order that continued to have some of the greatest income and wealth inequalities in the world). Similar to the situation in Europe, these leftist intellectual doctrines began to loosen their hold in the late 1970s and then declined dramatically in the 1980s and 1990s with the evident bankruptcy of the protectionist, import substitution model and ascendancy of neo-liberalism and the free market neoclassical economic paradigm. As a result, greater intellectual space and receptivity was opened for the field of industrial relations.

Also appearing after 1980 were several negative developments. The import substitution/protectionist economic model adopted by most Latin America countries in the 1950s and 1960s began to come apart in the 1970s amidst falling economic growth rates, rising inflation and mounting external debt burdens. In the early 1980s, these adverse developments led to a full-blown economic crisis in a number of countries, marked by hyperinflation, massive declines in the foreign exchange value of the currency and rapidly mounting unemployment (Bronstein, 1995). Latin Americans now call the 1980s "the lost decade". Under the military dictatorship of General Pinochet, Chile in 1973 had scrapped the import substitution/protectionist model and implemented a wide-ranging programme of market liberalization and deregulation (Ruiz-Tagle, 1989). Despite substantial short-term adjustment costs, the Chilean economy started to show significant long-term improvement, suggesting that a free market economic development strategy can deliver superior results. As a result, the neo-liberal policies implemented in Chile became a new model for the rest of Latin America, accepted in part voluntarily and in part under the pressure exerted by the American government, the IMF and other international financial agencies. The new neo-liberal package of reforms became known as the "Washington Consensus" (Amann and Baer, 2002).

On the face of it, the shift of Latin American countries to a less inter-ventionist and more open-market economic regime could have worked to the benefit of the industrial relations field by providing more autonomy and freedom of action for the principal actors in industrial relations, leading to a more decentralized labour relations system and greater scope for independent trade unionism, collective bargaining and workplace-level negotiation and dispute resolution. Indeed, a number of countries in the 1980s and 1990s introduced more flexibility into their labour codes and strengthened guarantees of freedom of association and trade union autonomy from government control (Cook, 1998; Aparicio-Valdez, 2003). But other events were working to negate these advantages. Bronstein (1995: 168) summarizes the paradox this way:

> A situation has thus emerged where, as far as industrial relations are concerned, there is a complete divergence between political and economic trends. Politically, the social actors (and notably the trade unions) have been given a measure of freedom of action unthinkable just 10 or 15 years ago; at the same time the exercise of this freedom has been limited by economic constraints. Indeed, while trade unions have gained opportunities for political expression, they have also lost some clout as their

membership has fallen with job losses in sectors most affected by adjustment. This is especially the case in the public sector. ... The political factor led to greater freedom of association, but the economic factor undermined the ideology of labour market regulation.

As Bronstein alludes to, while democratization and neo-liberal reforms gave greater opportunity for a decentralized, autonomous industrial relations system to evolve, in practice one of the parties to the industrial relations system – the trade unions – found itself in an increasingly weakened position in terms of size, power and ideological appeal. Domestic market liberalization, free trade agreements at the regional and hemispheric level (the MERCOSUR pact among the South American countries, the NAFTA pact among Canada, Mexico and the United States), and persistent anaemic economic growth rates in a number of Latin American countries led to millions of job losses among union members (Inter-American Development Bank, 2004). Not only did union density fall by one-half or more in many countries; in the new neo-liberal era unions lost a good deal of their ideological appeal as social movements for a better society and instead became bargaining agents for the relatively privileged group of workers who had coveted jobs in the formal private and public sectors (Bronstein, 1997). At the same time as union density was dramatically shrinking, a growing share of employment in Latin American countries – frequently accounting for the majority of total employment – was shifting to the informal economy where the practice of industrial relations in the traditional sense has little relevance (Aparicio-Valdez and Bernedo Alvarado, 2001; Amann and Baer, 2002).

At the end of the twentieth century, the picture for the industrial relations field in Latin America has to be judged as mixed. A number of encouraging signs can be discerned, not only for industrial relations but for the entire field of labour studies. Latin America's increasing influence and interest in the labour field is well illustrated, for example, by the fact that the current Secretary-General of the ILO, Juan Somavia, comes from Chile, while the current president of the IIRA, Aparicio-Valdez, is from Peru. Chile will also host in 2005 the Fifth IIRA Regional Congress of the Americas. One can also look around Latin America and see a variety of other signs of strength for industrial relations and labour studies.

With respect to industrial relations, at least 25 universities in Mexico offer some kind of programme or course of study in industrial relations (Sansberro, 2004). These programmes are frequently part of the field of business studies, reflecting the fact that in Mexico "industrial relations" continues to have a strong association with the corporate employment and labour relations function. Likewise, industrial relations is now offered at eight universities in Venezuela, including at the doctoral level at the University of Carabobo (Lucena, 2003). Similar to Mexico, these programmes tend to emphasize the personnel/HRM dimension of industrial relations. Industrial relations programmes have also been started in a number of other Latin American countries. In Chile, for example, the Università la República (a private university) recently created an Institute of International Labour Studies, directed by Emilio Morgado. Similarly, a major in industrial relations was created in 1995 at the National University in Uruguay under the direction of Oscar Ermida Uriarte and Juan Raso Delgue. Delgue is also the director of the new periodical *Relaciones Laborales*, the first journal in that part of Latin America to be devoted exclusively to industrial relations.

Also very positive in pushing forward the field of industrial relations in Latin America was a multi-year programme called RELASUR (Industrial Relations in the Southern Cone), funded jointly by the ILO and government of Spain. Headquartered in Montevideo, Uruguay, the programme sponsored numerous research studies, publications and seminars regarding industrial relations in Argentina, Brazil, Chile, Paraguay and Uruguay between 1991 and 1995. Seven books (e.g., *Relaciones Laborales en Argentina*) were published, as well as eight editions of the periodical *Revista de Relasur*.

The creation of these new industrial relations programmes and publications reflects, in part, a substantial growth of scholarly interest in the field of Latin American labour. Illustrative of the trend is a recent article by John French (2000), an American expert on Latin American labour studies, entitled "The Latin American labor studies boom". The boom spreads across several disciplinary areas, such as history, sociology and political science, and has been contributed to by several American industrial relations scholars, such as Maria Cook, Harley Shaiken and Russell Smith. In Latin America, sociology has been a particular area of renewed activity. Thirty years ago the contribution of sociology to labour studies was modest, both because the discipline was underdeveloped in Latin American universities and due to the heavy hand of government repression. Since the early 1980s, the sub-field of the sociology of work has experienced its own boom (de la Garza Toledo, 2002; Guimarães and de Paula Leite, 2002). In the early 1990s, a new association, the Latin American Association of Sociology of Work, was founded and now publishes a scholarly journal, *Revista Latinoamericana de Estudios del Trabajo*.

Less positive developments must also be acknowledged, however. To begin, one must note that in the larger picture the field of industrial relations occupies a relatively small niche area in Latin America. Frequently, the field is also less associated with a concrete body of knowledge and domain of academic research and more often regarded as an applied area of professional practice and consulting.

The future of the field also appears clouded. As has happened across most of the world, the trade union movements in Latin America have suffered a serious loss of membership and influence in the last two decades. On one hand, this development poses less of a threat to the industrial relations field in Latin America than in other regions. The reason is that the subject of industrial relations in Latin America continues to be defined broadly to include personnel/HRM, union–management relations and labour law. It is thus less dependent on the fate of the union movement than is the field in Canada and the United States, where the meaning of industrial relations to most people has narrowed in recent decades to "union–management relations".

Thinking of Latin American industrial relations as a three-legged stool, the weakening of its union–management leg is not so serious a blow, as it has never been its principal source of support. Unfortunately, the two more important legs – personnel/HRM and labour law – are also under threat.

Since industrial relations first came to Latin America in the 1920s it has been regarded as subsuming the corporate employment function that is now most popularly called HRM (Aldao-Zapiola and Hermida Martínez, 1995). As has happened in all other areas of the world, in the last two decades Latin American universities have given much more emphasis to business education and have founded and expanded numerous schools of business. In these business schools the popular term for the corporate employment function is no longer industrial relations but the management of human resources. In Mexico, where the greatest number of industrial relations programmes is found, the last 15 years has seen roughly a dozen universities replace the industrial relations label with that of HRM. Most likely this trend will continue both there and in other countries. Likewise, a number of employer groups have followed suit and have changed their names. The Association for Industrial Relations in Peru, for example, recently changed its name to Human Resources Association of Peru. If this action were simply a cosmetic name change it would entail little worry. The evidence, however, is that the shift from industrial relations to HRM is more than this – it also carries with it a perspective that is less academically balanced and inclusive (a stricter focus on management and less coursework in the social sciences), more narrowly regards workers as instruments of production (a "human resource") and brings with it a more overt managerialist ideology and set of values.

The third leg of the industrial relations stool is also a weaker source of support. In the last two decades the ascendancy of neo-liberalism has considerably weakened the intellectual case and government support for protective labour law. Social security programmes in Latin America are also under considerable stress and in some cases have been privatized. Also troubling the field of labour law in Latin America is the burgeoning growth of the informal sector of employment, where traditional labour law has less reach and relevance. Increasingly, the stance of labour law in Latin America has shifted from the traditional concern of balancing the interests of the social partners and protecting the weaker party to the employment relationship (the workers) and has moved towards promoting national competitiveness and finding ways to increase operational flexibility and reduce labour cost for employers (Aparicio-Valdez, 2003).

The field of industrial relations in Latin America thus appears in some danger of being slowly hollowed out, as has happened in North America. Reasons for optimism remain, nonetheless, although the root cause is quite grim. So far the evidence is that the neo-liberal strategy of free markets and labour deregulation has had a relatively disappointing record in promoting faster economic growth in Latin America, while job creation in the formal sector lags badly and social inequality grows more extreme (Bernedo Alvarado, 2004; the Inter-American Development Bank, 2004). Labour problems in Latin America are thus not only widespread but in a number of respects worsening (for example, the poverty rate increased from 40 per cent in 1980 to 44 per cent in 2003). As noted in Chapter 2, a principal reason the field of industrial relations was invented in the early 1920s was to analyse and solve the many serious and threatening labour problems of that era. If studying and solving labour problems is taken as a core mission of industrial relations, the future of the field not only in Latin America but across the world should be bright, albeit perhaps regrettably so.

THE IIRA AND CONTEMPORARY INDUSTRIAL RELATIONS: PROMOTING GLOBAL DIALOGUE   **11**

The last part of the story to tell in the global history of industrial relations is the recent activities and accomplishments of the IIRA. Chapter 6 described its birth and early years. This chapter picks up the narrative where Chapter 6 ended (the Fourth World Congress in 1976) and extends it to the present time. But before getting to the IIRA, some attention must first be given to developments at the ILO, since the ILO, IIRA and the field of industrial relations have been tightly connected from the very beginning.

The ILO

As earlier documented, the ILO and the industrial relations field grew out of the same intellectual ideas and historical events in the early part of the twentieth century. Indeed, of the various world organizations created during that century, none so accurately reflects the core positive and normative premises of industrial relations as the ILO. We have also seen how the ILO played a key role in carrying forward the ideas of industrial relations into the post-Second World War era and then propagating them throughout the world. The ILO has performed this function by putting on the world agenda the cause of improved labour conditions and human rights in the workplace; by actively promoting the adoption of improved conditions and human rights through standard setting, technical assistance and information outreach programmes; and by partnering the industrial relations research community in providing a headquarters and administrative support for the IIRA.

The ILO: Challenges and responses

Under Director-General Morse, the ILO experienced its own golden age. Through his leadership, the ILO was able to work out a compromise arrangement so that the Soviet Union and its Central and Eastern European satellite states could again become members of the Organization, thus helping bridge the political and ideological divisions between East and West and easing the tensions unleashed by the Cold War. During the 1950s and 1960s the ILO also became a major player in bringing economic development and improved labour conditions to the developing countries of Africa, Asia and Latin America. Using the principles enunciated in the Declaration of Philadelphia as a foundation, Morse and the ILO were also a major force in promoting increased respect for human rights in the workplace, such as freedom of association, an end to child labour, and equal opportunity for men and women.

In recognition of these achievements, the ILO was awarded the Nobel Peace Prize in 1969, on the occasion of its 50th anniversary. This award was a signal event for the Organization and clear testimony to its steady climb in stature and influence in the world community.

To the surprise of most people, in 1970 Morse resigned. His successor was Wilfred Jenks, a British labour law expert and long-time ILO professional. Jenks sought to move the ILO back toward greater emphasis on its historical role of raising labour standards through Conventions and Recommendations. Before he was able to fully accomplish this strategic redirection, Jenks unexpectedly died in 1974. He was then succeeded by Francis Blanchard from France (1974–89) and, later, Michel Hansenne from Belgium (1989–99).

We have seen in previous chapters that the field of industrial relations, and the labour institutions it studies, experienced a more turbulent and in most respects adverse economic and political climate after the early 1970s. The ILO was also caught up in these same currents (Cox, 1971a). Consideration of these events and developments is crucial to understand the evolution of ILO policy and programmes, and also provides lessons for industrial relations on possible directions for strategic change.

The centrepiece of the ILO's policy programme, for example, is achieving new and improved labour standards through application of Conventions and Recommendations. The economic idea behind ILO Conventions and Recommendations is taken directly from the early twentieth-century economic theories of the founders of the industrial relations field, Sidney and Beatrice Webb and John R. Commons. Their idea is to improve labour conditions by taking important elements of labour cost out of competition through the device of the common rule, thereby gradually raising the plane of competition and protecting workers from the ill effects of market failures and destructive competition. As pointed out in an earlier chapter, this strategy is at the heart of the industrial relations problem-solving programme and is why I have emphasized throughout the interconnectedness of the ILO and industrial relations. Emphasis on this point is provided by McIntyre and Ramstad (2002) who state that "Commons is the ILO's 'worldly philosopher'."

Essentially, both the ILO and industrial relations are engaged in the same task – establishing a floor of socially acceptable labour conditions and shielding workers from the excesses and anti-social effects of market competition and self-interested profit making. In the last three decades, however, this task has become considerably more complicated.

Part of the challenge facing the ILO has come from the political sphere. Most of the ILO member States up to the mid-1950s, for example, were Western industrial countries. After the mid-1950s, two new groups came into the ILO and both expressed greater reservation about the Organization's traditional programme of new labour standards through Conventions and Recommendations. The first group was the Soviet Union and Eastern bloc countries. They contended that the "socialist reality" of work life was so different from the capitalist reality that many of the ILO's standards, such as freedom of association, did not apply to them. The second group was the newly independent countries from the less developed regions of Africa and Asia. They also argued that many of the international labour standards did not apply to them, since at their low stage of economic development conditions necessitated practices, such as child labour and long work-hours, that the advanced countries could afford to give up. Some also charged that the ILO standards being promoted by the Western nations were a form of economic and cultural imperialism aimed at protecting the home market of the advanced countries and promoting alien social values of individualism and materialism (Brown, 2001).

Also adding to the political mix was the increasingly acrimonious split between the United States and the ILO in the 1970s. The United States government and the AFL–CIO became increasingly concerned that the ILO was being subverted by the communist and less developed nations to promote an anti-Western and anti-capitalist agenda (Galenson, 1981). Also leading to discontent was the American perception that the ILO was practising a double standard by avoiding direct criticism of human rights and labour standards violations in Soviet bloc countries. The person spearheading American objections was AFL–CIO president George Meany. Meany was deeply committed to free collective bargaining, bilateral employer–union regulation of labour standards, and voluntarism. He became increasingly critical of the ILO because he saw it as taking an (allegedly) soft line on communist-dominated unions and promoting greater government interference in labour–management relations through its principle of tripartism. A rupture came when Jenks unexpectedly appointed a Soviet official to serve as an Assistant Director-General. Unable to resolve the dispute, United States Secretary of Labor John

Dunlop recommended to President Ford that the country withdraw from the ILO. Congress approved this action and in 1977 the United States left the ILO. Although the United States returned in 1980, the political rift and loss of funding for the ILO seriously hampered its programmes and ability to move forward on new labour initiatives.

Yet another political event took place in 1989 that had widespread repercussions. That year the Berlin Wall fell and the communist governments of the Soviet Union began to collapse. Viewed broadly, the end of the communist regimes was a marked advance for the ILO's programme of human rights in the workplace and freedom of association. The new governments of the Russian Federation and the newly independent Central and Eastern European states also rapidly affirmed their support to ILO principles and extended much greater cooperation to the Organization. Paradoxically, however, the collapse of communism also had a downside. The ILO, like industrial relations, was born in 1919 as a response to worldwide labour unrest and the spectre of socialist revolution. Again, during the years of the Second World War after the League of Nations had collapsed and the ILO's existence was in question, the threat of labour radicalism and communist takeover in Central and Eastern Europe and Asia led to a renewed commitment to the ILO by the Western powers. When communism collapsed in 1989, so too did part of the threat that had motivated governments to pay attention to improving labour conditions and promoting social justice. In effect, industrial relations and the ILO were established by the capitalist countries after the First World War as a firewall and insurance policy against the Red Menace. When the Red Menace disappeared, suddenly part of the reason for the ILO and industrial relations went with it, at least to those with a short-sighted perspective.

A final factor that led to a weakening of political support for the ILO is the long-term decline in the trade union movement in the world economy. The ILO would never would have been established without the pressure exerted on their respective governments by the labour movements of the major industrial nations. And while employers often felt only lukewarm interest in the ILO, the international trade union movement steadfastly supported the Organization and exerted pressure on governments to maintain their participation. The decline of organized labour in many nations thus undermines this crucial pillar of political support.

If the political sphere became more difficult for the ILO, the economic sphere became doubly so. Here the ILO and industrial relations also shared a common fate. The post-war economic boom came to an end in the early 1970s. Inflation rates were ratcheting upwards in the industrial countries in the late 1960s and early 1970s, leading to greater monetary and fiscal tightening and slowing growth. Then, in a coup de grâce to the post-war boom, the 1973 Arab–Israeli war broke out, the Arab nations imposed an oil embargo on the West, and energy prices doubled in the space of a few weeks. Suddenly, mild inflation turned to an unprecedented case of stagflation as the world economy headed into steep recession with rising prices and mounting unemployment. This process was then repeated in 1979–80 with the Iranian Revolution, another energy crisis, and an even more serious bout of recession and stagflation.

These events made the job of the ILO considerably harder. A lesson of history is that periods of recession and unemployment not only make it very difficult to summon the political will to legislate higher labour standards but also undercut the willingness and ability of employers and governments to observe existing standards. The adverse economic climate of the 1970s and early 1980s thus inevitably pushed the ILO's standard-setting programme on the defensive. Also, the adverse economic climate threatened to undermine the gains achieved by the ILO's economic development programmes started in the 1960s. The most visible and ambitious was the World Employment Programme (WEP) launched in 1969. The WEP was envisioned as a multi-pronged, strategic initiative to generate additional employment opportunities through international, regional and national development programmes. Progress, however, was halted by the macroeconomic stagnation brought on by the energy crisis and other negative shocks.

A world slowdown in economic growth after 1973 was not the only macroeconomic problem to confront the ILO. Also appearing at the same time was the emergence and spread of globalization. Globalization, as it has come to be defined, means the integration and interconnectedness of national economies through the opening of markets and reduction of trade barriers, the marked expansion of cross-country trade, and relatively unimpeded flows of capital across national boundaries. Globalization has of course been a process under way since the age of exploration in the fourteenth and fifteenth centuries. According to most observers, however, the process of globalization dramatically gained speed after the 1970s, spurred by post-Second World War efforts of governments to promote free trade and the cumulative effects of recent innovations in transportation, communication and microelectronics. Together, these forces are gradually transforming the world from a large number of relatively autonomous, self-managed and often heavily state-directed economies to one large world economy composed of a network of national and regional economies connected by market forces and multinational corporations, all governed and regulated by an amalgam of domestic governments, a patchwork of international organizations, and the invisible hand of competition and self-interest.

In his famous "American shoemakers" article, Commons pointed out how the widening of markets introduces lower-cost producers and puts downward pressure on established wages and working conditions. The globalization of markets in the latter third of the twentieth century is a directly analogous process, except that the extension of markets is no longer to new territories within one country but to new nation states across the world economy. The consequence is the same, however. Unless the common rule can be extended across the wider market, demand and supply will put labour costs into competition and countries with high labour standards will experience greater pressure to lower their standards in order to keep production, capital and jobs from flowing to lower-cost foreign rivals. The pressure on nations to cut labour costs to preserve jobs is then heightened when worldwide labour markets have substantial unemployment and underemployment, since the excess supply of labour accentuates both the bidding-down process and the importance of preserving jobs. If allowed to persist, substantial excess supply of labour, combined with labour immobility and capital fluidity, can set off a process of destructive competition among nations and the proverbial race to the bottom. Within countries, the downdraught of market competition undermines high-road employers and all are forced toward the low road.

These labour market dynamics have a paradoxical effect. On one hand, an organization like the ILO becomes more important than ever in protecting nations and their workers from the anti-social effects of unrestrained competition and the downward pressure it exerts on wages and labour conditions. Further, destructive competition also leads to unfair competition, such as use of forced labour and child labour to gain a cost advantage in international trade.

These same conditions also make it more difficult for the ILO to gain nations' agreement and observance of existing standards and willingness to apply new standards. When every nation is in a struggle to maintain jobs and attract capital in a labour surplus environment, the idea of higher labour standards suffers diminished economic and social appeal: diminished economic appeal because higher standards appear to move nations up their labour demand curves and to cost jobs; diminished social appeal because for governments and their citizens, having jobs, even if bad ones, is often preferable to no jobs at all.

The mission of the ILO has also become more complicated and subject to challenge since the golden age of the 1960s because of the intellectual ascendancy of neoclassical economics and the neo-liberal political philosophy. As emphasized in earlier chapters, these theories and doctrines have gained considerable power and influence in intellectual and policy-making circles in the last three decades. Both emphasize individualism, the efficacy of free markets, the harmful effects of institutional interventions in labour markets, and the virtues of shifting economic resources and control from the public to private sector. Thus, neoclassical/neo-liberal critics of the ILO (and industrial relations) claim that a programme of labour standards is a misguided and often futile attempt to impose through legislative fiat a different (higher) set of labour outcomes than determined by free labour markets. Illustrative of this point of view, for example, is the recent comment of one economist (Gillingham, 2000: 244) that "[e]conomic theory provides little to support the utility of ILO methods" .

As I have emphasized throughout, the negative verdict of neoclassical economics on efforts to raise the conditions of labour reflects the theory's particular assumptions. I am not alone in this view. One of the most forceful and influential proponents of labour standards is economist and Nobel laureate Joseph Stiglitz. In an address to the IRRA (2000: 3), he commented, "it might seem as if the fundamental propositions of neoclassical economics were designed to undermine the rights and position of labor". One way it does so is by making economic efficiency the only welfare criterion for judging the merits of social policy; another is by portraying markets as largely self-regulating and free of market defects. Thus Stiglitz observes on this matter that "the central tenet of the Fundamental Theorems of Welfare Economics [holds] that issues of distribution could be separated from issues of efficiency; again, so long as property rights were well defined – and so long as none of a limited number of market failures, such as externalities arose – then the economy would be efficient". In other words, by well chosen and selective assumptions neo-classical economics is able to divorce equity from market exchange as a criterion for evaluating social welfare. In terms of the environment facing the ILO and industrial relations we now see a double liability – politics has removed the Red Threat and economic theory has removed Social Justice.

One further challenge facing the ILO requires mention. This challenge is also political and arises in the world economic policy-making community. In promoting improved labour standards the ILO faces other world organizations that have different agendas, priorities and philosophies. The organization that has gained the most attention in this regard is the World Trade Organization (WTO). The globalization of product markets, massive flows of financial capital across national boundaries, and political commitment of the world community to trade liberalization has greatly increased the power and visibility of the WTO. The WTO, given its mission, is primarily concerned with opening markets and removing trade barriers – an agenda and perspective that makes the WTO reluctant and relatively uninterested in getting involved in labour matters and inclined to take a sceptical view of international labour standards.

Not only has the ascendancy of the WTO presented the ILO with another challenge in pushing forward its programme of labour standards, it has also fuelled a substantial backlash among a variety of labour and social groups who feel that the policies of the WTO are "anti-labour", evidenced most starkly by the street riots at the 2000 WTO meeting in Seattle and subsequent meetings.

On the positive side, the programme of the ILO has gained support from a variety of other sources. The American government, beginning with President Clinton, has become a much more forceful proponent of labour standards. The American AFL–CIO, in turn, has played a significant role in rallying political support for the ILO. Equally strong support has come from the EU and the trade union federations of Europe. Other world organizations, such as the World Bank, have also taken a supportive position.

Also on the positive side, the ILO has developed new strategies and programmes to advance its mission in light of these political, economic and intellectual shifts. This initiative was begun under former Director-General Michel Hansenne and was then accelerated and taken in some new directions by the ILO's current Director-General, Juan Somavia. Somavia became Director-General in 1999 and is the first person elected to this position from a country (Chile) outside Europe and North America.

One prong of the ILO's strategy has been to identify from the universe of existing Conventions and Recommendations[1] a *core* of labour standards that can command widespread agreement and serve as a focal point for international social advancement. On this matter, Director-General Hansenne (1996: 234, emphasis in original), stated that countries "must abide by certain *fundamental rules* which apply to all countries irrespective of their level of development – and which in fact are a precondition for social development". In 1994, marking the ILO's 75th anniversary, a Governing Body Working Party on the Social Dimensions of the Liberalization of International Trade was established. Their deliberations led four years later to formal adoption of the ILO Declaration on Fundamental Principles and Rights at Work, 1998 (Kellerson, 1998) and to the establishment of the World Commission on the Social Dimension of Globalization in 2002. The Commission's report, *A fair globalization: Creating opportunities for all*, was issued in early 2004 and received worldwide attention.

With regard to the Declaration on Fundamental Principles and Rights at Work, four specific categories of principles and rights are identified and defined as fundamental: freedom of association and the effective recognition of the right to collective bargain, the elimination of all forms of forced or compulsory labour, effective abolition of child labour, and elimination of discrimination in employment and occupation. These four principles and rights are "expressed and developed" in eight core Conventions, which have been recognized as fundamental by the ILO and the international community.

Several aspects of the Declaration deserve mention. A problem of growing importance with the Conventions, for example, is that many member States fail to ratify them, or take many years to do so. The Declaration addressed this problem by declaring that all States, by simple act of membership in the ILO, commit themselves to respect, promote and realize the rights that are the subject of the core Conventions.

The ILO sought to give greater moral imperative to the fundamental rights and principles at work, and thus the core Conventions in which they are expressed, by linking them to fundamental human rights. Fundamental human rights, as stated in the United Nations Universal Declaration of Human Rights adopted in 1948, are universal and indivisible. If core labour standards are treated as a fundamental human right, this means they are not open to compromise or exception and are not fungible – that is, they cannot be broken into pieces and traded for money. Furthermore, fundamental human rights have the highest moral claim on all social actors and thus transcend lower-order concerns such as competitive advantage and national differences in political and social systems.

The ILO has also been successful in getting international endorsement of the core labour standards. The fundamental principles and rights at work were presented for consideration at the World Summit for Social Development in Copenhagen in 1995 and were endorsed by Heads of State, committing their nations to "pursue the goal of ensuring quality jobs, and safeguard the basic rights and interests of workers and to this end, freely promote respect for relevant International Labour Organization Conventions" (quoted in Kellerson, 1998: 222). These standards were also endorsed a year later at the Singapore meeting of the WTO.

The second major prong of the ILO's current strategy is the Decent Work Agenda, begun in 1999 by incoming Director-General Juan Somavia. The ILO recognized that the Declaration of Fundamental Principles and Rights at Work by itself is not sufficient to achieve the ILO's mission "to improve the situation of human beings in the world of work" (ILO, 1999: 3). What is also needed is "opportunities for women and men to obtain decent and productive work". Behind this statement is the realization that rights without jobs is a hollow victory and thus the pursuit of improved labour rights and standards cannot proceed on its own but must be embedded in a larger, integrated programme aimed at creating "decent work" for all people who want gainful employment. Although admittedly imprecise, the available data suggest that the world's economy is falling seriously short of meeting this goal. According to the ILO (2001), the decent work "deficit" is huge – roughly one out of six workers in the world are either completely without work or earning below US$1 per person per day.

The ILO has, of course, initiated and participated in large-scale economic development programmes in earlier years, such as the WEP of the 1970s. The Decent Work Agenda is different, however, on several counts. First, rather than treat labour rights and job expansion as two separate programmes, it seeks to integrate them, arguing that decent work is itself a fundamental human right. Second, the ILO has used the decent work theme to reorganize its numerous activities into a more compact, focused and synergistic set of programmes centred on four strategic areas: principles and rights at work, employment and income, social protection, and social dialogue. And, finally, the ILO has sought to emphasize not only the social case for decent work, but also the economic case and the linkages and synergies between the two. In this spirit, Somavia states (ILO, 1999: 8):

> The ILO has consistently maintained that economic and social development are two aspects of the same process which sustain and reinforce each other. The linkages are well illustrated by the four strategic objectives of the ILO. Principles and rights at work provide the ground rules and the framework for development; employment and income are the way in which production and output are translated into effective demand and decent standards of living. Social protection ensures human security and civic inclusion, and enables economic reform. Social dialogue links production with distribution, and ensures and participation in the development process.

The ILO and industrial relations

The ILO and industrial relations were born in nearly the same year, 1919 and 1920 respectively, and had the same parents – fear of the Labour Problem and socialist revolution on one side and a commitment to labour reform and social justice on the other. Not surprisingly, therefore, the subject of industrial relations was part of the ILO's activities and programmes from the very first year, as described in Chapter 3. And, as described in Chapter 6, the link between industrial relations and the ILO became even stronger in the immediate post-Second World War era under Director-General David Morse. Indeed, as Morse's *chef de cabinet*, Robert Cox (Cox and Sinclair, 1996: 442) later recalled, "From the late 1950s, a specifically American doctrine of industrial relations was given pride of place in the ILO and was a rationale for its programmes."

The ascendancy of industrial relations at the ILO in this period is related to several factors. Certainly one of these is that Morse was an American, had participated in the practice of industrial relations as a labour attorney, arbitrator and policy-maker, and knew John Dunlop and other major scholars in the field. But other factors were equally significant.

It must be recalled that the United States chose not to join the ILO until 1934 and, thus, the Organization's early approach to labour reform was largely determined by its European members. Although the United Kingdom was allied with the United States in its commitment to voluntarism in labour–management relations, the countries of continental Europe pushed a more juridical-based programme and gave greater emphasis to tripartite interest representation at peak levels. Thus, while the ILO always strongly supported the principle of freedom of association and the practice of collective bargaining, it did not get directly involved in labour relations but instead focused its efforts on legislating new labour standards through Conventions and Recommendations worked out between the trilateral partners: governments, employers and workers.

After the Second World War, political influence in the ILO swung over to the Americans and, naturally, ILO policy also took on an American slant. The Americans, and particularly the powerful AFL–CIO, had a strong preference in favour of free collective bargaining rather than legal enactment and sought to keep government out of direct involvement with labour–management relations as much as possible. The American preference was thus for decentralized bilateralism, not high-level trilateralism. All of these principles, of course, had also become assimilated into post-Second World War American industrial relations and, indeed, the field was not only the centre of study and practice of this form of labour regulation but was also the ideological mouthpiece for it. Thus, when the American influence became dominant in the ILO after the war, the field of industrial relations also took on a larger role. The rise in influence of industrial relations in the post-war period at the ILO is revealed in a number of ways. Chapter 6, for example, described how Morse used the Cole Report to expand the ILO's activities and programmes in labour–management relations. Morse was also the person responsible for the creation of the IILS at the ILO in 1960, with the plan for it to become the leading European-based industrial relations think-tank. The IILS was a close cousin to the American-style free-standing industrial relations institute, sponsored numerous industrial relations classes and research projects, and brought to Geneva many visiting industrial relations scholars from around the world. In the same chapter we also saw how Kerr, Dunlop, Harbison and Myers – the most influential American industrial relations scholars of the period – used the ILO as staging centre and research base for conduct of their Inter-University Study, and how their emphasis on economic development helped provide intellectual stimulus for Morse's decision to give greater emphasis at the ILO to economic development over legal enactment.

Finally, not described in Chapter 6 but very germane to the story being told here is the outcome of the internal reorganization undertaken at the ILO in the early 1970s. Twenty years earlier a division called Labour Law and Labour Relations had been created and was the location for many of the principal programmes of the ILO. In the early 1970s the structure was changed and a new department created. Its title was Industrial Relations and Labour Administration, and within it were several subunits (branches), the two most important of which were the Labour Law and Labour Relations branch (where the IIRA was housed after moving from the IILS) and the Labour Administration branch. More important, however, is the indication in these shifting labels that industrial relations was of growing visibility and importance at the ILO.

Through the mid-1990s industrial relations remained a central part of the ILO's organizational structure and activities. With regard to the latter, the industrial relations programme of the ILO encompassed a number of separate activities. One was research, conducted by both in-house staff and outside professionals. A number of industrial relations academics spent sabbaticals at the ILO and received grants for research projects.

Most of these led to books and articles, a well-recognized and regarded example being John Windmuller's *Collective bargaining in industrialized market economies: A reappraisal* (1987). Another significant activity of the industrial relations staff was researching and drafting new Conventions and Recommendations, while yet another was conducting numerous technical assistance programmes across the world on topics broadly related to industrial relations (such as collective bargaining and labour dispute resolution programmes).

We have seen that across the world industrial relations fell on hard times in the 1980s and 1990s. Industrial relations at the ILO did not completely escape this trend, although it took longer to materialize and has in some measure been more a matter of appearance than substance.

For example, if one looks at the organizational chart of the ILO and its major programmes today, the term industrial relations has disappeared. The ILO is now divided into four programme areas: Standards and Fundamental Principles and Rights at Work; Employment; Social Protection; and Social Dialogue. The Social Dialogue sector, in turn, is divided into four subunits: Bureau for Employers' Activities; Bureau for Workers' Activities; InFocus Programme on Social Dialogue, Labour Law and Labour Administration; and Sectoral Activities. The most important unit within Social Dialogue is the InFocus Programme and it is here where industrial relations used to be found. Note that the InFocus Programme still distinguishes Labour Law and Labour Administration as discrete areas, as was done in the 1980s. But industrial relations has been absorbed into Social Dialogue.

A second piece of evidence regarding the gradual disappearance of the term industrial relations from the official vocabulary of the ILO comes from its journal, the *International Labour Review*. From 1975 to 1984, five articles were published in the *International Labour Review* with the term industrial relations in the title, while from 1985 to 1995 the number was six. From 1996 to 2003, however, the *International Labour Review* did not feature a single article with industrial relations in the title.

To a significant degree, as indicated above, the sudden disappearance of the industrial relations term in the official publications of the ILO is a matter of shifting labels rather than shifting priorities and values, and not too much should be read into this trend. Thus, although the term industrial relations was not officially featured in the title of articles after 1995, a number of articles were published on the subject area of industrial relations, such as collective bargaining, strikes and developments in labour–management relations. Indeed, an entire issue of the *International Labour Review* (No. 2, 1998) was devoted to the 50th anniversary of the Convention on the Freedom of Association and Protection of the Right to Organise, 1948 (No. 87). Also, while the term industrial relations was noticeably slipping in usage, the term social dialogue was taking its place.

If social dialogue and industrial relations are more or less equivalent concepts, then the changing vocabulary at the ILO signals nothing of substance. One can make an argument on all sides of this matter and provide supporting evidence and, as I suggest below, the outcome depends significantly on the definition and interpretation of industrial relations. My judgement, however, is that industrial relations and social dialogue, while having substantial overlap, are distinct and substantively different constructs in several respects, and thus the disappearance of the one and rise of the other has more than purely cosmetic implications.

The ILO defines social dialogue as follows (www.ilo.org):

Social Dialogue is defined by the ILO to include all types of negotiation, consultation, or simply exchange of information between, or among, representatives of governments, employers, and workers, on issues of common interest relating to economic and social policy. It can exist as a tripartite process, with the government as an official party to the dialogue, or it may consist of bipartite relations only between labour and management (or trade unions and employers' organizations), with or without indirect government involvement. Concertation can be informal or institutionalized, and often it is a combination of the two. It can take place at the national, regional, or at enterprise level. It can be inter-professional, sectoral or a combination of these. The main goal of social dialogue itself is to promote consensus building and democratic involvement among the main stakeholders in the world of work.

Comparing the content of social dialogue with that of industrial relations is problematic, given the competing visions and definitions of industrial relations. Some authors, for example, define industrial relations as the study of the employment relationship (Heneman, 1969). Hyman (1995b: 10), on the other hand, defines industrial relations as "the social regulation of market forces", while Barbash (1993: 67) defines it as "the resolution of tension and conflict among the contending interests in the employment relationship, namely management efficiency, employee security and maintenance of economic stability and social peace by the state". Yet another common definition of industrial relations is that it centres on trade unions, collective bargaining, and labour–management relations (Whitfield and Strauss, 1998).

Defined as the study of the employment relationship, industrial relations is evidently much broader than social dialogue. But the comparison may not be meaningful since this definition of industrial relations centres on its science-building face (an academic area of study), while the concept of social dialogue embodies the problem-solving face (an applied method for resolving labour problems and promoting industrial peace).

The gap between social dialogue and industrial relations remains relatively large if Hyman's definition is used. The "social regulation of market forces" is a very expansive concept that includes within it alternative regimes of political economy, including state socialism, welfare state capitalism and laissez-faire capitalism. Social dialogue is far more narrowly construed, since "social partners" by definition do not exist in either socialism or laissez-faire capitalism. Likewise, Hyman's definition explicitly draws attention to the concept of "social regulation", which includes social dialogue as one method but also includes many other mechanisms of regulation, including culture, markets and law. Broadly speaking, Hyman's concept of industrial relations seems like a generalization of Kerr/Dunlop's "web of rules" and Flander's "job regulation". Viewed this way, social dialogue and industrial relations look like very different constructs – having some overlap but not much. For example, one can speak of an industrial relations system as a web of rules, but does it make equivalent sense to talk about a "social dialogue system"?

Some convergence occurs between social dialogue and Barbash's definition of industrial relations. Both definitions, for example, seem largely to equate industrial relations with a process – stated in the negative by Barbash (resolution of conflict and tension) and in the positive by the ILO (to promote consensus building and democratic involvement). But again there are differences. At least as officially defined, the social dialogue concept seems limited to negotiation, consultation and information exchange and expressly focuses on issues of common interest; Barbash's conceptualization, on the other hand, grounds industrial relations on conflicting interests and considerably expands the options for conflict resolution and tension reduction to also include the non-negotiated aspects of human resource management, protective labour law and macroeconomic policy. Social dialogue, by focusing on negotiation and information exchange between social partners, makes space for trade unions and the integrative aspects of negotiation and policy-making but does not seem to include many other parts of collective bargaining (strikes, union organizing) or most aspects of human resource management and labour law. (These subjects are of course still central to the ILO; the point is that they tend to fall outside the officially specified domain of social dialogue.) Also of note, Barbash's definition seems also to open up space for not only the process of conflict resolution but also the outcomes, such as efficiency, employee security and industrial peace. Social dialogue does not seem to contain the outcomes of the employment relationship, except perhaps for industrial peace, social stability and other related phenomena.

The gap between social dialogue and industrial relations closes considerably if one instead defines the latter as concerning trade unions, collective bargaining and labour–management relations. Indeed, now social dialogue is the broader concept and appears to subsume industrial relations. Thus in this guise both social dialogue and industrial relations involve forms of voice, information exchange, negotiation and bargaining in the work world. The difference between the two is that industrial relations primarily covers only employment situations with a formal, organized type of collective voice – typically a trade union, but also including works councils and other such representative bodies – and involves some form of bipartite or tripartite collective negotiation and/or bargaining, while social dialogue includes not only union–management structures but a variety of other voice and consultation methods. An example would be a national tripartite (employer, union, government) labour policy forum; another would be civic groups lobbying on behalf of workers' rights or environmental protection at the workplace. Illustrative of the intended broader reach of social dialogue is the Resolution Concerning Social Dialogue and Tripartism adopted at the 90th Session of the International Labour Conference of the ILO, in 2002. The resolution emphasizes using all forms of tripartite consultation and voice to promote not only traditional workplace goals concerning decent wages, hours and conditions, but a host of non-traditional objectives such as those related to HIV/AIDS in the labour force, social regulation of foreign direct investment, and greater provision of financial services to workers.

The message I take from this analysis is that the relationship between social dialogue and industrial relations depends on one's conception of industrial relations but, regardless of definition, the two concepts are not entirely equivalent. Going further, it appears that as defined by many industrial relations scholars the corpus of industrial relations is considerably broader than that of social dialogue. The substitution of social dialogue for industrial relations in the official vocabulary of the ILO can thus only appear problematic to those who take a broad and sympathetic view of industrial relations. But since the ILO by all accounts is itself completely sympathetic and committed to the broad agenda and programmes of industrial relations, how could this substitution of terms and concepts come about?

My answers to this conundrum are conjectural, but informed by opinions of people inside and outside the ILO. The number one reason that the ILO has quietly let go of the industrial relations name is, it appears, the same reason that university academic programmes, the Industrial Relations Research Association and corporate labour relations departments are also letting go the name. The opinion of many scholars notwithstanding, industrial relations now corresponds in the popular mind to the narrow "labour management" definition of the field and this model, unfortunately, is increasingly viewed as unduly narrow and out of date.

Central to this explanation is the long-term decline in union density across much of the world. Even 30 years ago, when the union movement was far larger, the ILO's model of formal tripartite interest representation through collective bargaining actually applied to no more than 7 per cent of the world's workforce (Cox and Harrod, 1972). By the late 1990s, this proportion had shrunk still further, reflecting not only the decline in the union movement in most countries but also the growth of jobs in areas outside the reach of traditional collective bargaining, such as the many fast-growing informal economies and the much greater number of contingent and part-time jobs. Thus the ILO's shift to social dialogue is an attempt to expand the model of representation and voice both vertically and horizontally – vertically by including more levels of voice (from shop floor to national policy-making) and horizontally by including a wider array of voice institutions.

A second trend behind the move from industrial relations to social dialogue is the growth in the number and influence of what the ILO calls "civil society groups". In earlier decades, the labour movement was the main representative and mouthpiece for workers. Today, however, workers are also using a variety of other groups and organizations to promote their interests and voice their concerns. Included in these are a myriad of non-governmental organizations (NGOs). These groups form around particular issues, such as civil rights, sweatshop labour and environmental protection, and perform more of a lobbying, agitation and political pressure function. Although in principle

NGOs can be incorporated into industrial relations as another pluralist interest group, in practice the historical focus of industrial relations on unions and labour–management relations suggests that a broader concept, such as social dialogue, might be more accommodative.

The third trend is a shift in the intellectual centre of gravity at the ILO from the Anglo-American governance model of industrial relations to a European-based governance model of social partnership. The Anglo-American model has not only declined substantially in coverage but its foundation on the principle of adversarial bargaining also looks increasingly at odds with the contemporary emphasis on cooperation at work. The European model of social partnership, on the other hand, remains vital (if challenged) and relatively widespread in coverage, while it emphasizes accommodation, consensus and commitment to social minima. Inevitably, the European model looks increasingly the more attractive and congruent with ILO goals and principles. Not surprisingly, therefore, the institutional models and nomenclature used by the ILO during the 1990s increasingly came from Europe, including unmistakably European terms such as social partners, social dialogue, social protection, social exclusion and social solidarity. Unfortunately, these terms and approaches to structuring the employment relationship are frequently unfamiliar and even alien to many people outside Europe. Thus, just as the concept and programme of industrial relations in the 1920s or 1950s seemed to many Europeans to be a non-transferable North American product, the concept of social dialogue strikes many people in North America as a similarly non-transferable product from Europe.

Is social dialogue a replacement concept for industrial relations? In my opinion, it is not. From an industrial relations scholar's perspective, and based on the history of the field presented in this volume, industrial relations is in fact the broader and more inclusive construct, while social dialogue seems significantly bound to European institutions and social democratic ideology. Does this then mean that the ILO should go back to industrial relations? As a proponent of industrial relations, I should of course say yes, and let the matter rest. But one must recognize that industrial relations today has also acquired a growing number of liabilities. So, we are left with a dilemma – industrial relations may no longer suffice to cover in a modern, appealing way the full range of workplace institutions and practices that conceptually fall within its domain, but then on the other hand neither does social dialogue. Evidently we have a lacuna here of growing proportions that industrial relations scholars need to resolve. Certainly the group best situated to lead this effort is the one that includes the leading industrial relations scholars from around the world. That group is the IIRA, to which I now turn.

The IIRA

In an earlier chapter we saw that up to the mid-1960s industrial relations was largely confined to the Anglophone countries and several of their former colonies. By the mid-1970s, however, the industrial relations field had established a global presence, marked by the creation of industrial relations associations and academic research and teaching programmes in Africa, southern and eastern Asia, the Middle East, continental Europe and Latin America. The most important event responsible for the global spread of the industrial relations field was the creation of the IIRA.

The IIRA enjoyed strong growth over its first decade of operation. From its original four founding associations, by 1976 the IIRA grew to 20 full members (national industrial relations associations), 44 institutional members (universities, institutes, etc.) and 394 individual members. It also hosted four world congresses in its first decade and the 1976 Congress in Geneva attracted nearly 400 registrants.

Since the mid-1970s, the field of industrial relations has experienced a number of challenges and, in several leading countries, suffered a significant decline in scholarly participation and influence. Not all developments have been on the negative side, however. Looking at the record of the IIRA from 1976 to 2003, one must conclude that it represents one of the bright spots and sources of growth for the field over this period. As the organization crossed into the twenty-first century, however, it also faced a time of reassessment and rethinking, sparked by the same environmental trends affecting industrial relations worldwide. Also worrisome for the IIRA is the industrial relations field's apparent diminished visibility and influence within the ILO, given that the latter is the IIRA's administrative home and source of significant resource support.

Since 1976, the IIRA has registered sizeable growth in membership, international participation, and programmes and activities. It has also played a significant role in promoting high-quality research, focusing the attention of scholars on new and emerging employment issues, and fostering an international research network and policy dialogue among industrial relations scholars across the world. Here is a brief overview.

Membership

During the last 20 years, individual, full and institutional membership in the IIRA all registered significant net growth. Statistics are provided below for three years, spaced roughly ten years apart.

	Full	Institutional	Individual
1984	23	26	279
1992	33	47	1269
2003	40	69	891

The number of full members (national industrial relations associations) has nearly doubled since 1984. Given the relatively adverse climate for the industrial relations field in many countries in the 1980s and 1990s, this increase in the number of industrial relations associations belonging to the IIRA is one of the most hopeful statistics to be found. Also positive is the breadth and diversity of countries represented: Argentina, Australia, Austria, Belgium, Brazil, Canada, Chile, Cyprus, Denmark, Finland, France, Germany, Greece, Hungary, India, Ireland, Israel, Italy, Japan, Korea, Netherlands, Nigeria, Norway, Peru, Philippines, Poland, Portugal, South Africa, Sweden, Taiwan (China), United Republic of Tanzania, Trinidad and Tobago, Turkey, United Kingdom, United States, Uruguay, Venezuela and Zimbabwe. Nineteen of these associations have over 100 members and, interestingly, 31 use English as the primary language.

The number of institutional members belonging to the IIRA has grown by more than two and a half times since 1984. Institutional members come from 28 countries, with the United States in the lead (9), followed by the United Kingdom (7), Canada, the Netherlands, India (4), Australia and South Africa (3).

Individual membership in the IIRA tripled between 1984 and 2003. In 2003 IIRA individual members came from 82 countries, located across all parts of the world. The United States led the list with 254, followed by Australia (76), Canada (68) and the United Kingdom (35). Approximately 15–20 per cent of the individual members are non-academic, including judges, labour ministry officials, arbitrators, and union and employer federation researchers.

Also evident, however, is a noticeable one-quarter drop in individual IIRA membership from 1,269 in 1992 to 891 in 2003. The actual highpoint in individual membership was 1,316, reached in 1997. Taken at face value, these numbers suggest a significant fall-off in the number of individual researchers belonging to the IIRA and, potentially, in the overall health of the organization. Although the exact trend is impossible to determine, much or possibly almost all of this decline is believed to be a statistical artifact. In 1999, the IIRA secretariat decided to purge the membership roll of more than 400 people listed as members but who had not paid annual dues for a number of years. The result was a substantial one-time drop in membership, followed by a resumption of growth in membership from 2000 to 2003.

World congresses

Following the Fouth World Congress in Geneva in 1976, the IIRA has continued to hold a world congress approximately every three years. In 2003 the Thirteenth World Congress was held in Berlin, hosted and organized by the German Industrial Relations Association. The locations of the world congresses since 1976 are provided below, along with attendance.

Year	Host city	Attendance
1979	Paris	350
1983	Kyoto	400+
1986	Hamburg	528
1989	Brussels	500+
1992	Sydney	900+
1995	Washington	998
1998	Bologna	1003
2000	Tokyo	1042
2003	Berlin	860
2006	Lima	

Noteworthy is the steady increase in attendance at the world congresses through the year 2000, leading to a more than threefold increase in participation between 1979 and 2000. Attendance, however, was down noticeably at the 2003 Berlin Congress. The major reason is that fewer home country nationals attended the Berlin Congress compared to the 2000 Tokyo Congress. Attendance from countries outside Germany was comparable and, indeed, the number of countries represented in Berlin (60) was significantly higher.

Regional congresses

Soon after its founding in 1966, the IIRA assisted various national associations in organizing and promoting regional industrial relations conferences. The first such conference was in North America in 1968, followed by Asia (1969), Europe (1969) and Latin America (1974).

Given the success of these events, and the desire of many IIRA members to meet more often than every world congress and to have an opportunity to meet in a smaller group and focus specifically on regional industrial relations issues, the Executive Committee decided to initiate IIRA-sponsored regional congresses, generally held in the two years between each world congress. These quickly grew in number and popularity, often attracting 300–500 participants from several dozen countries. A list of the regional congresses is provided below.

Year	Regional Congress	Host country
1984	First European	Austria
1987	Second European	Israel
1987	First Asian	Singapore
1988	First Americas	Canada
1988	First African	Nigeria
1990	Second Asian	Philippines
1991	Third European	Italy
1993	Second Americas	Venezuela
1994	Fourth European	Finland
1996	Third Asian	Taiwan, China
1997	Fifth European	Ireland
1997	Second African	Zimbabwe
1999	Third Americas	Peru
2001	Sixth European	Norway
2001	Fourth Asian	Philippines
2002	Third African	South Africa
2002	Fourth Americas	Canada
2004	Fifth Asian	Republic of Korea
2004	Seventh European	Portugal

Study groups

At the Sixth World Congress in Kyoto in 1983, incoming IIRA president Friedrich Fürstenberg proposed that "working groups" be established to promote research and scholarly collaboration in specific areas of interest within industrial relations. The initiative was approved on an experimental basis and members were invited to submit proposals. Six groups promptly formed, as shown in the table.

Study group	Chair (nationality)
Industrial Relations as a Field and Industrial Relations Theory	Barbash (USA)
Technological Change and Industrial Relations	Blanpain (Belgium)
Wage Structures and Regulations: Differences among Male and Female Workers	Gaudart (Austria)
Workers' Participation in Developing Countries	Grozdanic (Yugoslavia)
Industrial Conflict in International Perspective	Hanami (Japan)
Trilateral Concertation and Macroeconomic Policies	Treu (Italy)

The working groups proved quite popular and soon the IIRA set them up as official parts of the organization under the designation "study groups". Over time the number of study groups has grown until in 2004 there are 17.

Study group	Chair (nationality)
Industrial Relations as a Field and Industrial Relations Theory	Kaufman (USA); Kelly (UK)
Gender and Industrial Relations	Greene (UK); Kirton (UK)
Equality in Pay and Employment	Jain (Canada); Bellace (USA)
Workers' Participation	Markey (Australia)
Studies in the European Social Model	Demetriades (Ireland)
Public Policy and Industrial Relations	Negrelli (Italy); Verma (Canada)
Urban Labour Markets in Developing Countries	Scoville (USA)
Pay Systems	Mitchell (USA)
Flexible Work Patterns	Zeytinoglu (Canada)
The Future of Trade Unions	Kauppinen (Finland)
The Theory and Practice of Negotiations	Herman (USA); Pellegrini (Italy)
Human Resource Management	Zagelmeyer (UK); Marchington (UK)
Research Methods in Industrial Relations	Kelly (Australia); Whitfield (UK)
Industrial Relations in the Public Sector	Thompson (Canada); Keller (Germany)
The Comparative Industrial Relations Research and Teaching Society	Adams (Canada); Logan (UK)
Unemployment	Oaklander (USA)
Industrial Relations in Countries in Transition from Centrally Planned to Market Economies	Marinkovic (Serbia & Montenegro)

The study groups have proven to be very popular and active parts of the parent organization. They are smaller sized and more informal and thus conducive to personal interaction and dialogue. They also allow people to meet other scholars from around the world who are interested in the same area of research. A number of the study groups have spawned published volumes, with papers originally prepared for and presented at their meetings. A fairly comprehensive list of these books is provided later but three examples will indicate the nature of the contribution: *Industrial relations theory: Its scope and pedagogy* (Adams and Meltz, 1993); *Researching the world of work: Strategies and methods in studying industrial relations* (Whitfield and Strauss, 1998); and *Models of employee participation in a changing global environment* (Markey et al., 2001).

Presidents and secretaries

The IIRA is the only world organization for researchers and scholars interested in industrial relations. Its membership thus represents a large cross-section of the world's most active and talented people in the industrial relations field. At the apex of this group of scholars are the IIRA presidents. To date the IIRA has had twelve presidents, each a leading figure in the field.

IIRA President	Years	Country of origin
Ben Roberts	1967–73	United Kingdom
John Dunlop	1973–76	United States
Jean-Daniel Reynaud	1976–79	France
Mikio Sumiya	1979–83	Japan
Friedrich Fürstenberg	1983–86	Germany
Roger Blanpain	1986–89	Belgium
John Niland	1989–92	Australia
Thomas Kochan	1992–95	United States
Tiziano Treu	1995–98	Italy
Tadashi Hanami	1998–2000	Japan
Manfred Weiss	2000–2003	Germany
Luis Aparicio Valdez	2003–2005	Peru
Russell Lansbury (president-elect)		Australia

The IIRA presidents also illustrate the multidisciplinary nature of the field of industrial relations. Some are sociologists, such as Reynaud and Fürstenberg; others are economists, such as Roberts, Dunlop, Sumiya and Niland; yet others are from law, such as Blanpain, Treu, Hanami, Weiss and Aparicio-Valdez; while Kochan comes from a school of management.

The IIRA, as noted in an earlier chapter, has from its foundation been headquartered at the ILO in Geneva. Many benefits to the Association flow from this relationship. One is that the ILO serves as the secretariat of the IIRA and thus provides considerable organizational and administrative support. Although not a formal part of the IIRA constitution, a long-standing tradition developed (with one exception in the mid-1970s) that the secretary of the IIRA would normally be a senior ILO official and that this person would be responsible for the ongoing coordination and management of the organization. Over the nearly four decades of the IIRA's existence the secretaries have played an important role in the success of the organization.

IIRA Secretary	Years	Country of origin
Robert Cox	1967–70	United States
Kenneth Walker	1970–76	Australia
Ben Roberts	1976–79	United Kingdom
Efrén Córdova	1979–83	United States
Alfred Pankert	1983–84	Belgium
Alan Gladstone	1985–92	United States
William Simpson	1992–98	United Kingdom
Hông-Trang Perret-Nguyên	1998–2000	France
Tayo Fashoyin	2000–	Nigeria

Research themes

The programmes of the IIRA both reflect and shape the scholarly dialogue and debate in the industrial relations field. Each world congress typically (but not always) features five plenary session themes around which the conference is organized. Reproduced below are the session titles for each world congress from 1979 to 2003.

1979 World Congress
- Workers' Participation
- Forms of Protest and Settlement in Industrial Conflicts

- The Crisis of the Seventies in Developed Countries: Evaluation Studies
- The Changing Growth Models and their Effects on Industrial Relations

1983 World Congress

- Industrial Relations in Post-Industrial Societies
- Collective Bargaining and Incomes Policies in a Stagflation Economy
- Industrial Relations and Political Structures
- Industrial Relations in the Unorganized Sector
- Viability of the Japanese Model of Industrial Relations

1986 World Congress

- Technological Change and Labour Relations
- Institutional Forms of Workers' Participation, with special reference to the Federal Republic of Germany
- New Trends in Working-Time Arrangements
- Cooperation and Conflict in Public Service Labour Relations
- Labour Relations as a Strategic Factor in Development

1989 World Congress

- Labour Market Flexibility and New Employment Patterns
- Structural Change and Industrial Relations Strategies
- Aspirations and Expectations of a New Labour Force and Implications for Industrial Relations
- Equity and Equality of Treatment in Employment
- Recent Trends in Industrial Relations Studies and Theory

1992 World Congress

- The Role of the State in Industrial Relations
- Trade Unionism in the Future
- Human Resource Management – Implications for Teaching, Theory, Research and Practice in Industrial Relations
- Industrial Relations and Political Transformation
- The Macro/Micro Interface in Labour Market Policy and Practice

1995 World Congress

- The Global Human Resource Challenge: Managing Diversity in International Settings
- Emerging Models of Worker Participation and Representation
- The Challenge to Government Policy: Promoting Competitive Advantage with Full Employment and High Labour Standards

- New Models of Negotiation, Dispute Resolution, and Joint Problem-Solving
- Industrial Relations, Economic Development, and Democracy in the Twenty-first Century

1998 World Congress

- Turning Growth into Jobs: Efficiency and Equity in Training Policies
- Reconciling Multilateral Interests: The Restructuring of Employment Relations in Public Services
- Into the Unknown: Managing Human Resources in Small and Medium-Sized Business Units
- Squaring the Circle: Quality of Work and Family Life: Industrial Relations in a Wider Social Context
- Bargaining Globally: Labour–Management Relations in a Multinational Context: International Trade Agreements and Social Clauses
- Looking into the Next Century: Social Dialogue and Democratic Development: The Rediscovery of Pluralist Industrial Relations

2000 World Congress

- Exploring Trends in Employment Relations and New Approaches to Work in the Twenty-first Century
- The Impact of Globalization on National and Regional Systems of Industrial Relations and Employment Relations
- Search for Flexibility, Fairness, and Prosperity: Alternative Employment Policies in the Twenty-first Century
- Asia in the Twenty-first Century: Challenges and Opportunities in Work and Labour

2003 World Congress

- Enterprise Reorganization: Negotiated, Consultative, or Unilateral?
- Changing Contours of the Employment Relationship and New Modes of Labour Regulation
- Industrial Relations and Global Labour Standards
- Collective Actors in Industrial Relations: What Future?
- European Integration: Convergence or Diversity?

In looking over these conference session themes, one sees clear evidence of the fairly sharp division line between the "old" industrial relations and the emergence of the "new" industrial relations. The old industrial relations is evident in the programmes of 1979, 1983 and 1986 World Congresses. Here major topics of research were traditional industrial relations topics, such as industrial conflict, industrial democracy (workers' participation) and collective bargaining. Also included were topical subjects of that era, such as incomes policies, technological change and economic development.

The 1989 World Congress represents a transition point and then the 1992 and succeeding World Congresses show evidence of a distinct and ongoing shift in focus and content. One aspect of "new" industrial relations is more attention to the subject of human resource management. HRM appears for the first time on an IIRA programme in 1992 and the subject of human resources then reappears at the next two World Congresses.

New industrial relations continues to give attention to trade unionism and collective bargaining, but the focus shifts to the decline of these institutions, what the work world might look like without them, and alternative institutional methods for representation, voice and conflict resolution. Thus this subject is broached in the 1992 World Congress under the title "Trade Unionism in the Future". Then, the 1995 World Congress carries forward this theme with a session on "Emerging Models of Worker Participation and Representation" and "New Models of Negotiation, Dispute Resolution, and Joint Problem-Solving". In a similar vein, the 1998 World Congress explores social dialogue as an alternative form of pluralist industrial relations, while the 2000 World Congress explores new approaches to structuring and organizing work. These revisionist themes of new industrial relations reappear in even stronger form at the 2003 World Congress. One session considers "New Modes of Labour Regulation" and another poses the question "Collective Actors in Industrial Relations: What Future?" Perhaps this last session theme best illustrates the distance travelled since the mid-1970s by the industrial relations field, for surely no one in "old" industrial relations of the 1970s would have dreamed that this question could be more than idle academic speculation, with little application to the future of the field.

Another sign of the transition from old (post-Second World War) industrial relations to new industrial relations is the appearance of the substitute term "employment relations". It first appears in the programme of the 1998 World Congress and is used again in the 2000 World Congress. The 2003 World Congress also features a session on "Changing Contours of the Employment Relationship", again calling attention to the fact that the focus of the field is not "industry" (as in industrial relations) but all types of employment relationships, as the new term employment relations is meant to connote.

As earlier indicated, the programmes of the IIRA in part reflect wider trends in the industrial relations field, but they also in part shape the course of research and debate. Clearly, the leaders of the IIRA, in selecting session topics, are trying to move the industrial relations field in directions that explore important new trends and developments in the work world and new topics and problems shaping practice and policy.

In the area of policy and practice, for example, are sessions on quality of work life and family leave, flexible work arrangements and enterprise restructuring. Moving beyond these, certainly of all the challenges to modern industrial relations none is as important as the consequences of globalization. We see in the programmes of the IIRA a significant effort to address this subject in its manifold dimensions. At the 1995 World Congress, for example, this theme is addressed in the session "The Challenge to Government Policy: Promoting Competitive Advantage with Full Employment and High Labour Standards". Then, at the next world congress the theme of "Labour–Management Relations in a Multinational Context" is considered, followed at the next world congress by "The Impact of Globalization on National and Regional Systems of Industrial Relations".

In an interview, former IIRA president Thomas Kochan provided a particularly revealing example of how the Association has helped generate and move forward research in the field, especially in the comparative area. For more than three decades industrial relations scholars had been conducting individual country studies of industrial relations systems and their evolution through time. Kochan thought the next big step was to look at these national experiences in a comparative way, trying to draw out common trends and causal linkages. With colleagues from MIT, Michael Piore and Richard Locke, Kochan decided to organize a cross-national team of researchers to initiate a multi-year research programme combining comparative industrial relations and comparative politics (Thelen and Locke, 1995).

The IIRA played an important role in their project in several ways. Primarily, it provided a network of international scholars they could tap into to find the best people for the team. The 1995 World Congress provided an international forum to present the first wave of research, and with this momentum the project could be cascaded to include more people and countries, with a future wave of research to be presented at upcoming regional and world congresses. The initial output was the book *Employment relations in a changing world economy* (Locke, Kochan and Piore, 1995), with chapters by authors from ten countries. Then the focus was moved down to a cross-national analysis of employment relations patterns at the sector and industry level, yielding books such *After lean production: Evolving employment practices in the world auto industry* (Kochan, Lansbury and MacDuffie, 1997, eds.), *Telecommunications: Restructuring work and employment relations worldwide* (Katz, ed., 1997); and *From tellers to sellers: Changing employment relations in banks* (Regini, Kitay and Baethge, eds., 1999). Contemporaneously, research teams were formed in specific world regions, with conferences held in countries such as Singapore and the Republic of Korea. From this flowed other publications, such as *Employment relations in the growing Asian economies* (Verma, Kochan and Lansbury, eds. 1995). Commenting on the entire experience, Kochan (2003) stated that "the biggest payoff – and the one that motivated me to start this effort in the first place – was to build up the range of researchers and the quality of research that would be presented at the 1995 IIRA World Congress".

A final point worth noting is the evident attempt of the IIRA to strengthen its relationship and contribution to the ILO. Since 1995 each world congress has had one or more themes directly pertinent to the programmes and policy issues of the ILO. In 1995, for example, the subject of labour standards is a main theme, in 1998 social dialogue is featured, in 2000 alternative employment policies is considered, and in 2003 one of the five main congress themes is global labour standards.

Publications

One of the main contributions of the IIRA is to promote and disseminate scholarly research on industrial relations. It accomplishes this task in a variety of ways.

At each world congress 60 or more papers are presented and distributed as part of the main programme, and are then made available in print and/or electronic form. The proceedings of the 2000 World Congress, for example, comprised six printed volumes. An equally large number of papers are presented as part of the study group meetings after the completion of the main programme. Proceedings are also generally published from the various regional congresses.

In a number of cases, the world and regional congress papers and study group papers gain additional visibility when they appear later as symposia in academic journals or as edited books. Papers from the Tenth World Congress, for example, later appeared in five different academic journals. Although not a complete tally, I have endeavoured to compile a representative sample of books and symposia that have grown directly out of IIRA congresses and study groups from 1990 to 2002. It illustrates the breadth and depth of research generated by the Association.

Title	Date	Authors/editors
Comparative industrial relations research	2003	Roy Adams (ed.)
Flexible work arrangements: Conceptualizations and international experiences	2003	Isik Zeytinoglu (ed.)
Models of employee participation in a changing global environment	2001	Raymond Markey, Alain Chouraqui, Paul Gollan, Ann Hodgkinson, and Ulke Veersma (eds.)
"Equality in Employment: Issues and Policies", Symposium in *International Journal of Manpower*	2002	Harish Jain (guest ed.)
Strategic choices in reforming public service employment: An international handbook	2001	Carlo Ell'aringa, Giuseppe Della Rocca, and Berndt Keller (eds.)
Public service employment relations in Europe	1999	Stephen Bach, Lorenzo Bordogna, Giuseppe Della Rocca and David Winchester (eds.)
The impact of EMU on industrial relations in the European Union	1998	Timo Kauppinen (ed.)
Researching the world of work: Strategies and methods in studying industrial relations	1998	Keith Whitfield and George Strauss (eds.)
Theorizing in industrial relations: Approaches and applications	1997	Jack Barbash and Noah Meltz (eds.)
Changing employment relations in Australia	1997	Jim Kitay and Russell Lansbury (eds.)
Innovation and employee participation through works councils	1997	Raymond Markey and Jacques Monat (eds.)
"Workforce Strategies and Competitive Strategies: Human Resource Policies and Practices in the 1990s", Symposium in *International Journal of Manpower*	1996	Harish Jain and Anil Verma (guest eds.)
"Labor Market Discrimination", Symposium in *International Journal of Manpower*	1994	Harish Jain (guest ed.)
The future of industrial relations: Global change and challenges	1994	John Niland, Russell Lansbury and Chrissie Verevis (eds.)
Industrial relations theory: Its scope and pedagogy	1993	Roy Adams and Noah Meltz (eds.)

Labour relations in a changing environment	1992	Alan Gladstone and Hoyt Wheeler (eds.)
Theory, research, and teaching in international industrial relations	1992	Jack Barbash and Noah Meltz (eds.)
Industrial relations and African development	1992	Tayo Fashoyin (ed.)
Participation in public policy-making: The role of trade unions and employers' associations	1992	Tiziano Treu (ed.)
Workplace justice: Employment obligations in international perspective	1992	Hoyt Wheeler and Jacques Rojot (eds.)
Status influences in developing countries labour markets: Caste, gender and custom	1991	James Scoville (ed.)

The IIRA: An assessment

Looking back over the four decades of life of the IIRA, one can only judge that it has been quite successful in its original mission.

Before the IIRA was born, the field of industrial relations was limited to the Anglo-American part of the world and, indeed, had a significant, large-size presence only in the United States. To be sure, the study of work, employment, trade unions, labour law and national labour policy could be found in many universities, particularly in the more advanced industrial countries. But for the most part, research, teaching and dialogue on work-related subjects were fragmented and often parochial and ethnocentric, inhibited by barriers posed by disciplinary specialization, the difficulty of communicating and collaborating across national boundaries, and differences in national institutions, cultures and ideologies. Worse, in many other countries teaching and research on work-related subjects was practically absent from the universities, while in a number of nations the government or prevailing custom actively suppressed consideration of topics such as trade unions, strikes and workers' rights.

One looks at the 40 years since the founding of the IIRA and sees great progress across the world. Today the field of industrial relations has spread to all parts of the globe and is taught and researched at universities in Europe, Asia, Africa, Latin America, and the countries of the former Soviet Union and Eastern bloc. It is not an exaggeration to say, therefore, that the industrial relations field has "gone global". The evidence is found in numerous places – the publication of industrial relations journals in numerous countries and languages, the activities of over 40 national industrial relations associations, and the attendance of people from over 60 countries at the 2003 IIRA World Congress.

Many factors contributed to the global spread of industrial relations, but arguably the single most important for starting and sustaining this process was the International Industrial Relations Association. At its birth, the IIRA broadened the reach of industrial relations by bringing Japan into the group of four founding members. Shortly thereafter, the IIRA played an important role in starting industrial relations associations in Argentina, France, Poland, Taiwan (China) and numerous other countries and territories. Soon internationally recognized scholars from these countries, such as Reynaud from France, Fürstenberg from Germany and Sumiya from Japan, were serving as IIRA presidents. The process continues, as the presidency of the IIRA in 2003 passed to Aparicio Valdez from Peru. Behind each of these men, in turn, is a much larger group of scholars and researchers in dozens of countries across the world that is actively pushing forward knowledge, practice and policy-making in industrial relations.

Not only did the IIRA provide a valuable impetus for the birth and development of industrial relations outside the core Anglophone countries; it also provided a valuable forum for scholars and non-academic researchers from across the world to meet each other, discuss common topics of interest, and develop a more multicultural, multinational perspective on work institutions and problems. Without an international organization, most scholars and researchers will inevitably remain isolated in their individual countries, having at best only a modest and often narrow perspective on industrial relations in other parts of the world and small incentive and opportunity to acquire a broader knowledge. In less developed countries, an international organization often provides the crucial infrastructure for resident scholars to have contact with the wider body of teaching and research, given the lack of an internal domestic network of research institutions and scholars. In this regard, the IIRA greatly facilitates an international exchange of knowledge and experiences by bringing together people from across the world to meet face to face and to listen and learn from each other. Suddenly events and practices in a country half-way around the world, often viewed as remote and esoteric without any first-hand exposure, gain immediacy and interest upon hearing of them in person.

The IIRA has also played a significant role in generating and guiding research in the field of industrial relations. The programmes of the regional and world congresses help define the key topics around which research in the world industrial relations community is organized. To academics in the United Kingdom or United States this role is perhaps less obvious, since these countries have their own well-developed communities of scholars, self-generated research agendas, professional associations, and journals and other publishing outlets. Even here, however, the record of publications listed above suggests that the IIRA plays a valuable role in stimulating research, particularly of a comparative and cross-national nature. Also largely unseen by many scholars from the core industrial relations countries is the extent to which their papers presented at IIRA meetings are carried back by congress participants from less developed countries and used as basic materials for teaching and research. For the scholars in the many countries of the world where the industrial relations research infrastructure is less dense and developed, the IIRA serves as a valuable hub or network centre, setting research priorities and topics through its regional and world congresses and then stimulating research activity on these topics in dozens of countries. Without the IIRA, research on industrial relations in countries such as the Czech Republic, India, the Philippines, Nigeria and Venezuela would slide backwards for lack of a sponsor and venue. Also important to growing and sustaining industrial relations in these countries are the dozens of young scholars who have received scholarships from the IIRA to attend the world congresses.

I conclude, therefore, that the IIRA has played a valuable and almost indispensable role in helping propagate the field of industrial relations around the world. As we look to the future, this role only looks larger and more strategic. The field of industrial relations is currently beleaguered and in retreat in a number of core countries. The Association, in its role of the global representative and meeting place for academic industrial relations, stands as one of the most important assets the field has for sustaining growth and charting a new direction. As already indicated, the programmes of the IIRA in its world and regional congresses have steadily introduced new topics and moved the debate in the field in new directions, giving greater emphasis to management as a strategic actor, alternative forms of workplace voice and representation, and the challenge of protecting core labour standards in a globalizing economy. But more remains to be done and the IIRA is fit to lead the way.

In 2001, Director-General Juan Somavia of the ILO met with the IIRA president Manfred Weiss, past president Tadashi Hanami, incoming president Luis Valdez-Aparicio, and IIRA secretary Tayo Fashoyin. Somavia reiterated the ILO's strong support for the IIRA and emphasized the significant role the IIRA and global industrial relations research community continue to play in helping the ILO successfully move forward its mission of improved labour conditions and human rights in the workplace, particularly as enshrined in the Decent Work Agenda. This message was warmly received and greatly welcomed by all in attendance, for it not only affirms the historic bond between the ILO and IIRA but also provides a firm foundation for future growth and collaboration.

This message was particularly well received given several signs that the IIRA and field of industrial relations had in recent years possibly become less central to the activities and programmes of the ILO. Certainly both sides have much to gain from continued partnership. Indeed, it is difficult to imagine where the ILO could find another community of nearly 1,000 leading scholars who are so aligned with and supportive of its basic mission or that perform leading edge research that is so central to its aims and concerns. The ILO and industrial relations field were born together at the end of the First World War, shared a common philosophy and mission from the earliest years, and remain today partners in the quest for improved labour conditions and protection of basic human rights at work. In light of the many economic, political and intellectual forces working to undermine the gains of the past and block the advances of the future, partnership between the ILO and industrial relations becomes even more important.

Note
[1] There are 185 Conventions and 194 Recommendations as of 2004.

INDUSTRIAL RELATIONS: RETROSPECT AND PROSPECT   12

This volume has covered more than 200 years of history and has ranged across the globe in laying out the main lines of development in the field of industrial relations. Provided here is a relatively comprehensive account of the evolution of thought in industrial relations, a chronicle of the growth and institutionalization of the field around the world, a review of the recent challenges and vicissitudes confronting industrial relations, and a portrait of the field's global family tree of prominent contributors. Industrial relations comprises a worldwide community of scholars who are nonetheless separated by country, language, discipline and research interests. If nothing else, this volume helps introduce us to each other and promotes greater dialogue and mutual understanding. These goals, I note, are central to the mission of the IIRA, who commissioned this book, so nothing could be more appropriate.

In this concluding chapter I wish to do two things. The first, in keeping with word "retrospect" in the title, is to winnow and sift the mass of details contained in the previous 11 chapters and present in distilled form the central findings and conclusions concerning the historical origin and evolution of the industrial relations field. The second purpose, in keeping with the term "prospect" in the title, is to use these findings to draw some lessons and implications about the future of the field of industrial relations. As all participants know, the field of industrial relations is currently under significant challenge at both an intellectual and policy level and in a number of countries is in evident decline. A history of the field, besides being a useful record of what has happened in the past, allows us to see more clearly the path that has brought industrial relations to its current position. And, now that we know this path and the choices that put us on it, a window is opened so we may more easily peer into the future and see both what probably lies ahead if present trends continue and what different choices might be made so that industrial relations has brighter prospects in the years ahead.

The origin and purpose of industrial relations

The term industrial relations, although not entirely transparent in meaning, connotes the state of relations between employers and employees or, more macroscopically viewed, the relations between capital and labour. The adjective "industrial" was originally adopted because it was only in the context of industrial employment, such as in a mine, mill or factory, that the relations between employers and employees became problematic and worth studying. Today the term encompasses all paid employment and industrial subdivisions, such as the retail trade industry, mining industry and government. In other languages, the problematic meaning of the term industrial is finessed by using an alternative construction, such as the French term *relations professionnelles* (the work relations in trades and occupations) and the Spanish term *relaciones laborales*. In English-speaking countries, the substitute term "employment relations" is increasingly being used in order to better indicate that the field of study covers the entire gamut of employment relationships.

As I date it, industrial relations as an academic field of study first appeared in the United States in the year 1920, marked by the creation of a new "course" (concentration) in industrial relations in the Economics Department at the University of Wisconsin. The academic person most responsible for the birth and early development of the industrial relations field in the United States was Wisconsin professor John R. Commons. Commons, his mentor Richard Ely and numerous of their students comprised the Wisconsin school of labour economics and for many years the intellectual and policy programme of the Wisconsin school was at the heart of American industrial relations. Commons was also a co-founder of the American school of institutional economics and to this day in the United States industrial relations and institutional labour economics are virtually one and the same. An important topic of interest of Commons and the Wisconsin school was trade unions and collective bargaining, but they also devoted major attention to the management of labour, labour law, social insurance programmes and macroeconomic stabilization.

Industrial relations also emerged at the same time as a management function and vocational area of practice in American business firms, largely coterminous with what is today called personnel/HRM. In this period the practice of personnel management barely existed, the labour policy in most firms was quite informal and decentralized, and labour was typically treated as a commodity and dealt with in a relatively authoritarian and often insensitive manner. Industrial relations emerged as a reaction against the traditional system and the many problems it created, and emphasized gaining competitive advantage through scientific management of labour and practices

584

that create goodwill and a unity of interest. Although industrial relations was broadly conceived to cover all employment relations and was adopted by many non-union firms, a central programmatic and ideological premise of industrial relations was that some method for collective employee voice is highly desirable. Commons was the first and most influential early academic exponent of the new practice of industrial relations in industry, while wealthy industrialist John D. Rockefeller, Jr., and several business associates did the most to promote the institutionalization of industrial relations in North American universities and business firms.

Although industrial relations first emerged in America as a formal concept and institutionalized entity, the ideas and conditions that led to it had a long pre-history dating back to the dawn of the Industrial Revolution in the late eighteenth century. Central to the development of industrial relations was the emergence of large-scale capital-intensive industry; a wage-earning labour force separated from the land and other means of production; a business ethos that regarded labour as a commodity to be bought as cheaply as possible, used to the utmost, and then discarded; a skewed political and social system that favoured property owners, business interests and social elites and kept wage earners in a vulnerable, subordinated and sometimes exploited position; labour markets characterized by intense competition and frequent bouts of extensive unemployment; and a legal system that gave scant protection to workers' rights or security against workplace hazards such as accidents, unemployment and the infirmities of old age. Out of these conditions grew mounting labour unrest, militant trade unions and violent strikes, and radical working-class political movements espousing the replacement of capitalism with various forms of socialism, communism and syndicalism. As these symptoms of discontent and alienation came to a boil in the late nineteenth century, they became known throughout the world as the Labour Problem. From roughly 1880 to 1920 the Labour Problem grew in intensity and finally reached a peak during and immediately following the First World War, symbolized by the Bolshevik Revolution in Russia and workers' uprisings and general strikes in many other nations around the world. Not coincidentally, it was exactly at this moment in history that the industrial relations field was born and its "fraternal twin", the ILO, was created under the Treaty of Versailles at the Paris peace conference.

Although Commons was the first person to publish a scholarly work explicitly devoted to the new subject of industrial relations, many other people both inside and outside academia long preceded him in the more general analysis of the phenomena of industrial relations. A number of themes of industrial relations, for example, are contained in Adam Smith's *Wealth of nations* (1776), while English businessman Charles Morrison's book,

An essay on the relations between labour and capital (1854), is obviously apropos. Later in the nineteenth century, people began writing on labour and the Labour Problem in all the emerging industrial countries of the world, including not only the United Kingdom and the United States but also France, Germany and Japan: well-known names include Lujo Brentano, Emile Durkheim, Noburu Kanai, Alfred Marshall, Frederick Taylor and Max Weber.

Among these early writers, three people stand out as having had unsurpassed influence on the future field of industrial relations.

The first two are the English husband and wife team of Sidney and Beatrice Webb. The Webbs wrote two acclaimed books that lie at the core of industrial relations: *The history of trade unionism* (1894) and *Industrial democracy* (1897). Particularly in the latter, the Webbs developed theoretical ideas and a point of view that have become foundational for industrial relations. Going further, one may say that *Industrial democracy* still stands as the field's most towering intellectual work. Although the Webbs also founded the LSE in the mid-1890s, due to interesting circumstances (explored in Chapter 3) they did not actively encourage the study of labour at the LSE nor did they work toward the establishment of industrial relations as a separate field of study. Their ideas are so fundamental, however, and their influence on Commons and other labour scholars was so important that they and Commons, along with Rockefeller, together deserve the appellation "founders of industrial relations".

The other seminal writer is Karl Marx. Marx did not himself write on industrial relations and, indeed, would have been highly critical of both the idea and practice of industrial relations. Rather, his great influence was to present a vision of capitalist society so compellingly dire and dark that it moved the defenders of capitalism to mount a major counter-response.

Marx, in his master work *Capital*, derived a theory of capitalist economic development based on one fundamental and damning proposition – that the system is inherently unjust because it can only grow and reproduce by exploiting workers. The exploitation of workers arises from the fact that the wage they are paid is less than their contribution to production, with the residual (surplus value) being expropriated by the capitalist as unearned profit. Furthermore, Marx argued that the exploitation of the workers leads to a growing polarization of society into two antagonistic classes, the gradual immiseration of the working class as wages are driven down to the subsistence level, worsening unemployment and economic crises, and an eventual revolt by the workers and overthrow of capitalism, abolition of private property and takeover of the government by the proletariat.

While numerous other radical writers expounded many of the same themes in the late nineteenth and early twentieth centuries, Marx's vision gained particular attention since he claimed to show that it was the inevitable outcome of irreversible historical forces. Also helping Marx was the fact that in certain (but not all) respects capitalism was evolving in ways he predicted, such as a growing concentration of capital, longer periods of recession and depression (such as the 1870s and 1890s), and mounting labour unrest.

The defenders of capitalism advanced two intellectual arguments and policy programmes to rebut Marx and his apocalyptic scenario. The first was neoclassical economics and programme of a competitive laissez-faire market economy.

Neoclassical economics, as described in Chapter 1, grew out of English classical economics and was popularized in the late nineteenth century by economists such as Marshall, Menger and Walras. In a major triumph, American economist John B. Clark demonstrated with the newly developed marginal productivity theory that in a competitive market economy workers are not exploited under capitalism because as a class they receive a wage equal to the value of their contribution to production. Indeed, the neoclassical economists contended that a competitively organized economy leads to a double win – not only does competition lead to a just distribution of income (by the standard of "marginal productivity justice") but it also leads via Adam Smith's invisible hand to maximum economic efficiency. These conclusions were very influential because they seemed to discredit the Marxian critique, buttress the moral legitimacy of capitalism, and suggest that the "best of all possible worlds" is achievable not through socialism or workers' cooperatives but a competitive free market economy. Furthermore, the neoclassical theory seemed to reinforce the case for economic and political liberalism, the social virtues of free markets and free trade, and the harmful effects of all forms of monopoly and protectionism. In practice, the negative verdict on monopoly and protectionism fell more heavily on efforts to aid labour, such as trade unions and protective labour laws, since these were seen to reduce profit, capital investment and growth, while a measure of monopoly and protectionism for business could be rationalized as consistent with efficiency (due to economies of scale), a profit inducement to innovation and capital investment, or a means to stabilize production and preserve jobs.

The second intellectual argument and policy programme developed to rescue capitalism from the Marxian indictment and threatened apocalypse was what eventually evolved into the field of industrial relations. Industrial relations, and antecedent developments such as the German field of *Sozialpolitik*, took a position in between Marxism and neoclassicism and thus represented the "middle way" in solving the Labour Problem.

Like neoclassical economics, industrial relations also grew out of nineteenth-century political economy but with different roots. The intellectual and policy inspiration for industrial relations came from heterodox economics, particularly associated with German political economy and the historical–social school of economics that flourished in late nineteenth-century Germany, Japan, the United Kingdom and the United States. The German version was centred among the economists and sociologists of the Verein für Sozialpolitik, such as Schmoller, Brentano and Weber. It was soon imported into Japan and became very influential there. In the United Kingdom, the historical–social school of economics was centred among a loose collection of "dissidents", such as the Webbs and John Hobson, with its centre at the LSE. Meanwhile, in America people such as Ely (principal founder of the American Economics Association) imported German economics which, together with English heterodox theories and ideas drawn from law, psychology and sociology, metamorphosed into the American school of institutional economics, led by people such as Veblen, Mitchell and Commons.

Unlike the neoclassical economists, the historical–institutional economists agreed with Marx that the system of capitalism then existing was fundamentally unfair. They also thought it was glaringly wasteful and inefficient and thus suffered from a double liability. The problem with neoclassical economics, as seen by the historical–institutional economists, is that it rests on assumptions so narrow and unrealistic that its predictions and conclusions at best capture only a portion of reality and in other cases are flatly contradicted (e.g., the observed rigidity in wage rates going back centuries). Indeed, the core invisible-hand general-equilibrium version of the theory rests on a model of perfect people, perfect information, perfect markets and a perfect legal system that makes it fundamentally and perhaps dangerously utopian: similar in many respects to the equally utopian (and dangerous) theories of state socialism and communism. When more realistic assumptions are introduced into a theory of capitalist economy, such as bounded rationality, pervasive market imperfections, fixed costs, coordination failures and attendant recessions and depressions, highly unequal initial endowments and the corruption of legislators and judges by business interests, the implications and conclusions are more likely to be closer to Marx than to Clark.

In particular, in the context of early twentieth-century American industry, the historical–institutional economists thought efficiency suffered because of monopoly and restriction of output in product markets (recalling the rise of trusts and cartels in the late nineteenth century), waste in internal enterprise operations due to unprofessional and haphazard management, the productivity-sapping effect of workers' passive and overt resistance (working as little as possible, sabotage and striking), and the extensive idleness of capital and labour that accompanies extended periods of recession and depression.

Likewise, fairness and justice suffered in real-world capitalism because workers were placed in a distinctly inferior and vulnerable position in three crucial arenas. The first arena was external labour markets, where market imperfections and extensive unemployment undercut the individual worker's bargaining power in wage determination, leading to poverty-level wages, long hours and exploitative and onerous (sweatshop) conditions. The second arena was the internal governance structure of the firm, where master–servant legal doctrines, lack of alternative jobs, and the prevailing "commodity" view of labour gave employers a large measure of unchecked dictatorial power over workers ("the divine right of capitalists", similar to the divine right of kings claimed in medieval Europe). The third arena was in the national political process, where in many countries workers (and women and minorities) had limited or non-existent suffrage rights while capitalists and the rich and powerful dominated the political process and systematically engineered "rules of the game" to favour their interests (e.g., passing tariff legislation to protect manufacturers from foreign price competition but restricting trade unions and opening the borders to unlimited immigration in order to promote "competitive" wages). The result of all of these conditions was to foster among workers a collective sense of exclusion, inhumanity, exploitation, blighted opportunities and injustice, leading not unexpectedly to a growing Labour Problem and radical drift in trade unionism and politics.

All of these defects and problems notwithstanding, the historical–institutional economists and like-minded academics and social reformers did not agree with Marx that class polarization, working-class revolution and socialism were either inevitable or desirable. (The Webbs, I note, are a partial exception since they advocated an evolutionary form of democratic socialism.) Indeed, they were strongly opposed to Marxism in terms of both theory and politics. The historical–institutional economists thus sought to craft a pragmatic but progressive labour reform programme that was located between the neoclassical programme of free market capitalism and laissez-faire and the Marxian programme of class revolution and dictatorship of the proletariat. In a sentence, the essence of the industrial relations approach is to "save capitalism by making it good", to quote Commons.

The industrial relations reform programme sought to maintain capitalism in the belief that it is superior to all other alternative feasible systems of economic organization. At the same time the programme sought to "make capitalism good" by restructuring it to achieve not only the neoclassical goal of efficiency but also the equally important humanistic goals of equity (social justice) and opportunities for individual self-development. In their view, the end goal of an economy should be to advance the human condition. Efficiency is important to this goal since it promotes higher production and, thus, consumption of material goods and services. But efficiency can also be destructive of the very human condition it is meant to promote if allowed to proceed unconstrained by other fundamental human considerations. One such condition is the universal human demand that an economy also function in a way that meets reasonable standards of procedural and distributive justice – standards above and beyond the individualist and outcome-based neoclassical criterion of marginal productivity justice. A second condition is that the process by which material goods and services are created should enhance the capacity and life experience of the people who produce them, so extra well-being in one area of life – consumption – is balanced by greater well-being in another area – work. Without these constraints, efficiency may easily lead to numerous social evils, such as child labour, sixteen-hour workdays, riches for an elite and poverty for the masses, and an authoritarian workplace where workers have no voice and are discharged at will. Not only are these conditions an affront to fundamental human values; they also undermine the very efficiency of the market system, and if allowed to deteriorate far enough eventually lead to the Marxian overthrow of capitalism. Rather than a trade-off between efficiency and equity as presumed in neoclassical economics, from an industrial relations viewpoint equity is an indispensable ingredient to efficiency and over a range of situations the two are complements, not substitutes.

The middle road of industrial relations thus originated as a progressive programme of labour reform in industry and an intellectual rebuttal to and critique of Marxist and neoclassical theories of economic determinism. Its principal thrust was to solve the Labour Problem and promote the trilogy of efficiency, equity and human development by an effort to humanize, professionalize, democratize, stabilize and balance capitalism, accomplished through a synergistic set of new, improved and expanded institutions. Among these new, improved and expanded institutions were trade unions and pragmatic collective bargaining, personnel management, protective labour legislation, social insurance, countercyclical monetary and fiscal policies, labour mediation and arbitration services, and works councils and employee representation plans.

Developed to support and guide this reform effort, in turn, was an underlying base of theory and ethical/ideological principles. The (nascent) theory of early industrial relations at a "meta" (economy-wide) level came from American institutional economics and sought to explicate how institutions and attendant working rules coordinate and structure economic activity, and how policy through social engineering can reformulate these institutions and working rules to promote progressive improvement in efficiency, equity and human development. The "meso" (labour market and organizational) level of industrial relations theory was a blend of ideas from the Webbs, Commons and the Wisconsin school, Taylor and proponents of a "socialized" scientific management, and sociologists and psychologists such as Durkheim, Münsterberg and Weber. Complementing the base of theory in industrial relations was a widely shared set of normative principles. First among these was that labour should not be treated in production and market exchange as a commodity. Corollary principles included that workers' interests should count as well as consumers' interests in designing workplace practices and policies, all workplaces should provide and protect basic human and democratic rights, and workers should have access to collective forms of voice and representation if so desired.

Early industrial relations was thus not a unitary construct but had three different and partially divergent dimensions or "faces": an intellectual or science-building face; an applied or problem-solving face; and an ethical or ideological face. Further complicating matters, while these three faces all rested on a subset of generic ideas and practices found in many other countries, they nonetheless individually and collectively presented to the rest of the world a distinctly American look, for the field was born in the United States and remained a largely American development from the 1920s to the 1950s.

The evolution of industrial relations

During its first decade of existence in the 1920s the field of industrial relations was largely confined to a small academic base in the United States. Today, industrial relations is taught, researched and written on by scholars across the world, numbering several thousand in number. Also marking the progress of the field are the many institutions devoted to industrial relations, such as well-recognized schools and institutes of industrial relations, well over a dozen scholarly journals devoted to industrial relations, numerous specialized master's and doctoral programmes in industrial relations, over 40 national industrial relations associations, and an international association of industrial relations that counts members from more than 80 countries.

In this book, I have endeavoured to chart this globalization process and explain its pattern of development. One may view the birth and gradual expansion of industrial relations as analogous to an ink drop landing on a fibrous piece of paper and then expanding outward in uneven lines, quickly filling in certain areas but only slowly and perhaps spottily spreading to others (D. Kelly, 1999). Sometimes the ink also changes colour as it spreads. This analogy bears striking resemblance to the diffusion of industrial relations.

Although industrial relations appeared first in the United States, this was far from preordained or even the obvious choice at the time. The most likely candidate would have been the United Kingdom. It was home to the Industrial Revolution and the factory system, and by the late nineteenth century had the most mature and fully developed manufacturing base of any nation. It also had a far larger and more firmly institutionalized labour movement and was the first to enact factory act legislation to regulate undesirable labour conditions. When the world-renowned labour scholars Sidney and Beatrice Webb and the new LSE are added to the mix, all the ingredients necessary for the emergence of the industrial relations field seemed in place.

Germany was another top candidate to be the birthplace of industrial relations. Germany was a rapidly rising industrial power and by 1900 had surpassed the United Kingdom. The German labour movement was also greatly expanding and in partnership with the Social Democratic Party was widely regarded as the vanguard of the working class. And while the United Kingdom might have enacted the first factory act, Germany claimed the honour under Bismarck of crafting the world's first nationwide social insurance programmes for workers in the form of accident and old-age insurance plans. Then, on the academic front, Germany also had several advantages. German universities at the turn of the twentieth century were widely considered the world's finest. Germany also had more chairs of economics than any other country and was home to the major heterodox alternative to British classical and neoclassical economics – the German school of historical–social economics. Germany was also home to the world's first and most influential professional association of social scientists dedicated to the study of labour and social policy, the *Verein für Sozialpolitik*. Among *Verein* economists the Labour Question was widely debated and written on, while individual members such as Lujo Brentano wrote on trade unions (challenging the Webbs' theory of trade union development) and Max Weber wrote famous treatises on the theory of business organization and bureaucracy. And, finally, German academics and industrial practitioners shortly after the First World War developed the field of *Arbeitswirtschaft* (science of work) and the employment strategy of *Werksgemeinschaft* (enterprise community), both of which were close to the model of industrial relations.

Looking for a third candidate, one might next pick Japan. Japan was also a rapidly rising industrial power at the turn of the twentieth century and much concerned about growing industrial unrest and the threat to social stability posed by the emergence of trade unions and a working class. The Labour Problem was not only a concept much discussed in the Japanese press but also one that attracted the interest of academics and policy-makers. Numerous Japanese travelled to the West and returned, bringing the economic and social theories of people as diverse as Samuel Gompers, Karl Marx, Pierre Proudhon and Adam Smith. But among the Western nations the Japanese were most attracted to Germany and the German approach to social policy. Thus, after his return from studying in Germany, Noburu Kanai took the lead in founding in 1896 the Japan Social Policy Association and the theory of *Sozialpolitik* became a guiding influence in developing Japanese labour policy. As has happened in many other areas, the Japanese could easily have taken these Western ideas, improved and refined them, and come first to the academic marketplace with the new field of industrial relations.

Industrial relations did not appear first in any of these other countries, however. Instead, industrial relations was an American idea and only slowly rippled outward to other parts of the world. The main lines of development were also quite uneven, with industrial relations reaching the United Kingdom in the 1930s, Japan in the 1960s and Germany in the 1970s. Industrial relations did not reach other parts of the world, such as the former communist countries of Central and Eastern Europe, until the 1990s. Paradoxically, as the field was finally disseminating widely to Africa, Asia, Europe and Latin America, it went into a pronounced decline in the nation of its birth.

The birth of the industrial relations concept began in the United States in 1912 when President Taft appointed a high-level investigative body called the Commission on Industrial Relations. The concept next appeared in Canada in 1919 with the formation of the Royal Commission on Industrial Relations. Canadian William Lyon Mackenzie King played an influential role in the early development of industrial relations in the United States through his consulting work with industrialist John D. Rockefeller, Jr. When King moved back to Canada in 1919 and became prime minister in 1921, he naturally formed an important conduit for the transmission of industrial relations back to his home country. The first university unit devoted explicitly to industrial relations (at Queen's University) did not appear in Canada until 1937, however, and was largely the creation of American Clarence Hicks and Canadian Bryce Stewart – both connected with the Rockefeller consulting firm IRC, Inc. Hicks and Rockefeller, it should be noted, were also responsible for establishing the five other industrial relations units that appeared in American universities in the 1920s and 1930s: California Institute of Technology, Michigan, MIT, Princeton and Stanford.

During the 1920s, industrial relations moved beyond the borders of North America in two steps, but without much discernible effect on its institutional development in the short to medium term.

The most important step was the founding in 1919 of the ILO. The fact that both the ILO and industrial relations field emerged at practically the same time is not coincidence. They were born much like fraternal twins – having some differences in detailed appearance and personality but conceived by the same parents and highly similar in overall make-up.

The "parents" of the ILO and industrial relations were *fear* and *promise*. The fear factor came from the threat of the Labour Problem and Bolshevism, and the palpable feeling that the two might fuse together and usher in industrial civil war and socialist revolution. To head off this calamity, the industrial countries at the Paris peace conference at the close of the First World War made an unprecedented concession to labour and created the ILO, both as a visible symbol of labour's higher status in the new world order and as a tangible method to improve labour conditions and take some of the pent-up steam out of the Labour Problem. This same sense of threat and crisis came to a boil in the United States in 1919 and led to the creation of a new field of study and practice called industrial relations – chartered with the explicit mission of solving labour problems in order to maintain industrial peace and stability. The ILO and industrial relations can thus be viewed as the capitalist countries' defence against the Red Menace.

The other parent of the ILO and industrial relations was promise – the promise of permanently putting the industrial order on a higher plane to the benefit of all parties. Suddenly the traditional verities about the virtues of competition, individualism and laissez-faire looked quaint and outmoded, replaced by a new faith in science, human-built institutions and collective control. The ILO and industrial relations were embodiments of this new philosophy. Both borrowed from the Webbs and sought to constrain the worst excesses of competitive capitalism by encouraging trade unions and government protective labour laws in order to take labour conditions out of competition through market-wide "common rules". Both also looked to the promise of greater industrial efficiency, cooperation and security held out by new methods of scientific management and new programmes of social insurance.

Although very similar in mission and strategy, the ILO and the field of industrial relations nonetheless had only modest contact during the 1920s and 1930s. To a degree, it was as if the fraternal twins were separated at birth, one being raised in the United States and the other in Europe. Industrial relations was an American development, but the United States chose isolationism after the First World War and did not join the ILO until 1934. American industrial relations also emphasized bilateralism over trilateralism, collective bargaining over labour law, and gave greater attention to the role of individual employers in solving labour problems through methods such as personnel management. On the other side, the ILO was headquartered in Europe (Geneva, Switzerland) and mirrored in its programmes and activities the European preference for trilateralism and legal regulation of employment conditions, and emphasis on the collective activities of employers' associations rather than the personnel practices of individual companies. Given these geographic and programmatic differences, the ILO and industrial relations during the interwar period had only modest interaction (largely promoted at the American end by philanthropic funding from Rockefeller), the consequence of which was to slow down the international diffusion of industrial relations and keep the field largely confined to North America until after the Second World War.

Industrial relations also gained a second potential entrée to Europe in the 1920s through a little-known research and reform organization established in the Netherlands in 1925, the Industrial Relations Institute (IRI). As described in Chapter 3, the IRI was formed largely as an association of women personnel directors and welfare workers, co-directed by Mary van Kleeck (director of the Industrial Studies Department of the American Russell Sage Foundation) and Mary Fleddérus (personnel manager of the Dutch Leerdam Glassworks), and was dedicated to a programme of improved industrial relations through social Taylorism. Always a relatively small group, the IRI peaked in influence and visibility in the early 1930s and then ceased operation with the start of the Second World War. Despite holding several conferences in Europe, the IRI appears to have had little long-term influence in propagating the industrial relations field outside the United States.

Moving forward in the global evolution of industrial relations, the next significant extension of the field was to the United Kingdom in the early 1930s. Although the term industrial relations started to surface in the United Kingdom after the mid-1920s, it had practically no presence in British universities until three chairs of industrial relations were established at Cambridge, Cardiff and Leeds in 1933. Parallel to the North American experience, the entry of industrial relations into these universities was made possible by the philanthropy of a wealthy businessman, clothing manufacturer Montague Burton, who like Rockefeller was both socially conscious and concerned with promoting reconciliation between capital and labour. Industrial relations did not make further advance in British universities until after the Second World War.

Before carrying the evolution of the field into the 1940s, it is useful to pause and reflect on the reasons for the disparate pattern of growth in industrial relations in this early period. To return to an earlier metaphor, why did the ink drop fall on the United States, and why were its first lines of advance slow and largely limited to Canada, the United Kingdom, the ILO and IRI?

A number of explanatory variables account for this pattern. From a radical/Marxist point of view, the answer is relatively simple – industrial relations was an invention of the capitalist class meant to maintain its hegemony over labour and increase the extraction of surplus value. Industrial relations came first to the United States, in turn, because American capitalists were cleverer, more pragmatic and had more to lose, and were thus the first to realize that through modest concessions and adroit manipulation they could pacify labour, keep militant unions and the government out of the workplace and actually make greater profit. Viewed from this perspective, it is no wonder that Rockefeller, Jr. – son of the world's wealthiest capitalist – was the person most active in funding and promoting the new field of industrial relations and that middle-class professors anxious to avoid class revolution and steeped in the ethos of republicanism and voluntarism – such as Commons and colleagues – were willing allies in this cause.

This point of view must be given its due and at a broad level is surely part of the story. Anyone who believes in rational action and self-interest can hardly think otherwise. But there are also other explanatory variables. One notes, for example, that the United States was actually the least class-divided and contested society among the major industrial countries of that period. As a result, the Labour Problem in the United States could more nearly be divorced or separated from the larger Social Question that was still haunting continental Europe. While Europeans were deeply divided over capitalism versus socialism, Protestantism versus Catholicism, and democracy versus monarchy, these issues were far less contested in the United States (and the United Kingdom and Canada). As a result, Americans (and then the British and Canadians) were better able to treat capital–labour relations as a self-contained subject and carve it out in the social sciences as a separate area of study. Stated another way, in Europe labour policy was inextricably part of social policy and still had revolutionary potential, while in the United States labour policy could be backed out of social policy and treated as a self-contained social reform or business subject.

Yet other explanatory variables can also be cited. An obvious one is the level of industrialism. Industrial relations will not be an issue in countries that do not have a large urban-based wage-earning labour force. At the time of the First World War this largely limited the scope of industrial relations to North America, Western Europe and Japan.

Early industrial relations was avowedly aimed at preventing Marxist class struggle and promoting an accommodation between capital and labour in a capitalist economic system. Most segments of American (and British and Canadian) society accepted this vision – including the American labour movement (but less so the British unions). Large segments of the European working class and the dominant labour movements of the continent, on the other hand, were still committed to some type of socialist/Marxist programme of socialist transformation. For them industrial relations was not an attractive option. (Marxism did not come to Japan in any significant way until after the First World War, so this variable is a moot issue there.)

Another explanatory variable is the labour philosophy and business outlook of the employers. Industrial relations did not get started in the United States because of the labour movement (it was largely indifferent) but because a small but influential wing of employers backed the idea. These employers, largely from medium to large manufacturing firms, were distinguished by an outlook that was strategic, progressive and professional, and sought to gain competitive advantage through cooperation and goodwill with labour, not by grinding down workers or ruling with an iron fist. Every other industrial country also had a group of enlightened employers, but none had as large a group as the United States and, more importantly, none implemented enlightenment as part of a formal, strategically designed management model. The United States also had an egalitarian and democratic ethos which made it easier for managers to move away from the more rigid and distancing forms of elitism and command and control, whereas in Europe the French *patrons* and the British and German industrialists were separated from their workers by a larger divide of social status and commitment to unquestioned employer authority. Although more consensual and paternalistic in outlook, Japanese employers were no more willing to share power and status with workers than their European counterparts.

Attention must also be turned to differences in the university systems among countries. For a variety of reasons, American universities provided a more favourable environment for a new field such as industrial relations to take root and grow. The American system featured a very large number of competing colleges and universities, a very decentralized governance system, a pragmatic vocational and commercial orientation, and a large number of business schools – all of which facilitated introducing a new cross-disciplinary, business/social science and largely vocational subject. On the other hand, Canada had very few universities of any kind; the United Kingdom was dominated by two famous but very traditional universities (Cambridge and Oxford) that largely catered to training "gentlemen" for positions in Church, government and education; Germany had a number of excellent universities but embedded in a very bureaucratic and centralized governance system with a strong culture of compartmentalization among disciplines; while French universities (and *grandes écoles*) gave little attention to the social sciences and business and emphasized instead government administration and engineering.

Among all the other factors that could be cited, two deserve highlight. The first is the role of government funding and private foundations. Industrial relations started in the United States and grew over the years partly because it received tremendous financial support from a variety of foundations, in nearly all cases endowed by wealthy businessmen such as Rockefeller, Carnegie, Ford and Filene. Later, government funding for labour research was also an important catalyst for American industrial relations – a pattern repeated after the Second World War in nearly every country where industrial relations had a boom period. The final variable deserving mention is the English language. Industrial relations started in an Anglophone country and its outward rays of development for the next 40 years were to other English-speaking countries and outposts.

These variables explain the pattern of development of industrial relations before the Second World War. Let us now examine the evolution of the field in the post-Second World War period. The differences are marked.

To pick up the thread of the story we must return to the United States and the Depression years of the 1930s. Going into the Depression, the American industrial relations field had two identifiable, partially overlapping wings. The first wing, comprised largely of businessmen, consultants, industrial psychologists and like-minded people, was primarily interested in solving labour problems and improving employer–employee relations through new management programmes and initiatives. I have labelled this group the PM (Personnel Management) school. They promoted a unitarist approach to industrial relations and for the most part took a lukewarm attitude toward trade unions and government regulation. The home base of the PM school was the welfare capitalist employers, often equated in the public mind at home and abroad with Henry Ford and the model of Fordism (rationalized management, high wages, mass production, and integrating labour through higher real income, consumerism and middle-class status). While Ford practised elements of welfare capitalism, in actual fact other companies, such as Standard Oil, led the way and its distinguishing feature was the practice of employee representation (a form of non-union collective voice), regarded at the time as the "crown jewel" of the early PM industrial relations model.

The second wing of early industrial relations, comprised largely of academic institutional labour economists, like-minded researchers from law, sociology and history, and practitioners from social reform groups and the union movement, gave greater emphasis to solving labour problems through trade unionism and legal enactment. While they also advocated progressive management and were among the leading university scholars on the subject, members of this group often had sympathy for the cause of organized labour, believed that the nation needed more collective bargaining, and that progressive management was by itself capable of solving labour problems only among the minority of firms that were well managed and had a supportive economic environment. I have called this group the ILE (Institutional Labour Economics) school. They favoured a unitarist approach to industrial relations where possible, but believed that in many firms the large conflict of interests separating management and employees and the individual workers' lack of effective bargaining power and voice necessitated collective bargaining and a measure of government regulation, leading in this case to a pluralist model of arm's-length bargaining and negotiated compromise.

The 1920s in the United States was a period of prosperity, with business in the ascendancy and organized labour on the defensive. The epitome of the PM approach to industrial relations was the welfare capitalism movement, represented by several hundred companies in the progressive branch of the employer community and having its core in a Rockefeller-connected network of non-union firms practising employee representation. The heart of their employment model was what Commons called the goodwill and citizenship models of industrial relations. The results were impressive and many of the ILE proponents gradually shifted ground and concluded that the welfare capitalist programme of progressive management, supplemented by additional labour law, collective bargaining and macroeconomic stabilization, was an innovative and praiseworthy system of industrial relations.

The managerialist orientation of American industrial relations was further heightened in the late 1920s and early 1930s by the beginnings of the human relations movement. The human relations movement grew out of the Hawthorne experiments at the Western Electric Company, was led by Elton Mayo and colleagues of the Harvard Business School, and was at the time widely perceived to be part of the field of industrial relations. Human relations was in several respects a more radical challenge to the ILE school since it gave greater emphasis to psycho-social causes and solutions to labour problems, criticized economic theory of labour and downplayed the role of market, legal and other external factors, seemed to critics to rely on covert manipulation of workers through "touchy-feely" management practices, and appeared to some people to use unitarist methods in a way that was more overtly aimed at union prevention.

The Great Depression and New Deal labour policy of the Roosevelt administration fundamentally transformed American industrial relations. Indeed, if the term "transformation" is interpreted literally as "fundamentally different in character", then the 1933–45 period ranks as the first great transformation of American industrial relations, or the second if the First World War transformation in employment practices and relations is counted as the first. This transformation of the 1930s was a considerably greater shock to the system than the much-discussed transformation of the post-1970 period, which was centred around the decline of mass unionism and the New Deal model and re-emergence of a non-union employment system led by progressive companies practising a high-performance workplace model with antecedents in the 1920s. The Great Depression wrecked the welfare capitalist experiment on the reefs of massive unemployment and bankruptcy and led to severe public disillusionment with the business community and the PM approach. The monetary stabilization policy advocated by Commons also appeared discredited. When the Roosevelt administration entered office in 1933, it reversed course on labour policy and sought to fight the Depression and rejuvenate the mass production (Fordist) system through a neo-corporatist strategy of market cartelization and industrial self-government, using much-expanded trade unionism to stop deflationary wage cuts, redistribute income from capital to labour to spur purchasing power and aggregate demand, and bring democracy and joint governance to industry. The ILE academics for the most part abandoned the PM approach and swung in solid support of the New Deal model and helped craft its major labour initiatives – the National Labor Relations Act, Social Security Act and Fair Labor Standards Act. As widely interpreted, collective bargaining was now not only protected and encouraged by law but also the *preferred* wage-setting and workplace governance institution. To forcefully make this point, the National Labor Relations Act banned the welfare capitalist employee representation plan. At this time, American industrial relations started to split apart, with the dominant ILE wing committed to collective bargaining and labour law and suspicious of non-union employers, while the PM wing increasingly felt threatened and unwelcome. The ongoing development of human relations only exacerbated these tensions.

These fracture lines in American industrial relations were partially obscured by the tremendous boom experienced by the field in the 15 years following the Second World War. The period 1945–60 was the golden age in American industrial relations and up to the end of the 1950s industrial relations remained largely an American phenomenon. In response to the widespread unionization of industry and start-up problems of new collective bargaining arrangements, a mushroom growth in labour–management conflict and industry-stopping strikes and a sudden demand for thousands of trained labour relations specialists, American universities quickly rushed to set up new industrial relations schools, institutes and centres, while the state and federal governments pumped in large sums of money to finance applied research in industrial relations. Several dozen industrial relations programmes were set up offering undergraduate, master's and doctoral degrees or majors in industrial relations, two academic industrial relations journals were established (*Industrial and Labor Relations Review*, 1948, and *Industrial Relations*, 1961), and a new professional association (the IRRA, 1947) was established that soon had more than 1,000 members. Also a significant part of the golden age was the outpouring of groundbreaking, multidisciplinary research on a wide range of work and labour topics, and the active involvement of nationally recognized scholars from both the PM and ILE schools. The peak of the golden age was signalled by the publication of two books: *Industrial relations systems* (1958) by John Dunlop, and Clark Kerr et al.'s *Industrialism and industrial man* (1960). Dunlop's book has subsequently become the most cited theoretical work in the field of industrial relations.

As the golden age was unfolding in the United States, industrial relations for the first time began to sink solid roots in several other countries. For the first two decades after the Second World War, however, the spread of industrial relations was largely limited to select countries in the English-speaking part of the world, principally Canada in North America, the United Kingdom in Europe, and Australia in Asia-Pacific.

In Canada, a small number of industrial relations centres, institutes and schools were established during and immediately after the Second World War. The largest programmes were in Quebec, such as at Laval, Montreal and McGill Universities, but several new but smaller programmes in English-speaking Canada, such as at Toronto and Dalhousie, joined the existing Queen's industrial relations programme. Canada's first (and only) industrial relations journal (*Relations Industrielles/Industrial Relations*, 1945) was also started at Laval and in 1963 an industrial relations association was founded, the CIRA. The industrial relations programmes in English-speaking Canada were largely modelled and operated on American lines, while the programmes at French-speaking universities were influenced by the American model but pursued a largely autonomous course within Quebec.

The most significant developments in industrial relations in the 1945–60 period outside the United States took place in the United Kingdom. The three Burton chairs of industrial relations had not generated much activity and remained an isolated development until the end of the Second World War. Then several British universities added faculty positions in industrial relations in response to the same boom in union density and collective bargaining activity that had taken place in Canada and the United States. At the LSE, for example, Ben Roberts began teaching industrial relations, while Oxford brought on Hugh Clegg and Allan Flanders. Clegg and Flanders, together with German émigré and labour law scholar Otto Kahn-Freund, led the early development of British industrial relations and were principally responsible for giving it academic visibility and presence. Their group at Oxford developed a distinct research orientation and became known as the Oxford school. Another member of the school who later became a major leader in British industrial relations was sociologist Alan Fox.

An academic industrial relations association, the BUIRA, was formed in 1950 (under a modestly different name at first) and the United Kingdom's first academic industrial relations journal (*British Journal of Industrial Relations*, 1963) was founded little more than a decade later by Roberts at the LSE. These developments notwithstanding, the British industrial relations community remained relatively small into the 1960s (BUIRA academic membership was 88 in 1960, compared to over 600 in the American IRRA) and more narrowly structured in terms of subject matter and disciplinary representation. Throughout the 1950s the management-oriented PM wing, the human relations school and the subject of personnel management remained a visible part of American industrial relations, but British industrial relations had no similar management wing or association with personnel management and human relations. Human relations had a small presence in the United Kingdom, such as at the famous Tavistock Institute, but was typically viewed as separate from industrial relations and both personnel and human relations were regarded with some suspicion by British industrial relations scholars. Labour law and social insurance, also important topics in American industrial relations of this period, were largely absent from British industrial relations. Another difference was that labour economics was the centre of American industrial relations but in the United Kingdom sociology, history and political science bulked larger. The core of British industrial relations up to the mid-1960s was a relatively descriptive ("institutional") and historical research agenda centred on trade unions and the collective actors in the industrial relations system, or what amounts to the heart of the post-Second World War ILE approach.

The other country in which industrial relations established a visible foothold was Australia. Industrial relations courses and concentrations began to simultaneously appear at four Australian universities, introduced by Kingsley Laffer at the University of Sydney, Kenneth Walker at the University of Western Australia, Joe Isaac at Melbourne, and Bill Ford and William Hotchkiss at New South Wales. Given the lack of a national industrial relations community, early Australian industrial relations drew heavily from both the British and American models. Industrial relations in Australia emerged principally as a breakaway movement from economics, with the abovementioned faculty members feeling that traditional economic theory was too narrow and abstract to offer much value in understanding labour problems and work relations. Industrial relations thus started as applied labour economics but with significant addition of courses from other disciplines, such as psychology, management and law. The focus was on the institutions of the industrial relations system, particularly the relatively unusual Australian system of state and federal wage tribunals and arbitration councils. In 1959, Laffer founded Australia's first academic industrial relations journal (*The Journal of Industrial Relations*) and a few years later the practitioner–academic Industrial Relations Society of Australia was founded. Despite these advances, not until the 1970s did industrial relations in Australia gain a secure position in academia and relatively well-defined core subject area and research focus.

We now come to a major inflection point in the evolutionary development of industrial relations. As of 1960, industrial relations as a field of study had almost no formal presence outside the English-speaking world. A decade later more than a dozen new industrial relations associations were established and in operation in countries as diverse as Argentina, France, Israel and Japan, while numerous universities in Africa, Asia, Europe and Latin America added industrial relations courses and, sometimes, industrial relations majors or degree programmes. Another decade later the number of national industrial relations associations had doubled again, spreading to Chile, Nigeria, the Philippines, Sweden and many other countries in all corners of the world. Suddenly industrial relations had "gone global". What was the catalyst for this remarkable change?

A significant part of the answer is the founding of the IIRA and the events leading up to it. The IIRA was founded in 1966 as a joint endeavour of four organizations: the BUIRA in the United Kingdom, the American IRRA, the JIL in Japan and the IILS in Switzerland. The two people who took the lead in this effort were Ben Roberts of the LSE and Robert Cox, IILS director, with supporting help from Gerald Somers and Arthur Ross of the United States and Ichiro Nakayama of Japan and Jean-Daniel Reynaud of France.

The genesis of the IIRA can be traced back to the appointment of American David Morse as the new Director-General of the ILO in 1948. For a variety of reasons explained in Chapter 6, Morse sought to expand the strategy and programmes of the ILO by augmenting the enactment of new international labour standards through ILO Recommendations and Conventions with greater emphasis on improving labour conditions through economic development and labour–management relations programmes. It also happened that in the mid-1950s Kerr and colleagues Dunlop, Harbison and Myers were beginning their Ford Foundation sponsored Inter-University Study of Labour Problems in Economic Development. The ILO helped open doors for Kerr et al. at labour ministries, trade unions and employers' associations in the many countries they visited, and the scholars, in turn, gave a number of seminars, briefings and consultations at the ILO and with Morse. Out of this relationship, and due to other larger factors, industrial relations (in its broad 1950s, multidisciplinary, ILE-centred form) gradually became a central intellectual and ideological roadmap for the ILO after the late 1950s.

Morse was looking to make the ILO a more proactive, strategic player in the international community and he concluded that to accomplish this goal the Organization needed to be better connected with the leading scholars and research in the industrial relations field. Thus, in 1960 Morse created the IILS as a semi-autonomous research and training organization within the ILO. The IILS was broadly modelled on an American university industrial relations centre and brought labour and industrial relations scholars from a variety of countries to teach short classes, give seminars and spend sabbaticals doing research. A handicap in this effort, however, was that no international network of industrial relations scholars existed at this time and, indeed, the United Kingdom and the United States were the only two countries where industrial relations had a significant presence. In 1963, Roberts from the LSE was visiting at the ILO and the ILO's Cox (formerly Morse's *chef de cabinet*) had just been appointed the new director of the IILS. Roberts had travelled to Japan and a number of other countries and concluded that the industrial relations field, if it was to become a well-recognized and accepted branch of the social sciences, had to develop an international association to help transplant the field to other countries and establish an international community of scholars. On his part, Cox realized that an international association of industrial relations scholars would be a large asset for the IILS in terms of broadening and deepening the research talent available to the ILO. So the two men worked collaboratively to create a new international association. Their efforts bore fruit when the IIRA was launched in 1966 by the four organizations previously listed.

The founders of the IIRA decided to hold a world congress every third year. The first one was held in Geneva in 1967. Roberts was elected president. Apparently the time was ripe for such an organization because over 200 people from 39 countries attended. Equally important, the officers of the IIRA recruited attendees to return to their countries and start up industrial relations associations, university programmes and courses. In this effort they were quite successful for, by 1973, the IIRA had 19 "full" members (national industrial relations associations), 36 "institutional" members (e.g., university industrial relations centres) and 341 individual members. One may judge, therefore, that the founding of the IIRA precipitated a "global transformation" of industrial relations, for in 1965 the field was largely restricted to a handful of English-speaking countries and a decade later it had become established in several dozen other countries spanning Africa, Asia, Europe and Latin America.

Ironically, just as industrial relations appeared to be mounting the world stage clothed in success and promise for the future, some dark clouds were forming on the horizon and starting to move closer. And, adding to the irony, the first country they cast their shadow over was the birthplace and strongest redoubt of industrial relations, the United States.

Although not apparent at first, the field of industrial relations in the United States reached a peak in intellectual vitality and organizational strength at about the time Kerr et al. published *Industrialism and industrial man* (1960). Although for the next two decades the outward signs of growth, such as student enrolments, number of industrial relations academic programmes and IRRA membership, continued to trend upward, underneath this façade the foundations of the field were gradually weakening and eroding. When conservative Republican Ronald Reagan was elected president in 1980, suddenly the storm clouds closed in and industrial relations started to take a fierce buffeting. By the end of the 1980s the American union movement had lost two million members, a good deal of political power, and considerable support among academics and the public at large. The field of industrial relations, having earlier had the PM school and field of personnel/HRM break away, and now firmly tied to the fortunes of the labour movement, followed it down the steep road of decline. Although the election of a more labour-friendly Clinton administration in 1992 gave reasons for hope that the worst was over, such was not to be. Both the labour movement and academic industrial relations continued to haemorrhage members, calling into question their long-term survival prospects. Union membership in the private sector, a robust 35 per cent in the golden age of industrial relations, was an anaemic and still slumping 9 per cent as the nation entered the twenty-first century.

An influential line of thought in the United States portrays the gradual withering of the union sector and rise of the non-union employment relations model as a transformation of American industrial relations, while other observers have labelled the non-union HRM employment system as the "new industrial relations". Certainly compared to the situation as it existed in the 1950s these descriptions are accurate, although open to question is the relevant base period for comparison and the interpretation of these trends. From one point of view, the New Deal model of the 1930s–50s defines the baseline or "original" system of American industrial relations as envisioned by the founders of the field, and the decline of the union sector and rise of the non-union HRM model is thus interpretable as a distinct transformation to a new and historically dissimilar industrial relations system. An alternative interpretation is that the largely non-union welfare capitalist centred system of the 1920s defines the baseline or "original" model of American industrial relations; the mass unionism of the 1930s–50s was the result of a huge exogenous shock from the Depression and New Deal; and the subsequent decline of the union sector and rise of the non-union HRM model is thus less a unique transformation than a regression to the mean (i.e., gradual return to the 1920s base-line). In this view, the rise of the new non-union, high-performance workplace model of the 1980s–90s is less a distinctly new development than a rebirth and retooling of the original unitarist/goodwill employment relations model developed in the 1920s by the founders. The history sketched in this book suggests the second view has significant and under-appreciated validity but that in the spirit of the "composite model" developed in Chapter 2 the original American industrial relations problem-solving approach is best thought of as some combination of the approaches of the 1920s and 1930s.

Issues of interpretation aside, the significant decline of the New Deal model in industry in the post-1980 period had large and mostly negative ramifications for industrial relations in American academia. The industrial relations field witnessed the closing and downsizing of numerous university industrial relations centres and programmes, a 50 per cent shrinkage in IIRA academic membership, a flight from industrial relations to other fields by many of the field's most productive scholars, and an enveloping sense of crisis and marginalization among the people who stayed. Perhaps no action could more symbolically represent industrial relations' downward spiral in the United States than the announcement in 2003 that the University of Wisconsin was closing its industrial relations programme – the industrial relations programme that was the first in the nation and the home of Commons, the Wisconsin school of labour institutionalism and several generations of the most prominent industrial relations scholars in the nation and world.

How could American industrial relations fall so far? Chapter 7 identifies six reasons, detailed briefly below. Although in certain cases they relate mainly to the American situation, most have considerable relevance to the evolution of industrial relations in other countries.

The narrowing of industrial relations to labour–management relations

After 1960 the boundaries of the industrial relations field and its self-concept narrowed from "all aspects of employment" (employment relations) to unions and collective bargaining (labour–management relations), along with a substantial dose of applied labour economics. The narrowing of industrial relations arose, in part, from the decision of PM scholars and personnel practitioners to leave the industrial relations field and create two new and increasingly autonomous and rivalrous fields of study called, respectively, personnel/HRM and OB. The home of the PM school was now in business schools, management departments and management professional associations.

Industrial relations thus became largely identified with the ILE school and the social sciences (principally economics), although over time even the ILE component shrank as interest in management, social insurance and, to a lesser degree, labour law, declined. As a result, by the 1980s industrial relations in the public and academic mind meant unions and labour–management relations and, as described in Chapter 7, despite protestations to the contrary this was largely how industrial relations academics practised it. Having put most of its eggs in the labour–management basket, industrial relations then watched its fortunes sink as union density fell below 10 per cent in the private sector and interest in organized labour among academics and the public at large drained away.

The rise of HRM and OB

When the PM school started to drift away from industrial relations in the early 1960s it elicited little comment or concern. At the time, personnel management was held in low regard in both academia and industry, and most students majored in labour relations where the jobs were. OB had just been invented and was only starting to coalesce. Over the next several decades the situation changed dramatically. The intellectual and professional status of personnel management gradually improved, due in part to being renamed to HRM, greater infusion of theory and insights from the behavioural sciences, development of the strategic dimension of HRM, the development of a new high-performance work system that made substantial use of unitarist HRM practices, and a boom in business school enrolments and shift in jobs from labour relations to personnel/HRM. By 1980, personnel/HRM surpassed industrial relations and continued to move ahead to century's end, albeit still burdened by many of its long-standing conceptual and practical limitations (such as lack of theory and cost-driven and non-strategic operationalization at many companies).

The rise of neoclassical economics and neo-liberalism

At the same time as American industrial relations was losing the PM wing it was also losing its position among labour economists. The core of industrial relations in the 1950s were the "social science" labour economists, such as Dunlop, Kerr, Lester, Myers, Reynolds and Ross. In the 1950s these scholars and their neo-institutional perspective also dominated labour economics, creating significant intellectual synergies and organizational strength for industrial relations. The neo-institutional approach went into decline after 1960, however, and was gradually replaced by a rejuvenated neoclassical

607

school of labour economics with its intellectual centre at the University of Chicago. The rise of neoclassical economics, and its parallel political philosophy of neo-liberalism, proved to be quite detrimental to the fortunes of industrial relations in both the academic and policy worlds. Neoclassical economics rejects the historical, multidisciplinary, social-science and "go and see" approach of institutional labour economics (industrial relations) and instead practises disciplinary imperialism, formalist model building and a "stand-back" empirical strategy emphasizing econometric analysis of secondary data. It also uses a body of theory that tends to emphasize the virtues of free labour markets and downgrades the severity of labour problems and market failures. As neoclassical labour economics came to dominate the field, the base of labour economists active in industrial relations progressively shrunk, as did intellectual support for the field's favourite policy initiatives – regulation of labour markets through trade unions and labour law. By the end of the century, neoclassical economics and neo-liberalism ruled the field of labour, and labour policy and industrial relations was effectively shunted to one side. The Wisconsin brand of institutional economics also declined to the point of near disappearance in labour.

Neglect of the heterodox–left alternative

One would think that, as industrial relations was losing the PM wing and its central base of support in labour economics, the field would start to search for some new ideas and intellectual or policy soulmates. Three obvious places would have been other disciplines such as sociology, other heterodox areas of economics such as social, behavioural and new institutional economics, and various leftist/radical groups such as the Union for Radical Political Economy and the labour process group. None of these options was pursued, however, and instead the dwindling band of industrial relationists chose to stick with the status quo model and ride the downward escalator. One can argue that perhaps reaching out to these other groups would not have made much difference in the long run, but on the other hand the field had a chance to find new allies and practise what it preaches about a broader multidisciplinary, multi-method form of labour scholarship.

The rise of science building in universities

Next in this list of baleful events is the rise of science building in the American academic community. Lacking much of any formal theory, industrial relations' reason for being in academia has always been its usefulness for applied problem solving in the work world. The problem-solving orientation of the field meant that industrial relations professors had considerable real-world experience, often did consulting and arbitration, and pursued a line of research that was often relatively "prac-ademic". When they published in scholarly journals, which many did, the research was characterized by disciplinary breadth over depth; narrative description over model building, and case studies over econometric data analysis. This portfolio of skills and publications, while a winner in the 1950s and 1960s, increasingly became a loser thereafter. The culture and reward system in American universities increasingly turned away from problem solving, at least of the applied kind done in industrial relations, and instead gave greater emphasis to the research mission of professors and publication of research articles in highly rated journals. As the 1980s turned into the 1990s, pressures of publish or perish intensified, the competition to get in the best-rated journals ratcheted up, research increasingly became inward looking and "academic", and the entire research mode shifted sharply toward model building, hypothesis testing, and ever more sophisticated statistical techniques. This shift to science building inevitably led to a flight from industrial relations, not only because fewer people were interested in reading about the standard industrial relations subjects but also because industrial relations professors were put at a growing competitive disadvantage in the publication and fame game. They lacked a strong disciplinary base to support theorizing, there was a heavy discount applied to case study and "institutional" research, and universities tended to exclude industrial relations journals from the list of top-tier publication outlets used for rewarding faculty and determining department quality rankings. Adding further insult to injury, science building also caused the industrial relations scholarly journals to slowly lose distinctiveness and "field identity" – to the point where today they increasingly resemble a modestly eclectic second-tier journal in applied labour economics.

Ideological commitment to pluralism and unionism

The final factor contributing to American industrial relations' downward slide is its ideological and normative commitment to the pluralist employment model and trade unionism. When the industrial relations field started in the 1920s, it had a normative commitment to certain bedrock principles, among which are that labour is not a commodity and human rights have precedence over property rights, and that workers should enjoy basic democratic processes in workforce governance and freedom of association. Equally important are normative commitments that were *not* part of early industrial relations. For example, the early industrial relationists had a strong normative belief that workers should have the opportunity for some form of collective voice in the workplace, but they also believed that workers should have the ability to choose freely the kind of collective voice mechanism they want, whether it be an independent union, employee representation plan or no voice mechanism at all. Likewise, the early industrial relationists believed that where employees are at a power disadvantage and are taken advantage of they should have the benefit of collective bargaining, but this group also believed that unions are not necessary or even desirable where employers are able to create successfully a satisfied workforce through use of unitarist HRM methods. As a result of the New Deal and associated events, the ideology of industrial relations changed. The new ideology gave unions and collective bargaining preferred status, took conflict of interest and the need for pluralistic independent employee organizations as a normative principle rather than a fact to be determined, and regarded non-union employers and unitarist employment systems with varying degrees of aversion, suspicion and opprobrium. In effect, the industrial relations model of the 1920s was judged "guilty" and expunged from the field. This value set has persisted to the present time, with deleterious consequences. Among the reasons for this are that people who are interested in the subject of industrial relations, but hold non-ILE principles, are nonetheless effectively excluded from the field on ideological grounds. Moreover, the field stays locked into institutions and practices that, while often meritorious, are nonetheless in sharp decline. Lastly, the field is placed in the paradoxical position of ignoring or criticizing even the most progressive non-union employers, such as the numerous non-union firms listed in the "100 Best Places to Work", simply because they do not have a union or other independent collective voice mechanism.

Interestingly, as industrial relations started to stagnate in the United States in the 1960s and 1970s, the field grew and expanded in the rest of the world. Indeed, in marked contrast to the United States, industrial relations in countries such as Japan and the United Kingdom experienced a boom during this period and their own golden age. In other countries, such as Argentina, France, Germany, Israel and New Zealand, industrial relations took root, and steadily added new members and developed a formal institutional infrastructure.

So, one may ask whether the "American disease" was unique to that country. Unfortunately, it was not. The American pattern resembles an inverted V: a starting point in 1920, a peak about 1960 (or perhaps a plateau from about 1960 to 1970), and then an accelerating decline to the present time. Probably not coincidentally, this inverted V also broadly matches the historical pattern in American union density. When we look at other countries, many – but not all – exhibit this same inverted V pattern; the difference turns out to be one of timing.

The United Kingdom offers a particularly revealing case study. The history of British industrial relations also exhibits the same inverted V pattern, only it is more compressed and shifted forward in time. The beginning point of the upward slope in the United Kingdom is 1933 with the founding of the Burton chairs, although one could argue that for all intents and purposes the field did not really take root until 1945. From 1945 to 1979 industrial relations steadily expanded in the United Kingdom and from 1965 (the Donovan Commission) to 1979 enjoyed a golden age. The year 1979 represents the peak and abrupt turning point of the fortunes of industrial relations, coinciding with the "winter of discontent" and the election of Margaret Thatcher as prime minister. The election of Thatcher in the United Kingdom, as with Reagan in the United States, ushered in a dramatic negative turn in the economic environment and the policy and ideological stance of the government toward labour. As a result, both the union movement and industrial relations entered a period of significant decline (the "cold climate" described in Chapter 8), travelling down the inverted V. Unlike the situation in the United States, where industrial relations' descent continued into the new century, British industrial relations appears to have stabilized in the late 1990s and perhaps had a modest recovery, coinciding with the electoral victory of Tony Blair and the coming to power of the new Labour Party in 1997.

If the patterns between the United States and the United Kingdom are roughly similar, to what degree do the six explanatory variables identified above help explain the British experience? In most cases, relatively well.

Labour–management relations

The United Kingdom did not have a PM wing of the field in the early years as did the United States and, with only few exceptions, industrial relations was defined and operationalized around collective bargaining, the outcomes and problems thereof, and the institutions of the industrial relations system. For all practical purposes, therefore, British industrial relations started out after the Second World War with a relatively narrow conception of the subject oriented around the collective aspects of the employment relationship. And, as earlier noted, even the subjects of labour law and (especially) social insurance and social policy were largely on the periphery. This labour–management conception of the field was not a problem for the next three decades and, indeed, was perhaps a positive force *as long as* collective bargaining remained strong, publicly sanctioned and a source of important issues and problems commanding attention. These conditions were well met from 1945 to 1979. Not only did union density climb over this period, but effective union coverage was

70 per cent or more. Paradoxically, even as the collective bargaining system began to generate an increasing number of problems and dysfunctionalities (wage-push inflation amidst full employment and "anarcho-pluralism" on the shop floor), the immediate effect was to further stimulate growth and opportunities in industrial relations as the government formed investigative commissions and wage–price boards, and mounting strikes and shop-steward actions created new research opportunities and demand for academics to serve on arbitration and fact-finding panels. However, when Thatcher came to power, public and political opinion turned against the unions and globalization and neo-liberal economic policy shrunk private sector unionism in half, the industrial relations field began on its downward slope. In the United States, this decline continues but British industrial relations has apparently been able to halt this before hitting the bottom. The reasons appear to be twofold. The first is that the Blair government has enacted new legislation that has helped stabilize union membership, thus preventing the de-unionization seen in the United States. Also different from the United States, the United Kingdom has moved closer to Europe in social policy (the "third way") and British industrial relations has in the last ten years broadened its domain to give greater room to social policy – a good fit because the social policy debate involves both labour market institutions and the "externalist" perspective that are the forte of industrial relations. Employment and social policy in the United States, on the other hand, remains gridlocked and rightward drifting.

HRM and OB

The HRM/OB variable also has significant explanatory power in the British case. Part of the flattening out of American industrial relations that took place after 1960 was the result of the PM wing leaving the field. The United Kingdom had no comparable management group and thus this factor was not present to exert a negative drag on the British industrial relations field in the 1960s and 1970s. When HRM/OB arrived in full force in the United Kingdom in the mid-1980s (largely as an import from the United States), the initial effect was seriously to undermine the security and viability of industrial relations, witnessed by the surge in HRM research and establishment of new HRM journals, and the mushroom growth of MBA enrolments and displacement of industrial relations with HRM/OB courses. Again, several factors have moderated the negative effect of HRM/OB on British industrial relations. As noted in Chapter 8, for example, HRM/OB's relative lack of institutionalization in the United Kingdom gave industrial relations programmes and scholars greater opportunity to colonize the new invader; while American industrial relations increasingly neglected management during the 1960s and 1970s, British industrial relations did the opposite and thus was better positioned when the assault came; and the United Kingdom is more receptive to a critical perspective on management, which also plays to industrial relations' strength.

Neoclassical economics and neo-liberalism

Our third variable is the rise of neoclassical economics and neo-liberal social policy. As with HRM/OB, these factors were far less damaging to British industrial relations in the 1945–79 growth period and golden age. Neoclassical economics has not had the same hegemonic status in the post-war United Kingdom as in the United States, partly due to the stronger and longer-lasting legacy of Keynes and Robinson and their theories of imperfect capitalism. Ironically, the fact that institutional economics had little influence in the United Kingdom also helped, to the extent that its near demise had little overt negative effect on the vitality of industrial relations. This latter development reflects, in turn, that British industrial relations has been centred more in history and sociology, while American industrial relations in the post-1960 era has been largely dominated by economics. With the election of Thatcher, the neoclassical/neo-liberal influence swept over the United Kingdom and buffeted all collectivist-oriented social theories and programmes, certainly including industrial relations. Industrial relations lost access to the corridors of political power and policy-making, research and programme funding shrank, and the intellectual case for trade unionism and collective bargaining looked increasingly threadbare and anachronistic in the new era of enterprise and acquisitive individualism. The neoclassical/neo-liberal counter-revolution was, however, moderated by the United Kingdom's less thoroughgoing cultural embrace of individualism, the socially moderate "third way" political programme of the Blair government, and the fact that sociology and history continue to have a stronger presence in British industrial relations.

Neglect of the heterodox–left alternative

Although American industrial relations neglected the heterodox–left alternative, no such charge can possibly be levelled against British industrial relations. Part of the vibrancy and intellectual energy present in British industrial relations during its golden age came from the influential writings of a significant-sized group of radical/Marxist scholars, such as Paul Edwards, Richard Hyman and (in his later phase) Alan Fox. The writings of the radicals also helped keep British industrial relations more broadly focused than

American industrial relations, bringing industrial relations down to the shop-floor level (studies of shop stewards and the labour process) and up to the nation-state level (regimes of social regulation and political economy). Although the scholarship and critiques of the radicals and Marxists helped provide lift to British industrial relations in the golden age period, it did nothing to stop the downward slide set off by Thatcherism and, indeed, may have accelerated it to the extent that industrial relations became associated as a home of now unfashionable leftist collectivism. The role of this explanatory variable in the recent stabilizing of British industrial relations is uncertain. British industrial relations still has a good-sized radical/Marxist contingent, albeit one that has increasingly de-emphasized the formal concepts and rhetoric of classical Marxism. On the plus side, they bring a theoretical perspective and empirical approach that help keep the field more broadly focused and grounded in real-life issues (as opposed to debates over the specification of regression equations) and also serve as a natural bridge to the social democratic dialogue and policy debates of continental Europe and the EU. On the downside, the radical/Marxist segment of British industrial relations continues to position the field to the left of the mainstream of public and political sentiment, probably hastens the separation of HRM from industrial relations, and is not a natural fit in business school programmes, where British industrial relations is increasingly centred.

Science building

British universities have also seen a shift toward science building. The difference relative to the United States is one of timing and degree. Science building in the United Kingdom arrived later (the 1990s) and so far has been more moderate in effect. As a result, the British industrial relations research model – long noted for its emphasis on case studies, historical and sociological modes of analysis, and empirical investigation of institutions, has been better able to survive, adapt and even move forward in the new environment. Furthermore, industrial relations has developed a reputation in the United Kingdom of being a centre of excellence for social science research, and industrial relations journals are highly ranked and considered more prestigious than competing management journals. For these reasons, university administrators see a good reason to support industrial relations as they seek to build institutional recognition and government funding (government funding is partly tied to research rankings determined through the Research Assessment Exercise). On net, therefore, science building has not undermined industrial relations in the United Kingdom to the same extent as in the United States – at least not yet.

On the other hand, a discernible trend toward more American-style research is clearly evident in the mainline British industrial relations journals, aided and abetted in part by the availability of new secondary data sets such as the WERS. Whether British industrial relations can maintain a distinctive intellectual and methodological identity amidst the trend toward formalization and statistical hypothesis testing remains an open issue.

Ideology and values

The sixth explanatory variable is an ideological commitment or "leaning" toward trade unions and industrial pluralism/collectivism. This value commitment has characterized both British and American industrial relations but more strongly so in the former. The collectivist normative stance of American industrial relations caused it to become increasingly isolated from the main current of public and scholarly opinion. Certainly British industrial relations suffered the same liability during the cold climate period of Conservative government rule (1980–97). While modal American opinion continues to drift toward individualism and political conservatism, thus further isolating and marginalizing industrial relations, British public opinion seems to have made some move away from the Thatcher ideology and back toward a centrist position. While the old days of collectivism and shop-steward control may be gone forever, the more centrist political culture in the United Kingdom nonetheless contributes to and helps explain the modest rebound in recent years experienced by British industrial relations.

I judge, therefore, that these six variables have considerable explanatory power in accounting for comparative trends in the status of industrial relations in both the United Kingdom and the United States. I cannot repeat this exercise for the many other countries examined in this volume, but will extend the analysis in three respects.

The first is to note that the inverted V pattern is found in many other countries, although in few is it as sharp and dramatic as the United Kingdom and the United States. Industrial relations in Canada, for example, had a gradual but sustained period of growth into the late 1980s and then a modest declining trend in the 1990s and early 2000s. Australia, France, India, Mexico and New Zealand exhibited much the same pattern, although particularly in New Zealand the contraction was considerably sharper in the 1990s. We also see this pattern in eastern Asia. Industrial relations started in Japan in the early 1960s and enjoyed a golden age into the 1970s, thereafter going into decline. The same is true of the Republic of Korea, although industrial relations did not really get established until after the end of military rule in the late 1980s. The field then had a quick build-up, coinciding with the spurt of unionism and labour unrest, followed by a downturn beginning in the mid-1990s. Clearly, each national case has unique, country-specific factors that exert an important influence on the rise, fall and pace of change in industrial relations. But the ubiquity of the inverted V pattern across countries and continents suggests a set of common factors are at work – perhaps themselves part of a larger evolutionary transformation in industrial societies to a post-modern age.

The second extension of this analysis is to note that the inverted V pattern does not characterize a large group of countries. Three sub-groups are identifiable.

The first sub-group includes countries that have not yet developed a significant-sized industrial sector and modern urban-based wage labour force. Representative are many of the countries in the Middle East and Africa, some in Central and Southeast Asia, and a number in South and Central America and the Caribbean. Most of these countries have pockets of modern industry but with the great bulk of employment in traditional areas, such as agriculture, handicrafts and trade, and in the informal economy. When and if they begin the upward climb of industrialization, labour problems and industrial relations will undoubtedly follow.

The second sub-group comprises the former communist countries of Central and Eastern Europe and Asia. Under the communist governments, industrial relations was off limits in universities, banned on the argument that industrial relations was only relevant to capitalist countries where capital exploits labour. With the fall of these regimes (with the exception of Cuba and the Democratic People's Republic of Korea), a vast new territory has opened up for industrial relations, symbolized by the economy of China with one-sixth of the world's population. In nearly all cases, however, industrial relations has at best gained only a very modest toehold in these countries and in many cases remains largely an unknown entity, owing to a variety of factors across countries – continued political repression of independent trade unions and labour activists in some, a low stage of industrial development in others, and the ill effects of economic disarray and high unemployment in others. These countries, like those in the first sub-group, have yet to put together the modern, stable political and economic systems and significant-sized labour movements that have so far been the prerequisites for the emergence and growth of industrial relations.

The third sub-group that has not exhibited the inverted V pattern are the countries in the Germanic (Rhineland) and Scandinavian regions of western Europe. Industrial relations did not gain a strong foothold in these countries until the early 1970s and for the next two decades grew relatively slowly. Even into the 1980s, industrial relations was often a concept and field of study known only to those European scholars who travelled to international industrial relations conferences or participated in an international network of researchers interested in labour and employment issues. Coincident with the formation of the EU in 1992, however, activity and interest in industrial relations began to quicken and the field developed a broader presence in Europe. As documented in Chapter 9, this upward trend is revealed in a number of indicators. Examples include the founding of new industrial relations journals devoted to Europe (e.g., *Industrielle Beziehungen – The German Journal of Industrial Relations*, 1994), a steadily rising number of books on industrial relations published by European scholars, a similar growth in European-based conferences on industrial relations, and rising membership from European countries in the IIRA. Also symbolic is the creation of the EIRO. The Observatory is funded by the EU, headquartered in Ireland, and pursues an extensive range of publishing and research activities on industrial relations in all the member EU countries.

The interesting question for comparative analysis is why industrial relations appears to be holding its own and even growing in a number of the countries of the EU while in many other parts of the world it is in decline. Brief examination of the six explanatory variables highlighted above reveals part of the answer – all six remain more favourably positioned in Europe than in most other parts of the world.

I noted in Chapter 9, for example, that the concept of industrial relations used in Europe has remained more broadly conceived than is common in the United States and other countries. Although trade unions and collective bargaining also represent the core subject of industrial relations in Europe, the dominant trend among European writers is nonetheless to frame the subject as a study of alternative regimes of social regulation of employment. Doing so broadens the scope of industrial relations by permitting consideration of alternative regulatory regimes (e.g., "varieties of capitalism") and creating more intellectual space to consider different levels of regulation within a particular regime, such as tripartite concertation at the state level, bargaining at the industry and sector level, enterprise regulation through works councils, and shop-floor regulation of the labour process. Also positive is that neither HRM/OB nor neoclassical economics – two of the principal intellectual threats to industrial relations – are as strongly established in Europe. Both have less applicability and appeal in Europe because management and market forces are more constrained by social regulation operating through law, trade unions and works councils. Industrial relations in Europe is also strengthened and protected by a larger and more influential intellectual community on the centre-left, an academic environment less consumed with narrow empiricism and more open to broad issues of political economy, and a continuing cultural and

617

ideological commitment in these nations to the social concept, such as social democracy, social partnership, social market economy and social justice.

Above and beyond all these particularistic considerations, one gets closer to the root of the explanation by simply noting three facts about Europe (western and northern in particular): union density remains the highest in the world, the ethos of collectivism and social solidarity is still "in", and the supranational organs of the European Union are moving in the direction of greater social regulation of employment rather than less as in North America. Examined in this light, it is not surprising that industrial relations is badly deteriorated in the United States but alive and well in the EU.

This last observation leads to our final stop on the evolutionary tour of industrial relations – the ILO and IIRA. These two organizations have been key actors in the growth and evolution of industrial relations and have done much to give the field a global presence. To discern the present status and future direction of the industrial relations field, therefore, one must give attention to recent events and trends at both organizations.

As earlier described, industrial relations and the ILO were born together at the end of the First World War and have grown together through the twentieth century, carrying forward a common commitment to improving the conditions of labour and promoting greater human rights and social justice in the world of work. However, in pursuing this common programme they have differed along three important dimensions: the principal instrument of the ILO has been legal enactment, while industrial relations has emphasized collective bargaining; the ILO's centre of gravity has tended to be in continental Europe, while industrial relations has been more North American centred; and the ILO emphasizes applied policy and practice over scholarly research, while industrial relations has the opposite commitment. Although these differences have always been present, they have waxed and waned over the years with the social and political currents, narrowing most notably under Director-General David Morse in the 1950s and 1960s when industrial relations became a de facto guiding intellectual framework for the ILO.

After Morse resigned, the distance between the two gradually started to widen as a product of the ILO's drift back toward a more European juridical strategy of legal enactment, the decline in vitality and reach of organized labour and the North American industrial relations model, and the political estrangement between the ILO and the United States and the latter's decision to temporarily leave the Organization. In 1999, the ILO made at least a symbolic break with industrial relations when the department and programmes carrying the name industrial relations were re-titled with the European term "social dialogue". Operationally, many of the programmes and activities carried out by the ILO under the name industrial relations continued when the new name social dialogue was adopted. Furthermore, the ILO remains as committed as ever to the core principles of industrial relations, such as freedom of association and right to collective bargain. So, one may argue that the name change was largely cosmetic. But, as described in Chapter 11, the concept of social dialogue and concept of industrial relations are not equivalent and, in fact, connote significantly different modes of labour regulation, labour relations and labour policy. Trilateralism, concertation and social partnership are core components of social dialogue, while bilateralism, voluntarism and adversarial collective bargaining are core components of Anglo-American industrial relations.

One must conclude, therefore, that in terms of core principles and objectives the ILO and field of industrial relations remain largely identical (like the "fraternal twins" metaphor) but at the level of applied practice and policy they have drifted apart and industrial relations has become a less visible presence at the ILO. Can one thus conclude that the inverted V pattern has also appeared at the ILO? Yes, perhaps, although the relationship may well get closer again in the future. What can be stated with certainty is a twofold proposition. The first part of the proposition is the observation that the ILO and industrial relations community have over the last 80 years been the two groups most single-mindedly united and committed to an agenda of improved labour conditions, social justice and human rights in the workplace. The second part of the proposition is that both groups need each other, and can synergistically benefit each other more than at any time in the past, given their common objectives and the challenging intellectual, economic and political environment confronting all advocates of improved labour conditions.

If the ILO and industrial relations are fraternal twins, surely the most visible sign of this close connection is the IIRA, founded with the support and cooperation of the ILO and currently headquartered with the ILO in Geneva. The purpose of the IIRA, as stated in its constitution, is to "promote the study of industrial relations throughout the world in the several academic disciplines". This objective was seen by the founders as valuable in its own right – pushing outward the frontiers of science and practical knowledge in industrial relations – but also one that serves the interests of the ILO by helping develop an external "think tank" of labour scholars it can draw upon for expertise and research.

As the IIRA nears its fortieth anniversary, one must judge that it has succeeded as well as its founders could ever have hoped in achieving the original goal. Looking back to the early 1960s, industrial relations was well established in the United Kingdom and the United States and had a modest toehold in Australian and Canadian universities. So low was the number of national industrial relations associations that Cox and Roberts were able to form an organizing committee of only three, representing Japan, the United Kingdom and the United States. Only a few years after the founding of the IIRA, the number of national associations had jumped to 20, while nearly three dozen new industrial relations teaching programmes and research centres had been established at universities around the world. Nor was this a one-time spike. Since the 1970s, the industrial relations field has continued to expand to all parts of the globe. Today, for example, 40 national industrial relations associations belong to the IIRA and members come from 80 countries. The IIRA has also promoted the study of industrial relations by providing a growing network of opportunities for researchers to meet and collaborate, such as the IIRA world congresses, regional congresses and study groups. The world congresses have grown from meetings of 200–300 people to 800–1,000, while the Regional Congresses regularly attract 200–400 people in Africa, the Americas, Asia and Europe. Also very successful and popular are the IIRA study groups, which have grown from the original six groups in 1983 to 17 today. Out of these various venues has come a long list of books and other publications (see Chapter 11), a number of which are widely cited in the literature of industrial relations.

Without the IIRA, industrial relations might well have shrunk over the long term rather than expanded, given that the centre of the field was the United States and the sharp deterioration that has withered American industrial relations over the last 25 years. Fortunately, as the American part of the field stalled in the 1960s and 1970s and then declined in the 1980s and 1990s, industrial relations expanded in the other parts of the world, due in some significant degree to the activities and programmes of the IIRA. Not only did the globalization of industrial relations keep the field growing in size and numbers, it also had the beneficial effect of broadening and diversifying the field's intellectual and problem-solving base so that it was less identified with and parochially tied to its original American roots.

As we move into the first decade of the twenty-first century, however, a nagging question emerges with growing force. Is it possible that the global expansion of industrial relations came to an end in the 1990s and now the global forces of contraction are gathering strength? Or, framed another way, has the global field of industrial relations now embarked on the first downward leg of the inverted V pattern, and was the decline of the American industrial relations field merely a harbinger for what was to follow in other countries? Alternatively, one may frame the issue this way: was industrial relations and the trade union movement it studied and promoted only a particular stage of capitalist development, now increasingly obsolete and receding into history? These are the big questions in the global evolution of industrial relations that await a final answer. In the next and concluding section, I end with some thoughts on these questions.

The future of industrial relations

Industrial relations started out as a small niche area in American universities eight decades ago and has since spread to all parts of the world. This is an impressive accomplishment. Looking forward, one wonders what the next one, two or eight decades holds for the field. Reasons for both optimism and pessimism exist, although probably the scales tilt in the direction of the latter. The verdict one renders on this issue, however, is undoubtedly influenced by country of origin. A person looking at industrial relations from Germany or the United Kingdom is likely to see more hope for the future, while a person looking at the same issue from the United States has a difficult time avoiding doom and gloom. Whether looking forward or backward, comparative industrial relations is, as Hyman (2004) reminds us, inherently subject to the selective interpretation of social reality due to ethnocentricity.

Given this caveat, I think most people would readily agree that the last two decades of the twentieth century represented a particularly difficult and challenging time for industrial relations. Indeed, in light of recent trends many knowledgeable observers of industrial relations question the field's long-term survival prospects. Illustrative are comments of two former IIRA presidents, John Niland (Australia) and Thomas Kochan (United States). Niland (1994: 463) stated in his presidential address, "It is not being overly dramatic to wonder whether the discipline will survive much beyond the year 2000", while Kochan (1998: 31) has more recently said, "the field of industrial relations is in a state of profound crisis". Not everyone accepts these dire portraits, but the fact that prominent scholars state them is indicative of the general trend in the status and health of the field.

As I noted in the Introduction, for a field that continues to claim formal jurisdiction over "all aspects of employment" the fall into crisis is certainly ironic and paradoxical. After all, who today would say that the subject of employment and contemporary developments in the world of work is *less* important today than two or three decades ago? Few, I wager, and most would probably say the opposite – that the world of work is more important than ever for peoples and nations across the globe. So, apparently somewhere in the past industrial relations and the main current of events and ideas in the world of work and employment started to travel different paths, one leading up and the other down. One could say that this entire book has been devoted to retracing and rediscovering these fateful steps.

A field of study in the academic world earns its keep in one of three ways: it provides theory or research tools that are productive in pushing ahead science building; it helps solve important social problems through professional training and applied research; and/or it addresses a subject deemed important for political or ethical reasons. The current problem for industrial relations is that all three criteria have significantly weakened, albeit some more than others and with considerable diversity across countries.

By common agreement, industrial relations does not have a well-developed integrative theoretical base. Several have been advanced, such as Dunlop's industrial relations systems model, but none have moved beyond the stage of classification and description. Of the theories and models used in industrial relations, nearly all come from outside the field, such as economics, sociology and organizational behaviour. Indeed, a number of people in industrial relations have denied that an integrative theory is feasible or even desirable, given the vast range of subjects and institutions that fall with the domain of "all aspects of employment" and the difficulty of theory construction across countries and disciplinary lines. Lacking an integrative theory, industrial relations has instead sought to develop theoretical generalizations at a lower level of abstraction, such as so-called "middle range" theories. But even here a candid assessment must be that the results have so far been meagre. Concepts of "job regulation" and "social regimes of market regulation" or models of strategic choice and the efficiency/equity trade-off are suggestive and have insight but have not to date provided the theoretical basis for an advancing research programme. Perhaps most indicative of the state of theorizing in the field is that many scholars judge that the two enduring theoretical insights in industrial relations come from a century ago – the Webbs' notion of taking labour cost out of competition through a market-wide "common rule" and Commons' complementary theory of market extension and union development.

Largely lacking theory, industrial relations then has to seek competitive advantage in science building based on the superior productivity of its research methods. One such method that has long provided a fundamental rationale for the field is the interdisciplinary (or plura-disciplinary) perspective; a second is close contact with real life through case studies, ethnographic studies and other "go and see" techniques. Unfortunately, industrial relations has not itself practised the interdisciplinary method with much verve or success, while most other academics give it favourable lip service but steer the other way, toward disciplinary specialization where stronger theory exists. Nor is the "go and see" method of industrial relations highly valued today and, indeed, the favoured approach in the higher reaches of academia is the opposite – to stand back from social reality and use sophisticated mathematics, computers, statistics and large secondary data sets to "let the numbers tell the story".

The second way in which industrial relations earns its keep as a field of study is in contributing to the solution of significant social problems. In this respect, industrial relations is no different from numerous other applied subject areas in universities, such as international relations, nursing and actuarial science. In the main, the justification for each is not intellectual but practical – to train people and develop procedures and policies that help resolve real-world problems, be they wars, sickness or insurance against risk. The mission of industrial relations is to solve labour problems in industry and the number one labour problem that lies at the heart of the field is conflict between employer and employees and the social and economic disorder it can unleash if allowed to fester and grow. In this respect, industrial relations is simply international relations transferred to the industrial realm, and the wars it seeks to prevent and end are not between nation states but industrial classes. Like international relations, the field booms when relations become particularly problematic and conflicts and wars threaten large-scale disaster, while it recedes and even atrophies when peace and tranquillity rob it of a mission and raison d'être.

In the United States, where industrial relations was born and got its start, the field came into the universities primarily on the basis of its potential to solve labour problems and, particularly, restore and maintain industrial peace. As we seek to understand the recent decline in vitality and academic status of industrial relations (the downward path), the problem-solving face of the field is the key point of access. The central insight from the historical analysis in this volume is that the problem-solving approach of industrial relations narrowed both over time and as it moved outward to other countries.

Originally, industrial relations pertained to all employment relationships and sought to solve labour problems through a four-pronged approach of trade unionism, progressive management, government protective labour legislation and social insurance, and (to a lesser degree) macroeconomic stabilization. The field was in these early years sometimes called *employment relations*, and one could legitimately interpret this term to connote the entirety of employment relationships in the economy. Over time, the field of industrial relations gradually started to shed or lose academic jurisdiction over all of these three subdivisions except trade unionism and labour–management relations. In part this divestiture arose as a natural by-product of growing academic division of labour in the social sciences and business schools. In 1920 in the United States the study of work and employment was sufficiently undeveloped that trade unionism, personnel management and labour law (but not macroeconomic stabilization) could be housed within industrial relations for teaching and research purposes. A half-century later employment management (personnel /HRM) was spun off to management departments and business schools for more intensive, in-depth treatment while the various aspects of employment policy were increasingly taken over by economics, law and public administration. Also in part, the divestiture of employment management and employment policy (particularly the former) came from the post-New Deal intellectual and ideological commitment of many people in industrial relations to favour trade unionism and collective bargaining over the other two approaches to solving labour problems, and their concomitant suspicion toward non-union employers. By the time industrial relations started to develop in the United Kingdom after the Second World War, the field started from the first without the employment management division and only a truncated version of the employment policy division.

By the 1960s, therefore, industrial relations in its two major home countries had largely narrowed from "all employment relationships" to "union–management relationships". As long as the union sectors of their economies remained large and important and industrial conflict continued to flare up, many labour problems demanded attention and universities saw good reason to establish and grow industrial relations programmes and to hire new faculty members to teach students and conduct research. However, when the union movements went into decline, strikes plummeted and public policy turned indifferent and sometimes hostile toward collective bargaining, student enrolments and research funding began to dwindle and industrial relations started to lose its major rationale for existence. Soon, retrenchment and cutbacks hit industrial relations, gathering speed in proportion to the decline in the labour movement. In Europe, on the other hand, industrial relations avoided much of this agony, partly because trade unionism remained strong and more stable, partly because industrial relations was defined more broadly to include employment policy, and partly because the field was less institutionalized and thus less locked into old patterns. Of course, industrial relationists in the United Kingdom and the United States sought belatedly to recapture the broad definition of industrial relations by bringing back into the fold employment management and employment policy, but this effort was only partially successful since these subjects were now claimed by others and industrial relations "problem solvers" were not always well equipped or suited to compete effectively in these new topic areas.

As we search for the reason industrial relations has taken the downward path, the narrowing of the term industrial relations and the concomitant decline of the labour movement in most countries is a significant part of the story. But there is more. Also important is the growing mismatch between the institutional solutions offered by industrial relations and the nature of today's labour problems. The essence of industrial relations as a problem-solving field is to work out new institutional arrangements (or web of rules) to solve labour problems. Over the last three decades in all industrial countries the type of labour problems that demand public attention has changed dramatically, reflecting underlying demographic shifts (working women, dual earner couples, workforce diversity, etc.), economic transformations (decline of manufacturing, rise of white-collar and service jobs, more informal employment, etc.), and social developments (decline of communitarian values, drugs and HIV/AIDS, etc.). Indeed, some of the largest labour problems are not even within individual nations but between nations, such as migration policy and the growing gap between rich and poor countries. Certainly part of the decline of industrial relations in the Anglo-American world, and most particularly in the United States, is the public perception that the programmes and policies associated with industrial relations, such as collective bargaining and extensive formal rule-bound employment contracts, are not well suited or particularly relevant to solving these new problems. In effect, industrial relations has fallen out of step with the modern workplace because its toolkit of institutional "fixes" is no longer regarded as very effective, further reducing the incentive for universities to protect and maintain industrial relations as a field of study.

The third way industrial relations earns its keep as a field of study is to cover a subject that for political or ethical reasons universities consider is sufficiently important that teaching and/or research space must be made available for it. When industrial relations was created, the field was deliberately intended to improve the social status and economic conditions of labour and, in particular, was dedicated to the principle that labour should not be treated as a commodity. For this reason, industrial relations was regarded by many people as "labour friendly" and deserved a place in universities as the place where the interests and viewpoint of workers get representation. After the Second World War, the ideological orientation of industrial relations shifted further and the field became more widely associated with an ideological commitment to not only "labour" in the lower case but "Labour" in the upper case, meaning organized labour and the trade union movement. This ideological orientation worked for and against the field. When unions are strong and in favour, universities feel political and ideological pressure to provide curricular and research space for the mission and programme of organized labour, creating a rationale for having an industrial relations programme. Certainly this pressure was intensely felt in the United States during the 1945–65 period, as well as in other countries such as Australia, Japan and the United Kingdom. However, when the labour movement goes into decline and loses public/political support, one of the props under industrial relations programmes is weakened and universities see less reason to maintain them, particularly in the face of declining student enrolments. Certainly part of the decline of the industrial relations field since 1980 owes its origins to this phenomenon.

Industrial relations has thus suffered from lack of a solid theoretical foundation and an intellectually compelling research programme, a decline in the relevance and usefulness of its problem-solving programme, and declining ideological support for the cause of organized labour. As a result, industrial relations has lost the support of three main sponsors or "customers" – universities, business firms and government. Universities will make room for industrial relations if it has something intellectually interesting and important to say, or if it can fill classrooms with students, or if the labour movement cares enough about the field and exerts sufficient pressure on key officials. As just described, all of these conditions are weakening and universities are increasingly scaling back or dropping industrial relations.

Likewise, a growing number of employers have also deserted industrial relations. Cynics will perhaps say that employers never embraced industrial relations in the first place, so they have nothing to walk away from. But this is a misreading of the history of the field. Certainly in North America, employers were in the vanguard of the new industrial relations field in the 1920s and, even in the 1950s, were frequently well disposed to industrial relations. Indeed, as pointed out in Chapter 9, one reason many European intellectuals in earlier years wanted nothing to do with industrial relations was because it was too managerialist. Now, 30 and 40 years later, industrial relations has shed most traces of managerialism and is largely associated with trade unions and, to a degree, government regulation. Where union density remains high, employers continue to accept industrial relations, but in countries and industries where decentralization and de-unionization have arrived the attitude of employers has notably hardened and turned antagonistic. As a result, no John D. Rockefeller, Jrs., Montague Burtons and J.R.D. Tatas are on the contemporary scene to endow new industrial relations centres and fund faculty research.

Nor are governments as interested in industrial relations as they used to be, and some have turned hostile towards it. During the years of the post-war "social accord", industrial relations was an integral part of social policy in practically every industrial nation. Large-sized and institutionally secure labour movements, along with a well-developed welfare state, were accepted by public opinion and mainstream political parties as the inevitable and desired historical trajectory of modern capitalism. The actual experience with widespread collective bargaining in many countries, particularly outside corporatist Northern Europe, gradually proved disappointing, however. Unions seemed to shift from protectors of the weak and shields of justice to narrow interest groups that used their power to win outsize economic gains and a host of restrictive practices benefiting union members but at the cost of saddling the community with strikes, higher inflation, lower productivity and a more politicized and disruptive workplace. Inevitably, a reaction set in, symbolized by the election of Thatcher, Reagan and other conservative governments around the world and the movement toward neo-liberalism, market deregulation, trimming back the welfare state and reducing the immunities and power of organized labour. In such an environment, few government policy-makers see industrial relations as contributing answers to their most pressing problems and, thus, see few reasons to support industrial relations through grants, research projects and institutional support. Even the ILO, which is industrial relations' soulmate and long-time partner, has in a quiet and unobtrusive way downgraded the priority given to the field. The EU is the largest exception to this phenomenon and is an important reason why European industrial relations is in a relatively robust condition.

Industrial relations, like every social institution, can only survive if it attracts outside resources from sponsors or "paying customers" to cover ongoing costs of operation. Increasingly, three of its major sponsors have backed away and allocated their resources elsewhere. Every social institution, to survive, must also provide sufficient benefits to members to keep them from leaving for better opportunities. Industrial relations is also in danger of failing this test, witnessed by declining membership in some industrial relations associations, falling circulation among some prominent industrial relations journals, and declining attendance at some industrial relations conferences. As we peer into the future, therefore, we must conclude that it looks less than bright.

For better or worse, as things stand today the fate of industrial relations is heavily bound up with the fate of organized labour. Like the world's glaciers, labour movements across the globe are slowly retreating and shrinking. One can argue that this is undesirable and should not be the case. Or a reasonable argument is that the contradictions of capitalism and tendency of employers to overreach will bring about a new Labour Problem and resurgence of unions. Alternatively, perhaps industrial relations and trade unionism have performed their historic mission of containing the Labour Problem and Red Threat and social injustice in early capitalism and can now shuffle off the stage – public-spirited victims of their own success.

These are large questions that defy a ready answer. In the here and now, however, the facts are plain to see – unions are declining, despite much effort at union renewal, and significant new sources of growth are not on the horizon. Thus organized labour may be able to hold its own in some countries, but overall union density is likely to continue to diminish across the world – absent some unforeseen economic or social shock that causes widespread Depression-era job insecurity and deprivation, major war-time disruption and economic controls, and/or a major liberalization of labour law to promote more unionism. As it declines, industrial relations seems fated to follow in the same direction, albeit slowly and with continued pockets of strength given that the "shrinking" institution of trade unionism still has over 50 million members worldwide and much larger effective coverage.

If union membership does rebound, then industrial relations may be able to go back to "business as usual". If it does not, then we have to ask the long-run question: is it possible to have industrial relations without unions? The answer is yes, but getting there is not necessarily easy.

At a conceptual level, relations between employers and employees, and the labour problems that emanate from these relations, remain a live issue and worthy of study even without unions. Indeed, conflict of interest between employers and employees is inherent to the relationship, so even if unions are no longer the institution to mediate this tension, there must be some other institution that performs this role. Likewise, even without unions many firms will find a need for some form of collective voice, such as a works council or employee involvement programme. Viewed from this perspective, as long as employers and employees exist, the relations between them will be problematic, sometimes conflictual, and always in need of mechanisms for dialogue, adjustment and regulation. Industrial relations – as the study of employer–employee relations – is thus generic and in no way dependent on any particular institution.

The same conclusion can be reached by an alternative route. A popular way to think about industrial relations is as the study of alternative regimes of labour market regulation and workforce governance. Collective bargaining is one such regulatory regime; the invisible hand of market forces in general equilibrium theory is another. Again, industrial relations is generic.

At a practical level, however, the difficulties in sustaining industrial relations as a formal entity without a significant union presence (or, alternatively, productive body of theory for science building) are considerable. Other disciplines and fields of study, such as economics, management and law, have already appropriated alternative modes of labour market regulation as their specialty areas, so without a significant trade union movement industrial relations may well have nothing unique to feature in its textbooks, courses, academic journals and research conferences, and thus only modest rationale for a separate institutional infrastructure (which generates costs someone has to deem worthwhile to bear). Promoting an integrative, plura-disciplinary perspective remains as one such rationale even in a (conjectural) union-less world, but recent trends suggest it is a weak reed. Furthermore, one can reasonably surmise that even without unions, and the associated labour institutions and policies, the *Industrial and Labor Relations Review* and *British Journal of Industrial Relations* will still find plenty of articles to publish on labour. However, the question still must be asked: what does the label "industrial relations" then connote beyond a rather vacuous "all aspects of employment"? Likewise, researchers will continue to find many interesting labour problems to investigate, but what comparative advantage does someone in industrial relations have when it comes to issues such as work–family balance, poverty, or worker retraining?

The bottom line appears to be that industrial relations must have either a compelling toolkit of theory and methods to justify its existence or a compelling set of real-life problems to solve for which it has a comparative expertise. Both are in question at the moment, so the short-term future could well be judged as relatively gloomy. Then, of course, there is also the problem of the name of the field – the fact that *industrial relations* sounds increasingly old-fashioned and wedded to a smokestack blue-collar economy, and whether some new term, such as *employment relations*, can serve as a popular and effective substitute.

Perhaps with some naiveté, I feel there are actually significant rays of hope for industrial relations, or whatever the field is labelled. I see hope on both the fronts of theory building and problem solving.

My impression is that institutional economics – and institutionalism in sociology and political science – after having a near-death experience, are making a substantial comeback. Combined with equally interesting work in socio-economics, behavioural economics and other heterodox fields, the possibility exists for constructing a much stronger theoretical base for industrial relations. With a stronger base of theory, industrial relations will be better positioned not only to promote interesting science building but will also be able to better advance and defend its policy programme against the inevitable neoclassical and neo-liberal attack. To the degree that a resuscitated institutional economics yields interesting insights and implications about alternative modes of regulation and working rules in the employment sphere, industrial relations gains a valuable conceptual tool for thinking about new institutional architectures for workplace governance and new labour policies that better match the new economy and new workforce. Alternatively, if through institutional economics industrial relations can develop an integrative theory of the employment relationship, the field will be well-positioned to reclaim its original broad territory in the social sciences as "the study of all aspects of employment".

Rays of hope also emanate from world of current events. Among the many propositions that come from industrial relations, I see five as fundamental:

- labour cannot be treated as a commodity without serious social repercussions,
- achieving and maintaining economic efficiency is impossible without also maintaining a minimum of social justice and individual economic security,
- labour markets are inherently imperfect and incapable of self-regulation,
- unemployment is capitalism's gravest defect and most serious labour problem,
- social welfare is advanced not only by providing consumers with plentiful low-priced goods and services but also by providing workers with decent wages and good jobs.

Neoclassical economics and the neo-liberal political paradigm that now dominate academic research and economic policy-making minimize, neglect, or deny the importance of these propositions. Any form of policy intervention to improve the condition of labour above what the free market provides is immediately labelled "protectionism" and cast under a cloud of suspicion. If this blind spot were limited to scholastic debates among academics, little of consequence would result. Due, however, to a confluence of events and developments – globalization, deregulation, privatization, lax legal enforcement, decline of unions, and the erosion of the social safety net protecting workers and their families – the world economy is headed in the direction of a more competitive, deregulated and de-institutionalized labour market. These trends, coupled with the growing inequality between advanced industrial countries and stagnating economies of the developing countries, is creating conditions that challenge all five propositions. That is, labour is being commodified across the world economy, inequality and insecurity are on the rise, global market forces are undermining national regulatory regimes, one out of six workers in the world economy are jobless or seriously underemployed, and workers' interests are increasingly subordinated to consumers' interests.

These trends in the world economy may well be throwing up the ultimate test of the relevance and intellectual value of industrial relations. According to neoclassical economists and neo-liberal political strategists, these developments are either not serious social problems or are best solved by promoting free trade and flexible labour markets. Doing so, they believe, will promote rising living standards, create more jobs and higher wages, put the unemployed back to work, and provide maximum incentives to acquire more skills and education. But will they? Industrial relations offers a more qualified answer.

Viewed from the perspective of industrial relations, the answer is an unambiguous Yes for a minority of people and countries in the world community. It may well be a Yes even for the large majority in the long run. But, as Keynes said, in the long run we are all dead. For most working people, it is wages, hours, conditions and treatment in the here and now that really count. And it is at this point, if one believes in the five propositions of industrial relations cited above, where the fundamental contradiction of neoclassical economics and neo-liberalism lies. Simply put, free labour markets – without the balance, fairness, social protection and macroeconomic guidance offered by the institutions of industrial relations and the visible hand of state management – will necessarily create or perpetuate conditions that undermine their own effectiveness and survival. That is, free markets will heighten insecurity, lead to growing inequality, fail to automatically eliminate unemployment through flexible price movements, create sub-standard working conditions, fail to give workers adequate voice and protection against arbitrary and discriminatory treatment, and contribute to a variety of other evils that collectively imperil efficiency, social justice and human development and call into question the very legitimacy of the market system and capitalist order. This proposition, as I see it, is the fundamental theorem of industrial relations and is the one upon which the existence and utility of the field ultimately rest.

Industrial relations is not anti-capitalist or anti-market; in fact, part of its purpose is to make the market system and capitalism work better. To accomplish this goal, industrial relations seeks to humanize, stabilize, professionalize, democratize and balance the market system through new and expanded institutions. Of course, this worthy agenda may be carried to excess, subverted to serve the vested interests of various producer groups, or used to promote sectarian ideological or political objectives, so balance and pragmatic realism are also required in all phases of industrial relations. But, broadly viewed, we can nonetheless assert that industrial relations *must* have a future because real-life capitalism cannot survive without it. This lesson had to be learned the hard way in the first age of globalization a century ago; it is hoped that it will not have to be re-learned in the same way during the second age of globalization we are now passing through.

REFERENCES

Abraham, D. 1982. "Economic democracy as a labor alternative to the growth strategy in Weimar Germany", in A. Markovits (ed.): *The political economy of West Germany: Modell Deutschland* (New York, Praeger), pp. 116–40.

Ackers, P. 2002. "Reframing employment relations: The case for neo-pluralism", in *Industrial Relations Journal*, Vol. 33, No. 1, pp. 2–19.

——— ; Wilkinson, A. 2003. "Introduction: The British industrial relations tradition – Formation, breakdown, and salvage", in P. Ackers and A. Wilkinson (eds.): *Understanding work and employment* (Oxford, Oxford University Press), pp. 1–27.

Adams, G. 1966. *Age of industrial violence 1910–1915* (New York, Columbia University Press).

Adams, J.S. 1963. "Toward an understanding of inequity", in *Journal of Abnormal Psychology*, Vol. 67, Nov., pp. 422–36.

Adams, R. 1988. "Desperately seeking industrial relations theory", in *International Journal of Comparative Labour Law and Industrial Relations*, Vol. 4, No. 1, pp. 1–10.

———. 1989. "North American industrial relations: Divergent trends in Canada and the United States", in *International Labour Review*, Vol. 128, No. 1, pp. 47–64.

———. 1993a. "'All aspects of people at work': Unity and division in the study of labor and labor management", in Adams and Meltz (eds.), 1993, pp. 119–60.

———. 1993b. "Understanding, constructing, and teaching industrial relations theory", in Adams and Meltz (eds.), 1993, pp. 1–16.

———. 1995a. *Industrial relations under liberal democracy* (Columbia, University of South Carolina Press).

———. 1995b. "Industrial relations in Europe and North America: Some contemporary themes", in *European Journal of Industrial Relations*, Vol. 1, No. 1, pp. 47–62.

——— ; Meltz, N. (eds.). 1993. *Industrial relations theory: Its scope and pedagogy* (Metuchen, New Jersey, Scarecrow Press).

Adams, T.; Sumner, H. 1905. *Labor problems* (New York, Macmillan).

Addison, J.; Siebert, W.S. 1979. *The market for labor: An analytic treatment* (Santa Monica, Goodyear).

——— ; ———. 1992. "The social charter: Whatever next?", in *British Journal of Industrial Relations*, Vol. 30, No. 4, pp. 495–513.

Agarwala, A. 1947. *Indian labour problems* (Allahabad, Kitabistan).

Alba, V. 1968. *Politics and the labor movement in Latin America* (Stanford, Stanford University Press).

Albeda, W. 1977. *Arbeidsverhoudingen in Nederland* (Alphen, Samson).

Albert, M. 1993. *Capitalism vs. capitalism: How America's obsession with individual achievement and short-term profit has led it to the brink of collapse* (New York, Four Walls Eight Windows).

Alchon, G. 1991. "Mary van Kleeck and social economic planning", in *Journal of Policy History*, Vol. 3, No. 1, pp. 1–23.

——. 1992. "Mary van Kleeck and scientific management", in D. Nelson (ed.): *A mental revolution: Scientific management since Taylor* (Columbus, Ohio State University), pp. 102–29.

Alcock, A. 1971. *History of the International Labour Organization* (New York, Octagon Books).

Aldao-Zapiola, C. 2000. "Human resource management in Latin America", in M. Warner (ed.): *Management in the Americas* (New York, Thomson Learning), pp. 138–49.

—— ; Hermida Martínez, D. 1995. *Relaciones industriales y recursos humanos en América Latina* (Buenos Aires, de Indusgraf).

Alexander, R. 1962. *Labor relations in Argentina, Brazil, and Chile* (New York, McGraw-Hill).

——. 2003. *A history of organized labor in Argentina* (Westport, CT, Praeger).

Allen, C. 1964. *Law in the making* (Oxford, Clarendon Press).

Allen, V. 1971. *The sociology of industrial relations* (London, Longman).

——. 1972. *Future industrial relations: English-speaking Africa* (Geneva, International Institute for Labour Studies).

Amadieu, J.F. 1995. "Industrial relations: Is France a special case?", in *British Journal of Industrial Relations*, Vol. 33, No. 3, pp. 345–51.

Amann, E.; Baer, W. 2002. "Neoliberalism and its consequences in Brazil", in *Journal of Latin American Studies*, Vol. 32, pp. 945–59.

Annan, L. 1975. "The university in Britain", in M. Stephens and G. Roderick (eds.): *Universities for a changing world* (New York, Wiley), pp. 19–33.

Aparicio-Valdez, L. 2003. "Modernization of labour law and industrial relations in Latin America", in R. Blanpain and M. Weiss (eds.): *Changing industrial relations and modernization of labour law: Liber amicorum in honour of Professor Marco Biagi* (New York, Kluwer Law International).

—— ; Bernedo Alvarado, J. 2001. "Latin America", in R. Blanpain (ed.): *The evolving employment relationship and the new economy* (New York, Kluwer Law International), pp. 89–101.

Appelbaum, E.; Berg, P.; Kalleberg, A.; Bailey, T. 2000. *Manufacturing advantage: Why high-performance work systems pay off* (Ithaca, Cornell University Press).

—— ; Bernhardt, A.; Murnane, R. 2003. *Low-wage America: How employers are reshaping opportunity in the workplace* (New York, Russell Sage).

Araki, T. 2002. "Labor law scholarship in Japan", in *Comparative Labor Law and Policy Journal*, Vol. 23, No. 3, pp. 735–48.

Araujo Guimarães, N.; de Paula Leite, M. 2002. "Brazil", in D. Cornfield and R. Hodson (eds.): *Worlds of work: Building an international sociology of work* (New York, Kluwer), pp. 23–46.

Arensberg, C. 1951. "Behavior and organization: Industrial studies", in J. Rohrer and M. Sherif (eds.): *Social psychology at the crossroads* (New York, Harper), pp. 324–52.

——— ; Barkin, S.; Chalmers, W.E.; Wilensky, H.; Worthy, J.; Dennis, B. 1957. *Research in industrial human relations* (Madison, IRRA).

——— ; Tootle, G. 1957. "Plant sociology: Real discoveries and new problems", in M. Komarovsky (ed.): *Common frontiers of the social sciences* (Glencoe, Free Press), pp. 310–37.

Argyris, C. 1957. *Personality and organization* (New York, Harper and Row).

Armstrong, E. 1969. *Industrial relations: An introduction* (London, Harrap).

Arthurs, H. 2002. "National traditions in labor law scholarship: The Canadian case", in *Comparative Labor Law and Policy Journal*, Vol. 23, No. 3, pp. 645–78.

Ascher, A. 1963. "Professors as propagandists: The politics of the *Kathedersozialisten*", in *Journal of Central European Affairs*, Vol. 23, No. 3, pp. 282–302.

Auer, P.; Gazier, B. 2002. *The future of work, employment, and social protection: The dynamics of change and the protection of workers* (Geneva, IILS).

Ayusawa, I. 1966. *A history of labor in modern Japan* (Honolulu, East–West Center Press).

Babbage, C. 1832. *On the economy of machinery and manufactures* (London, Charles Knight).

Bach, S.; Sisson, K. (eds.). 2000. *Personnel management: A comprehensive guide to theory and practice* (Oxford, Blackwell Business).

Bain, G. 2003. Telephone interview.

——— ; Clegg, H. 1974. "A strategy for industrial relations research in Great Britain", in *British Journal of Industrial Relations*, Vol. 12, No. 1, pp. 91–113.

——— ; Woolven, G. 1979. *A bibliography of British industrial relations* (Cambridge, Cambridge University Press).

Baker, R. 1904. "Parker and Roosevelt on labor", in *McLure's Magazine*, Issue 24, Nov., pp. 41–52.

Bakke, E. 1946. *Mutual survival: The goals of unions and management* (New York, Harper).

——— . 1950. *Bonds of organization: An appraisal of corporate human relations* (New York, Harper).

——— . 1958. *The human resource function* (New Haven, Yale Labor-Management Center, Yale University).

——— ; Kerr, C.; Anrod, C. (eds.). 1967. *Unions, management, and the public*, 3rd ed. (New York, Harcourt, Brace & World).

Balderston, C. 1935. *Executive guidance of industrial relations* (Philadelphia, University of Pennsylvania Press).

Balfour, W.C. 1955. "Discussion", in IRRA: *Proceedings of the Seventh Annual Meeting* (Madison), pp. 88–9.

Barbalet, J. 1983. *Marx's construction of social theory* (London, Routledge).

Barbash, J. 1967. "John R. Commons and the Americanization of the Labor Problem", in *Journal of Economic Issues*, Vol. 1, No. 3, pp. 161–7.

——— . 1979. "The American ideology of industrial relations", in IRRA: *Proceedings of the 1979 Spring Meeting* (Madison), pp. 453–7.

——— . 1984. *The elements of industrial relations* (Madison, University of Wisconsin Press).

_____ . 1989. "Introduction", in J. Barbash and K. Barbash (eds.): *Theories and concepts in comparative industrial relations* (Columbia, University of South Carolina Press), pp. 3–6.

_____ . 1991. "Industrial relations concepts in the USA", in *Relations Industrielles/Industrial Relations*, Vol. 46, No. 1, pp. 91–118.

_____ . 1993. "The founders of the field of industrial relations as a field of study: An American perspective", in Adams and Meltz (eds.), 1993, pp. 67–80.

_____ . 1994. "Americanizing the Labor Problem: The Wisconsin school", in C. Kerr and P. Staudohar (eds.): *Labor economics and industrial relations: Markets and institutions* (Cambridge, MA, Harvard University Press), pp. 41–65.

_____ ; Meltz, N. (eds.). 1997. *Theorizing in industrial relations: Approaches and applications* (Sydney, ACIRRT, University of Sydney).

Baritz, L. 1960. *The servants of power: A history of the use of social sciences in American industry* (Middletown, CT, Wesleyan University Press).

Barnard, C. 1938. *The functions of the executive* (Cambridge, MA, Harvard University Press).

Barnes, G. 1920. "The scope and purpose of international labour legislation", in E.J. Solano (ed.): *Labour in the international economy* (London, Macmillan), pp. 3–40.

Barnes, H. 1925. *The history and prospects of the social sciences* (New York, Knopf).

Barnes, W. 1886. *The Labor Problem: Plain questions and practical answers* (New York, Harper).

Barnett, G. 1933. "American trade unionism and social insurance", in *American Economic Review*, Vol. 23, Mar., pp. 1–15.

Barry, B. 1989. "Management education in Great Britain", in W. Byrt (ed.): *Management education: An international survey* (London, Routledge), pp. 56–77.

Basle, M. 2001. "Acknowledged and unacknowledged institutionalist antecedents of *régulation* theory", in Boyer and Saillard (eds.), 2001, pp. 21–7.

Batstone, E. 1988. *The reform of workplace industrial relations: Theory, myth and evidence* (Oxford, Clarendon Press).

_____ ; Boraston, I.; Frenkel, S. 1977. *Shop stewards in action: The organization of workplace conflict and accommodation* (Oxford, Blackwell).

Battacharya, S. 2002. *Paradigms in the historical approach to labour studies*, V.V. Giri Memorial Lecture, 44th Annual Conference, Indian Society of Labour Economics (Amritsar, Punjab, Guru Nanak Dev University).

Beardwell, I. 1996. "'How do we know how it really is?' An analysis of the new industrial relations", in I. Beardwell (ed.): *Contemporary industrial relations: A critical analysis* (Oxford, Oxford University Press), pp. 1–10.

Beaumont, P. 1995. *The future of employment relations* (London, Sage).

Beaumont, R. 2003. "In conclusion: Transitioning from the past to the future", in B. Kaufman, R. Beaumont and R. Helfgott (eds.), 2003, pp. 448–72.

_____ ; Becker, D.; Robertson, S. 2003. "HR today and tomorrow: Organizational strategy in global companies", in B. Kaufman, R. Beaumont and R. Helfgott (eds.), 2003, pp. 403–17.

Beauville, C. 1988. "Towards a renewal of French unionism?", in *Proceedings of the Forty-First Annual Meeting* (Madison, IRRA), pp. 351–60.

Beck, H. 1995. *The origins of the authoritarian welfare state in Prussia* (Ann Arbor, University of Michigan Press).

Becker, G. 1957. *The economics of discrimination* (Chicago, University of Chicago Press).

———. 1976. *The economic approach to human behavior* (Chicago, University of Chicago Press).

Beer, M.; Spector, B. 1984. "Human resources management: The integration of industrial relations and organizational development", in K. Rowland and G. Ferris (eds.): *Research in personnel and human resource management*, Vol. 2 (Greenwich, CT, JAI Press), pp. 261–97.

Behrend, H. 1963. "The field of industrial relations", in *British Journal of Industrial Relations*, Vol. 1, No. 3, pp. 383–94.

Beinin, J. 1994. "Will the real Egyptian working class please stand up?", in Z. Lockham (ed.): *Workers and working classes in the Middle East* (Albany, State University of New York Press), pp. 247–70.

Bélanger, J.; Edwards, P.; Haiven, L. 1994. *Workplace regulations and the global challenge* (Ithaca, Cornell University Press).

Belcher, T. 1965. "United States foreign policy and social change", in W. Form and A. Blum (eds.): *Industrial relations and social change in Latin America* (Gainsville, University of Florida Press), pp. 121–34.

Bellace, J. 1994. "The role of the state in industrial relations", in J. Niland, R. Lansbury and C. Verevis (eds.): *The future of industrial relations: Global change and challenges* (London, Sage), pp. 19–40.

Bendix, D.W. 1978. "Research and teaching in labour relations: Old wine in new bottles?", in *South African Journal of Labour Relations*, Vol. 2, No. 4, pp. 25–31.

Bendix, R. 1956. *Work and authority in industry* (New York, Wiley).

———; Fisher, F. 1949. "The perspectives of Elton Mayo", in *Review of Economics and Statistics*, Vol. 31, Nov., pp. 312–21.

Bendix, S. 1989. *Industrial relations in South Africa*, 4th ed. (Cape Town, Juta Publishers).

Benjamin, H. 1965. *Higher education in the American republics* (New York, McGraw-Hill).

Bennett, J.; Kaufman, B. 2002. "Conclusion: The future of private sector unionism in the US – Assessment and forecast", in J. Bennett and B. Kaufman (eds.): *The future of private sector unionism in the United States* (Armonk, M.E. Sharpe), pp. 339–86.

———; Taylor, J. 2002. "Labor unions: Victims of their own political success?", in J. Bennett and B. Kaufman (eds.): *The future of private sector unionism in the United States* (Armonk, M.E. Sharpe), pp. 245–59.

Bercuson, D. 1973. "Introduction", in W.L. Mackenzie King: *Industry and humanity* (Toronto, University of Toronto Press).

Berenstein, A. 1995. *Origin and development of the International Society for Labour Law and Social Security* (Geneva, ISLLSS).

Berger, S. 2000. *Social democracy and the working class in nineteenth and twentieth century Germany* (London, Longman).

Berghahn, V.; Karsten, D. 1987. *Industrial relations in West Germany* (Hamburg, Berg).

Bernedo Alvarado, J. 2004. "2002: The Peruvian labour field", in R. Blanpain and L. Aparicio-Valdez (eds.): *Labour relations in the Asia-Pacific countries* (New York, Kluwer Law International), pp. 131–46.

Bernstein, I. 1960. *The lean years* (Boston, Houghton Mifflin).

———. 1970. *The turbulent years* (Boston, Houghton Mifflin).

Berridge, J.; Goodman, J. 1988. "The British Universities Industrial Relations Association: The first thirty-five years", in *British Journal of Industrial Relations*, Vol. 26, No. 2, pp. 155–77.

Berquist, C. 1986. *Labor in Latin America: Comparative essays on Chile, Argentina, Venezuela, and Colombia* (Stanford, Stanford University Press).

Bertrand, H. 2001. "The wage–labour nexus and the employment system", in Boyer and Saillard (eds.), 2001, pp. 80–86.

Beveridge, Lord. 1960. *The London School of Economics and its problems 1919–1937* (London, Allen & Unwin).

Beveridge, W. 1945. *Full employment in a free society* (London, Norton).

Bewley, T. 1999. *Why wages don't fall during a recession* (Cambridge, MA, Harvard University Press).

Bhowmik, S. 2002. "India", in D. Cornfield and R. Hodson (eds.): *Worlds of work: Building an international sociology of work* (New York, Kluwer), pp. 131–52.

Biernacki, R. 1995. *The fabrication of labor* (Berkeley, University of California Press).

Birk, R. 2002. "Labor law scholarship in France, Germany, and Italy: Some remarks on a difficult question", in *Comparative Labor Law and Policy Journal*, Vol. 23, No. 3, pp. 679–700.

Bladen, V. 1978. *Bladen on Bladen: Memoirs of a political economist* (Toronto, Scarborough College of the University of Toronto).

Blain, N.; Plowman, D. 1987. "The Australian industrial relations literature, 1970–1986", in *Journal of Industrial Relations*, Vol. 29, No. 3, pp. 295–320.

Blanpain, R. 2002. "National styles in labor law and social science scholarship: A personal view", in *Comparative Labor Law and Policy Journal*, Vol. 23, No. 3, pp. 727–34.

——— ; Biagi, M. 1993. *Industrial relations in small and medium-sized enterprises* (Boston, Kluwer).

Blaug, M. 1997. *Economic theory in retrospect*, 5th ed. (Cambridge, Cambridge University Press).

Bloomfield, M. 1917. "The new profession of handling men", in *Industrial Management*, Jan., pp. 441–6.

Blum, S. 1925. *Labor economics* (New York, Henry Holt).

Boivin, J. 1989. "Industrial relations: A field and a discipline", in J. Barbash and K. Barbash (eds.): *Theories and concepts in comparative industrial relations* (Columbia, University of South Carolina Press), pp. 91–108.

——— . 1991. "The teaching of industrial relations in Canadian universities", unpublished paper (Montreal, Laval University).

——— . 1996. "La constitution d'un champ d'étude? Trajectoires dans l'étude des relations professionelles", in Murray, Morin and da Costa (eds.), 1996, pp. 93–9.

——— . 2003. Personal interview.

Booth, A. 1995. *Economics of the trade union* (Cambridge, Cambridge University Press).

Booth, C. 1902. *Life and labor of the people in London* (New York, AMS Press).

Bose, R. 1956. *Gandhian technique and tradition in industrial relations* (Calcutta, All-India Institute of Social Welfare and Business Management).

Bossard, J.; Frederick Dewhurst, J. 1931. *University education for business* (Philadelphia, University of Pennsylvania Press).

Boulding, K. 1957. "A new look at institutionalism", in *American Economic Review*, Vol. 47, May, pp. 1–12.

Bourdieu, P.; Passeron, J.C. 1967. "Sociology and philosophy in France since 1945: Death and resurrection of a philosophy without subject", reprinted in P. Hamilton (ed.), 1990: *Emile Durkheim: Critical assessments*, Vol. 6 (London, Routledge), pp. 141–73.

Boxall, P.; Dowling, P. 1990. "Human resource management, employee relations and the industrial relations tradition in Australia and New Zealand", in G. Griffin (ed.): *Current research in industrial relations, Proceedings of the 5th AIRAANZ Conference* (Melbourne, University of Melbourne), pp. 152–9.

Boyer, G.; Smith, R. 2001. "The development of the neoclassical tradition in labor economics", in *Industrial and Labor Relations Review*, Vol. 54, No. 2, pp. 199–223.

Boyer, R.; Saillard, Y. (eds.). 2001. Régulation *theory: The state of the art* (London, Routledge).

Brandeis, L. 1918. "Efficiency by consent: To secure its active cooperation labor must be consulted and convinced in regard to changes", in *Industrial Management*, Vol. 2, pp. 108–9.

Braverman, H. 1974. *Labor and monopoly capital: The degradation of work in the twentieth century* (New York, Monthly Review Press).

Brentano, L. 1870. *On the history and development of gilds, and the origins of trade-unions* (London, Trübner & Co.).

Breuilly, J. 1992. *Labour and liberalism in nineteenth century Europe* (New York, Manchester University Press).

Briggs, A. 1954. "Social background", in Flanders and Clegg (eds.), 1954, pp. 1–41.

Brock, C.; Lawlor, H. 1985. *Education in Latin America* (London, Croom Helm).

Brody, D. 1980. *Workers in industrial America: Essays on the twentieth century struggle* (New York, Oxford University Press).

——. 1989. "Labor history, industrial relations, and the crisis of American labor", in *Industrial and Labor Relations Review*, Vol. 43, No. 1, pp. 7–18.

Bronfenbrenner, M. 1971. *Income distribution theory* (Chicago, Aldine).

Bronstein, A. 1995. "Societal change and industrial relations in Latin America: Trends and prospects", in *International Labour Review*, Vol. 134, No. 2, pp. 163–87.

——. 1997. "Labour law reform in Latin America: Between state protection and flexibility", in *International Labour Review*, Vol. 136, No. 1, pp. 5–27.

Brosnan, P. 1978. "Industrial relations teaching at Victoria University of Wellington", in D. Turkington (ed.): *Proceedings of the Australia and New Zealand Conference of Teachers of Industrial Relations, 10–12 May 1978* (Wellington, Victoria University of Wellington, Industrial Relations Centre), pp. 116–21.

Brown, D. 2001. "Labor standards: Where do they belong on the international trade agenda?", in *Journal of Economic Perspectives*, Vol. 15, No. 3, pp. 89–103.

Brown, H.P. 1959. *Growth of British industrial relations: A study from the standpoint of 1906–1914* (London, St. Martin's Press).

Brown, J.; Knight, A. 1992. *The Mexican petroleum industry in the twentieth century* (Austin, University of Texas Press).

Brown, J.A.C. 1954. *The social psychology of industry: Human relations in the factory* (New York, Penguin).

Brown, J.D. 1976. *The Industrial Relations Section of Princeton University in World War II: A personal account* (Princeton, Princeton University, Industrial Relations Section).

Brown, R. 1981. "Sociologists and industry: In search of a distinctive competence", in *Sociological Review*, Vol. 29, No. 2, pp. 217–35.

Brown, W. 1973. *Piecework bargaining* (London, Heinemann).

——. 1978. "Transforming the miraculous into the natural: Current trends in industrial relations research in Britain", in D. Turkington (ed.): *Proceedings of the Australia and New Zealand Conference of Teachers of Industrial Relations, 10–12 May 1978* (Wellington, Victoria University of Wellington, Industrial Relations Centre), pp. 1–23.

——. 1993. "The contraction of collective bargaining in Britain", in *British Journal of Industrial Relations*, Vol. 31, No. 2, pp. 189–200.

——. 1997. "The high tide of consensus, *The system of industrial relations in Great Britain* (1954) revisited", in *Historical Studies in Industrial Relations*, Vol. 4, Sep., pp. 135–49.

——. 1998. "Funders and research: The vulnerability of the subject", in Whitfield and Strauss (eds.), 1998, pp. 267–86.

——. 2000. "Putting partnership into practice in Britain", in *British Journal of Industrial Relations*, Vol. 38, No. 2, pp. 299–316.

——; Wright, M. 1994. "The empirical tradition in workplace bargaining research", in *British Journal of Industrial Relations*, Vol. 32, No. 2, pp. 153–64.

Bruce, K. 2004. "Early labour economics: Its links to applied management", unpublished paper (Bristol Business School, University of the West of England).

Budd, J. 2004. *Employment with a human face: Balancing efficiency, equity, and voice* (Ithaca, Cornell University Press).

Bugler, J. 1968. "The new Oxford group", in *New Society*, Vol. 15, Feb., pp. 221–2.

Burawoy, M. 1979. *Manufacturing consent: Changes in the labor process under monopoly capitalism* (Chicago, University of Chicago Press).

Burns, T. 1967. "The sociology of industry", in A. Welford et al. (eds.): *Society: Problems and methods of study* (London, Routledge), pp. 188–218.

Burton, J.; Mitchell, D. 2003. "Employee benefits and social insurance: The welfare side of employee relations", in B. Kaufman, R. Beaumont and R. Helfgott (eds.), 2003, pp. 172–219.

Busch, G. 1983. *The political role of international trade unions* (New York, St. Martin's Press).

Butler, H. 1927. *Industrial relations in the United States*, Series A, No. 27 (Geneva, ILO).

Cain, G. 1976. "The challenge of segmented labor market theories to orthodox theory: A survey", in *Journal of Economic Literature*, Vol. 14, Dec., pp. 1215–57.

——. 1993. "Labor economics", in R. Lampman (ed.): *Economists at Wisconsin: 1892–1992* (Madison, University of Wisconsin, Department of Economics), pp. 234–46.

Caine, S. 1963. *The history of the foundation of the London School of Economics and Political Science* (London, Bell & Sons).

Caire, G. 1973. *Les relations industrielles* (Paris, Dalloz).

——. 1996. "Forces et faiblesses de l'approche française des relations industrielles: Mise en perspective historique", in Murray, Morin and da Costa (eds.), 1996, pp. 24–63.

Caldera, R. 1939. *Derecho del trabajo* (Caracas, Tipografia la Nación).

Callus, R. 1991. "The making of the Australian workplace industrial relations survey", in *Journal of Industrial Relations*, Vol. 31, Dec., pp. 450–67.

——— ; Morehead, R.; Cully, A.; Buchanan, J. 1991. *Industrial relations at work* (Canberra, AGPS).

Campbell, J. 1989. *Joy in work, German work* (Princeton, Princeton University Press).

Cappelli, P. 1985. "Theory construction in IR and some implications for research", in *Industrial Relations*, Vol. 24, No. 1, pp. 90–112.

——— . 1991. "Is there a future for the field of industrial relations in the United States?", in R. Lansbury (ed.): *Industrial relations teaching and research: International trends* (Sydney, ACIRRT, University of Sydney), pp. 3–40.

Carey, H. 1837. *Principles of political economy* (Philadelphia, Carey, Lea, and Blanchard).

Carmi, O. 2003. Telephone interview.

Carnegie, A. 1884. *The gospel of wealth* (Garden City, Doubleday).

Carreras, S. 1899. *Cuestiones sociales* (Buenos Aires).

Carrière, J.; Haworth, N.; Roddick, J. 1989. *The State, industrial relations and the labor movement in Latin America*, Vol. 1 (New York, St. Martin's Press).

Cella, G. 1995. "Between conflict and institutionalization: Italian industrial relations in the 1980s and early 1990s", in *European Journal of Industrial Relations*, Vol. 1, No. 3, pp. 385–404.

——— ; Treu, T. 1982. *Relazioni industriali: Manuale per l'analisi dell'esperienza italiana* (Bologna, il Mulino).

Chamberlain, N. 1948. *The union challenge to management control* (New York, Harper).

——— . 1951. *Collective bargaining* (New York, McGraw-Hill).

——— . 1960. "Issues for the future", in IRRA: *Proceedings of the Thirteenth Annual Meeting* (Madison), pp. 101–9.

——— . 1961. "Review of *Industrialism and industrial man*", in *American Economic Review*, Vol. 51, June, pp. 475–80.

——— ; Kuhn, J. 1965. *Collective bargaining*, 2nd ed. (New York, McGraw-Hill).

Champlin, D.; Knoedler, J. (eds.). 2004. *The institutional tradition in labor economics* (Armonk, M.E. Sharpe).

Charles, R. 1973. *The development of industrial relations in Britain 1911–1939* (London, Hutchison).

Chasse, D. 2004. "John R. Commons and his students: The view from the end of the twentieth century", in Champlin and Knoedler (eds.), 2004.

Chaykowski, R.; Weber, C. 1993. "Alternative models of industrial relations graduate programs in Canadian and US universities", in *Relations Industrielles/Industrial Relations*, Vol. 48, No. 1, pp. 86–98.

Chester, N. 1986. *Economics, politics, and social studies in Oxford, 1900–1985* (London, Macmillan).

Child, J. 1969. *British management thought* (London, Allen & Unwin).

Ching, C. 1953. *Review and reflection* (New York, Forbes).

Church, R. 1974. "Economists as experts: The rise of an academic profession in America 1870–1917", in L. Stone (ed.): *The university in society*, Vol. II (Princeton, Princeton University Press), pp. 571–610.

Clay, H. 1929. *The problem of industrial relations, and other lectures* (London, Macmillan).

_____ . 1930. *Report on industrial relations in Southern Rhodesia* (Salisbury, Government Printer).

Clegg, H. 1972. *The system of industrial relations in Great Britain*, 2nd ed. (Oxford, Basil Blackwell).

_____ . 1975. "Pluralism in industrial relations", in *British Journal of Industrial Relations*, Vol. 13, No. 3, pp. 309–16.

_____ . 1976. *Trade unionism under collective bargaining* (Oxford, Basil Blackwell).

_____ . 1979. *The changing system of industrial relations in Great Britain* (London, Basil Blackwell.

_____ . 1983. "Otto Kahn-Freund and British industrial relations", in L. Wedderburn, R. Lewis and J. Clark (eds.): *Labour law and industrial relations: Building on Kahn-Freund* (Oxford, Clarendon Press), pp. 14–28.

_____ . 1985. *A history of British trade unions since 1889* (Oxford, Clarendon Press).

_____ . 1990. "The Oxford School of Industrial Relations", Warwick Papers in Industrial Relations (Coventry, Industrial Relations Research Unit).

Clower, R.; Howitt, P. 1997. "Foundations and economics", in A. d'Autume (ed.): *Is economics becoming a hard science?* (Brookfield, Edward Elgar), pp. 17–34.

Coase, R. 1937. "The nature of the firm", in *Economica*, Vol. 4, Nov., pp. 386–405.

Cochrane, J. 1979. *Industrialism and industrial man in retrospect* (Ann Arbor, University of Michigan Press).

Coghlan, T. 1918. *Labour and industry in Australia* (London, Oxford University Press).

Cohen, L. 1990. *Making a new deal: Industrial workers in Chicago, 1919–1939* (New York, Columbia University Press).

Cole, D. 1956. "Improving labour–management co-operation: A proposed plan of action for the International Labour Office", in *International Labour Review*, Vol. 73, No. 5, pp. 483–500.

Cole, G.D.H. 1918. *An introduction to trade unionism* (London, Allen & Unwin).

_____ . 1925. *Short history of the British working class movement* (London, Allen & Unwin).

_____ . 1929. *The next ten years of British social and economic policy* (London, Macmillan).

Cole, R. 1989. *Strategies for learning: Small-group activities in American, Japanese, and Swedish industry* (Berkeley, University of California Press).

Commons, J. 1909. "American shoemakers, 1648–1895", in *Quarterly Journal of Economics*, Vol. 24, No. 4, pp. 39–83.

_____ . 1911. "Organized labor's attitude toward industrial efficiency", in *American Economic Review*, Vol. 1, Sep., pp. 463–72.

_____ . 1913. *Labor and administration* (New York, Macmillan).

_____ . 1918. *History of labor in the United States*, Vols. 1 and 2 (New York, Macmillan).

_____ . 1919a. "Labor demands secure jobs", newspaper article, reel 19 of the John R. Commons Papers, microfilm version (Madison, State Historical Society of Wisconsin).

_____ . 1919b. *Industrial goodwill* (New York, McGraw-Hill).

_____ . 1920. "Management and unionism", in IRRA: *Proceedings of the Industrial Relations Association of America* (Chicago).

_____ . 1921a. *Trade unionism and labor problems*, 2nd series (New York, Augustus Kelley).

_____ . 1921b. *Industrial government* (New York, Macmillan).

——. 1922. "Tendencies in trade union development in the United States", in *International Labour Review*, Vol. 5, No. 6, pp. 855–87.

——. 1924. *Legal foundations of capitalism* (New York, Macmillan).

——. 1934a. *Institutional economics: Its place in political economy* (New York, Macmillan).

——. 1934b. *Myself* (Madison, University of Wisconsin Press).

——. 1950. *The economics of collective action* (Madison, University of Wisconsin Press).

——; Andrews, J. 1916. *Principles of labor legislation*, 4th ed. (New York, Harper, 1936).

——; Phillips, U.; Gilmore, E.; Sumner, H.; Andrews, J. 1910. *A documentary history of American industrial society* (New York, Arthur Clark).

Compa, L.; Diamond, S. 1996. *Human rights, labor rights, and international trade* (Philadelphia, University of Philadelphia Press).

Comte de Paris, Louis-Philippe-Albert d'Orléans. 1869. *The trades unions of England* (London, Smith, Elder and Company).

Conner, V. 1983. *The National War Labor Board: Stability, social justice, and the voluntary state in World War I* (Chapel Hill, University of North Carolina Press).

Conrad, W. 1981. "Federal Republic of Germany", in A. Blum (ed.): *International handbook of industrial relations* (Westport, CT, Greenwood Press), pp. 209–38.

Cook, M. 1998. "Toward flexible industrial relations? Neo-liberalism, democracy, and labor reform in Latin America", in *Industrial Relations*, Vol. 37, No. 3, pp. 311–36.

Cooney, S. 1999. "Testing times for the ILO: Institutional reform for the new international economy", in *Comparative Labor Law and Policy Journal*, Vol. 20, No. 3, pp. 365–99.

Cooper, L. 1932. "The American labor movement in prosperity and depression", in *American Economic Review*, Vol. 22, Dec., pp. 641–59.

Cowdrick, E. 1924. "The expanding field of industrial relations", in *American Management Review*, Dec., pp. 3–5.

Cox, R. 1971a. "International labor in crisis", in *Foreign Affairs*, Vol. 49, No. 3, pp. 519–33 (signed as N.M.).

——. 1971b. "Approaches to the futurology of industrial relations", in *Bulletin of the Institute of Labour Studies*, Vol. 8, pp. 139–64.

——. 1971c. "Approaches to a futurology of industrial relations on a global scale", in *Proceedings of the 1971 Asian Regional Conference on Industrial Relations* (Tokyo, Japan Institute of Labor), pp. 275–98.

——. 1974. "ILO, limited monarchy", in R. Cox and H. Jacobson (eds.): *The anatomy of influence: Decision making in international organizations* (New Haven, Yale University Press), pp. 102–38.

——. 2003. "Note concerning the origins and early years of the IIRA", personal correspondence.

——; Harrod, J. 1972. *Future industrial relations: An interim report* (Geneva, International Institute for Labour Studies).

——; Sinclair, T. 1996. *Approaches to world order* (Cambridge, Cambridge University Press).

Craig, A.W.J. 1983. *The system of industrial relations in Canada* (Scarborough, Ontario, Prentice-Hall).

Craig, J. 1984. *Scholarship and nation building* (Chicago, University of Chicago Press).

Crispo, J. 1978a. *The Canadian industrial relations system* (Toronto, McGraw-Hill).

———. 2003. Telephone interview.

Crouch, C. 1993. *Industrial relations and European state traditions* (Oxford, Clarendon Press).

———. 1995. "Exit or voice: Two paradigms for European industrial relations after the Keynesian welfare state", in *European Journal of Industrial Relations*, Vol. 1, No. 1, pp. 63–81.

———; Pizzorno, A. 1978. *The resurgence of class conflict in Europe since 1968* (London, Holmes and Meier).

———; Streeck, W. 1997. *Political economy of modern capitalism* (London, Sage).

Crouzet, F. 2001. *A history of the European economy, 1000–2000* (Charlottesville, University of Virginia Press).

Cummings, L. 1982. "Comment", in *Industrial Relations*, Vol. 21, No. 1, pp. 78–83.

Cummins, E.; DeVyver, F. 1947. *The labor problem in the United States* (New York, Van Nostrand).

Da Costa, I. 1996. "L'étude des relations industrielles, passé, présent, avenir", in Murray, Morin and da Costa (eds.), 1996, pp. 106–20.

———. 2003. "Notes on the industrial relations field in France", unpublished correspondence.

Dabscheck, B. 1980. "The Australian system of industrial relations: An analytical model", in *Journal of Industrial Relations*, Vol. 22, No. 2, pp. 196–218.

———. 1989. *Australian industrial relations in the 1980s* (Oxford, Oxford University Press).

———. 1994. "A new province for law and order: The Australian experiment with industrial tribunals", in J. Niland, R. Lansbury and C. Verevis (eds.): *The future of industrial relations: Global change and challenges* (London, Sage), pp. 63–75.

———. 1995. *The struggle for Australian industrial relations* (Oxford, Oxford University Press).

Dahrendorf, R. 1959. *Class and class conflict in industrial societies* (Stanford, Stanford University Press).

———. 1995. *LSE: A history of the London School of Economics and Political Science* (Oxford, Oxford University Press).

Damachi, U. 1985. *Industrial relations: A development dilemma* (Lagos, Lagos University Press).

Daniel, C. 1998. *The MBA: The first decade* (Lewisburg, PA, Bucknell University Press).

Davidson, R. 1985. *Whitehall and the labour problem in late-Victorian and Edwardian Britain* (London, Croom Helm).

Davies, P.; Freedland, M. 2002. "National styles in labor law scholarship: The United Kingdom", in *Comparative Labor Law and Policy Journal*, Vol. 23, No. 3, pp. 765–88.

Dávila, C.; Miller, R. 1999. *Business history in Latin America: The experiences of seven countries* (Liverpool, Liverpool University Press).

Davis, H. 1950. *Social science trends in Latin America* (Washington, DC, American University Press).

Davis, L. 1966. "The design of jobs", in *Industrial Relations*, Vol. 6, No. 1, pp. 21–45.

Dawson, K. 1972. *The Industrial Revolution* (London, Pan).

Dawson, W. 1973. *Bismarck and state socialism* (New York, Fertig).

Debs, E. 1948. *The writings and speeches of Eugene V. Debs* (New York, Hermitage Press).

De la Garza Toledo, E. 2002. "Mexico", in D. Cornfield and R. Hodson (eds.): *Worlds of work: Building an international sociology of work* (New York, Kluwer), pp. 69–86.

Delaney, J.; Godard, J. 2001. "An industrial relations perspective on the high-performance workplace", in *Human Resource Management Review*, Vol. 11, No. 4, pp. 395–430.

Denker, J. 1981. *Unions and universities: The rise of the new labor leader* (Montclair, NJ, Allanheld, Osmun).

Dennison, H. 1935. "Testimony", in National Labor Relations Board: *Legislative hearings on the National Labor Relations Act, 1935* (Washington, DC, Government Printing Office, 1985).

Derber, M. 1967. *Research in labor problems in the United States* (New York, Random House).

——. 1970. *The American idea of industrial democracy* (Urbana-Champaign, University of Illinois Press).

——. 1982. "Comment", in *Industrial Relations*, Vol. 21, No. 1, pp. 84–91.

——; Young, E. 1957. *Labor and the New Deal* (Madison, University of Wisconsin Press).

Derossi, F. 1971. *The Mexican entrepreneur* (Paris, OECD).

Desmarez, P. 2002. "France–Belgium", in D. Cornfield and R. Hodson (eds.): *Worlds of work: Building an international sociology of work* (New York, Kluwer), pp. 201–20.

Devanna, M.; Fombrun, C.; Tichy, N.; Warren, L. 1982. "Strategic planning and human resource management", in *Human Resource Management*, Vol. 21, spring, pp. 11–16.

Deveali, M. 1953. "La empresa y las relaciones de trabajo", in *Derecho del Trabajo*, Vol. 13, pp. 321–40.

Dickman, H. 1987. *Industrial democracy in America* (LaSalle, IL, Open Court).

Disraeli, B. 1845. *Sybil: Or the two nations* (London, Colburn).

Doeringer, P.; Piore, M. 1971. *Internal labor markets and manpower analysis* (Lexington, Lexington Books).

Domhoff, W. 1990. *The power elite and the state: How policy is made in America* (New York, Aldine de Gruyter).

——. 1996. *State autonomy or class dominance: Case studies on policy making in America* (New York, Aldine de Gruyter).

Donnelly, J. 1935 "Testimony", in National Labor Relations Board: *Legislative hearings on the National Labor Relations Act, 1935* (Washington, DC, Government Printing Office, 1985).

Dore, R. 1973. *British factory–Japanese factory: The origins of national diversity in industrial relations* (Berkeley, University of California Press).

——. 2000. *Stock market capitalism: Welfare capitalism, Japan and Germany versus the Anglo-Saxons* (Oxford, Oxford University Press).

Dorfman, J. 1959. *The economic mind in American civilization 1918–1933*, Vol. 4 (New York, Viking).

Doshi, K. 1993. "India", in M. Rothman et al. (eds.): *Industrial relations around the world* (Berlin, de Gruyter), pp. 173–86.

Douglas, P. 1934. *The theory of wages* (New York, Macmillan).

Dow, G. 1997. "The new institutional economics and employment regulation", in B. Kaufman (ed.): *Government regulation of the employment relationship* (Madison, IRRA), pp. 57–90.

Drucker, P. 1954. *The practice of management* (New York, Harper).

Dufour, C.; Hege, A. 1997. "The transformation of French industrial relations: Glorification of the enterprise and disaffection on the streets", in *European Journal of Industrial Relations*, Vol. 3, No. 3, pp. 333–56.

Dulebohn, J.; Ferris, G.; Stodd, J. 1995. "The history and evolution of human resource management", in G. Ferris, S. Rosen and J. Stodd (eds.): *Handbook of human resource management* (New York, Blackwell), pp. 18–41.

Dunlop, J. 1950. "Framework for the analysis of industrial relations: Two views", in *Industrial and Labor Relations Review*, Vol. 3, No. 3, pp. 383–93.

——. 1954. "Research in industrial relations: Past and future", in IRRA: *Proceedings of the Seventh Annual Meeting* (Madison), pp. 92–101.

——. 1958. *Industrial relations systems* (New York, Holt).

——. 1960. "Consensus and national labor policy", in IRRA: *Proceedings of the Thirteenth Annual Meeting* (Madison), pp. 2–17.

——. 1961. *The potential of the American economy: Essays in honor of Sumner H. Slichter* (Cambridge, MA, Harvard University Press).

——. 1977. "Policy decisions and research in economics and industrial relations", in *Industrial and Labor Relations Review*, Vol. 30, No. 3, pp. 275–82.

——. 1988. "Labor markets and wage determination: Then and now", in B. Kaufman (ed.): *How labor markets work: Reflections on theory and practice by John Dunlop, Clark Kerr, Richard Lester, and Lloyd Reynolds* (Lexington, Lexington Books), pp. 47–87.

——. 1993. *Industrial relations systems*, revised ed. (Cambridge, MA, Harvard Business School Press).

——. 1994. "Organizations and human resources: Internal and external markets", in C. Kerr and P. Staudohar (eds.): *Labor economics and industrial relations: Market and institutions* (Cambridge, MA, Harvard University Press), pp. 375–400.

——. 2003. Personal interview.

——; Harbison, F.; Kerr, C.; Myers, C. 1975. *Industrialism and industrial man reconsidered* (Princeton, Inter-University Study of Labor Problems in Economic Development).

Dunn, R. 1926. *American company unions* (Chicago, Trade Union Educational League).

Dunn, S. 1990. "Root metaphor in the old and new industrial relations", in *British Journal of Industrial Relations*, Vol. 28, No. 1, pp. 1–31.

——. 1993. "From Donovan to ... wherever", in *British Journal of Industrial Relations*, Vol. 31, No. 2, pp. 169–87.

Dunnette, M.; Bass, B. 1963. "Behavioral scientists and personnel management", in *Industrial Relations*, Vol. 3, No. 2, pp. 115–30.

Durkheim, E. 1893. *The division of labor in society* (New York, Free Press).

Eberwein, W.; Tholen, J.; Schuster, J. 2002. *The Europeanization of industrial relations: National and European processes in Germany, United Kingdom, Italy, and France* (Burlington, Ashgate).

Ebke, W.; Finkin, M. (eds.). 1996. *Introduction to German law* (New York, Kluwer).

Economic Commission for Latin America. 1968. *Education, human resources and development in Latin America* (New York, United Nations).

Edwards, P. 1995. "From industrial relations to the employment relationship", in *Relations Industrielles/Industrial Relations*, Vol. 50, No. 1, pp. 39–65.

———. 2003a. "The future of industrial relations", in P. Ackers and A. Wilkinson (eds.): *Understanding work and employment* (Oxford, Oxford University Press), pp. 337–58.

———. 2003b. "The promising future of industrial relations: Developing the connections between theory and relevance", paper presented at the 2003 meeting of the British University Industrial Relations Association.

———. 2003c. "The employment relationship and the field of industrial relations", in P. Edwards (ed.): *Industrial relations: Theory and practice*, 2nd ed. (London, Blackwell), pp. 1–36.

———; Scullion, H. 1982. *The social organization of industrial conflict* (Cambridge, Blackwell Business).

Edwards, R. 1979. *Contested terrain: The transformation of work in the twentieth century* (New York, Basic Books).

Eisner, J.M. 1967. *William Morris Leiserson: A biography* (Madison, University of Wisconsin Press).

Ekelund, R.; Hébert, R. 1997. *A history of economic theory and method* (New York, McGraw-Hill).

Elvander, N. 2002. *Industrial relations: A short history of ideas and learning* (Stockholm, National Institute for Working Life).

Ely, R. 1886. *The labor movement in America* (New York, Thomas Crowell).

———. 1938. *Ground under our feet: An autobiography* (New York, Macmillan).

Endres, A.; Fleming, G. 1996. "International economic policy in the interwar years: The special contribution of ILO economists", in *International Labour Review*, Vol. 135, No. 2, pp. 207–225.

Endruweit, G.; Gaugler, E.; Staehle, W.H.; Wilpert, B. 1985. *Handbuch der Arbeitsbeziehungen: Deutschland, Österreich, Schweiz* (Berlin, de Gruyter).

Engels, C.; Weiss, M. 1998. *Labour law and industrial relations at the turn of the century* (London, Kluwer).

Engerman, S. 2003. "The evolution of labor standards", in K. Basu, H. Horn, L. Román and J. Shapiro (eds.): *International labor standards: History, theory, and policy options* (London, Blackwell), pp. 7–83.

Engles, F. 1844. *The condition of the working class in England in 1844* (New York, Lovell).

Epstein, E. 1989. *Labor autonomy and the state in Latin America* (Boston, Unwin Hyman).

Esping-Andersen, G. 1985. *Politics against markets: The social democratic road to power* (Princeton, Princeton University Press).

Estey, J. 1928. *The Labor Problem* (New York, McGraw-Hill).

European Industrial Relations Observatory. 2002. *Towards a qualitative dialogue in industrial relations* (Dublin).

Evans, R. 1982. *The German working class, 1888–1933* (New York, Barnes and Noble).

Ewing, K. 2003. "Labour law and industrial relations", in P. Ackers and A. Wilkinson (eds.): *Understanding work and employment* (Oxford, Oxford University Press), pp. 138–60.

Farber, H.; Western, B. 2002. "Accounting for the decline of unions in the private sector", in J. Bennett and B. Kaufman (eds.): *The future of private sector unionism in the United States* (Armonk, M.E. Sharpe), pp. 28–58.

Fashoyin, T. 1980. *Industrial relations in Nigeria: Development and practice* (London, Longman).

———. 1992. *Industrial relations and African development* (New Delhi, South Asian Publishers).

———. 2003. "The development of the field of industrial relations in Africa", unpublished paper.

Faucher, A. 1988. *Cinquante ans de sciences sociales à l'Université Laval: L'histoire de la faculté de sciences sociales, 1938–1988* (Sainte-Foy, Quebec, Laval University).

Federal Task Force on Part I of the Canada Labour Code. 1996. *Seeking a balance* (Ottawa, Minister of Public Works and Government Services).

Feis, H. 1927. "International labor legislation in the light of economic theory", in *International Labour Review*, Vol. 15, No. 4, pp. 491–518.

Ferner, A.; Hyman, R. 1992. *Industrial relations in the New Europe* (London, Blackwell).

———. 1998. *Changing industrial relations in Europe*, 2nd ed. (London, Blackwell).

Ferris, G.; Barnum, B.; Rosen, S.; Holleran, L.; Dulebohn, J. 1995. "Toward business–university partnerships in human resource management: Integration of science and practice", in G. Ferris, S. Rosen and D. Barnum (eds.): *Handbook of human resource management* (New York, Blackwell), pp. 1–16.

Feuer, L. 1959. *Marx and Engels: Basic writings on politics and philosophy* (New York, Doubleday).

Findlay, J. 1921. "Industrial peace in New Zealand", in *International Labour Review*, Vol. 4, No. 1, pp. 32–45.

Fine, M. 1972. "Toward corporatism: The movement for labor–capital collaboration in France, 1914–1936", unpublished Ph.D. dissertation (Madison, University of Wisconsin).

Fine, S. 1956. *Laissez-faire and the general-welfare state* (Ann Arbor, University of Michigan Press).

———. 1995. *Without blare of trumpets* (Ann Arbor, University of Michigan Press).

Fischer, W. 1973. "Social tensions at early states of industrialization", in J. Sheehan (ed.): *Industrialization and industrial labor in nineteenth-century Europe* (New York, Wiley), pp. 101–19.

Fisher, D. 1993. *Fundamental development of the social sciences: Rockefeller philanthropy and the United States Social Science Research Council* (Ann Arbor, University of Michigan Press).

Fishlow, A. 1988. "The state of Latin American economics", in C. Mitchell (ed.): *Changing perspectives in Latin American studies: Insights from six disciplines* (Stanford, Stanford University Press), pp. 87–120.

Fitzgerald, R. 1988. *British labour management and industrial welfare, 1846–1939* (London, Croom Helm).

Flanders, A. 1964. *The Fawley productivity agreements* (London, Faber and Faber).

———. 1965. *Industrial relations: What is wrong with the system? An essay on its theory and future* (London, Faber and Faber).

———. 1968. "Collective bargaining: A theoretical analysis", in *British Journal of Industrial Relations*, Vol. 6, No. 1, pp. 1–26.

———. 1970. *Management and unions* (London, Faber and Faber).

———; Clegg, H. (eds.). 1954. *The system of industrial relations in Great Britain* (Oxford, Basil Blackwell).

Fleddérus, M. 1930. *Rational organization and industrial relations: A symposium of views from management, labour and the social sciences* (The Hague, International Industrial Relations Institute).

———. 1932. *World economic planning: The necessity for planned adjustment of production capacity and standards of living* (The Hague, International Industrial Relations Institute).

Flexner, A. 1930. *Universities: American, English, German* (New York, Oxford University Press).

Floud, R.; McCloskey, D. 1994. *The economic history of Britain since 1700: Vol. 2, 1860–1939*, 2nd ed. (New York, Cambridge University Press).

Foenander, O. de. 1928. "The forty-four hours case in Australia, 1926–27", in *Quarterly Journal of Economics*, Vol. 23, pp. 307–27.

———. 1937. *Towards industrial peace in Australia* (Melbourne, University Press).

———. 1954. *Better employment relations and other essays in labour* (Sydney, Law Book Co. of Australia).

Fogarty, M. 1955. "Industrial relations: Studies in the Universities", in *The Times Review of Industry*, Jan., pp. 17–18.

———. 1957. *Christian Democracy in Western Europe 1820–1953* (Notre Dame, IN, University of Notre Dame Press).

Fohlen, C. 1978. "Entrepreneurship and management in France in the nineteenth century", in P. Mathias and M. Postan (eds.): *The Cambridge economic history of Europe*, Vol. VII (London, Cambridge University Press), pp. 347–81.

Follett, M. 1925a. "Psychological foundations: Business as an integrative unity", in H. Metcalf (ed.): *Scientific foundations of business administration* (Baltimore, Williams and Wilkins), pp. 150–70.

———. 1925b. "Psychological foundations: Constructive conflict", in H. Metcalf (ed.): *Scientific foundations of business administration* (Baltimore, Williams and Wilkins), pp. 114–31.

Follows, J. 1951. *Antecedents of the International Labour Organization* (Oxford, Clarendon Press).

Fones-Wolf, E. 1994. *Selling free enterprise: The business assault on labor and liberalism, 1945–60* (Urbana, University of Illinois Press).

Foulkes, F. 1975. "The expanding role of the personnel function", in *Harvard Business Review*, Vol. 53, No. 2, pp. 71–84.

———. 1980. *Personnel policies at large nonunion companies* (Englewood Cliffs, Prentice-Hall).

Fox, A. 1966. *Industrial sociology and industrial relations*, Royal Commission on Trade Unions and Employers' Associations Research Papers 3 (London, Her Majesty's Stationery Office).

———. 1973. "Industrial relations: A social critique of pluralist ideology", in J. Child (ed.): *Man and organization* (London, Allen & Unwin), pp. 185–233.

———. 1974. *Beyond contract: Work, power, and trust relations* (London, Faber and Faber).

———. 1985. *History and heritage: The social origins of the British industrial relations system* (London, Allen & Unwin).

———. 1990. *A very late development: An autobiography* (Chippenham, Wiltshire, Antony Rowe).

Franke, W. 1987. "Accommodating to change: Can IR learn from itself?", in IRRA: *Proceedings of the Fortieth Annual Meeting* (Madison), pp. 474–81.

Freeman, R. 1992. "Is declining unionization of the United States good, bad, or irrelevant?", in L. Mishel and P. Voos (eds.): *Unions and economic competitiveness* (Armonk, M.E. Sharpe), pp. 143–72.

——. 1998. "Spurts in union growth: Defining moments and social processes", in M. Bordo, C. Goldin and E. White (eds.): *The Great Depression and the American economy in the twentieth century* (Chicago, University of Chicago Press), pp. 265–96.

——; Medoff, J. 1984. *What do unions do?* (New York, Basic Books).

——; Rogers, J. 1999. *What workers want* (Ithaca, Cornell University Press).

Frege, C. 2002. "Scientific knowledge production in the United States and Germany: The case of industrial relations research", in *Comparative Labor Law and Policy Journal*, Vol. 23, No. 3, pp. 865–94.

——. 2003. "Industrial relations in Continental Europe", in P. Ackers and A. Wilkinson (eds.): *Understanding work and employment* (Oxford, Oxford University Press), pp. 242–64.

French, J. 2000. "The Latin American labor studies boom", in *International Review of Social History*, Vol. 45, pp. 279–308.

——. 2003. "The laboring and middle-class peoples of Latin America and the Caribbean: Historical trajectories and new research directions", unpublished paper (Raleigh, Duke University).

French, W. 1964. *The personnel management process: Human resources administration* (New York, Houghton Mifflin).

Frey, B.; Eichenberger, R. 1992. "Economics and economists: A European perspective", in *American Economic Review*, Vol. 82, No. 2, pp. 216–20.

——; Frey, R. 1995. "Is there a European economics?", in *Kyklos*, Vol. 48, No. 2, pp. 185–6.

Fried, A. 1987. *Industrial Relations Research Institute: A brief history, 1947–1987* (Madison, University of Wisconsin, Industrial Relations Research Institute).

Friedlaender, H.; Oser, J. 1953. *Economic history of Europe* (New York, Prentice-Hall).

Friedman, M. 1953. *Essays in positive economics* (Chicago, University of Chicago Press).

Furner, M. 1975. *Advocacy and objectivity: A crisis in the professionalization of American social science, 1865–1905* (Lexington, University of Kentucky Press).

Furniss, E. 1925. *Labor problems* (Boston, Houghton Mifflin).

Fürstenberg, F. von. 1969. "Industrial relations", in *Woerterbuch der soziologie* (Stuttgart, Enke), pp. 451–3.

——. 1975. *Industrielle Arbeitsbeziehungen: Untersuchungen zu Interessenlagen und Interessenvertretungen in der Modern Arbeitswelt* (Vienna, Manz).

Furubotn, E.; Richter, R. 1997. *Institutions and economic theory* (Ann Arbor, University of Michigan Press).

Fusfeld, D. 1956. *The economic thought of Franklin D. Roosevelt and the origins of the New Deal* (New York, Columbia University Press).

Fynes, R. 1873. *The miners of Northumberland and Durham* (Blyth, Northumberland, Richardson).

Galenson, W. 1981. *The International Labour Organization: An American view* (Madison, University of Wisconsin Press).

Galin, A. 1993. "Israel", in M. Rothman et al. (eds.): *Industrial relations around the world* (Berlin, de Gruyter), pp. 187–205.

Garon, S. 1996. "Social knowledge and the State in industrial relations of Japan (1882–1940) and Great Britain (1870–1914)", in D. Rueschemeyer and T. Skopcol (eds.): *States, social knowledge, and the origins of modern social policies* (Princeton, Princeton University Press), pp. 264–95.

Geare, A.J. 1977. "The field of study of industrial relations", in *New Zealand Journal of Industrial Relations*, Vol. 19, Sep., pp. 274–85.

——. 2004. Personal interview.

Geary, D. 1981. *European labour protest, 1848–1939* (New York, St. Martin's Press).

Geck, L.H.A. 1931. *Die Sozialen Arbeitsverhältnisse im Wandel der Zeit* (Berlin, Springer).

Gemelli, G. 1996. "American influence on European management education: The role of the Ford Foundation", in R. Amdam (ed.): *Management education and competitiveness: Europe, Japan, and the United States* (London, Routledge), pp. 38–68.

Gennard, J. 1986. "Ben Roberts: An appreciation", in *British Journal of Industrial Relations*, Vol. 24, No. 1, pp. 3–23.

Ghebali, V.Y. 1989. *The International Labour Organization: A case study on the evolution of UN specialized agencies* (Boston, Martinus Nijhoff).

Gibb, G.; Knowlton, E. 1956. *The resurgent years: 1911–1927* (New York, Harper & Bros.).

Gilbert, R. 1993. "Workplace industrial relations 25 years after Donovan: An employer's view", in *British Journal of Industrial Relations*, Vol. 31, No. 2, pp. 235–53.

Giles, A. 1989. "Industrial relations theory, the state, and politics", in J. Barbash and K. Barbash (eds.): *Theories and concepts in comparative industrial relations* (Columbia, University of South Carolina Press), pp. 123–53.

——; Bélanger, J. 2002. "Canada", in D. Cornfield and R. Hodson (eds.): *Worlds of work: Building an international sociology of work* (New York, Kluwer Academic), pp. 47–68.

——; Murray, G. 1988. "Toward an historical understanding of industrial relations theory in Canada", in *Relationelles Industrielles/Industrial Relations*, Vol. 43, No. 4, pp. 780–811.

——; ——. 1997. "Industrial relations theory and critical political economy", in Barbash and Meltz (eds.), 1997, pp. 77–120.

Gillespie, R. 1991. *Manufacturing knowledge: A history of the Hawthorne experiments* (Cambridge, Cambridge University Press).

Gillingham, J. 2000. "The many lives of the International Labour Organization (ILO)", in R. Tilly and P. Welfends (eds.): *Economic globalization, international organizations and crisis management* (Berlin, Springer-Verlag), pp. 237–54.

Gilman, N. 1899. *A dividend to labor: A study of employers' welfare institutions* (New York, Houghton Mifflin).

Gilson, M. 1940. *What's past is prologue: Reflections on my industrial experience* (New York, Harper).

Giri, V. 1959. *Labour problems in Indian industry* (New York, Asia Publishing House).

——. "Beginning of an era – I", in T. Papola et al.: *Labour, employment and industrial relations in India* (Delhi, B.R. Publishing), pp. 19–25.

Gislain, J.J. 1998. "Sismondi and the evolution of institutions", in G. Faccarello (ed.): *Studies in the history of French political economy* (London, Routledge), pp. 229–53.

Gitelman, H. 1988. *The legacy of the Ludlow Massacre: A chapter in American industrial relations* (Philadelphia, University of Pennsylvania Press).

Giugni, G. 1981. "The Italian system of industrial relations", in P. Doeringer et al. (eds.): *Industrial relations in international perspective* (New York, Holmes and Meier), pp. 324–64.

Gladstone, A. et al. 1989. *Current issues in labour relations: An international perspective* (Berlin, de Gruyter).

Glickman, L. 1997. *A living wage: American workers and the making of consumer society* (Ithaca, Cornell University Press).

Godard, J. 1998. "An organizational theory of variation in the management of labor", in D. Lewin and B. Kaufman (eds.): *Advances in industrial and labor relations*, Vol. 8 (Greenwich, CT, JAI Press), pp. 25–65.

——. 2000. *Industrial relations, the economy, and society*, 2nd ed. (New York, Captus Press).

Godfrey, M. 2003. *Employment dimensions of decent work: Trade-offs and complementarities*, Discussion Paper (Geneva, International Institute for Labour Studies).

Gold, M.; Weiss, M. 1999. *Employment and industrial relations in Europe* (Cambridge, MA, Kluwer Law International).

Goldthorpe, J. 1977. "Industrial relations in Great Britain: A critique of reformism", in T. Clarke and L. Clements (eds.): *Trade unions under capitalism* (London, Fontana), pp. 184–224.

Gonce, R. 1996. "The social gospel: Ely, and Commons' initial stage of thought", in *Journal of Economic Issues*, Vol. 30, No. 3, pp. 641–65.

Gordon, A. 1985. *The evolution of labor relations in Japan: Heavy industry, 1853–1955* (Cambridge, MA, Harvard University Press).

Gordon, C. 1994. *New deals: Business, labor, and politics in America, 1920–1935* (New York, Cambridge University Press).

Gordon, M. 1987. *The origins of the First World War* (London, Longmans).

Gordon, R.; Howell, J. 1959. *Higher education for business* (New York, Columbia University).

Gorz, A. 1976. "The tyranny of the factory, today and tomorrow", in A. Gorz (ed.): *The division of labor: The labor process and class-struggle in modern capitalism* (Atlantic Highlands, New Jersey, Humanities Press), pp. 55–62.

Gospel, H. 1983. "New managerial approaches to industrial relations; Major paradigms and historical perspectives", in *Journal of Industrial Relations*, Vol. 25, No. 2, pp. 162–76.

——. 1992. *Markets, firms, and the management of labour in modern Britain* (Cambridge, Cambridge University Press).

——; Palmer, G. 1993. *British industrial relations*, 2nd ed. (London, Routledge).

Gould, W. 2001. "Labor law for a global economy: The uneasy case for international labor standards", in *Nebraska Law Review*, Vol. 80, No. 4, pp. 715–53.

Gourevitch, P.; Lange, P.; Martin, A. 1981. "Industrial relations and politics", in P. Doeringer (ed.): *Industrial relations in international perspective* (New York, Holmes and Meier), pp. 401-16.

Grant, N. 1973. "Structure of higher education: Some international comparisons", in R. Bell and A. Youngson (eds.): *Present and future in higher education* (London, Tavistock), pp. 29–46.

Grebing, H. 1969. *The history of the German labour movement* (London, Wolff).

Greeley, H. 1856. *The Social Problem* (Boston, Shepherd, Clark).

Greene, A.M. 2003. "Women and industrial relations", in P. Ackers and A. Wilkinson (eds.): *Understanding work and employment* (Oxford, Oxford University Press), pp. 305–15.

Grinberg, L.L. 1991. *Split corporatism in Israel* (Albany, State University of New York).

Grossekettler, H. 1989. "On designing an economic order: The contributions of the Freiburg school", in D. Walker (ed.): *Perspectives on the history of economic thought, Volume II: Twentieth century economic thought* (Northampton, Edward Elgar), pp. 38–84.

Gruenberg, G.; Najita, J.; Nolan, D. 1997. *The National Academy of Arbitrators: Fifty years in the world of work* (Washington, DC, Bureau of National Affairs).

Guest, D. 1987. "Human resource management and industrial relations", in *Journal of Management Studies*, Vol. 24, pp. 503–21.

—. 1991. "Personnel management: The end of orthodoxy?", in *British Journal of Industrial Relations*, Vol. 29, No. 2, pp. 149–75.

—; Hoque, K. 1996. "Human resource management and the new industrial relations", in I. Beardwell (ed.): *Contemporary industrial relations: A critical analysis* (Oxford, Oxford University Press), pp. 11–36.

Guille, H.; Sappey, D.; Water, M. 1989. "Can industrial relations survive without unions?", in M. Bray and D. Kelly (eds.): *Issues and trends in Australasian industrial relations: Proceedings of the fourth biennial meeting of the AIRAANZ* (Wollongong, AIRAANZ), pp. 31–48.

Guillén, M. 1994. *Models of management: Work, authority, and organization in a comparative perspective* (Chicago, University of Chicago Press).

Guimarães, N.A.; de Paula Leite, M. 2002. "Brazil", in D. Cornfield and R. Hodson (eds.): *Worlds of work: Building an international sociology of work* (New York, Kluwer), pp. 23–46.

Gunderson, M. 2001. "The economics of human resource management", in *Human Resource Management Review*, Vol. 11, No. 4, pp. 431–52.

—; Ponak, A.; Taras, D. 2001. *Union–management relations in Canada*, 4th ed. (Toronto, Addison-Wesley).

—; Verma, A. 2003. "Industrial relations in the global economy", in B. Kaufman, R. Beaumont and R. Helfgott (eds.), 2003, pp. 330–52.

Günter, H.; Leminsky, G. 1978. "The Federal Republic of Germany", in J. Dunlop and W. Galenson (eds.): *Labor in the twentieth century* (New York, Academic Press), pp. 149–96.

Haas, E. 1964. *Beyond the nation state: Functionalism and international organization* (Stanford, Stanford University Press).

Haber, S. 1964. *Efficiency and uplift: Scientific management in the progressive era, 1890–1920* (Chicago, University of Chicago Press).

Hall, P.; Soskice, D. 2001. *Varieties of capitalism: The institutional foundations of comparative advantage* (Oxford, Oxford University Press).

Hamilton, A. 2000. "Max Weber's *Protestant ethic and the spirit of capitalism*", in S. Turner (ed.): *The Cambridge companion to Weber* (Cambridge, Cambridge University Press), pp. 151–71.

Hamilton, W. 1919. "The institutional approach to economic theory", in *American Economic Review*, Vol. 9, No. 1, pp. 309–18.

Hanami, T. 1971. "The role and functions of industrial relations centres in Japan", in *Sophia Law Review*, Vol. 14, No. 2, pp. 1–21.

———. 1994. "Industrial relations and the future of the ILO: Changing issues and actors", in International Labour Organization: *Visions of the future of social justice* (Geneva, ILO), pp. 125–8.

———. 2002a. "Was the modern labor law accepted in postwar Japan?", in *Comparative Labor Law and Policy Journal*, Vol. 23, No. 3, pp. 749–52.

———. 2002b. Telephone interview.

———. 2003. Telephone interview.

Hancock, K. 1998. "Joe Isaac", in *Journal of Industrial Relations*, Vol. 40, No. 4, pp. 483–507.

———; Rawson, D. 1993. "The metamorphosis of Australian industrial relations", in *British Journal of Industrial Relations*, Vol. 31, No. 4, pp. 489–513.

Hanke, J.; Mense-Petermann, U. 2001. "Industrial relations in the transformation process: The cases of Poland and the Czech Republic", in Széll (ed.), 2001, Vol. 2, pp. 131–48.

Hansenne. M. 1996. Cited in "Perspectives", in *International Labour Review*, Vol. 135, No. 2, pp. 225–38.

Harbison, F.; Ibrahim, I. 1958. *Human resources for Egyptian enterprises* (New York, McGraw-Hill).

Hardach, K. 1980. *The political economy of Germany in the twentieth century* (Berkeley, University of California Press).

Hardin, B. 1977. *The professionalization of sociology: A comparative study, Germany–USA* (New York, Campus-Verlag).

Hare, A.E.C. 1946. *Industrial relations in New Zealand* (London, J.M. Dent).

———. 1958. *The first principles of industrial relations* (London, Macmillan).

Harris, H. 1982. *The right to manage: Industrial relations policies of American business in the 1940s* (Madison, University of Wisconsin Press).

———. 2000. *Bloodless victory: The rise and fall of the open shop in the Philadelphia metal trades* (New York, Cambridge University Press).

Harris, J. 1977. *William Beveridge: A biography* (Oxford, Clarendon Press).

Harrison, R. 2000. *The life and times of Sidney and Beatrice Webb, 1858–1905: The formative years* (London, Palgrave).

Harvard University. 1929. *Wertheim lectures on industrial relations* (Cambridge, MA).

Harvey, C. 1982. "John D. Rockefeller, Jr., and the social sciences: An introduction", in *Journal of the History of Sociology*, Vol. 4, No. 2, pp. 1–31.

Hawkins, C. 1965. "The ORIT and the American trade-unions: Conflicting perspectives", in W. Form and A. Blum (eds.): *Industrial relations and social change in Latin America* (Gainesville, University of Florida Press), pp. 87–104.

Hawley, E. 1966. *The New Deal and the problem of monopoly: A study in economic ambivalence* (Princeton, Princeton University Press).

Hazama, H. 1997. *The history of labour management in Japan* (New York, St. Martin's Press).

Heclo, H. 1995. "The Social Question", in K. McFate et al. (eds.): *Poverty, inequality, and the future of social policy* (New York, Russell Sage), pp. 665–91.

Helfgott, R. 2003. "The United States in the 1920s: Breaking with European traditions", in B. Kaufman, R. Beaumont and R. Helfgott (eds.), 2003, pp. 19–30.

Heneman, H. 1968. "Contributions of current research", in IRRA: *The role of industrial relations centers: Proceedings of a Regional Meeting of the Industrial Relations Research Association* (Madison), pp. 49–58.

——. 1969. "Toward a general conceptual system of industrial relations: How do we get there?", in G. Somers (ed.): *Essays in industrial relations theory* (Ames, Iowa State University), pp. 3–24.

—— et al. 1960. *Employment relations research: A summary and appraisal* (Madison, IRRA).

Herbst, J. 1965. *The German historical school in American scholarship: A study in the transfer of culture* (Ithaca, Cornell University Press).

Herkner, H. 1895. *Die Arbeiterfrage* (Berlin, J. Gutentag).

Hetzler, H.W. 1995. "25 Jahre Deutsche Sektion der International Industrial Relations Association – Erinnerungen, Erfahrungen und Erwartungen", in *Industrielle Beziehungen*, Vol. 2, No. 3, pp. 312–34.

Hichens, W. 1919. *A new spirit in industrial relations* (London, Nisbett).

Hicks, C. 1941. *My life in industrial relations: Fifty years in the growth of a profession* (New York, Harper).

Hicks, J. 1932. *The theory of wages* (New York, Macmillan).

Hicks, J.C.R. 2003. "Balance y prospectiva de las relaciones industriales en México", unpublished presentation (Guanajuato, Governor's Office).

Higgens, H. 1915. "A new province for law and order: Industrial peace through minimum wage and arbitration, Part I", in *Harvard Law Review*, Vol. 29, Nov., pp. 13–39.

Hill, S. 1976. "The new industrial relations?", in *British Journal of Industrial Relations*, Vol. 14, No. 2, pp. 214–19.

Hills, S. 1995. *Employment relations and the social sciences* (Columbia, University of Columbia Press).

Hince, K. 1991. "Industrial relations teaching and research in New Zealand", in R. Lansbury (ed.): *Industrial relations teaching and research: International trends* (Sydney, ACIRRT, University of Sydney), pp. 72–100.

——; Vranken, M. 1991. "A controversial reform of New Zealand labour law: The Employment Contracts Act 1991", in *International Labour Review*, Vol. 130, No. 4, pp. 475–93.

Hobsbawm, E.J. 1964. *Labouring men: Studies in the history of labour* (London, Weidenfeld and Nicolson).

Hodgson, G. 2001. *How economics forgot history* (London, Routledge).

Hoerr, J. 1988. *And the wolf finally came* (Pittsburgh, University of Pittsburgh Press).

Hoeveler, J.D. 1976. "The university and the social gospel: The intellectual origins of the 'Wisconsin Idea'", in *Wisconsin Magazine of History*, Vol. 59, No. 4, pp. 282–98.

Hovenkamp, H. 1990. "The first great law and economics movement", in *Stanford Law Review*, Vol. 42, Apr., pp. 993–1058.

Hofer, S. 2000. "Jurisprudence, history, national economics after 1850", in P. Koslowski (ed.): *The theory of capitalism in the German economic tradition* (Berlin, Springer-Verlag), pp. 467–503.

Hoffman, R.; Jacobi, O.; Keller, B.; Weiss, M. 2003. *European integration as a social experiment in a global world* (Düsseldorf, Hans Böckler).

Hoffman, J.; Hoffman, R.; Kirton-Darling, J.; Rampeltshammer, L. 2003. *The Europeanization of industrial relations in a global perspective: A literature review* (Dublin, European Industrial Relations Observatory).

Hoffstadter, R. 1963. *The progressive era: 1900–1915* (Englewood Cliffs, Prentice-Hall).

Hollander, S. 1987. *Classical economics* (New York, Basil Blackwell).

Hollingsworth, J.R.; Boyer, R. (eds.). 1997. *Contemporary capitalism: The embeddedness of institutions* (Cambridge, Cambridge University Press).

Hotchkiss, W. 1923. "Industrial relations management", in *Harvard Business Review*, Vol. 1, July, pp. 438–50.

Houser, J.D. 1927. *What the employer thinks* (Cambridge, MA, Harvard University Press).

Howard, W. 1991. "John Niland", in *Journal of Industrial Relations*, Vol. 33, Dec., pp. 435–6.

Howell, G. 1878. *Conflicts of labour and capital historically and economically considered* (London, Chatto and Windus).

Howlett, C. 1993. *Brookwood Labor College and the struggle for peace and social justice in America* (Lewiston, Edwin Mellen Press).

Hoxie, R. 1915. *Scientific management and labor* (New York, Appleton).

Humphreys, G. 1986. *Taylorism in France: The impact of scientific management on factory relations and society* (New York, Garland).

Huthmacher, J. 1968. *Senator Robert F. Wagner and the rise of urban liberalism* (New York, Athenaeum).

Hutt, W.H. 1954. *The theory of collective bargaining* (Glencoe, The Free Press).

Hyman, R. 1975. *Industrial relations: A Marxist introduction* (London, Macmillan).

_____ . 1982. "Comment", in *Industrial Relations*, Vol. 21, No. 1, pp. 100–113.

_____ . 1989. *The political economy of industrial relations: Theory and practice in a cold climate* (London, Macmillan).

_____ . 1994a. "Introduction, economic restructuring, market liberalism and the future of national industrial relations systems", in R. Hyman and A. Ferner (eds.): *New frontiers in European industrial relations* (London, Blackwell), pp. 1–14.

_____ . 1994b. "Book review symposium", in *Journal of Industrial Relations*, Vol. 36, Mar., pp. 156–61.

_____ . 1995. "Industrial relations in theory and practice", in *European Journal of Industrial Relations*, Vol. 1, No. 1, pp. 17–46.

_____ . 2001a. *Understanding European trade unionism: Between market, class, and society* (London, Sage).

_____ . 2001b. "The Europeanisation – or the erosion – of industrial relations", in *Industrial Relations Journal*, Vol. 32, No. 4, pp. 280–94.

_____ . 2003. "The historical evolution of British industrial relations", in P. Edwards (ed.): *Industrial relations: Theory and practice*, 2nd ed. (Oxford, Blackwell), pp. 37–57.

_____ . 2004. "Is industrial relations theory always ethnocentric?", in B. Kaufman (ed.): *Theoretical perspectives on work and the employment relationship* (Champaign, IRRA), forthcoming.

Ichniowski, C.; Kochan, T.; Levine, D.; Olson, C.; Strauss, G. 1996. "What works at work: Overview and assessment", in *Industrial Relations*, Vol. 35, No. 3, pp. 356–74.

Industrial Relations Counselors, Inc. 1949. *Industrial relations work at certain universities*, Parts 1–3 (New York, Industrial Relations Counselors).

Industrial Relations Institute. 1935. *Ten years I.R.I.: Report of the International Industrial Relations Institute* (The Hague, Holland).

Inter-American Development Bank. 2004. *Good jobs wanted: Labor markets in Latin America* (Washington, DC, Johns Hopkins University Press).

International Labour Organization. 1931. *The International Labour Organization: The first decade* (London, Allen & Unwin).

_____ . 1938. *Historical survey of the contributions of the International Labour Organization to the study of management* (Geneva).

_____ . 1956. *Report of the Meeting of Experts on Industrial and Human Relations*, 2–11 July 1956 (Geneva).

_____ . 1965. *Labour faces the new age: Purposes, structure and work of the ILO* (Geneva).

_____ . 1974. *Collective bargaining in industrialized market economies*, Studies and Reports, New Series No. 80 (Geneva).

_____ . 1999. *Decent work*, Report of the Director-General, International Labour Conference, 87th Session, 1999 (Geneva).

_____ . 2001. *Reducing the decent work deficit: A global challenge*, Report of the Director-General, International Labour Conference, 89th Session, 2001 (Geneva).

Isaac, J. 1980. "Foreword", in D. Plowman and S. Deery: *Australian industrial relations* (Sydney, McGraw-Hill), pp. vii–ix.

_____ . 1993. "Kingsley Middleton Laffer 1911–1993", in *Journal of Industrial Relations*, Vol. 35, No. 3, pp. 375–8.

_____ . 1998. "Australian labour market issues: An historical perspective", in *Journal of Industrial Relations*, Vol. 40, No. 4, pp. 690–715.

_____ . 2003. Personal correspondence.

Isbester, A.F.; Coates, D.; Williams, C.B. 1965. *Industrial and labour relations in Canada: A selected bibliography* (Kingston, Queen's University).

Iwuji, E. 1979. "Industrial relations in Kenya", in U. Damachi, H. Seibel and L. Trachtman (eds.): *Industrial relations in Africa* (New York, St. Martin's Press).

Jacobi, O. 2001. "Supranational industrial relations in Europe – A literature review", in G. Széll (ed.): *European labour relations*, Vol. I (Aldershot, Gower), pp. 262–79.

Jacoby, S. 1985. *Employing bureaucracy: Managers, unions, and the transformation of work in American industry, 1900–1945* (New York, Columbia University Press).

_____ . 1990. "The new institutionalism: What it can learn from the old", in *Industrial Relations*, Vol. 29, No. 2, pp. 316–40.

_____ . 1991. "Pacific ties: Industrial relations and employment systems in Japan and the United States", in H. Harris and N. Lichtenstein (eds.): *Industrial democracy in America: The ambiguous promise* (New York, Cambridge University Press), pp. 206–48.

_____ . 1997. *Modern manors: Welfare capitalism since the New Deal* (Princeton, Princeton University Press).

_____ . 2003. "A century of human resource management", in B. Kaufman, R. Beaumont and R. Helfgott (eds.), 2003, pp. 147–71.

_____ ; Nason, E.; Saguchi, K. 2004. "The role of senior HR executives in Japan and the United States: Employment relations, corporate governance, and values", in *Industrial Relations*, Vol. 43, forthcoming.

Jacques, M. 1976. "Consequences of the General Strike", in J. Skelley (ed.): *The General Strike 1926* (London, Lawrence and Wishart), pp. 375–404.

Jamieson, S. 1957. *Industrial relations in Canada* (Ithaca, Cornell University Press).

Jarley, P.; Chandler, T.; Faulk, L. 2001. "Maintaining a scholarly community: Casual authorship and the state of IR research", in *Industrial Relations*, Vol. 40, No. 2, pp. 348–47.

Jenkins, L.; Lansbury, R.; Westcott, M. 1991. "Extending the boundaries: Industrial relations and research and teaching in Australia", in R. Lansbury (ed.): *Industrial relations teaching and research: International trends* (Sydney, ACIRRT, University of Sydney), pp. 104–42.

Johnston, G. 1929. "Rationalisation and industrial relations", in *International Labour Review*, Vol. 20, No. 5, pp. 619–40.

Jonas, G. 1989. *The circuit riders: Rockefeller money and the rise of modern science* (New York, Norton).

Kadish, A. 1993. "Oxford economics in the later nineteenth century", in A. Kadish and K. Tribe (eds.): *The market for political economy: The advent of economics in British university culture, 1850–1905* (London, Routledge), pp. 42–77.

Kahn-Freund, O. 1954. "Legal framework", in Flanders and Clegg (eds.), 1954, pp. 42–127.

_____ . 1983. "Labour law and industrial relations in Great Britain and West Germany", in Lord Wedderburn, R. Lewis and J. Clark (eds.): *Labour law and industrial relations: Building on Kahn-Freund* (Oxford, Clarendon Press), pp. 1–13.

Kannappan, S. 1959. "The Tata steel strike: Some dilemmas of industrial relations in a developing country", in *Journal of Political Economy*, Vol. 67, Oct., pp. 489–507.

Kasper, W.; Streit, M. 1998. *Institutional economics: Social order and public policy* (Northampton, Edward Elgar).

Kassalow, E. 1968. "The comparative labor field", in *Bulletin of the International Institute of Labour Studies*, Vol. 5, Nov., pp. 92–107.

Katz, H. (ed.). 1997. *Telecommunications: Restructuring work and employment relations worldwide* (Ithaca, ILR Press).

_____ ; Darbishire, O. 2000. *Converging divergences: Worldwide changes in employment systems* (Ithaca, Cornell University Press).

Kaufman, B. 1988. "The postwar view of labor markets and wage determination", in B. Kaufman (ed.): *How labor markets work: Reflections on theory and practice by John Dunlop, Clark Kerr, Richard Lester, and Lloyd Reynolds* (Lexington, Lexington Books), pp. 145–204.

_____ . 1989. "Labor's inequality of bargaining power: Changes over time and implications for public policy", in *Journal of Labor Research*, Vol. 10, No. 3, pp. 285–98.

_____ . 1993. *The origins and evolution of the field of industrial relations in the United States* (Ithaca, ILR Press).

_____ . 1994. "The evolution of thought on the competitive nature of labor markets", in C. Kerr and P. Staudohar (eds.): *Labor economics and industrial relations: Markets and institutions* (Cambridge, MA, Harvard University Press), pp. 145–88.

———. 1996. "Why the Wagner Act? Re-establishing contact with its original purpose", in D. Lewin, B. Kaufman and D. Sockell (eds.): *Advances in industrial and labor relations*, Vol. 7 (Greenwich, CT, JAI Press), pp. 15–68.

———. 1997a. "Labor markets and employment regulation: The view of the 'Old Institutionalists'", in B. Kaufman (ed.): *Government regulation of the employment relationship* (Madison, IRRA), pp. 11–55.

———. 1997b. "The growth and development of a nonunion sector in the southern paper industry", in R. Zieger (ed.): *Southern labor in transition* (Knoxville, University of Tennessee Press), pp. 295–329.

———. 1998a. "John R. Commons: His contributions to the development of the field of personnel/HRM", in IRRA: *Proceedings of the Fiftieth Annual Meeting* (Madison), pp. 328–41.

———. 1998b. "An interview with Herbert R. Northrup", in *Journal of Labor Research*, Vol. 19, No. 4, pp. 669–93.

———. 1999a. "The future of collective bargaining and its impact on dispute resolution", in J. Grenig and S. Briggs (eds.): *Proceedings of the Fifty-Second Annual Meeting, National Academy of Arbitrators* (Washington, DC, Bureau of National Affairs), pp. 11–29.

———. 1999b. "Expanding the behavioral foundations of labor economics", in *Industrial and Labor Relations Review*, Vol. 52, No. 3, pp. 361–92.

———. 1999c. "Emotional arousal as a source of bounded rationality", in *Journal of Economic Behavior and Organization*, Vol. 38, No. 2, pp. 135–44.

———. 2000a. "The early institutionalists on industrial democracy and union democracy", in *Journal of Labor Research*, Vol. 21, No. 2, pp. 189–209.

———. 2000b. "Personnel/human resource management: Its roots as applied economics", in R. Backhouse and J. Biddle (eds.): *Toward a history of applied economics* (Durham, Duke University Press), pp. 229–56.

———. 2000c. "The case for the company union", in *Labor History*, Vol. 41, No. 3, pp. 321–50.

———. 2001a. "Human resource management and industrial relations: Commonalities and Differences", in *Human Resource Management Review*, Vol. 11, No. 4, pp. 339–74.

———. 2001b. "The theory and practice of strategic HRM and participative management: Antecedents in early industrial relations", in *Human Resource Management Review*, Vol. 11, No. 4, pp. 505–34.

———. 2001c. "An interview with Steelworkers' president Lynn Williams", in *Journal of Labor Research*, Vol. 22, No. 1, pp. 145–71.

———. 2002a. "Reflections on six decades in industrial relations: An interview with John Dunlop", in *Industrial and Labor Relations Review*, Vol. 55, No. 2, pp. 324–48.

———. 2002b. "The role of economics and industrial relations in the development of the field of personnel/human resource management", in *Management Decisions*, Vol. 40, No. 10, pp. 962–79.

———. 2003a. "Industrial relations counselors: Its history and significance", in B. Kaufman, R. Beaumont and R. Helfgott (eds.), 2003, pp. 31–112.

———. 2003b. "The quest for cooperation and unity of interest in industry", in B. Kaufman, R. Beaumont and R. Helfgott (eds.), 2003, pp. 115–46.

———. 2003c. "John R. Commons and the Wisconsin school on industrial relations strategy and policy", in *Industrial and Labor Relations Review*, Vol. 57, No. 1, pp. 3–30.

_____ . 2003d. "The organization of economic activity: Insights from the institutional theory of John R. Commons", in *Journal of Economic Behavior and Organization*, Vol. 52, No. 1, pp. 71–96.

_____ . 2003e. "Sumner Slichter on personnel management and employee representation in the pre-New Deal era", in D. Lewin and B. Kaufman (eds.): *Advances in industrial and labor relations*, Vol. 12 (New York, Elsevier), pp. 223–69.

_____ . 2004a. "What unions do: Insights from economic theory", in *Journal of Labor Research*, Vol. 25, summer, pp. 351–82.

_____ . 2004b. "Historical insight: The early institutionalists on trade unions and national labor policy", in *Journal of Labor Research*, forthcoming.

_____ . 2004c. "The institutional and neoclassical schools in labor economics", in D. Champlin and J. Knoedler (eds.): *The institutional tradition in labor economics* (Armonk, M.E. Sharpe), forthcoming.

_____ . 2004d. "Employment relations and the employment relations system: A guide to theorizing", in B. Kaufman (ed.), 2004f, pp. 41–75.

_____ . 2004e. "Toward an integrative theory of human resource management", in B. Kaufman (ed.), 2004f, pp. 321–66.

_____ . (ed.). 2004f. *Theoretical perspectives on work and the employment relationship* (Champaign, IRRA), forthcoming.

_____ . 2004g. "The impossibility of a competitive labor market", unpublished paper (Atlanta, Georgia State University).

_____ ; Beaumont, R.; Helfgott, R. (eds.). 2003. *Industrial relations to human resources and beyond: The evolving process of employee relations management* (Armonk, M.E. Sharpe).

_____ ; Taras, D. (eds.). 2000. *Nonunion employee representation: History, contemporary practice, and policy* (Armonk, M.E. Sharpe).

Kawada, H. 1969. "The role of industrial relations centers", in *The changing patterns of industrial relations in Asian countries: Proceedings of the Asian Regional Conference on Industrial Relations* (Tokyo, Japan Institute of Labor), pp. 245–58.

Kawakami, H. 1917. *Binbo monogatan* (Kyoto, Kobundo Shobo).

Kay, J.P. 1970. "Working class conditions in the 1830s: Seen in Manchester by a social reformer", in *The Industrial Revolution in Britain: Triumph or disaster?* (New York, Heath), pp. 6–10.

Kearney, H. 1973. "Universities and society in historical perspective", in R. Bell and A. Youngson (eds.): *Present and future in higher education* (London, Tavistock Publications), pp. 1–12.

Keeble, S. 1992. *The ability to manage: A study of British management, 1890–1990* (Manchester, Manchester University Press).

Keenoy, T. 1991. "The roots of metaphor in the old and new industrial relations", in *British Journal of Industrial Relations*, Vol. 29, No. 2, pp. 313–28.

_____ ; Kelly, D. 1998. *The employment relationship in Australia*, 2nd ed. (Sydney, Harcourt).

Keller, B. 1991. *Einführung in die Arbeitspolitik: Arbeitsbeziehungen und Arbeitsmarkt in Sozialwissenschaftslicher Perspektive* (Munich, Oldenbourg).

_____ . 1996. "The German approach to industrial relations: A literature review", in *European Journal of Industrial Relations*, Vol. 2, No. 2, pp. 199–210.

_____ . 2002. Telephone interview.

____ ; Platzer, H.W. 2003. *Industrial relations and European integration: Trans- and supranatural developments and prospects* (Burlington, Vermont, Ashgate).

Kellerson, H. 1998. "The ILO Declaration of 1998 on Fundamental Principles and Rights: A challenge for the future", in *International Labour Review*, Vol. 137, No. 2, pp. 221–7.

Kelly, D. 1999. "Academic industrial relations in Australia: An historical overview", unpublished Ph.D. dissertation (Wollongong, NSW, University of Wollongong).

____ . 2003a. "A shock to the system? The impact of HRM on academic IR in Australia in comparison with USA and UK, 1980–95", in *Asia Pacific Journal of Human Resources*, Vol. 41, No. 2, pp. 149–71.

____ . 2003b. "A continuous association: The first 20 years of the Association of Industrial Relations Academics of Australia and New Zealand", unpublished paper (Wollongong, NSW, University of Wollongong).

____ . 2004. "The transfer of ideas in industrial relations: Dunlop and Oxford in the development of Australian industrial relations thought, 1960–1980", in D. Lewin and B. Kaufman (eds.): *Advances in industrial and labor relations*, Vol. 13, forthcoming.

Kelly, J. 1998. *Rethinking industrial relations: Mobilization, collectivism and long waves* (London, Routledge).

____ . 1999. "The Cold War never happened, or how not to write industrial relations history", in *Historical Studies in Industrial Relations*, Vol. 8, pp. 127–36.

____ . 2000. "Social democracy and anti-communism: Allan Flanders and the history of the field of industrial relations in Britain", unpublished manuscript (London, LSE).

Kelly, L. 1987. "Industrial relations at Queen's: The first fifty years", in *Relations Industrielles/Industrial Relations*, Vol. 42, No. 3, pp. 475–99.

Kendall, W. 1975. *The labour movement in Europe* (London, Allen Lane).

Kennedy, D. 1919. "Employment management and industrial relations", in *Industrial Management*, Vol. 58, No. 5, pp. 353–8.

Kerr, C. 1955. "Industrial relations and the liberal pluralist", in IRRA: *Proceedings of the Seventh Annual Meeting, Industrial Relations Research Association* (Madison), pp. 2–16.

____ . 1983. "A perspective on industrial relations research – Thirty-Six Years Later", in IRRA: *Proceedings of the Thirty-Sixth Annual Winter Meeting, Industrial Relations Research Association* (Madison), pp 14–21.

____ . 1988. "The neoclassical revisionists in labor economics (1940–1960) – RIP", in B. Kaufman (ed.): *How labor markets work* (Lexington, Lexington Books), pp. 1–46.

____ . 1994. "The social economics revisionists: The 'real world' study of labor markets and institutions", in C. Kerr and P. Staudohar (eds.): *Labor economics and industrial relations: Markets and institutions* (Cambridge, MA, Harvard University Press), pp. 66–108.

____ . 2003. *The gold and blue: A personal memoir of the University of California, 1949–1967* (Berkeley, University of California Press).

____ ; Dunlop, J.; Harbison, F.; Myers, C. 1955. "The Labour Problem in economic development: A framework for a reappraisal", in *International Monthly Review*, Vol. 71, Mar., pp. 223–35.

____ ; ____ ; ____ ; ____ . 1960. *Industrialism and industrial man* (Cambridge, MA, Harvard University Press).

_____ ; Fisher, L. 1957. "Plant sociology: The elite and the aborigines", in M. Komarovski (ed.): *Common frontiers of the social sciences* (Glencoe, Free Press), pp. 281–309.

_____ ; Siegel, A. 1955. "The structuring of the labor force in industrial society: New dimensions and new questions", in *Industrial and Labor Relations Review*, Vol. 8, No. 2, pp. 151 68.

Ketteler, W. 1864. *Die Arbeiterfrage und das Christenthum* (Mainz, Kircheim).

Keynes, J. 1936. *The general theory of employment, interest, and money* (New York, Harcourt Brace.

Keyserling, L. 1945. "Why the Wagner Act?", in L. Silverberg (ed.): *The Wagner Act: After ten years* (Washington, DC, Bureau of National Affairs), pp. 3–33.

Kindleberger, C. 1990. *Historical economics: Art or science?* (Berkeley, University of California Press).

King, W.L.M. 1918. *Industry and humanity* (Toronto, University of Toronto Press).

Kinzley, W.D. 1991. *Industrial harmony in Japan: Invention of a tradition* (London, Routledge).

Kipping, M.; Bjarnar, O. 1998. *The Americanization of European Business: The Marshall Plan and the transfer of US management models* (New York, Routledge).

Kirkaldy, H. 1947. *The spirit of industrial relations* (Oxford, Oxford University Press).

Kleiner, M.; Block, R.; Myron, R.; Salsburg, S. (eds.). 1987. *Human resources and the performance of the firm* (Madison, IRRA).

Knight, F. 1932. "The newer economics and the control of economic activity", in *Journal of Political Economy*, Vol. 40, No. 4, pp. 433–76.

Knight, M.; Barnes, H.; Flugel, F. 1928. *Economic history of Europe* (Boston, Houghton Mifflin).

Kochan, T. 1980. *Industrial relations and collective bargaining: From theory to policy and practice*, 2nd ed. with H. Katz, 1988 (Homewood, IL, Irwin).

_____ . 1993. "Teaching and building middle range industrial relations theory", in Adams and Meltz (eds.), 1993, pp. 353–80.

_____ . 1998. "What is distinctive about industrial relations research?", in Whitfield and Strauss (eds.), 1998, pp. 31–50.

_____ . 2000. "Building a new social contract at work: A call for action", in IRRA: *Proceedings of the 52nd Annual Meeting* (Champaign), pp. 1–25.

_____ . 2003. Telephone interview.

_____ ; Barocci, T. 1985. *Human resources management and industrial relations* (Boston, Little, Brown).

_____ ; Katz, H.; McKersie, R. 1986. *The transformation of American industrial relations* (New York, Basic Books).

_____ ; Lansbury, R.; MacDuffie, J.P. (eds.). 1997. *After lean production: Evolving employment practises in the world auto industry* (Ithaca, ILR Press).

_____ ; Osterman, P. 1994. *The mutual gains enterprise* (Boston, Harvard Business School Press).

Kocka, J. 1978. "Entrepreneurs and managers in German industrialization", in Mathias and Postan (eds.), 1978, pp. 492–89.

_____ . 1999. *Industrial culture and bourgeois society: Business, labor, and bureaucracy in modern Germany* (New York, Berghahn Books).

Koot, G. 1987. *English historical economics, 1870–1926* (Cambridge, Cambridge University Press).

Kornhauser, A. 1948. "The contribution of psychology to industrial relations research", in IRRA: *Proceedings of the First Annual Meeting* (Madison), pp. 172–88.

——— ; Ross, A.; Dubin, R. 1954. *Industrial conflict* (New York, McGraw-Hill).

Korpi, W. 1981. "Sweden: Conflict, power, and politics in industrial relations", in P. Doeringer (ed.): *Industrial relations in international perspective* (New York, Holmes and Meier), pp. 185–217.

Koshiro, K. 1980. "Japanese studies in labor economics: A survey", in *Japanese Economic Studies*, summer, pp. 42–81.

——— . 2000. *A fifty-year history of industry and labor in postwar Japan* (Tokyo, Japan Institute of Labor).

——— . 2003. "A short note on labor studies in Japan", unpublished paper (Yokohama, Yokohama National University).

Koslowski, P. 1995. *The theory of ethical economy in the historical school* (Berlin, Springer-Verlag).

Kronman, A. 1983. *Max Weber* (Stanford, Stanford University Press).

Kulemann, W. 1890. *Die Gewerkschaftsbewegung* (Jena, G. Fischer).

Kume, I. 1998. *Disparaged success: Labor politics in postwar Japan* (Ithaca, Cornell University Press).

Kuwahara, Y. 1989. *Industrial relations system in Japan: A new interpretation* (Tokyo, Japan Institute of Labor).

Laffer, K. 1968. "Industrial relations: Its teaching and scope, an Australian experience", in *Bulletin of the International Institute of Labour Studies*, Vol. 5, Nov., pp. 9–26.

——— . 1974. "Is industrial relations an academic discipline?", in *Journal of Industrial Relations*, Vol. 16, Mar., pp. 62–73.

Laistner, M. 1923. *Greek economics* (London, J.M. Dent).

Landsberger, H. 1958. *Hawthorne revisited*, Cornell Studies in Industrial and Labor Relations, Vol. IX (Ithaca, Cornell University Press).

Lane, C. 1994. "Industrial order and the transformation of industrial relations: Britain, Germany and France compared", in R. Hyman and A. Ferner (eds.): *New frontiers in European industrial relations*, 2nd ed. (Oxford, Blackwell), pp. 166–95.

Lane, R. 1991. *The market experience* (New York, Cambridge University Press).

Lange, W.H. 1928. *The American Management Association and its predecessors*, Special Paper No. 17 (New York, American Management Association).

Langguth, G. 1995. *In search of security: A socio-psychological portrait of today's Germany* (Westport, CT, Praeger).

Lansbury, R.; Westcott, M. 1992. "Researching Australian industrial relations: Dawn or twilight of a golden age?", in *Journal of Industrial Relations*, Vol. 34, No. 3, pp. 396–419.

——— ; Michelson, G. 2003. "Industrial relations in Australia", in P. Ackers and A. Wilkinson (eds.): *Understanding work and employment: Industrial relations in transition* (Oxford, Oxford University Press), pp. 227–41.

Laroque, P. 1938. *Les rapports entre patrons et ouvriers* (Paris, F. Aubier).

Larson, S. 1975. *Labor and foreign policy: Gompers, the AFL, and the First World War, 1914–1918* (Rutherford, Fairleigh Dickinson University Press).

Latham, A. 1930. *The Catholic and national unions of Canada* (Toronto, Macmillan).

Lazear, E. 1999. "Personnel economics: Past lessons and future directions", in *Journal of Labor Economics*, Vol. 17, No. 2, pp. 199–36.

———. 2000. "Economic imperialism", in *Quarterly Journal of Economics*, Vol. 115, No. 1, pp. 99–145.

Leavitt, H. 1961. "Toward organizational psychology", in B. von Haller Gilmer (ed.): *Walter van Dyke Bingham Memorial Program* (Pittsburgh, Carnegie Institute of Technology).

Lecher, W.; Platzer, H.W. 1998. *European Union – European industrial relations?* (London, Routledge).

Lederer, E.; Marschak, J. 1927. "Die Klassen auf dem Arbeitsmarkt und ihre Organisationen", in *Grundriss der Nationalökonomik*, Vol. IX, Part II (Verlag von J.C.B. Mohr (Paul Siebeck), Tübingen), pp. 120–41.

Lee, E. 1994. "The Declaration of Philadelphia: Retrospect and prospect", in *International Labour Review*, Vol. 133, No. 4, pp. 466–84.

Lee, J. (ed.). 1928. *Dictionary of Industrial Administration*, Vol. 1 (London, Pitman & Sons).

Lee, M.B. 1993. "Korea", in M. Rothman, D. Briscoe and R. Nacamulli (eds.): *Industrial relations around the world* (Berlin, de Gruyter), pp. 245–69.

——— ; Lee, Y.M.. 2004. "The development of the industrial relations field in Korea", unpublished paper (Seoul, LG Corporation and Dongguk University).

——— ; Rhee, Y. 1996. "Bonuses, unions, and labor productivity in South Korea", in *Journal of Labor Research*, Vol. 17, spring, pp. 219–38.

Lehmbruch, G. 2001. "The institutional embedding of market economies: The German 'model' and its impact on Japan", in Streeck and Yamamura (eds.), 2001, pp. 39–93.

Leiserson, W. 1922. "Constitutional government in American industry", in *American Economic Review*, Vol. 12, supplement, pp. 56–79.

———. 1929. "Contributions of personnel management to improved labor relations", in *Wertheim lectures on industrial relations* (Cambridge, MA, Harvard University Press), pp. 125–64.

———. 1938. *Right and wrong in labor relations* (Berkeley, University of California Press).

Leisink, P. 1996. "Dutch and Flemish industrial relations: Theory and practice", in *European Journal of Industrial Relations*, Vol. 2, No. 1, pp. 69–92.

Lenel, H.O. 1971. "Does Germany still have a social market economy?", reprinted in Peacock and Willgerodt (eds.), 1989, pp. 261–72.

Lens, S. 1974. *The labor wars* (New York, Anchor).

Lescohier, D. 1919. *The labor market* (New York, Macmillan).

———. 1960. *Don Divance Lescohier: My story for the first seventy-seven years* (Madison, Art Brush).

Lester, R. 1952. "A range theory of wage differentials", in *Industrial and Labor Relations Review*, Vol. 5, No. 4, pp. 483–500.

———. 1958. *As unions mature* (Princeton, Princeton University Press).

———. 1988. "Wages, benefits, and company employment systems", in B. Kaufman (ed.): *How labor markets work: Reflections on theory and practice* (Lexington, Massachusetts, Lexington Books), pp. 89–116.

Levenstein, A. 1912. *Die Arbeiterfrage* (Munich, E. Reinhardt).

Levine, S. 1978. "Doctrine, theory, and teaching in industrial relations: A comment", in D. Turkington (ed.): *Industrial relations teaching and research in Australia and New Zealand: Proceedings of the Australia and New Zealand Conference of Teachers of Industrial Relations, 10–12 May 1978* (Wellington, Victoria University of Wellington, Industrial Relations Centre), pp. 54–7.

——— ; Kawada, H. 1980. *Human resources in Japanese industrial development* (Princeton, Princeton University Press).

Lewin, D. 1987. "Industrial relations as a strategic variable", in Kleiner et al. (eds.), 1987, pp. 1–41.

——— . 2004. *Human resources and business performance: Theory, evidence, and assessment* (New York, Oxford University Press).

——— ; Mitchell, D. 1995. *Human resources management: An economic approach* (Cincinnati, Southwestern).

——— ; ——— ; Zaidi, M. 1997. *The human resource management handbook* (Greenwich, CT, JAI Press).

Lewis, H.G. 1956. "Hours of work and hours of leisure", in IRRA: *Proceedings of the Ninth Annual Meeting* (Madison), pp. 192–206.

——— . 1963. *Unions and relative wages in the United States* (Chicago, University of Chicago Press).

Lewisohn, S. 1926. *The new leadership in industry* (New York, Dutton).

Lichtenstein, N.; Harris, H. 1993. *Industrial democracy: The ambiguous promise* (New York, Oxford University Press).

Lieberman, S. 1986. *Labor movements and labor thought: Spain, France, Germany, and the United States* (New York, Praeger).

Ling, C. 1965. *The management of personnel relations, history and origins* (Homewood, IL, Irwin).

Lipset, S.M. 1986. "North American labor movements: A comparative perspective", in S. Lipset (ed.): *Unions in transition: Entering the second century* (San Francisco, Institute for Contemporary Studies), pp. 431–51.

List, F. 1841. *The national system of political economy* (London, Longmans, Green & Co.).

Lloyd, D. 1965. *Introduction to jurisprudence*, revised ed. (New York, Praeger).

Locke, R.; Kochan, T.; Piore, M. (eds.). 1995. *Employment relations in a changing world economy* (Cambridge, MIT Press).

——— ; Piore, M.; Kochan, T. 1995. "Employment relations in a changing world economy", in R. Locke, T. Kochan and M. Piore (eds.), 1995, pp. xiii–xxix.

Lockman, Z. 1994. "'Worker' and 'working class' in pre-1914 Egypt: A rereading", in Z. Lockman (ed.): *Workers and working classes in the Middle East* (Albany, State University of New York Press), pp. 71–110.

Lodge, G. 1962. *Spearheads of democracy: Labor in the developing countries* (New York, Harper and Bros.).

Logan, H.A. 1928. *The history of trade union organization in Canada* (Chicago, University of Chicago Press).

——— . 1948. *Trade unions in Canada* (Toronto, Macmillan).

Logan, J. 2004. "Labor's 'last stand' in national politics? The campaign for striker replacement legislation, 1988–1996", in D. Lewin and B. Kaufman (eds.): *Advances in industrial and labor relations*, Vol. 13, forthcoming (New York, Elsevier).

Looise, J.; van Riemsdijk, M. 2001. "Globalization and human resource management: The end of industrial relations", in Széll (ed.), 2001, Vol. 1, pp. 280–96.

Lorenz, E. 2001. *Defining global justice* (Notre Dame, University of Notre Dame Press).

Lorwin, L. 1929. *Labor and internationalism* (New York, Macmillan).

——. 1955. "Recent research on Western European labor movements", in IRRA: *Proceedings of the Seventh Annual Meeting* (Madison), pp. 69–80.

Love, J. 1990. "The origins of dependency analysis", in *Journal of Latin American Studies*, Vol. 22, No. 1, pp. 143–68.

Lucena, H. 1980. "Industrial relations in an enclave economy: The case of Venezuela", in *Labour and Society*, Vol. 5, No. 4, pp. 341–54.

——. 2003. "The industrial relationship as study field of investigation", unpublished paper (Venezuela, University of Carabobo).

Lutz, M.; Lux, K. 1979. *The challenge of humanistic economics* (Menlo Park, Benjamin-Cummings).

Lyddon, D. 2003. "History and industrial relations", in P. Ackers and A. Wilkinson (eds.): *Understanding work and employment* (Oxford, Oxford University Press), pp. 89–118.

Lynd, R.; Lynd, H. 1937. *Middletown in transition: A study in cultural conflicts* (New York, Harcourt Brace).

MacDowell, L.S. 2000. "Company unionism in Canada, 1915–1948", in B. Kaufman and D. Taras (eds.), 2000, pp. 96–120.

Machin, S. 2000. "Union decline in Britain", in *British Journal of Industrial Relations*, Vol. 38, No. 4, pp. 631–45.

Mack, M. 1969. *A Bentham reader* (New York, Praeger).

Magat, R. 1999. *Unlikely partners: Philanthropic foundations and the labor movement* (Ithaca, Cornell University Press).

Mahoney, T.; Deckop, J. 1986. "Evolution of concept and practice in personnel administration/human resource management", in *Journal of Management*, Vol. 12, pp. 223–41.

Maier, C. 1970. *Recasting bourgeois Europe* (Princeton, Princeton University Press).

——. 1979. "Between Taylorism and technocracy: European ideologies and the vision of industrial productivity in the 1920s", in *Journal of Contemporary History*, Vol. 5, No. 2, pp. 27–61.

Maier, J.; Weatherhead, R. 1979. *The Latin American university* (Albuquerque, University of New Mexico Press).

Malhorta, P. 1949. *Indian labour movement: A survey* (Delhi, Chand & Co.).

Mandel, E. 1968. *Marxist economic theory* (New York, Monthly Review).

Manicas, P. 1987. *A history and philosophy of the social sciences* (New York, Basil Blackwell).

Manning, A. 2003. *Monopsony in motion* (Princeton, Princeton University Press).

Mantzavinos, C. 2001. *Individuals, institutions and markets* (New York, Cambridge University Press).

Margerison, C. 1969. "What do we mean by industrial relations?", in *British Journal of Industrial Relations*, Vol. 7, No. 4, pp. 273–86.

Marginson, P.; Wood, S. 2000. "WER98 special issue: Editor's introduction", in *British Journal of Industrial Relations*, Vol. 38, No. 4, pp. 489–96.

Markey, R. et al. 2001. *Models of employee participation in a changing global environment* (Burlington, VT, Ashgate).

Marsden, D. 1999. *A theory of employment relations systems: Micro-foundations of diversity* (New York, Oxford University Press).

Marsden, R. 1982. "Industrial relations: A critique of empiricism", in *Sociology*, Vol. 16, No. 2, pp. 232–50.

Marsh, A. 1968. "Research and teaching in industrial relations: The United Kingdom experience", in *Bulletin of the International Institute of Labour Studies*, Vol. 5, Nov., pp. 64–78.

Marshall, A. 1890. *Principles of economics*, 9th ed., 1961 (London, Macmillan).

———. 1896. *Elements of economics of industry*, 2nd ed. (London, Macmillan).

Marshall, B. 1978. "Academic factionalism in Japan: The case of Todai Economics Department, 1919–1939", in *Modern Asian Studies*, Vol. 12, No. 4, pp. 529–51.

Marsland, S. 1989. *The birth of the Japanese labor movement: Takano Fusataro and the Rodo Kumiai Kiseikai* (Honolulu, University of Hawaii Press).

Martens, G. 1979. "Industrial relations and trade unionism in French-speaking West Africa", in U. Samachi, D. Seibel and L. Trachtman (eds.): *Industrial relations in Africa* (New York, St. Martin's Press), pp. 16–72.

Martin, J. 1975. "The influence of the behavioral sciences on management literature", in *Personnel Journal*, Vol. 54, Mar., pp. 150–53.

Martin, R. 1998. "The British tradition of industrial relations research: The contribution of W.E.J. Lord McCarthy", in *British Journal of Industrial Relations*, Vol. 36, No. 1, pp. 83–97.

Mathewson, S. 1931. *Restriction of output among unorganized workers* (New York, Viking).

Mathias, P.; Postan, M. 1978. *The Cambridge economic history of Europe*, Vol. VII (London, Cambridge University Press).

Matthews, D.; Apthorpe, R. 1958. *Social relations in Central African industry* (Lusaka, Rhodes–Livingston Institute).

May, T. 1987. *An economic and social history of Britain, 1760–1970* (London, Longman).

Mayo, E. 1933. *The human problems of an industrial civilization* (New York, Macmillan).

———. 1945. *The social problems of an industrial civilization* (Cambridge, MA, Harvard University Press).

McCarthy, C. 1912. *The Wisconsin idea* (New York, Macmillan).

McCarthy, W. Lord. 1994. "The involvement of academics in British industrial relations", in *British Journal of Industrial Relations*, Vol. 32, No. 2, pp. 201–17.

McCartin, J. 1997. *Labor's great war: The struggle for industrial democracy and the origins of modern American labor relations, 1912–1921* (Chapel Hill, University of North Carolina Press).

McCawley, T. 1924. *Industrial arbitration* (Brisbane, Government Printing).

McCormick, J. 1986. "Introduction", in M. Maurice, F. Sellier and J.J. Silvestre: *The social foundations of industrial power: A comparison of France and Germany* (Cambridge, MIT Press), pp. vii–xi.

McGivering, I.; Matthews, D.; Scott, W. 1960. *Management in Britain* (Liverpool, Liverpool University Press).

McGregor, D. 1960. *The human side of enterprise* (New York, McGraw-Hill).

McIlwee, T. 2001. "Collective bargaining", in Széll (ed.), 2001, Vol. 1, pp. 14–26.

McIntyre, R.; Ramstad, Y. 2002. "John R. Commons and the problem of international labor rights", in *Journal of Economic Issues*, Vol. 36, No. 2, pp. 293–302.

McIvor, A. 2001. *A history of work in Britain, 1880–1950* (New York, Palgrave).

McNulty, P. 1980. *The origin and development of labor economics* (Cambridge, MIT Press).

Mehrotra, S.N. 1949. *Labour movement in India* (New Delhi, S. Chand).

Meidner, R. 1997. "The Swedish model in an era of mass unemployment", in *Economic and Industrial Democracy*, Vol. 18, No. 1, pp. 87–97.

Meltz, N. 1989. "Industrial relations, balancing efficiency and equity", in J. Barbash and K. Barbash (eds.): *Theories and concepts in comparative industrial relations* (Columbia, University of South Carolina Press), pp. 109–14.

——. 1993. "Industrial relations systems as a framework for organizing contributions to industrial relations theory", in Adams and Meltz (eds.), 1993, pp. 161–82.

Merkle, J. 1980. *Management and ideology: The legacy of the international scientific management movement* (Berkeley, University of California Press).

Metcalf, D. 1999. "The British national minimum wage", in *British Journal of Industrial Relations*, Vol. 37, No. 2, pp. 171–201.

Metcalf, H.; Urwick, L. 1942. *Dynamic administration* (New York, Harper).

Meyer, H. 1976. "Personnel directors are the new corporate heroes", in *Fortune*, Issue 93, Feb., pp. 84–8, 140.

Meyers, F. 1967. "The study of foreign labor and industrial relations", in S. Barkin et al. (eds.): *International labor* (Madison, IRRA), pp. 15–32.

——. 1981. "France", in A. Blum (ed.): *International handbook of industrial relations* (Westport, CT, Greenwood), pp. 169–208.

Middlemas, K. 1980. *Power and the party: Changing faces of communism in Western Europe* (London, André Deutsch).

Miller, D.; Form, W. 1951. *Industrial sociology* (New York, Harper).

Millis, H. 1935. "Testimony", in National Labor Relations Board: *Legislative history of the National Labor Relations Act, 1935* (Washington, DC, Government Printing Office).

——; Montgomery, R. 1945. *Organized labor* (New York, McGraw-Hill).

Millward, N.; Marginson, P.; Callus, R. 1998. "Large-scale national surveys for mapping, monitoring, and theory development", in Whitfield and Strauss (eds.), 1998, pp. 135–56.

Mirowski, P. 1989. *More heat than light: Economics as social physics, physics as nature's economics* (Cambridge, Cambridge University Press).

Mishell, L.; Bernstein, J.; Boushby, H. 2002. *The state of working America, 2002–2003* (Washington, DC, Economic Policy Institute).

Mitchell, D. 1986. "Inflation, unemployment and the Wagner Act: A critical appraisal", in *Stanford Law Review*, Vol. 38, Apr., pp. 1065–95.

——. 2001. "IR journal and conference literature from the 1960s to the 1990s: What can HR learn from it? Where is it headed?", in *Human Resource Management Review*, Vol. 11, No. 4, pp. 375–94.

——; Erickson, C. 2004. "De-unionization and macro performance: What Freeman and Medoff didn't do", in *Journal of Labor Research*, Vol. 25, forthcoming.

——; Zaidi, M. 1997. "The Dunlop Commission's omissions on American labor market policy", in *Contemporary Economic Issues*, Vol. 15, No. 2, pp. 105–14.

___ ; ___ ; Lewin, D. 1997. *Human resource management handbook* (Greenwich, CT, JAI Press).

Mitchell, J. 1903. *Organized labor* (Philadelphia, American Book and Bible).

Montgomery, D. 1993. "Industrial democracy or democracy in industry? The theory and practice of the labor movement", in Lichtenstein and Harris (eds.), 1993, pp. 20–42.

Morató, O. 1911. *Problemas sociales* (Montevideo, Talleres Gráficos).

Morawski, W. 2001. "Trade unions in Poland: Dilemmas of dependence, independence and relative autonomy", in G. Schienstock, P. Thompson and F. Traxler (eds.): *Industrial relations: Between command and market* (New York, Nova), pp. 45–72.

Morgado, E. 2004. Personal interview (Santiago, Universidad de la República).

Morris, J. 1966. *Elites, intellectuals, and consensus: A study of the social questions and the industrial relations system in Chile* (Ithaca, New York State School of Industrial and Labor Relations).

___ ; Córdova, E. 1967. *Bibliography of industrial relations in Latin America* (Ithaca, New York State School of Industrial and Labor Relations).

Morris, R. 1987. "The early uses of the industrial relations concept", in *Journal of Industrial Relations*, Vol. 29, No. 4, pp. 532–8.

___ . 1997. "The old concept of employment relations and its modern renaissance", in R. Morris (ed.): *Essays in employment relations theory* (Nepean, University of Western Sydney, Centre for Employment Relations), pp. 67–86.

Morris-Suzuki, T. 1989. *A history of Japanese economic thought* (London, Routledge).

Morrison, C. 1854. *An essay on the relations between labour and capital*, 1972 reprint (New York, Arno Press).

Morse, D. 1969. *The origin and evolution of the ILO* (Ithaca, Cornell University Press).

Moss, D. 1996. *Socializing security: Progressive-era economists and the origins of American social policy* (Cambridge, MA, Harvard University Press).

Müller-Jentsch, W. 1986. *Soziologie der industriellen Beziehungen: Eine Einführung* (Frankfurt, Campus-Verlag).

___ . 2002. "Germany", in D. Cornfield and R. Hodson (eds.): *Worlds of work: Building an international sociology of work* (New York, Kluwer), pp. 221–52.

___ . 2003. "Notes on the German field of industrial relations", unpublished correspondence.

___ . 2004. "Theoretical approaches to industrial relations", in B. Kaufman (ed.), forthcoming.

___ ; Weitbrecht, H. 2003. *The changing contours of German industrial relations* (Munich, Rainer Hampp).

Müller-Vogg, H. 1987. "Federal Republic of Germany", in B. Roberts (ed.): *Industrial relations in Europe* (London, Rowe), pp. 75–99.

Munsterberg, H. 1913. *Psychology and industrial efficiency* (Boston, Houghton Mifflin).

Murray, G.; Morin, M.L.; da Costa, I. 1996. *L'état des relations professionnelles: Traditions et perspectives de recherche* (St. Nicolas, Octares).

___ . 2002. Telephone interview.

Murray, J. 2001. *Transnational labour regulation: The ILO and EC compared* (London, Kluwer).

Myers, C. 1958. *Labor problems in the industrialization of India* (Cambridge, MA, Harvard University Press).

_____ ; Kannappan, S. 1970. *Industrial relations in India* (New York, Asia Publishing House).

_____ ; Pigors, P. 1951. *Personnel administration: A point of view and a method* (New York, McGraw-Hill).

_____ ; _____ ; Malm, F. 1964, *Management of human resources: Readings in personnel administration* (New York, McGraw-Hill).

Nadler, D.; Gerstein, M.; Shaw, R. 1992. *Organizational architecture* (San Francisco, Jossey-Bass).

Nakayama, I. 1960. *Industrialization of Japan and industrial relations* (Tokyo, Nihon Roudoukyoukai).

_____ . 1975. *Industrialization and labor–management relations in Japan* (Tokyo, Japan Institute of Labor).

Naphtali, F. (ed). 1928. *Wirtschaftsdemokratie: Ihr Wesen, Weg und Ziel* (Berlin, Verlags-Gesellschaft des Allgemeinem Deutschen Gewerkschaftsbundes).

National Civic Federation. 1919. *The labor situation in Great Britain and France* (New York, E.P. Dutton).

National Industrial Conference Board. 1931. *Industrial relations: Administration of policies and programs* (New York).

Nel, P.S. 1997. *South African industrial relations: Theory and practice* (Pretoria, van Schaik).

Nelson, D. 1975. *Managers and workers: Origins of the new factory system in the United States, 1880–1920* (Madison, University of Wisconsin).

_____ . 1997. *Shifting fortunes: The rise and decline of American labor from the 1820s to the present* (Chicago, Ivan Dee).

_____ . 2000. "The AFL and the challenge of company unionism, 1915–1937", in B. Kaufman and D. Taras (eds.), pp. 61–75.

Newcomb, S. 1886. *A plain man's talk on the Labor Question* (New York, Harper).

Nicholls, A.J. 1994. *Freedom with responsibility: The social market economy in Germany, 1918–1963* (Oxford, Clarendon Press).

Niland, J. 1994. "Change and the international exchange of ideas", in J. Niland, R. Lansbury and C. Verevis (eds.): *The future of industrial relations: Global change and challenges* (London, Sage), pp. 451–72.

Nishizawa, T. 2001. "Lujo Brentano, Alfred Marshall, and Tokuzo Fukuda: The reception and transformation of the German historical school in Japan", in Shionoya (ed.), 2001, pp. 155–72.

Nivens, M. 1967. *Personnel management 1913–1963* (London, Institute of Personnel Management).

Nolan, M. 1986. "Economic crisis, state policy, and working-class formation in Germany, 1870–1900", in I. Katznelson and A. Zolberg (eds.): *Working class formation* (Princeton, Princeton University Press), pp. 352–96.

_____ . 1994. *Visions of modernity: American business and the modernization of Germany* (New York, Oxford University Press).

Nyland, C. 1998. "Taylorism and the mutual gains strategy", in *Industrial Relations*, Vol. 37, No. 4, pp. 519–42.

Oberschall, A. 1965. *Empirical social research in Germany* (Paris, Mouton).

Ojeli, D. 1976. *Industrial relations in English-speaking West Africa*, Conference Paper (Accra, IILS).

Okochi, K. 1936. *A history of thought on social policy in Germany* (Tokyo, Nihonhyouron-sha).

———. 1943. *Smith and List: Economic ethics and economic theory* (Tokyo, Nihonhyouron-sha).

———. 1950. *The actual condition of the postwar labour unions* (Tokyo, Nippon Hyoron Sha).

———; Karsh, B.; Levin, S. 1973. *Workers and employers in Japan: The Japanese employment relations system* (Princeton, NJ, Princeton University Press).

Osterman, P. 1987. "Choice of employment systems in internal labor markets", in *Industrial Relations*, Vol. 26, No. 1, pp. 46–67.

———; Kochan, T.; Locke, R.; Piore, M. 2001. *Working in America: Labor market policies for the new century* (Cambridge, MA, MIT Press).

Otter, C. von. 2002. "Sweden", in D. Cornfield and R. Hodson (eds.): *Worlds of work: Building an international sociology of work* (New York, Kluwer), pp. 325–45.

Palmer, G. 1991. "Commentary", in R. Lansbury (ed.): *Industrial relations teaching and research: International trends* (Sydney, University of Sydney, ACIRRT), pp. 66–71.

Pankoke, E. 1970. *Sociale Bewegung – Sociale Frage – Sociale Politik* (Stuttgart, Jahrhundert).

Papola, T.; Ghosh, P.; Sharma, A. 1993. "Editors' Introduction", in T. Papola et al.: *Labour, employment and industrial relations in India* (Delhi, B.R. Publishing), pp. 1–18.

Park, Y.; Leggett, C. 1998. "Employment relations in Korea", in G. Bamber, R. Lansbury and N. Wailes (eds.): *International and comparative employment relations* (London, Sage), pp. 275–93.

Parkin, F. 1992. *Durkheim* (Oxford, Oxford University Press).

Pastore, J.; Skidmore, T. 1985. "Brazilian industrial relations: A new era?", in H. Juris, M. Thompson and W. Danield (eds.): *Industrial relations in a decade of change* (Madison, IRRA), pp. 73–114.

———; Zylberstajn, H. 1987. *A administração do conflito trabalhista no Brasil* (São Paulo, Instituto de Pesquisas Econômicas).

Peabody, F. 1900. *Jesus Christ and the Social Question* (London, Macmillan).

Peacock, A.; Willgerodt, H. 1989. *Germany's social market economy: Origins and evolution* (London, Macmillan).

Perlman, M.; McCann, C. Jr. 1998. *The pillars of economic understanding: Ideas and traditions* (Ann Arbor, University of Michigan Press).

Perlman, S. 1926. "Greetings to the League", in League for Industrial Democracy: *Twenty years of social pioneering* (New York), 1926, p. 51.

———. 1928. *A theory of the labor movement* (New York, Macmillan).

Perry, A.L. 1878. *Elements of political economy* (New York, Scribner's).

Peters, T.; Waterman, R. 1982. *In search of excellence* (New York, Harper and Row).

Peukert, H. 2000. "Walter Eucken (1891–1950) and the historical school", in P. Koslowski (ed.): *The theory of capitalism in the German economic tradition: Historicism, ordo liberalism, critical theory, solidarism* (Berlin, Springer-Verlag), pp. 93–145.

Phelps Brown, E.H. 1959. *The growth of British industrial relations* (London, Macmillan).

———. 1990. The counter-revolution of our time", in *Industrial Relations*, Vol. 29, No. 1, pp. 1–14.

Phillips, G.A. 1976. *The General Strike: The politics of industrial conflict* (London, Weidenfeld and Nicolson).

Pignon, D.; Querzola, J. 1976. "Dictatorship and democracy in production", in A. Gorz (ed.): *The division of labour: The labour process and class-struggle in modern capitalism*, (Atlantic Highlands, NJ, Humanities Press), pp. 63–102.

Pigou, A. 1905. *Principles and methods of industrial peace* (London, Macmillan).

Pillbeam, P. 2000. *French socialists before Marx* (Montreal, McGill–Queen's University Press).

Piore, M. 1995. *Beyond individualism* (Cambridge, MA, Harvard University Press).

——— ; Sabel, C. 1984. *The second industrial divide: Possibilities for prosperity* (New York, Basic Books).

Pipkin, C. 1927. *The idea of social justice* (New York, Macmillan).

Plowman, D.; Deery, S.; Fisher, C. 1981. *Australian industrial relations* (New York, McGraw-Hill).

Polanyi, K. 1944. *The great transformation* (New York, Farrar and Rinehart).

Potts, J. 2000. *The new evolutionary economics* (Northampton, Edward Elgar).

Powell, D. 1992. *British politics and the Labour Question, 1868–1990* (New York, St. Martin's Press).

Price, L. 1999. *Economics: The culture of a controversial science* (Chicago, University of Chicago Press).

Price, L.L. 1887. *Industrial peace* (London, Macmillan).

Princeton University, Industrial Relations Section. 1986. *The Industrial Relations Section of Princeton University, 1922–1985* (Princeton).

Purcell, J. 1993. "The end of institutional industrial relations", in *Political Quarterly*, Vol. 64, No. 1, pp. 6–23.

Pyle, K. 1974. "Advantages of followership, German economics and Japanese bureaucrats, 1890–1925", in *Journal of Japanese Studies*, Vol. 1, No. 1, pp. 127–64.

Rader, B. 1966. *The academic mind and reform: The influence of Richard T. Ely in American life* (Lexington, University of Kentucky Press).

Radosh, R. 1969. *American labor and United States foreign policy* (New York, Random House).

Raff, D.; Summers, L. 1987. "Did Henry Ford pay efficiency wages?", in *Journal of Labor Economics*, Vol. 5, No. 4, Part 2, pp. 57–86.

Ratnam, C.S.V. 1997. "Teaching of industrial relations in India", in Indian Industrial Relations Association: *National Workshop for Faculty Members on Industrial Relations Teaching and Research* (New Delhi), pp. 1–8.

Rawson, S. 1978. "Research in industrial relations in New Zealand: Comment", in D. Turkington (ed.): *Proceedings of the Australia and New Zealand Conference of Teachers of Industrial Relations, 10–12 May 1978* (Wellington, Victoria University of Wellington, Industrial Relations Centre), pp. 107–12.

Reder, M. 1982. "Chicago economics, permanence and change", in *Journal of Economic Literature*, Vol. 20, No. 1, pp. 1–38.

Regini, M. 1994. "Human resource management and industrial relations in European countries", in J. Niland, R. Lansbury and C. Vervis (eds.): *The future of industrial relations: Global change and challenges* (London, Sage), pp. 256–69.

——— . 2003. "Tripartite concertation and varieties of capitalism", in *European Journal of Industrial Relations*, Vol. 9, No. 3, pp. 251–63.

———; Kitay, J.; Baethge, M. (eds.). 1999. *From tellers to sellers: Changing employment relations in banks* (Cambridge, MA, MIT Press).

Reglia, I.; Regini, M. 1995. "Between voluntarism and industrialization: Industrial relations and human resource practices in Italy", in R. Locke, T. Kochan and M. Piore (eds.), 1995, pp. 131–64.

Reinalda, B. 1998. "Organization theory and the autonomy of the International Labour Organization: Two classic studies still going strong", in B. Reinalda and B. Verbeek (eds.): *Autonomous policy making by international organizations* (London, Routledge), pp. 42–61.

Reisman, D. 1995. *Thorstein Veblen* (New Brunswick, Transaction).

Reynaud, J.D. 1963. *Les syndicats en France* (Paris, Armand Colin).

———. 1980. "Industrial relations and political systems: Some reflections on the crisis in industrial relations in Western Europe", in *British Journal of Industrial Relations*, Vol. 18, No. 1, pp. 1–13.

———. 2003. Telephone interview.

———; Eyraud, F.; Saglio, J.; Paradeise, C. 1990. *Les systèmes de relations professionnelles: Examen critique d'une théorie* (Lyon, CNRS).

Reynolds, L. 1949a. "The role of a university in industrial relations", in *The universities and industrial relations* (Montreal, McGill University), pp. 10–22.

———. 1949b. *Labor economics and labor relations*, 1st ed. (Englewood Cliffs: Prentice-Hall).

———. 1951. *The structure of labor markets* (New York, Harper).

———. 1988. "Labor economics then and now", in B. Kaufman (ed.): *How labor markets work* (Lexington, Lexington Books), pp. 117–44.

———; Taft, C. 1956. *The evolution of wage structure* (New Haven, Yale University Press).

Ricardo, D. 1817. *Principles of political economy and taxation* (London, J. Murray).

Richardson, J. 1929. "Recent developments in industrial co-operation in the United States and Canada", in *International Labour Review*, Vol. 20, July, pp. 67–83.

———. 1933. *Industrial relations in Great Britain*, Series A, No. 36 (Geneva, ILO).

———. 1954. *An introduction to the study of industrial relations* (London, Allen & Unwin).

Richardson, T.; Fisher, D. 1999. *The development of the social sciences in the United States and Canada: The role of philanthropy* (Stamford, CT, Ablex).

Ridley, F. 1970. *Revolutionary syndicalism in France: The direct action of its time* (Cambridge, Cambridge University Press).

Rimmer, M. 2003. Personal correspondence.

Ringer, F. 1969. *The decline of the German mandarins: The German academic community, 1890–1933* (Cambridge, MA, Harvard University Press).

Ringrose, H. 1951. *Trade unions in Natal* (New York, Oxford University Press).

Robbins, L. 1932. *The nature and significance of economic science* (London, Macmillan).

Roberts, B. (ed.). 1968. *Industrial relations: Contemporary issues* (London, Macmillan).

———. 1970. "Presidential address to the Second World Congress", unpublished paper (Geneva, IIRA).

———. 1972. "Affluence and disruption", in W. Robson (ed.): *Man and the social sciences* (London, Allen & Unwin), pp. 245–72.

———. 1973. "Presidential address to the Third World Congress", unpublished paper (Geneva, IIRA).

———. 2002. Personal interview.

Robinson, D. 1981. "British industrial relations research in the sixties and seventies", in P. Doeringer (ed.): *Industrial relations in international perspective* (New York, Holmes and Meier), pp. 145–84.

Rockefeller, J.D., Jr. 1923. *The personal relation in industry* (New York, Boni and Liverwright).

Rodgers, D. 1998. *Atlantic crossings: Social politics in a progressive era* (Cambridge, MA, Harvard University Press).

Roethlisberger, F., Dickson, W. 1939. *Management and the worker* (Cambridge, MA, Harvard University Press).

Rojot, J. 1989. "The myth of French exceptionalism", in J. Barbash and K. Barbash (eds.): *Theories and concepts in comparative industrial relations* (Columbia, University of South Carolina Press), pp. 76–88.

Romero, F. 1992. *The United States and the European trade union movement, 1944–1951* (Chapel Hill, University of North Carolina Press).

Romualdi, S. 1947. "Labor and democracy in Latin America", in *Foreign Affairs*, Vol. 25, Apr., pp. 477–89.

Roscher, W. 1843. *Grundriss zu Vorlesungen über die Staatswirthschaft: nach geschichtlicher Methode* (Göttingen, Druck und Verlag der Dieterischschen Buchhandlung).

Rose, M. 1979. *Servants of post-industrial power? Sociologie du travail in modern France* (Armonk, M.E. Sharpe).

Ross, A. 1948. *Trade union wage policy* (Berkeley, University of California Press).

———. 1961. "Introduction to a new journal", in *Industrial Relations*, Vol. 1, No. 1, pp. 5–7.

———. 1965. "The new industrial relations", in *The changing patterns of industrial relations: Proceedings of the International Conference on Industrial Relations* (Tokyo, Japan Institute of Labor), pp. 142–65.

———; Hartman, P. 1960. *Changing patterns of industrial conflict* (New York, Wiley).

Ross, D. 1991. *The origins of American social science* (Cambridge, Cambridge University Press).

Rossi, W.; Rossi, D. 1925. *Personnel administration: A bibliography* (Baltimore, Williams and Wilkins).

Rostow, W. 1978. *The world economy: History and prospect* (Austin, University of Texas Press).

Roethlisberger, F.; Dickson. W. 1939. *Management and the worker* (Cambridge, MA, Harvard University Press).

Rothstein, B. 2002. "The universal welfare state as a social dilemma", in B. Rothstein and S. Steinmo (eds.): *Restructuring the welfare state: Political institutions and policy change* (New York, Palgrave), pp. 206–22.

Routh, G. 1959. *Industrial relations and race relations* (Johannesburg, South Africa Institute of Race Relations).

Royal Commission on Industrial Relations, Canada. 1919. *Report of Commission*. Reprinted in *Labour Gazette*, July 1919 (Ottawa, Department of Labour).

Royal Commission on Labour, Great Britain. 1894. *Final Report* (London, Her Majesty's Stationery Office).

Rudé, G. 1964. *Crowd in history: A study of popular disturbances in France and England, 1730–1848* (New York, Wiley).

Rueschemeyer, D.; van Rossem, R. 1996. "The *Verein für Sozialpolitik* and the Fabian Society: A study in the sociology of policy-relevant knowledge", in D. Rueschemeyer and T. Skopcol (eds.): *States, social knowledge, and the origins of modern social policies* (Princeton, Princeton University Press), pp. 117–64.

Ruiz-Tagle, J. 1989. "Trade unionism and the State under the Chilean military", in E. Epstein (ed.): *Labor autonomy and the State in Latin America* (Boston, Unwin Hyman), pp. 73–100.

Russell Sage Foundation. 1919. "Industrial relations: A selected bibliography", in *Bulletin of the Russell Sage Foundation Library*, Vol. 35 (New York).

Ryberg, L.; Bruun, N. 1996. "An overview of industrial relations research in the Nordic countries: Institutions and trends", in *European Journal of Industrial Relations*, Vol. 2, No. 1, pp. 93–112.

Ryner, M. 1999. "Neoliberal globalization and the crisis of Swedish social democracy", in *Economic and Industrial Democracy*, Vol. 20, No. 1, pp. 39–79.

Samuels, W. 2000. "Institutional economics after one century", in *Journal of Economic Issues*, Vol. 34, No. 92, pp. 305–15.

Sansberro, S. 2004. Personal interview (Guanajuato, Universidad de Guanajuato).

Saposs, D. 1956. Rebirth of the American labor movement", in IRRA: *Proceedings of the Eighth Annual Meeting* (Madison), pp. 16–30.

Sarma, A. 1984. *Industrial relations: Conceptual & legal framework* (Bombay, Himalaya Publishing).

Sauvé, P.; Subramanian, A. 2001. "Dark clouds over Geneva? The troubled prospects of the multilateral trade system", in R. Porter et al. (eds.): *Efficiency, equity, and legitimacy: The multilateral trading system at the millennium* (Washington, DC, Brookings Institution), pp. 16–33.

Scharpf, F. 1991. *Crisis and choice in European social democracy* (Ithaca, Cornell University Press).

Schatz, R. 1998. "A portrait of the IRRA's founders as young men", in *Labor Law Journal*, Vol. 49, No. 7, pp. 1157–62.

Scheinberg, S. 1986. *The development of corporation labor policy, 1900–1940* (New York, Garland).

Schienstock, G.; Traxler, F. 1997. "A comparative approach to socialist and postsocialist industrial relations", in Schienstock, Thompson and Traxler (eds.), 1997, pp. 1–24.

——; Thompson, P.; Traxler, F. (eds.). 1997. *Industrial relations between command and market: A comparative analysis of Eastern Europe and China* (New York, Nova).

Schmid, A. 1987. *Property, power, and public choice* (New York, Praeger).

Schmidtke, O. 2002. *The Third Way transformation of social democracy* (London, Ashgate).

Schmitter, P.; Lehmbruch, G. 1979. *Trends towards corporatist intermediation* (London, Sage).

Schregle, J. 1981. Comparative industrial relations: Pitfalls and potentials", in *International Labour Review*, Vol. 120, No. 1, pp. 15–28.

Schrickel, C. 1966. *Personnel practices of United States manufacturing firms operating in Colombia, Ecuador, Peru, and Venezuela*, Ph.D. dissertation (Columbus, Ohio State University).

Schwanholz, M. 2001. "The social dimension of the European integration process – History, status quo, perspectives", in Széll (ed.), 2001, Vol. 1, pp. 137–66.

Schumpeter, J. 1954. *History of economic analysis* (New York, Oxford University Press).

Searle, G. 1971. *The quest for national efficiency* (Berkeley, University of California Press).

Seear, N. 1967. "Industrial research in Britain", in A. Welford et al. (eds.): *Society: Problems and methods of study* (London, Routledge), pp. 175–87.

Segal, M. 1986. "Post-institutionalism in labor economics: The forties and fifties revisited", in *Industrial and Labor Relations Review*, Vol. 39, No. 3, pp. 388–403.

Selekman, B.; van Kleeck, M. 1924. *Employees' representation in coal mines* (New York, Russell Sage).

Sellier, F. 1968. "Teaching and research in industrial relations in France", in *Bulletin of the International Institute of Labour Studies*, Vol. 5, Nov., pp. 47–63.

——— . 1972. *Future industrial relations: France, Italy, Portugal and Spain* (Geneva, IILS).

——— . 1978. "France", in J. Dunlop and W. Galenson (eds.): *Labor in the twentieth century* (New York, Academic Press), pp. 197–240.

——— ; Maurice, M.; Silvestre, J. 1982. *The social foundations of industrial power: A comparison of France and Germany* (Cambridge, MA, MIT Press).

Semmel, B. 1960. *Imperialism and social reform* (Cambridge, MA, Harvard University Press).

Servais, J.M. 1989. "The social clause in trade agreements: Wishful thinking or an instrument of social progress?", in *International Labour Review*, Vol. 128, No. 4, pp. 423–32.

Sewell, W. 1986. "Artisans, factory workers, and the formation of the French working class, 1789–1848", in I. Katznelson and A. Zolberg (eds.): *Working class formation* (Princeton, Princeton University Press), pp. 45–70.

Shalev, M. 1983. "The social democratic model and beyond: Two generations of comparative research on the welfare state", in *Comparative Social Research*, Vol. 6, pp. 315–51.

——— . 1996. "The labor movement in Israel: Ideology and political economy", in E. Goldberg (ed.): *The social history of labor in the Middle East* (Boulder, Westview), pp. 131–62.

Shanahan, W. 1954. *German Protestants face the social question* (Notre Dame, IN, University of Notre Dame Press).

Sheehan, J. 1966. *The career of Lujo Brentano: A study of liberalism and social reform in imperial Germany* (Chicago, University of Chicago Press).

Shionoya, Y. (ed.). 2001. *The German historical school* (London, Routledge).

Siegel, J. 1998. "Industrial relations research and the American policy-making process", in Whitfield and Strauss (eds.), 1998, pp. 257–66.

Sigsworth, E. 1990. *Montague Burton: The tailor of taste* (Manchester, Manchester University Press).

Simon, H. 1982. *Models of bounded rationality*, Vol. 2 (Cambridge, MA, MIT Press).

Singh, N. 2003. "The theory of international labor standards", in K. Basu, H. Horn, L. Román and J. Shapiro (eds.): *International labor standards: History, theory and policy options* (London, Blackwell), pp. 105–81.

Sisson, K. 1993. "In search of HRM", in *British Journal of Industrial Relations*, Vol. 31, No. 2, pp. 201–10.

Skidelsky, R. 1992. *John Maynard Keynes: The economist as savior, 1920–1937,* Vol. 2 (New York, Penguin).

Slichter, S. 1928. "What is the Labor Problem?", in J. Hardman (ed.): *American labor dynamics in light of post-war developments* (New York, Harcourt Brace), pp. 287–91.

——. 1929. "The current labor policies of American industries", in *Quarterly Journal of Economics*, Vol. 43, May, pp. 393–435.

——. 1931. *Modern economic society*, 2nd ed. (New York, Henry Holt).

——; Healy, J.; Livernash, R. 1960. *The impact of collective bargaining on management* (Washington, DC, Brookings Institution).

Slomp, H. 1990. *Labor relations in Europe: A history of issues and developments* (New York, Greenwood).

——. 1996. *Between bargaining and politics* (London, Praeger).

Smelser, N.; Swedberg, R. 1994. *The handbook of economic sociology* (Princeton, Princeton University Press).

Smith, A. 1776. *An inquiry into the nature and causes of the wealth of nations* (New York, Modern Library).

Smith, D. 1978. "Research in industrial relations in New Zealand: Comment", in D. Turkington (ed.): *Proceedings of the Australia and New Zealand Conference of Teachers of Industrial Relations, 10–12 May 1978* (Wellington, Victoria University of Wellington, Industrial Relations Centre), pp. 213–17.

Smith, E. 1994. *The German economy* (London, Routledge).

Smith, J. 1955. "The scope of industrial relations", in *British Journal of Sociology*, Vol. 6, Mar., pp. 80–85.

Smith, P.; Morton, G. 2001. "New Labour's reform of Britain's employment law: The devil is not only in the detail but in the values and policy too", in *British Journal of Industrial Relations*, Vol. 29, No. 1, pp. 119–38.

Smith, S. 1949. "The university and business", in *The universities and industrial relations* (Montreal, McGill University), pp. 1–9.

Smith, W. 1959. *Confucianism in modern Japan* (Tokyo, Hokuseido Press).

Social Science Research Council (UK). 1980. *Industrial Relations Research Unit: The first ten years, 1970–1980* (Coventry, University of Warwick).

Social Science Research Council (US). 1928. *Survey of research in the field of industrial relations* (New York).

Solano, E.J. 1920. *Labour as an international problem* (London, Macmillan).

Solow, R. 1997. "How did economics get that way and what way did it get?", in *Daedalus*, Vol. 126, No. 1, pp. 39–58.

Somers, G. 1969. "Bargaining power and industrial relations theory", in G. Somers (ed.): *Essays in industrial relations theory* (Ames, Iowa State University Press), pp. 39–54.

——. 1975. "Collective bargaining and the social-economic contract", in IRRA: *Proceedings of the Twenty-Eighth Annual Winter Meeting* (Madison), pp. 1–7.

Spates, T. 1960. *Human values where people work* (New York, Harper).

Spencer, E. 1984. *Management and labor in Imperial Germany: Ruhr industrialists as employers, 1896–1914* (New Brunswick, Rutgers University Press).

Stanley, A. 1998. *From bondage to contract* (London, Cambridge University Press).

Stanojevic, M. 2003. "Workers' power in transition economies: The cases of Serbia and Slovenia", in *European Journal of Industrial Relations*, Vol. 9, No. 3, pp. 283–302.

Stavenhagen, R.; Zapata, F. 1972. *Future industrial relations: Latin America* (Geneva, IILS, ILO).

Stevenson, R. 2002. "The ethical basis of institutional economics", in *Journal of Economic Issues*, Vol. 36, No. 2, pp. 263–78.

Stiglitz, J. 2000. *Democratic development as the fruits of labor*, address to the 2000 Meeting of the IRRA (Champaign, IRRA).

———. 2002. "Employment, social justice and societal well-being", in *International Labour Review*, Vol. 141, No. 1–2, pp. 9–29.

Stockton, F. 1932. "Personnel management in the collegiate school of business", in *Personnel Journal*, Vol. 12, Dec., pp. 220–27.

Stolberg, B. 1933. "The government in search of a labor movement", in *Scribner's Magazine*, Issue 6, Dec., pp. 345–50.

Storey, J. 1992. *Developments in the management of human resources: An analytical review* (London, Blackwell).

Strauss, G. 1970. "Organizational behavior and personnel relations", in W. Ginsberg et al. (eds.): *A review of industrial relations research*, Vol. 1 (Madison, IRRA), pp. 145–206.

———. 1982. "Comment", in *Industrial Relations*, Vol. 21, No. 1, pp. 95–99.

———. 1984. "Industrial relations: Time of change", in *Industrial Relations*, Vol. 23, No. 1, pp. 1–15.

———. 1989. "Industrial relations as an academic field: What's wrong with it?", in J. Barbash and K. Barbash (eds.): *Theories and concepts in comparative industrial relations* (Columbia, University of South Carolina Press), pp. 241–60.

———. 1993. "Present at the beginning: Some personal notes on OB's early days and later", in A. Bedeian (ed.): *Management laureates: A collection of autobiographical essays*, Vol. 3 (Greenwich, CT, JAI Press), pp. 145–90.

———. 1994. "Reclaiming industrial relations academic jurisdiction", in IRRA: *Proceedings of the Forty-Sixth Annual Meeting* (Madison), pp. 1–11.

———. 1998. "Research methods in industrial relations", in Whitfield and Strauss (eds.), 1998, pp. 5–30.

———. 2001. "HRM in the USA: Correcting some British impressions", in *International Journal of Human Resource Management*, Vol. 12, No. 6, pp. 873–97.

———; Feuille, P. 1978. "Industrial relations research: A critical analysis", in *Industrial Relations*, Vol. 17, No. 3, pp. 259–77.

———; ———. 1981. "Industrial relations research in the United States", in P. Doeringer (ed.): *Industrial relations in international perspective* (New York, Holmes and Meier), pp. 76–144.

———; Sayles, L. 1960. *Personnel: The human problems of management* (Englewood Cliffs, Prentice-Hall).

——— et al. 1974. *Organizational behavior: Research and issues* (Madison, IRRA).

Streeck, W. 1992. *Social institutions and economic performance: Studies of industrial relations in advanced capitalist economies* (London, Sage).

———. 1993. "The rise and decline of corporatism", in L. Ulman, B. Eichengreen and W. Dickens (eds.): *Labor and integrated Europe* (Washington, DC, Brookings Institution), pp. 80–101.

———. 1994. "European social policy after Maastricht: The social dialogue and subsidiarity", in *Economic and Industrial Democracy*, Vol. 15, No. 2, pp. 151–77.

_____ ; Yamamura, K. 2001. *The origins of nonliberal capitalism: Germany and Japan in comparison* (Ithaca, Cornell University Press).

Stromholm, S. 1985. *A short history of legal thinking in the West* (Stockholm, Norstedt).

Sturdy, A.; Knight, D.; Willmott, H. 1992. *Skill and consent: Contemporary studies in the labour process* (London, Routledge).

Sturmthal, A. 1951. *The tragedy of European labour: 1918–1939* (New York, Columbia University Press).

_____ . 1953. *Unity and diversity in European labor: An introduction to contemporary labor movements* (Glencoe, Free Press).

_____ . 1964. *Workers councils: A study of workplace organization on both sides of the Iron Curtain* (Cambridge, MA, Harvard University Press).

_____ . 1972. *Comparative labor movements* (Belmont, Wadsworth).

_____ . 1983. *Left of center: European labor since World War II* (Urbana, University of Illinois Press).

Sumiya, M. 1981. "The Japanese system of industrial relations", in P. Doeringer (ed.): *Industrial relations in international perspective* (New York, Holmes and Meier), pp. 324–64.

_____ . 1990. *The Japanese industrial relations reconsidered* (Tokyo, Japan Institute of Labor).

Summers, C. 1958. "The public interest in union democracy", in *Northwestern Law Review,* Vol. 53, Nov., pp. 110–25.

Sutcliffe, J. 1921. *A history of trade unionism in Australia* (Melbourne, Macmillan).

Swart, S. 1978. "Labour relations training at South African universities", in *South African Journal of Labour Relations*, Vol. 2, No. 4, pp. 2–5.

Széll, G. (ed.). 2001. *European labour relations*, 2 vols. (Burlington, Vermont, Gower).

Tabb, J.; Ami, Y.; Shaal, G. 1961. *Labor relations in Israel* (Tel Aviv, Devir).

Taras, D.G. 1997. "Collective bargaining regulation in Canada and the United States: Divergent cultures, divergent outcomes", in B. Kaufman (ed.): *Government regulation of the employment relationship* (Madison, IRRA), pp. 295–342.

_____ . 2000. "Contemporary experience with the Rockefeller Plan: Imperial Oil's Joint Industrial Council", in B. Kaufman and D. Taras (eds.), 2000, pp. 231–58.

_____ . 2003. "Voice in the North American workplace: From employee representation to employee involvement", in B. Kaufman, R. Beaumont and R. Helfgott (eds.), 2003, pp. 293–329.

Taylor, F. 1895. "A piece-rate system: Being a partial solution to the Labor Problem", reprinted in D. Wren (ed.): *Early management thought* (Brookfield, Dartmouth), 1997, pp. 245–72.

_____ . 1911. *The principles of scientific management* (New York, Harper).

Taylor, G. 1948. *Government regulation of industrial relations* (New York, Prentice-Hall).

Taylor, R. 2003. *Social democratic trade unionism: An agenda for action* (London, Catalyst).

Tead, O.; Metcalf, H. *Personnel administration: Its principles and practice* (New York, McGraw-Hill).

Tezuka, M. 2001. "The economic reconstruction plan of Alfred Müller-Armack: What is the social market economy?", in Y. Shinoya (ed.), 2001, pp. 202–17.

Thakur, C.P. 2003 "Emerging patterns of industrial relations: From reality check to some speculation", in *Indian Journal of Labour Economics*, Vol. 46, No. 4, pp. 637–49.

Thelen, K.; Locke, R. 1995. "Apples and oranges revisited: Contextualized comparisons and the study of comparative labor politics", in *Politics and Society*, Vol. 23, No. 3, pp. 337–68.

Thomas, A. 1921. "The International Labour Organization: Its origins, development and future", in *International Labour Review*, Vol. 1, No. 1, pp. 5–22.

Thompson, E.P. 1964. *The making of the English working class* (New York, Pantheon).

Thompson, M.; Taras, D. 2003. "Employment relations in Canada", in G. Bamber, R. Lansbury and N. Wailes (eds.): *International and comparative employment relations*, 4th ed. (London, Sage), pp. 91–118.

Thompson, P.; Newsome, K. 2004. "Labour process theory: Work and the employment relationship", in B. Kaufman (ed.), forthcoming.

Thurley, K.; Woods, S. (eds.). 1983. *Industrial relations and management strategy* (Cambridge, Cambridge University Press).

Thurow, L. 1975. *Generating inequality* (New York, Basic Books).

———. 1983. *Dangerous Currents: The state of economics* (New York, Random House).

———. 1988. "Producer economics", in IRRA: *Proceedings of the Forty-First Annual Meeting* (Madison), pp. 9–20.

Tietmeyer, H. 1999. *The social market economy and monetary stability* (London, Economica).

Tipton, J. 1959. *Participation of the United States in the International Labour Organization* (Champaign, University of Illinois).

Tiraboschi, M. 2003. "Marco Biagi: The man and the master", in R. Blanpain and M. Weiss (eds.): *Changing industrial relations and modernization of labour law: Liber amicorum in honour of Professor Marco Biagi* (New York, Kluwer Law International), pp. 1–16.

Toennies, F. 1897. "Der Hamburger Streik von 1896/97", in *Archiv für Sozialwissenschaft*, Vol. 10, pp. 173–238.

Tone, A. 1997. *The business of benevolence* (Ithaca, Cornell University Press).

Tonn, J. 2003. *Mary P. Follett: Creating democracy, transforming management* (New Haven, Yale University Press).

Totten, G. 1967. "Collective bargaining and works councils as innovations in industrial relations in Japan during the 1920s", in R. Dore (ed.): *Aspects of social change in modern Japan* (Princeton, Princeton University Press), pp. 203–44.

Towers, B. 2003a. "Forward, industrial relations: Time to move on?", in P. Ackers and A. Wilkinson (eds.): *Understanding work and employment* (Oxford, Oxford University Press), pp. xii–xvi.

———. 2003b. "Dons, dockers and miners alike ... Industrial relations and the *IRJ*, 1970–2002", in *Industrial Relations Journal*, Vol. 34, No. 1, pp. 4–14.

Tremblay, L.M. 1968. "Industrial relations research in Canada", in *Bulletin of the Institute of International Labour Studies*, Vol. 5, Nov., pp. 27–46.

Treu, T. 2002. Telephone interview.

Tribe, K. 1995. *Strategies of economic order: German economic discourse, 1750–1950* (Cambridge, Cambridge University Press).

Trist, E. 1981. *The evolution of socio-technical systems* (Toronto, Ontario Quality of Working Life Centre).

_____; Murray, H. 1990. "Historical overview: The foundation and development of the Tavistock Institute", in E. Trist and H. Murray (eds.): *The social engagement of social science*, Vol. 1 (Philadelphia, University of Pennsylvania Press), pp. 1–36.

Trow, M. 1993. "Comparative perspectives on British and American higher education", in S. Rothblatt and B. Wittrock (eds.): *The European and American university since 1800* (Cambridge, Cambridge University Press), pp. 280–302.

Troy, L. 1999. *Beyond unions and collective bargaining* (Armonk, M.E. Sharpe).

Trudeau, P. 1956. *The asbestos strike*, translated by James Boake (Toronto, James, Lewis, and Samuel).

Tsutsui, W. 1998. *Manufacturing ideology: Scientific management in twentieth century Japan* (Princeton, Princeton University Press).

Turner, J.; Beeghley, L.; Powers, C. 1989. *The emergence of sociological theory*, 2nd ed. (Chicago, Dorsey).

Turner, L. 1998. *Fighting for partnership* (Ithaca, Cornell University Press).

Ulrich, D. 1998. "A new mandate for human resources", in *Harvard Business Review*, Vol. 76, No. 1, pp. 124–34.

Underhill, E.; Rimmer, M. 1998. "Industrial relations", in Australian Research Council: *Challenges for the social sciences and Australia* (Canberra), pp. 147–55.

Undy, R. 1999. "New Labour's 'industrial relations settlement': The Third Way?", in *British Journal of Industrial Relations*, Vol. 37, No. 2, pp. 315–36.

United Kingdom Committee on Industry and Trade. 1926. *Survey of industrial relations* (London, Her Majesty's Stationery Office).

United States Bureau of Labor Statistics. 1921. *Personnel Research Agencies*, Bulletin No. 299 (Washington, DC, Government Printing Office).

_____. 1930. *Personnel Research Agencies*, Bulletin No. 518 (Washington, DC, Government Printing Office).

United States Commission on Industrial Relations. 1916. *Industrial relations: Final report and testimony*, Vol. 1 (Washington, DC, Government Printing Office).

United States Senate Committee on Education and Labor. 1939. *Violations of free speech and rights of labor: Hearings before a Subcommittee of the Committee on Education and Labor*, Part 45 (Washington, DC, Government Printing Office).

University of Natal, Economics Department. 1950. *The African worker: A sample study of the life and labour of the urban African worker* (New York, Oxford University Press).

Vaid, K. 1966. "Editor's note", in Shriram Centre for Industrial Relations. *Books, journals, and periodicals on labour and industrial relations in India* (New Delhi).

_____. 1969. "A study of industrial relations centres in India", in *The changing patterns of industrial relations in Asian countries: Proceedings of the Asian Regional Conference on Industrial Relations* (Tokyo, Japan Institute of Labor), pp. 259–75.

Valentine, R. 1915. "The progressive relation between efficiency and consent", in *Bulletin of the Taylor Society*, Vol. 1, Nov., pp. 3–7.

Valticos, N. 1969. "Fifty years of standard setting activities by the International Labour Organization", in *International Labour Review*, Vol. 100, No. 3. [Reprinted in *International Labour Review*, 1996, Vol. 135, No. 3–4, pp. 393–413].

_____. 1998. "International labour standards and human rights: Approaching the year 2000", in *International Labour Review*, Vol. 137, No. 2, pp. 132–47.

van Kleeck, M. 1928. "Recent gains in industrial relations", in K. Page (ed.): *Recent gains in American civilization* (New York, Harcourt Brace), pp. 49–70.

Veblen, T. 1899. *The theory of the leisure class* (New York, Modern Library).

———. 1904. *The theory of business enterprise* (New York, Scribner's).

Venkata, R.C.S. 1997. "Teaching of industrial relations in India", in Indian Industrial Relations Association and International Management Institute: *National Workshop for Faculty Members on Industrial Relations Teaching and Research* (New Delhi), pp. 1–8.

Verma, A.; Cutcher-Gershenfeld, J. 1993. "Joint governance in the workplace: Beyond union–management cooperation and worker participation", in B. Kaufman and M. Kleiner (eds.): *Employee representation: Alternatives and new directions* (Madison, IRRA), pp. 197–234.

———; Kochan, T.; Lansbury, R. 1995. *Employment relations in the growing Asian countries* (London, Routledge).

Vetter, E.G. 1972. "Role of trade unions in a market economy", reprinted in Peacock and Willgerodt (eds.), 1989, pp. 140–51.

Visser, J. 2001. "Industrial relations and social dialogue", in P. Auer (ed.): *Changing labour markets in Europe: The role of institutions and policies* (Geneva, ILO), pp. 184–242.

Wagner, P.; Wittrock, B. 1991. "States, institutions, and discourses: A comparative perspective on the structuration of the social sciences", in P. Wagner, B. Wittrock and R. Whitley (eds.): *Discourses on society: The shaping of the social sciences* (Boston, Kluwer), pp. 331–58.

Wagner, R. 1935. "Testimony", in National Labor Relations Board: *Legislative hearings on the National Labor Relations Act, 1935* (Washington, DC, Government Printing Office), 1985, pp. 22–26.

———. 2001. *Globalization and labour management relations* (New Delhi, Response).

Wajcman, J. 2000. "Feminism facing industrial relations in Britain", in *British Journal of Industrial Relations*, Vol. 38, No. 2, pp. 183–201.

Walker, K. 1956. *Industrial relations in Australia* (Cambridge, MA, Harvard University Press).

———. 1968. "Summary of discussions", in *Bulletin of the International Institute for Labour Studies*, Vol. 5, Nov., pp. 108–35.

———. 2003. Telephone interview.

Walras, L. 1874 (English translation, 1954). *Elements of pure economics* (Homewood, Irwin).

Walsh, P. 1994. "Industrial relations research in New Zealand: The state of a discipline", in *New Zealand Journal of Industrial Relations*, Vol. 19, No. 2, pp. 161–74.

Walton, R. 1985. "From control to commitment in the workplace", in *Harvard Business Review*, Vol. 63, No. 92, pp. 76–84.

———; McKersie, R. 1965. *A behavioral theory of labor negotiations* (New York, McGraw-Hill).

Watkins, G. 1922. *An introduction to the study of labor problems* (New York, Thomas Crowell).

———. 1928. *Labor management* (New York, McGraw-Hill).

———; Dodd, P. 1940. *Labor problems*, 3rd ed. (New York, Thomas Crowell).

Watson, T. 1997. "Human resource management, industrial relations, and theory: Standing back and starting again", in *New Zealand Journal of Industrial Relations*, Vol. 22, Apr., pp. 7–21.

Webb, B. 1926. *My apprenticeship* (London, Longmans, Green & Co.).

_____ . 1948. *Our partnership* (London, Longmans, Green & Co.).

Webb, S. 1918. *The works manager to-day* (London, Longmans, Green & Co.).

_____ . 1897. *Industrial democracy* (London, Longmans, Green & Co.).

_____ . 1920. *A constitution for the socialist commonwealth of Great Britain* (London, London School of Economics and Political Science).

_____ . 1923. *Decay of capitalist civilization* (Westminster, The Fabian Society).

_____ ; Webb, B. 1894. *The history of trade unionism* (London, Longmans, Green & Co.).

Weber, A. 1910. *Der Kampf zwischen Kapital und Arbeit* (Tübingen, Mohr).

Weber, A. 1987. "Industrial relations and higher education", in D. Mitchell (ed.): *The future of industrial relations* (Los Angeles, UCLA Institute of Industrial Relations), pp. 8–28.

Weber, M. 1904. *The Protestant ethic and the spirit of capitalism* (Leipzig, Mohr).

_____ . 1968. *Economy and society* (New York, Bedminster).

Wedderburn, Lord. 1983. "Otto Kahn-Freund and British labour law", in Lord Wedderburn, R. Lewis and J. Clark (eds.): *Labour law and industrial relations: Building on Kahn-Freund* (Oxford, Clarendon Press), pp. 29–80.

Weiss, D. 1973. *Relations industrielles: Acteurs, auteurs, faits, tendances* (Paris, Sirey).

Weiss, M. 1987. *Labour law and industrial relations in the Federal Republic of Germany* (Deventer, Kluwer).

_____ . 2002. Telephone interview.

Weitbrecht, H. 1969. *Effectivität und Legitimität der Tarifautonomie* (Berlin, Duncker & Humblot).

Wells, H. 1906. *The future in America: A search after realities* (New York, Harper).

Whalen, C. 1991. "Saving capitalism by making it good: The monetary economics of John R. Commons", in *Journal of Economic Issues*, Vol. 27, No. 4, pp. 1155–79.

Wharton School Industrial Research Unit and Labor Relations Council. 1989. *Report on Progress* (Philadelphia, University of Pennsylvania).

Wheeler, H. 1985. *Industrial conflict: An integrative theory* (Columbia, University of South Carolina Press).

_____ ; McClendon, J. 1991. "The individual decision to unionize", in G. Strauss et al. (eds.): *The state of the unions* (Madison, IRRA), pp. 47–83.

Whitehead, T. 1936. *Leadership in a free society* (Cambridge, MA, Harvard University Press).

Whitfield, K.; Strauss, G. 1998. *Researching the world of work: Strategies and methods in studying industrial relations* (Ithaca, Cornell University Press).

Whyte, W.F. 1944. "Pity the personnel man", in *Advanced Management*, Vol. 19, No. 4, pp. 154–8.

_____ . 1965. "A field in search of a focus", in *Industrial and Labor Relations Review*, Vol. 18, No. 3, pp. 305–22.

_____ . 1994. *Participant observer: An autobiography* (Ithaca, ILR Press).

Wiarda, H. 1976. *The corporative origins of the Iberian and Latin America labor relations system* (Amherst, University of Massachusetts, Labor Relations and Research Center).

Wiebe, R. 1962. *Businessmen and reform: A study of the progressive movement* (Chicago, Quadrangle).

Wilcox, W. 1975. "The university in the United States of America", in M. Stephens and G. Roderick (eds.): *Universities for a changing world* (New York, Wiley), pp. 34–50.

Wilensky, H. 1954. *Syllabus of industrial relations* (Chicago, University of Chicago Press).

Wilkerson, B. 1994. "The Korea labour 'problem'", in *British Journal of Industrial Relations*, Vol. 32, No. 3, pp. 339–58.

Williams, C. 1859. *The great Social Problem: Four lectures on labour, capital, and wages* (Manchester, Heywood).

Williams, H. 1927. "High wages and prosperity", in *Industrial Management*, Vol. 33, No. 6, pp. 325–27.

Williamson, O. 1985. *The economic institutions of capitalism* (New York, Free Press).

Wilson, M. 1978. "Research in industrial relations in New Zealand", in D. Turkington (ed.): *Proceedings of the Australia and New Zealand Conference of Teachers of Industrial Relations, 10–12 May 1978* (Wellington, Victoria University of Wellington, Industrial Relations Centre), pp. 191–206.

Winchester, D. 1983. "Industrial relations research in Britain", in *British Journal of Industrial Relations*, Vol. 21, No. 1, pp. 100–114.

——. 1991. "The rise and fall of the golden ages: The British experience of industrial relations research and teaching", in R. Lansbury (ed.): *Industrial relations teaching and research: International trends* (Sydney, University of Sydney, ACIRRT), pp. 48–65.

Windmuller, J. 1987. *Collective bargaining in industrialized market economies: A reappraisal* (Geneva, ILO).

Witte, E. 1947. "The university and labor education", in *Industrial and Labor Relations Review*, Vol. 1, No. 1, pp. 3–17.

——. 1954. "Institutional economics as seen by an institutional economist", in *Southern Economic Journal*, Vol. 21, Oct., pp. 131–40.

——. 1963. *The development of the Social Security Act* (Madison, University of Wisconsin Press).

Wittrock, B. 1993. "The modern university: The three transformations", in S. Rothblatt and B. Wittrock (eds.): *The European and American university since 1800* (Cambridge, Cambridge University Press), pp. 303–62.

——; Wagner, P. 1996. "Social science and the building of the modern welfare state", in D. Rueschemeyer and T. Skopcol (eds.): *States, social knowledge, and the origin of modern social policies* (Princeton, Princeton University Press), pp. 90–114.

Wolman, L. 1961. *Reminiscences of Leo Wolman* (New York, Columbia University, Oral History Research Office).

Wood, S. 1982. "The study of management in British industrial relations", in *British Journal of Industrial Relations*, Vol. 13, No. 2, pp. 51–61.

——. 2000. "The *BJIR* and industrial relations in the new millennium", in *British Journal of Industrial Relations*, Vol. 38, No. 1, pp. 1–5.

—— et al. 1975. "Industrial relations system concept as a basis for theory in industrial relations", in *British Journal of Industrial Relations*, Vol. 13, No. 3, pp. 291–308.

Woods, H.D. 1949. "Foreword", in *The universities and industrial relations* (Montreal, McGill University), pp. i–ii.

_____ ; Goldenberg, S. 1981. "Industrial relations research in Canada", in P. Doeringer (ed.): *Industrial relations in international perspective* (New York, Holmes and Meier), pp. 22–75.

Woods, H.; Carruthers, A.; Crispo, J.; Dion, G. 1968. *Canadian industrial relations: The report of the task force on labour relations* (Ottawa, Information Centre).

World Commission on the Social Dimension of Globalization. 2004. *A fair globalization: Creating opportunities for all* (Geneva, ILO).

Wren, D. 1994. *The evolution of management thought*, 4th ed. (New York, Wiley).

Wright, A.W. 1979. *G.D.H. Cole and socialist democracy* (Oxford, Clarendon Press).

Yamawaki, N. 2001. "Walter Eucken and Wilhelm Röpke: A reappraisal of their economic thought and the policy of ordoliberalism", in Y. Shionoya (ed.), 2001, pp. 188–201.

Yeo, Eileen. 1996. *The contest for social science: Relations and representations of gender and class* (London, Rivers Oram).

Yesufu, T.M. 1962. *An introduction to industrial relations in Nigeria* (Oxford, Oxford University Press).

Yoder, D. 1931. "Introductory courses in industrial relations", in *Personnel*, Vol. 7, Feb., pp. 123–7.

_____ . 1959. *Personnel principles and polices: Modern manpower management* (Englewood Cliffs, Prentice-Hall).

_____ ; Heneman, H.G.; Turnbull, J.G. 1958. *Handbook of personnel management and labor relations* (New York, McGraw-Hill).

Yonay, Y. 1998. *The struggle for the soul of economics: Institutionalist and neoclassical economists in American between the wars* (Princeton, Princeton University Press).

Young, A. 1935. "Testimony", in National Labor Relations Board: *Legislative history of the National Labor Relations Act, 1935* (Washington, DC, Government Printing Office), 1985.

Zapata, F. 1981. "Mexico", in A. Blum (ed.): *International handbook of industrial relations* (Westport, Greenwood), pp. 351–92.

Zegarra Garnica, F. 1994. "Desarrollo actual de las relaciones industriales", in *Análisis Laboral,* Dec., pp. 18–19.

Zieger, R. 1995. *The CIO: 1935–1955* (Chapel Hill, University of North Carolina Press).

INDEX

Other ILO publications

Fundamental rights at work and international labour standards

Respect for fundamental rights at work is at the core of the ILO's Decent Work strategy. This important new book offers valuable insight on the application of the ILO's fundamental international labour standards – on freedom of association, collective bargaining, the abolition of forced and compulsory labour, equality of opportunity and treatment, and the protection of children and young people – by governments, employers and workers across the globe. The book offers a detailed description of each instrument and its principles, along with specific problems encountered in applying that instrument at a national level. It also contains information about the application of the standards in practice, as well as the ILO's supervisory system.

ISBN 92-2-113375-3   [2003]   27.50 Swiss francs

Organized labour in the 21st century

Edited by A.V. Jose

This volume explores through a number of country case studies the experiences of trade unions responding to globalization. It highlights the importance of organizational strategies to enable unions to exercise voice and influence policy. It reveals that the major challenge for unions in all countries, notably developing countries, is the representation of non-traditional constituents and the provision of new services. In addition, it shows that changes in the world of work and in social attitudes are leading to union alliances and coalitions with other civil society actors for common goals.

Examining industrialized, middle-income and developing economies, this book offers a wider understanding of the role and changing priorities of organized labour. It provides insightful reflection and analysis for the formulation of effective policies and strategies for labour movements in the years to come.

ISBN 92-9014-642-7   [2002]   30 Swiss francs

Changing labour markets in Europe. The role of institutions and policies

Edited by Peter Auer

Labour market institutions are a stabilizing force in the face of continuous structural and technological change. They are necessary for shaping the behaviour of firms and workers, and are a precondition for the efficient functioning of labour market systems. Drawing on the experience of four small European economies (Austria, Denmark, Ireland and the Netherlands), this timely book analyses four important policy areas in terms of their potential contribution to employment success: macroeconomics, industrial relations, working time and equal opportunities.

ISBN 92-2-111385-X   [2001]   35 Swiss francs

The Committee of Freedom of Association: Its impact over 50 years

Eric Gravel, Isabelle Duplessis and Bernard Gernigon

On the occasion of the 50th anniversary of the Committee on Freedom of Association of the Governing Body of the ILO, this volume demonstrates, based on a selection of examples from the past 25 years, the manner in which this body carries out its supervisory role. It also shows the Committee's influence on the application of ILO standards and principles in the field of freedom of association. An assessment is made of the impact of the Committee through the analysis of various cases, with a view to identifying lessons for the future.

ISBN 92-2-112667-6   [2002]   10 Swiss francs

Prices subject to change without notice.
Order ILO publications securely online at www.ilo.org/publns

The International Labour Organization

The *International Labour Organization* was founded in 1919 to promote social justice and, thereby, to contribute to universal and lasting peace. Its tripartite structure is unique among agencies affiliated to the United Nations; the ILO's Governing Body includes representatives of government, and of employers' and workers' organizations. These three constituencies are active participants in regional and other meetings sponsored by the ILO, as well as in the International Labour Conference – a world forum which meets annually to discuss social and labour questions.

Over the years the ILO has issued for adoption by member States a widely respected code of international labour Conventions and Recommendations on freedom of association, employment, social policy, conditions of work, social security, industrial relations and labour administration, among others.

The ILO provides expert advice and technical assistance to member States through a network of offices and multidisciplinary teams in over 40 countries. This assistance takes the form of labour rights and industrial relations counselling, employment promotion, training in small business development, project management, advice on social security, workplace safety and working conditions, the compiling and dissemination of labour statistics, and workers' education.

ILO Publications

The *International Labour Office* is the Organization's secretariat, research body and publishing house. The *Publications Bureau* produces and distributes material on major social and economic trends. It publishes policy studies on issues affecting labour around the world, reference works, technical guides, research-based books and monographs, codes of practice on safety and health prepared by experts, and training and workers' education manuals. It also produces the *International Labour Review* in English, French and Spanish, which publishes the results of original research, perspectives on emerging issues, and book reviews.

You may purchase ILO publications and other resources securely on line at http://www.ilo.org/publns; or request a free catalogue by writing to the Publications Bureau, International Labour Office, CH-1211 Geneva 22, Switzerland; fax (41 22) 799 6938; email: pubvente@ilo.org